Tuscany

**Neal Bedford
Damien Simonis
Imogen Franks**

LONELY PLANET PUBLICATIONS
Melbourne • Oakland • London • Paris

TUSCANY

FLORENCE
The treasures of the Uffizi,
Renaissance architecture from
the dome of the Duomo to the
Basilica di San Lorenzo, and
Michelangelo's sublime David

AREZZO
The fresco cycle at the Chiesa di San
Francesco and the magnificent facade
of the Pieve di Santa Maria

THE CHIANTI REGION
A patchwork quilt of vineyards, fallow
fields and olive groves, with seams
of cypress and pine

LUNIGIANA
Lush valleys, rugged terrain
and isolated villages in this
little-visited corner of Tuscany

APUANE ALPS
Breathtaking views and some
of the region's best walking

PISA
Romanesque splendour and the
gravity-defying Leaning Tower

SAN GIMIGNANO
Medieval hill-top Manhattan
with commanding views
of fertile countryside

SIENA
Home of the famous Palio horse race and
one of Italy's greatest Gothic cathedrals

Adriatic Sea

San Marino

EMILIA-ROMAGNA

LE MARCHE

UMBRIA

LIGURIA

Ligurian Sea

Ravenna

Forlì

Faenza

Bologna

To Ferrara (30km)

To Modena (20km)

Vignola

To Parma (32km)

Pontremoli

Passo Cerreto

Fivizzano

Aulla

La Spezia

Carrara

Massa

Pietrasanta

Seravezza

Viareggio

Livorno

Cecina

Rosignano Marittimo

Castelnuovo di Garfagnana

Barga

Borgo a Mozzano

Lucca

Pisa

Ponsacco

Pontedera

Abetone

San Marcello Pistoiese

Pistoia

Montecatini Terme

Monsummano

Prato

Florence (Firenze)

Fiesole

Empoli

Certaldo

Castelfiorentino

San Gimignano

Volterra

Pomarance

Saline di Volterra

Poggibonsi

Siena

Asciano

The Crete

Monte San Savino

Castiglion Fiorentino

Cortona

Arezzo

Montevarchi

Poppi

Bibbiena

Sansepolcro

Pieve Santo Stefano

Borgo San Lorenzo

Firenzuola

Dicomano

Rufina

Pontassieve

Impruneta

San Casciano in Val di Pesa

Greve in Chianti

Radda in Chianti

Alpe della Luna

Monte Falterona (1654m)

Alpe di S Benedetto

Pania della Croce (1858m)

Monte Pisanino (1945m)

Pizzo d'Uccello (1781m)

Chianti

Casentino

Monti del Chianti

Monti Albano

Parco Nazionale delle Foreste Casentinesi, Monte Falterona e Campigna

Parco Regionale delle Alpi Apuane

Riserva Naturale dell'Orecchiella

Parco Naturale Migliarino San Rossore Massaciuccoli

Parco Nazionale dell'Arcipelago

Gorgona

ROME

Fiumicino

Cerveteri

Viterbo

Civitavecchia

Tarquinia

Montefiascone

LAZIO

Lago di
Bolsena

Chiusi

Montepulciano

Pienza

Abbadia San Salvatore

MONTALCINO
Home of the famous Brunello
wine and an inviting hilltop
town in its own right

PITIGLIANO
Extraordinary town of tiny
winding lanes, rising
dramatically from a
rocky outcrop

Montalcino

Monte Amiata
(1738m)▲

Pitigliano

Massa
Marittima

Grosseto

Monti
dell'Uccellina

Parco Regionale
della Maremma

Lagoon
Orbetello

Lago di
Burano

Orbetello

Porto S Stefano

Monte
Argentario

Il Telegrafo
(635m)▲

Giglio Porto

Giglio

Giannutri

Parco Nazionale
dell'Arcipelago

PARCO REGIONALE DELLA MAREMMA
The forest-covered Monti dell' Uccellina and
a magnificent stretch of unspoilt coastline

Tyrrhenian Sea

*Golfo
di
Follonica*

Populonia

Piombino

Rio Marina

Porto Azzurro

Monte Calamita
(413m)▲

Portoferraio

Elba

Parco Nazionale
dell'Arcipelago

Montecristo

Parco Nazionale
dell'Arcipelago

*Golfo di
Baratti*

ELBA
Idyllic little beaches and coves and
stunning views from Monte Capanne

Monte Capanne
(1018m)▲

Pianosa

Capraia

Monte Arpagna
(41m)▲

Parco Nazionale
dell'Arcipelago

*To Corsica,
Sardinia & Sicily*

40km

20   20mi

0   10

ELEVATION

1500m
1000m
500m
200m
100m
0

*National
Park*

*National
Marine
Park*

Tuscany
2nd edition – March 2002
First published – July 2000

Published by
Lonely Planet Publications Pty Ltd ABN 36 005 607 983
90 Maribyrnong St, Footscray, Victoria 3011, Australia

Lonely Planet offices
Australia Locked Bag 1, Footscray, Victoria 3011
USA 150 Linden St, Oakland, CA 94607
UK 10a Spring Place, London NW5 3BH
France 1 rue du Dahomey, 75011 Paris

Photographs
Many of the images in this guide are available for licensing from
Lonely Planet Images.
email: lpi@lonelyplanet.com.au
Web site: www.lonelyplanetimages.com

Front cover photograph
A leaning towards pizza in Pisa (Jon Davison)

ISBN 1 86450 357 2

text & maps © Lonely Planet Publications Pty Ltd 2002
photos © photographers as indicated 2002

Printed by The Bookmaker International Ltd
Printed in China

Contents – Text

2 Contents – Text

Contents – Maps

4 Contents – Maps

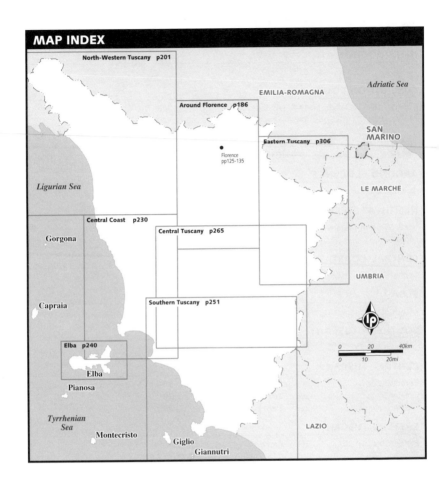

The Authors

Neal Bedford
Born in Papakura, New Zealand, Neal gave up an exciting career in accounting after university to experience the mundane life of a traveller. With the urge to move, travel led him through a number of countries and jobs, ranging from an au pair in Vienna, life-guard in the USA, fruit picker in Israel and lettuce-washer at rock concerts. Deciding to give his life some direction, he well and truly got his foot stuck in the door by landing the lucrative job of packing books in Lonely Planet's London office. One thing led to another and he managed to cross over to the mystic world of authoring. He has worked on a number of books for Lonely Planet.

Damien Simonis
With a degree in languages and several years' reporting and sub-editing on Australian newspapers (including *The Australian* and the *Age*), Sydney-born Damien left Australia in 1989. He has since lived, worked and travelled extensively throughout Europe, the Middle East and North Africa. Since 1992, Lonely Planet has kept him busy writing *Jordan & Syria*, *Egypt & the Sudan*, *Morocco*, *North Africa*, *Italy*, *Florence*, *Venice*, *Spain*, *The Canary Islands*, *Barcelona*, *Madrid* and *Catalunya & the Costa Brava*. He has also written and snapped for other publications in Australia, the UK and North America. When not on the road, Damien resides in splendid Stoke Newington, deep in the heart of north London.

Imogen Franks
Thanks to her father's job and her mother's love of travel, Imogen was on the road in Sudan by the tender age of three months and was living in Indonesia at three. Young habits die hard and Imogen hasn't stopped seeing the world since. One memorable trip led her from her home in the north of England to Lonely Planet's London office where she now works as an editor. From there she occasionally jumps over the fence to authoring and back again, and she now has a few select Lonely Planet titles tucked firmly under her writing arm.

FROM THE AUTHORS
Neal Bedford
First I'd like to thank Damien for all his advice, direction and superb knowledge of Tuscany. It was a pleasure once again to follow in his footsteps. Special thanks to Maria Christina, Werner and their two daughters for their insight into the Tuscan way of life, and for having to put up with my English and broken German!

A big *grazie* goes out to all the tourist offices throughout Tuscany, which supplied me with more information than I could carry and made my life on the road that much easier. Once again my heartfelt appreciation goes out to Christina, whose support and guidance helped me more than she will ever know. I hope in some way it always will.

Damien Simonis

A big thank you to Silvia Mosconi, who in spite of exam pressure went out of her way to welcome me back into local life after a long absence from the city of the Medici. It was fun hanging out and meeting up with the likes of Enrico, Paolo and Francesca. Also to Michela and Fabbiana – good to see you again!

Kristina Nordahl had some handy hints on the nocturnal scene and several soothing ales were had with Gerard Collon, with whom many words were spilled. A couple of glasses of fine wine and the odd beer also emptied themselves in the company of Mariah and Joe, who happened to be passing through just when I was in Florence researching. I would like to know what the odds against us simply bumping into each other in Standa were!

Marco of Hotel Dalí helped me out of a lodging crisis and would no doubt have done more had I not been in such a rush – best of luck and until next time around!

Meanwhile, thanks also go to some of the Milan crew for bringing that much-needed element of pleasurable confusion into an already haphazard existence. Particular thanks this time around go to Anna Cerutti, Paola Brussa, Lucia Spadaro and Maurizio Gallotti for *piacevoli momenti ed anche un po' di casini*. After all, all work and no fun can prove exceedingly dull.

As always, LP authors in the same country help each other by trading and pooling information. I owe a particular debt of thanks on this score to Sally Webb, my colleague on LP's *Italy*.

Imogen Franks

Many thanks are due to Neal for his useful pointers as well as his youthful wit and cynicism, as always. Thanks also to the people at the regional statistics office in Florence and to Rachel Suddart, Leonie Mugavin and Tammy Fortin for giving the Getting There & Away information a thorough 'once over'. Thanks are also due to Paul Piaia for help above and beyond the call of duty and to Luisella Arzani for knowing her trip hop from her hip hop. And last but never least, *grazie mille* to one particular travel information buff who puts a smile on my face every day.

This Book

Neal Bedford updated this 2nd edition of Lonely Planet's *Tuscany*, with help from Damien Simonis who updated the Florence chapter, and Imogen Franks who updated the Facts about Tuscany and Getting There & Away chapters. The 1st edition was researched and written by Damien Simonis.

FROM THE PUBLISHER

This edition of *Tuscany* was produced in Lonely Planet's London office. Abigail Hole was the coordinating editor. Jolyon Philcox handled the design and layout and produced the maps with help from Liam Molloy, Rachel Beattie and Jimi Ellis. Liam also drew the decorative borders, chapter ends and the climate chart. Arabella Shepherd, Sam Trafford and Jenny Lansbury helped with editing and proofreading. Andrew Weatherill designed the cover and Lachlan Ross drew the back cover map. The illustrations were drawn by Jane Smith and the photographs were provided by Lonely Planet Images. Thanks to Quentin Frayne for his work on the Language chapter, Paul Clifton for his help with the Gay & Lesbian section, Emma Sangster for help with the Health section and Leonie Mugavin, Rachel Suddart and Tammy Fortin for assisting with the Getting There & Away chapter. Thanks are also due to Amanda Canning, Paul Piaia and Michala Green for all their expert help along the way.

ACKNOWLEDGMENTS

Thanks to Edizioni La Mandragora for permission to reprint the Panzanella and Pappa al Pomodoro recipes from *Florence – The Art of Cookery* by Sandra Rosi, and to Agenzia Per Il Turismo Costa Degli Etruschi for permission to reprint the Cacciucco recipe from the *Discovering the Local Flavours* booklet.

THANKS

Many thanks to the travellers who used the last edition and contacted us with helpful hints, advice and interesting anecdotes:

Bas Blij, Joanne Bullin, Roger Colebrook, Esther Y Iwanaga, Katrine Gilje Krogh, David Laming, Phylis Maiden, Amanda Mc-Naught, Eric A Michrowski, Bob Miller, Beata Paulusse, Bronwyn Wyatt, Justin Zaman.

Foreword

ABOUT LONELY PLANET GUIDEBOOKS

The story begins with a classic travel adventure: Tony and Maureen Wheeler's 1972 journey across Europe and Asia to Australia. There was no useful information about the overland trail then, so Tony and Maureen published the first Lonely Planet guidebook to meet a growing need.

From a kitchen table, Lonely Planet has grown to become the largest independent travel publisher in the world, with offices in Melbourne (Australia), Oakland (USA), London (UK) and Paris (France).

Today Lonely Planet guidebooks cover the globe. There is an ever-growing list of books and information in a variety of media. Some things haven't changed. The main aim is still to make it possible for adventurous travellers to get out there – to explore and better understand the world.

At Lonely Planet we believe travellers can make a positive contribution to the countries they visit – if they respect their host communities and spend their money wisely. Since 1986 a percentage of the income from each book has been donated to aid projects and human rights campaigns, and, more recently, to wildlife conservation.

Although inclusion in a guidebook usually implies a recommendation we cannot list every good place. Exclusion does not necessarily imply criticism. In fact there are a number of reasons why we might exclude a place – sometimes it is simply inappropriate to encourage an influx of travellers.

UPDATES & READER FEEDBACK

Things change – prices go up, schedules change, good places go bad and bad places go bankrupt. Nothing stays the same. So, if you find things better or worse, recently opened or long-since closed, please tell us and help make the next edition even more accurate and useful.

Lonely Planet thoroughly updates each guidebook as often as possible – usually every two years, although for some destinations the gap can be longer. Between editions, up-to-date information is available in our free, quarterly *Planet Talk* newsletter and monthly email bulletin *Comet*. The *Upgrades* section of our website (**w** www.lonelyplanet.com) is also regularly updated by Lonely Planet authors, and the site's *Scoop* section covers news and current affairs relevant to travellers. Lastly, the *Thorn Tree* bulletin board and *Postcards* section carry unverified, but fascinating, reports from travellers.

Tell us about it! We genuinely value your feedback. A well-travelled team at Lonely Planet reads and acknowledges every email and letter we receive and ensures that every morsel of information finds its way to the relevant authors, editors and cartographers.

Everyone who writes to us will find their name listed in the next edition of the appropriate guidebook, and will receive the latest issue of *Comet* or *Planet Talk*. The very best contributions will be rewarded with a free guidebook.

We may edit, reproduce and incorporate your comments in Lonely Planet products such as guidebooks, websites and digital products, so let us know if you don't want your comments reproduced or your name acknowledged.

How to contact Lonely Planet:
Online: **e** talk2us@lonelyplanet.com.au, **w** www.lonelyplanet.com
Australia: Locked Bag 1, Footscray, Victoria 3011
UK: 10a Spring Place, London NW5 3BH
USA: 150 Linden St, Oakland, CA 94607

Introduction

If the requirements for nationhood were cultural wealth, variety of landscape, quality of food, natural beauty, fashion and industriousness, Tuscany would probably be counted among the great nations. Like a fine wine, Tuscany has been some time in the making. More than 10,000 years of history have gone into shaping this, perhaps one of the most representative and varied of the Italian regions.

The Etruscans left behind them an impressive artistic tradition that Rome could do little more than copy and adapt. Cities that sprang out of the landscape thousands of years ago still thrive today. From Arezzo to Volterra, the Etruscan origins of the region are never far out of sight.

Out of the confusion of the early Middle Ages emerged a series of fiercely independent city states that spent centuries engaged in a deadly game of one-upmanship. Of these, Florence emerged the victor and capital of Tuscany. Today it is possibly the single greatest repository of Renaissance art in the world – its palaces, churches, galleries and cloisters hold a seemingly endless treasure trove of extraordinary paintings and sculpture.

Where to begin beyond the banks of the Arno? From the haunting Gothic majesty of Florence's most bitter rival, Siena, through to the Romanesque splendour of the one-time maritime power Pisa, the roll call of *città d'arte* (cities of art) in Tuscany is daunting. Arezzo, Cortona and Lucca are among the more striking of the other cities.

Strike out beyond the main urban centres, and an extraordinary Tuscany appears. Centuries-old villages huddle for protection

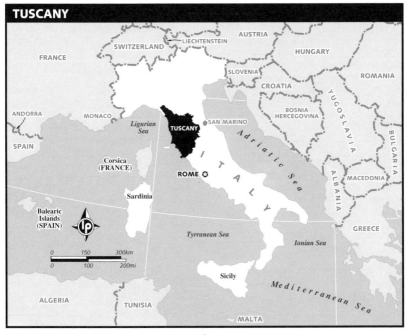

atop lonely hills. Sprawling churches lie scattered about in the most unlikely places. From the patchwork-quilt hills of the Chianti region to the rain-swept heights of the Apuane Alps, from the plains of the Maremma to the rugged gorges around Pitigliano, the variety of the Tuscan countryside seems endless. And Tuscany is home to some of the finest wines and most exquisite virgin olive oil in the world. Whether at the end of the day or at lunchtime, both will accompany wonderful meals. Simple and honest fare means that you can generally be sure of eating well – Tuscans are obsessive about using only the freshest ingredients and cooking them just right.

While in the countryside, leave the roads and get into your stride. Country lanes and mule tracks criss-cross much of the region, offering the walker unlimited options for wandering in fields, across rolling hills, or for the more serious walker, amongst the peaks of the Apuane Alps. The patient walker can also indulge in a little bird and animal watching – the remarkable variety of birds, in winter especially, makes excursions to some of the region's nature reserves worthwhile.

Tuscany also offers enough beach activity to keep summer holiday-makers happy. The best of the beaches are on the islands, led by the former home of the exiled Emperor Napoleon, Elba. Come winter, something a little warmer is in order. Tuscany's hot springs are the perfect answer, and the choice ranges from plush spas to open springs and waterfalls.

Many have suggested that, by the manner in which Tuscans have shaped and moulded their land, they have long displayed an innate artistic sensibility. That thought reflects what at least seems like a real local affinity with beauty. There is no doubt that Tuscans like to present well, and they always have done. And even today, Tuscany and its people have lost none of their seductive power.

Facts about Tuscany

HISTORY
Etruria Rules

More than two million years ago, the site where Florence now stands was virtually on the coast. As the waters receded, life came to the region that we now know as Tuscany (Toscana).

Evidence suggests the first Neolithic tribes, Ligurians from northern Italy, moved into the area around the 10th century BC. They were later joined by other tribes, among them the Etruscans, who appear to have founded settlements as early as the 9th century BC. By the beginning of the 6th century the Etruscans had become the dominant power in central Italy. Territory in their control stretched from Rome in the south to the Apennines (Appennini).

Etruria, encompassing much of modern Tuscany and parts of Latium (the Latin name for Lazio) and Umbria, was by no means a monolith. The Etruscan settlements were largely independent of one another and they are said to have formed a league, the 12-city Dodecapolis, for the celebration of annual religious festivities more than anything else. In times of conflict with other tribes they generally helped each other out.

The senior members of the league included Fiesole (the northernmost town), Chiusi, Cortona, Arezzo, Roselle, Populonia, Volterra, Sovana, Saturnia, Vetulonia, Tarquinia and Veii (the last two in Latium). Each city was ruled by a chief, or *lucumones*.

Just where the Etruscans came from remains a 64,000 dollar question. The Greek historian Herodotus claimed they migrated in waves from Asia Minor in the wake of the Trojan Wars. Linguistic evidence, based largely on funerary inscriptions, suggests their language was neither Indo-European (like English, Latin, Greek, etc) nor Semitic (like Arabic, Hebrew, Aramaic, etc). It was still spoken until the 2nd century AD, enabling the Roman emperor Claudius to write a history of Etruria. Unfortunately the manuscript has not survived.

A more recent theory has the Etruscans, along with the Basques (in northern Spain) and other tribes, migrating from northern Africa as long as 6000 years ago in the face of worsening desertification. These tribes, according to the theory, headed for the Canary Islands, the Iberian peninsula, Italy, Sicily and Sardinia.

To the Greeks the Etruscans came to be known as the Tyrsenoi or Tyrrhenoi, a name that survives in that of the Tyrrhenian Sea, off Italy's west coast. The Romans, who in the 6th century BC had barely embarked on the urbanisation of what would be the most powerful city in the world, called the Etruscans' homeland Tuscia, from which comes to us the regional name of Tuscany.

Etruria on the March

Starting in the late 7th century BC, the Etruscans embarked on repeated campaigns of conquest across the peninsula. They marched south into Latium, taking the village of Rome and proceeding into Campania, where they were brought to a halt by the Greeks at Cumae in 535 BC.

In the same period, Etruscan warrior bands marched across the Apennines and burst into the Po valley, where they quickly came to rule the roost. With help from Carthage (the Phoenician outpost in North Africa) they also ousted the Greeks from Corsica.

Etruria had by now reached the apogee of its power. In Rome, the Etruscans were in complete control and furnished at least three of its kings. The backward Latin tribes had much to learn from their culturally superior Etruscan overlords.

The Romans Rebel

Rome owed a considerable debt to the Etruscans. Not only did the Etruscans reform the military, creating a disciplined infantry organised into heavily armed centuries (units of 100 men), they also passed on knowledge of engineering and tunnelling techniques. The classic Roman town plan, based on two perpendicular main streets, the *decumanus* and *cardo,* is said to have been inherited from the Etruscans – as is the Roman toga and the she-wolf symbol of Rome. Furthermore, the art and architecture of the Etruscans heavily influenced that of the Romans.

However, the Romans weren't too worried about honouring their debts. The Roman Republic was established in 509 BC and within 10 years Rome was head of the Latin League (a loose alliance of towns in Latium) with the Etruscans as public enemy number one.

In 392 BC the Romans took Veii, an Etruscan stronghold about 15km north of Rome. This marked the start of a limited campaign of conquest and soon all of southern Etruria was under Roman influence. Several attempts to regain control of southern Etruria failed and in 351 BC the Etruscans sued for peace.

But this didn't stop them trying to win back lost territories. Over the next century, as Rome experienced mixed successes against the Samnites in Campania, the Etruscan cities broke their peace treaties with Rome in vain attempts to regain what was lost. They always came off second best and by 265 BC all of Etruria was firmly bound to Rome through the Roman system of compulsory alliances.

Upheaval and civil war around 88 BC impelled Rome to grant full Roman citizenship, which entitled the holders to full rights and privileges as members of the Roman Republic, to subordinate territories – including Etruria – throughout much of the Italian peninsula. While citizenship assured the few Etruscans who had survived the carnage equal rights, it also spelled the final stage in the eradication of local culture and language (although the latter hung on for another couple of centuries).

Another result of the civil wars was a policy of Roman colonisation. As the Republic gave way to the Empire, Caesar founded Florentia (the Roman name for today's Florence) in 59 BC as a military settlement for war veterans, choosing a trading post on the narrowest crossing of the River Arno as the site. In 20 BC, Romans began to arrive at the military colony of Saena Julia (today's Siena). Other towns founded by the Romans included Pisa (an important river port), Lucca (base of the triumvirate of Julius Caesar, Crassus and Pompey), Pistoia and Empoli. The next 400 years of relative stability in the Roman Empire allowed these towns to flourish and Christianity to spread (before long Florence had its own martyr, San Miniato).

The Early Middle Ages

Towards the end of the 3rd century AD, the system of tetrachy (the division of power between two emperors) was introduced to the Empire and with it came the reorganisation of the administration of the peninsula. As part of this, the province of Regio VII Etruria was converted into the Regio Tuscia et Umbria. Thus the name Etruria was consigned to the dustbin of history.

The Romans themselves were not far behind. By the 6th century their mighty empire had collapsed into an ignominious heap and most of central Italy had been put to the torch by the criss-crossing barbarian and Byzantine armies. The latter were sent in by Justinian, the eastern emperor in Constantinople (now Istanbul), to retake Italy and unify the great empire again. Tuscia came under their control but this state of affairs didn't last long – the invading Lombards wrested control of Tuscia from Byzantine forces in AD 570. They turned it into a duchy with its capital in Lucca and remained in control until 774. Little documentation from this period survives, but it appears Tuscia was relatively peaceful through these centuries. One thing we do know, however, is that in the last century of Lombard rule, the Via Francigena (entering Tuscia at the Cisa pass and dropping south through the Lunigiana to Lucca and on to San Gimignano and Siena) was one of the busiest pilgrim routes to Rome in the country.

But this period of peace and pilgrimages was not long-lasting. The Lombards were soon ousted by the Franks, who formed a canny (but not so durable) alliance with the papacy under Charlemagne to create the Holy Roman Empire in 800. Charlemagne installed as lieutenants a series of margraves – counts – to rule for him, and by the end of the 11th century, particularly under the administration of Countess Matilda Canossa, the duchy had achieved considerable independence from the Empire. Florence, with a population of 20,000, had supplanted Lucca as a robust and flourishing regional capital.

When hostilities broke out between Emperor Henry IV and Pope Gregory VII, Matilda allied herself with the pope, setting a precedent that would long resonate through Florentine history. Henry tried to have the pope deposed in 1077, but instead found himself at Matilda's castle at Canossa, in Emilia, imploring him to lift an order of excommunication.

Influential as the state may have been under Matilda, her death in 1115 spelled the end of Tuscany as a political unit as disputes over the ownership of her lands led to the cities of Florence, Siena and Lucca declaring independence and the other lands coming under papal rule.

The City States

Over the following years, the principle of a sovereign city state firmly established itself in Tuscia. Officially, these states had their jurisdiction limited by the Holy Roman Emperor, who was in charge of the surrounding lands. In reality, they paid him little attention.

Pisa, given control of the coast from Portovenere (in Liguria) to Civitavecchia (in Lazio) and also of the island of Sardinia, flourished as it competed with Genoa and Venice for Mediterranean trade. In this time of ascendance, many of the great Pisan monuments were completed. The cathedral had already been started, the Leaning Tower was begun and artisans flocked to this flourishing port.

Siena, meanwhile, had become the dominant city of central Tuscany, slowly extending its power southwards into the Maremma.

And last but not least, the *comunes* (city councils) of Prato and Pistoia became independent with the promulgation of their own statutes in 1140 and 1117. Lucca followed suit and would remain an independent republic until the age of Napoleon.

However, the city states of Tuscia all wanted a bigger slice of the pie, and it was Florence that managed to tuck into the lion's share.

The Rise & Rise of Florence

Only eight years after the death of Matilda, Florence's city fathers undertook the conquest of nearby Fiesole. They then turned their attentions to Siena. Although skirmishes had been taking place for years between Florence and Siena in the Chianti region, it was not until the bloody Battle of Monteaperti in 1260 that the two sides clashed head on.

By this time Florence and many other Tuscan cities had been divided into two main factions, the pro-empire Ghibellines and the pro-pope Guelphs. Supposedly the division was between those who backed imperial influence in Italy and those who preferred papal supremacy. Often, however, the papal-imperial conflict was more of a pretext for local feuding than anything else. The Ghibellines dominated Florence until 1250, when the Guelphs turfed them out.

The Battle of Monteaperti, although a resounding defeat for Guelph Florence, was only a temporary setback. Within 10 years Florence had managed to impose a Guelph governorship on Siena, after the Battle of Colle di Val d'Elsa.

Florence got lucky with Pisa too. The port town was heavily defeated at sea by Genoa at the Battle of Meloria in 1284, signalling the end of Pisa as a dominant trading city and weakening it enough for Florence to have a Guelph in power there too. Five years later, Florentine Guelph troops, Dante among them, crushed Arezzo. It and other Tuscan towns were all soon obliged to accept Guelph leadership.

By the turn of the century Florence counted 100,000 inhabitants, making it one of the five biggest cities in Europe. Pisa, Siena and Lucca each had fewer than half that number.

Although Florence was emerging as the leading city in Tuscany, its bigger rivals were not exactly subordinate, Guelph governors or not. In 1335, for instance, Siena completed the takeover of Grosseto and Massa Marittima.

Indeed, this was Siena's golden age, a period in which much of the cathedral was completed, the Torre del Mangia was raised in the Palazzo Pubblico and many of the fine works of art by Duccio and others were commissioned. In short, it was in this period that the Gothic masterpiece you see today was largely formed.

In 1348 disaster struck. The Black Death swept across Tuscany, decimating urban populations and stunning the countryside. It was a blow from which Siena would never really recover, while Florence managed to bounce back and capture Prato just three years later. In 1384 Florence simply bought Arezzo.

In the meantime, the Visconti rulers of Milan had brought Pisa and Siena into their orbit and so threatened to complete their domination of Tuscany by encircling Florence. This city had more lives than a cat, however, and the problem was solved by the timely death in 1402 of Gian Galeazzo Visconti.

Only four years later, Florence had taken control of Pisa, Livorno, Cortona and Montepulciano. Siena remained one of the few significant Tuscan centres not under direct Florentine control.

Enter the Medicis

The attempt at democratic republican rule in Florence had always been something of a farce. The city governors, or priors, were elected every two months, but tended to be carefully selected and elections gerrymandered by the competing wealthy merchant and banking families who called the shots in Florence by the end of the 14th century.

One of these families was the Medici clan. Having successfully become God's bankers (being the Vatican's top financiers), this family had risen to be among the most powerful in the city by the time Cosimo de' Medici was in charge of its affairs in 1429. Although discreet, Cosimo's desire to rule by proxy was clear enough to some and the rival Albizi clan plotted his removal. The move backfired and by the time Cosimo returned from a brief exile in 1434, Florence was effectively his.

The Medici family crest was made up of six *palle* (balls), which must have been cause for some mirth through the years as Medici supporters would clatter around on horseback crying out: 'Balls! Balls! Balls!'

The word has the same less than decorous meaning in Italian as it does in English. Be that as it may, the Medicis were here to stay and their balls can be seen on stone coats of arms in towns across Tuscany to this day.

Cosimo tended to remain in the background, believing discretion to be the better part of valour. Few were fooled. In the 1450s, Pope Pius II actually dubbed Cosimo 'master of all Italy'. The Medici clan kept the government stacked with its own people and, when dissenting voices were raised, found indirect means to silence them, such as special taxes and other rulings to ruin their opponents financially. The Medicis were not beyond tinkering with the constitution to head off potential opposition.

Foreign policy came close to undoing Cosimo. His unswerving allegiance to the Milanese usurper, Francesco Sforza, brought upon Florence the enmity of Venice and of the kingdom of Naples. Opposition to the ensuing war was strong and things were looking a trifle dodgy when Neapolitan forces breached the Tuscan frontier in 1450. Cosimo remained unperturbed and the doubters were proved wrong. Venice was too concerned with threats from Turkey, and the other Italian states worried lest a French army march into Italy to aid Florence. As so often in the peninsula, the boys put away their toys and signed a pact in 1454 aimed at creating unity in the face of potential outside aggression. Ten years of peace followed.

It was also under Cosimo, a passionate patron of the arts, that the humanist revolution in thinking and the accompanying *Rinascimento* (Renaissance) in the visual arts took off. The process had been under way since the previous century, as witnessed by the work of artists such as Giotto, but the generous patronage of the Medici family was a catalyst that would turn Florence into the most innovative centre of the arts in all of Europe.

Lorenzo il Magnifico (the Magnificent) continued his grandfather's work, expanding the city's power and maintaining its primacy in the artistic realm. See the boxed text 'The Magnificent Medici' for more details.

His death and his succession by his nasty son Piero in 1492, the year Columbus

The Magnificent Medici

It's not many rulers who earn the title of magnificent, so what exactly did Lorenzo do to make both his subjects and the history books like him so much?

At a time when freedom of expression was not always encouraged by the ruling elite, Lorenzo created a climate of tolerance in which the great Renaissance artists and scholars could flourish. Among others, he gave patronage and protection to Michelangelo, Botticelli and Leon Battista Alberti. He was himself a poet and is credited by some as saying 'Whoever wants to be happy, let him be so: about tomorrow there's no knowing'.

But his wisdom didn't stop at art and literature. Lorenzo's diplomatic skills brought a much-needed period of peace to the region when, soon after taking power, he managed to negotiate with the king of Naples, averting war and earning himself the respect of the Florentines into the bargain. For the rest of his rule, he slowly reinforced, through peaceful means, the position of Florence as a great city-state.

Just as his popularity was coming under

'Balls! Balls! Balls!' The Medici family crest – still seen on buildings in Florence

fire from the miserable Savonarola, Lorenzo died. The outpouring of grief in Florence marked the beginning of a new era as relative peace and prosperity gave way to political uncertainty, economic gloom and an artistic downturn. No wonder they called him magnificent.

discovered the Americas, spelled the temporary end of Medici rule and the start of heated times for Florence.

Ups & Downs

In 1494, Piero abjectly bowed to an invading force led by the diminutive French king Charles VIII. Piero and his family, increasingly disliked by the people of Florence, fled the city and, once Charles VIII left, were replaced by the rather humourless theocracy of a dour, droopy-lipped Dominican monk by the name of Girolamo Savonarola, an ally of the French king.

Savonarola's spiritual austerity programme and slavish pro-imperialism went down fine for a while. But as the city's econ-

omy stagnated and Savonarola, in a taste of what was to come with Martin Luther and the Reformation in the following century, directed a growing portion of his fire-and-brimstone sermons at papal and Church corruption, he found himself increasingly friendless. So much so that he ended up on an Inquisitorial bonfire in 1498. Over the following 14 years Florence reverted to a republic along pre-Medici lines – but this family was not so easily discouraged.

It took some time and a good deal of bloodshed, but Giovanni de' Medici returned home in 1512 backed by a Spanish-led army. He set about restoring the position of his family in Florence, which should have been further strengthened when he was elected Pope

Leo X three years later. But the Medici name had lost much of its lustre. Florence was not the same city as in the days of Cosimo. Most of its banks had failed and business was not so good. A series of Medici lads, culminating in the illegitimate (and utterly useless) Ippolito and Alessandro, managed to so alienate the Florentines that when Pope Clement VII (another Medici) was cornered in Rome by Holy Roman Emperor Charles V's uncompromising imperial army, the people rejoiced and threw the Medicis out.

Of course deals were done and the imperial forces subsequently promised to reinstate the Medicis in Florence if the pope recognised imperial suzerainty of all Italy. Florence, which had enjoyed a few short Medici-free years, was weakened by siege in 1530. Alessandro and Ippolito returned and the former was made duke, bringing to an end even the pretence of a republic. The jealousy of an unhinged cousin, Lorenzino, saved Florence from too protracted a rule by Alessandro: Lorenzino killed him and ran away. Florence breathed a sigh of relief and waited for the next exciting instalment in the Medici soap opera.

The Grand Duchy of Tuscany

Cosimo (a descendant of the original Cosimo's brother) succeeded Alessandro in 1537. Although in many respects Florence and its Tuscan dominions had by now been eclipsed on the European stage by the emergence of powerful nation states such as France, Cosimo was determined to keep a key role for Florence in the affairs of a still-fractured Italy.

A crucial moment came in 1555 when a Florentine army entered Siena after a year-long siege. The city and all its possessions across southern Tuscany passed into Florentine hands. Four years later Cosimo's victory was confirmed by the Peace of Cateau-Cambrésis. And in 1569 Pope Pius V conferred upon Cosimo the title of Cosimo I, grand duke of Tuscany.

Florence was now the capital of most of Tuscany. Only Lucca and its modest possessions in the Garfagnana, the Lunigiana (held by the Hapsburg Empire), Piombino and most of Elba (together forming a separate principality) and the coastal area around Orbetello and Monte Argentario (the Spanish-controlled *presidios,* or military outposts) remained out of the grand duke's control.

In his long reign (1537–74), Cosimo I was no doubt a despot – but he was a comparatively enlightened one. He sorted out the city's finances, built a fleet (which participated in the crushing defeat of the Turkish navy in the Battle of Lepanto in 1571) and promoted economic growth across Tuscany with irrigation programmes for agriculture and mining. He was a patron of the arts and sciences, and also reformed the civil service, building the Uffizi in Florence to house all government departments in a single, more easily controlled building. He and his family also acquired and moved into the Palazzo Pitti.

The Medicis of the Grand Duchy

From the death of Cosimo I until that of the dissolute lout Gian Gastone de' Medici in 1737, the once glorious family continued to rule over Tuscany with uneven results.

Cosimo I's two immediate successors, Francesco and Ferdinando I, between them managed to keep Tuscany out of trouble and go some way to stimulating the local economy and promoting agriculture, building hospitals and bringing some relief to the poor. Cosimo II invited Galileo Galilei to Florence, where the scientist could continue his research under Tuscan protection and undisturbed by the bellyaching of the Church.

Ferdinando II was ineffectual if well meaning – during the three terrible years of plague that scourged Florence from 1630, he stayed behind when anyone else who could was hightailing it to the countryside.

Next in line was Cosimo III, a dour, depressing man if ever there was one. Perhaps he had read his Savonarola. Not exactly a fun date, he was also an ill-educated bigot. Persecution of the Jews was one of his contributions to Tuscan society and he also backed the Inquisition in its opposition to virtually any kind of scientific learning. Inevitably, sex was one of his biggest bugbears. A little stretch on the rack was the prescribed tonic for horizontal jogging outside marriage, while buggery was punished with decapitation.

But while Cosimo III was busy overseeing the mores of his subjects, they were either dying or going hungry. The population of Tuscany was in decline, the economy was a mess, taxes were skyrocketing and the Medici clan were losing their grip.

Before the next in the Medici line, the drunkard Gian Gastone, had kicked (or rather stumbled over) the bucket, the European powers had decided the issue of the 'Tuscan succession' and appointed Francis, Duke of Lorraine and husband of the Austrian empress Maria Theresa, grand duke of Tuscany in 1737.

The last significant act of the Medicis was six years after the death of Gian Gastone. His sister Anna Maria, who died in 1743, bequeathed all the Medici property and art collections to the grand duchy of Tuscany, on condition that they never leave Florence.

Austrians in Charge

The imperial Austrian couple popped down for a three-month sojourn in Florence and liked it well enough, but from then until 1765 the grand duchy was to be ruled by the *Reggenza* (regents).

The regents brought a feeling of (mostly) quiet discontent to their subjects. It is true that much-needed reforms swept away glaring inequities in taxation, somewhat streamlined the civil administration and bridled the Inquisition. At the same time, however, the regents' main task seemed to be the systematic plunder of Tuscany's resources for the greater glory of the Austrian Empire.

Things looked up a little in 1765, when Pietro Leopoldo, heir to the Austrian throne, became grand duke and moved down from Vienna. He threw himself into his task with considerable vim and vigour. The list of his reforms and initiatives is impressive, even if some proved less than satisfactory. The grand duke abolished torture and the death penalty, suppressed the Inquisition, embarked on a school building programme for the poor, busied himself with agricultural issues and prodded Florence's city council

to clean up the city, improve lighting and introduce street names. He also saw to it that at least some of the art and furnishings that had been removed to Austria under his predecessor were returned.

However, on the death of his brother Emperor Josef II in 1790, Pietro Leopoldo was recalled to Vienna, leaving Tuscany under the control of a Regency Council (until Grand Duke Ferdinando III arrived the following year) that within weeks found itself struggling to put down food riots in Florence.

Napoleon

The revolutionary events that had so profoundly rocked France in the meantime could not fail to have an impact, sooner or later, on the rest of Europe. Napoleon Bonaparte marched into Italy at the head of his ill-equipped but highly motivated republican army in 1796 and on 24 March 1799 occupied Florence. Within a couple of days Grand Duke Ferdinando III had been courteously handed his hat and the French tricolour was flying over Palazzo Pitti.

This first round of French occupation of the northern half of Italy was as fleeting as the invasion had been spectacular. By the end of July, Ferdinando III was again grand duke, although he was hedging his bets back in Vienna.

Good job really, because the following year Napoleon was back, not as a republican general but as consul and virtual ruler of France. He retook Florence and made it capital of his newly coined kingdom of Etruria. For the following nine years, it was run by Louis, son of the Bourbon duke of Parma, and his wife, the Infanta Maria Luisa of Spain.

In 1809 Napoleon, by now emperor, handed Tuscany over to his sister Elisa, who remained grand duchess for the five years left to Napoleon as warrior emperor. Before the year 1814 was out, Grand Duke Ferdinando III was back in charge – third time lucky.

Towards Italian Unity

Grand Duke Ferdinando III proved to be one of the more popular of the Tuscan overlords.

He pushed through a raft of reforms at every level of city and grand-ducal administration and by all accounts was an all-round good fellow. He eschewed many of the trappings of his position and mingled freely with his subjects.

His death in 1824 was greeted with dismay, not least because no-one knew what to expect from his gloomy son Leopoldo. But Grand Duke Leopoldo II proved more up to the task than many had thought. Under his rule the first long-distance rail line (Florence-Pisa-Livorno) and the first telegraphic link (Florence-Pisa) were both opened in the 1840s. In 1847, he had the pleasure of seeing Lucca transferred to the control of the grand duchy, ending centuries of Luccan independence.

It was in this period that some of the most important infrastructural reforms in Tuscany took place. The road system was improved (often using plans laid out under Napoleonic rule) and the drainage and population of much of the lowland coast, especially the Maremma, was accelerated. (For centuries the coast had been sparsely populated for several reasons, including malaria and fear of attack by North African pirates – the last such assault by Tunisian raiders took place on the Monte Argentario coast as late as 1815!)

Meanwhile, political change was afoot. The independence of the grand duchy was menaced not only by more direct interference from Vienna, but also by growing calls for a united Italian state. After mass demonstrations were held against him and in favour of a unified Italy, Leopold left the grand duchy. And not a minute too soon.

A whirlwind of plotting and a few turns of the wheel of fortune brought events to a head in 1859, when a combined French-Piedmontese army marched against the Austrians and defeated them in two bloody battles at Magenta and Solferino in June. The Austrians were forced to give up their Italian territories and, left to their own devices, the territories began to ally with each other.

On 15 March 1860, the provisional government in Florence announced the adhesion of the grand duchy to what was still the Savoy kingdom of Sardinia. After other parts of the peninsula also joined, a united Italy under a constitutional monarch was born in the following year.

Rome was still to be wrenched from Papal hands and Turin, the initial residence of the national government, was deemed too far north to remain capital, so the job fell to Florence. In February 1865, King Vittorio Emmanuele and an 'army' of 30,000, including bureaucrats and their families, descended on Florence, a city of around 115,000.

The incorporation of Rome into the kingdom and the end of fighting throughout the peninsula finally came in 1870 and the government shifted there the following year, leaving behind them a region in a pitiful state.

Tuscany, economically weak by the end of the Medicis, was kept in check by the wars and crises, the tendency towards heavy taxation and the consequent lack of local investment in any kind of production for the following century and a half. By 1892, a report on Florence suggested that 72,000 of a total population of 180,000 were officially poor.

In the 10 years prior to the outbreak of WWI, Florence became something of a cultural cauldron in Italy. Numerous literary, political and free-thinking newspapers and reviews opened at this time.

Florentine politics was becoming more radical too. By 1914 the Socialists had almost 3000 party members in Florence and the previous year, when universal male suffrage was granted, almost 30% of Tuscan votes went to the Socialists. Tuscany was also turning into a fulcrum of anarchist activity.

WWI & Fascism

Italy's decision to enter WWI on 24 May 1915 initially had little direct impact on Tuscany, tucked far away from the front lines in the north. Like the rest of the country, however, Tuscany paid a high price in the lives of its young men sacrificed as cannon fodder.

By 1917, the situation on Italy's home front had become grim too. All basic products were strictly rationed and that winter, a harsh one, brought intense hardship as heating fuel was virtually unavailable.

Italy, like the rest of Europe, emerged from the war in a state of collective shock. The fighting had cost the fledgling country dear in lives and resources and the political turmoil that ensued was inevitable.

By 1920, Benito Mussolini's Blackshirts had established branches in Florence, which in less than two years would become one of the Fascists' key strongholds. Tuscany became one of the single biggest sources of card-carrying Fascist members.

Almost perversely, in 1921 Livorno was the site of the ill-fated Italian Socialist Party's congress, where a split led to the birth of the Partito Comunista Italiano (PCI; the Italian Communist Party).

On 28 October 1922, Mussolini rolled the dice and marched on Rome. Had the king been truly opposed to the Fascists, it is likely they would have failed in this endeavour, but in the event Mussolini emerged the victor at the head of the world's first Fascist regime.

The Florentine version of Fascism was particularly virulent. In 1924, after the assassination in Rome of the Socialist Giacomo Matteotti had particularly aroused anti-Fascist sentiment, Blackshirt *squadre* (squads) set about terrorising anyone suspected of antipathy towards their glorious movement. The violence in Florence became so alarming that Mussolini sent people in to shake out the local organisation and put a brake on the bloodshed.

WWII

For Italy, the real tragedy began in June 1940, when Mussolini decided to take the plunge and join Hitler's European tour. One disaster led to another and by 8 September 1943, when Italy surrendered to the Allies, the latter's troops were about to land at Salerno, south of Naples. But the Allies were a long way from Tuscany, which now became occupied territory under the Germans and a nasty band of die-hard Italian Fascists.

Resistance groups began to operate in Tuscany almost immediately and the mountainous and hilly countryside was frequently the stage for partisan assaults and German reprisal. Allied bombers meanwhile caused heavy damage to coastal cities such as Piombino and Livorno. Pisa too was badly bombed, while raids on Florence were comparatively light.

By July 1944, Free French troops occupied the island of Elba. At the same time, Allied forces approached the German lines near Florence. At this point, the German high command decided to blow the city's bridges, sparing only the Ponte Vecchio (some say it was Hitler who ordered it be spared). Allied troops moved into the city later that day, and Pisa and Lucca both fell to the Allies in the first days of September.

The Germans, meanwhile, had fallen back to one of their planned defensive lines, the so-called Gothic Line, which stretched from the Versilia coast across the Apuane Alps and Garfagnana, and on across the Apennines to Rimini on the Adriatic coast. The Allies first breached the line in heavy fighting in November and December, but winter delayed their advance and they did not finally break through to the Po valley and force the Germans north until April 1945.

To the Present

In the 1946 referendum on whether to institute a republic or a monarchy, 71.6% of Tuscans voted, along with most of Italy, for a republic. Since then the people of Tuscany have watched the comings and goings of national governments (59 since WWII) from a distance, concerned primarily with what's happening in their region. For more information on Tuscan politics since WWII, see Government & Politics later in this chapter.

Disaster struck in November 1966 when the River Arno burst its banks in Florence after torrential rain. Some 14,000 families were left homeless and the impact on the city's art treasures was incalculable. The clean-up process was long and arduous, but more complex still was the restoration of monuments, paintings and manuscripts that had been damaged but not lost. Funds and experts poured in from around the world to help out. If anything good can be said to have resulted from the flood, then it was the great advances made in art restoration. Florence remains a world centre in this field to this day.

Twenty years later, Florence again hit the international headlines when Lando Conti, the city's mayor, was killed by the left-wing Red Brigades. Terrorism called again in 1993 when a car bomb killed five people, injured 37 and damaged the Uffizi gallery, destroying several works of art in the process. In 2000, top Mafia bosses Leoluca Bagarella and Filippo Graviano were imprisoned for their part in the bombing. A third, Bernardo Provenzano, remains on the run but was sentenced in his absence.

The same year saw Florence in the diplomatic spotlight as NATO ministers converged on the city to discuss defence tactics, including somewhat controversial plans for a rapid reaction force.

But while newsworthy events may centre on the region's famous capital, Tuscany itself has become known on the international stage as a tourist destination – and a popular one at that. Although tourism obviously brings its benefits, namely in the form of the tourist dollar, the impact of thousands of visitors streaming through famous monuments and small villages is, inevitably, changing the face of Tuscany forever.

GEOGRAPHY

If you regard Tuscany's coast as the base, the region forms a rough triangle covering 22,992 sq km. Crammed within that triangle is a remarkable variety of land forms, from mountains in the north and east to flat plains in the south, from islands off the coast to hill country in the interior sliced up by river valleys.

Much of the coast facing the Tyrrhenian and Ligurian seas is flat, with the major exception of a stretch immediately south of Livorno and parts of the Monte Argentario peninsula.

The northern flank of the region, which runs roughly from east to west (with a gradual southwards drop), is closed off by the Apennines, which it shares with Emilia (part of the Emilia-Romagna region) and the Apuane Alps. These latter mountains in the north-western corner of the region are renowned for their white marble deposits (see Carrara in the North-Western Tuscany chapter).

Lower hill ranges rise farther south in the region, such as those of Monte Albano south of Pistoia and Monte Pratomagno in Arezzo province to the east. Separating them is a series of low river valleys, the most important of which is the Arno. In all, two-thirds of Tuscany is mountainous or hilly.

The most extensive lowlands are the Maremma Pisana, one-time swamps south of Pisa and in from the coast, and its southerly extension, the Maremma, which covers a wide area down to the regional boundary with Lazio.

The River Arno, at 240 windy kilometres long, is Tuscany's main river, although it is hardly one of the world's great natural wonders. It rises in Monte Falterona in the Apennines, flows south to Arezzo and then meanders north-west for a while. By the time it passes through Florence it is on a westwards course towards Pisa and finally the Ligurian Sea. Once an important trade artery, traffic on the river today is virtually nonexistent.

Of the seven islands scattered off Tuscany's coast, the central and eastern parts of Elba, along with Giannutri and parts of Giglio, are reminders of a great Apennine wall that collapsed into the sea millions of years ago. Capraia, Montecristo, western Elba and parts of Giglio are the creation of volcanic activity. The islands are surprisingly varied, from the unexciting flatness of Pianosa to the rugged and rocky coastline of much of Elba, broken up here and there by small but often enchanting little coves and beaches.

CLIMATE

Tuscan summers can be hot and oppressive. Inland especially the heat can be suffocating. The Chianti hills and the valleys are the worst. Being in Florence in July and August is akin to sticking your head into a smelter oven. Temperatures along the coast are marginally lower. Some hill and mountain areas are also cooler.

The Vallombrosa and Camaldoli forests and especially the Apuane Alps can be a real relief from the heat – although even here you can easily strike very hot weather.

In general, daytime highs of 35°C are more the norm than the exception. You can expect this kind of weather from late June to well into September.

Spring and autumn are the most delightful times of year, although the latter can be wet. Rainfall in October and especially November is heavy. Average daytime highs of around 20 to 25°C are pleasant and ideal for countryside walks, such as in the Chianti region.

On the subject of walking, the Apuane Alps tend to be cooler than much of the rest of the region. They also happen to be the wettest zone in Tuscany, receiving up to 3000mm a year. The south-western side of this range enjoys a predominantly Mediterranean climate, warm in summer and mild in winter. The northern side and the Apennines, on the other hand, are colder in winter, with the temperature frequently plunging below zero, bringing regular snowfalls.

On the subject of winter, it is generally pretty chilly across the region – more than you might expect. Snowfalls and minimum temperatures around and below zero are common in inland hilly areas (such as Siena and Cortona). The coast enjoys a milder climate and Florence doesn't get snow too often.

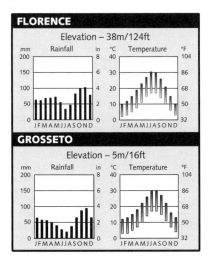

ECOLOGY & ENVIRONMENT

One of the greatest ecological headaches in Tuscany is the question of marble extraction in the mountains of the Apuane Alps. The great white scars (that from the seaside almost look like snowfalls) are the result of many centuries' work.

But never has the stone been removed at such a pace as today. Approximately 1.5 million tonnes per year are scraped away and trundled down to the coast on heavy trucks. Before WWII, the level of incursion was much slighter and marble miners eased blocks down to nearby villages with complex pulley systems. The extraction is disfiguring part of what is considered a nature reserve, the waste produced is creating disposal problems and the heavy truck traffic is itself an ecological disaster. Everyone knows this but no one dares seriously object to one of Tuscany's prestige industries. Carrara marble is sought after worldwide by everyone from architects to sculptors.

Heavy industry never really came to Tuscany, so the problems of air and water pollution associated with industry elsewhere in Italy are not as great as here. That said, the medium- and light-industrial areas of Livorno, Piombino, suburban Florence and along the River Arno are far from hazard free. Heavy road traffic makes clean air a distant dream in Florence and in much of the heavily populated Prato-Pistoia area. Noise pollution can also be a problem in the cities.

The landscape of Tuscany has long seemed something of a work of art, with farmers alternating a patchwork quilt of farmland with stretches of forest. The postwar crisis in agriculture saw many farmers leave the land and in more remote spots, where wringing results from the earth was always a challenge at best, forest or scrub is reclaiming its territory. Sometimes this uncontrolled regrowth has a downside, helping propagate bushfires as occurred in the summers of 1998 and 2001.

FLORA & FAUNA
Flora

Tuscan farmland has long been appreciated as a visual treat, a pleasing mix of orderly human intervention and natural 'chaos'. In among the ubiquitous olive groves (olives were introduced in Etruscan times from the Middle East) and vineyards, a feast of trees and smaller plants thrives.

Tall, slender cypress and the odd flattened *pino marittimo* (or cluster pines, mainly on the coast) are among the most striking of Tuscany's call-sign trees. Driving down a cypress-lined country road on the way to a little village or vineyard is one of those pleasant daydreams that frequently become reality for the cross-country tourist in Tuscany. The cypress was introduced from Asia Minor in Roman times precisely for its decorative qualities.

Beech trees are common in the mountainous territory of the Apuane Alps, often competing for attention with chestnuts. Hunting for chestnuts is a favourite pastime on November weekends. Heating them up for eating is the next stage. In the Casentino and Vallombrosa areas of eastern Tuscany, deep, thick forests of pine, oak (one species of which is the cork, whose bark is all-important to the wine industry) and beech still cover important tracts of otherwise little-touched land. Other species include maple, hazelnut, alder and imported eucalyptus.

Springtime is obviously the brightest time of year, when whole valley floors and upland plains are bathed in a technicolour sea of wildflowers. They can include jonquils, crocuses, anemones, gentians and orchids.

Coastal and island areas boast typical Mediterranean *macchia,* or scrub.

Flower spotters should equip themselves with specialist books such as *Mediterranean Wild Flowers,* by M Blamey and C Grey Wilson.

Fauna

Cinghiale, or wild boar, has been on Tuscan menus since the days of the Etruscans, and the hills and coastal areas of the region still teem with these beasts. The only difference is that today most of them are the offspring of eastern European boar imported to make up for the depletion of local species. Although common enough, you will probably not spot them on walks in the countryside.

They are busy avoiding their nastiest enemy – the Tuscan hunter.

Among other animals fairly common in the Tuscan countryside are squirrels, rabbits, foxes, martens, weasels and hares. The badger and the black-and-white-quilled *istrice,* a porcupine supposedly imported from North Africa by the ancient Romans, for whom it was a particularly tasty morsel, are rarer. In parks such as the Parco Regionale della Maremma roe deer are frequently spotted, especially at dawn or dusk.

Wolves purportedly still roam the hills between Volterra and Massa Marittima, but some locals think they are actually only wild dogs. Either way, sightings are incredibly rare and you'd be very lucky to spot them. The wild cat is another predator that roams the scarcely populated areas of Tuscany, but because there are very few they are hardly ever seen.

On a more slithery note, you can encounter several kinds of snake. Most are harmless and, if you are walking, will glide out of your way if you give them warning (by treading heavily as you approach them). The only poisonous customer is the viper, which can be identified by its diamond markings. Rocky areas and the island of Elba are among its principal habitats.

Birdlife is varied in Tuscany. The best time of year for fully appreciating that variety is from November to around March, when many migratory species hang about in nature reserves along the coast, including Lago di Burano, Laguna di Orbetello and Monti dell'Uccellina. As many as 140 species of our winged friends call Tuscany home or use it as a stopover. They include the blackbird, black-winged stilt, buzzard, crow, dove, falcon, hawk, hoopoe, jay, kestrel, kingfisher, osprey, thrush, tit, woodpecker and wren.

The hunting season extends from early September to sometime in January. The opening and closure dates depend in part on what you want to hunt. Limits are imposed on how many of any given type of bird or animal you can bag in one day, and hunters are required to arm themselves with a licence and practise the activity in designated areas. Some game animals, such as wild boar, are considered pests in some areas and culled as such.

National Parks

Tuscany can claim two of Italy's 20 national parks: the Parco Nazionale dell'Arcipelago Toscano, Europe's largest marine park, and the Parco Nazionale delle Forest Casentinesi Monte Falterona Campigna on the border with Emilia-Romagna.

The region also has three regional parks, one in the Apuane Alps, one in the Maremma and one on the heavily urbanised coast near Livorno.

For more information on these parks, visit W www.parks.it.

GOVERNMENT & POLITICS

At the time of writing, Italy's president is Carlo Azeglio Ciampi and the prime minister is the somewhat controversial Silvio Berlusconi (a media-magnate who is enjoying his second spell in office), who heads up Italy's 59th government since 1945.

From unification in 1861 until 1948, Italy was governed as a centralised state. When the parliamentary republic was formed in 1948, five regions (Friuli-Venezia Giulia, Sicily, Sardinia, Trentino-Alto Adige and Valle d'Aosta) were given special autonomous statutes on either ethnic or particular political grounds. They thus gained wide administrative powers, albeit within limits set by the state. The other 15 regions, Tuscany included, had to wait until 1970 and then only gained limited powers.

The PCI – the Italian Communist Party – won the first regional assembly elections in 1970 with 42.3% of the votes. The Democristiani (Christian Democrats), who until the late 1980s dominated Italian national politics, came in second with 30.6% of the vote, and the Socialists third with 8.8%. Indeed, while Florence often votes right, the region tends to lean to the red.

The *giunta regionale* (regional government) is headed by the Presidente della Regione and is formed after elections (every four years) to the *consiglio regionale* (regional parliament). It has no revenue-raising powers and receives funds from the state. It legislates on a limited range of issues, such as tourism and the hospitality industry, agriculture and forests, museums and libraries, some areas of professional training, markets and fairs and so on, and tends to act primarily as a coordinator between the state and the region. The current Presidente della Regione is Claudio Martini.

The Tuscans, with their strong regional loyalties and distrust of the central state, believe that more power should be devolved to the region. Since the 1990s the region, along with others, has been campaigning to this effect and with some success. It is now envisaged that more powers, including the crucial ability to raise revenue, will be slowly and quietly handed over to the regions.

The region of Tuscany is subdivided into 10 provinces, which are in turn separated into a total of 287 *comuni* (town or city councils). If the regional government is the coordinator, the *consiglio provinciale* (provincial government) does all the nuts-and-bolts work, in conjunction with its town councils. The latter function much as local governments anywhere, providing local transport, civic services (such as rubbish collection and street cleaning) and so on. The *giunta comunale* (town council's government) is headed up by a *sindaco* (mayor).

ECONOMY

Tuscany hit its economic peak in the Middle Ages. The countryside profited by supplying many of the raw materials, from farm produce and meat through to metals and marble, needed by the cities, while the cities became, to a greater or lesser extent, thriving trade and banking centres.

Florence emerged as the front runner, but Siena, until crushed by its jealous rival, was also a flourishing banking centre (the Monte dei Paschi di Siena bank remains one of Italy's senior financial institutions). Smaller towns thrived as well. Prato, for instance, became, and long remained, an important wool and textile centre, while Arezzo was famed for its gold.

The gradual eclipse of Florence as a power in the wake of the Renaissance brought overall decline to Tuscany too. By the 18th century, Tuscany had largely been reduced to a rural backwater. At the end of the 19th century, 57% of the workforce worked the land, mostly along traditional lines. The bulk of *mezzadri* (farmers) worked the big landholders' land, taking a share of the profit. Farm machinery had been tried out but largely failed to take off, partly due to the difficulty of the terrain in some areas. Even in the flatlands of the Maremma, drained and reclaimed over the previous two centuries, agriculture remained largely labour-intensive, mostly because landowners did not wish to invest in machinery and the farmers themselves could not afford to.

Industry was noticeable mostly by its absence, although mining (iron on Elba, marble in the Apuane Alps and copper, mercury, lignite and other raw materials around the region) benefited from a growing demand, especially from more rapidly industrialising countries abroad.

All told, however, Tuscany remained a predominantly agricultural economy until the mid-1950s. Even then, although small-scale manufacturing spread (the main areas being the suburbs of Florence, the north-western towns and Livorno on the coast), heavy industry never really came to Tuscany.

Instead, the 'Tuscan model' was born. Amid much doom-mongering on the part of trade unions and business groups, small light-industrial firms established themselves across the region. The pessimists, who might have hoped for massive industrialisation and phalanxes of smoke stacks, saw in this phenomenon a precarious and short-term solution to Tuscany's undoubted backwardness. But, at a time when agriculture was in crisis and a flood of labour flowed towards the urban centres and the coast, this micro-industrial expansion saved Tuscany's bacon.

In the period from the end of WWII to 1970, employment in the non-agricultural sector grew by 70%, industrialisation by 115%, and the Tuscan model spread to other parts of central and north-eastern Italy, leaving the heavy industry to the north-west.

As if in recognition of a centuries-old tradition of family business, small- and medium-size enterprises became the motor of Tuscany's economic regeneration. Tradition wasn't the only spur, however. Heavy state interference in big industry and a desire to sidestep militant unionism through diffusion of employment also influenced the tendency.

For most observers, Tuscany was already a 'post-industrial' society by the end of the 1970s. For alongside small-scale industry, the service sector was growing fast. Fashion, tourism, financial services and the like began to make up a growing slice of the income pie.

Tourism is one of the central pillars of the modern Tuscan economy. Florence alone received 3.75 million visitors in 2000 (compared with 2.9 million in 1998), generating €2.25 billion in related business turnover. Other sources of income include the production and export of quality textiles, clothes and shoes, leather goods, furniture and jewellery. Quality agricultural products, including wine and olive oil, are also up there. In Florence other light-industrial products that power the local economy include food-processing, rubber goods and chemicals.

Total exports out of the region in 2000 were approximately 24% higher than imports, but relied largely on the success of the fashion, textiles and leather industries.

Bearing in mind that at the close of WWII farming was still the centrepiece of the Tuscan economy, it is a measure of how radical change has been that now only 3.7% of the Tuscan pool of labour works the land. The light-industrial sector takes up 34%, while the rest of the 1.4-million-strong workforce are occupied in other sectors (principally tourism, banking and other services). Unemployment stood at 6.5% of the total workforce in 2000.

POPULATION & PEOPLE

The total population of Tuscany was just over 3.5 million at the last count (1999), including 80,000 foreigners who have made Tuscany their home and one million people living in the regional capital. Most people live in the north-west in an area bounded by Florence, Livorno, Massa and Pistoia. Prato province is the most crowded, with 614 people per square kilometre.

By comparison, the centre, south and east have a good deal more breathing space. Siena province has 66 people per square kilometre, while Grosseto has just 48.

The make-up of the family unit is perhaps surprising in view of the traditional child-friendliness associated with Italians in general. In line with a national trend, approximately a third of Tuscan families are childless (Italy's birth rate is one of the lowest in Europe).

In recent years Italy has become popular with immigrants from North Africa, Albania and Kosovo, and Tuscany, Florence particularly, is no exception. Internal migration also takes place. Although migrants from the south traditionally favour northern cities such as Milan and Turin, Florence is also a popular spot.

EDUCATION

Italy's state school system is free of charge and compulsory up the age of 14; the nationwide literacy rate of 97% is in line with the European average.

The Italians have a long tradition of further education and Tuscany is no exception. The main university centres are Florence, Siena and Pisa. The latter is the oldest of the three and can claim Galileo Galilei as one of its former masters, while Siena is famous today for its Università per Stranieri (University for Foreigners; see Siena in the Central Tuscany chapter for more details on the courses available).

Florence's main centre of study is the Università degli Studi di Firenze. It traces its history back to the Studium Generale established in 1321. Pope Clement VI granted this institution permission to issue full degrees in 1349, after the universities of Bologna and Paris. Italy's first theology faculty was also founded in Florence. In successive centuries the various faculties were split up and spread across the city and Pisa. In 1860, the Istituto di Studi Pratici e di Perfezionamento (Institute for Practical Studies and Further Education) was established in Florence under the auspices of the newly united Italy. It was finally elevated officially to university status in 1923.

SCIENCE & PHILOSOPHY

Tuscany, indeed Italy in general, are not readily associated with dramatic scientific discovery but the region does boast some very famous names in this field.

Although he considered himself first and foremost an artist (see Leonardo da Vinci under Painting later for more details), Tuscan-born Leonardo da Vinci (1452–1519) was perhaps the greatest polymath of his time. His curiosity led him into a vast array of fields of knowledge, including anatomy, zoology, botany, geology, optics, aerodynamics and hydrodynamics.

Anxious to win greater insight into the human body in order to be better able to portray it, he carried out numerous dissections which he recorded as striking anatomical drawings. For the time they were a unique and insightful medical tool.

An architect and engineer, Leonardo was also at home with mechanics. His biggest contribution to scientific progress was the systematic use of diagrams to illustrate engineering principles. He also envisaged flying machines and even armoured vehicles centuries before they would become reality.

Perhaps less famous today but certainly more controversial during his lifetime was Galileo Galilei (1564–1642), a Pisan who became Mathematician and Natural Philosopher to the Grand Duchy of Tuscany before facing the wrath of the Church. See the boxed text 'The World Turns' later in this chapter for more details.

Other famous sons include Leon Battista Alberti and Filippo Brunelleschi, both of whom applied mathematical principles to the art of building and made significant contributions to the development of architecture and the role of the architect as both an artist and a scientist.

And Tuscan minds have also contributed to the field of philosophy. Humanism, the intellectual movement of the Renaissance, was based on Greek and Latin classical learning and placed man at the centre of human interests, activities and concerns. Over time, this way of thinking would spread its influence far and wide. On a political note, Niccolò Machiavelli's writings on government and

The World Turns

'*Eppur si muove*', Galileo is supposed to have mut-
tered after having been compelled to recant his
teachings on astronomy before the Inquisition in
Rome in 1633. 'And yet it does move'. He was re-
ferring to the Earth, whose exalted position at the
centre of the universe he so inconveniently maintained
was a falsehood. The Earth, along with other planets,
rotated around the Sun, just as Copernicus had claimed.

JANE SMITH

As long ago as 1616 Galileo had been ordered not to push
this theory, which conservative Vatican elements not overly
well disposed to the 'new learning' saw as a potential threat to
the Church. If long-established teachings about the position of
the world in God's universe were condemned as balderdash, the
long-established place of the Church in society would be ques-
tioned. The growing insistence on humankind's capacity to
reveal what makes things tick, rather than simply remaining
awestruck by the divine majesty of it all, was singularly inconvenient to those intent on maintaining the Church's position of pre-eminence in worldly and spiritual affairs.

Galileo was born in Pisa on 15 February 1564, the son of a musician. He received his early education at the monastery of Vallombrosa near Florence and later studied medicine at the University
of Pisa. During his time there he became fascinated by mathematics and the study of motion, so
much so that he is regarded as the founder of experimental physics. He became professor of mathematics in Pisa and then moved to Padua for 18 years to teach and research there.

Having heard of the invention of the telescope in 1609, he set about making his own version, the
first used to scan the night skies. In the coming years he made discoveries that led him to confirm
Copernicus' theory that the planets revolve around the Sun. In 1610 he moved to Florence, where
the Grand Duke had offered him permanent residence to continue his research. Galileo had many
supporters but not enough to prevent his works on the subject being placed on the index of banned
books in 1616.

For the next seven years he continued his studies in Florence, where he lived mainly at Bellosguardo. The 1616 edict declaring his teachings on astronomy blasphemous was softened in 1624
to the extent that he was given permission to write an 'objective study' of the various proposed
models. His study was a triumph of argumentation in favour of his own theory, culminating nevertheless in the obligatory disclaimer that remained imposed on him. It was in the wake of this that
the first Inquisition summoned him to Rome in 1632. From then on he was confined to internal exile
in Florence until his death in 1642. Until his last days, even after blindness had beset him in 1637,
he continued to study, experiment, correspond with other scientists across Europe and write books.
He lies buried in the Basilica di Santa Croce.

the realities of power in *Il Principe* (The
Prince; 1532) were a turning point in political philosophy, in that he was concerned with
how to maintain power rather than how to
justify power in the first place. See the boxed
text 'Machiavell's Manoeuvres' later in this
chapter for more details.

ARTS

The undisputed beauty of the Tuscan countryside is matched by the extraordinary
artistic output of its people. From the Middle Ages through to the Renaissance in particular, Tuscany's cities were hives of such
creativity that it is hardly surprising they

have not been able to match, in either quality or quantity, the output of those troubled but glorious centuries. From the visual arts to literature, although less so in music, the Tuscans left an indelible mark on the culture of Italy, and indeed all Europe.

Architecture

Etruscan & Roman Comparatively few ancient reminders of Etruscan and Roman civilisation remain today in Tuscany.

Of the Etruscans, the most common reminders of their presence are tombs scattered about the Tuscan countryside, particularly in the south. A rare exception is the archaeological site of Poggio Civitate, near Murlo (south of Siena), consisting of a couple of buildings – one dating back to the 7th century BC (the site is closed to visitors).

Of the tombs, two general types emerge. The first is cut deep into a rock wall, with a steep declining walkway or steps to the entrance. The tomb is generally formed of an atrium and burial chamber. Others created more in the open were surrounded by a low wall and covered with a low dome or vault, above which was heaped a mound of earth. Good examples of both can be seen in Populonia, on the coast just north of Piombino. Another well-known site is Sorano, in southern Tuscany.

It is perhaps more surprising that so little evidence of Roman times remains. In Volterra, Arezzo and Fiesole you can admire Roman amphitheatres but that's about it. Virtually nothing remains of Roman Florentia (today's Florence).

Romanesque Out of the confusion of the collapse of the Roman Empire and the early medieval centuries of barbarian invasion and foreign rule, several fairly simple building styles emerged in Italy. One such style was Romanesque, which had its roots in the simple defensive designs of the Roman Empire. It emerged in the northern Lombard plains and was readily adopted by Tuscan architects.

Of course, we're not talking about the average citizen's humble abode, which was usually flimsy, precarious wooden housing, but about monumental buildings such as churches, government palaces and mansions for the rich and powerful. Of these, few nonreligious buildings survive, so the best examples of the Romanesque style tend to be churches or cathedrals. Tuscan countryside and villages are littered with Romanesque churches of greater or lesser beauty.

The standard church ground plan, generally composed of a nave and two aisles, no transept and between one and five apses, topped by a simple dome, followed that used in Roman-era basilicas. Initially, at any rate, churches tended to be bereft of decoration except for the semi-circular apses and arches above doorways and windows. Such churches were most commonly accompanied by a free-standing square-based bell tower, also adorned with layers of semi-circular arched windows.

In Tuscany, the early rediscovery of that favourite of Roman building materials, marble, led to a rather more florid decorative style, the best examples of which you can see in Pisa and Lucca. The key characteristics of the Tuscan variant are the use of two-tone marble banding and complex rows of columns and loggias in the facade. The cathedral in Carrara, begun in the 11th century, was one of the first medieval buildings to be constructed entirely of marble from the Apuane Alps.

The Battistero (Baptistry; see later in this chapter) in Florence, embellished in its marble casing, is a fine example of the pure lines of the Romanesque style. Compare it with the Gothic mass of the Duomo (Cathedral) next door. Also in Florence, the Chiesa di San Miniato al Monte is a splendid example of the style. The Pieve di Santa Maria in Arezzo is another fine version, although in this instance lacking the refinement of a marble facing.

Gothic The transition across Europe from Romanesque to the massive forms of the Gothic was uniformly spectacular but extraordinarily varied in its results. Compared with their humble Romanesque predecessors the Gothic versions are colossal. The process began in the Île de France area around Paris, where the first truly Gothic churches were built from the 12th century – at a time when elsewhere in Europe Romanesque was still the predominant style.

The one element most Gothic structures have in common is their great height. Soaring structures, it was felt, would lift mortal eyes to the heavens and at the same time remind people of their smallness compared with the greatness of God. These complex structures were perfected using pillars, columns, arches and vaulting of various kinds to support high ceilings. Rather than relying on the solidity of mass and building thick, heavy walls, priority was given to an almost diaphanous light pouring though tall pointed windows. The whole thing was topped by a virtually obsessive desire to decorate. These churches are bedecked with pinnacles, statues, gargoyles and all sorts of baubles – the busier the better.

However, the Tuscan version of Gothic is somewhat different to the improbable lace stonework of the great Gothic cathedrals of northern Europe, such as Notre Dame in Paris. Although still of the epic proportions that are the trademark of the Gothic style, Gothic churches in Tuscany are comparatively unadorned. Instead, they are characterised by rich marble decoration. In terms of volume they are every bit as impressive as their Northern counterparts, as the cathedrals of Florence and Siena, plus the churches of Santa Croce and Santa Maria Novella in Florence, will testify.

Florence's Duomo was designed by Arnolfo di Cambio (1245–1302), the first great master builder in Florentine architectural history. Arnolfo was also responsible for applying the Gothic style to one of Florence's great civic structures, the Palazzo Vecchio. Built of *pietra forte* (literally 'hard stone') with the rusticated surface typical of many later grand buildings in Florence, it is one of the most imposing of the medieval Italian city state government buildings.

It is easily matched by Siena's Palazzo Pubblico which, with its slender Torre del Mangia, is one of the finest examples of civic Gothic construction in Tuscany. Built at the turn of the 14th century, this elegant

seat of Sienese government was expanded in the following decades.

Bad Boy Brunelleschi Enter Filippo Brunelleschi (1377–1446), one of the hotter tempers in the history of Italian architecture. After failing to win the 1401 competition to design a set of bronze doors for Florence's Battistero, Brunelleschi left in a creative huff for Rome. His intention had been to study and continue with sculpture, but his interests moved to mathematics and architecture. He and his sculptor pal Donatello spent much of their time taking measurements of ancient Roman monuments, research that later would come to spectacular fruition. Locals, however, thought they were using bizarre divining methods to look for buried treasure!

Brunelleschi launched the architectural branch of the Renaissance in Florence. It manifested itself in a rediscovery of simplicity and purity in classical building, with great attention paid to perspective and harmonious distribution of space and volume. His single most remarkable achievement was solving the conundrum of the dome in Florence's Duomo. He proposed to build the octagonal-based dome without the aid of scaffolding, unheard of at the time. Brunelleschi's double-skinned dome, raised in sections, was the greatest feat of its kind since ancient times. In later years Michelangelo, when commissioned to create the dome for St Peter's in Rome, observed with undisguised admiration, *'Io farò la sorella, già più gran ma non più bella'* – I'll make its (the Brunelleschi dome's) sister, bigger yes, but no more beautiful.

That feat alone was tremendous but Brunelleschi's importance goes beyond the splendid dome. He 'created' the role of architect. Rather than act as a foreman, guiding construction as it progressed and to some extent making it up as he went along, Brunelleschi devised formulae of perspective and balance that allowed him to create a completed concept at the drawing board.

Other examples of Brunelleschi's keen sense of proportion, all in Florence, include the portico of the Spedale degli Innocenti

(Hospital of the Innocents; 1419), considered the earliest work of the Florentine Renaissance, the Sagrestia Vecchia (Old Sacristy) in the Basilica di San Lorenzo (1428) and the Cappella dei Pazzi in Santa Croce (1430).

Perhaps more importantly, Brunelleschi was also called upon to design the Basilica di San Lorenzo (1420) and the Basilica di Santo Spirito (designed in 1436). A quick wander inside both might lead you to think they are identical. The use of Corinthian columns, simple arches, a coffered ceiling over the wide nave (merely painted in Santo Spirito) and two-tone (grey *pietra serena,* literally 'tranquil stone', and white plaster on the trim) colouring are common elements, but closer inspection soon reveals differences. Brunelleschi had planned for Santo Spirito to be lined with semi-circular chapels jutting out into the square around it, but these were walled in by his successors. Santo Spirito is an altogether heavier, more massive church in its feel, while San Lorenzo oozes a light elegance.

Brunelleschi more than once flounced out of meetings and dropped projects if he did not get his own way. But it was he who launched a new era in building design and philosophy, so he can probably be forgiven his short fuse.

Florence & the Renaissance Brunelleschi did little outside Florence and, under the patronage of the Medici and other senior families, it was in Florence that the Tuscan Renaissance flourished. Not that things weren't happening elsewhere in the region, but the growing power of Florence in the coming centuries effectively meant that most of the artistic impulses came from what was to become the capital.

Other cities remained immune to the Renaissance for some time. Well into the 15th century, for example, Siena's architects and artists were still well rooted in the Gothic.

It was in Florence, thus, that the Renaissance truly took off. It is generally accepted that Michelozzo di Bartolomeo Michelozzi (1396–1472) was commissioned by Cosimo de' Medici to build a new residence that was in keeping with the family's importance (Palazzo Medici-Riccardi). Three

hefty storeys, with the air of a fortress, are topped by a solid roof with eaves jutting far out from the walls. The lowest storey features rustication (which can also be seen on the Palazzo Vecchio). This describes the rough-hewn, protruding blocks of stone used to build it, as opposed to the smoothed stone of the upper storeys. This set the tone for civic building in Florence.

The acclaimed theorist of Renaissance architecture and art was Leon Battista Alberti, author of *De Re Aedificatoria* (On Architecture; 1452–72) as well as treatises on painting and sculpture. Born in Genoa into an exiled Florentine family, he contributed the facade of the Palazzo Rucellai, a development of the style started with Michelozzo.

Other Renaissance palaces represent variations on the style and lend Florence its uniquely stern yet elegant feel. One example is the palace of the Strozzi family, designed by Benedetto da Maiano (1442–97) with facade work by Giuliano da Sangallo (1445–1516). This particular aspect of Florentine Renaissance building was echoed in buildings in other parts of Tuscany, especially the nearby northern towns of Prato, Pistoia and Pisa – and often many years after the Renaissance had been left behind.

Francesco di Giorgio (1439–1502) was about the only architect of any note to come out of Siena during the Renaissance. An accomplished painter and sculptor as well, his only lasting building is the Chiesa di Santa Maria del Calcinaio, a few kilometres outside Cortona. His was an original vision – he dropped the use of pillars and columns to separate aisles from a central nave. Instead, the building is a solid, two-storey construction with tabernacle windows on the second level.

Michelangelo Born into a poor family, Michelangelo Buonarroti (1475–1564) got a lucky break early on, entering the Medici household as a privileged student of painting and sculpture. In later years he also turned his attention to building design, although his architectural activities in Florence were not extensive. Indeed, much of his greatest work was done in Rome, where the majesty of the High Renaissance left even Florence gasping in the dust.

In Florence, Michelangelo worked on the Sagrestia Nuova (New Sacristy) in the Basilica di San Lorenzo, intended as part of the funerary chapels for the Medici family. Although not completed as planned, this was as close as Michelangelo got to realising one of his architectural-sculptural whims.

Another of Michelangelo's tasks in the same church was the grand staircase and entrance hall for the Biblioteca Medicea Laurenziana (Laurentian Library). Michelangelo never saw it completed, as he returned to Rome. It is a startling late-Renaissance creation, with columns recessed into the walls (and thus deprived of their natural supporting function) and other architectural oddities since seen as precursors of Mannerism.

Mannerism The High Renaissance ended around 1520. Certainly by 1527, with the sack of Rome by Charles V's imperial forces, it was all over, if only because war and suffering had depleted the funds and snuffed out the desire to continue creating in such quantity.

What followed is generally called Mannerism, although this intermediate phase between the Renaissance and Baroque is not easily defined. For many, Michelangelo's work in San Lorenzo is a clear precursor to the Mannerist period. For others, the Mannerists were a fairly unimaginative lot, fiddling around the edges of what had been the core of Renaissance thinking in architecture without making substantive innovations.

Antonio da Sangallo il Giovane (1485–1546), son of another Florentine architect and sculptor, Antonio da Sangallo il Vecchio (1455–1534), worked mostly in Rome, although he returned briefly to Florence to build the Fortezza da Basso in 1534 for Alessandro de' Medici. His father had worked on several projects in Rome and around Tuscany, including the Chiesa della Madonna di San Biagio and several civic buildings in Montepulciano, as well as the Fortezza Vecchia in Livorno.

Bartolomeo Ammannati (1511–92) expanded Florence's Palazzo Pitti into a suburban palace for the Medici dukes and designed the Ponte Santa Trinita. He also had a hand in the design of the Giardino di Boboli.

Arezzo-born Giorgio Vasari (1511–74) left his mark in Florence with the creation of the Uffizi and the Corridoio Vasariano that links Palazzo Vecchio with Palazzo Pitti across the Arno. Bernardo Buontalenti (1536–1608) succeeded Vasari as architect to the Grand Duke of Tuscany. He designed the Forte di Belvedere and the Palazzo Nonfinito on Via del Proconsolo, which differs from Renaissance predecessors principally in decorative flounces on the facade.

Don't Baroque the Boat The 17th century saw a construction slowdown throughout Tuscany. This was the era of Baroque, which often had more impact on decor than on architectural design. At its most extreme, particularly in Rome, such decoration was sumptuous to the point of giddiness – all curvaceous statuary, twisting pillars and assorted baubles.

These are the exception rather than the norm in Tuscany, but some examples of the style can be found in the region, for example, the villas near Lucca, the cathedral in Pescia and the frenzied interior of the Basilica di Santa Maria del Carmine in Florence. The regional capital also boasts the Chiesa di San Gaetano and the facade for the Chiesa d'Ognissanti. The former, finished by Gherardo Silvani (1579–1675), is considered the finest piece of Baroque in Florence and a demonstration of the restraint typical of the city.

Urban Renewal The first tentative moves towards urban renewal in some Tuscan cities came early in the 19th century. Under Napoleon's representative, Elisa Baciocchi, for instance, Lucca's walls were turned into the velvet green garden area surrounding the old city that you see today.

In Florence, public works programmes also got under way. The space around the southern flank of the Duomo was cleared and fronted by neoclassical buildings. The architect behind that project was Gaetano Baccani (1792–1867). East and west of the town centre two new bridges went up on the

Mostly Madonnas

As so much of the art of medieval and Renaissance Europe falls into distinct thematic groups, the titles of many paintings in particular are nearly always the same. You will rarely see such stock titles translated into English in Tuscany, so a handful of clues follows.

A *Crocifissione* (Crucifixion) represents the crucifixion of Christ, one of the most common subjects of religious art. Another is the *Deposizione* (Deposition), which depicts the taking down of the body of Christ from the cross, while the *Pietá*, a particularly popular subject for sculptors, shows the lifeless body of Christ in the arms of his followers – the characters can vary, but the theme remains the same. Before all the nastiness began, Christ managed to have an *Ultima Cena*, or Last Supper, with the Apostles.

Perhaps the most favoured subject is the *Madonna col Bambino/Bimbo* (Virgin Mary with Christ Child). The variations on this theme are legion. Sometimes they are depicted alone, sometimes with various *santi* (saints), *angeli* (angels) and other figures. The *Annunciazione* (Annunciation) is yet another standard episode, when the Angel Gabriel announces to Mary the strange honour that has been bestowed on her. When the big event occurred, lots of people, including the *Magi* (Wise Men) came to participate in the *Adorazione* (Adoration) of the newly born Christ.

Arno, the Ponte San Niccolò and the Ponte Vittoria.

By the end of the century the walls had been torn down and replaced by a series of *viali* (boulevards) that still carry the bulk of the city's traffic today. Perhaps worst of all, the core of old Florence, around what had been the Roman forum, was flattened to make way for the grandiloquent Piazza della Repubblica in the 1890s.

The Mercato Centrale (finished in 1874) is a rare Florentine example of the late-19th-century passion for iron-and-glass structures, designed by Giuseppe Mengoni (1829–77), the Bologna-born architect responsible for Milan's Galleria.

To the Present To the Italians, the Art Nouveau style that took hold of the architectural imagination in Europe from the 1880s through to the interwar period is known as Liberty (after the London store of that name). Examples of it are dotted about the main cities of Tuscany although often they are rather modest. One exception is Viareggio, which is crammed with Liberty buildings. In an area stretching back four or five blocks from the seashore the buff can feast on 40 or so edifices with at least some Liberty traces. In central Florence one of the best examples is the Casa Galleria by

Giovanni Michelazzi (1879–1920), at Borgo Ognissanti 26.

If you're determined to seek these examples out, pick up a copy of *Le Stagioni del Liberty in Toscana* (available in several languages), a pink booklet available in tourist offices around the region.

Mussolini's rise to power also left its stamp on the architecture of the region, most notably in the grandiose buildings of Florence's train station and main football stadium.

Sadly for a region so rich in the architecture of the past, Tuscany has seen little flourishing of architectural talent or visionary town planning since WWII. Cities and towns such as Livorno, which were heavily damaged during WWII, were generally at the receiving end of an unsympathetic postwar reconstruction boom. Florence, as Tuscany's capital, has been plagued by uncontrolled urban sprawl, particularly to the west. Nothing could be further from the ideals of Brunelleschi's finest structures than the soulless, fast-buck housing and light-industrial zones that now virtually fill the area between Florence and Prato.

Painting

The painting to emerge in medieval Europe – and Tuscany was no exception – was not so much a response to an aesthetic need, as a means of keeping alive in the minds of the faithful the stories of the Bible and teachings of the church. Art was devotional and instructive, as most people, even among the wealthiest classes, were illiterate or as near as dammit. For this reason, as you will soon come to notice the more you study the paintings that fill churches and galleries across Tuscany, many themes became standard and crop up repeatedly. The bulk of Romanesque, Byzantine and Gothic art was commissioned (although not always paid for) by the Church for religious institutions. The clergy generally had a clear idea of what they wanted and gave precise instructions to painters. The latter were viewed much as tradespeople are today. There was little exaltation of their skills and until the dawn of the Renaissance few artists even signed their work.

As greater individuality and an aesthetic appreciation of painting, apart from its didactic or devotional purposes, emerged with the Renaissance, so its practitioners gained in social standing. In Florence especially, but also elsewhere in Tuscany and beyond, lay people began to commission art, either for public places or their own homes. This promoted a broadening of themes such as battle scenes, portraits (generally busts) and scenes from classical mythology, but even through the Renaissance and beyond, much of the output remained faithful to a series of frequently stock religious icons. Innovation was not always easy under such conditions.

Renaissance Florence was the uncontested centre of Tuscan art and for a while could be said to have held primacy in all Italy. With the passing of the Renaissance, Florence and Tuscany as a whole stagnated and the great revolutions in Western art, whether in painting or sculpture, took place on other stages. That remains the case to this day.

Antiquity It is difficult to talk of 'Etruscan art' and perhaps more appropriate to view it as art created in Etruscan territory. What has been preserved comes largely from tombs. Painted ceramics, statues and the like from around the 8th century BC are all marked by an eastern predilection for geometrical designs.

Greek influence was also strong, particularly along the southern coast of Etruria (modern Tuscany and into Lazio), where there was direct contact with Greek traders. Fresco painting in tombs seems to have started in Tarquinia (Lazio) and was later developed in the Chiusi area. It is worth noting that the greatest concentration of Greek ceramics found in Italy turned up on Etruscan territory.

As Roman expansion gathered pace, Etruscan artistic activity declined, although it knew one final creative spurt in the last two centuries BC. The Romans were a rather coarse lot – they only began to embark on artistic endeavours around the 2nd century BC. Heavily influenced by the Etruscans and, hence, indirectly by the Greeks, there was little original about their early output. In any case, precious little has been left to us in Tuscany. The great frescoes of Pompeii or mosaics of Roman towns from Sicily to Syria are but a distant dream.

Emerging from the Middle Ages Not until the 13th century does any original artistic activity seem to get underway again in Tuscany. As the cities freed themselves from imperial or feudal control in the course of the 12th century, so art seems to have begun to free itself from the inherited rigidity of Romanesque and Byzantine norms.

Lagging behind sculptural activity (described later in the chapter), the earliest surviving paintings appeared in churches ranging from Lucca's San Michele in Foro to Santa Croce in Florence. Other works began to appear in Arezzo, Siena and smaller centres such as Pescia. The Florentine Coppo di Marcovaldo (c.1225–80), imprisoned in Siena, ended up painting his *Madonna del Bordone* in the Chiesa di Santa Maria dei Servi before moving on to Orvieto and Pistoia.

In Tuscany Pisa was in the ascendant. Master of Sardinia and a busy sea trade port, Pisa was more open to external influences and artistic interchange than inland cities such as Florence. The first artist of note to make an impact in Florence was Cimabue (c.1240–1302). He began in Pisa

RUSSELL MOUNTFORD

Flowers and vines front a Sienese farmhouse.

JENNY JONES

Amazing glaze – Sienese ceramics

JOHN HAY

The Chianti region – huddled medieval villages amid forests, vineyards and olive groves

Typical farm and cypresses on the Pienza road

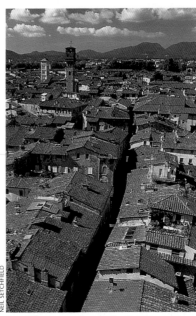

Lovely Lucca was founded by the Etruscans.

Relax on beaches and coves around Elba.

Early passion at a Fiorentina-Verona game

but later travelled all over Tuscany. Vasari identifies him as the catalyst for change in painting from the rigidity of Gothic and Byzantine models. In Florence, his *Maestà* (Majesty; in the Uffizi) amply demonstrates the transition from Byzantine-style iconography to a fresh exploration of expression and life-like dimension.

Giotto di Bondone (c.1266–1337), born in the Mugello north of Florence, was the key figure in the artistic revolution that was gathering pace in the run-up to the Renaissance explosion. Most of his Florentine contemporaries were to some degree influenced by him, and his is one of the pivotal names in the Italian artistic pantheon.

In Giotto's work the move from the symbolic, other-worldly representations of Italo-Byzantine and Gothic religious art to something more real, more directly inspired by observed truth than the desire to teach 'truths', is clear. His figures are essentially human and express feeling, something alien to earlier phases of art in Christian Europe.

He is better known for his work in towns such as Assisi (Basilica di San Francesco) and Padua (Cappella degli Scrovegni). However, several works are in Florence, among the most important of which are the frescoes in the Peruzzi and Bardi chapels in the Basilica di Santa Croce. Fresco painting involves painting watercolours directly onto wet plaster, a tricky business.

The Sienese School Although the focus of artistic life in Tuscany was already shifting to Florence, its southern rival, Siena, enjoyed a brief period of glory.

Guido da Siena (active in the second half of the 13th century), who seems to have been influenced by Coppo di Marcovaldo, left behind few works. The only signed one was the *Madonna col Bambino* in the Palazzo Pubblico.

The only artist in Siena to hold a candle to Giotto was Duccio di Buoninsegna (c.1255–1318). Although still much attached to the Byzantine school, he mixed the style with Gothic ideas and introduced a degree of fluidity and expressiveness that have led some to compare him with Cimabue. Various examples of his work can be seen in Siena cathedral and Florence's Uffizi. Duccio's star pupil was Simone Martini (c.1284–1344). Perhaps his most celebrated work is the *Annunciazione*, created for the cathedral in Siena but now hanging in the Uffizi.

Other artists of note in Siena included the brothers Pietro (c.1290–c.1348) and Ambrogio Lorenzetti (died c.1348). Both worked in Siena and elsewhere – Pietro was particularly active in Assisi. Ambrogio's best-known work is the startling *Effetti del Buon e del Cattivo Governo* (Allegories of Good and Bad Government) in Siena's Palazzo Pubblico.

As you trawl through the palazzi and galleries of Siena, it will sooner or later hit you that, for all the beauty of the masterpieces by Siena's greatest artists, they seem to stand still in time. While the Renaissance and subsequent movements gripped Florence, Siena remained supremely indifferent and plugged on with largely Byzantine and Gothic models. You can see this in the work of such painters as Taddeo di Bartolo (1362–1422) and even Giovanni di Paolo (1395–1482), who remained anchored in late Gothic, while in Florence people such as Uccello, Verrocchio and Filippo Lippi were turning painting on its head.

Giotto's Successors Confirmation of Giotto's influence comes in the work of several other painters active at the same time. Maso di Banco's (active prior to 1348) *Storie di San Silvestro* (Stories of St Sylvester) series (in Florence's Basilica di Santa Croce) reflects in its luminosity and simplicity the long shadow of his master, Giotto. The human faces also have a fullness and naturalness of expression that one might expect from Giotto, although they retain a Gothic stiffness in movement.

Andrea di Cione Orcagna (active from 1343 to 1368) represents something of a Gothic throwback. His most important remaining works are the tabernacle and other statuary inside the late-Gothic Orsanmichele and a polyptych in the Basilica di Santa Maria Novella. Flattened profiles and garish colouring fly in the face of the groundwork laid by Giotto.

Indeed, Gothic was anything but dead as the new century dawned and the two tendencies appeared in direct competition. One of Gothic's principal exponents in the first quarter of the 15th century in Florence was the Sienese painter Lorenzo Monaco (c.1370–c.1424). Several of his works are in the Uffizi.

Il Quattrocento & the Renaissance The

young Masaccio (1401–28) can probably be given a good deal of the credit for the definitive break with Gothic in Florentine painting. Born in an Arno village at the dawn of the 15th century (what the Italians call the Quattrocento, or the 'four hundreds'), his brief but dynamic career made him to painting what his older contemporaries, Brunelleschi and Donatello, were to architecture and sculpture. His genius is immediately apparent in his Florentine masterpieces, such as his frescoes in the Cappella Brancacci (Basilica di Santa Maria del Carmine), to recognise his genius. His best-known image, the *Cacciata dei Progenitori* (Expulsion) in the Cappella Brancacci, depicts all the anguish and shame of Adam and, especially, Eve. Such raw and believable human emotion was a novelty in painting.

Following in Masaccio's footsteps were two masters who in temperament could not have been more different from one another. Fra Angelico (c.1395–1455), a Dominican monk later known as Beato (Blessed) Angelico for his noted piety, for a while dominated the Florentine art world. His work, much of it done for the Convento di San Marco, is suffused with a diaphanous light aimed at emphasising the good in humankind. Although a friar, Fra Filippo Lippi (c.1406–69) had an appetite for sex, drink and general carousing that left him the father of two by a nun. Fra Filippo left some fine pieces behind in Florence. A *Madonna col Bambino e due Angeli* in the Uffizi and another in Palazzo Pitti (in the Sala di Prometeo) demonstrate his mastery of light and shadow, a weighty reality about the characters and an eye for detail.

A strange bird was Paolo Uccello (1397–1475). More preoccupied with perspective studies than making a living, Uccello did manage to crank out a few lasting pieces. They include the *Il Diluvio* (Great Flood) fresco in the Basilica di Santa Maria Novella and the *Battaglia di San Romano* (Battle of San Romano) done for the Medici family and now (in part) in the Uffizi.

Antonio del Pollaiuolo (c.1431–98) had a predilection for scenes of tension or struggle. His *Ercole e Anteo* (Hercules and Anteus), now in the Uffizi, amply demonstrates the emphasis on human movement, expressed with a freedom rarely witnessed until then.

The painting of Andrea del Verrocchio (1435–88), who is perhaps better known for his sculpture (see Sculpture later in this chapter), presents difficulties as it is often impossible to distinguish his work from that of his pupils. Among the latter was Leonardo da Vinci, with whom Verrocchio did the *Battesimo di Cristo* (now in the Uffizi).

Born in the remote south-east Tuscan town of Sansepolcro, Piero della Francesca (c.1415–92) went to Florence to learn from his predecessors and contemporaries but did the bulk of his work in his own neck of the woods, particularly in Arezzo and the Montefeltro court in Urbino (Le Marche). His *Leggenda della Vera Croce* (Legend of the True Cross) fresco cycle in the Chiesa di San Francesco in Arezzo is a masterpiece.

Luca Signorelli (1450–1523), born in Cortona, was a pupil of Piero della Francesca. He went on to become one of the great figures of the late Renaissance, specialising above all in grand, complex works, of which his fresco cycle in the cathedral in Orvieto (Umbria) is the uncontested masterpiece.

Sandro Botticelli (1445–1510) is remembered most for works such as *Nascita di Venere* (Birth of Venus) and *Allegoria della Primavera* (Allegory of Spring), both in the Uffizi. In these and other paintings of this ilk, flowing, ethereal figures seem to float serenely across the canvas in an idealised evocation of classical Greece.

Fra Filippo's son, Filippino Lippi (1457–1504), worked in Botticelli's workshop for a time but Lippi was more directly influenced by Leonardo da Vinci and Flemish artists. His frescoes of *Storie di San Giovanni Evangelista e San Filippo* (Stories of St John and St Philip) in the Cappella Strozzi in the Basilica di Santa Maria Novella reveal a move away from the humanist ideals of quattrocento painting.

Leonardo da Vinci Born in a small town west of Florence, Leonardo da Vinci (1452–1519) stands apart from all his contemporaries. How do you categorise a man who hardly belonged in his own time? Painter, sculptor, architect, scientist and engineer, Leonardo brought to all fields of knowledge and art an original touch, often opening up whole new branches of thought. If one had to sum up what made him tick, it might be 'seeing is believing'. In the thousands of notes he left behind, he repeatedly extolled the virtue of sight and observation. Paying little heed to received wisdoms, either Christian or classical, Leonardo barrelled along with unquenchable curiosity.

All his studies took up much of Leonardo's time, but he found plenty more to devote to what he saw as the noblest art, painting. Leonardo did much of his work outside Florence (he stayed in Milan for 20 years). One of his outstanding early works, the *Annunciazione,* now in the Uffizi, already revealed his concern with light and shadow, and with its representation through chiaroscuro.

Michelangelo While Leonardo was in Milan, Michelangelo Buonarroti (1475–1564) was asserting himself as a rival painter, albeit of a very different ilk. In contrast to Leonardo's smoky, veiled images, Michelangelo demonstrated a greater clarity of line. As a young lad he was taken in by Lorenzo de' Medici, who could spot talent when it presented itself. His greatest painting project was the ceiling of the Sistine Chapel in Rome. In Florence relatively little of his work can be seen, but the *Tondo Doni* (tondo means circular and Doni was the patron) in the Uffizi provides stunning insight into his craft. Details of his sculpture are given later in this chapter.

High Renaissance to Mannerism Fra Bartolomeo (1472–1517) stands out for such paintings as the *Apparizione della Vergina a San Bernardo* (Vision of St Bernard), now in the Galleria dell'Accademia, Florence. A follower of Savonarola, Fra Bartolomeo's is a clearly devotional art, with virtually all incidental detail eliminated in favour of the central subject. Piero di Cosimo (c.1461–1521), on the other hand, was interested in nature and mythology. Several of his works can be seen in Florence's Palazzo Pitti.

The torment associated with the likes of Jacopo Pontormo (1494–1556) makes his work emblematic of Mannerism, that troubled search for a freer expression. In his *Visitazione* (Visitation) in the SS Annunziata in Florence, the figures seem almost furtive or preoccupied.

Il Rosso Fiorentino (Florentine Redhead; 1494–1540) also worked on the SS Annunziata frescoes and several other projects elsewhere in Tuscany before heading to Rome. In his works, too, one detects a similar note of disquiet, although his style is different. The flashes of contrasting light and dark create an unreal effect in his characters.

Il Bronzino (1503–72), a student of Pontormo, begins to move away from Mannerism in his later works. Employed by the Medici family, his approach lacked the agitation evident in his master. Rather he fixed images in a static fashion, reflecting perhaps his employers' desire to convey the sureness of their sovereignty, however spurious. His greatest achievement was the chapel for Eleonora de Toledo in the Palazzo Vecchio.

Down in Siena, Domenico Beccafumi (c.1484–1551) was perhaps one of the leading exponents of Tuscan Mannerism. Among his better-known works, the *Caduta degli Angeli* (Fall of the Angels) is replete with disquiet and movement – to the point of blurring his images. It can be seen in the Pinacoteca Nazionale in Siena. Around the same time, Il Sodoma (1477–1549) was producing works of an altogether smokier style. Some critics see in him a follower, initially at least, of Leonardo da Vinci and later of Raffaello – his paintings have a matt quality suffused with Mediterranean light. You can compare several of his works with those of Beccafumi in Siena's Pinacoteca Nazionale.

The works of Giorgio Vasari (1511–74) and his students litter Florence, some better than others. His particular boast seems to have been speed – with an army of helpers he was able to plough through commissions for frescoes and paintings with great alacrity, if not always with equal aplomb. He is perhaps most important in the history of Renaissance art as the author of *Lives of the Artists,* a rich compendium of fact and fiction about Italian art up to his own day. Vasari & co were largely responsible for the decoration of the Palazzo Vecchio.

Baroque & Neoclassicism Flocks of artists continued to work in Florence as the new century wore on, but few of enormous note. Giovanni da San Giovanni (1592–1636) was the leading light of the first half of the century and some of his frescoes remain in the Palazzo Pitti. One much under-estimated painter of the period was Cecco Bravo (1601–60), whose canvasses combine Florentine tastes of the period with a rediscovery of the soft, nebulous colours of Venice's Titian.

The arrival of artists from out of town, such as Pietro da Cortona and the Neapolitan Luca Giordano (1634–1705), brought the winds of Baroque taste to Florence. Where the Mannerists had searched, often rather stiffly, for ways of breaking with Renaissance conventions, Baroque artists bounded headlong into a hedonistic riot of colour and movement, leaving any semblance of reality behind.

At any rate, Florence was by now no longer the centre of artistic creation it had been.

The Macchiaioli The Florentine art scene remained sterile until the first signs of Impressionism wafted across from Paris, around the middle of the 19th century. In Florence anti-academic artists declared that painting real-life scenes was the only way forward. Their Macchiaioli movement lasted until the late 1860s and received its name (which could be translated as the

'stainers' or 'blotchers') in a disparaging newspaper article in 1862.

The Macchiaioli released Florentine, indeed Italian, art from the sclerosis that had set in over the previous century. They abandoned the religious and historical themes to which painting, no matter how innovative in style, had largely been bound for centuries. Then they dropped chiaroscuro effects in favour of playful use of colour plus light and/or colour plus shade.

Although the hub of their activity was Florence, a good number of the Macchiaioli had come from all over Italy. You can see some of the works of various of these artists, such as Livorno-born Giovanni Fattori (1825–1908), Neapolitan Giuseppe Abbati (1836–68) and the Emission painter Silvestro Alga (1826–95), in Florence's Galleria d'Arte Moderna.

By 1870 the movement had run out of steam. Splinter tendencies emerged separating realism from questions of style.

To the Present Florence's decline as a centre of artistic ferment seems to have been compounded during the 20th century. Futurism had little impact here in the years before WWI, while the Novecento movement, which preached a return to order in the wake of various avant-garde tendencies, also bore precious little fruit in Tuscany.

Indeed, the focus on painting in Tuscany seems to have turned from artistic creativity to the restoration of great works already painted. In the wake of the devastating 1966 flood, Florence has gained a worldwide reputation in this field.

One of the few Tuscan stars of the 20th-century international art scene was undoubtedly the Livorno-born Amedeo Modigliani (1884–1920), although he spent most of his adult life in Paris. His portraits and nudes are often a celebration of strong colour and are the best-known part of his opus. See also Livorno in the Central Coast chapter.

Sculpture
Etruscans & Romans Although bronze sculptures found in Etruscan tombs go back to the 8th century BC, production of greater

quality and in increased quantity dates to the 5th century BC. It is to this period that such fine pieces as the Arezzo *Chimera* (now housed in the Museo Archeologico in Florence) can be dated. Another good place to see Etruscan bronze work is Volterra.

Although Etruscan cities began to fall to Rome at about this time, it took centuries to extinguish local culture completely. From the 4th century BC onwards, the Etruscans were making terracotta and, later, terracotta funerary urns and sarcophagi. You can see a fine collection in Florence's Museo Archeologico. A close look at the relief sculptures on these reveals that influences from the Eastern Mediterranean and even beyond seem still to have made their way across to Etruria.

As with painting, the Romans took most of their cues from elsewhere, initially from the Greek-influenced Etruscans and later directly from the Greeks. Comparatively little has been found in Tuscany. Much of the Roman statuary collected by the Medici (and on show in the Uffizi and the Loggia della Signoria in Florence) came from Rome. In the archaeological museums of Florence, Siena, Arezzo and elsewhere you can see some modest examples of Roman bronze and stone statuary.

Medieval Sculptors As the straightforward simplicity of Romanesque began to give way to the grandeur of Gothic, so the first of the Tuscan master sculptors began to emerge.

Nicola Pisano (c.1215–c.1278), who left behind some of his best work in the baptistry in Pisa and the pulpit in Siena cathedral, was something of a master to all who followed in Tuscany. Despite his nickname (Pisano) he was actually born in southern Italy. He was succeeded by his son Giovanni Pisano (c.1248–c.1314), who worked on the cathedral in Siena.

Arnolfo di Cambio (c.1245–1302), a student of Nicola Pisano, is best known as the architect of the Duomo and Palazzo Vecchio in Florence. He also had the task of decorating the facade of the Duomo. Some of this sculpture remains in the Museo dell'Opera del Duomo, but the bulk of his

work was destroyed in the 16th century when the cathedral was remodelled.

Another outstanding sculptor was Andrea Pisano (c.1290–c.1348), who left behind him the bronze doors of the south facade of the Florence Battistero. The realism of the characters combines with the fine linear detail of a Gothic imprint, revealing that this century was one of transition.

Il Quattrocento (15th Century) In 1401 Lorenzo Ghiberti (1378–1455) won a competition to design a second pair of doors for the Florence Battistero. He was later called on to do another set of doors on the eastern side and ended up dedicating 17 years of his career to what an admiring Michelangelo (and it was not his wont to admire anything much) would later dub the Porta del Paradiso (Heaven's Door).

Ghiberti's workshop was a prestige address in Florence, and one of the lucky young hopefuls to be apprenticed there was Donatello (c.1386–1466). As the Renaissance gathered momentum in the 1420s and '30s, Donatello burst his banks and produced a stream of sculpture hitherto unparalleled in its dynamism and force. The results swing from his rather camp bronze *David,* the first nude sculpture since classical times (Palazzo del Bargello), to the racy *Cantoria,* a marble and mosaic tribune where small choirs could gather, created for the Duomo (now in the Museo dell'Opera del Duomo).

Meanwhile, Siena's Jacopo della Quercia (1374–1438) was cutting a temperamental swathe across Tuscany, working above all in Lucca and Siena, where he designed the Fonte Gaia (Happy Fountain) in Il Campo.

Although he would subsequently be best known for his decorative, glazed terracotta, Luca della Robbia (c.1400–82) for a while showed promise as a sculptor, as examination of his exquisite *Cantoria*, now in Florence's Museo dell'Opera del Duomo, will reveal. His nephew Andrea (1435–1525) and the latter's son Giovanni (1469–1529) continued the successful family terracotta business. The pretty terracotta medallions and other more complex pieces adorning buildings all over Florence and beyond came to be known as *robbiane*. A collection can be admired in the Bargello.

Desiderio da Settignano (c.1430–64) was a master of marble. Little of his work remains in Florence aside from the tomb of Carlo Marsuppini in the Basilica di Santa Croce. A pupil of Desiderio, Mino da Fiesole (1429–84) was busy in Florence and as far afield as Naples. His most important work was a new tomb for Ugo, the early medieval count of Tuscany, in Florence's La Badia.

Although also active as a painter, Andrea del Verrocchio is best remembered for his sculpture. His virtuosity can be admired in the tomb monument to Piero and Giovanni de' Medici in the Basilica di San Lorenzo in Florence. His masterpiece, however, is the bronze equestrian statue of Colleoni in Venice.

More Michelangelo! A passionate republican, Michelangelo Buonarroti was most prolific as a sculptor. And while he painted and built in Florence, his greatest gifts to the city were those he crafted from stone.

After a stint in Rome, where he carved the remarkable *Pietà,* Michelangelo returned to Florence in 1501 to carry out one of his most striking commissions, the colossal statue of *David*. By now, Michelangelo had long established himself as the champion of full nudity. The body, he argued, was a divine creation and its beauty without peer.

In 1516, after another long stint in Rome, Michelangelo was back in Florence. Among his last great works, not quite completed, are the wonderful statues in the Sagrestia Nuova of San Lorenzo.

Il Cinquecento (16th Century) Other sculptors during Michelangelo's lifetime included Benvenuto Cellini (1500–71) and Bartolommeo Ammannati (1511–92). The former, trained as a goldsmith, produced the bronze *Perseo e Medusa* (now standing in the Loggia della Signoria in Florence) – technically fine, but it lacks life. Ammannati is perhaps best known for the nearby *Fontana del Nettuno* (Neptune Fountain) in Piazza della Signoria.

Another name associated with Florence was Giambologna (Jean de Boulogne; 1529–1608). Some consider him the herald of Baroque. He was at any rate the dominant force in Florentine sculpture towards the end of the 16th century. His *Ratto della Sabina* (Rape of a Sabine), placed in the Loggia della Signoria, is one of his best known efforts. It is typical of his lust for movement – the figures seem to be caught up in a veritable whirlwind.

Lean Centuries One of Florence's senior court sculptors, Giovanni Battista Foggini (1652–1725), immersed himself in the Baroque circles of Rome when sent there by the Medicis to copy statues of antiquity. He returned and put to use his new found knowledge in reliefs and other decoration in several churches, among them the Basilica di Santa Maria del Carmine.

One of the dominant figures in the 19th century was Lorenzo Bartolini (1777–1850). Born in Prato, he studied in France before settling in Florence, where he became the grand man of sculpture. He and his contemporaries, however, were to some extent bound up in the rediscovery of the masters of the 15th century and so produced little that was exciting or innovative.

To the Present Possibly even more so than with painting, Tuscan sculpture has remained in the doldrums. Perhaps the awe-inspiring legacy of the great masters has been too great a burden to shake off.

This is not to say activity ground to a complete halt. The Pescia-born Libero Andreotti (1875–1933) and the tormented Florentine Evaristo Boncinelli (1883–1946) were among the prominent figures in the first half of the century, while Pistoia-born Marino Marini (1901–80) is doubtless the torch-bearer of 20th-century Tuscan sculpture. You can admire his work in the museum dedicated to him in Florence.

Literature
First Stirrings Long after the fall of Rome, Latin remained the language of learned discourse and writing throughout Italy. The

elevation of local tongues to literary status was a long and weary process, and the case of Italian was no exception.

In the mid-13th century, Tuscan poets started to experiment with verse and song in the local tongue, inspired by the troubadours of Provence and a Sicilian tradition that had grown out of the Provençal experience. Such early poets included Chiaro Davanzati (died 1303) and Guittone d'Arezzo (c.1235–94), whose writings also included political and moral treatises in verse. Brunetto Latini (1212–94) was not only recognised as one of Florence's finer poets, he was Dante's instructor.

Dante the Master Most of the poetry, song, didactic and religious literature of 13th-century writers in Tuscany, and indeed beyond, would appear to shrink before the genius of Dante Alighieri (1265–1321). Born in Florence in 1265 to a wealthy family, Dante received an excellent education, became active in Florentine politics as a white Guelph and began to write in a number of different styles and genres, covering everything from philosophy to politics to love. He was exiled from Florence in 1301 when the opposing faction took the reigns of power and spent the rest of his life, during which he wrote the *Divina Commedia* (Divine Comedy), wandering Europe.

Dante wrote on many subjects and often in Latin, but when he decided to compose the *Divina Commedia* in the 'vulgar' tongue of his countrymen, he was truly inspired. The protagonist is escorted on a journey through hell, purgatory and heaven in a work so dense with subtext that scholars are still beavering away at it today. At once a religious work and cautionary tale, it also operates on a far more complex level.

The gloomy circles of Dante's hell do not serve merely to warn of the wages of sin. Far more interestingly, they become an uneasy resting place for a parade of characters, many of them his contemporaries, whom he judged worthy of discomfort in the next life. In his vision of purgatory and heaven, political and religious figures of all persuasions get short shrift; others come out better.

Dante himself would not take all the credit. He was full of praise for the poet Guido Cavalcanti (c.1250–1300), inventor of the *dolce stil nuovo* (sweet new style) in Tuscan that Dante turned into the tool of his most exalted writings.

Dante's extraordinary capacity to construct and tell stories within stories would have ensured him a place in the pantheon of scribblers regardless of his language of delivery. But his decision to write in the Tuscan dialect was a bold step. In doing so he catapulted Italian, or at least a version of it, to the literary stage. Scholars have been enthusing ever since that Italian was 'born' with Dante's *Commedia*.

Dante died in Ravenna in 1321. He is buried there and Florence still supplies the oil for the lamp in his tomb, as penance for having exiled him.

Petrarch & Boccaccio Dante does not stand completely alone. Together with two fellow Tuscans, they form the triumvirate that laid down the course for the development of a rich Italian literature.

Petrarch (Francesco Petrarca; 1304–74), born in Arezzo to Florentine parents who had been exiled from their city at about the same time as Dante, actually wrote more in Latin than in Italian. *Il Canzoniere* is the distilled result of his finest poetry. Although the core subject is the unrequited love for a girl called Laura, the whole breadth of human grief and joy is treated with a lyrical quality hitherto unmatched. So striking was his clear, passionate verse, filtered through his knowledge of the classics, that a phenomenon known as *petrarchismo* emerged across Europe – the desire of writers within and beyond Italy to emulate him.

Contemporary and friend of Petrarch was the Florentine Giovanni Boccaccio (1303–75), who ended his days in Certaldo, outside Florence. His masterpiece was the *Decameron,* written in the years immediately following the plague of 1348, which he survived in Florence. His 10 characters each recount a story in which a vast panorama of personalities, events and symbolism is explored.

The Renaissance Even as the Renaissance in the fine arts was getting under way, writers were amusing themselves with language too. Burchiello (1404–49), a Florentine barber, would play host to writers, painters and other creative types in his shop, where they fooled around with verse. The sonnets that have remained often seem to make little sense, leaping from one subject to another, with references to people and events by now unknown even to scholars. The importance of his verse lies more in the extent to which it shows writers actively searching for new forms of expression. Such a search fits in nicely with the age.

The Medici Lorenzo the Magnificent dominated the second half of the 15th century in Florence and was handy with a pen himself. His enlightened approach to learning and the arts created a healthy atmosphere for writers.

Angelo Ambrogini (1454–94), born in Montepulciano and known as Il Poliziano, is considered one of Italy's most important 15th-century poets in Latin and Italian. His major work in the latter is the allegorical tale in verse *Stanze per la Giostra* (Verses for the Joust) penned to celebrate the victory of Giuliano de' Medici at such a contest.

Another outstanding writer of the Florentine Renaissance is Niccolò Machiavelli (1469–1527). He is known above all for his work on power and politics, *Il Principe* (see also the boxed text 'Machiavelli's Manoeuvres' later in this chapter). But he was a prolific writer in many fields. His *Mandragola* is a lively piece of comic theatre and a virtuoso example of Italian literature.

A little more staid is the principal work of Francesco Guicciardini (1483–1540), a wily statesman and historian. His *Storia d'Italia* (History of Italy) might never have been written had Cosimo I de' Medici not dispensed with his services shortly after becoming duke in 1537.

17th to 19th Centuries Few writers of great standing emerged in these centuries, although the occasional name is worthy of mention.

Theatre The first signs of change in theatre away from the Commedia dell'Arte, which had become something of a fixture in the Italian repertoire since the early 16th century, emerged in Florence. Giovanni Battista Fagiuoli (1660–1742) was among those who made the first tentative steps away from the old forms, but it would fall to the Venetian Carlo Goldoni to start a true revolution in the theatre.

Novels Although plenty of lesser scribblers were busy over the course of these centuries, Tuscany cannot really claim to have produced any outstanding names. There is, as usual, at least one exception to the rule. Carlo Lorenzini (1826–90), better known to Italians of all ages under the pseudonym of Carlo Collodi, was the creator of *Le Avventure di Pinocchio*. Outside Italy Pinocchio has come to be known more in his saccharine Walt Disney guise, but in Italy this children's best seller has been a source of amusement and instruction for both children and adults for generations.

Considerably less well known to posterity are writers such as Renato Fucini (1843–1921) and Mario Pratese (1842–1921), both of whom tend to be classed with realist novelists.

Poetry Giosue Carducci (1835–1907) was one of the key figures of 19th-century Tuscan literature. Born in the Maremma, he actually spent the second half of his life in Bologna. Probably the best of his poetry was written in the 1870s. It ranged in tone from pensive evocation of death (such as in *Pianto Antico*) or memories of youthful passion *(Idillio Maremmano)* to a kind of historic nostalgia. In many of these latter poems he harked back to the glories of ancient Rome.

Early 20th Century Florence's Aldo Palazzeschi (1885–1974) was in the vanguard of the Futurist movement during the pre-WWI years. In 1911 he published arguably his best (although at the time little appreciated) work, *Il Codice di Perelà* (Perelà's Code), an at times bitter allegory that in part becomes a farcical imitation of the life of Christ.

A contemporary of Palazzeschi's, now all but forgotten, was Ardengo Soffici (1879–1964), a painter and writer who, after some hesitation, embraced Futurism. After WWI he moved closer to Fascism.

The Mussolini Years By the 1920s and '30s Florence was bubbling with activity as a series of literary magazines flourished, at least for a while, in spite of the Fascist regime. Magazines such as *Solaria,* which lasted from 1926 to 1934, its successor *Letteratura* (which began circulating in 1937) and *Il Frontespizio* (1929–40) gave writers from across Italy a platform from which to launch and discuss their work.

These were not the easiest of times, and most of the magazines, including Vasco Pratolini's short-lived *Campo di Marte,* fell prey sooner or later to censorship. That some lasted as long as they did is remarkable enough.

One of the founding authors of *Letteratura* was Alessandro Bonsanti (1904–84), much of whose writings are in essays and criticism. A contributor on *Letteratura* was Guglielmo Petroni (born 1911), from Lucca. Although a poet of some note in his day, his novel *Il Mondo è una Prigione* (The World is a Prison, 1948), a vivid account of political prison, was thought to be one of the best accounts of the Italian Resistance. Mario Tobino (born 1910), from Viareggio, uses his experience as director of a lunatic asylum to great effect in *Le Donne Libere di Magliano* (Free Women of Magliano), which looks at life inside one such institution.

One of the most controversial figures in Italian letters of these years was Prato-born Curzio Malaparte (1898–1957). An early member of the Fascist party, from which he was later turfed out, Malaparte was a showy and tempestuous character. His most enduring works were novels, including *Maledetti Toscani* (Damned Tuscans), written in and about the tough immediate postwar period.

To the Present Few Tuscan writers of the 20th century gained a particularly high profile. One exception was Vasco Pratolini (1913–91), son of a manual labourer and self-taught writer who dabbled successfully in theatre and cinema as well as the novel and poetry. Among his most enduring works is the trilogy *Una Storia Italiana* (Italian Story), whose first part, *Metello,* set off a heated debate in Italian literary circles. Those who liked this novel saw in it a mature departure from neo-realism to a more robust realism. Pratolini's detractors considered him still caught in a rigid and limited ideological trap. The trilogy follows the lives of working- and middle-class Florentines, through whom Pratolini analyses a variety of political, social and emotional issues.

A minor novelist is Catholic writer Carlo Cocciolo, born in Livorno in 1920, whose themes recall those of Georges Bernanos. Arrigo Benedetti (1910–76) in such novels as *Il Passo dei Longobardi* (Passage of the Lombards), showed a keen eye for day-to-day detail, which he mixed with a sense of the fantastic and mythological.

One of Italy's leading postwar poets was the Florentine Mario Luzi (born 1914). His poetry concentrates on the anguish arising from the contrast between the individual and the broader universe.

Few women writers have reached the limelight in Tuscany but an important exception was Anna Banti (1895–1985). Her prose approach is psychological, delving deep into the minds of her characters and analysing the position of women in society.

Dacia Maraina (born 1936) is with little doubt Tuscany's most prominent contemporary female author, with some 10 novels to her credit. An interesting one is *Voci* (Voices), in which the main character, a female journalist, embarks on the investigation of a murder. It is a mystery laced with disturbing social comment.

Pisa-born Antonio Tabucchi (born 1943) is emerging as a writer of some stature, with more than a dozen books to his name. Possibly one of his most endearing works is *Sostiene Pereira,* set in prewar Lisbon and made into a charming film starring Marcello Mastroianni.

Machiavelli's Manouveres

JANE SMITH

Born in 1469 into a poor branch of what had been one of Florence's leading families, Niccolò Machiavelli got off to a bad start. His father was a small-time lawyer whose practice had been all but strangled by the city authorities as he was a debtor.

Young Niccolò missed out on the best schools and could consider himself lucky that his father was at least rich in books. His prospects were not sparkling.

Somehow he managed to swing a post in the city's second chancery at the age of 29, and so embarked on a colourful career as a Florentine public servant. His tasks covered a range of internal dealings in Florence and some aspects of foreign affairs and defence. Our man must have shown early promise, as by 1500 he was in France on his first diplomatic mission. A couple of years later he married Marietta Corsini, with whom he would have five children in the following 12 years.

Impressed by the marshal success of Cesara Borgia and the centralised state of France, Machiavelli came to the conclusion that Florence needed a standing army. The city, like many others across the length and breadth of the Italian peninsula, had a habit of employing mercenaries to fight their wars. The problem with this system was that mercenaries had few reasons to fight – or die – for anyone. They took their pay and as often as not did their level best to avoid mortal combat.

Machiavelli managed to convince his rulers of the advantages of an army raised to defend hearth and home, and so in 1506 formed a conscript militia. In 1509 he got to try it out on the rebellious city of Pisa, whose fall was in large measure attributed to the troops led by the wily statesman. He was back in Pisa two years later to dismantle a French-backed schismatic council there.

Florence, however, was not Rome's flavour of the month and troops from the Holy See and its allies marched on the city. Machiavelli was now defending not only his hearth but his future – to no avail.

The return to power of the Medici family was a blow for Machiavelli, who was promptly removed from all posts. Suspected of plotting against the Medici, he was even thrown into the dungeons in 1513 and tortured. He maintained his innocence and was freed, but reduced to penury as he retired to his little property outside Florence.

It was in these years that he produced his greatest writing. *Il Principe* (The Prince) is his classic treatise on the nature of power and its administration. In it he developed his theories not only on politics and power but also on history and human behaviour. Thus Machiavelli turned what was a thoroughly demoralising time to good account for generations to come. This work and other writings reflect the confusing and corrupt times in which he lived, and his desire for strong and just rule – in Florence and beyond.

He ached to get back into active public life, but this was never to be truly satisfied. He was commissioned to write an official history of Florence, the *Istorie Fiorentine*, and towards the end of his life appointed to a defence commission to improve the city walls and join a papal army in its ultimately futile fight against imperial forces. By the time the latter had sacked Rome in 1527, Florence had again rid itself of the Medici. Machiavelli hoped that he would be restored to a position of dignity but by now he was as suspected by the Medici's opponents as he had been years before by the Medici. He died frustrated and, as in his youth, on the brink of poverty in 1527.

Music

While Florence may have been the epicentre of the greatest explosion in the world of fine arts and the birthplace of literary Italian, music was not as strong a point either there or elsewhere in Tuscany.

The Roman-born composer Jacopo Peri (1561–1633) moved to Florence in 1588 to serve the Medici court. He and Florentine writer Ottavio Rinuccini (1562–1621) are credited with having created the first opera in the modern sense, *Dafne,* in 1598. They and Giulio Caccini (1550–1618) also wrote *Euridice* a couple of years later. It is the oldest opera for which the complete score still exists. All three men were part of a Florentine group of intellectuals known as the Camerata, which worked to revive and develop ancient Greek musical traditions in theatre.

Florence's next musical contribution was a key development, although it came at the hands of a Paduan resident on the Arno. In 1711 Bartolomeo Cristofori (1655–1731) invented the pianoforte.

In 1632, Giovanni Battista Lulli was born in Florence. That may not ring too many bells until we add that he moved to France where he would dominate the musical life of the court of Louis XIV as Jean-Baptiste Lully. With Molière he created new dramatic genres such as the comedy-ballet. He also gave instrumental suites their definitive form.

Another Florentine export to Paris was the composer Luigi Cherubini (1760–1842), who somehow managed the tricky feat of keeping his head attached to his torso through the French Revolution, the Napoleonic era and the Restoration.

Giacomo Puccini (1858–1924), the man behind such well-loved opera classics as *Madame Butterfly, Tosca* and *La Bohème,* was born in Lucca.

Contemporary Music On a quite different note, one of Italy's former leading pop bands, Litfiba, were a Florentine product – their ex-singer, Pero Pelù, now continues solo – and both Jovanotti, the country's most popular rap singer, and the singer Irene Grandi are also Tuscan. Siena-born Gianna Nannini is an extremely popular, internationally aclaimed and politically active Italian artist whose work ranges from rock albums to film soundtracks.

Indeed, Tuscany has produced plenty of bands and musicians, ranging from Marasco – a gritty, folksy singer from Florence who was big in the 1950s, through to Dirotto Su Cuba, a trip hop band that has attracted a lot of attention around the country.

Film

The Italian cinema has known periods of enormous productivity and contributed some of Europe's proudest gems on film. Most people think of the postwar period of neo-realism as the apogee of Italian filmmaking, and there is no doubting the richness of the output at that time. It didn't end there and Italy has continued to produce good directors ever since.

Tuscany has contributed some famous names to the Italian industry and can even claim to have invented the projector before the Lumière brothers patented theirs in Paris. Poor Filoteo Alberini created his *kinotegrafo* (cinema projector) in 1895, a year before the Lumière brothers, but no-one in Florence was interested and Alberini moved to Rome. There he created the Cines, which would grow to command the stage of Italian cinema.

Another film entrepreneur from Tuscany was a Florentine gent by the name of Giovanni Montalbano who set up studios in Rifredi in the 1920s to create historical blockbusters. The enterprise pumped out some pretty poor flicks and soon went belly up.

An early Florentine film-maker of note was Gianni Franciolini (1910–60). After spending about 10 years in France learning journalism and then film, Franciolini returned to Italy in 1940, from which time he turned out a film almost every year until his death. An early effort, *Fari Nella Nebbia* (Headlights in the Mist; 1941) shows the French influence on his ideas but also presages the prolific period of Italian film-making that lay just around the corner – neo-realism.

The biggest name to come out of Tuscany is with little doubt Franco Zeffirelli (born 1923). His career took him from radio and theatre to opera productions and occasional stints as aide to Luchino Visconti on several films. His film-directing days began in earnest in the 1970s, and you might remember his TV blockbuster *Jesus of Nazareth* (1977). Many of his productions have been non-Italian. A couple of his more interesting ones were *Romeo and Juliet* (1968), *Young Toscanini* (1988) and *Hamlet* (1990), a British-US production with Mel Gibson and Glenn Close heading an all-star cast. He filmed *Tea with Mussolini,* starring Maggie Smith, in his hometown of Florence (1999).

Neri Parenti (born 1950) started directing in 1979. Since 1980 he has been kept busy directing the comedian Paolo Villaggio in a seemingly endless stream of films starring Fantozzi, Villaggio's best-known comic character – a sort of thinking man's cross between Mr Bean and Benny Hill. The humour can swing pretty low but he's popular.

Two of Italy's modern success stories are Tuscan. Light-hearted comedy is a forte of Leonardo Pieraccioni (born 1965). His *Il Ciclone* (Cyclone; 1996), about the effects of the arrival of a small flamenco troupe on the lads of a small Tuscan town, was a big hit.

Humour with considerably greater depth is, however, the department of Roberto Benigni (born 1952). Long established as one of Italy's favourite comedic actors, he must be the first director to try to get a laugh out of the Holocaust – and succeed. He picked up three Oscars in 1999, including Best Actor, an honour rarely bestowed by Hollywood upon anyone but its own, for his *La Vita è Bella* (Life is Beautiful; 1998). The flick, which he directed and starred in, is the story of an Italian Jewish family that ends up in the camps, where the father tries to hide its horrors from his son by pretending it's all a game. Arezzo-born Benigni was already known to cinema-goers outside Italy for his appearances in Jim Jarmusch's *Down by Law* and *Night on Earth*. Charlie Chaplin's daughter, Geraldine, declared months after the Oscars that Benigni had inherited her father's cinematic poetry. Quite an accolade.

SOCIETY & CULTURE

Tuscans are particularly attached to their home ground and family. These ties continue to influence how people do things in this part of the world. Many businesses are relatively small, family enterprises. From the great names in wine, such as the Antinori, through to the flower-producing industry of Pescia, most 'industries' are run by families who pass on the business from generation to generation. In some respects this has contributed to a degree of immobility in Tuscan society. The readiness with which Anglo-Saxons seem disposed to shift from one city or one country to another often leaves Tuscans perplexed – mind you, their home ground is a pretty tough one to leave!

This is not to say they don't move around. Ever since the Middle Ages, when urban Tuscan families were at the head of some of the most advanced and dynamic of European trading and banking enterprises, living and working abroad was for many a rite of passage. Most, however, sooner or later returned home.

The family remains the cornerstone of Tuscan society. Although the big extended families of the past are in most cases little more than a distant memory, family ties remain tight. Children still typically remain at home with their parents until they reach their 30s, often only leaving when they get married. And from then on, weekly visits home to *mamma* and *babbo* are the norm for most.

The stereotypical perceptions foreigners tend to have of Italians, while they inevitably contain a grain of truth, do not tell much of the story. The image of an animated, gesticulating people seemingly with plenty of time to kill is some distance from the truth.

If anything the Tuscans have more in common with the image many have of the Scots – who can become pretty animated themselves! Thrifty and hard-working, the Tuscans can also be a fairly reserved lot. To be swept up into Tuscan social life (as opposed to circles of resident Italians from other parts of the country) is no mean feat and a sign of considerable success.

Dos & Don'ts

Tuscans, perhaps even more than other Italians, take particular pride in their dress and appearance. To many outsiders such concerns can seem a trifle overdone. In some cases, however, those outsiders seem to abandon any standards they might normally adhere to at home as soon as they hit the holiday trail.

Leaving aside the sartorial spectacle of the loud-shirts-and-shorts brigade, there are those who seem to think walking around with precious little on is the only way to fly. Your average Tuscan in heavily touristed centres such as Florence has grown accustomed to the odd ways of the *stranieri* (foreigners) but in restaurants, cafes and bars it doesn't hurt to at least put your shirt back on!

Many churches will not allow you entry if you are deemed to be inadequately attired (generally shorts or skirts above the knees and sleeveless tops are out). No one's suggesting you bring your Sunday best along but a little common sense and sensitivity go a long way.

Topless sunbathing, while not uncommon on some Tuscan beaches, is not *de rigueur* – women should look around before dropping their tops. Nude sunbathing is likely to be offensive anywhere but on appropriately designated beaches (there are a couple on Elba).

The standard form of greeting is the handshake. Kissing on both cheeks is generally reserved for people who already know one another. There will always be exceptions to these rules, so the best thing on being introduced to locals is probably not to launch your lips in anyone's general direction unless you are pretty sure they are welcome. If this is the case, a light brushing of cheeks will do.

The police *(polizia* and *carabinieri)* have the right to arrest you for 'insulting a state official' if they believe you have been rude or offensive – so be diplomatic in your dealings with them! (See also Dangers & Annoyances in the Facts for the Visitor chapter.)

RELIGION

As elsewhere in Italy, Catholicism is the dominant religion. It became the state religion of the new Italian nation when unity was completed in 1871. Only when the 1929 Lateran Treaty between the Vatican and the Italian state was modified in 1985 did Catholicism lose that status.

Still, as many as 85% of Italians profess to be Catholic and roughly the same figure can probably be applied to Tuscany. There is also a small Protestant population, made up of various denominations and consisting mostly of the expat community. Florence, interestingly, is one of the country's biggest centres of Buddhism, which has about 5000 followers throughout Tuscany.

Religiosity among the Italians appears often to be more a matter of form. First communions, church weddings and religious feast days are an integral part of Italian ritual. In the same way the Royal Family is a part of the ritual scenery in the life of many Britons, so the Papacy is a kind of royal family to Italians.

LANGUAGE

As with all regions of Italy, the people of Tuscany speak Italian. See the Language chapter for an introduction to the language and vocabulary.

Many Italians speak some English because they studied it at school. Clearly in heavily touristed centres such as Florence and, to a lesser extent, Pisa and Siena, you will find that many hotel, restaurant and shop staff members speak at least a little English. In 'Chiantishire' you will often come across locals with some knowledge. Nevertheless, in these places as elsewhere in Tuscany you will be better received if you at least attempt to communicate in Italian.

Facts for the Visitor

SUGGESTED ITINERARIES

You could organise yourself to cover quite a bit of ground, especially with your own vehicle, in as little as a week, although ideally you would need at least two weeks to make the most of the following suggestions. Taking Florence as a natural focal point, various itineraries spring to mind.

After a few days in Florence (to do the place any justice at all you need at least four days), you could set out southwards. Your main objective would be Siena, with a detour en route to San Gimignano and Volterra, south-west of Florence. Next, from Siena you could scoot east to Cortona and then head south-west to the charming towns of Montepulciano, Pienza, Montalcino and a series of abbeys scattered about the Sienese countryside.

At a more leisurely pace, you could easily spend a few days weaving your way south to Siena through Chianti, stopping in at Greve, Radda, Monteriggioni and so on.

Another fairly obvious option from Florence would be to move westwards to take in the towns of Prato, Pistoia, Lucca and Pisa, making one of the latter two an overnight stop. From Pisa you might want to pop along to one of the beaches around nearby Viareggio. Although nothing amazing, they certainly bring relief to the heat of a summer's day. Carrara, the centre of Tuscany's white marble industry, is a worthwhile stop and in the north-western corner of the region you could easily lose yourself for several days. The main attraction is the walking in the Garfagnana, the mountains of the Apuane Alps and in the still less visited Lunigiana.

If you have ended up in Pisa, you could choose to take the coastal option. This might see you travelling along the ridge inland from the coast south towards Piombino. The road gets more interesting the further you go; towns such as Suvereto and Campiglia Marittima are highlights. One of the prettiest spots along the Tuscan coast is the Golfo di Baratti, backed by the Etruscan

Highlights

Top 10

Tuscany's single greatest quality is perhaps the fact that it offers a little of everything. The visitor can put together a 'package' that ranges from the splendours of the cities to the comparative wildness of the mountains. It all depends on what you want. Some top choices might include:

1   Siena
2   The Apuane Alps
3   Florence
4   Islands of Elba and Capraia
5   Pitigliano and the nearby
    Etruscan towns
6   Parco Regionale della Maremma
7   The countryside and wine of the
    Chianti region
8   Pisa
9   Populonia and the Golfo di Baratti
10 Tuscan cuisine

Bottom 10

In a region as densely packed with goodies as Tuscany, it might seem near impossible that there could be anything remotely on the downside. Some of the following you could skip and not be noticeably much poorer for it:

1   Piombino
2   Queues to see the sights in
    Florence
3   Beaches in August
4   Bologna–Florence autostrada
5   Grosseto
6   Touchy-feely men's pickup lines
7   Traffic and trying to park in Florence
8   Monte Argentario on a summer
    weekend
9   Livorno
10 Saltless Tuscan bread

ruins of Populonia and the likenamed medieval *borgo* nearby. With a few days more to spare, it is tempting and easy to proceed to Piombino and get the ferry for Napoleon's one-time island of exile, Elba.

Heading into the little-travelled east you could happily spend a week or so exploring the Vallombrosa area and the remoter still Casentino, with a swing south to Arezzo and Cortona.

In the south, several days or more could be profitably spent moving from the Monte Argentario peninsula on the coast inland through relatively untouristed country, bespattered with ancient Etruscan sites around the hill towns of Magliano in Toscana, Manciano, Pitigliano, Sovana and Sorano.

PLANNING
When to Go
The best time to visit Tuscany is in the low season, from April to June and in September/October, when the weather is usually good, prices are lower and there are fewer tourists. Late July and August is the time to avoid the place: the sun broils, prices are inflated and you can't see the place for the swarms of holiday-makers. Most of Italy goes on vacation in August, abandoning the cities (and leaving many shops, hotels and restaurants closed) and packing out the coast and mountains. Finding a place to stay by the sea or in the hills without booking months in advance can be especially difficult at this time.

June and September are the best months for walking in the Apuane Alps (like everything else, walking trails and *rifugi*, mountain huts, are crowded in August). During these months the weather is generally good, although you should allow for cold snaps.

You may prefer to organise your trip or itinerary to coincide with one or more of the many festivals that festoon the Tuscan calendar – an obvious choice is Il Palio in Siena. To help start planning around such events, see Special Events later in this chapter.

What Kind of Trip
Apart from simply making a tour of the main towns and cities, several other approaches suggest themselves. Many people choose to rent a villa in the countryside for a week or two. Generally in this case you should hire a car to allow you to potter around the area and visit some of the surrounding towns and cities that interest you.

More energetic types might opt to build their visit around walking routes. The most challenging walking is in the Apuane Alps, but for gentler walking there are plenty of trails criss-crossing the Chianti region and other parts of Tuscany. Cycling (for the fit – there is not a great deal of flat country in Tuscany) is another option.

Tuscany is really not beach country. If you are looking for an essentially sea and sun holiday, this is not the place to come.

Some visitors opt to build their stay around some kind of course, whether language, cooking or art history. Such courses abound in Florence and to a lesser extent in other towns, and in various cases in the countryside too.

Maps
Road Atlases If you are driving around Tuscany and beyond, the AA's *Big Road Atlas – Italy*, is available in the UK for UK£9.99, is scaled at 1:250,000 and includes 39 town maps. In Italy, de Agostini's *Atlante Stradale d'Italia* (1:600,000) contains city plans and sells for €11.40. For €20.20 the same publisher offers the more comprehensive *Atlante Turistico Stradale d'Italia* (1:250,000). The Touring Club Italiano (TCI) publishes an *Atlante Stradale d'Italia* (1:200,000), which is divided into three parts – Nord, Centro and Sud. Each costs €17.55. It also produces a comprehensive edition including all three parts and a CD-Rom for €51.15.

Regional & Provincial Maps Michelin's map No 430, *Italia Centro* (1:400,000), selling for €6.20, includes Tuscany and parts of surrounding regions.

The TCI produces a regional map of Tuscany at a scale of 1:200,000 (€6.20), while several other publishers do the region at 1:250,000. For greater scale detail, you have to revert to provincial maps (the region is divided up into 10 provinces). Edizioni Multigraphic Firenze publishes a series of provincial maps. Ask for the *Carta Stradale Provinciale* of the province(s) you want. They are scaled at 1:100,000. Beyond that they subdivide into road maps at 1:50,000 *(Carta Turistica e Stradale)* and, for walkers (see also later), the *Carta Turistica dei Sentieri e Rifugi* (Tourist Trails and Refuges Map). These maps are scaled at 1:50,000 and 1:25,000 (€5.15). Various other publishers produce comparable maps.

City Maps City maps in this book, combined with tourist office maps, are generally adequate. But more detailed maps are available at good bookshops (such as Feltrinelli) or newspaper stands.

The quality of city maps available commercially varies considerably, depending on the city. Most tourist offices stock free maps of the city they cover, and commercial maps of larger cities are available from newsstands and bookstores. Edizioni Multigraphic Firenze and Studio FMB Bologna both produce quality maps, generally scaled at 1:10,000 (around €5.15). For suggestions on the maps for the main cities covered in this book, refer to each destination.

Walking Maps Information on maps useful for walkers is given in the Tuscany on Foot chapter.

What to Bring

Pack as little as possible. A backpack is an advantage since petty thieves tend to prey on luggage-laden tourists with no free hands. Backpacks whose straps and openings can be zipped inside a flap are less awkward and more secure than the standard ones.

Suitcases with portable trolleys may be fine in airports but otherwise you won't get far on foot with them. If you must carry a suitcase/bag, make sure it is lightweight and not too big. Remember that most everyday necessities can be found easily in Italy – there is no need to stock up in advance and drag it all around with you.

A small backpack (with a lock) for day trips and sightseeing is far preferable to a handbag or shoulder bag. It's more practical and secure.

Clothes Tuscany is hot in summer but can be ice cold in winter, especially at higher altitudes. You probably won't need so much as a light jacket in July and August, but in winter you will need a decent coat, hat, gloves and scarf.

Italians dress up just to do the daily food shopping, so if you plan to hang around in cafes and bars or enjoy some of the nightlife you'll feel more comfortable with a set of casually dressy clobber. Jeans and T-shirts will give you the decided air of a bum by local standards.

You'll need a pair of hardy, comfortable walking shoes with rubber soles – trainers are fine except for going out, so something a little more presentable, though casual, might cover all bases.

People planning to hike in the mountains should bring the necessary clothing and equipment, in particular a pair of walking boots (lightweight and waterproof). Even in high summer you would be advised to have some warm clothing on long hikes – it can get chilly high up.

Unless you plan to spend large sums in dry-cleaners and laundries (laundries are few and far between anyway), pack a portable clothesline. Many *pensioni* (boarding houses) and hotels ask guests not to wash clothes in the rooms, but such rules are rarely enforced. Consider packing a light travel iron or crease-proof clothes.

Useful Items Apart from any special personal needs, consider taking the following:

- an under-the-clothes money belt or shoulder wallet, useful for protecting your money and documents in cities
- a towel and soap, often lacking in cheap accommodation
- a small Italian dictionary and/or phrasebook
- a Swiss army knife (including cork screw)
- a medical kit
- a padlock or two to secure your luggage to racks and to lock hostel lockers
- an adapter plug for electrical appliances
- a torch (flashlight)

- a sleeping sheet to save on sheet rental costs if you're using youth hostels (a sleeping bag is unnecessary unless you're camping)
- an alarm clock
- sunglasses and hat
- a universal sink plug

Basic drugs are widely available and indeed many items requiring prescriptions in countries such as the USA can be obtained easily over the counter in Italy. If you require specific medication, it's easier to bring it with you. Condoms can cost €15.50, or more, for 12 but as little as €6.20 in supermarkets.

RESPONSIBLE TOURISM

When visiting monuments, treat them with respect. At ancient sites such as the Roman amphitheatre in Fiesole or Etruscan tombs and similar locations, don't go clambering over everything where you are asked not to or have no need to. By leaving things alone you do your little part to help preserve them.

Don't use the flash when photographing artworks in museums, churches and so on. The burst of light only damages the art.

The sheer volume of people visiting a place such as Florence, and to a slightly lesser extent towns such as Siena, San Gimignano, Cortona and Pisa, puts enormous pressure on the infrastructure of those places. For a local trying to get anything done in central Florence it can be a nightmare. Try to be aware while wandering around and staring at things that some people around you are trying to get places!

Being stuck behind a rubber-necker on the road can infuriate the most patient driver. Be aware that not everyone is taking a leisurely drive in the beautiful countryside, and to avoid any grief (or accident) pull over and let other cars past.

The moral is, simply, respect the monuments and works of art, the towns and their people, as you would your own most prized possessions. Tread softly and enjoy.

TOURIST OFFICES
Local Tourist Offices

The regional tourist office for Tuscany (☎ 055 438 51 35, **W** www.regione.toscana .it) can be found at Via di Novoli 26, Florence. Azienda di Promozione Turistica (APT) offices, in all the provincial capitals, generally provide information only on that province, usually including the city itself, but little or nothing on the rest of the region.

In Florence you have a choice of three different offices, but the main APT on Via Cavour is the best stocked – it's amazing what they dig up for you if you ask the right questions. Since tourism isn't exactly new to Tuscany you'll generally find English spoken, and sometimes other languages as well.

The next rung down are local city or town tourist offices. These come under various names but most commonly are known as Pro Loco. They may deal with a town only, or in some cases the surrounding countryside.

Things you may want to ask for include: a *pianta della città* (map); *elenco degli alberghi* (a list of hotels); and *informazioni sulle attrazioni turistiche* (information on the major sights). Many will help you find a hotel.

The bigger APT offices will often respond to written and telephone requests – for example, information about hotels or apartments for rent.

The addresses, telephone numbers and email addresses of offices are listed under the relevant towns and cities throughout this book.

Tourist Offices Abroad

Information on the Tuscan region is available from the Italian State Tourist Office (check out their Web site at **W** www.enit.it) in the following countries:

Australia
(☎ 02-9262 1666, **e** enitour@ihug.com.au) Level 26, 44 Market St, Sydney, NSW 2000
Austria
(☎ 09000-970 228, **e** enit-wien@aon.at) Kaerntnerring 4, 1010 Vienna
Canada
(☎ 416-925 4882, **e** enit.canada@on.aibn .com) Suite 907, South Tower, 175 Bloor St East, Toronto, Ontario M4W 3R8

FACTS FOR THE VISITOR

France
(☎ 01 42 66 66 68, e enit.parigi@
wanadoo.fr) 23 rue de la Paix, 75002 Paris
Germany
Berlin: (☎ 030-247 83 98, e enit-berlin@
t-online.de) Karl Liebknecht Strasse 34,
D-10178 Berlin
Frankfurt: (☎ 069-25 91 26, e enit.ffm@
t-online.de) Kaiser Strasse 65, D-60329
Frankfurt-am-Main
Munich: (☎ 089-53 13 17, e enit-muenchen@
t-online.de) Goethe Strasse 20,
D-80336 Munich
The Netherlands
(☎ 020-616 82 44, e enitams@wirehub.nl)
Stadhouderskade 2, 1054 ES Amsterdam
Spain
(☎ 91 559 9750, e italiaturismo@retemail.es)
Gran Via 84, Edificio Espagna 1-1, 28013
Madrid
Switzerland
(☎ 01-211 79 17, e enit@bluewin.ch) Urania
Strasse 32, 8001 Zürich
UK
(☎ 020-7355 1439, e enitlond@globalnet
.co.uk) 1 Princes St, London W1R 8AY
USA
Chicago: (☎ 312-644 0996, e enitch@italian
tourism.com) 500 North Michigan Ave, Suite
2240, Chicago, IL 60611
Los Angeles: (☎ 310-820 1898) 12400
Wilshire Blvd, Suite 550, Los Angeles, CA
90025
New York: (☎ 212-245 5095, e enitny@
italiantourism.com) Suite 1565, 630 Fifth Ave,
New York, NY 10111

Italian cultural institutes in major cities
throughout the world have extensive information on study opportunities in Italy. For
more information see also Useful Organisations later in this chapter.

VISAS & DOCUMENTS
Passport
Citizens of the European Union (EU) member states can travel to Italy with their
national identity cards alone. People from
countries that do not issue ID cards, such as
the UK, must have a valid passport. All
non-EU nationals must have a full valid
passport. If your passport is stolen or lost
while in Italy, notify the police and obtain a
statement, and then contact your embassy
or consulate as soon as possible.

Visas
Italy is one of 15 countries that have signed
the Schengen Convention, an agreement
whereby all EU member countries (except
the UK and Ireland) plus Iceland and Norway have agreed to abolish checks at
internal borders. The other EU countries
are Austria, Belgium, Denmark, Finland,
France, Germany, Greece, Luxembourg, the
Netherlands, Portugal, Spain and Sweden.
Legal residents of one Schengen country do
not require a visa for another Schengen
country. In addition, nationals of a number of
other countries, including the UK, Canada,
Ireland, Japan, New Zealand and Switzerland do not need visas for tourist visits of up
to 90 days to any Schengen country.

Various other nationals not covered by the
Schengen exemption can also spend up to 90
days in Italy without a visa. These include
Australian, Israeli and US citizens. However
all non-EU nationals entering Italy for any
reason other than tourism (such as study or
work) should contact an Italian consulate as
they may need a specific visa. They should
also insist on having their passport stamped
on entry as, without a stamp, they could encounter problems when trying to obtain a
permesso di soggiorno (see under Permits
later in this section). If you are a citizen of
a country not mentioned in this section, you
should check with an Italian consulate
whether you need a visa.

The standard tourist visa issued by Italian
consulates is the Schengen visa, valid for up
to 90 days. A Schengen visa issued by one
Schengen country is generally valid for
travel in all other Schengen countries. However individual Schengen countries may
impose additional restrictions on certain na-
tionalities. It is therefore worth checking
visa regulations with the consulate of each
Schengen country you plan to visit.

It's mandatory that you apply for a visa in
your country of residence. You can apply for
no more than two Schengen visas in any
12-month period and they are not renewable
inside Italy.

Study Visas Non-EU citizens who want to
study at a university or language school in

Italy must have a study visa. These visas can be obtained from your nearest Italian embassy or consulate. You will normally need confirmation of your enrolment and payment of fees as well as proof of adequate funds to support yourself. The visa will then cover only the period of the enrolment. This type of visa is renewable within Italy but, again, only with confirmation of ongoing enrolment and proof that you are able to support yourself – bank statements are preferred.

Permits

EU citizens supposedly do not need any permits to live, work or start a business in Italy. They are, however, advised to register with a *questura* (police station) if they take up residence – in accordance with an anti-Mafia law that aims at keeping a watch on everyone's whereabouts in the country. Failure to do so carries no consequences, although some landlords may be unwilling to rent out a flat to you if you cannot produce proof of registration. Those considering long-term residence will want to get a permesso di soggiorno, a necessary first step to acquiring a *carta d'identità*, or residence card (see the Residence Permits section). While you're at it, you'll need a *codice fiscale* (tax file number) if you wish to be paid for most work in Italy.

Work Permits Non-EU citizens wishing to work in Italy will need to obtain a *permesso di lavoro* (work permit). If you intend to work for an Italian company and will be paid in euros, the company must organise the permesso and forward it to the Italian consulate in your country – only then will you be issued an appropriate visa.

If non-EU citizens intend to work for a non-Italian company or will be paid in foreign currency, or wish to go freelance, they must organise the visa and permesso in their country of residence through an Italian consulate. This process can take many months – so look into it early.

Some foreigners prefer simply to work 'black' in areas such as teaching English, bar work and seasonal jobs. See the section on Work later in this chapter.

Residence Permits Visitors are technically obliged to report to a questura if they plan to stay at the same address for more than one week (this does not apply to holiday-makers), to receive a *permesso di soggiorno* (residence permit). Tourists who are staying in hotels are not required to do this, because hotel-owners are required to register all guests with the police.

A permesso di soggiorno only becomes a necessity if you plan to study, work (legally) or live in Italy. Obtaining one is never a pleasant experience, although for EU citizens it is straightforward. Other nationals will find it involves enduring long queues, rude police officers and the frustration of arriving at the counter (after a two-hour wait) to find that you don't have all the necessary documents.

The exact requirements, such as documents and official stamps *(marche da bollo)*, vary from year to year. In general, you will need a valid passport, containing a visa stamp indicating your date of entry into Italy; a special visa issued in your own country if you are planning to study; four passport-style photographs; and proof of your ability to support yourself financially.

It is best to go to the questura to obtain precise information.

Travel Insurance

Don't, as they say, leave home without it. It will generally cover theft, loss and medical problems. Some policies offer lower and higher medical-expense options; the higher ones are chiefly for countries such as the USA, which have extremely high medical costs. There is a wide variety of policies available, so check the small print.

Some policies specifically exclude 'dangerous activities', which can include scuba diving, motorcycling, and even trekking. A locally acquired motorcycle licence is not valid under some policies.

Paying for your ticket with a credit card often provides limited travel accident insurance, and you may be able to reclaim the payment if the operator doesn't deliver. Ask your credit card company what it will cover.

You may prefer a policy that pays doctors or hospitals directly rather than your having to pay on the spot and claim later. If you have to claim later make sure you keep all documentation.

Check that the policy covers ambulances or an emergency flight home.

Driving Licence & Permits

EU member states' driving licences are recognised in Italy. The only exception is the old-style green UK licence, which is not valid in Italy without the accompaniment of an International Driving Licence. If you hold a licence from other countries you are supposed to obtain an International Driving Permit too. See under Car & Motorcycle in the Getting There & Away chapter for more information.

Hostel Cards

A valid HI hostelling card is required in all associated youth hostels (Associazione Italiana Alberghi per la Gioventù; **W** www .hostels.aig.org) in Italy. You can get this in your home country or at youth hostels in Italy. In the latter case you apply for the card and must collect six stamps in the card at €2.60 each. You pay for a stamp on each of the first six nights you spend in a hostel. With six stamps you are considered a full international member. HI is on the Web at **W** www.iyhf.org.

Student, Teacher & Youth Cards

These cards can get you worthwhile discounts on travel, and reduced prices at some museums, sights and entertainments. The International Student Identity Card (ISIC), for full-time students, and the International Teacher Identity Card (ITIC), for full-time teachers and professors, are issued by more than 5000 organisations around the world – mainly student travel-related, and often selling student air, train and bus tickets too.

Student travel organisations such as STA (Australia, UK & USA), Council Travel (UK & USA) and Travel CUTS/Voyages Campus (Canada) can issue these cards. See under Air in the Getting There & Away chapter for some addresses, phone numbers and Web sites.

Anyone under 26 can get a Euro26 card. This gives similar discounts to the ISIC and are issued by most of the same organisations. The Euro26 has a variety of names including the Under 26 Card in England and Wales.

CTS (Centro Turistico Studentesco e Giovanile) youth and student travel organisation branches in Italy can issue ISIC, ITIC and Euro26 cards.

Seniors Cards

Seniors over 60 or 65 (depending on what they are seeking a discount for) can get many discounts simply by presenting their passport or ID card as proof of age. For discounted international rail travel in Europe, you could apply for a Rail Europe Senior card. Check out the Rail Europe Web site at **W** www.raileurope.com for details.

Copies

Make photocopies of important documents, especially your passport. Other documents to photocopy might include your airline ticket and credit cards. Also record the serial numbers of your travellers cheques (cross them off as you cash them in). Leave extra copies with someone reliable at home. If your passport is stolen or lost, notify the police and obtain a statement, and then contact your embassy or consulate as soon as possible.

It's also a good idea to store details of your vital travel documents in Lonely Planet's free online Travel Vault in case you lose the photocopies or can't be bothered with them. Your password-protected Travel Vault is accessible online anywhere in the world – you can create it at **W** www.ekno .lonelyplanet.com.

EMBASSIES & CONSULATES

It's important to realise what your own embassy – the embassy of the country of which you are a citizen – can and can't do to help you if you get into trouble.

Generally speaking, it won't be much help in emergencies if the trouble you're in is remotely your own fault. Remember that you are bound by the laws of the country you are in. Your embassy will not be sympathetic if you end up in jail after committing a crime locally, even if such actions are legal in your own country.

In genuine emergencies you might get some assistance, but only if all other channels have been exhausted. For example, if you need to get home urgently, a free ticket home is exceedingly unlikely – the embassy would expect you to have insurance. If you have all your money and documents stolen, the embassy might assist with getting a new passport, but not with a loan for onward travel.

Some embassies used to keep letters for travellers or have a small reading room with home newspapers, but these days the mail holding service has usually been stopped and even newspapers tend to be out of date.

Italian Embassies & Consulates

The following is a selection of Italian diplomatic missions abroad. As a rule, you will need to approach a consulate rather than an embassy (where both are present) on visa matters. Also bear in mind that in many of the countries listed below there are further consulates in other cities.

Australia
Embassy: (☎ 02-6273 3333, fax 6273 4223, e embassy@ambitalia.org.au) 12 Grey St, Deakin, Canberra, ACT 2600
Consulate: (☎ 03-9867 5744, fax 9866 3932, e itconmel@netlink.com.au) 509 St Kilda Rd, Melbourne, Vic 3004
Consulate: (☎ 02-9392 7900, fax 9252 4830, e itconsydn@itconsyd.org) Level 43, The Gateway, 1 Macquarie Place, Sydney, NSW 2000

Austria
Embassy: (☎ 01-712 51 21, fax 713 97 19, e ambitalviepress@via.at) Metternichgasse 13, Vienna 1030
Consulate: (☎ 01-713 56 71, fax 715 40 30) Ungarngasse 43, Vienna 1030

Canada
Embassy: (☎ 613-232 2401, fax 233 1484, w www.italyincanada.com) 21st floor, 275 Slater St, Ottawa, Ontario K1P 5H9
Consulate: (☎ 514-849 8351, fax 499 9471, w www.italconsul.montreal.qc.ca) 3489 Drummond St, Montreal, Quebec H3G 1X6
Consulate: (☎ 416-977 1566, w www.toronto.italconsulate.org) 136 Beverley St, Toronto, Ontario M5T 1Y5

France
Embassy: (☎ 01 49 54 03 00, fax 01 45 49 35 81, e ambasciata@amb-italie.fr) 47 rue de Varenne, Paris 75007

Consulate: (☎ 01 44 30 47 00, fax 01 45 25 87 50) 5 blvd Augier, Paris 75016

Germany
Embassy: (☎ 030-25 44 00, w www.botschaft-italien.de) Dessauer Strasse 28–29, 10963 Berlin
Consulate: (☎ 069-753 10, e italia.consolato.francoforte@t-online.de) Beethovenstrasse, 17, D 60325 Frankfurt-am-Main

Ireland
Embassy: (☎ 01-660 1744, fax 668 2759, e italianembassy@eircom.net) 63–65 Northumberland Rd, Dublin 4

The Netherlands
Embassy: (☎ 070-302 1030, fax 361 4932, e italemb@worldonline.nl) Alexanderstraat 12, 2514 JL The Hague

New Zealand
Embassy: (☎ 04-473 53 39, fax 472 72 55, e ambwell@xtra.co.nz) 34 Grant Rd, Thorndon, Wellington

Slovenia
Embassy: (☎ 061-426 21 94, fax 425 33 02) Snezniska Ulica 8, Ljubljana 61000

Spain
Embassy: (☎ 91 423 3300, fax 91 575 7776, e ambitalsp@cempresarial.com) Calle de Lagasca 98, Madrid 28006
Consulate: (☎ 93 467 7305, fax 93 487 0002, e cgbarcconsolare@infonegocio.com) Carrer de Mallorca 270, Barcelona 08037

Switzerland
Embassy: (☎ 031-352 41 51, fax 351 10 26 e ambital.berna@spectraweb.ch) Elfenstrasse 14, Bern 3006
Consulate: (☎ 022-839 67 44, fax 839 67 45) 14 rue Charles Galland, Geneva 1206

UK
Embassy: (☎ 020-7312 2200, fax 7312 2230, e emblondon@embitaly.org.uk) 14 Three Kings Yard, London W1Y 2EH
Consulate: (☎ 020-7235 9371, fax 7823 1609) 38 Eaton Place, London SW1X 8AN

USA
Embassy: (☎ 202-612 4400, fax 518 2155, e stampa@itwash.org) 1601 Fuller St, NW Washington, DC 20009
Consulate: (☎ 213-826 6207, fax 820 0727, e cglos@conlang.com) Suite 300, 12400 Wilshire Blvd, West Los Angeles, CA 90025
Consulate: (☎ 212-737 9100, fax 249 4945, e italconsulnyc@italconsulnyc.org) 690 Park Ave, New York, NY 10021-5044
Consulate: (☎ 415-931 4924, fax 931 7205) 2590 Webster St, San Francisco, CA 94115

Embassies & Consulates in Rome

Most countries have an embassy (and often a consulate) in Rome, many also maintain consulates elsewhere in the country. Passport enquiries should be addressed to the Rome-based offices:

Australia
  Embassy: (☎ 06-85 27 21) Via Alessandria 215
Austria
  Embassy: (☎ 06-844 01 41) Via Pergolesi 3
Canada
  Embassy: (☎ 06-44 59 81) Via G B de Rossi 27
France
  Embassy: (☎ 06-68 60 11) Piazza Farnese 67
Germany
  Embassy: (☎ 06-49 21 31) Via San Martino della Battaglia 4
Ireland
  Embassy: (☎ 06-697 91 21) Piazza Campitelli 3
The Netherlands
  Embassy: (☎ 06-322 11 41) Via Michele Mercati 8
New Zealand
  Embassy: (☎ 06-441 71 71) Via Zara 28
Slovenia
  Embassy: (☎ 06-808 10 75) Via L Pisano 10
Spain
  Embassy: (☎ 06-580 01 44) Via Garibaldi 35
Switzerland
  Embassy: (☎ 06-80 95 71) Via Barnarba Oriani 61
UK
  Embassy: (☎ 06-482 54 41) Via XX Settembre 80a
USA
  Embassy: (☎ 06-4 67 41) Via Vittorio Veneto 119a-121

Consulates in Florence

It may be handier for some to go to their consulate in Florence. Quite a few countries have consular reps here, including:

France
  (☎ 055-230 25 56) Piazza Ognissanti 2
Germany
  (☎ 055-29 47 22) Lungarno Vespucci 30
Switzerland
  (☎ 055-22 24 34) Piazzale Galileo 5
UK
  (☎ 055-28 41 33) Lungarno Corsini 2
USA
  (☎ 055-239 82 76) Lungarno Vespucci 38

CUSTOMS

Duty-free sales within the European Union (EU) no longer exist. Under the rules of the single market, goods bought in and exported within the EU incur no additional taxes, provided duty has been paid somewhere within the EU and the goods are for personal consumption.

Travellers who are coming from outside the EU, on the other hand, are permitted to import, duty free: 200 cigarettes, 1L of spirits, 2L of wine, 60mL of perfume, 250mL of toilet water, and other goods up to a total value of €175; anything over this limit must be declared on arrival and the appropriate duty paid (it is advisable to carry all receipts).

MONEY
Currency

In January 2002, the hassle of exchanging money when travelling between many EU countries became a thing of the past. On this date, the euro became Italy's currency and the currency throughout much of the EU – Denmark, Sweden and the UK are the only nations that didn't join the party.

Since 28 February 2002, the euro has been Italy's sole currency. Banks will still accept lira for 10 years beyond that date, but will only issue euros.

The euro is divided into 100 cents. Coin denominations are one, two, five, 10, 20 and 50 cents, €1 and €2. The notes are €5, €10, €20, €50, €100, €200 and €500. All euro notes of each denomination are identical on both sides in all EU countries, and the coins are identical on the side showing their value, but there are also 12 different obverses, each

Prices Quoted

This book was researched during the transition period, when not all prices were available in euros. Prices quoted (for example, by hotels, restaurants and entertainment venues) in the national currency have been converted to euros at the fixed conversion rate (€1 is equal to 1936.27L). These may undergo further change as the euro comes into use.

representing one of the 12 euro-zone countries. For more information check out the Web site Ⓦ www.europa.eu.int/euro.

Exchange Rates

country	unit		euros
Australia	A$1	=	€0.58
Canada	C$1	=	€0.71
Japan	¥100	=	€0.89
New Zealand	NZ$1	=	€0.47
UK	UK£1	=	€1.61
USA	US$1	=	€1.12

Exchanging Money

If you need to change cash or travellers cheques, be prepared to queue (this is when you'll wish you had a credit/debit card to stick in the nearest friendly ATM!).

You can change money in banks, at the post office or in special change offices. Banks are generally the most reliable and tend to offer the best rates. However, you should look around and ask about commissions. These can fluctuate considerably and a lot depends on whether you are changing cash or cheques. While the post office charges a flat rate of €0.60 per cash transaction, banks charge €1.55 or even more. Travellers cheques attract higher fees. Some banks charge €0.50 per cheque with a €1.55 minimum, while the post office charges a maximum €2.60 per transaction. Other banks will have different arrangements again, and in all cases you should compare the exchange rates too.

Cash Don't bring wads of cash from home (travellers cheques and plastic are much safer). Wandering around with pounds and dollars in your pockets is just asking to be made instantly poor by rubbery fingers. It is, however, an idea to keep an emergency stash separate from other valuables in case you should lose your travellers cheques and credit cards. You will need cash for many day-to-day transactions – many pensioni (small hotels), eateries and shops take cash only.

Travellers Cheques These protect your money because they can be replaced if they are lost or stolen. They can be cashed at most banks and exchange offices. American Express (Amex), Thomas Cook and Visa are widely accepted brands. If you lose your Amex cheques, you can call a 24-hour freephone number (☎ 800 87 20 00) anywhere in Italy. For Thomas Cook or Mastercard cheques call ☎ 800 872 050 and for Visa cheques call ☎ 800 874 155.

It may be preferable to buy travellers cheques in euros rather than another currency (UK pounds or US dollars) as they are less likely to incur commission on exchange. Amex and Thomas Cook do not charge commission, but other exchange places have various charges so check first. Get most of the cheques in largish denominations to save on per-cheque exchange charges.

It's vital to keep your initial receipt, and a record of your cheque numbers and the ones you have used, separate from the cheques themselves. You must take your passport with you when you are going to cash travellers cheques.

Credit/Debit & ATM Cards The simplest way to organise your holiday funds is to carry plastic (whether a credit/debit or ATM card). You don't have large amounts of cash or cheques to lose, you can get money after hours and at weekends and the exchange rate is sometimes better than that offered for travellers cheques or cash exchanges. By arranging for payments to be made into your card account while you are travelling, you can avoid paying interest.

Major credit/debit cards, for example, Visa, MasterCard, Eurocard, Cirrus and Eurocheque cards, are accepted throughout Italy.

They can be used for many purchases (including in some supermarkets) and in hotels and restaurants (although pensioni and smaller trattorias and pizzerias tend to accept cash only). Credit cards can also be used in ATMs *(bancomat)* displaying the appropriate sign or (if you have no PIN number) to obtain cash advances over the counter in many banks – Visa and Master-Card are among the most widely recognised for such transactions. Check charges with your bank but, as a rule, there is no charge for purchases on major cards and a minimum charge on cash advances and ATM transactions in foreign currencies. In cases of larger withdrawals this charge will rarely exceed 1.5%.

It is not uncommon for ATMs in Italy to reject foreign cards. Don't despair or start wasting money on international calls to your bank. Try a few more ATMs displaying your credit card's logo before assuming the problem lies with your card rather than with the local system.

If your credit card is lost, stolen or swallowed by an ATM, you can telephone 24-hours and free of charge to have an immediate stop put on its use. For MasterCard the number in Italy is ☎ 800 87 08 66, or make a reverse-charge call to St Louis in the USA on ☎ 314-275 66 90; for Visa, phone ☎ 800 87 72 32 in Italy. Amex is widely accepted but it is not as common as Visa or Mastercard.

International Transfers One reliable way to send money to Italy is by 'urgent telex' through the foreign office of a large Italian bank, or through major banks in your own country, to a nominated bank in Italy. It is important to have an exact record of all details associated with the money transfer. The money will always be held at the head office of the bank in the town to which it has been sent. Urgent-telex transfers should take only a few days, while other means, such as telegraphic transfer, or draft, can take weeks.

It is also possible to transfer money through Amex and Thomas Cook.

A speedier option is to send money through Western Union (freephone ☎ 800 46 44 64). The sender and receiver have to turn up at a Western Union outlet with passport or other form of ID and the fees charged for the virtually immediate transfer depend on the amount sent. This service functions through several outlets in Tuscany.

Security
Keep only a limited amount as cash, and the bulk in more easily replaceable forms such as travellers cheques or plastic. If your accommodation has a safe, use it. If you have to

leave money in your room, divide it into several stashes and hide them in different places.

For carrying money on the street the safest thing is a shoulder wallet or under-the-clothes money belt. An external money belt attracts rather than deflects attention from your valuables.

Costs
Tuscany's popularity makes it expensive. Accommodation charges (especially in the high season) and high entrance fees for many sights keep daily expenditure high. A *very* prudent backpacker might scrape by on around €45 a day, but only by staying in youth hostels, eating one simple meal a day (at the youth hostel), buying a sandwich or pizza slice for lunch, travelling slowly to keep transport costs down and minimising visits to museums and galleries.

One rung up, you can get by on €80 per day if you stay in the cheaper pensioni or small hotels, and keep sit-down meals and museum visits to one a day. Lone travellers may find even this budget hard to maintain.

If money is no object, you will find a plethora of ways to burn it. In the cities especially there's no shortage of luxury hotels, expensive restaurants and shops to wave wads at. Realistically, a traveller wanting to stay in comfortable, lower to mid-range hotels, eat two square meals daily, not feel restricted to one museum a day and be able to enjoy the odd drink and other minor indulgences should reckon on a minimum daily average of €130 per day – more if you have a car.

Ways to Save If you could it would be nice to avoid paying the extra charged by many pensioni for compulsory breakfast – a coffee and brioche in a cafe cost less and are better. The sad reality is that most places only offer the one price on rooms that automatically includes breakfast.

In bars, prices can double (sometimes even triple) if you sit down and are served at the table. Stand at the bar to drink your coffee or eat a sandwich.

Read the fine print on menus (usually posted outside eating establishments) to check the *coperto* (cover charge) and *servizio* (service fee).

Aerograms (on sale only at the post office for €0.50) are the cheapest way to send international mail.

Tipping
You are not expected to tip on top of restaurant service charges, but it is common to leave a small amount. If there is no service charge, the customer might consider leaving a 10% tip, but this is by no means obligatory. In bars, Italians often leave any small change as a tip, often only a few small coins. Tipping taxi drivers is not common practice, but you should tip the porter at higher class hotels.

Taxes & Refunds
Value-added tax, known as IVA (Imposta di Valore Aggiunto) is slapped onto just about everything in Italy and hovers around 19%. Tourists who are residents of countries outside the EU may claim a refund on this tax if the item was purchased for personal use and cost more than €155. The goods must be carried with you and you must keep the fiscal receipt.

The refund only applies to items purchased at affiliated retail outlets displaying a 'Tax-free for tourists' sign. Otherwise, ask the shopkeeper. You must complete a form at the point of purchase and have the form stamped and checked by Italian customs when you leave the country. You then return it by mail within 60 days to the vendor, who will make the refund, either by cheque or to your credit card. At major airports and some border crossings you can get an immediate cash refund at specially marked booths.

Receipts
Laws aimed at tightening controls on the payment of taxes in Italy mean that the onus is on the buyer to ask for and retain receipts for all goods and services. This applies to everything from a litre of milk to a haircut. Although it rarely happens, you could be asked by an officer of the Guardia di Finanza (Fiscal Police) to produce the receipt immediately after you leave a shop. If you

don't have it, you may be obliged to pay a fine of up to €155.

POST & COMMUNICATIONS
Post
Italy's postal service is notoriously slow, unreliable and expensive.

Francobolli (stamps) are available at post offices and authorised tobacconists (look for the official *tabacchi* sign: a big 'T', often white on black). Main post offices in the bigger cities are generally open from around 8am to at least 5pm. Many open on Saturday morning too. Tobacconists keep regular shop hours.

Rates Postcards and letters up to 20g sent air mail cost €0.80 to Australia and New Zealand, €0.70 to the USA and €0.40 within Europe. Aerograms are a cheap alternative, costing only €0.50 to send anywhere. They can be purchased at post offices only.

The *posta prioritaria* (priority post) service, similar to the UK's 1st-class post, is used by most. Postcards and letters up to 20g posted to destinations within Europe cost €0.60, and €0.75 anywhere else.

If you want to post more important items by registered mail *(raccomandato)* or by insured mail *(assicurato)*, remember that they will take as long as normal mail. Raccomandato costs €2.60 on top of the normal cost of the letter. The cost of assicurato depends on the value of the object being sent (€5.15 for objects up to €52 value) and is not available to the USA.

Sending Mail If you choose not to use posta prioritaria (see Rates) an air-mail letter can take up to two weeks to reach the UK or the USA, while a letter to Australia will take between two and three weeks.

The service within Italy is not much better: local letters take at least three days and up to a week to arrive in another city.

Pacchetti (parcels) can be sent from any post office. You can buy posting boxes or padded envelopes from most post offices. *Cartolerie* (stationery shops) and some tobacconists also sell padded envelopes. Don't tape up or staple envelopes – they should be

FACTS FOR THE VISITOR

sealed with glue. Your best bet is not to close the envelope or box completely and ask at the counter how it should be done. Parcels usually take longer to be delivered than letters. A different set of postal rates applies.

Express Mail Urgent mail can be sent by the post office's express mail service, known as *posta celere* or CAI Post. Letters up to 500g cost €15.50 in Europe, €23.75 to the USA and €35.10 to Australia. A parcel weighing 1kg will cost €17.55 in Europe, €27.90 to the USA and Canada, and €41.30 to Australia and New Zealand. CAI post is not necessarily as fast as private services. It will take three to five days for a parcel to reach the USA, Canada or Australia and one to three days to European destinations. Ask at post offices for addresses of CAI post outlets.

Couriers Several international couriers operate in Italy: DHL has the freephone number ☎ 800 34 53 45; for Federal Express call freephone ☎ 800 83 30 40; for UPS call freephone ☎ 800 82 20 54. Look in the telephone book for addresses. Note that if you are having articles sent to you by courier in Italy, you might be obliged to pay IVA of up to 20% to retrieve the goods.

Receiving Mail Poste restante is known as *fermo posta*. Letters marked thus will be held at the counter of the same name in the main post office in the relevant town. Poste restante mail should be addressed as follows:

> John SMITH
> Fermo Posta
> Posta Centrale
> 50100 Florence
> Italy

Postcodes are provided throughout this guide. You will need to pick up your letters in person and present your passport as ID.

Amex card or travellers cheque holders can use the free client mail-holding service at Amex offices. Take your passport when you go to pick up mail.

Emergency Numbers

Military Police (Carabinieri)	☎ 112
Police (Polizia)	☎ 113
Fire Brigade (Vigili del Fuoco)	☎ 115
Highway Rescue (Soccorso Stradale)	☎ 116
Ambulance (Ambulanza)	☎ 118

Telephone

The privatised Telecom Italia is the largest phone company in the country and its orange public pay phones are liberally scattered all over the place. The most common accept only *carte/schede telefoniche* (telephone cards), although you will still find some that accept cards and coins. Some card phones now also accept special Telecom credit cards and even commercial credit cards.

Phones can be found in the streets, train stations and some big stores as well as in unstaffed Telecom centres.

You can buy phonecards at post offices, tobacconists, newspaper stands and from vending machines in Telecom offices. To avoid the frustration of trying to find fast-disappearing coin telephones, always keep a phonecard on hand. They come with a value of €2.60, €5.15 and €25.80. Remember to snap off the perforated corner before using them.

Public phones operated by private telecommunications companies, Infostrada and Albacom, can be found in airports and train stations. These phones accept Infostrada or Albacom phonecards (available from post offices, tobacconists and newspaper stands), which come with a value of €2.60 or €5.15. Rates are slightly cheaper than Telecom's for long-distance and international calls.

Costs Rates, particularly for long-distance calls, are among the highest in Europe. The cheapest time for domestic calls is 10pm to 8am. It is a little more complicated for international calls but, basically, the cheapest off-peak time is 10pm to 8am and all of Sunday.

A *comunicazione urbana* (local call) from a public phone will cost €0.10 for three to six minutes, depending on the time of day you call. Peak call times are 8am to 6.30pm Monday to Friday and 8am to 1pm Saturday.

Rates for *comunicazione interurbana* (long-distance calls) within Italy depend on the time of day and the distance involved. At the worst, one minute will cost about €0.20 in peak periods.

If you need to call overseas, beware of the cost – even a call of five minutes to Australia after 10pm will cost around €4.15 from a private phone (more from a public phone). Calls to most of the rest of Europe cost about €0.25 per minute and closer to €0.60 from a public phone.

Travellers from countries that offer direct dialling services paid for at home country rates (such as AT&T in the USA and Telstra in Australia) should think seriously about taking advantage of them.

Domestic Calls Telephone area codes all begin with 0 and consist of up to four digits. The area code is followed by a number of anything from four to eight digits.

Area codes are an integral part of all telephone numbers in Italy, even if you are calling within a single zone. For example, any number you ring in Florence will start with 055, even if it's next door.

Numeri verdi (freephone numbers) usually begin with 800 (some start with 199 and 848). Mobile-telephone numbers begin with a three-digit prefix such as 330, 335, 347, etc. For directory enquiries within Italy, dial ☎ 12.

International Calls Direct international calls can easily be made from public telephones by using a phonecard. Dial 00 to get out of Italy, then the relevant country and city codes, followed by the telephone number.

Useful country codes are: Australia 61, Canada and the USA 1, New Zealand 64 and the UK 44. Codes for other countries in Europe include: France 33, Germany 49, Greece 30, Ireland 353 and Spain 34. Other codes are listed in Italian telephone books.

To make a reverse charge (collect) international call from a public telephone, dial ☎ 170.

Easier, and often cheaper, is using the Country Direct service in your country. You dial the number and request a reverse charge call through the operator in your country. Numbers for this service include the following:

Australia (Optus)	☎ 172 11 61
Australia (Telstra)	☎ 172 10 61
Canada	☎ 172 10 01
France	☎ 172 00 33
Germany	☎ 172 00 49
Ireland	☎ 172 03 53
The Netherlands	☎ 172 00 31
New Zealand	☎ 172 10 64
UK (BT)	☎ 172 00 44
UK (BT Chargecard)	☎ 172 01 44
USA (AT&T)	☎ 172 10 11
USA (IDB)	☎ 172 17 77
USA (MCI)	☎ 172 10 22
USA (Sprint)	☎ 172 18 77

For international directory enquiries call ☎ 176.

eKno Communication Service Lonely Planet's eKno global communication service provides low-cost international calls – for local calls you're usually better off with a local phonecard. eKno also offers free messaging services, email, travel information and an online travel vault, where you can securely store all your important documents. You can join eKno online at **W** www.ekno.lonelyplanet.com or by dialling ☎ 800 875691 within Tuscany. Once you have joined, to use eKno from Tuscany dial ☎ 800 875683.

Your Mobile Phone Abroad

Italy uses GSM 900/1800, which is compatible with the rest of Europe and Australia but not with the North American GSM 1900 or the totally different system in Japan (though some North Americans have GSM 1900/900 phones that do work here).

If you have intend to use your mobile phone here, check with your service provider about using it in Italy, and beware of calls being routed internationally (very expensive for a 'local' call).

International Phonecards A growing army of private companies now distribute international phonecards, some linked to US phone companies such as Sprint and MCI. The cards come in a variety of unit sizes and are sold in some bars, tobacconists, newspaper stands and other shops – look out for signs advertising them.

Telecom itself has brought out its Welcome Card, which costs €13 for 100 units and is certainly cheaper than making international calls on a standard phonecard, but may not stand up to some of the competition. Other new Telecom cards can be used in several countries as well as Italy.

Call Centres Privately run call centres are a further possibility for long-distance calls. One such option is Yellow Point which has established itself at Via Santa Elisabetta 5 in Florence. You pay for a card to use in one of their phones. When you have finished, they check what you have left on the card and pay you the difference. They claim the rates work out cheaper than dialling with Telecom. At other call centres cards are not used; you just make the call in a private booth and pay for it once you've finished.

Calling Tuscany from Abroad Call the international access code (00 in most countries), followed by the code for Italy (39) and the full number – remember to include the initial zero (for example – ☎ 00-39-055 555 55 55).

Fax

There is no shortage of fax offices in Italy and prices vary considerably from one office to another. However, in general, to send a fax within Tuscany you can expect to pay €1.55 for the first page and €1.05 for each page thereafter, plus €0.03 a second for the actual call. International faxes can cost from €3.10 for the first page and €2.10 per page thereafter, plus €0.05 a second for the actual call, depending on the destination. Faxes can also be sent from some Telecom public phones. It usually costs about €0.50 per page to receive a fax.

Email & Internet Access

Italy has been a little slower than some parts of Western Europe to march down the information highway. Nevertheless, email has definitely arrived. If you plan to carry your notebook or palmtop computer with you, buy a universal AC adapter, which will enable you to plug it in anywhere without frying the innards. You'll also need a plug adapter – it's easiest to buy these before you leave home.

Your PC-card modem also may or may not work once you leave your home country – and you won't know for sure until you try. The safest option is to buy a reputable 'global' modem before you leave home, or buy a local PC-card modem if you're spending an extended time in Italy. The telephone socket will sometimes be different from that at home, so have at least a US RJ-11 telephone adapter that works with your modem. You can almost always find an adapter that will convert from RJ-11 to the local variety. For more information on travelling with a portable computer, see Ⓦ www.teleadapt.com or Ⓦ www.warrior .com. Major Internet service providers (ISPs), such as AOL (Ⓦ www.aol.com), CompuServe (Ⓦ www.compuserve.com) and AT&T (Ⓦ www.attbusiness.net), have dial-in nodes in Italy; download a list of the dial-in numbers before you leave home – and read the fine print. Often you pay an extra fee for use of a local node.

Some Italian servers can provide short-term accounts for Internet access. Agora (☎ 800 304 999, Ⓦ www.agoratelematica.it) is one that has English-speaking staff.

If you intend to rely on cybercafes, you'll need to carry three pieces of information with you to enable you to access your Internet mail account: your incoming (POP or IMAP) mail server name, your account name and your password. Your ISP or network supervisor will be able to give you these. Armed with this information, you should be able to access your Internet mail account from any Net-connected machine in the world. Another option to collect mail through cybercafes is to open a free eKno Web-based email account online at Ⓦ www.ekno.lonelyplanet.com. You can then access your email from anywhere in the world from any Net-connected machine that's running a standard browser.

You'll find plenty of cybercafes in Florence, and they are slowly catching on in other parts of Tuscany. Expect to pay from €2.60 to €6.20 an hour.

DIGITAL RESOURCES

The World Wide Web is a rich resource for travellers. You can research your trip, hunt down bargain air fares, book hotels, check on weather conditions or chat with locals and other travellers about the best places to visit (or avoid!).

One of the best places to start your Web explorations is the Lonely Planet Web site (W www.lonelyplanet.com). Here you'll find succinct summaries on travelling to most places on earth, postcards from other travellers and the Thorn Tree bulletin board, where you can ask questions before you go or dispense advice when you get back. You can also find travel news and updates to many of our most popular guidebooks, and the subWWWay section links you to the most useful travel resources elsewhere on the Web. Many towns and provinces have their own Web sites which are listed throughout this book. Other useful sites include:

ATAF Online All you ever wanted to know, and probably quite a few things you didn't, about Florence's public transport system.
W www.ataf.net

Chianti A useful site devoted to this popular wine region.
W www.chianti.it

Chiantinet An excellent site with lots of information about the Chianti area and links to other sites.
W www.chiantinet.it

Citylife A site full of more or less useful listings information and a host of links.
W www.firenze.net

CTS Village Useful information from CTS, Italy's leading student travel organisation. Italian only.
W www.cts.it

Excite Reviews Call this site up and key in Italy and it will give you a long selection of sites related to Italy, as well as brief reviews and ratings.
W www.excite.com

Excite Travel This site contains a farefinder and booking facilities and links to maps, restaurant tips and the like.
W travel.excite.com

Ferrovie dello Stato This is the official site of the Ferrovie dello Stato, the Italian railways. You can look up fare and timetable information here, although it can be a little complicated to plough through.
W www.fs-on-line.com

Go Tuscany This site is aimed at the expat community and English-speaking visitors to the region. It contains tips on places to stay and eat in and outside Florence, itineraries in Tuscany, classified ads and an events calendar.
W www.firenze.net/events

Internet Cafe Guide At this site you can get a list of Internet cafes around Italy. It's not as up to date as you might expect such a site to be, but it is a start.
W www.netcafeguide.com

Parks.it This is the place to look for basic information on all of Italy's national and regional parks, along with any other protected areas. Naturally all of Tuscany's parks are here.
W www.parks.it

Siena All From this page you can fan out in search of all sorts of Siena- and Tuscany-related links. Everything from books to events, museum timetables to notes on the life of Santa Caterina can be located here. Italian only.
W www.novamedia.it/sienall

Siena Online At this address you can open a series of Web pages and search links for items on Siena.
W www.sienaol.it

Siena Tourist Office The provincial Siena tourist office site has useful info on tourist offices throughout the province, as well as other items of interest. Italian only.
W www.siena.turismo.toscana.it

BOOKS

Most books are published in different editions by different publishers in different countries. As a result, a book might be a hardcover rarity in one country while it is readily available in paperback in another. Your local bookshop or library is best placed to advise you on the availability of the following recommendations.

Lonely Planet

If you intend to spend most of your time in Florence, Lonely Planet's *Florence*, with more in-depth information on the city, may be useful. Travellers planning to move around more widely should consider *Italy*. The *Italian phrasebook* lists all the words and phrases you're likely to need when travelling in Italy. A good source of information on walking in both Tuscany and Italy is *Walking in Italy*, with details on tracks, walking times and accommodation.

Lonely Planet's *World Food Italy* is a full-colour book with information on the whole range of Italian food and drink. It includes a useful language section, with the definitive culinary dictionary and a handy quick-reference glossary.

Other books on Italy by Lonely Planet include *Milan, Turin & Genoa, Rome, Rome Condensed, Sardinia, Sicily* and *Venice*.

On a more general note, there are lots of handy tips in Cathy Lanigan's *Travel with Children*, and *Travel Photography: A Guide to Taking Better Pictures* is written by internationally renowned travel photographer, Richard I'Anson. It's designed to take on the road and is full colour throughout.

Guidebooks
If you like density, the ultimate guides are the red hardbacks published in Italian by the Touring Club Italiano. Look for *Toscana* and *Firenze e Provincia*. To give you an idea of what you are in for, the latter is some 800 closely printed pages. The TCI, perhaps realising that not everyone can get their heads around this sort of thing, also puts out a much more user-friendly, green-covered, paperback series.

Travel
An endless stream of foreign wallahs has poured into Tuscany over the centuries to soak in the beauty and express an opinion. Many barely got past the expat communities of Florence and some of their opinions are remarkable more for their pomposity than for any insight. Numerous exceptions confirm that harsh rule.

Two Grand Tour classics are Johann Wolfgang von Goethe's *Italienische Reise* (Italian Journey), and Henry James' *Italian Hours*. DH Lawrence wrote three short travel books while living in Italy, now combined in one volume entitled *DH Lawrence and Italy*. The relevant one is *Etruscan Places*, in which Lawrence fairly writhes in ecstasy over this ancient people.

A brief, readable, insightful and highly opinionated account of Florence, its past and its foibles is *The Stones of Florence*, by Mary McCarthy.

If you like that sort of thing, the popular *Under the Tuscan Sun* by Frances Maye details the joys and woes of setting up an expat residence in Tuscany.

Italian History & People
Edward Gibbon's *History of the Decline and Fall of the Roman Empire* (available in six hardback volumes, or an abridged, single-volume paperback) remains the masterwork on that subject in English.

For a general look at Italy, try *History of the Italian People*, by Giuliano Procacci. Other options to help you get started include *Italy: A Short History*, by Harry Hearder, and *Concise History of Italy*, by Vincent Cronin. *A History of Contemporary Italy: Society and Politics 1943–1988*, by Paul Ginsburg, is an absorbing analysis of the country's post-WWII travails.

Tuscan History & People
It is damned near impossible to find a general history of Tuscany. Time and again you will be offered histories of Florence. It is even fairly difficult to come across histories of other Tuscan cities. The following will get you started.

As its title suggests, Pier Francesco Listri's *Tuscany – From Etruscans to Year 2000* takes you on a whirlwind tour of Tuscany from Etruscan times to the present day. Christopher Hibbert's *The Rise and Fall of the House of Medici* is an acknowledged classic on the fortunes of Florence's most famous family. For a more general history of the city, try his *Biography of Florence*, which sweeps you along at a brisk pace through the political, social and artistic highs and lows of the city. Hibbert's racy narrative style makes both books a good initial investment.

Leaning more to the artistic side of the story of Florence is Michael Levey's *Florence – A Portrait*. Not as full of intriguing anecdote as Hibbert's books, it is still an excellent and highly readable treatment.

A rather more ponderous general history of the city is Marcello Vanuzzi's multi-volume *Storia di Firenze*. The quirky text has been condensed into an English version, *The History of Florence*. The information is in there, but the often overly lyrical style is a little peculiar, not to say highly irritating at some points.

Ferdinand Schevill's *Siena – The History of a Medieval Commune* was penned at the beginning of the 20th century. Some of the writer's assertions should be read with a pinch of salt, but it remains one of the only accounts of the city in English.

For an excursion into the day-to-day life of a Tuscan merchant family, get hold of Iris Origo's *The Merchant of Prato*, a splendid synthesis of the reams of documentation that have survived from the 14th century.

Art & Architecture

An attractive coffee-table book with serious content is *History of Italian Renaissance Art*, by Frederick Hartt. He concentrates on Florence, but does not overlook art and architecture elsewhere in Tuscany. He of course also deals with the greats of Roman and Venetian art. Hartt was one of the most distinguished authorities on Renaissance art in the 20th century.

A good general reference work covering the Renaissance in all its facets is JR Hale's *Concise Encyclopedia of the Italian Renaissance*.

Charles Avery's *Florentine Renaissance Sculpture* is a comprehensive study of this aspect of Florence's glittering artistic legacy.

Bruno Nardini's *Incontro con Michelangiolo* has been translated as *Michelangelo – Biography of a Genius*, a compelling account of the artist's life.

If you think you are up to it, you can pick up Leon Alberti's Renaissance masterpiece *On Painting*, or Giorgio Vasari's classic *Le Vite de' Eccellenti Architetti, Pittori, et Scultori Italiani, da Cimabue, insino a' Tempi Nostri*, better known to English readers simply as Lives of the Artists, available in several editions and translations.

Fiction

The beauty of Tuscany not only captivated a multitude of travellers but also inspired a number of well-known authors to pen novels set among its rolling hills and hilltop towns. Some of the more famous novels set in Tuscany include *Room with a View* and *Where Angels Fear to Tread* by EM Forster (set in Florence and San Gimignano respectively), *Portrait of a Lady* by Henry James, *Romola* by George Eliot, *The English Patient* by Michael Ondaatjie, *Innocence* by Penelope Fitzgerald and *Summer's Lease* by John Mortimer.

Children

Bambini alla Scoperta di Florence (translated as Florence for Kids) is a brightly presented book for young people obliged by their elders to explore the city. It is an entertaining, informative approach, with quizzes and other learning prompts. Adults can learn quite a lot about the city too. It is published by Fratelli Palomb Editori.

Cathy Lanigan's *Travel with Children* gives practical information and advice to make travel as stress-free as possible.

Cuisine

The Food of Italy, by Waverley Root, is an acknowledged classic covering Italian cuisine in general. For more specifically Tuscan cooking, you could try *Il Libro della Cucina Fiorentina e Toscana*, a prettily illustrated job by Elisabetta Piazzesi that has been translated into several languages – you can find it in bookshops in Florence. For information on *World Food Italy*, Lonely Planet's guide to Italian cuisine, see under Lonely Planet earlier in this section.

Stephanie Alexander and Maggie Beer's *Tuscan Cooking* is a beautifully illustrated coffee-table tome. Another more suited to the coffee table than the kitchen is Jeni Wright's *Tuscan Food and Folklore*.

For some fine traditional recipes, foodies will enjoy Slow Food Editore's *Ricette di*

Osterie di Firenze e Chianti – if you read some Italian.

Wine buffs will appreciate Luca Maroni's *Guide to Italian Wines* or *Italian Wines*.

Walking

For information on books describing walking in Tuscany, see the Tuscany on Foot chapter.

FILMS

Although Tuscany hasn't loomed large on the silver screens of moviedom, it's still provided a number of fine directors and of course, superb backdrops (for more on Tuscan film directors see the Facts About Tuscany chapter).

Some films well known to the English-speaking world that have taken advantage of Tuscany's countless period-settings include James Ivory's *A Room with a View*, Bertolucci's *Stealing Beauty*, Kenneth Branagh's *Much Ado About Nothing*, Jane Campion's *The Portrait of a Lady*, Anthony Minghella's *The English Patient*, Roberto Benigni's *Life is Beautiful*, and Ridley Scott's *Gladiator* and *Hannibal*.

NEWSPAPERS & MAGAZINES

You can easily find a wide selection of national daily newspapers from around Europe and the UK at newsstands all over central Florence and in most towns of consequence throughout Tuscany. The *International Herald Tribune*, *Time*, *Newsweek*, the *Economist*, *Le Monde*, *Der Spiegel* and a host of other international magazines are also available.

Italian National Press

There is no 'national' paper as such, but rather several important dailies published out of the major cities. These include Milan's *Corriere della Sera*, Turin's *La Stampa* and Rome's *La Repubblica*. This trio forms what could be considered the nucleus of a national press, publishing local editions up and down the country. Politically speaking, they range from centre-left *(La Repubblica)* to establishment right *(La Stampa)*.

Local Press

The Florence-based *La Nazione* is the main regional broadsheet. Compared with the likes of the *Corriere della Sera* it is pretty poor on both national and foreign news, but if you are more interested in what's happening locally, it's probably the paper of choice. It is published in provincial editions, so the one you buy in Florence won't be exactly the same as the one you pick up in Grosseto. You will find a fairly decent cinema and theatre listings section in it too. Along the coast you will see *Il Tirreno*, again with local editions. Most provinces have at least one other local competition rag.

Useful Publications

The multi-lingual *Chianti News* and *Tuscany News* sometimes have interesting articles but are directed more at local expats than passing interlopers.

RADIO

You can pick up the BBC World Service on medium wave at 648kHz, short wave at 6195kHz, 9410kHz, 12095kHz, 15575kHz, and on long wave at 198kHz, depending on where you are and the time of day. Voice of America (VOA) can usually be found on short wave at 15205kHz.

There are three state-owned stations: RAI-1 (1332 AM or 89.7 FM), RAI-2 (846 AM or 91.7 FM) and RAI-3 (93.7 FM). They combine classical and light music with discussion programmes and news broadcasts.

Many of the local stations are a little bland. For a good mix of contemporary music you could try Controradio on 93.6 AM, or Nova Radio on 101.5 FM in Florence.

TV

The three state-run stations, RAI-1, RAI-2 and RAI-3 are run by Radio e Televisione Italiane. Historically, each has been in the hands of one of the main political groupings in the country, although those waters have been muddied in the past few years of musical chairs down in Rome.

Of the three, RAI-3 tends to have some of the more interesting programmes. Generally, however, these stations and the private Canale 5, Italia 1 and Rete 4, tend to serve up a diet of indifferent news, tacky variety hours (with lots of near-naked tits and bums,

Chianti grapes ready for harvesting: Tuscany mostly produces red wine, though not exclusively.

Some of the best wine is aged in small barrels.

Chianti – both distinctive and distinguished

Visit the vines by following Strada del Vini, wine trails through rural Tuscany.

Florence's Mercato Centrale was built in 1874.

Antipasti – the 'pre-meal' or a meal in itself?

Local cuisine relies on fresh herbs such as basil.

Traditional unsalted Tuscan bread

Temple-like delicatessens are a Tuscan treat.

appalling crooning and vaudeville humour), game shows and dire soaps. Talk shows, some interesting but many nauseating, also abound.

VIDEO SYSTEMS

If you want to record or buy video tapes to play back home, you won't get a picture if the image registration systems are different. TVs and nearly all prerecorded videos on sale in Italy use the PAL (Phase Alternation Line) system that is common to most of Western Europe and Australia; PAL is incompatible with France's SECAM system or the NTSC system used in North America and Japan.

PHOTOGRAPHY & VIDEO
Film & Equipment

The major Italian airports are all fully equipped with modern inspection systems that do not damage most film or other photographic material that is carried in hand luggage.

A roll of 100 ASA Kodak film *pellicola* costs around €3.60/4.10 for 24/36 exposures. Developing costs around €5.70/7.25 for 24/36 exposures in standard format. A roll of 36 slides *diapositive* costs €5.15 to buy and €4.10 for development.

Restrictions

Photography is not allowed in many churches, museums and galleries. Look out for signs with crossed-out camera symbols as you go in.

TIME

Italy operates on a 24-hour clock. Daylight-saving time starts on the last Sunday in March, when clocks are put forward one hour. Clocks are put back an hour on the last Sunday in October.

European countries such as France, Germany, Austria and Spain are on the same time as Italy. Greece, Egypt and Israel are one hour ahead. When it's noon in Florence, it's 11am in London, 6am in New York, 3am in San Francisco, 6am in Toronto, 9pm in Sydney, 7pm in Perth and 11pm in Auckland.

ELECTRICITY
Voltages & Cycles

Electric current in Florence is 220V, 50Hz, as in the rest of continental Europe. Several countries outside Europe (such as the USA and Canada) have 60Hz, which means that appliances from those countries with electric motors (such as some CD and tape players) may perform poorly. It is always safest to use an adapter.

Plugs & Sockets

Plugs have two round pins, again as in the rest of continental Europe.

WEIGHTS & MEASURES

The metric system is used (see the inside back cover for a conversion chart). Basic terms for weight include *un etto* (100g) and *un chilo* (1kg). Like other continental Europeans, the Italians indicate decimals with commas and thousands with points.

LAUNDRY

Coin laundrettes, where you can do your own washing, are slowly catching on in Italy. You'll find plenty in Florence and one or two in Siena and Pisa and along the coast. A load will cost from €3.10. *Lavasecco* (dry-cleaning) charges range from around €3.10 for a shirt to €6.20 for a jacket.

TOILETS

Public toilets are not exactly widespread in Italy. Most people use the toilets in bars and cafes – although you might need to buy a coffee first!

HEALTH
Medical Services

If you need an ambulance anywhere in Italy call ☎ 118.

The quality of medical treatment in public hospitals varies in Italy. Simply put, the farther north, the better the care.

Private hospitals and clinics throughout the country generally provide excellent services but are expensive for those without medical insurance. That said, certain treatments in public hospitals may also have to be paid for and can be equally costly.

Medical Kit Check List

Following is a list of items you should consider including in your medical kit – consult your pharmacist for brands available in your country.

- ☐ **Aspirin or paracetamol (acetaminophen in the USA)** – for pain or fever
- ☐ **Antihistamine** – for allergies, eg, hay fever; to ease the itch from insect bites or stings; and to prevent motion sickness
- ☐ **Cold and flu tablets, throat lozenges and nasal decongestant**
- ☐ **Multivitamins** – consider for long trips, when dietary vitamin intake may be inadequate
- ☐ **Loperamide or diphenoxylate** –'blockers' for diarrhoea
- ☐ **Prochlorperazine or metaclopramide** – for nausea and vomiting
- ☐ **Rehydration mixture** – to prevent dehydration, which may occur, for example, during bouts of diarrhoea; particularly important when travelling with children
- ☐ **Insect repellent, sunscreen, lip balm and eye drops**
- ☐ **Calamine lotion, sting relief spray or aloe vera** – to ease irritation from sunburn and insect bites or stings
- ☐ **Antifungal cream or powder** – for fungal skin infections and thrush
- ☐ **Antiseptic (such as povidone-iodine)** – for cuts and grazes
- ☐ **Bandages, Band-Aids (plasters) and other wound dressings**
- ☐ **Water purification tablets or iodine**
- ☐ **Scissors, tweezers and a thermometer** – note that mercury thermometers are prohibited by airlines

Your embassy or consulate in Italy can provide a list of recommended doctors in major cities. If you have a specific health complaint, it would be wise to obtain the necessary information and referrals for treatment before leaving home.

The public health system is administered along provincial lines by centres generally known as Unità Sanitarie Locali (USL) or Unità Soci Sanitarie Locali (USSL). Increasingly they are being reorganised as Aziende Sanitarie Locali (ASL). Through them you find out where your nearest hospital, medical clinics and other services are. Look under 'U' or 'A' in the telephone book (sometimes the USL and USSL are under 'A' too, as Azienda USL).

Under these headings you'll find long lists of offices – look for Poliambulatorio (Polyclinic) and the telephone number for Accetazione Sanitaria. You need to call this number to make an appointment: there is no point in just rolling up. Clinic opening hours vary widely, with the minimum generally being about 8am to 12.30pm Monday to Friday. Some open for a couple of hours in the afternoon and on Saturday mornings too.

Each ASL/USL area has its own Consultorio Familiare (Family Planning Centre) where you can go for contraceptives, pregnancy tests and information about abortion (legal up to the 12th week of pregnancy).

For emergency treatment, go straight to the *pronto soccorso* (casualty) section of a public hospital, where you can also get emergency dental treatment. Sometimes hospitals are listed in the phone book under Aziende Ospedaliere. In major cities you are likely to find English-speaking doctors, or a volunteer translator service. Often first aid is also available at train stations, airports and ports.

Medical Cover

Citizens of EU countries are covered for emergency medical treatment in Italy on presentation of an E111 form. Treatment in private hospitals is not covered and charges are also likely for medication, dental work and secondary examinations, including X-rays and laboratory tests. Ask about the E111 at your local health services department a few weeks before you travel (in the UK, the form is available free of charge at post offices). However, the E111 is not a substitute for medical and travel insurance.

Australia also has a reciprocal arrangement with Italy so that emergency treatment is covered – Medicare in Australia publishes a brochure with the details. The USA, Canada and New Zealand do not have reciprocal arrangements and citizens of these countries will be required to pay for any treatment in Italy themselves.

Advise medical staff of any reciprocal arrangements *before* they begin treating you. Most travel insurance policies include medical cover. See Travel Insurance under Visas & Documents earlier in this chapter.

General Preparations

Make sure you are healthy before you leave home. If you are embarking on a long trip, make sure your teeth are OK, because dental treatment is particularly expensive in Italy.

If you wear glasses, take a spare pair and your prescription. If you lose your glasses, you will be able to have them replaced within a few days by an *ottico* (optician).

Travellers who require a particular medication should take an adequate supply as well as the prescription, with the generic rather than the brand name. Basic drugs are widely available and indeed many items requiring prescriptions in countries such as the USA can be obtained over the counter in Italy. Tampons and condoms are available in pharmacies and supermarkets.

No vaccinations are required for entry into Italy though it's recommended that everyone keep up-to-date with diphtheria, tetanus, measles and polio vaccinations.

Basic Rules

Stomach upsets are the most likely travel health problem, but in Tuscany the majority of these will be relatively minor and probably due to overindulgence in the local food. Some people take a while to adjust to the regular use of olive oil in the food.

Water Tap water is drinkable throughout Tuscany, although locals themselves have taken to drinking the bottled stuff. The sign *acqua non potable* tells you that water is not drinkable (you may see it in trains and at some camping grounds). Water from drinking fountains is safe unless there is a sign telling you otherwise.

Travel Health Guides

Travel with Children from Lonely Planet includes advice on travel health for younger children. There are also a number of excellent travel health sites on the Internet. From the Lonely Planet home page there are links at W www.lonelyplanet.com/weblinks /wlheal.htm to the World Health Organization and the US Centers for Disease Control & Prevention.

Medical Problems & Treatment

Self-diagnosis and treatment can be risky, so you should always seek medical help. An embassy, consulate or five-star hotel can usually recommend a local doctor or clinic. Although we do give drug dosages in this section, they are for emergency use only. Correct diagnosis is vital. In this section we have used the generic names for medications – check with a pharmacist for brands available locally.

Environmental Hazards

Heatstroke This serious and sometimes fatal condition can occur if the body's heat-regulating mechanism breaks down and the body temperature rises to dangerous levels. Long, continuous periods of exposure to high temperatures can leave you vulnerable to heatstroke. Avoid excessive alcohol consumption or strenuous activity when you first arrive in Italy during mid-summer.

The symptoms of heatstroke are feeling unwell, not sweating much or at all and a high body temperature (39 to 41°C or 102 to 106°F). Where sweating has ceased, the skin becomes flushed. Severe, throbbing headaches and lack of coordination will also occur. The sufferer may become confused or aggressive. Eventually the victim will become delirious or convulse. Hospitalisation is essential and, meanwhile, get patients out of the sun, remove their clothing, cover them with a wet sheet or towel and then fan them continuously.

Heat Exhaustion & Prickly Heat Dehydration and salt deficiency can cause heat exhaustion and can lead to severe heatstroke (see the previous section). Take time to acclimatise to high temperatures, drink sufficient liquids such as tea and drinks rich in mineral salts (such as clear soups, and fruit and vegetable juices), and do not do anything too physically demanding. Salt deficiency is characterised by fatigue, lethargy, headaches, giddiness and muscle cramps; salt tablets may help, but adding extra salt to your food is better.

Prickly heat is an itchy rash caused by excessive perspiration trapped under the skin. It usually strikes people who have just arrived in a hot climate. Keeping cool by bathing often, using a mild talcum powder or even resorting to air-conditioning may help until you acclimatise.

Sunburn At higher altitudes you can get sunburn surprisingly quickly, even through cloud. Use a sunscreen, a hat and some barrier cream for your nose and lips. Calamine lotion is good for soothing mild sunburn. Protect your eyes with good-quality sunglasses.

Infectious Diseases

Diarrhoea Despite all your precautions, you may still have a mild bout of travellers' diarrhoea. Dehydration is the main danger with any diarrhoea, particularly for children and the elderly, so fluid replenishment is the number-one treatment. Weak black tea with a little sugar, soda water or soft drinks allowed to go flat and half-diluted with water are all good.

With severe diarrhoea, a rehydrating solution is necessary to replace minerals and salts and you should see a doctor. Stick to a bland diet as you recover.

Hepatitis Hepatitis is a general term for inflammation of the liver. The symptoms are fever, chills, headache, fatigue, feelings of weakness and aches and pains, followed by loss of appetite, nausea, vomiting, abdominal pain, dark urine, light-coloured faeces, jaundiced (yellow) skin and the whites of the eyes may turn yellow. People who have had hepatitis should avoid alcohol for some time after the illness as the liver needs time to recover.

Hepatitis A is transmitted by contaminated food and drinking water. You should seek medical advice but there is not much you can do apart from resting, drinking lots of fluids, eating lightly and avoiding fatty foods. Hepatitis E is transmitted in the same

way as hepatitis A; it can be particularly serious in pregnant women.

Hepatitis B is spread through contact with infected blood, blood products or body fluids – for example, through sexual contact, unsterilised needles, blood transfusions or contact with blood via small breaks in the skin. Other risk situations include getting a tattoo and body piercing with contaminated equipment. The symptoms of hepatitis B may be more severe than type A and the disease can lead to long term problems such as chronic liver damage, liver cancer or a long-term carrier state. Hepatitis C and D are spread in the same way as hepatitis B and can also lead to long-term complications.

HIV & AIDS Infection with the human immunodeficiency virus (HIV) may lead to acquired immune deficiency syndrome (AIDS), which is a fatal disease. Any exposure to blood, blood products or body fluids may put the individual at risk. The disease is often transmitted through sexual contact or dirty needles – vaccinations, acupuncture, tattooing and body piercing can be potentially as dangerous as intravenous drug use. Blood used for transfusions in European hospitals is screened for HIV and should be safe. ☎ 1678 61061) is the national help and information line dedicated to HIV-related problems, and the Consultorio per la Salute Omosessuale, a centre in Florence (☎ 055 47 65 57, Via San Sanobi 54) provides various services relating to AIDS & HIV.

The Linea Verde Aids (freephone ☎ 1678 61061) is the national help and information line dedicated to HIV-related problems, and the Consultorio per la Salute Omosessuale, a centre in Florence (☎ 055 47 65 57, Via San Sanobi 54) provides various services relating to AIDS & HIV.

Sexually Transmitted Infections (STIs)

HIV/AIDS and hepatitis B can be transmitted through sexual contact – see the relevant sections earlier for more details. Other STIs include gonorrhoea, herpes and syphilis; sores, blisters or rashes around the genitals and discharges or pain when urinating are common symptoms. In some STIs, such as wart virus or chlamydia, symptoms may be less marked or not observed at all, especially in women. Chlamydia infection can cause infertility in men and women before any symptoms have been noticed. Syphilis symptoms eventually disappear completely but the disease continues and can cause severe problems in later years. While abstinence from sexual contact is the only 100% effective prevention, using condoms is also effective.

Insect-Borne Diseases

Leishmaniasis This is a group of parasitic diseases transmitted by sandflies and found in coastal parts of Tuscany. Cutaneous leishmaniasis affects the skin tissue, causing ulceration and disfigurement; visceral leishmaniasis affects the internal organs. Seek medical advice, as laboratory testing is required for diagnosis and correct treatment. Avoiding sandfly bites by covering up and using repellent is the best precaution against this disease. Bites are usually painless, itchy and yet another reason to cover up and apply repellent.

Lyme Disease Lyme disease is an infection transmitted by ticks that can be acquired in Europe, including in forested areas of Tuscany. The illness usually begins with a spreading rash at the site of the tick bite and is accompanied by fever, headache, extreme fatigue, aching joints and muscles and mild neck stiffness. If untreated, these symptoms usually resolve over several weeks but, over subsequent weeks or months, disorders of the nervous system, heart and joints may develop. Treatment works best early in the illness. Medical help should be sought.

Bites & Stings

Jellyfish Tuscan beaches are occasionally inundated with jellyfish. Their stings are painful but not dangerous. Dousing in vinegar will deactivate any stingers that have not fired. Calamine lotion, antihistamines and analgesics may reduce the reaction and relieve the pain. If in doubt about swimming, ask locals if any jellyfish are in the water.

Snakes Italy's only dangerous snake, the viper, is found throughout Tuscany. To minimise your chances of being bitten, always wear boots, socks and long trousers when walking through undergrowth where snakes may be present. Don't put your hands into holes and crevices and do be careful when collecting firewood.

Viper bites do not cause instantaneous death and an antivenene is widely available in pharmacies. If someone is bitten by a snake that could be venomous, keep the victim calm and still, wrap the bitten limb tightly, as you would for a sprained ankle, and attach a splint to immobilise it. Then seek medical help, if possible with the dead snake for identification. Don't attempt to catch the snake if there is even a remote possibility of being bitten again. Tourniquets and sucking out the poison are now comprehensively discredited.

Ticks Always check your body if you have been walking through a potentially tick-infested area. In recent years there have been several reported deaths in Sardinia related to tick bites. Health authorities have yet to pinpoint the cause.

Less Common Diseases

Rabies Rabies is still found in Italy, but only in isolated areas of the Alps. It is transmitted through a bite or scratch by an infected animal. Dogs are noted carriers. A bite, scratch or even lick from a mammal in an area where rabies does exist should be cleaned immediately and thoroughly. Scrub with soap and running water and then clean with an alcohol or iodine solution. Medical help should be sought immediately. A course of injections may then be required in order to prevent the onset of symptoms and death.

WOMEN TRAVELLERS

Tuscany is not a dangerous region for women, but women travelling alone will sometimes find themselves plagued by unwanted attention from men. This attention usually involves catcalls, hisses and whistles and, as such, is usually more annoying than threatening.

As in many parts of Europe, lone women may at times also find it difficult to be left alone. It is not uncommon for Italian men to harass foreign women in the street, while drinking a coffee in a bar or trying to read a book in a park. Usually the best response is to ignore them, but if that doesn't work, politely tell them that you are waiting for your *marito* (husband) or *fidanzato* (boyfriend) and, if necessary, walk away. Florence can be a pain in this way, especially in the bars. It can also be an issue in some of the coastal resorts and on Elba.

Avoid becoming aggressive as this almost always results in an unpleasant confrontation. If all else fails, approach the nearest member of the police or *carabinieri* (military police force).

Basically, most of the attention falls into the nuisance/harassment category. However, women on their own should use their common sense. Avoid walking alone on deserted and dark streets and look for centrally located hotels within easy walking distance of places where you can eat at night. Lonely Planet does not recommend hitchhiking, and women travelling alone should be particularly wary of doing so.

Recommended reading is the *Handbook for Women Travellers*, by M & G Moss.

GAY & LESBIAN TRAVELLERS

Homosexuality is legal in Italy and well tolerated in the northern half of the country. The legal age of consent is 16 years.

Gay discos and the like can be tracked down through local gay organisations (see later) or the national monthly gay magazine *Pride* (€3.10). Be warned, however, that outside Florence's limited scene there ain't a lot happening on this front in Tuscany. There's a Web site at W www.gay.it/pinklily, with lots of information on activities and places to go, but it was last updated in 1999.

International gay and lesbian guides worth tracking down are the *Spartacus Guide for Gay Men*, published by Bruno Gmünder Verlag, Mail Order, PO Box 61 01 04, 10921 Berlin; and *Places for Women*, published by Ferrari Publications, Phoenix, AZ, USA.

Organisations

The national organisation for gay men is ArciGay (☎ 051 644 70 54, fax 051 644 67 22); ArciLesbica is its equivalent for lesbians. They are based at Piazza di Porta Saragozza 2, 40123 Bologna.

You'll find any number of Italian gay sites on the net, but some are all but useless. ArciGay (W www.gay.it, Italian only) has general information on the gay and lesbian scene in Italy and plenty of useful links.

The organisation Azione Gay e Lesbica Finisterrae (☎/fax 055 67 12 98, W www .azionegayelesbica.it – Italian only) is at Via Manara 12 in Florence.

DISABLED TRAVELLERS

Tuscany isn't exactly the easiest place for disabled travellers. Cobblestone streets, common in many towns, can be a nuisance for the wheelchair-bound, and many buildings (including hotels) don't have lifts.

The Italian State Tourist Office in your country may be able to provide advice on Italian associations for the disabled and what help is available in the country. It may also carry a small brochure, *Services for Disabled People*, published by the Italian railways, which details facilities at stations and on trains. Some of the better trains, such as the ETR460 and ETR500, have a carriage for passengers in wheelchairs and their companions.

Organisations

The UK-based Royal Association for Disability & Rehabilitation (Radar; ☎ 020-7250 3222, W www.radar.org.uk), Unit 12, City Forum, 250 City Rd, London EC1V 8AS, publishes a useful *Holiday Fact Pack*, which provides a good overview of facilities available to disabled travellers throughout Europe.

Another organisation that's worth calling is Holiday Care Service (☎ 01293-774535, W www.holidaycare.org.uk). They produce an information pack on Italy for disabled people and others with special needs.

In Italy itself you may also be able to get help. COIN (Cooperative Integrate) is a national voluntary group with links to the government and branches all over the country. They have information on accessible accommodation, transport and attractions. COIN (☎ 06 23 26 75 05, W www.coinsociale.it, e turismo@coinsociale.it) is at Via Enrico Giglioli 54a, Rome.

Promotur – Accessible Italy (☎ 011 309 63 63, Ⓦ www.tour-web.com/accessibleitaly/), Piazza Pitagora 9, 10137 Turin, is a private company that specialises in holiday services for the disabled, ranging from tours to the hiring of adapted transport.

SENIOR TRAVELLERS

Senior citizens are entitled to discounts on public transport and on admission fees at some museums in Tuscany. It is always important to ask. The minimum qualifying age is generally 60 or 65 years. You should also seek information in your own country on travel packages and discounts for senior travellers, through senior citizens' organisations and travel agents.

TRAVEL WITH CHILDREN

Italy's attitude to children is quite the opposite of some European countries (we won't mention them here, they know who they are) where dogs are more welcome in restaurants and bars. Most places are quite happy to accommodate the young ones and it's not uncommon to see children out until 11pm or midnight.

Successful travel with children can require a special effort. Don't try to overdo things by packing too much into the time available, and make sure activities include the kids as well. Remember that visits to museums and galleries can be tiring, even for adults. Allow time for the kids to play, either in a park or in the hotel room.

Discounts are available for children (usually under 12 years of age) on public transport and for admission to museums, galleries, etc.

Always make a point of asking at tourist offices if they know of any special family or children's activities and for suggestions on hotels that cater for kids. Families should book accommodation in advance, where possible, to avoid inconvenience.

Farmacie (chemists) sell baby formula in powder or liquid form as well as sterilising solutions, such as Milton. Disposable nappies are widely available at supermarkets, chemists (where they are more expensive) and sometimes in larger stationery stores. A pack of around 30 disposable nappies

(diapers) costs around €9.30. Fresh cow's milk is sold in cartons in bars (which have a 'Latteria' sign) and in supermarkets. If it is essential that you have milk you should carry an emergency carton of UHT milk, since bars usually close at 8pm. In many out-of-the-way areas the locals use only UHT milk.

For more information, see Lonely Planet's *Travel with Children.*

USEFUL ORGANISATIONS

With branches all over the world, Istituto Italiano di Cultura (IIC; Ⓦ www.italcult.net) is a government-sponsored organisation aimed at promoting Italian culture and language. They put on classes in Italian and provide a library and information service. This is a good place to start your search for places to study in Italy. The library at the London branch – 39 Belgrave Square, London SW1 (☎ 020-7235 1461) – has an extensive reference book collection, with works on the arts and history, a range of periodicals and videos. Other international IIC branches include:

Australia
(☎ 03-9866 5931, Ⓦ www.iicmelau.org) 233 Domain Rd, South Yarra, Melbourne, Vic 3141
(☎ 02-9392 7939) Level 45, Gateway 1, Macquarie Place, Sydney, NSW 2000
Canada
(☎ 416-921 3802, Ⓦ www.iicto-ca.org) 496 Huron St, Toronto, Ontario M5R 2R3
(☎ 514-849 3473) 1200 Penfield Drive, Montreal, Quebec H3A 1A9
France
(☎ 01 44 39 49 39, Ⓦ www.italynet.com /cultura/istcult) Hôtel Galliffet, 50 rue de Varenne, 75007 Paris
Germany
(☎ 030-261 7875) Hildebrandstrasse 1, 10785 Berlin
(☎ 089-764563) Hermann Schmidt Strasse 8, 80336 Munich
Ireland
(☎ 01-676 6662) 11 Fitzwilliam Square, Dublin 2
Switzerland
(☎ 01-202 4846) Gotthardstrasse 27, 8002 Zürich
USA
(☎ 212-879 4242) 686 Park Ave, New York, NY 10021-5009

(☎ 310-443 3250) 1023 Hildegard Ave, Los Angeles, CA 90024

(☎ 202-328 3840) 1717 Massachussets Ave S104, NW, Washington, DC 20036

DANGERS & ANNOYANCES
Theft

This is the main problem for travellers in Tuscany, although it is not as troublesome as in other parts of the country.

Pickpockets and bag-snatchers operate in the most touristy parts of the bigger cities and some of the coastal resort towns. Paying a little attention should help you avoid unpleasantness.

Wear a money belt under your clothing. Keep all important items, such as money, passport, other papers and tickets, in your money belt at all times. If you are carrying a bag or camera, wear the strap across your body and have the bag on the side away from the road to deter snatch thieves who operate from motorcycles and scooters. Thankfully motorcycle bandits aren't common in Tuscany, even in Florence.

In Florence especially you should also watch out for groups of dishevelled-looking women and children. They generally work in groups of four or five and carry paper or cardboard which they use to distract your attention while they swarm around and riffle through your pockets and bag. Never underestimate their skill – they are as fast as lightning and very adept.

Parked cars are also prime targets for thieves, particularly those with foreign number plates or rental company stickers. *Never* leave valuables in your car – in fact, try not to leave anything in the car if you can help it.

In case of theft or loss, always report the incident at the questura within 24 hours and ask for a statement, otherwise your travel insurance company won't pay out.

Traffic

Italian traffic can at best be described as chaotic, at worst downright dangerous, for the unprepared tourist. Drivers are not keen to stop for pedestrians, even at pedestrian crossings, and are more likely to swerve. Italians simply step off the footpath and walk

through the (swerving) traffic with determination – it is a practice which seems to work, so if you feel uncertain about crossing a busy road, wait for the next Italian. In many cities, roads that appear to be for one-way traffic have special lanes for buses travelling in the opposite direction, and it's not uncommon to see cyclists peddling or motoring the wrong way on one-way streets – always look both ways before stepping out.

LEGAL MATTERS

For many Italians, finding ways to get around the law (any law) is a way of life. They are likely to react with surprise, if not annoyance, if you point out that they might be breaking a law. Few people pay attention to speed limits, many motorcyclists and drivers don't stop at red lights – and certainly not at pedestrian crossings. No-one bats an eyelid about littering or dogs pooping in the middle of the footpath – even though many municipal governments have introduced laws against these things. But these are minor transgressions when measured up against the country's organised crime, the extraordinary levels of tax evasion and corruption in government and business.

The average tourist will probably have a brush with the law only after being robbed by a bag snatcher or pickpocket.

Drugs

Italy's drug laws are lenient on users and heavy on pushers. If you're caught with drugs that the police determine are for your own personal use, you'll be let off with a warning (and, of course, the drugs will be confiscated). If, instead, it is determined that you intend to sell the drugs, you could find yourself in prison. It's up to the police to determine whether or not you're a pusher, since the law is not specific about quantities. The sensible option is to avoid illicit drugs altogether.

Drink Driving

The legal limit for blood alcohol level is 0.08% and breath tests are now in use. See Road Rules in the Getting Around chapter for more information.

Police

To call the *polizia* (police) dial the freephone emergency number ☎ 113 or the carabinieri on ☎ 112. Addresses of police stations are given in destination sections throughout the book.

The police are a civil force and take their orders from the Ministry of the Interior, while the carabinieri fall under the Ministry of Defence. There is a considerable duplication of their roles, despite a 1981 reform intended to merge the two forces.

The carabinieri wear a dark-blue uniform with a red stripe and drive dark-blue cars with a red stripe. They are well trained and tend to be helpful. Their police station is called a *caserma* (barracks).

The police wear powder-blue trousers with a fuchsia stripe and a navy-blue jacket and drive light blue cars with a white stripe, with 'polizia' written on the side. Tourists who want to report thefts, and people wanting to get a residence permit, will have to deal with them. Their headquarters are called the questura.

Other varieties of police in Italy include the *vigili urbani*, basically traffic police, who you will have to deal with if you get a parking ticket, or your car is towed away; and the *guardia di finanza*, who are responsible for fighting tax evasion and drug smuggling.

Your Rights Italy has some anti-terrorism laws on its books that could make life difficult if you happen to be detained by the police. You can be held for 48 hours without a magistrate being informed and you can be interrogated without the presence of a lawyer. It is difficult to obtain bail and you can be held legally for up to three years without being brought to trial.

BUSINESS HOURS

Generally shops are open 9am to 1pm and 3.30pm to 7.30pm (or 4pm to 8pm) Monday to Friday. Some stay closed on Monday mornings. Big department stores, such as Coin and Rinascente, and most supermarkets have continuous opening hours, from 9am to 7.30pm Monday to Saturday. Some

even open 9am to 1pm on Sunday. Smaller shops will open on Saturday morning until about 1pm.

Banks tend to open 8.30am to 1.30pm and 3.30pm to 4.30pm Monday to Friday (hours can vary). They are closed at weekends, but it is always possible to find an exchange office open in the larger cities and in major tourist areas.

Major post offices open 8.30am to 5pm or 6pm Monday to Friday and to 1pm or 2pm Saturday. Smaller post offices generally open 8.30am to 2pm Monday to Friday and 8.30am to midday on Saturday.

Pharmacies are usually open from 9am to 12.30pm and 3.30pm to 7.30pm. They always close on Sunday and usually on Saturday afternoon. When closed, pharmacies are required to display a list of those in the area that are open.

Bars (in the Italian sense, ie, coffee-and-sandwich places) and cafes generally open 7.30am to 8pm, although some stay open after 8pm and turn into pub-style drinking and meeting places. Discos and clubs might open around 10pm, but often there'll be no-one there until midnight. Restaurants open roughly midday to 3pm and 7.30pm to 11pm. Restaurants and bars are required to close for one day each week, which varies between establishments.

Museum and gallery opening hours vary, although there is a trend towards continuous opening hours from around 9.30am to 7pm. Many close on Monday.

PUBLIC HOLIDAYS

Most Tuscans take their annual holidays in August, deserting the cities for the cooler seaside or mountains. This means that many businesses and shops close for at least a part of the month, particularly during the week around Ferragosto (Feast of the Assumption) on 15 August. Cities such as Florence are left to the tourists, who may be frustrated that many restaurants and shops are closed until early September. The Easter break (Settimana Santa) is another busy holiday period for Italians.

Italian national public holidays include the following:

New Year's Day (Anno Nuovo) 1 January – the celebrating takes place on New Year's Eve (Capodanno)

Epiphany (Befana) 6 January

Good Friday (Venerdì Santo) March/April

Easter Monday (Pasquetta/Giorno dopo Pasqua) March/April

Liberation Day (Giorno della Liberazione) 25 April – marks the Allied victory in Italy and the end of the German presence and Mussolini

Labour Day (Giorno del Lavoro) 1 May

Feast of the Assumption (Ferragosto) 15 August

All Saints' Day (Ognissanti) 1 November

Feast of the Immaculate Conception (Concezione Immaculata) 8 December

Christmas Day (Natale) 25 December

St Stephen's Day (Boxing Day, Festa di Santo Stefano) 26 December

Individual towns also have public holidays to celebrate the feasts of their patron saints. See the following Special Events section for details.

SPECIAL EVENTS

Tuscany's calendar is full to bursting with events, ranging from colourful traditional celebrations, with a religious and/or historical flavour, through to festivals of the performing arts, including opera, music and theatre. Some appear in the following list:

February

Carnevale During the period before Ash Wednesday many towns stage carnivals and enjoy their last opportunity to indulge before Lent. The popular carnival celebrations held at Viareggio are among the best known in all Italy, second only to the extravaganza of Venice.

April

Pasqua (Easter) Holy Week in Tuscany is marked by solemn processions and passion plays. In Florence the Scoppio del Carro is staged in the Piazza del Duomo at noon on Easter Saturday. This event features the explosion of a cart full of fireworks – a tradition dating back to the Crusades and seen as a good omen for the city if the explosion works.

May

Maggio Musicale Fiorentino Starting in late April and spilling over into June, Florence's Musical May was inaugurated in 1933. It is a high point on the musical calendar, with top names performing opera, ballet and classical music at venues across the city. Tickets can be hard to come by.

Palio della Balestra The Palio of the Crossbow, held in Gubbio (Umbria) on the last Sunday in May, is a crossbow contest between the men of Gubbio and Sansepolcro, who dress in medieval costume and use antique weapons. There is a rematch at Sansepolcro on the second Sunday in September.

Balestro del Girifalco This crossbow competition takes place in Massa Marittima on the first Sunday after 19 May.

June

Regatta di San Ranieri This boat race, held on 16–17 June, in Pisa is preceded by the *Luminaria*, a torchlit procession.

Festa di San Giovanni The spectacular *fuochi artificial* (fireworks) that are set off in Piazzale Michelangelo on 24 June, the feast day of Florence's patron saint, are the culmination of the city's festivities. In the four or five preceding days, teams from the city's four historical districts battle it out in the Gioco del Calcio Storico (Historical Soccer Game). On the first day the game is preceded by a procession of hundreds of people in traditional costume in Piazza Santa Croce, which becomes the football pitch for the matches.

Palio delle Quattro Antiche Repubbliche Marinare (Historical Regatta of the Four Ancient Maritime Republics) This event sees a procession of boats and a race between the four historical maritime rivals – Pisa, Venice, Amalfi and Genoa. The event rotates between the four rival towns and is due next to take place in Pisa in 2002.

Giostra del Saracino (Joust of the Saracen) On the second last Sunday of June, four ancient quarters of the city of Arezzo present teams of knights armed with lances who compete in Piazza Grande for the Lanza d'Oro (the Golden Lance). The joust has its origins in the early 16th century and in its present form commemorates Christian efforts to hold back the tide of Islam in the 14th century. The joust is staged again in September.

Gioco del Ponte (Game of the Bridge) Two groups in medieval costume contend for the Ponte di Mezzo, a bridge over the Arno River, in Pisa on the third Sunday of the month.

July

Il Palio (The Banner) Siena's pride and joy, this famous traditional event, held on 2 July, sees the town's beautiful central square, Piazza del Campo, turned into a scene of equine mayhem.

It involves a dangerous bareback horse race around the piazza, preceded by a parade of supporters in traditional costume. There is a replay in August.

Giostro dell'Orso Pistoia hosts this so-called Joust of the Bear on 25 July.

Anfiteatro delle Cascine Nightly free concerts to keep Florence humming through the summer. It largely attracts a young crowd.

Festa di San Paolino This torchlit procession in Lucca is accompanied by a crossbow competition on the third Sunday of the month.

Florence Dance Festival A series of performances of dance – from classical ballet to modern – held in Piazzale Michelangelo.

Pistoia Blues One of Italy's bigger music events, held in Pistoia around the middle of the month.

August

Il Palio 16 August sees a repeat of Siena's famous horse race.

Bravio delle Botti The streets of Montepulciano rattle and thunder to the sound of barrel races on the last Sunday of August.

September

Festa delle Rificolone (Festival of the Paper Lanterns) Processions, mostly of lantern-bearing children, converge on Florence's Piazza Santissima Annunziata to celebrate the eve of Our Lady's birthday on 7 September. A food fair is held in the same square in the week prior to the festival.

Giostro del Saracino Good old-fashioned medieval jousting in Arezzo on the first Sunday of the month; this is a re-run of the June event.

Festa degli Omaggi A parade in traditional dress through the streets of Prato, this is held on 8 September.

Luminaria di Santa Croce This is a torchlit procession through Lucca on 14 September.

Palio della Balestra A rematch of the crossbow competition between Gubbio and Sansepolcro is held at Sansepolcro on the second Sunday of the month.

October

Rassegna Internazionale Musica dei Popoli Local and international musicians come together in Florence to perform traditional and ethnic music from all over the world. The festival goes on for most of the month.

November

Festa di Santa Cecilia A series of concerts and exhibitions takes place in Siena to honour the patron saint of musicians.

ACTIVITIES

If the museums, galleries and sights are not enough for you there are numerous options for getting off the beaten tourist track.

Walking

The Apuane Alps have well-marked and challenging trails for the serious walker. If you want something a little more easy-going, there is plenty of pleasant walking in the Chianti area or out towards San Gimignano. See the Tuscany on Foot chapter for more details.

Cycling

This is a good option for people who can't afford a car but want to see some of the more out-of-the-way places. The only problem is that much of Tuscany is hilly, so you will need some stamina and a good bike. You can either bring your own bike or buy or hire one in Tuscany. For further information, see Bicycle in the Getting Around chapter.

Popular areas are those near Florence and Siena, from where you could explore the hills around Fiesole, San Gimignano and in the Chianti, just to name a few possibilities.

Water Sports

Windsurfing and sailing are extremely popular in Italy, and at most Tuscan beach resorts it is possible to rent boats and equipment. On Elba you will find plenty of outfits willing to take your money for diving courses and windsurfing instruction.

Skiing

The Tuscan skiing option is centred on Abetone, on the border with the region of Emilia-Romagna. Bear in mind that the slopes are not exactly first rate and pretty packed on winter weekends – but you could combine a week of skiing with excursions to the great cities of Florence, Pisa, Lucca and so on. For more information turn to Abetone in the North-Western Tuscany chapter.

COURSES

Studying Italian in Tuscany is big business. Universities and private schools all over the region offer tuition, although the two main magnets are Florence and Siena. It's a great way to get a feel for the place.

Individual schools and universities are listed under the relevant towns throughout this book. The handy Web site W www.it-schools.com lists a plethora of schools in Tuscany, and all of Italy. Accommodation can usually be arranged through the school.

Many schools also offer courses in painting, art history, sculpture, architecture and cooking; however, all these courses can be expensive at an average of €310 to €465 per month.

It is also possible to undertake serious academic study at a university, although obviously only if you have a solid command of the language.

Italian cultural institutes (see Useful Organisations earlier in this chapter) will provide information about study in Tuscany, as well as enrolment forms to some schools.

In England, there is an organisation called Vallicorte (☎/fax 020-7680 1377, W www.vallicorte.com), Box 15, 78 Wapping High St, London E1W 2NB, that organises small-group courses in art and architecture, painting, cooking and wine near Lucca and Florence. Courses run in spring and autumn and start at £585 for four days, including food and accommodation.

For the hefty sum of around €2910 per week you can learn the art of Tuscan cuisine in various grandiose villas and historic buildings (☎ 0577 74 94 98, fax 0577 74 92 35, W www.cuisineinternational.com).

At a more moderate €620 you can spend five days in a restored Chianti stone farm house combining a cookery and wine course with language lessons. For information contact: Podere Le Rose (☎ 055 29 45 11, fax 055 239 68 87), Poggio San Polo 2, 53010 Lecchi-Gaiole (SI), Italia.

WORK

It is illegal for non-EU citizens to work in Italy without a work permit, but trying to obtain one can be time consuming. EU citizens are allowed to work in Italy, but they still need to obtain a permesso di soggiorno from the main questura in the town where they have found work. See the Visas & Documents section earlier in this chapter for more information about these permits.

Au Pair Work

Babysitting is a possibility, as is au pair work, organised before you come to Tuscany. A useful guide is *The Au Pair and Nanny's Guide to Working Abroad*, by S Griffith & S Legg. *Work Your Way Around the World*, by Susan Griffith, is also useful.

English Tutoring

The easiest source of work for foreigners is teaching English, but even with full qualifications an American, Australian, Canadian or New Zealander might find it difficult to secure a permanent position. Most of the larger, more reputable schools will hire only people with a permesso di lavoro, but their attitude can become more flexible if demand for teachers is high and they come across someone with good qualifications. The more professional schools will require at least a TEFL (Teaching English as a Foreign Language) certificate. It is advisable to apply for work early in the year, in order to be considered for positions available in October (language-school years correspond roughly to the Italian school year: late September to the end of June).

Some schools hire people without work permits or qualifications, but the pay is usually low (around €7.75 per hour). It is more lucrative to advertise your services and pick up private students (although rates vary wildly, ranging from as low as €7.75 up to €25.80 per hour). Although you can get away with absolutely no qualifications or experience, it might be a good idea to bring along a few English grammar books (including exercises) to help you at least appear professional.

Most people get started by placing advertisements in shop windows and on university notice boards.

Street Performers

Busking is common although, theoretically, buskers require a municipal permit. Italians tend not to stop and gather around street performers, but they are usually quite generous all the same.

Other Work

There are plenty of markets around the country where you can set up a stall and sell your wares, although you may need to pay a fee. Selling goods on the street is illegal unless you have a municipal permit and it is quite common to see municipal police moving people along. Another option is to head for beach resorts in summer, particularly if you have handicrafts or jewellery to sell.

Some people manage to swing work in the kitchens of more touristy restaurants, particularly in Florence.

ACCOMMODATION

Prices for accommodation quoted in this book are intended as a guide only. There is generally a fair degree of fluctuation in hotel prices, depending on the season and whether establishments raise prices when they have the opportunity. It is not unusual for prices to remain fixed for years on end, and in some cases they even go down. But it is more common that they rise by around 5 or 10% annually. Always check room charges before putting your bags down.

Reservations

It's a good idea to book a room if you are planning to travel during peak tourist periods such as summer. Hotels usually require confirmation by fax, email or letter, as well as a deposit. Tourist offices will generally send out information about hotels, camping, apartments and so on, if you need more suggestions than we provide here. Another option is to use one of the Florence-based hotel booking services.

Camping

Most camping facilities in Tuscany are major complexes with swimming pools, tennis courts, restaurants and shops. Even the most basic camp sites can be surprisingly dear once you add up the various charges for each person, a site for your tent or caravan and a car, but they generally still work out cheaper than a double room in a one-star hotel. Prices range from around €5.15 to €10.30 per adult, €3.10 to €7.75 for children aged under 12, and €5.15 to €10.30 for a site.

You'll also often have to pay to park your car and there is sometimes a charge for use of the showers, usually around €1.05.

In the cities camp sites are often a long way from the historic centre. The inconvenience, plus the additional cost of needing to use public transport, should be weighed up against the price of a hotel room. Some, but by no means all, camp sites are in pleasant country or beachside locations.

Independent camping is generally not permitted and you might find yourself disturbed during the night by the carabinieri. But, out of the main summer tourist season, independent campers who choose spots not visible from the road, don't light fires, and who try to be inconspicuous, shouldn't have too much trouble. Always get permission from the landowner if you want to camp on private property. Camper vans are popular in Italy (see under Car & Motorcycle in the Getting There & Away chapter for more details).

The Touring Club Italiano publishes an annual book listing all camp sites in Italy, *Campeggi in Italia* (€18.50), and the Istituto Geografico de Agostini publishes the annual *Guida ai Campeggi in Europa*, sold together with *Guida ai Campeggi in Italia* (€16).

Hostels

Ostelli per la Gioventù, of which there are nine in Tuscany, are run by the Associazione Italiana Alberghi per la Gioventù (AIG), which is affiliated to Hostelling International (HI). You need to be a member, but can join at one of the hostels. For details on how to get a card see under Hostel Cards in the Visas & Documents section earlier in this chapter. Nightly rates vary from €9.30 to €16.50 including breakfast. A meal will cost €7.75.

Accommodation is in segregated dormitories, although some hostels offer family rooms (at a higher price per person).

Hostels are generally closed from 10am to 3.30pm, although the Florence and Marina di Massa ones open all day. Check-in is from 6pm to 10.30pm, although some hostels will allow you a morning check-in, before they close for the day – it is best to confirm beforehand. Curfew is 11.30pm or midnight. It is usually necessary to pay before 9am on the day of your departure, otherwise you could be charged for another night.

Pensioni & Hotels

Prices quoted in this book are intended as a guide only. Hotels and pensioni are allowed to increase charges twice a year, although many don't. Travellers should always check on prices before committing to stay in a place. Make a complaint to the local tourist office if you believe you're being overcharged. Many proprietors employ various methods of bill-padding, such as charging for showers, or making breakfast compulsory.

There is often no difference between a pensione and an *albergo* (or hotel); in fact, some establishments use both titles. However, a pensione will generally be of one to three-star quality, while an albergo can be awarded up to five stars. *Locande* (similar to pensioni) and *alloggi*, also known as *affittacamere*, are generally cheaper, but not always. Locande and affittacamere are not included in the star classification system.

Quality of accommodation can vary a great deal. One-star alberghi/pensioni tend to be basic and usually do not have an en-suite bathroom. Standards at two-star places are often only slightly better, but rooms will generally have a private bathroom. Once you arrive at three stars you can assume that standards will be reasonable, although quality still varies dramatically. Four- and five-star hotels are sometimes part of a group of hotels and offer facilities such as room service, laundry and dry-cleaning.

Prices are highest in Florence and on Elba (in July and August).

A *camera singola* (single room) will always be expensive. Although there are a few pokey exceptions, you should reckon on a minimum of €28.80. In Florence you will generally not pay less than €31. A double room with twin beds *(camera doppia)*, and a double with a double bed *(camera matrimoniale)* cost from around €36.15. It is much cheaper to share with two or more people.

Proprietors will often charge no more than 15% of the cost of a double room for each additional person.

Tourist offices have booklets that list all pensioni and hotels, including prices (although they might not always be up to date). Ask about locande and affittacamere too.

Agriturismo

This is a holiday on a working farm and is particularly popular in Tuscany. Traditionally the idea was that families rented out rooms in their farmhouses, and it is still possible to find this type of accommodation. However, more commonly it is a restaurant in a restored farm complex, with rooms available for rent. All *agriturismo* establishments are operating farms and you will usually be able to sample the local produce.

Increasingly this is becoming a popular choice with travellers wanting to enjoy the peace of the countryside. Generally you need to have your own transport to get to and away from these places.

In Florence three organisations can provide information on this kind of accommodation in Tuscany: Agriturist Toscana (☎ 055 28 78 38, ⓔ agritosc@confagricoltura.it), at Piazza San Firenze 3, who publish a book of listings for the whole country (*Agriturist 2002*, €22), Terranostra (☎ 055 324 50 11, ⓦ www.terranostra.it/toscana), at Via della Villa Demidoff 64/d, and Turismo Verde Toscano (☎ 055 234 49 25, ⓔ cia-toscana@ interbusiness.it), at Via Verdi 5.

Convents & Monasteries

Many of the more than 50 convents and monasteries scattered about Tuscany offer some form of accommodation to outsiders. The standard is usually quite good, but the rooms can be rather spartan and often single sex. As a rule the institutions are looking for guests hoping to plug into their religion more closely or at least spiritually recharge their batteries. In many cases you are asked to take part in monastic life and respect the hours and practices of the order while you stay. Tourists just looking for a cheap sleep are not generally welcome. Of course there are exceptions to the rule, so don't disregard all of them if you're not religiously inclined.

You generally need to call ahead rather than just turn up. A handy book available in good travel bookshops in Tuscany is *Guida ai Monasteri d'Italia*, by Gian Maria Grasselli and Pietro Tarallo. To get the best out of it you really need to read Italian. In the worst case you can at least make out the phone numbers and call to see whether you can get into your chosen monastery.

Rifugi

If you are planning to hike in the Apuane Alps, obtain information on the network of *rifugi* (mountain huts). The most common are those run by the Club Alpino Italiano (CAI; W www.cai.it/rifugi) and accommodation is generally in bunk rooms sleeping anything from two to a dozen or more people. Half board (dinner, bed and breakfast) includes a set evening meal prepared by the gestore (manager) and their assistants. Food is plentiful and good. A night's accommodation can cost up to €20.65, while lunch can cost up to €11.35.

In addition to CAI rifugi there are some private ones and the occasional bivacchio, a basic, unstaffed hut. In general, rifugi remain open from mid-June to mid-September, but some at lower altitudes may remain open longer.

If you are counting on staying in a rifugio, always call ahead or have someone do so for you to check it is open and has room for you. Where possible, let staff know approximately when you expect to arrive.

Student Accommodation

People planning to study in Italy can usually organise accommodation through the school or university they will be attending. Options include a room with an Italian family, or a share arrangement with other students in an independent apartment.

Rental Accommodation

Finding rental accommodation in the cities can be difficult and time-consuming, but not impossible. Rental agencies will assist, for a fee. A one-room apartment with kitchenette in Florence's city centre will cost from €310 to €516.50 a month (long term). Renting in other towns can be considerably cheaper.

Villas among the Vines

If you have money to burn and desire a bit of luxury in the Tuscan countryside, a villa just may be the ticket for you. It's become quite a popular accommodation option and villas can be found in most corners of Tuscany. People wanting to rent a villa in the countryside can seek information from specialist travel agencies in their own country, or contact an organisation in Italy directly. One major Italian company with villas in Tuscany is Cuendet. This reliable firm publishes a booklet listing all the villas in its files, many with photos. Prices for a villa for four to six people range from around €460 a week in winter up to €1300 week in August. For details, write to **Cuendet & Cie spa** (☎ 0577 57 63 10, fax 0577 30 11 49, W www.cuendet.com, Strada di Strove 17, 53035 Monteriggioni, Siena).

In the UK, you can order Cuendet's catalogues and make reservations by calling ☎ 0800 891 573 freephone. In the USA, Cuendet bookings are handled by **Rentals in Italy** (☎ 805-987 5278, fax 482 7976, 1742 Calle Corva, Camarillo, CA 93010).

Invitation to Tuscany (☎ 01481-727298, fax 713473, W www.invitationtotuscany.com, PO Box 527, TSB House, Le Truchot, St Peter Port, Guernsey GY1 3AA, Channel Islands, UK) is another reputable purveyor of self-catering villas. Properties, many with a pool, can cost anything from UK£400 to UK£1200 per week for four to eight people. They have representatives in the UK, USA, Australia and New Zealand.

Cottages to Castles (☎ 01622-726883, fax 729835, W www.cottagestocastles.com, 351 Tonbridge Rd, Maidstone, Kent ME16 8NH, UK; in Australia ☎ 03-9853 1142, fax 9853 0509, e cottages@vicnet.net.au, 11 Laver St, Kew, Victoria 3101) also has an enticing collection of properties to choose from. Their prices are comparable to those of Invitation to Tuscany.

CIT offices throughout the world also have lists of villas and apartments available for rent in Tuscany.

You can look for rental ads in the advert rags such as Florence's *La Pulce* and *Panorama*. You'll find few ads for shared accommodation though. Short-term rental is more expensive, but many locals are keen to rent to foreigners for brief periods.

FOOD

Eating is one of life's great pleasures for Italians and Tuscany is no exception. For a food glossary, see the Language chapter towards the end of this book, or check out Lonely Planet's *World Food Italy*. See the special section 'The Tuscan Table' for information on when, where and what to eat in Tuscany, as well as some pointers on the region's wine.

Vegetarian Food

Vegetarians will have few problems eating in Tuscany, although vegans may make heavier weather of it. While few restaurants are strictly vegetarian, vegetables are a staple of the Italian diet. Most eating establishments serve an impressive selection of *antipasti* and *contorni* (vegetable side orders prepared in a variety of ways).

Self-Catering

If you have access to cooking facilities, it is best to buy fruit and vegetables at open markets, and salami, cheese and table wine at *alimentari*, which are a cross between grocery stores and delicatessens. *Salumerie* and *pizziccherie* sell sausages, meats and sometimes cheeses. For quality wine, search out an *enoteca*. Fresh bread is available at a *forno* or *panetteria* (bakeries that sell bread, pastries and sometimes groceries) and usually at alimentari. Most towns also have supermarkets.

DRINKS
Nonalcoholic Drinks

Coffee The first-time visitor to Italy is likely to be confused by the many ways in which the locals consume their caffeine. As in other Latin countries, Italians take their coffee seriously. Consequently they also make it complicated!

First is the pure and simple espresso – a small cup of very strong black coffee. A *doppio espresso* is a double shot of the same. You could also ask for a *caffè lungo*, but this may end up being more like the watered down version with which Anglos will be more familiar. If you want to be quite sure of getting the watery version, ask for a *caffè americano*.

Enter the milk. A *caffè latte* is coffee with a reasonable amount of milk. To most locals it is a breakfast and morning drink. The stronger version is a *caffè macchiato*, basically an espresso with a dash of milk. Alternatively, you can have *latte macchiato*, a glass of hot milk with a dash of coffee. The cappuccino is basically a frothy version of the caffè latte. You can ask for it *senza schiuma* (without froth), which is then scraped off the top. It tends to come lukewarm, so if you want it hot, ask for it to be *molto caldo*.

In the summer, the local version of an iced coffee is a *caffè freddo*, a long glass of cold coffee, sometimes helped along with ice cubes.

A Snail's Place?

From fast food to the global village in one small step, the Slow Food movement has spawned a whole new campaign – that of the *cittá slow*, or slow city. Coordinated by the mayor of the small Tuscan town of Greve, Paolo Saturnini, there are now over 30 Italian towns and cities going slow.

But it's not just about taking life at a more gentle pace. Slow Cities emphasise local traditions while actively promoting a healthy way of living that includes eating organic produce, minimising noise pollution levels and introducing ecologically friendly transport systems. These cities seek a balance between progress and maintaining their individuality in a world where regional, national and international differences are increasingly less pronounced. The perfect antidote to globalisation.

For more information, pay a leisurely visit to the Slow Food Web site at [W] www.slowfood.com.

To warm up on those winter nights, try a *corretto* – an espresso 'corrected' with a dash of grappa or some other spirit. Some locals have it as a heart starter.

After lunch and dinner it wouldn't occur to Italians to order either caffè latte or a cappuccino – espressos, macchiatos and correttos are perfectly acceptable. Of course, if you want a cappuccino there's no problem – but you might have to repeat your request a couple of times to convince disbelieving waiters that they have heard correctly.

Tea Italians don't drink a lot of *tè* (tea) and generally only in the late afternoon, when they might take a cup with a few *pasticcini* (small cakes). You can order tea in bars, although it will usually arrive in the form of a cup of warm water with an accompanying tea bag. If this doesn't suit your taste, ask for the water *molto caldo* or *bollente* (boiling). Good-quality packaged teas, such as Twinings tea bags and leaves, as well as packaged herbal teas, such as camomile, are often sold in alimentari and some bars. You can find a wide range of herbal teas in a *erboristeria* (herbalist's shop), which sometimes will also stock health foods.

Granita Granita is a drink made of crushed ice with fresh lemon or other fruit juices, or with coffee topped with fresh whipped cream. It is a Sicilian speciality but you will see it around Tuscany in the summer months too.

Soft Drinks The usual range of international soft drinks are available in Tuscany, although they tend to be expensive. There are some local versions too, along with the rather bitter, acquired taste of Chinotto.

Water While tap water is reliable throughout the country, most Italians prefer to drink bottled *acqua minerale* (mineral water). It will be either *frizzante* (sparkling) or *naturale* (still) and you will be asked in restaurants and bars which you would prefer. If you want a glass of tap water, ask for *acqua dal rubinetto*, although simply asking for *acqua naturale* will also suffice.

Alcoholic Drinks

Beer The main Italian labels are Peroni, Dreher and Moretti, all very drinkable and cheaper than the imported varieties.

Italy also imports beers from throughout Europe and the rest of the world. Several German beers, for instance, are available in bottles or cans; English beers and Guinness are often found *alla spina* (on tap) in *birrerie* (bars specialising in beer).

Wine See the special section 'The Tuscan Table' at the end of this chapter for details of the region's wine.

Liquors & Liqueurs After dinner try a shot of grappa, a strong, clear brew made from grapes. It originally comes from the Grappa area in the Veneto region of northeastern Italy, but they now make it in Tuscany too. Or you could go with an *amaro*, a dark liqueur prepared from herbs. If you prefer a sweeter liqueur, try an almond-flavoured *amaretto* or the sweet, aniseed *sambuca*.

ENTERTAINMENT
Bars & Pubs

Unlike various other European destinations, Italians cannot be said to have a 'drinking culture' but, in the bigger cities especially, you'll find plenty of bars. You can get a beer, wine or anything else at practically any bar. They range from workaday grungy through to chic places where it's all about seeing and being seen.

Those places operating first and foremost as nocturnal drinking establishments can be expected to stay open until about 1am in most cases, sometimes later.

The Italian version of the English/Irish pub has taken off in a big way. Basically places where you can get Guinness on tap or select from a wide range of international beers, they can be found in most large cities.

Perhaps one reason why Italians don't tend to wander out of bars legless is the price of a drink. A tiny glass of beer can start at around €2.10! For a pint you are looking at an average of €4.20.

Discos & Clubs

Discos (what Brits think of as clubs) are expensive: entrance charges hover around from €10.35 to €15.50, which sometimes includes a drink. Tuscany is not the most happening clubland in Europe, but you'll find some reasonable places in Florence and coastal spots such as Viareggio. Some are enormous, with several dance spaces catering to a variety of tastes.

Outside Florence and the summer resorts such as Viareggio, the pickings are slim. Often the clubs are well out in the countryside and if you aren't in the know and don't have wheels they can remain pretty much out of reach. The theory appears to be that at least the city and town dwellers don't have their sleep ruined.

Live Music

Rock The world's major performers are constantly passing through Italy and sometimes poke their noses into Tuscany. Keep an eye on local newspapers.

In June and early July Arezzo stages Arezzo Wave, a rock festival featuring some known acts and emerging bands. Lucca's Summer Festival is held in July. It attracts some class acts, which in 2001 featured Neil Young & Crazy Horse, George Benson and the Eagles.

Jazz Italians love jazz and in Tuscany the biggest jazz event is Siena Jazz, held in July and August.

Classical The main concert seasons are usually during the winter months, although there are always plenty of classical music concerts included in major summer entertainment festivals.

Cinemas

There is no shortage of cinemas in Tuscany, but quite a dearth of original language ones. In Florence several cater to an extent to the market for subtitled, original language (mostly English) movies, but even there the choice is usually limited. Beyond Florence your chances are close to zero. It costs around €7 to see a movie, although that can come down to €3.50 on the cheap day, which is often Wednesday.

Theatre

If you can understand Italian, you'll have several options in places such as Florence, Pisa and Siena. Performances in languages other than Italian are scarce. Tourist offices should be able to help out with information.

SPECTATOR SPORTS
Football (Soccer)

Il calcio excites Italian souls more than politics, religion, good food and dressing up all put together. Tuscany's only Serie A (premier league) reps are Florence's Fiorentina. They finished ninth in the 2000/01 season but won the Italian Cup. They have a fanatical fan base so getting tickets for home games may prove difficult.

SHOPPING

Shopping in Tuscany is probably not what you are used to back home. Most shops are small businesses, and large department stores and supermarkets tend to be thin on the ground.

If you need necessities such as underwear, tights, pyjamas, T-shirts or toiletries head for one of the large retail stores such as COIN or Rinascente. Otherwise, you can pick up underwear, tights and pyjamas in a *merceria* (haberdashery), toiletries and condoms in a *farmacia* (chemist) or sometimes in an alimentari, and items such as T-shirts in a normal clothing store. Supermarkets also stock toiletries and condoms. For airmail paper, note pads, pens, greeting cards, etc, try a *cartoleria* (stationer's).

Ceramics

You'll find plenty of locally made stuff and if you get the chance you should visit Montelupo, west of Florence, which has been a famed centre of ceramics production since medieval times. Cortona, in the south-east, is another good place to look for pottery.

Clothing & Leather

Italy is synonymous with elegant, fashionable and high-quality clothing. The problem is that most of the better quality clothes are very expensive. However, if you can manage to be in the country during the summer sales in July and August and the winter sales in December and January, you can pick up incredible bargains. By mid-sale, prices are often slashed by up to 60 or 70%.

In Tuscany, Florence is probably the place to be. All the big-name stylists have outlets there, although what's on offer tends to stick to the straight and narrow. For deals, try Gucci's and Prada's wholesale outlets on the road linking Florence and Arezzo (see Shopping in the Florence chapter).

Florence is also known for leather goods. You can spend a fortune on shoes, bags, wallets and just about anything else that can conceivably be fashioned from animal hides. It was always said that you could pick up good stuff cheaply too, but prices have tended to sneak upwards over the years. In Florence's San Lorenzo street market there is plenty of cheap and cheerful stuff on sale, but you need to watch the quality.

Shoes are a big attraction to the compulsive shopper, but expect to have a little trouble finding larger sizes. Again, the time to be looking is during the sales.

Jewellery
Popular jewellery tends to be chunky and cheap-looking, but if they can afford it, Italians love to wear gold. The best-known haunt for tourists wanting to buy gold in Tuscany is the Ponte Vecchio in Florence, lined with tiny shops full of both modern and antique jewellery.

That said, the gold capital of Tuscany is actually Arezzo.

Souvenirs & Handicrafts
The beautiful Florentine paper goods, with their delicate designs, are reasonably priced and make wonderful gifts. Specialist shops are dotted around Florence, although it is possible to buy these paper goods in stationery and specialist shops throughout the region.

FACTS FOR THE VISITOR

THE TUSCAN TABLE

For some, arrival in Tuscany means having reached the pearly gates of food heaven. For others, Tuscan cuisine is rather overrated.

The truth lies somewhere between the two. As with many (but not all) of the Mediterranean cuisines, it is essentially the result of poverty. Simple, wholesome ingredients have traditionally been thrown together to produce healthy but hardly fascinating meals. The extraordinary excesses we read about of the tables of medieval barons or later on those of the Medicis and their pals were not passed down to us through the ages. One can only drool and dream about what concoctions must have been served up at such Bacchanalian feasts.

Most common folk had to make do with limited ingredients. This is what has come down to us today, although the cuisine has been refined and enriched, particularly with other dishes and combinations from more widely flung parts of Italy. And all told it is very good – one of the keys remains the quality and freshness of the ingredients, upon which great store is placed. The use of herbs, such as basil, thyme, parsley and rosemary, is liberal. And let's not forget olive oil. Tuscany produces some of the best Italy has to offer.

Gourmets will miss something though – adventure. In Tuscany as elsewhere in Italy, tradition still controls much of what the cook does. Many can solemnly state exactly what sauce goes with which pasta – any deviation from the rules meets with scorn. They can tweak and fiddle (perhaps best exemplified in a growing daring in the preparation of pasta sauces), but all in all must remain faithful to the old ways. Undoubtedly many of these 'rules' are sound, but at times they are merely oppressive.

Carping aside, it is unlikely that you will quickly get sick of Tuscan cuisine. Add to the food some of the finest wines produced in the country and you will want to come with your taste buds fully braced for action.

For information about books on Tuscan cuisine, see under Books in the Facts for the Visitor chapter.

Meals in Tuscany

When & What to Eat Italians rarely eat a sit-down *colazione* (breakfast). It's generally a quick affair taken at a bar counter on the way to work. They tend to drink a cappuccino, usually *tiepido* (warm), and eat a croissant *(cornetto)* or other type of pastry (generically known as a brioche).

Bars (in the Italian sense, ie, coffee-and-sandwich places) and cafes generally open from 7.30am to 8pm, although some stay open after 8pm and turn into pub-style drinking and meeting places. A few serve filling snacks with lunchtime and pre-dinner drinks. At others you can pick up reasonable *panini* (filled rolls or sandwiches).

You'll also find numerous outlets where you can buy pizza *a taglio* (by the slice) Another option is to go to an *alimentari* (delicatessen) and ask them to make a *panino* with the filling of your choice. At a *pasticceria* (cake shop) you can buy pastries, cakes and biscuits.

For *pranzo* (lunch), restaurants usually operate from 12.30pm to 3pm, but many are not keen to take orders after 2pm. It's the main meal of the day and many shops and businesses close for two or three hours every afternoon to accommodate it. People generally start sitting down to dine around 7.30pm for *cena* (dinner). You will be hard-pressed to find a place still serving after 10.30pm. It's traditionally a simpler affair, but is becoming a fuller meal because of the inconvenience of travelling home for lunch every day.

Many restaurants and bars shut one or two days per week, but others don't. In some parts of Italy at least one day off is mandatory but ultimately the decision on whether or not to enforce that rule rests with the comune. The Florence comune, for instance, does not care what restaurateurs do (unless they close for three days or more in a week) so that some skip the weekly break altogether.

A full meal consists of an *antipasto*, *primo piatto* and *secondo piatto*, which is usually accompanied by a *contorno* (vegetable side dish); see Tuscan Cuisine later in this section for more details. *Insalate* (salads) have a strange position in the order here. They are usually ordered as separate dishes and in some cases serve as a replacement for the primo.

Numerous restaurants offer a *menù turistico* or *menù a prezzo fisso*, a set price lunch that can cost as little as €7.75 (usually not including drinks). Generally the food is breathtakingly unspectacular with limited choices. From your tastebuds' point of view (if you are not overly hungry) you'd be better off settling for a good primo or secondo at a decent restaurant. On the other hand, if you look at lunch as a mere refuelling stop, this could be the way to go.

Where to Eat Quality restaurants abound in Tuscany and making a choice can sometimes be a little daunting. Be sure not to judge an eatery by its tablecloth. You may well have your best meal at the dingiest little establishment imaginable.

Also worth noting are 'Slow Food' restaurants – establishments highly rated by the Slow Food Movement (for more information see the boxed text 'A Snail's Place' in the Facts for the Visitor chapter). Every two years the movement publishes *Osterie d'Italia*, which rates what they believe to be the top restaurants in the country. You'll spot them by the 'Slow Food' sticker proudly displayed outside.

Some bars known as *vinai* are good places to either snack or put together a full meal from a range of enticing options on display. This is more of a lunchtime choice than for your evening meal.

The standard name for a restaurant is *ristorante*. Often you will come across something known as a *trattoria*, by tradition, at least, a cheaper, simpler version of a ristorante. On pretty much the same level is the *osteria*. The *pizzeria* needs no explanation.

A *fiaschetteria* may serve up small snacks, sandwiches and the like, usually at the bar while you down a glass of wine or two. It is a particularly Tuscan phenomenon. A *tavola calda* (literally 'hot table') usually offers cheap, pre-prepared meat, pasta and vegetable dishes in a buffet.

Wine lovers should look out for their local *enoteca* (wine bar). These places offer snacks and sometimes full meals to accompany a selection of wines. Their primary business is the latter – food is viewed as an accompaniment (and often only cold dishes are available) to your chosen tipple(s). Generally the idea is to try the wines by the glass.

The problem with all this is that nowadays all the names seem to have become interchangeable. In all cases, it is best to check the menu, usually posted by the door, for prices. Occasionally you will find places with no written menu. This usually means they change the menu daily. Inside there may be a blackboard or the waiter will tell you what's on – fine if you speak Italian, a little disconcerting if you don't. Try to think of it as a surprise. If you encounter this situation in an overtly touristy area, you should have your rip-off antenna up.

Tuscan Cuisine

Staples In the dark years of the barbarian invasions of what was left of the Roman Empire, times got exceedingly difficult for the bulk of the people in Tuscany. Salt became a scarce commodity and *pane sciocco* (unsalted bread) became the basis of nutrition. Or at least that is one story. Unsalted bread has in any case remained a feature of local cooking ever since.

The other single most important staple product is olive oil. Some of the best extra virgin olive oil, with its limpid emerald appearance, looks good enough to drink. Since Etruscan times farmers have grown olives. Harvest time is around late November, and certainly not later than 13 December (the Festa di Santa Lucia). In Tuscany olives are still largely harvested by hand and sent to presses. After an initial crushing, the resulting mass is squeezed. The most prized oil is extra virgin, extracted on the first round of squeezing and without any additives.

Antipasti (Starters) You have the option of starting a meal with a 'pre-meal', which can vary from vegetables to a small offering of fried seafood. The classic in Tuscany is *crostini*, lightly grilled slices of unsalted bread traditionally covered in a chicken liver pâté. Other toppings have become equally popular – diced tomato with herbs, onion and garlic is a popular version virtually indistinguishable from the Pugliese *bruschetta*.

The other classic is *fettunta*, basically a slab of toasted bread rubbed with garlic and dipped in olive oil. Another favourite, *prosciutto e melone* (ham and rockmelon), is known well beyond the confines of Tuscany. Other cured meats and sausages are popular too.

Primi Piatti (First Courses) The primo piatto often consists of a pasta, risotto or soup dish. You may be surprised to learn that pasta does not occupy a place of honour in traditional Tuscan menus. Some believe it was the Arabs who introduced pasta to Sicily in the early Middle Ages. By the 14th century its use had definitely spread to Florence, but without displacing local favourites.

A light summer dish is *panzanella* (mixed salad with breadcrumbs; see under Recipes later in this section) and its winter equivalent is *ribollita*, another example of making use of every last scrap. A vegetable stew, again with bread mixed in, it's a hearty dish for cold winter nights. *Pappa al pomodoro* is another traditional Tuscan first course (see Recipes later in this section). Along the Maremma coast water was for centuries about the only thing in abundance in the swamps, and so *acqua cotta* (literally 'cooked water') was the mainstay of the average peasant family: a few vegetable leaves, onion, stale bread bits and a grating of pecorino cheese thrown together to make a thin broth. The modern restaurant version is considerably tastier, with a richer variety of elements.

Pasta did take hold in Tuscany, and among the dishes that have long kept locals munching happily are: *pappardelle sulla lepre* (ribbon pasta with hare), *pasta e ceci* (a pasta and chickpea broth) and *spaghetti allo scoglio* (spaghetti with seafood – pretty much a national dish). *Ravioli* and *tortelli*, both kinds of filled pasta, are also popular. Try the Maremma version of tortelli, large packets of fresh pasta filled with spinach and ricotta cheese and bathed in a sauce of your choice (*burro e salvia* – butter and sage – is a good match). In Siena and other parts of central Tuscany you will come across *pici* or *pinci*, a rough, thick version of spaghetti. Their greater consistency allows cooks to match them up with heavier sauces and you feel like you are getting your teeth into something more substantial than with standard spaghetti. *Testaroli*, a speciality of the Lunigiana region, is a pancake-like pasta usually served with pecorino cheese, olive oil or pesto.

Secondi Piatti (Second Courses) Secondo piatti are meat or fish dishes, and in keeping with the simplicity for which local cuisine is known, meats and fish tend to be grilled. Meat eaters will sooner or later want to try *bistecca alla fiorentina*, a slab of Florentine steak. It should not cost more than €26 to €31 per kilogram, which is usually sufficient for two. Traditionally the meat was taken from bovines in the Val di Chiana, but often this is no longer the case.

Cuisines born of poverty found a use for everything. As a result, offal became an integral part of the local diet. *Rognone*, a great plate of kidneys, is one favourite, although you might find it a little much. Tripe is particularly prized by some, and a common dish is *Trippa alla fiorentina*, prepared with carrot, celery, tomato and onion mix. For true tripe fans, locals distinguish between various parts of the gut. One particular part of the tripe is known as *lampredotto*, just in case you are contemplating having some on a roll without knowing what it is.

Tuscany is hunting territory, and *cinghiale* (wild boar) along with other game meats finds its way to many restaurant tables. Indeed for some the game meats form the basis of the best in Tuscan cooking.

Among the possible choices of side order are *fagiolini alla fiorentina*, string beans prepared with tomatoes, fennel seeds, onion and garlic. *Fagioli all'uccelletto*, white *cannellini* beans cooked with sage, garlic, oil and tomatoes, is another.

Not surprisingly, seafood dominates along the coast and on the islands. One dish that stands out is *cacciucco* (see under Recipes later in this section). When dining in this part of Tuscany ask if the seafood is fresh – if it is, stick with seafood pasta dishes and mains. The meat dishes you can try out when you are farther inland.

Dolci (Desserts) You will find no shortage of house desserts and regional specialities.

Almond-based biscuits are a Tuscan tradition, such as Siena's *cantucci* or *biscottini di Prato*, best chomped while you sip Vin Santo (see Tuscan Wines later in this chapter). Lighter but also using almonds are *brutti ma buoni* (literally 'ugly but good'). *Schiacciata con l'uva* is a kind of flat pastry covered in crushed red grapes.

Panforte is a classic of the Tuscan table. It's a dense tart made of an almond base but bursting with other ingredients including walnuts, figs, mixed dried fruits such as orange and lemon, mixed spices including cinnamon, coriander, and even white pepper, honey and cocoa. Done properly, the result is divine and seems purpose designed for the region's Vin Santo. From Pontremoli in the Lunigiana comes a vaguely similar pie filled with a chocolate and almond mix.

Zuppa Inglese, invented by Sienese cooks and originally known as *zuppa ducale*, is a sugar bomb of chocolate, cream, rum and *savoiardi* biscuits. It acquired its present name because in the Florence of the 18th century it was a favourite among British expats who used to gobble it down at Caffè Doney (long gone).

Instead of opting for a house dessert, at least once or twice (or once or twice a day, the stuff is so good!) you should head for the nearest *gelateria* (ice-cream parlour) to round off the meal with some excellent *gelati*, followed by a *digestivo* (digestive liqueur) at a bar. This is by no means a Tuscan phenomenon, but is enjoyed the length and breadth of Italy.

Recipes

Panzanella

This simple dish is basically a cold mixed salad with bread crumbs. Its success depends wholly on two things: the bread, which has to be unsalted and left for at least a day (preferably two) and the ingredients, which need to be fresh and tasty.

6 servings
Preparation: 2 hours

12 slices of unsalted bread
1 cucumber
50g rocket leaves
2 large tomatoes
1 spring onion
Basil leaves
Extra virgin oil (to taste)
Salt

Olio
di
Olivia

JANE SMITH

Soak bread slices in cold water for half an hour, then squeeze out excess water and crumble into a bowl. Wash vegetables, and after chopping finely, add to bowl. Next add the oil and salt, and toss well. Leave in the fridge for about an hour before serving.

Pappa al Pomodoro
This thick soup is also mixed with bread, but as its name indicates, tomatoes form its base.

6 servings
Preparation: 45 minutes

400g peeled and chopped tomatoes
6 slices hard unsalted bread
1 onion
1 leek
1 carrot
1 stick celery
4 tablespoons extra virgin olive oil
Sage, basil and salt

Chop onion, leek, carrot and celery and fry with oil in a deep pan. Add salt, tomatoes, sage and basil and cook for 10 minutes. Cut bread into cubes, add to tomato mixture and cook for another 10 minutes until it becomes smooth and creamy. Add water to the mixture to obtain the right consistency. Serve immediately.

Cacciucco
Traditionally a hot-pot stew of whatever seafood came to hand, when prepared well nowadays it can be a cornucopia of delights from the depths.

6 servings
Preparation: 1½ hours

500g squid
500g octopus
300g fresh dog fish
500g white fish for stock
500g mixed shellfish
500g shrimps or prawns
1½ cups tomatoes
12 slices unsalted bread, rubbed with
garlic and pepper
¾ cup white wine
1 cup extra virgin olive oil
6 cloves crushed garlic
1 chopped red chilli
Sage

Heat oil in a deep pan, add garlic, sage and chilli and fry gently for one minute. Chop squid and octopus into pieces and add to pan, then mix in white wine and tomatoes.

Cook for 20 minutes, stirring occasionally. Add fish, cut into pieces. (Optionally, cook fish heads in well-seasoned stock in a separate pot, and add broth to pan for extra body and flavour). Continue to cook on low heat until squid and octopus are tender. Add shellfish and shrimps and cook for six to seven minutes until shells open.

Serve dish on bread arranged on a wide soup plate. Accompany with a young red wine.

Wine

Wine in Italy *Vino* (wine) is an essential accompaniment to any meal. Tuscans are justifiably proud of their wines and it would be surprising for dinner-time conversation not to touch on the subject at least for a moment.

Prices are reasonable and you will rarely pay more than €7.75 for a drinkable bottle of wine, although prices range up to more than €21 for the better stuff. If you want an exceptional *riserva* (aged wine) you can pay up to €100.

For something to merely wash down your meal, you will generally be perfectly safe spending €4.15 or so in a supermarket, which will buy you something reasonable enough.

Since the 1960s, wine in Italy has been graded according to four main classifications. *Vino da tavola* indicates no specific classification; *Indicazione Geografica Tipica* (IGT) means that the wine is typical of a certain area; *Denominazione di Origine Controllata* (DOC) wines are produced subject to certain specifications (regarding grape types, method and so on); and *Denominazione d'Origine Controllata e Garantita* (DOCG), which shows that wine is subject to the same requirements as normal DOC but that it is also tested by government inspectors. These indications appear on labels.

A DOC label can refer to wine from a single vineyard or an area. DOC wines can be elevated to DOCG after five years' consistent excellence. Equally, wines can be demoted; the grades are by no means set in stone.

Further hints come with indications such as *superiore*, which can denote DOC wines above the general standard (perhaps with greater alcohol or longer ageing). *Riserva* is applied only to DOC or DOCG wines that have aged for a specified amount of time.

In general, however, the presence or absence of such labels is by no means a cast-iron guarantee of anything. Many notable wines fly no such flag. Many a vino da tavola or IGT wine is so denominated simply because its producers have chosen not to adhere to the regulations governing production. These sometimes include prestige wines.

Your average trattoria will generally only stock a limited range of bottled wines, but better restaurants present a carefully chosen selection from around the country. Some osterie in particular concentrate more on presenting a range of fine wines than on the food. *Enoteche* (wine bars) usually present you with an enormous range of wines and a limited food menu.

Generally if you simply order the *vino della casa* (house wine) by the glass, half litre or litre you will get a perfectly acceptable table wine to accompany your food.

Tuscan Wines Wine enthusiasts arriving in Tuscany will think they have died and gone to heaven. Bacchus' elixir is produced from one end of the region to the other and many of Italy's top wines come from here.

Tuscany produces five of Italy's DOCG wines. They are Brunello, Carmignano, Chianti and Chianti Classico, Vernaccia di San Gimignano (the only white) and Vino Nobile di Montepulciano. Tuscany also boasts some 38 DOC wines.

There was a time when the bulk of wine coming out of Tuscany was rough and ready, if highly palatable, Chianti in flasks. The Chianti region remains the heartland of Tuscan wine production, but for a good generation winemakers have been concentrating more on quality rather than quantity.

The best of them, Chianti Classico, comes from seven zones in many different guises. The backbone of the Chianti reds is the Sangiovese grape, although other grape types are mixed in varyingly modest quantities to produce different styles of wine. Chianti Classico wines share the Gallo Nero (Black Cock) emblem that once symbolised the medieval Chianti League. Chianti in general is full and dry, although ageing requirements differ from area to area and even across vineyards.

The choice doesn't stop in the Chianti region. Among Italy's most esteemed and priciest drops is the Brunello di Montalcino (in Siena province). Until not so long ago only a handful of established estates produced this grand old red, but now over 140 vineyards are at it. The finished product varies a great deal and depends on soil, microclimate and so on. Like the Chianti reds, the Sangiovese grape is at the heart of the Brunello. It is aged in casks for four years and then another two years after in bottles.

Another Sangiovese-based winner is Vino Nobile di Montepulciano, another hilltop town in Siena province. The grape blend and conditions here make this a quite distinctive wine too, but it is not aged for as long as the Brunello.

Tuscany is largely, but not exclusively, about reds. Easily the best-known white is the Vernaccia of San Gimignano. Some of the best is aged in *barriques* (small barrels), while others are sometimes oaked.

An important development since the end of the 1980s has been the rise of Super Tuscans, a long-lived wine of high quality. Departing from the norms imposed by DOC and DOCG requirements, certain vineyards are finally doing the kind of thing that Australian and Californian vintners have been doing for ages – experimenting with different mixes. So now alongside the Sangiovese they are growing Sauvignon, Merlots, Syrahs and other grape varieties and mixing them with the Sangiovese. These wines are then aged in barriques – another break from Tuscan tradition, but a process used all over the world for many modern premium wines.

Super Tuscan was a nickname given to the first red wines produced this way, and the name has stuck. This kind of experimentation has resulted in some first class wines that have been giving DOC and DOCG wines a run for their money – and often winning. Common names in the field of Super Tuscans include Sassicáia, Summus, Excelsus, Tignanello and Sammarco, some of which have been classed among the best wines in all Italy. Although Super Tuscans have sprung up all over Tuscany, they are generally found in and around Chianti Classico. Indeed, many Chianti producers have a Super Tuscan label in their portfolios.

A regional speciality that'll appeal to the sweet tooth is *vinsanto* (holy wine), a dessert wine also used in Mass. Malvasia and Trebbiano grape varieties are generally used to produce a strong, aromatic and amber-coloured wine, ranging from dry to very sweet (even the dry retains a hint of sweetness). The wine takes four years to mature and a good one – which will set you back at least €13 for a 350ml bottle – will last years; it is traditionally served with almond-based Cantucci biscuits.

For hints on particular vineyards you might want to invest in a wine guide. Burton Anderson's hardback pocket guide, *Wines of Italy*, is a handy little tool to have with you. For more information on books about wine, see under Books in the Facts for the Visitor chapter.

Strada del Vini (Wine Roads) The kind wine-folk of Tuscany have made life that much easier for those with a healthy interest in wine by creating Strada del Vini, wine trails through rural Tuscany. These trails generally follow back roads, passing by a plethora of vineyards where you can taste, buy and immerse yourself in wine (not literally though). It's a rewarding way to combine sampling a few wines and getting a glimpse of wine production and traditional farming life.

Each *strada* has its own distinct emblem which you'll see on sign-posts in towns and the countryside, but all are marked with a common logo of the *Strada del Vino di Toscana*, a Pegasus atop six balls forming a downward-pointing triangle (much like a bunch of grapes).

To date 14 strada have been marked out, which criss-cross famous wine-production areas such as Rufina and Montepulciano, to the not-so-famous such as Massa Marittima and the Lunigiana. You can pick up maps and information at tourist offices or contact the organisations direct:

Consorzio Strada del Vino Costa Degli Etruschi
(☎ 0565 7497 68, W www.lastradadelvino.com) Località San Guido 45, 57020 Bolgheri

Strada del Vino Chianti Colli Fiorentini
(☎ 055 324 57 50, e c.collifiorentini@fi.flashnet.it) Viale Belfiore 9, 50144 Firenze

Strada dei Vini Chianti Rufina e Pomino
(☎ 055 324 56 80, W www.chiantirufina.com/stradadeivini) Viale Belfiore 9, 50144 Firenze

Strada del Vino Colli di Candia e di Lunigiana
(☎ 0585 81 65 74, e attprod@zia.ms.it) Via Crispi 11, 54100 Massa

Strada del Vino Colli di Maremma
(☎ 0564 50 73 81) Piazza del Pretorio 4, 58054 Scansano, Grosseto

Strada del Vino Colline Lucchesi e Montecarlo
(☎ 0583 41 75 41, W www.provincia.lucca.it) Via Barsanti e Matteucci 208, 55100 Lucca

Strada del Vino delle Colline Pisane
(☎ 050 92 96 28, e lestradedelvino@mail.valdera.org) Piazza Vittorio Emanuele II 14, 56100 Pisa

Strada del Vino di Montecucco
(☎ 0564 96 96 11, e emmaiuno@amiata.net) Zona I/1 area Grossetana, Località San Lorenzo, 58031 Arcidosso, Grosseto

Strada del Vino di Montespertoli
(☎ 0571 65 75 79, e ctm@leonet.it) Via Sidney Sonnino 19, 50025 Montespertoli, Firenze

Strada del Vino Monteregio di Massa Marittima
(☎ 0566 90 27 56, w www.stradavino.it) Via Parenti 22, 58024 Massa Marittima

Strada del Vino Nobile di Montepulciano
(☎ 0578 75 78 12, w www.vinonobiledimontepulciano.it) Piazza Grande 7, 53045 Montepulciano

Strada del Vino Terre di Arezzo
(☎ 0575 91 47 67, w www.provincia.arezzo.it/servizi) Piazza della Libertà 3, 52100 Arezzo

Strada del Vino Vernaccia di San Gimignano
(☎ 0577 94 01 08, w www.vernaccia.it) Via Villa della Rocca, 53037 San Gimignano

Strada Medicea dei Vini di Carmignano
(☎ 055 871 24 68, e lucettamaria@tiscalinet.it) Piazza Emanuele II 2, 59015 Carmignano

Getting There & Away

If you're coming from outside Europe, competition on intercontinental routes between the airlines means you should be able to pick up a reasonably priced fare, even if you are coming from as far away as Australia. If you live in Europe, you can go overland to Tuscany easily enough, but don't ignore the flight option, as enticing deals frequently pop up. You can fly to Tuscany from elsewhere within Italy, but the overland options usually offer better value for money. In particular, journeys from Milan and Rome are both cheaper and just as easy (indeed often more convenient) by train.

AIR
Airports & Airlines

Tuscany's main hub is Pisa's Galileo Galilei Airport (W www.pisa-airport.com), which is where the bulk of European scheduled and charter flights for the area land. Intercontinental flights use Rome's Leonardo da Vinci (Fiumicino) Airport, to the south of Tuscany. The small Amerigo Vespucci Airport (W www.safnet.it), just outside Florence, takes some European flights. Both the Florence and Pisa airports are used for domestic flights from other parts of Italy as well as international ones.

Many European and international carriers compete with the country's national airline, Alitalia.

Note that, in response to the threat of terrorim, airport security is tighter than ever. Check with your airline how long you need to allow for check-in and what you can carry in hand luggage.

Buying Tickets

With a bit of research – ringing around travel agents, checking Internet sites, perusing the travel ads in newspapers – you can often get yourself a good travel deal. Start early as some of the cheapest tickets need to be bought well in advance and popular flights can sell out.

Full-time students and those aged under 26 years (under 30 in some countries) have access to better deals than other travellers. You have to show a document proving your date of birth, or a valid International Student Identity Card (ISIC) when buying your ticket.

Generally, there is nothing to be gained by buying a ticket direct from the airline. Discounted tickets are released to selected travel agents and specialist discount agencies, and these are usually the cheapest deals going.

One exception to this rule is the expanding number of 'no-frills' carriers, which sell direct to travellers. Unlike the 'full-service' airlines, no-frills carriers often make one-way tickets available at around half the return fare, meaning that it is easy to put together an open-jaw ticket.

The other exception is booking on the Internet. Many airlines, full-service and no-frills, offer some excellent fares to Web surfers. They may sell seats by auction or simply cut prices to reflect the reduced cost of electronic selling.

Many travel agencies around the world have Web sites, which can make the Internet a quick and easy way to compare prices. There are also an increasing number of online agents, such as W www.travelocity.co.uk and W www.deckchair.com, that operate only on the Internet. On-line ticket sales work well if you are doing a simple one-way or return trip on specified dates. However, on-line superfast fare generators are no substitute for a travel agent who knows all about special deals, has strategies for avoiding stopovers and can offer advice on everything from which airline has the best vegetarian food to the best travel insurance to bundle with your ticket.

You may find the cheapest flights are advertised by obscure agencies. Most such firms are honest and solvent, but there are some rogue fly-by-night outfits around. Paying by credit card generally offers protection, as most card issuers provide refunds if you can prove you didn't get what

Air Travel Glossary

Alliances Many of the world's leading airlines are now intimately involved with each other, sharing everything from reservations systems and check-in to aircraft and frequent-flyer schemes. Opponents say that alliances restrict competition. Whatever the arguments, there is no doubt that big alliances are the way of the future.

Courier Fares Businesses often need to send urgent documents or freight securely and quickly. Courier companies hire people to accompany the package through customs and, in return, offer a discount ticket which is sometimes a bargain. However, you may have to surrender all your baggage allowance and take only carry-on luggage.

Fares Airlines traditionally offer 1st class (coded F), business class (coded J) and economy class (coded Y) tickets. These days there are so many promotional and discounted fares available that few passengers pay full fare.

Lost Tickets If you lose your airline ticket, an airline will usually treat it like a travellers cheque and, after inquiries, issue you with another one. Legally, however, an airline is entitled to treat it like cash and if you lose it then it's gone forever. Take very good care of your tickets.

Onward Tickets An entry requirement for many countries is that you have a ticket out of the country. If you're unsure of your next move, the easiest solution is to buy the cheapest onward ticket to a neighbouring country or a ticket from a reliable airline which can later be refunded if you do not use it.

Open-Jaw Tickets These are return tickets where you fly out to one place but return from another. If available, this can save you backtracking to your arrival point.

Overbooking Since every flight has some passengers who fail to show up, airlines often book more passengers than they have seats. Usually excess passengers make up for the no-shows, but occasionally somebody gets 'bumped' onto the next available flight. Guess who it is most likely to be? The passengers who check in late. If you do get 'bumped', you are normally offered some form of compensation.

Reconfirmation Some airlines require you to reconfirm your flight at least 72 hours prior to departure. Check your travel documents to see if this is the case

Restrictions Discounted tickets often have various restrictions on them – such as needing to be paid for in advance and incurring a penalty to be altered or cancelled. Others are restrictions on the minimum and maximum period you must be away.

Round-the-World Tickets RTW tickets give you a limited period (usually a year) in which to circumnavigate the globe. You can go anywhere the carrying airlines go, as long as you don't backtrack. The number of stopovers or total number of separate flights is decided before you set off and they usually cost a bit more than a basic return flight.

Ticketless Travel Airlines are gradually waking up to the realisation that paper tickets are unnecessary encumbrances. On simple one-way or return trips, reservations details can be held on computer and the passenger merely shows ID to claim their seat.

Transferred Tickets Airline tickets cannot be transferred from one person to another. Travellers sometimes try to sell the return half of their ticket, but officials can ask you to prove that you are the person named on the ticket. On an international flight, tickets are compared with passports.

you paid for. Similar protection can be obtained by buying a ticket from a bonded agent, such as one covered by the Air Travel Organiser's Licence (ATOL; [W] www.atol .org.uk) scheme in the UK. Agents who only accept cash should hand over the tickets straight away and not tell you to 'come back tomorrow'. After you've made a booking or paid your deposit, call the airline and confirm that the booking was made. It's generally not advisable to send money (even cheques) through the post unless the agent is very well established – some travellers have reported being ripped off by fly-by-night mail-order ticket agents.

Many travellers change their routes halfway through their trips, so think carefully before you buy a ticket which is not easily refunded.

Travellers with Special Needs

If they're warned early enough, airlines can often make special arrangements for travellers, such as wheelchair assistance at airports or vegetarian meals on the flight. Children under two years travel for 10% of the standard fare (or free on some airlines) as long as they don't occupy a seat. They don't get a baggage allowance. 'Skycots', baby food and nappies should be provided by the airline if requested in advance.

Children aged between two and 12 can usually occupy a seat for half to two-thirds of the full fare, and do get a baggage allowance.

There's an airline directory that provides information on the facilities offered by various airlines on the disability-friendly Web site at [W] www.everybody.co.uk.

Youth Passes

Alitalia offers people aged under 26 (and students aged under 31 with a valid ISIC) a Europa Pass from London and Dublin. The pass is valid for up to six months and allows unlimited one-way flights to the airline's European and Mediterranean destinations for UK£62 per flight, with a minimum of four flights. The first flight must be *to* Italy and the last flight back to the UK or Ireland *from* Italy. Internal flights in Italy on this pass cost UK£45 a pop.

Lufthansa Airlines, British Midland and Scandinavian Airlines (SAS) have a similar pass called Young Europe Special (YES). Eight Italian destinations are included in the programme. The Alitalia deal is better if you plan to do most of your flying and travelling in Italy.

For further details on both passes, contact STA Travel in the UK (see under The UK & Ireland later in this section for contact details).

The Rest of Italy

Travelling by plane is expensive within Italy and it generally makes much better sense to use the efficient and considerably cheaper train and bus services. In any case, only a few domestic airports offer flights to Florence. Alitalia (☎ 800 05 03 50, [W] www .alitalia.it – in Italian, [W] www.alitalia.co.uk – in English) and Meridiana (☎ 199 11 13 33, [W] www.meridiana.it) are the domestic airlines.

There are flights from Bari, Bergamo, Cagliari, Catania, Milan, Olbia, Palermo and Rome into Florence's Amerigo Vespucci Airport. You can get to Pisa from Alghero, Catania, Milan, Olbia, Palermo and Rome. Domestic flights can be booked through any travel agency, details of which are given in the regional chapters of this guide, or by contacting the airline direct.

Alitalia offers a range of discounts for young people, families, the elderly and weekend travellers, and both Alitalia and Meridiana have occasional promotional fares. It should be noted that airline fares fluctuate and that very specific restrictions usually apply to special deals.

With Alitalia, you can fly to Florence or Pisa from pretty much anywhere in Italy. There are three or four daily flights to each airport from either Rome or Milan.

Sample standard return fares to Florence (Vespucci) and Pisa (Galileo Galilei) with Alitalia are given on the next page. Meridiana fares tend to be pretty similar. You may be able to find cheaper fares by buying internal flights at the same time as a flight into the country, or by booking while you are actually in Italy.

route	cost (€)	duration
Bari to Florence	350	2 hours via Rome
Cagliari to Florence	350	2¼ hours via Rome
Catania to Pisa	415	2 hours via Rome
Milan to Florence	230	55 minutes
Milan to Pisa	220	1¼ hours
Rome to Florence	230	1¼ hours
Rome to Pisa	230	1 hour

The UK & Ireland

Discount air travel is big business in London. Advertisements for many travel agencies appear in the travel pages of the weekend broadsheets, in *Time Out*, the *Evening Standard* and the free magazine *TNT*.

For students and for travellers aged under 26, a popular travel agency in the UK includes STA Travel (☎ 020-7361 6161, W www.statravel.co.uk), 86 Old Brompton Rd, London SW7. It has branches throughout the UK and sells tickets to all travellers, but caters especially for young people and students.

Other recommended discount travel agents include Trailfinders (☎ 020-7937 1234, W www.trailfinders.co.uk), 215 Kensington High St, London W8; Bridge the World (☎ 020-7734 7447, W www.b-t-w.co.uk), 4 Regent Place, London W1; and Flight-bookers (☎ 020-775 72000, W www.ebook ers.com), 177–178 Tottenham Court Rd, London W1.

No-frills airlines (see Buying Tickets earlier) are big business for travel between the UK and Ireland and Italy. They increasingly serve minor airports as well as a few main ones and encourage you to book flights on line. The best deals are usually to be had if you travel mid-week and book early.

The Irish airline Ryanair (☎ 0870 333 1231 in the UK, ☎ 199 11 41 14 in Italy, W www.ryanair.com) is the only no-frills airline that flies directly to Tuscany, with two flights daily to Pisa from London Stansted airport. At the time of writing the one-way fare was around UK£50 but silly deals as low as UK£10 are frequently available.

If you're happy to fly to Rome or Milan and take the train or bus to Tuscany from there, you can get good deals with the various other no-frills airlines such as Go (☎ 0870 607 6543 in the UK, ☎ 848 88 77 66 in Italy, W www.go-fly.com), Buzz (☎ 0870 240 7070 in the UK, ☎ 02 696 82 222 in Italy, W www.buzzaway.com) and Virgin Express (☎ 020-7744 0004 in the UK, ☎ 800 09 70 97 in Italy, W www .virgin-express.com). At the time of writing, standard one-way fares from London to Rome or Milan with these airlines ranged from UK£40 to UK£90.

The two principal full-service airlines linking the UK and Italy are British Airways (BA; ☎ 0845 7733 377, W www.british-airways.com), 156 Regent St, London W1R, and Alitalia (☎ 0870 544 8259, W www .alitalia.co.uk), 4 Portman Square, London W1. British Airways flies direct to Pisa from London Gatwick twice daily; return fares at the time of writing were UK£130. Alitalia offers regular flights to both Pisa, via Milan Malpensa, and to Florence. Return fares from London start at UK£130 to Pisa and UK£180 to Florence.

The Charter Flight Centre (☎ 020-7282 1090, W www.charterflights.co.uk), 19 Denbigh St, London SW1, has return flights to Pisa for around UK£150.

If you're coming from Ireland, it might be worth comparing the cost of flying direct with the cost of travelling to London first and then flying on to Italy.

Continental Europe

Air travel between the rest of continental Europe and Italy is worth considering if you are pushed for time. Short hops can be expensive but good deals are available from some major hubs.

Several airlines, including Alitalia, Qantas Airways and Air France, offer cut-rate fares on legs of international flights between European cities. These are usually cheap but often involve flying at night or early in the morning.

France It's easy to fly from France to Tuscany, but if you're on a budget it may be worth considering the longer but cheaper option of the train.

The student travel agency OTU Voyages (☎ 08 20 81 78 17, W www.otu.fr) has a central Paris office at 39 ave Georges-Bernanos as well as many offices around the country. It's a safe bet for good student deals and cut-price travel.

Air Littoral (☎ 08 03 83 48 34 in France, ☎ 035 23 30 04 in Italy, W www.air-littoral.fr) operates flights between Nice and Florence twice daily and offers connections from other airports in France.

At the time of writing, return fares from Paris to Florence with Alitalia were around €300. It is possible to get better deals but you'll need to search around and be flexible in your travel plans.

Germany If you're looking for a cheap deal, Munich is a haven of bucket shops and more mainstream budget travel outlets. Council Travel (☎ 089-39 50 22), Adalbert-strasse 32, near the university, is one of the best.

STA Travel (☎ 01805 456 422, W www.statravel.de) is at Goethestrasse 73 in Berlin and has branches across the country.

Germany has a number of online travel agents that are worth checking out. You might want to try W www.lastminute.de and W www.justtravel.de.

At the time of writing, Lufthansa was offering return fares from Munich to Florence and Pisa for €250.

The Netherlands There are plenty of discount travel agents along Amsterdam's Rokin, but shop around to compare prices before deciding. One recommended travel agent, Holland International (☎ 070 307 6307), has offices in most cities in the Netherlands. Online try W www.budgettravel.com or W www.airfair.nl.

At the time of writing, standard returns to Florence with Meridiana airline started at €263.

Belgium For student and youth travel, it's worth trying Connections (☎ 02-55 00 100, W www.connections.be) at 19–21 rue du Midi in Brussels. Another recommended travel agent is Nouvelle Frontières (☎ 02-547 44 22, W www.nouvelles-frontieres.be), 2 blvd Maurice Lemmonier, 1000 Brussels, which also has branches in Anvers, Bruges, Liège and Gand.

At the time of writing, return fares from Brussels to Florence with Lufthansa were around €185.

The USA & Canada

The North Atlantic is the world's busiest long-haul air corridor and the flight options are bewildering. Flights from the USA to either Florence or Pisa are possible with Alitalia and with other European airlines such as Lufthansa and Air France. Whichever you opt for, you will almost certainly have to change flights. You might also want to consider flying to Rome and taking the train from there. This will increase your flight options but be aware that often the difference in ticket prices is negligible.

Discount travel agencies in the USA are known as consolidators. San Francisco is the ticket-consolidator capital of America, although some good deals can be found in Los Angeles, New York and other big cities. Consolidators can be found through the *Yellow Pages* or the major daily newspapers. The *New York Times*, the *Los Angeles Times*, the *Chicago Tribune* and the *San Francisco Examiner* all produce weekly travel sections in which you will find a number of travel agency ads. Watch out for their SOT number – if they have one of these they are probably legitimate. Ticket Planet is a leading ticket consolidator in the USA and is recommended (W www.ticketplanet.com).

America's largest student travel organisation is Council Travel (☎ 1 800 2COUNCIL, W www.counciltravel.com), with around 60 offices in the USA. STA Travel (☎ 1 800 781 4040, W www.statravel.com) has offices in Boston, Chicago, Miami, New York, Philadelphia, San Francisco and other major cities.

Fares vary wildly depending on season, availability and a little luck. At the time of writing, low season fares to Florence were around US$515 from New York and around

US$564 from Los Angeles. In the high season you can be looking at anything from an extra US$300 upwards. Note these fares will often involve one, or maybe two, changes. After March, prices begin to rise rapidly and availability declines.

Discount and rock-bottom options from the USA include charter, stand-by and courier flights. Stand-by fares are often sold at 60% of the normal price for one-way tickets.

A courier flight from America to Italy can cost a third to two-thirds of the standard price. Now Voyager (☎ 212-431 1616), Suite 307, 74 Varrick St, New York, NY 10013, specialises in courier flights but you must pay an annual membership fee (around US$50) that entitles you to take as many courier flights as you like.

Also well worth considering are Europe by Air coupons (☎ 1 888 387 2479, W www .europebyair.com). You purchase a minimum of three US$99 coupons before leaving North America. Each coupon is valid for a one-way flight within the combined system of more than 30 participating regional airlines in Europe (exclusive of local taxes, which you will be charged when you make the flight). The coupons are valid for 120 days from the day you make your first flight. A few words of caution – using one of these coupons for a one-way flight won't always be better value than local alternatives, so check them out before committing yourself to any given flight. The same company offers two- and three-week unlimited flight passes and sells one-off air fares too.

If you can't find a particularly good deal, it's always worth considering a cheap transatlantic hop to London to trawl through the bargains there. See The UK & Ireland section earlier in this chapter.

Canadian discount air-ticket-sellers are also known as consolidators and their fares tend to be about 10% higher than those sold in the USA. Both Alitalia and Air Canada have direct flights to Rome and Milan from Toronto and Montreal. Scan the budget travel agencies' ads in the *Toronto Globe & Mail*, the *Toronto Star* and the *Vancouver Province*.

Travel CUTS (☎ 1 866 246 9762, W www .travelcuts.com) is Canada's national student travel agency, with offices in all major cities. It is known as Voyages Campus in Quebec.

Low-season return fares from Montreal to Florence start from around C$825, while a high-season ticket could cost C$1378. From Vancouver you'd be looking at C$1083 and C$1536 respectively.

Australia & New Zealand

Two well-known agents for cheap fares are STA Travel (☎ 1300 360 960, W www .statravel.com.au) and Flight Centre (☎ 133 133, W www.flightcentre.com.au). STA Travel has its main office at 224 Faraday St, Carlton, in Melbourne, and other offices in all major cities and on many university campuses. Flight Centre has a central office at 82 Elizabeth St, Sydney, and there are dozens of offices throughout Australia.

Quite a few travel offices specialise in discount air tickets. Some travel agencies, particularly smaller ones, advertise cheap air fares in the travel sections of weekend newspapers.

For flights from Australia to Europe, there are a number of competing airlines and a wide variety of air fares. Most of the cheaper flights go via South-East Asia, involving stopovers in Kuala Lumpur, Bangkok or Singapore. If a long stopover between connections is necessary, transit accommodation is sometimes included in the price of the ticket. If it's not included, it may be worth considering a more expensive ticket that does cover accommodation.

On some flights between Australia and Europe, airlines throw in a return flight to another European city – so, for instance, if you have a return fare to London, a London-Rome-London flight will be included in the price. Check with your travel agent about such deals.

Low-season return fares from Sydney or Melbourne to Florence are around A$1,600, but shop around, as cheaper deals are sometimes available. High-season returns start from around A$2100 to A$2500. Flights from Perth are usually a few hundred dollars cheaper.

Flight Centre (☎ 09-309 6171) has a large central office in Auckland at National

Bank Towers, on the corner of Queen and Darby Sts, and many branches throughout the country. STA Travel (☎ 0800 874 773, W www.statravel.com.nz), 10 High St, Auckland, has other offices in Auckland as well as in Hamilton, Palmerston North, Wellington, Christchurch and Dunedin.

From New Zealand, round-the-world (RTW) tickets are generally good value as they can sometimes be cheaper than a normal return. Otherwise, you can fly from Auckland to pick up a connecting flight in Melbourne or Sydney. Standard return low-season fares from New Zealand to Florence (change in Rome) are around NZ$2500 but some airlines (try Thai International and Malaysia Airlines) may offer cheaper deals.

LAND

There are plenty of options for reaching Tuscany by train, bus or private vehicle. Bus is generally the cheapest, but services are usually less frequent and considerably less comfortable than the train.

If you are travelling by bus, train or car to Italy, remember to check whether you require visas for the countries you intend to pass through.

Bus

Eurolines (W www.eurolines.com), a consortium of European coach companies, operates international coach services across Europe. Their Italian headquarters (☎ 055 35 71 10, fax 055 35 05 65) are at Via Mercadante 2/b, 50144 Florence. Tickets can be bought at the Lazzi office (see The Rest of Italy later in this section).

Bus Passes Eurolines offers the Eurolines Pass, a useful option for travellers planning to pack in a lot of kilometres touring Europe. A pass valid for 15/30/60 days in the high season (June to mid-September) costs UK£120/179/195 for those aged under 26 (those aged over 26 have only the 30-/60-day options at UK£222/259). In the low season the pass costs about 25% less. It allows unlimited travel between up to 46 European cities, including Florence, Milan, Naples, Rome and Venice.

Another option if you plan to travel a lot beyond Italy is Busabout (☎ 020-7950 1661, fax 7950 1662, W www.busabout.com), 258 Vauxhall Bridge Rd, London SW1V 1BS. This company offers passes of varying duration allowing you to use their hop-on hop-off bus network in Western and Central Europe. The frequency of departures and the number of stops available goes up between April and October (when buses pass through each stop once every two days). There are 14 stops in Italy and you can book onward travel and accommodation on the bus or at their Web site. Busabout's passes cost UK£169/229 for 15/21 days, and UK£309/479/589/699 for one/two/three/seven months. Students and young people with appropriate ID (such as ISIC, GO25 and Euro>26) pay UK£149/209 and UK£279/429/529/629 respectively.

The Rest of Italy Long-haul travel is generally more comfortably done by train, particularly if you're travelling around the north of Italy or from Rome and Naples. If you're travelling from the south, where train services are often non-existent or painfully slow, the bus is sometimes a sensible alternative.

Lazzi (☎ 055 36 30 41, W www.lazzi.it) is responsible for long-haul bus services from other parts of Italy. SITA (☎ 800 37 37 60 or 055 4 78 21, W www.sita-on-line.it) also offers a handful of long-distance services, mostly to southern Italy.

Generally you must book these tickets in advance. Sample fares from Florence are €49.50 to Messina in Sicily (12 hours, three weekly) and €15 to Milan (3½ hours, five daily).

In collaboration with SITA, Lazzi also operates a winter service called Alpi Bus, which runs extensive routes to the Alps. These buses depart from numerous cities and towns throughout Tuscany, Lazio, Umbria and Emilia-Romagna for most main resorts in the Alps. Destinations likely to interest travellers in Tuscany are hardly numerous. A brochure detailing the service is available from the Lazzi office.

The same company also operates the Freccia dell'Appennino (Apennine Arrow) service, with buses connecting

Florence, Siena and Montecatini with destinations in Le Marche (such as Ascoli Piceno) and in Abruzzo (such as Chieto and Pescara). These services tend to stop in Perugia, where you sometimes have to change bus.

See Lazzi's Web site for further details. Alternatively try calling ☎ 0577 28 32 03.

The UK Eurolines (☎ 0870 514 3219), 52 Grosvenor Gardens, Victoria, London, runs buses to Florence (30 hours, two to five times weekly). The one-way/return fares are UK£69/106 (UK£63/96 for those under 26 and senior citizens). Fares rise by around UK£10 in the peak period (July, August and the week before Christmas). If you book in advance, you can often get a good deal. For example, at the time of writing, a standard return could be had for UK£79 by booking in advance.

Buses leave from Victoria Coach Station, a few blocks from the Eurolines office.

Continental Europe The Eurolines network covers all of Europe. Check out the Web site (**W** www.eurolines.com) for details of offices, timetables and fares in each country. We've listed three of the main offices here along with sample fares current at the time of research.

France (☎ 08 36 69 52 52) 28 ave du Général de Gaulle, Paris. A standard return fare from Paris to Florence costs €155.
Germany (☎ 089-5458 7000) Deutsche Touring GmbH, Arnulfstrasse 3 (Stamberger Bahnhof), Munich. A standard return fare from Munich to Florence costs €138.
The Netherlands (☎ 020-560 8788) Julianaplein 5, 1097 Amsterdam. A standard return fare from Amsterdam to Florence costs €150.

Train

Florence is an important rail hub so it's easy to get to Tuscany from European destinations and elsewhere in Italy.

The *Thomas Cook European Timetable* (UK£9.50) has an extensive listing of train schedules. It is updated monthly and available from Thomas Cook offices and agents worldwide.

On overnight hauls you can book a *cuccetta* (couchette) for around €15 to €23 on most international trains. In 1st class there are four bunks per cabin and in 2nd class there are six.

It is always advisable, and sometimes compulsory, to book seats on international trains to and from Italy.

Some of the main international services include transport for private cars – an option worth examining to save wear and tear on your vehicle before it arrives in Italy.

The Rest of Italy The principal north-south train line into Tuscany passes through Florence on a route that runs from Milan through Bologna and on to Rome via Arezzo. Another line from Rome hugs the coast as it heads into Tuscany, before passing through Grosseto, Follonica (branch to Piombino), Livorno, Pisa (branch to Florence), Viareggio and on along the coast to La Spezia and Genoa (Liguria).

Information For information on trains you can call ☎ 848 88 80 88 (in Italian) anywhere in Italy, or visit **W** www.fs-on-line.com (in Italian, English, Dutch, French *and* Spanish). In train stations in Tuscany you can sometimes find the handy *In Treno* (€2) booklet of timetables, which covers journeys to other parts of Italy from Florence. It is possible to get a timetable outside Italy as well. In the UK, for instance, you can find it at Italwings (☎ 020-7287 2117), 162/168 Regent St, London W1 for UK£9.

Main train timetables generally display *arrivi* (arrivals) on a white background and *partenze* (departures) on a yellow one. Imminent arrivals and departures also appear on electronic boards. You will notice a plethora of symbols and acronyms on the main timetables, some of which are useful for identifying the kind of train concerned (see Types of Train below).

Types of Train A wide variety of trains circulate around Italy. They start with slow all-stops *locali*, which generally don't travel much beyond their main city of origin or province. Next come the *regionali*, which also tend to be slow but cover greater distances, sometimes going beyond their region of origin. *Interregionali* cover greater distances still and don't necessarily stop at every station.

From this level there is a leap upwards to InterCitys (IC), faster long-distance trains operating between major cities and for which you generally have to pay a *supplemento* on top of the normal cost of a ticket. Services using top-of-the-range locos are now collectively known as Eurostar Italia (ES).

Notturne (night trains) are either old *espressi* or, increasingly, InterCity Notte (ICN) services. You generally have the option of a couchette (one of four or six fold-down bunkbeds in a compartment) or a proper bed in a *vagone letto* (sleeping car), which tends to be much more expensive. The international version is the EuroNight (EN).

Passes & Discounts Eurail, InterRail, Europass and Flexipass tickets are valid on the national rail. Possible local passes include the Railpass, Flexipass and Euro-Domino pass, all of which can be bought in Italy and abroad. They allow you unlimited rail travel for varying periods of time. None of these passes is much use unless you plan to travel extensively in Italy.

People aged between 12 and 26 can acquire the Carta Verde and people aged 60 and over the Carta d'Argento. Both cost €23.25, are valid for a year and entitle holders to 20% off ticket prices. Children aged between four and 12 years are automatically entitled to a 50% discount; those under four travel free.

The Offerta Famiglia allows groups of three to five people travelling together to get a discount of 20% on their travel (a combined ticket for everyone travelling is issued). This offer is not valid in July, August, December, the first half of January or the period from Palm Sunday to Easter.

Tickets There are many ticketing possibilities. Apart from the standard division between 1st and 2nd class on the faster trains (generally you can get only 2nd-class seats on locali and regionali), you usually have to pay a supplement for travelling on a fast train.

As with tickets, the price of the supplement is in part calculated according to the length of the journey. You can pay the supplement separately from the ticket. Thus, if you have a 2nd-class return ticket from Florence to Rome, you might decide to avoid the supplement one way and take a slower train but pay a supplement for the return trip to speed things up a little. Whatever you decide, you need to pay the supplement before boarding the train.

You can buy rail tickets (for major destinations on fast trains at least) from most travel agents. If you choose to buy them at the station, there are automatic machines that accept cash. If you queue at the windows, watch out for those displaying the Eurostar sign – they will only sell you tickets on ES trains.

It is advisable, and in some cases obligatory, to book long-distance tickets in advance, whether international or domestic. In 1st class, booking is often mandatory (and free). Where it is optional (which is more often, but not always, the case in 2nd class), you may pay a €2.60 booking fee. Tickets can be booked at the windows in the station or at most travel agencies. It is also possible to book your tickets over the phone (☎ 199 16 61 77) with a credit card.

The following prices are approximate, standard, 2nd-class, one-way fares (including supplement) on IC trains from Florence. ES fares are higher, and the trains are faster and make fewer stops.

destination	cost (€)	duration
Bologna	10.70	1 hour
Milan	24.70	3 hours 20 minutes
Naples	37	4 hours
Rome	25	1 hour 55 minutes
Venice	21.75	3 hours

Other long-haul destinations within Italy for which there is at least one direct connection from Florence include Bolzano, Palermo, Reggio Calabria, Siracusa, Trieste and Udine.

Rules & Fines When you buy a ticket you are supposed to stamp it in one of the yellow machines scattered about all stations (usually with a *convalida* sign on them).

Failure to do so will be rewarded with an on-the-spot fine. This rule does not apply to tickets purchased outside Italy. If you buy a return ticket, you must stamp it each way (each end of the ticket). One of the several Italian verbs for this operation of stamping your ticket is *obliterare* – it makes for a wonderful translation into English: 'Ladies and gentlemen, please obliterate your tickets before boarding the train.'

The ticket you buy is valid for two months until stamped. Once stamped it is valid for 24 hours if the journey distance (one-way) is greater than 200km, six hours if it is less. For a return ticket, the time is calculated separately for each one-way journey (that is, on a short return trip you get six hours from the time of stamping on the way out and the same on the way back).

All seats on ES trains on Friday and Sunday must be booked in advance. On other days wagons for unbooked seats are set aside. If you board an ES train on a Friday or Sunday without a booking, you pay a €5.15 fine.

The UK Land travel possible between Britain and continental Europe is made possible by the Channel Tunnel. The Eurostar passenger train service (☎ 0870 518 6186, W www .eurostar.com) travels between London and Paris and London and Brussels. The Euro-tunnel vehicle service travels between Folkestone and Calais (see the Car & Motorcycle section later in this chapter for details).

Alternatively, you can get a train ticket that includes the Channel crossing by ferry or SeaCat hovercraft. After that, you can travel via Paris and southern France or by heading from Belgium down through Germany and Switzerland.

The cheapest standard return fare from London to Florence, via Paris (on Eurostar), on offer at the time of writing was UK£220.

For information on international rail travel (including Eurostar services), contact Rail Europe (☎ 0870 584 8848, W www.rail europe.co.uk), 179 Piccadilly, London W1.

Continental Europe Train lines cross the Italian frontier at several points from France, Switzerland, Austria and Slovenia. Unless you are following the coast from France, in which case you can get to Florence via Genoa (Liguria) and Pisa, you will almost certainly end up heading to Florence from Bologna. The main high-speed international runs follow the Milan-Bologna-Florence-Rome route. If you are approaching from Austria or Eastern Europe, you will either join the line at Bologna or have to change trains there.

France Your quickest option from Paris to Florence is a morning departure on a TGV to Milan, changing there for the onward trip. You are looking at around €225 for a standard return and about 10½ hours' travel.

As many as three trains do an overnight run from Paris, either direct to Florence or with early-morning changes at either Milan or Pisa. A couchette on a night train cost around €215 at the time of writing.

Switzerland, Germany & Austria The comfiest way by rail from Switzerland into Italy is with the modern Cisalpino (CiS) service. The bulk of these services go to Milan, starting at Basle, Bern, Geneva or Zürich. One service connects Zürich directly with Florence, via Milan. That trip costs €165 and takes a little less than seven hours.

Coming from Germany, it is possible to get a Cisalpino from Stuttgart to Milan via Zürich. You can also take a direct train from Innsbruck (Austria) and Munich to Florence via the Brenner Pass. Elsewhere in Austria, you can travel from Vienna to Florence via Venice and Bologna.

Car & Motorcycle

From the UK, you can take your car across to France by ferry or by the Channel Tunnel car train, Eurotunnel (☎ 0870 535 3535, W www.eurotunnel.com). The latter runs between terminals in Folkestone and Calais round the clock, with crossings lasting 35 minutes. You pay for the vehicle only and fares vary according to time of day and season. You can be looking at as much as UK£297, but good deals are often available. At the time of writing you could travel for as little as UK£23.

The main points of entry to Italy are the Mt Blanc tunnel from France at Chamonix, which connects with the A5 for Turin and Milan; the Grand St Bernard tunnel from Switzerland, which also connects with the A5; and the Brenner Pass from Austria, which connects with the A22 to Bologna. Mountain passes in the Alps are often closed in winter and sometimes in autumn and spring, making the tunnels a less scenic but more reliable way to arrive in Italy (though there are safety concerns following the fires in the Mt Blanc and Gotthard tunnels). Make sure you have snow chains in winter.

Europe is made for motorcycle touring and Tuscany is no exception. Motorcyclists literally swarm in during the summer to tour the winding, scenic roads. Motorcyclists rarely have to book ahead for ferries. You will be able to enter restricted traffic areas in Italian cities without any problems and Italian traffic police generally turn a blind eye to motorcycles parked on footpaths.

Roads are generally good throughout Italy and there is an excellent network of *autostrade* (motorways). The main north-south link, which skirts Florence, is the Autostrada del Sole, extending from Milan to Reggio di Calabria (called the A1 from Milan to Naples and the A3 from Naples to Reggio di Calabria). The A11 heads west via Pistoia and Lucca towards Pisa and Livorno and meets the A12 to La Spezia and Genoa. As well as the A1, you can take the SS1 south from Livorno to Rome via Grosseto. Where it is single carriageway it can be hairy, but progress on the parallel A12 extension continues.

Several back mountain roads cross the Apennines from Emilia-Romagna in more picturesque style. One example is the SS302, or Via Faenza, from that town south to Borgo San Lorenzo in the Mugello. From there you are a fairly short drive from Florence. From Perugia (Umbria), the SS75b west along the north of Lago Trasimeno puts you on the road to Siena, intersecting the A1 on the way.

Drivers usually travel at high speeds in the left-hand fast lane on the *autostrada*, so use that lane only to pass other cars. You have to pay a toll to use the autostrada, which generally can be paid by credit card (including Visa, MasterCard, American Express and Diners Club). Another way to pay is to buy a Viacard (available in €25.80, €51.65 and €77.47 denominations at toll booths and some service stations and tourist offices – check W www.autostrade.it for details). You present it to the attendant as payment or insert it into the appropriate Viacard machine as you exit an autostrada. Left-over credit is not refundable on leaving Italy.

Travellers with time to spare could consider using the system of *strade statali* (state roads), which are sometimes multi-lane dual carriageways and are toll-free. They are represented on maps as 'S' or 'SS'. The *strade provinciali* (provincial roads) are sometimes little more than country lanes, but provide access to some of the more beautiful scenery and the many towns and villages. They are represented as 'SP' on maps.

An interesting Web site loaded with advice for people planning to drive in Europe is W www.ideamerge.com/motoeuropa. If you want help with route planning, try out W www.euroshell.com.

For information on road rules within Italy see the Getting Around chapter.

Paperwork & Preparations Proof of ownership of a private vehicle should always be carried (Vehicle Registration Document for UK-registered cars) when driving through Europe. All EU member states' driving licences (not the old-style UK green licence) are fully recognised throughout the Union, regardless of your length of stay. Those with a non-EU licence are supposed to obtain an International Driving Permit (IDP) to accompany their national licence. In practice you will probably be OK with national licences from countries such as Australia, Canada and the USA. Your national automobile association usually issues IDPs.

Third-party motor insurance is a minimum requirement in Italy and throughout Europe. The Green Card, an internationally recognised proof of insurance obtainable from your insurer, is mandatory. Ask your insurer for a European Accident Statement form, which can simplify matters in the event of an accident. Never sign statements you can't read or understand – insist on a translation and sign that only if it's acceptable.

A European breakdown assistance policy is a good investment, such as the AA Five Star Service (☎ 0870 550 0600) or the RAC's Eurocover Motoring Assistance (☎ 0870 572 2722). In Italy, assistance can be obtained through the Automobile Club Italiano. See Road Assistance under Car & Motorcycle in the Getting Around chapter for details.

Every vehicle travelling across an international border should display a nationality plate of its country of registration. A warning triangle (to be used in the event of a breakdown) is compulsory throughout Europe. Recommended accessories are a first-aid kit, a spare-bulb kit and a fire extinguisher.

Rental There is a mind-boggling variety of special deals and terms and conditions attached to car rental. Here are a few pointers to help you through.

Multinational agencies – Hertz, Avis, Budget and Europe's largest rental agency, Europcar – will provide a reliable service and good standard of vehicle. However, if you walk into an office and ask for a car on the spot, you will always pay high rates, even allowing for special weekend deals. National and local firms can sometimes undercut the multinationals but be sure to examine the rental agreement carefully.

Planning ahead and pre-booking a rental car through a multinational agency before leaving home will enable you to find the best deals. Pre-booked and pre-paid rates are always cheaper. If you don't know exactly when you will want to rent, you could call back home from Italy (more or less affordable to the UK and the USA) and reserve through an agency there. This way you get the benefits of booking from home. Fly/drive packages are worth looking into – ask your travel agency for information or contact one of the major rental agencies.

Make sure you understand what is included in the price (unlimited kilometres, tax, insurance, collision damage waiver and so on) and what your liabilities are. Insurance can be a thorny issue. Are you covered for theft, vandalism and fire damage? Check

whether or not you have car insurance with your credit card provider and what the conditions are. The extra cover provided may pick up the slack in any local cover. The minimum rental age in Italy is 21 years.

Holiday Autos sometimes has good rates for Europe, for which you need to pre-book – its main office is in the UK (☎ 0870 400 0099, ⓦ www.holidayautos.co.uk). At the time of writing they were charging UK£433 (all-inclusive) for a small car (such as a Fiat Punto) for two weeks. Car Rental Direct (☎ 020-7625 7166, ⓦ www.globcars.com) is another possibility.

Motorcycle rental is possible in Tuscany, for example, there are several specialist rental agencies in Florence.

See the Car & Motorcycle section under Getting Around in the Florence chapter for more information on rental.

Purchase It is illegal for nonresidents to purchase vehicles in Italy. The UK is probably the best place to buy second-hand cars (prices there are not competitive for new cars though). Bear in mind that you will be getting a left-hand-drive car (with the steering wheel on the right).

If you want a right-hand-drive car and can afford to buy new, prices are relatively low in Belgium, the Netherlands and Luxembourg. Paperwork can be tricky wherever you buy.

SEA

Ferries connect Italy with countries all over the Mediterranean but if you want to reach Tuscany directly by sea, the only options are the ferry crossings to Livorno from Sardinia and Corsica. See Livorno in the Central Coast chapter for more details.

ORGANISED TOURS

Options for organised travel to Tuscany abound. The Italian State Tourist Office (see under Tourist Offices Abroad in the Facts for the Visitor chapter) can provide a list of tour operators and what each specialises in. Such tours can save you hassles but they rob you of independence and do not generally come cheap.

Warning

The information in this chapter is particularly vulnerable to change: prices for international travel are volatile, routes are introduced and cancelled, schedules change, special deals come and go, and rules and visa requirements are amended. Airlines and governments seem to take a perverse pleasure in making price structures and regulations as complicated as possible. You should check directly with the airline or a travel agent to make sure you understand how a fare (and ticket you may buy) works. In addition, the travel industry is highly competitive and there are many lurks and perks.

The upshot of this is that you should get opinions, quotes and advice from as many airlines and travel agents as possible before you part with your hard-earned cash. The details given in this chapter should be regarded as pointers and are not a substitute for your own careful, up-to-date research.

General

A couple of big, established specialists in the UK are Magic of Italy (☎ 0870 546 2442, W www.magictravelgroup.co.uk) and Alitalia's subsidiary, Italiatour (☎ 01883-621900, W www.alitour.com). They offer a wide range of Tuscan tours, city breaks and resort-based holidays.

Short Breaks

In London, Kirker Travel Ltd (☎ 020-7231 3333, W www.kirkerholidays.com), 3 New Concordia Wharf, Mill St, London SE1 2BB, specialises in short breaks from the capital. The cost (higher in summer) usually includes accommodation, air fare, transfers and breakfast.

Walking & Cycling

There are several companies offering organised walking tours in Tuscany. One of them is Explore Worldwide (☎ 01252-760000,

W www.exploreworldwide.com). Also in the UK, Alternative Travel Group (☎ 01865-315678, W www.atg-oxford.co.uk) offers a series of escorted and unescorted walking and cycling tours. With the unescorted version, accommodation is pre-booked and luggage forwarded on while you walk or cycle.

Headwater (☎ 01606-813333, W www.headwater.com) also does walking and cycling tours in Tuscany.

Cooking & Wine

More focused possibilities abound. For one-week trips led by cooking instructors, try Tasting Places (☎ 020-7460 0077, W www.tastingplaces.com), Unit 40, Buspace Studios, Conlan St, London W10 5AP. You cook and eat your way to a better understanding of Tuscany. You won't get much change from UK£1350. See also under Courses in the Facts for the Visitor chapter.

Under-35s

A range of coach tours for young people, aimed at a high-speed, party-minded crowdd, are offered by Top Deck Travel (☎ 020-7370 4555, W www.topdecktravel.co.uk), 131–135 Earls Court Rd, London SW5 9RH, and Contiki Travel Ltd (☎ 020-7637 0802, W www.contiki.com), c/o Royal National Hotel, Bedford Way, London WC1H 0DG.

In the USA, New Frontiers (☎ 800 366 6387, W www.newfrontiers.com), 12 East 33rd St, New York, offers rail-travel packages and other tours in Italy.

Seniors

Saga Holidays offers holidays for the over 50s, from cheap coach tours to luxury cruises. You will find offices in Britain (☎ 0800 300456, W www.holidays.saga.co.uk), Enbrook Park, Folkestone, Kent CT20 3SE; the USA (freephone ☎ 1 877 265 6862, W www.sagaholidays.com), 222 Berkeley St, Boston, MA 02116; and Australia (☎ 02-9957 4266), Level 1, Suite 2, 110 Pacific Highway, North Sydney, NSW 2061.

Getting Around

AIR

There are no direct flights between cities in Tuscany.

BUS

Unless you have your own wheels, bus is often the only way to get around Tuscany. Where there is a train, you should probably take it, but there are some exceptions. One of them is the Florence-Siena run, which is much quicker and more convenient by rapid SITA bus. Other buses also run from Florence and Siena to Colle di Val d'Elsa, where there are connecting buses to San Gimignano and Volterra.

Direct buses run from Florence to Arezzo, Castellina in the Chianti region, Marina di Grosseto and other smaller cities throughout Tuscany as well.

Lazzi has buses from Florence to parts of Tuscany, mostly in the north-west, including Pisa, Lucca and Pistoia. The CAP and COPIT companies serve towns in the north-west.

In general, separate bus companies operate services in each province, radiating from the provincial capital. Frequently services overlap into neighbouring provinces.

Services can be frequent on weekdays but between smaller towns often drop to a few or even none on Sundays and public holidays. If you are depending on buses to get around, always keep this in mind, as it is easy to get stuck in smaller places at the weekend.

To give you an idea of the cost and time involved for making bus journeys around Tuscany, a few sample one-way trips from Florence follow. Further information appears in the destination chapters throughout the guide.

destination one-way	cost (€)	duration
Arezzo	5.10	2½ hours
Greve in Chianti	2.60	1 hour
Lucca	4.45	1¼ hours
Marina di Carrara	6.30	3 hours
Pisa	5.80	3 hours
Pistoia	2.60	50 minutes
Poggibonsi	3.80	1¼ hours
Prato	1.80	45 minutes
Radda in Chianti	3.20	1¾ hours
San Gimignano (change at Poggibonsi)	5.15	1½ hours
Siena	4.15	2¼ hours
Siena *(rapido)*	6.20	1¼ hours
Viareggio	6.50	1½ hours
Volterra *(rapido)*	6.30	1¼ hours

TRAIN

Note that all tickets must be validated *before* you board your train. Simply punch them in the yellow machines installed at the entrance to all train platforms. If you don't validate them, you risk a large fine.

Some of the long-distance trains that run across the country can be used to get around Tuscany. Destinations such as Arezzo and Chiusi, on the Bologna-Florence-Rome line, are easily reached this way.

The lines radiating west towards Pisa (and on to Livorno) and Viareggio are also fairly reliable, with regular services.

The Florence-Pisa run is a good example of where you should choose rail over bus. The train via Empoli takes little over an hour, while the bus stops frequently and takes up to three hours (and costs more into the bargain).

The Viareggio line is the one to take for Prato, Pistoia and Lucca. If you get an all-stops commuter train on either of these lines, the going can be a little slow.

The coastal rail line (between Rome and Genoa) is the easiest way to reach most major points along the Tuscan coast (and a branch line cuts inland to Florence). To proceed to smaller towns a little way inland you will often need to make a bus connection.

Several minor lines spread out across the Tuscan countryside too, but services can be limited and slow. The Florence-Siena service is a good example. Others include Siena-Grosseto, Siena-Chiusi, Arezzo-Sinalunga, Lucca-Pisa and Volterra-Cecina (with a couple of connections to Pisa). Another line winds north from Pontassieve, via Borgo San Lorenzo, across the north-east of the region to Faenza in Emilia-Romagna.

An added inconvenience of numerous Tuscan towns is their hilltop position. When you arrive at the train station in places such as Siena, Cortona and Volterra, you still have to get a local bus to take you up to the town.

Some sample one-way, 2nd-class fares and times follow. Bear in mind that times vary considerably depending on what kind of train you end up on and the number of stops made (for information on types of trains see the section under Land in the Getting There & Away chapter):

from	to	cost (€)	duration
Florence	Arezzo	4.45	1½ hours
Florence	Borgo San Lorenzo	2.95	55 minutes
Florence	Empoli	2.50	40 minutes
Florence	Grosseto	9.35	3 hours
Florence	Lucca	4.30	1¼ hours
Florence	Montecatini	3.10	50 minutes
Florence	Montelupo	1.95	25 minutes
Florence	Pisa (via Empoli)	4.70	1 hour
Florence	Pistoia	2.50	40 minutes
Florence	Prato	1.45	25 minutes
Florence	Siena	5.10	1½ hours
Florence	Viareggio	5.50	1¾ hours
Siena	Chiusi	4.45	1¼ hours
Siena	Grosseto	5.40	1¼ hours

CAR & MOTORCYCLE

Touring Tuscany with your own wheels gives you maximum flexibility. The main highways are good if often busy. The traffic around Florence, on the *autostrade* (four- to six-lane motorways) and the *superstrade* (up to four-lane motorways) between Florence and Siena can be intense (to say the least).

Remember that the autostrade are toll roads. There aren't too many of these. The A1 (aka Autostrada del Sole) from Bologna heads down through northern Tuscany to swing in a wide loop to the west and south of Florence before veering south-east to pass (at some distance) Arezzo, Cortona and Chiusi before proceeding on to Rome. The

A12 slithers down the Ligurian coast from Genoa and La Spezia through Viareggio and Pisa to Livorno. It will eventually go to Rome, but at this point peters out just south of Rosignano Marittima. The A11 connects Florence with Pisa and the A12.

There are a couple of four-lane, toll-free superstrade as an alternative to the autostrade. The SS1 (Via Aurelia) along the coast is four lanes almost all the way from Livorno Sud (south) to Tuscany's border with Lazio. From Livorno Nord (north) it's mostly two-lane only and often clogged with traffic. The SGC highway (also known as the Fi-Pi-Li) connects Florence, Pisa and Livorno. The other important one is the SS2, which links Florence with Siena.

When you get away from the main centres, the smaller back roads offer frequently pretty drives, but be prepared to take your time. Progress around the winding hill country of Tuscany can be slow. The most congested areas are in the north-west, in and around the towns of Florence, Prato, Pistoia, Lucca, Pisa and Viareggio.

JANE SMITH

Maximum flexibility and flair on a *motorino*

Road Distances (km)

	Arezzo	Carrara	Cortona	Empoli	Florence (Firenze)	Grosseto	Livorno	Lucca	Massa	Orbetello	Pisa	Pistoia	Prato	Siena	Viareggio	Volterra
Arezzo	---															
Carrara	202	---														
Cortona	29	231	---													
Empoli	115	90	144	---												
Florence (Firenze)	80	122	109	35	---											
Grosseto	135	207	143	135	140	---										
Livorno	195	72	224	54	115	135	---									
Lucca	155	52	184	40	75	180	45	---								
Massa	195	7	184	83	115	200	65	43	---							
Orbetello	175	247	183	173	180	40	175	216	240	---						
Pisa	175	57	204	49	95	150	20	21	50	190	---					
Pistoia	115	92	144	35	35	175	85	45	85	215	65	---				
Prato	99	109	128	27	19	154	125	62	97	199	67	17	---			
Siena	65	153	66	63	70	70	130	140	160	122	110	105	91	---		
Viareggio	180	30	197	71	105	170	41	25	24	216	21	69	86	131	---	
Volterra	111	135	125	70	75	114	53	83	128	154	65	105	97	55	86	---

The Car & Motorcycle section of the Getting There & Away chapter covers paperwork and ways of getting your car to Tuscany from other parts of Italy and abroad.

Road Maps & Atlases
See Maps in the Facts for the Visitor chapter for information on road maps.

Road Rules
In general, standard European road rules apply. In built-up areas the speed limit is usually 50km/h, rising to 90km/h on secondary roads, 110km/h (caravans 80km/h) on main roads and up to 130km/h (caravans 100km/h) on autostrade.

Motorcyclists must use headlights at all times. Crash helmets are obligatory on bikes of 125cc or more.

Vehicles already on a roundabout often have right of way. However, this is not always the case and working out which type of roundabout you are confronted with is best done by paying careful attention to local example!

The blood-alcohol limit is 0.08%. Random breath tests are conducted – penalties range from on-the-spot fines to confiscation of your driving licence.

Petrol
Petrol *(benzina)* in Italy is among the dearest in Western Europe. At the time of writing, super cost €1.20 per litre; unleaded *(senza piombo)* €1.10 per litre; and diesel (or *gasolio*) €0.85 per litre.

If you are driving a car that uses liquid petroleum gas (LPG), you will need to buy a special guide to service stations that have *gasauto* or GPL. By law these must be located in nonresidential areas and are usually in the country or on city outskirts, although you'll find plenty on the autostrade. GPL costs around €0.55 per litre.

You can pay with most credit cards at the great majority of service stations. Those on

Sign Language

You can save yourself some grief in Tuscany by learning what some of the many road signs mean:

entrata – entrance (for example, onto an autostrada)
incrocio – intersection/crossroads
lavori in corso – roadworks ahead
parcheggio – car park
passaggio a livello – level crossing
rallentare – slow down
senso unico – one-way street
senso vietato – no entry
sosta autorizzata – parking permitted (during times displayed)
sosta vietata – no stopping/parking
svolta – bend
tutte le direzioni – all directions (useful when looking for town exit)
uscita – exit (for example, from an autostrada)

the autostrade open 24 hours a day. Otherwise, opening hours are generally from around 7am to 12.30pm and 3.30pm to 7.30pm (7pm in winter). Up to 75% are closed on Sundays and public holidays, and those that open then close on Monday. Don't assume you can't get petrol if you pass a station that is closed. Quite a few have self-service pumps that accept banknotes. It is illegal to carry spare fuel in your vehicle.

Road Assistance

As a rule, holders of motoring insurance with foreign organisations such as the RAC, AA (UK) or AAA (USA) will be provided with an emergency assistance number to use while travelling in Italy – check with your motoring organisation that a reciprocal agreement exists before you leave. You can also get road assistance and a tow with the Automobile Club Italia (ACI) by calling ☎ 116. If you have the appropriate insurance you should probably be covered. It is

likely in any case that, whichever number you use, an ACI truck will arrive.

City Driving

As a rule of thumb, in most cities you will want to park your car and forget about it. Driving in the historic centre of most towns is either banned or restricted, and finding a legal parking spot can be a nightmare. Until you know your way around, park in a designated meter-parking area or car park. If you leave the car farther away from the centre you can generally find free street parking.

When you do drive around in the cities, you'll probably find it a little chaotic and unnerving initially. Road rules and traffic lights are generally respected though.

Never leave anything visibly unattended in your car. Where possible, never leave anything in the car at all.

Rental

All the big car rental companies have outlets in the main cities and at the airports. Generally, you won't find much below €46.50 a day. This can drop to as low as €31 if you rent for a week. The Internet may cough up cheaper deals, so if you have time do a bit surfing. Alinari (☎ 055 28 05 00, Via Guelfa 85r) in Florence rents motorbikes for up to €93 a day. Bruno Bellini (☎ 0577 94 02 01, Via Roma 41) rents bikes for €52 a day in San Gimignano.

If you decide to rent a motorhome, one of Italy's few rental outlets specialising in these is based near Florence. Caravan Mec (☎ 055 31 19 28, W www.caravanmec.it), at Via della Cupola 281 in Peretola, has rates starting at €207 for a week's rental in the low season. Note that you have to pay a €1291.25 deposit.

BICYCLE

If you plan to bring your own bike, check with the airline about any hidden costs. It will have to be disassembled and packed for the journey.

Cycle touring across Tuscany is becoming increasingly popular. UK-based cyclists planning to give it a try could contact the Cyclists' Touring Club (☎ 01483-417217,

W www.ctc.org.uk), Cotterell House, 69 Meadow, Godalming, Surrey GU7 3HS, UK. It can supply information to members on cycling conditions, itineraries and cheap insurance. Route and information sheets include: *Emilia-Romagna & Tuscany*; *Tuscany & Umbria*; *Circular Tour of Tuscany*; and *Day Rides from Sambuca*. Membership costs UK£25 per annum.

Once in Italy, it is possible to transport your bicycle on many trains. Those marked on timetables with a bicycle symbol have a carriage set aside for the transport of bicycles. Otherwise you need to dismantle it and pack it. You may not take your bike on Eurostar Italia services that require a booking. In all cases where you are allowed to take the bike, you must pay a *supplemento* of €5.15.

You can hire bicycles, including mountain bikes, from several outlets in Florence and other towns around the region (see regional chapters for details).

HITCHING
Hitching is never entirely safe and we don't recommend it. Travellers who decide to hitch should understand that they are taking a small but potentially serious risk. People who do choose to hitch will be safer if they travel in pairs and let someone know where they are planning to go.

To get out of Florence you need to start at one of the highway exits. The chances of anyone stopping for you on autostrade are close to zero – try the more congested toll-free highways (such as the SS2 heading south towards Siena, the SS65 north to Bologna or the SS435 west to Lucca).

BOAT
Regular ferries connect Piombino with Elba. In summer, excursions depart from Portoferraio on Elba for the island of Capraia, and from Marina di Campo to the tiny island of Pianosa. From Livorno ferries run to Capraia via the prison island of Gorgona. You can reach the islands of Giglio and Giannutri (May to September only) from Porto Santo Stefano. See the relevant chapters for more details.

LOCAL TRANSPORT
All Tuscan cities and major towns have a reasonable local bus service (local buses are generally orange). Usually you won't need to use them, as most towns are compact, with sights, hotels, restaurants and long-distance transport stations within walking distance of each other. The only probable exceptions are be Florence, Siena and Pisa.

Buses and trains connect Pisa's Galileo Galilei airport with Pisa and Florence, while buses link Amerigo Vespucci airport with central Florence.

ORGANISED TOURS
Guided tour options of individual cities abound (local tourist offices generally have details; see the relevant chapters for details). They can be illuminating, but generally you can get around any of the towns under your own steam with no difficulty. From cities such as Florence and Siena it is possible to join tours of towns and areas (such as the Chianti region) in the vicinity.

GETTING AROUND

Tuscany on Foot

When Mother Nature created Tuscany, she obviously didn't have cars in mind. Tuscany is eminently suited to walking. The beautiful patchwork countryside of the centre, the wilder valleys and hills of the east, south and north-west and finally the Apuane Alps and Apennine ranges offer a colourful variety of opportunities to the traveller with time and a desire to move on foot. A truly ambitious walker could undertake the 24-stage Grande Escursione Appenninica, an arc that takes you from the Due Santi pass above La Spezia south-east to Sansepolcro.

People have been traipsing across Tuscany since Adam was a boy, creating paths and trails as they went. One of the most important pilgrim routes in Europe during the Dark Ages was known as the Via Francigena (or Via Romea), which turned into something of a highway across Tuscany. Starting down the River Magra valley through the wild Lunigiana territory of the north-west, the trail hugged the coast for a while before cutting inland to Siena via San Gimignano and then turning south to the Christian capital, Rome. Parts of the route can still be walked today.

For a few suggestions on walks scattered across Tuscany, read on.

WHEN TO WALK

It is possible to walk parts of Tuscany throughout the year, but not all.

The most pleasant (and safest) time to go walking in the Apuane Alps and other mountain areas (such as Monte Cetona in the south-east, or the small Orecchiella reserve in the north) is summer. August is perhaps not ideal, as many locals are on holiday and trails get busy.

Depending on your experience, weather conditions and where exactly you walk, you can probably get away with some walks well into the autumn, but by November you risk dealing with snow and ice, not to mention limited light – a not particularly happy combination.

Conversely, walking at low altitude or even on the Chianti hills and similar terrain is pretty much a year-round option. Obviously in the depths of winter you are unlikely to be keen on difficult day-long walks, but plenty of pleasant country strolls of a few hours are often just the ticket on a bright crisp winter's day.

The height of summer is not the ideal time for such walks. Inland (especially) the heat is oppressive, making even a crawl to the nearest air-conditioned bar a bit of a strain.

Spring is undoubtedly the prettiest period, especially when the wild flowers are in full bloom. Easter and holidays around 25 April and 1 May are to be avoided if at all possible.

The colours of autumn have their own special attraction. Given that summertime continues into late October, you have lots of light for longer walks. After Tuscany's mad summer tourist rush, things begin to ease off by late September – all the more so out in the countryside.

WHAT TO TAKE

For your average walks in the Chianti area and in many of the parks you will need only a minimum of items. Firstly, a good pair of comfortable trainers (gym shoes) should be sufficient, although of course there is nothing to stop you taking along your walking boots. A change of socks is handy for the end of the day. A small daypack could contain an extra layer of clothing should temperatures drop and some kind of wet-weather gear (such as a poncho). Depending on the season, sunblock, sunglasses and a hat are recommended. Obviously you need a map of the area you are walking in and a compass should be a standard item in any walker's pack.

If you are not sure how long you will be out and about, a water flask and some food are essential. Mixed nuts and dried fruit are good, although you may want to prepare a picnic lunch for day-long walks, especially if you cannot be sure of happening on an eatery at the right moment.

You may laugh, but if you encounter difficulties while off the beaten track a mobile phone can come in handy.

In the Apuane Alps and other mountainous areas things are a little tougher and you need to kit yourself out properly. This means first and foremost sturdy walking boots. You can find yourself in loose scree and other tough terrain where a pair of trainers will be of no use at all. All-weather clothing and a reasonable level of fitness are also advisable.

Free camping is not permitted in the mountains. That may seem like bad news to some, because you need to plan your overnight stops around the availability of beds in *rifugi* (see Walking in the North-West later in this chapter). The upside is that you can leave tents, cooking gear and the like at your base accommodation. Bring your sleeping bag along as extra insurance against the cold.

On the subject of cold, you need to be prepared for all kinds of weather in the mountains. You may start the day in splendid sunshine and heat, but that can easily change to cold and wet – bear in mind that the Apuane Alps get the greatest concentration of rainfall in Tuscany. Take a pair of soft shoes to change into at the end of the day's march.

INFORMATION
Maps
Nothing like the UK's Ordnance Survey maps really exists in Italy. Several publishers produce maps of varying quality that cover certain parts of Tuscany.

First off, the best regional map is probably the Touring Club Italiano's (TCI's) 1:200,000 scale map. It is detailed and a more than sufficient tool for navigating around the region on wheels.

The next level down, but still not detailed enough for walking, are individual provincial maps (there are 10 provinces in Tuscany). Edizioni Multigraphic Firenze publishes a series. Ask for the *Carta Stradale Provinciale* of the province(s) you want. They are scaled at 1:100,000.

Edizioni Multigraphic also publishes a couple of series designed for walkers and mountain-bike riders (*mulattiere*, or mule trails, are especially good for mountain bikes), which are scaled at 1:50,000 and 1:25,000. Where possible you should go for the latter. Ask for the *Carta dei Sentieri e Rifugi* or *Carta Turistica e dei Sentieri*.

Another publisher is Kompass, which produces 1:25,000 scale maps of various parts of Italy, including Tuscany. In some cases it covers areas that Edizioni Multigraphic does not. Occasionally you will come across useful maps put out by the Club Alpino Italiano (CAI) as well. As a rule of thumb, you can get hold of good walking maps for the area you are in at local newsstands and bookshops, and occasionally tourist offices.

Books
You are unlikely to want to have too many books with you. An excellent one that includes over 50 walks and hikes of a not-too-strenuous nature is *Walking in Tuscany*, by Gillian Price (the text spills over into neighbouring Umbria and Lazio). This covers an ample selection taking you from Chianti country to the island of Elba, and to plenty of lesser explored parts of the Tuscan region as well.

Price does not cover the more arduous trekking possibilities in the Apuane Alps in Tuscany's north-west. A couple of good suggestions for this area appear in Lonely Planet's specialist guide, *Walking in Italy*, along with several other walks in Tuscany. *The Alps of Tuscany*, by Franceso Greco, in English, describes in detail a good number of walks in the Apuane Alps, the Cinque Terre and Portofino (the last two outside Tuscany). Tim Jepson's *Wild Italy* has some information on the Apuane Alps, but if your Italian is up to it you should go for one of several Italian guides on the mountains, such as *Alpi Apuane: Guida al Territorio del Parco*, by Frederick Bradley and Enrico Medda. The series of *Guide dei Monti d'Italia*, grey hardbacks published by the TCI and Club Alpino Italiano (CAI), are exhaustive walking guides containing maps. You might also like to consult the A Piedi... series, which includes *A Piedi nel Chianti* and *A Piedi in Toscana*.

TUSCANY ON FOOT

Responsible Walking

The popularity of walking is placing great pressure on the natural environment. Please consider the following tips when walking and help preserve the ecology and beauty of Tuscany.

- Don't light fires unless you're absolutely sure it's safe.
- Don't pick Alpine wild flowers – most of them are protected.
- Take all rubbish away with you, including cigarette butts, unless there are rubbish bins in the area. Don't bury your rubbish.
- Leave the local wildlife alone.
- Don't make too much noise.
- Be careful about where you go to the toilet and be sure to bury your bodily waste.
- Ensure that you close gates after you have passed through.
- Be attentive when passing through fields, particularly during periods of cultivation. Stick to the edges or obvious tracks and don't trample on crops.
- Keep to existing tracks to avoid causing erosion by disturbing the natural lay of the land.
- Don't pick grapes or olives on your way through vineyards or olive groves.
- Take note of and observe any rules and regulations particular to the national or state reserve that you are visiting.

Walking and Eating in Tuscany and Umbria, by James Lasdun and Pia Davis provides 40 varied itineraries across these two central regions of Italy.

Where to Walk

The areas listed below are some of the most popular for walking in Tuscany. By no means is it a complete list of places to walk – much of Tuscany is perfect for a day's outing and you may easily find places more suitable to you.

The following walks described in detail are generally half-day walks on some well-established trails that provide a glimpse of the varied terrain Tuscany has to offer. Note that they were undertaken by a rather unfit, 30-year-old with a long stride so please adjust times to fit your own build!

WALKING IN THE CHIANTI REGION & AROUND

The walking options in this gentle and blessed country are virtually limitless and in most cases require only a moderate level of fitness. SELCA puts out a map in several languages, *The Black Rooster Roads*, at 1:70,000, which covers the Chianti Classico region and has many trails marked out for you to follow. It also has member vineyards of the Chianti Classico consortium shown, which make for a very pleasant diversion from your walk.

The classic walk would take you rambling over several days (perhaps as many as five or six) from Florence to Siena. The variations on this theme are numerous, so you can expand or contract it as suits. One option starts at Strada in Chianti, heads south to Badia di Passignano and then turns east to Greve in Chianti. A route dropping roughly south and then edging south-east would keep you in mild hill country, on country lanes and passing through such villages as Panzano and Radda in Chianti. Another, longer walk would follow the walking route from, say, San Donato in Collina and wind across several low hill ranges and valleys to Greve and then by one of several routes south to Siena.

Away from Chianti territory, another popular option is to walk from San Gimignano to Volterra. The start and end points are fascinating medieval towns (see the Central Tuscany chapter) with good transport links and plenty of accommodation. Most tend to walk *from* San Gimignano, but there is no reason not to do it in reverse. It is about 30km, so it's advisable to split it into a two-day walk (a further one-day extension would add the stretch between San Gimignano and Certaldo to the north). The *Dolce Campagna Antiche Mura* map, produced by SELCA and scaled at 1:50,000, is a good walking companion.

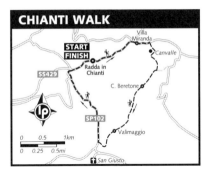

CHIANTI WALK

Villa Miranda
START
FINISH
Canvalle
Radda in Chianti
SS429
C. Beretone
SP102
Valimaggio
San Giusto

0   0.5   1km
0   0.25   0.5mi

Lonely Planet's *Walking in Italy* guide has extensive coverage of the walk from Certaldo to Volterra, as well as a pleasant three-day walk through the Chianti Classico region.

Circular Walk from Radda in Chianti

Location:	Chianti Senese
Duration:	2 ¾ hours
Difficulty:	Easy
Terrain:	Rolling hills, vineyards and woods – classic Chianti country

Starting at the eastern end of the village, continue east on the SS429 towards Gaiole in Chianti. The road is well used by cars and trucks so take some care. After about 20 minutes you come to a crossroads; continue heading east past a petrol station, for another 10 minutes, until you come to Villa Miranda, where a small paved road at the far end of the building cuts right towards vineyards. Here you'll spot red and white signs for the No 68 trail. Follow these signs, which lead you along the paved road past a couple of *agriturismo* and the ancient tower of Canvalle on your right as you head uphill. After 1km the road becomes a dirt track, which winds its way uphill through woods.

After about 15 minutes' walk uphill you come to a fork in the path; head right, then straight. The path soon levels out and after another 10 minutes you pass a small wooden cross encircled by cypress trees. Continue straight, making sure not to deviate to the left

or right (the path is clearly marked with red and white paint). The path becomes even and gentle, and you'll have fine views of Radda to your right and wooded hills to your left. After 30 minutes you come to a small clearing, and from here the dirt path starts to descend. Ten minutes on you come to a fork in the path; take the right arm which continues downhill through more cultivated land and past a couple of buildings on your left. It soon becomes a dirt road which passes through woodland and olive groves.

Twenty minutes on from the last junction you come to the SP102, a tar-sealed road running north to south. Turn right (uphill) onto the SP102, which heads north towards Radda. Here you'll have views of vineyards and olive groves to your right. The road is not too busy but the occasional car may whizz by. After 30 minutes you come to a junction of roads; turn right onto the SS429 and after 10 minutes you reach the western outskirts of Radda.

WALKING IN THE MUGELLO

The varied topography of this area allows the walker to experience from gentle rolling hills to high mountain passes and deep ravines.

Sorgenti Firenze Trekking (SO.F.T., Florence Springs Trekking), are a network of trails criss-crossing the Mugello that are well marked out and easy to follow. One central ring circumnavigates the area, passing through the lowlands to the south and follows an alpine ridge to the north. You could easily spend 10 days completing this trail. Twenty-two secondary trails branch off from this main circle, and are generally great for a day or half-day walk. Tourist offices in the region stock the handy booklet *Mugello, a Holiday in Tuscan Countryside*, which describes a few of these secondary walks and also has a list of accommodation possibilities along the way, ranging from camp sites to country houses. One of the best sources of information on walks is the *Mugello, Alto Mugello, Val di Sieve* map at 1:70,000, produced by SELCA. All SO.F.T. trails are clearly marked, as are many of the CAI trails.

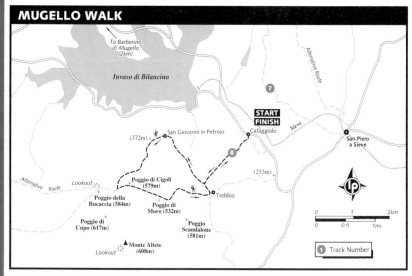

MUGELLO WALK

Cafaggiolo-Trebbio-Cafaggiolo

Location:	South-west Mugello
Duration:	3½ hours
Difficulty:	Easy–medium
Terrain:	Farmland and wood land

This walk is track No 8 on the *Mugello, Alto Mugello, Val di Sieve* map. The path is generally marked with yellow paint (occasionally with white and red paint).

Facing the Cafaggiolo Villa (226m), take the small farm track that heads left and after 100m turn right at the very first junction. This path skirts around the back of the houses surrounding the villa and past a stone wall with a yellow marker and a private property sign (related to the chicken pens, not the path!).

Past the stone wall the dirt path soon starts its steep ascent towards Trebbio (435m), passing through thick woods. After five minutes' climb you come to a junction; ignore any deviations and continue straight on. There are no views to be had but you'll undoubtedly spot rabbits, pheasants and annoying horse flies (bring some insect repellent for these critters). After another 30 minutes of uphill slog Trebbio appears on

your left. Soon after the path splits; take the right-hand arm that brings you past a private dwelling and out into farmland north-west of Trebbio. Take the dirt road to your right, heading downhill away from Trebbio. This road leads you through farmland and north towards the hamlet of San Giovanni. Be sure to stick to the road and not deviate from it, as there are plenty of paths leading left and right. Here you'll have fine views of Invaso di Bilancino, a manmade lake, and the northern hills of the Mugello. After about 20 minutes you pass a vineyard and another 10 minutes on you come to San Giovanni itself.

At the last house in the village you have the choice of continuing straight on or turning left. Take the path to the left and after about five minutes it forks again, just past a small horse-training ring. Turn left away from the lake. This path is rather unused and leads you back into denser vegetation and past fields of sunflowers. After 15 minutes you come to an abandoned house and another junction in the path. Head straight on into thick undergrowth and woods, and after five minutes the path splits once more; take the left path. Continue for 20 minutes on the steep uneven, rocky path until you come to a T-junction, where track No 8 joins the No 19. Turn left and follow the well-kept No 19 path.

Here the path becomes even and gentle and passes through untouched woods. After 10 minutes you reach its highest point, Poggio di Moro (532m). Soon afterwards you come to a small clearing; continue straight on. From here you enter forested pine woods and after another 10 minutes you come to a junction of paths. Take the path to the left, which leads out of the pine woods back into farmland and towards Trebbio. Fifteen minutes on you enter the village of Trebbio. Here you can turn left and take the path back to the private dwelling you passed on your way up from Cafaggiolo and follow the path back down. Another option is to continue straight on past Trebbio and take the dirt road downhill for 2.4km, then turn left onto the tar-sealed road which leads back to Cafaggiolo.

WALKING IN THE NORTH-WEST

The most serious walking you can hope to undertake in Tuscany is in the north-west, particularly in the Apuane Alps. To a lesser extent, the Apennine region bordering the region of Emilia is also promising, especially in the Reserva Naturale dell'Orecchiella.

The Apuane Alps offer a variety of walking possibilities, from relatively easy strolls to challenging treks that can even require alpine and rock-climbing skills. A good map for the area, which clearly marks roads, villages, trails (all 94 of them), and *rifugi* is the *Carta dei Sentieri e Rifugi Alpi Apuane* by Edizioni Multigraphic scales at 1:25,000.

One of the best-known objectives is the **Pania della Croce** peak (1858m) in the southern reaches of the park. The tree line is made up mainly of beech, above which the stony ground, in some areas with surface karst, creates a dramatic, stark walking environment. Another exciting area to consider for walking is around the **Pizzo d'Uccello** peak (1781m) in the north of the park.

You can take on the services of guides in the park, but they don't come cheap. You are generally looking at €103.30 per day for the guide, plus accommodation and food

costs if the walk lasts more than a day. Lists of accredited guides are available at the information centres for the park.

Where to Sleep

Walks in the Apuane Alps won't take you higher than around 1800m, but many walkers tend to spend a few days on the trails in these mountains. The only sleeping options are *rifugi* (mountain refuges) or *bivacchi* (huts), mostly operated by the CAI and generally only open from June to September. A rifugio can be quite cosy with beds, a restaurant and a small supplies store. A bivacchio is generally an extremely basic option to doss down in for the night, often without a guardian.

The CAI operates eight rifugi and four bivacchi in the Apuane Alps. One non-CAI rifugio also operates in the same area. Non-CAI members pay up to double what members pay to sleep in these rifugi. Fees vary depending on the type of *rifugio* and the services provided. You can be looking at anything up to €18.55 per night for a bed with blankets. A heating supplement of up to €3.60 per person may apply. A meal can cost anything up to €15.50. As a rule, lights-out is between 10pm and 6am. It's a good idea to call ahead to find out if they are open and have space for you. You can obtain information on the park, including a list of rifugi, from the parks visitor centres (see the Garfagnana and La Versilia sections in the North-Western Tuscany chapter for more information, or check out the parks Web site at ⓦ www.parks.it/parco.alpi.apuane).

Stazzema–Rifugio Forte dei Marmi–Stazzema

Location:	Southern Apuane Alps
Duration:	2½ hours
Difficulty:	Medium
Terrain:	Lush woods and alpine slopes

Starting from the centre of Stazzema (443m), head east out of town along the main alleyway. You soon hit a tar-sealed road that heads uphill to connect with another tar-sealed road. Turn left and follow this new road around a

TUSCANY ON FOOT

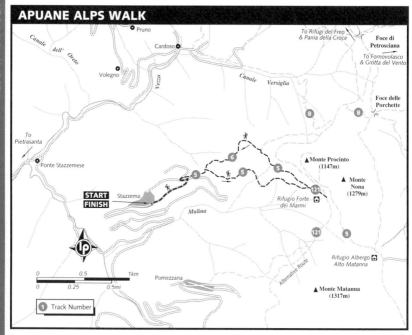

APUANE ALPS WALK

Pruno

Cardoso

Canale dell' Oreto

Volegno

Vezza

Canale Versiglia

To Rifugi del Freo & Pania della Croce

Foce di Petrosciana

To Fornovolasco & Grotta del Vento

Foce delle Porchette

8

8

To Pietrasanta

Ponte Stazzemese

6

5

5

▲ Monte Procinto (1147m)

▲ Monte Nona (1279m)

START FINISH

Stazzema

Rifugio Forte dei Marmi

121

Mulina

121

5

Alternative Route

Rifugio Albergo Alto Matanna

Pomezzana

▲ Monte Matanna (1317m)

0   0.5   1km
0   0.25   0.5mi

LP

1 Track Number

sweeping bend to the right, past a wood shed on your right. After a few minutes' walk a well signposted path to your right appears. This is track No 5, which leads to Rifugio Fonte dei Marmi (868m; ☎ 0584 77 70 51), an hour's climb from Stazzema.

A few hundred metres after leaving the road the track divides. Track No 6 heads left but take track No 5, which continues its way uphill to the right. The track is well kept and hugs the contours of the hillside on its climb to the rifugi. The vegetation is lush alpine wood, through which you'll catch glimpses of the valley below. After 40 minutes you hit the junction with track No 121, where there's a stone shelter and a spring which fills into a stone tank. Two hundred metres to the right is the rifugio, perfectly situated under the peaks of Monte Procinto (1147m) and Monte Nona (1279m). It's fitted out with a bar, restaurant and 52 beds.

From here you have numerous walking options. Immediate goals are Monte Procinto

and Nona, both only an hour's (albeit steep) climb from the rifugio, and both offering fantastic views. Monte Nona is conquered from the south-west while a tough track circumnavigates the tower of Monte Procinto. You could also continue south on track No 5 for 50 minutes to Rifugio Alto Matanna (☎ 0584 77 60 05; 1030m), from where you can tackle the 30-minute climb to Monte Matanna (1317m). Heading north on track No 121, you come to Foce di Petrosciana (913m), where you can continue northwards to Rifugio Del Freo (☎ 0584 77 80 07; 1200m) and an assault on Pania della Croce (1858m), or turn eastwards to the village of Fornovolasco and the caves of Grotta del Vento.

Returning to the junction of track No 5 and 121, take the 5/bis northwards away from the rifugio. Monte Procinto is to your right as the path hugs steep slopes. After 20 minutes you come to a junction; take the path to the left which heads downhill. Within a few minutes the 5/bis joins track No 6; once again, take the path to the left. Here the path descends rather rapidly and after a 25-minute downhill walk you arrive at the original junction between tracks 5 and 6, from where you can re-trace your steps to Stazzema.

WALKING IN ELBA

The island is a splendid little spot to undertake some comparatively short walks and is becoming increasingly popular for such activities. You will generally be able to plan your own routes quite easily, or in any case arrange it so that you arrive somewhere where accommodation is assured or buses can be caught to a more central point.

Walkers should get a copy of *Elba Between Sea and Sky*, which has details of walking trails, along with rock climbing and mountain biking. You can also get information on hiking at Il Genio del Bosco – Centro Trekking Isola d'Elba (☎ 0565 93 08 37) at Portoferraio. For comprehensive map coverage with clearly marked trails, try Vivalda Editori's *Isola d'Elba*, which is scaled at 1:35,000 and comes with a booklet describing 10 walks, six mountain-bike trails and four rock-climbing excursions in German and English.

The island's western half, dominated by Monte Capanne, boasts some of the most attractive walking (and mountain-biking) country. Other areas that attract are the south-eastern corner around Capoliveri and Monte Cala-mita, and the rougher and comparatively neglected north-eastern corner to the north of Rio nell'Elba. The GTE, a path running from near Cavo in the north-east, across the central lowlands, up to Monte Cappane and down to the coastal town of Pomonte in the south-west, is a rewarding walk, taking at least two days.

Marciana–Monte Capanne–Marciana
Location:	Western Elba
Duration:	4½ hours
Difficulty:	Medium
Terrain:	Lush woods and barren mountain slopes

The route begins in the village of Marciana (355m), at the Fortezza Pisana. Follow the

sealed road uphill, which soon becomes gravel. After 150m follow the sign pointing right to Santuario della Madonna. The path soon joins the Via Crucis (see the Elba chapter) which leads directly to the Santuario. At the fourth station track No 10 leads off to the left, passing through pine trees and after five minutes entering a small picnic area. Stick to track 10, which passes straight over the picnic area and starts to climb into quite barren territory. Climbing steadily the path follows the contours of the steep, mountainous slopes. Towering above you to your right are the peaks of Monte Giove (853m) and La Stretta (806m), and to your left are views of Marciana and the coast.

Thirty minutes on from the Via Crucis the path divides; take track No 6 which veers to the left. After 10 minutes it once again drops below the tree line and levels out. The views to the coast are breathtaking (or maybe it's just the exertion). Follow the path for another 10 minutes, where it then splits again. Take

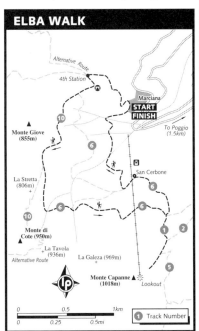

the right path, which continues to follow the ridgeline above you. After about 20 minutes you come to another junction of tracks. Track No 1, which ascends Monte Capanne (1018m), heads off directly to your right. This is the path you need to take.

The path climbs steeply for 15 minutes, where it's joined by track No 2. From here to the summit is the hardest part of the climb, with much of the track exposed to the elements, passing over slate rock, making switch backs and becoming rather steep. After 30 minutes you reach your goal. The views here sweep across the whole island, and on a good day you can easily make out the mainland and the mountains of Corsica.

After a well-deserved break head back down to the junction of track Nos 1 and 6. Instead of returning the way you came, continue downhill on track No 6 for about 15 minutes, when you'll come to the small hermitage San Cerbone, sheltered in a shady chestnut grove. Pass to the left of the hermitage and continue downhill through lush woods until you hit a fork in the path; follow the arm that heads downhill. From here it's a very gentle 30-minute stroll back to Marciana.

WALKING IN THE PARCO REGIONALE MAREMMA
This blessed stretch of coastline in Southern Tuscany is perfect for a day's walk, and the terrain of the park is varied enough to suit all capabilities. Walks range from easy beach strolls to more strenuous climbs through the hilly Monti dell'Uccellina, visiting secluded beaches, caves and abandoned castles and monasteries. And it's very likely you will spot plenty of natural wildlife going about its daily business.

Of the six walks accessible from Alberese (named A1 to A7; see the Southern Tuscany chapter for details), four are by guided tour only and are reached using the park's private bus service which drops you in the heart of the park. The three leaving from Talamone (called T1 to T3), at the southern end of the park, are unguided. During summer (mid-June to September) only two guided treks are open (A1 and A2; adult/child €7.75/ 5.15). Tours leave at 7.30am, 8.30am, 9am (Friday only – in English, booking essential), 4pm and 4.30pm (Wednesday only – in German, booking essential). All guided walks (A1 to A4) are open over the winter period. Both trail A5 to A6 (€5.15/3.60), which meanders through the countryside near Alberese, and A7 (€2.05), which explores the mouth of the Ombrone River at the northern end of the park, are open year round. Trails T1 to T3 (€5.15/3.60) also open year round but are inaccessible from 1pm to 4pm during summer. Night walks are also available, and cost €18.05 per person (reservations essential).

Florence (Firenze)

postcode 50100 • pop 461,000

Situated on the banks of the Arno River valley and set among low hills covered with olive groves and vineyards, Florence is immediately captivating. Cradle of the Renaissance and sometime home of Machiavelli, Michelangelo and the Medicis, the city seems unfairly burdened with art, culture and history.

Despite the implausible traffic, stifling summer heat, pollution and industrial sprawl on the city's outskirts, Florence attracts millions of tourists each year. The French writer Stendhal was so dazzled by the magnificence of the Basilica di Santa Croce that he was barely able to walk for faintness. He is apparently not the only one to have felt thus overwhelmed by the beauty of Florence – they say Florentine doctors treat a dozen cases of 'stendhalismo' a year.

You will need at least four or five days to do Florence any justice at all.

HISTORY

Controversy still reigns over who founded Florence. The commonly accepted story held that Julius Caesar founded Florentia around 30 BC, making of it a strategic garrison on the narrowest crossing of the Arno, whose purpose was to control the Via Flaminia linking Rome to northern Italy and Gaul. Archaeological evidence suggests that an earlier village may have been founded on the site, perhaps by the Etruscans of Fiesole, as early as 200 BC.

Along with the rest of northern Italy, the city suffered during the barbarian invasions of the Dark Ages. In the early 12th century it became a free *comune* (city state) and by 1138 was ruled by 12 consuls, assisted by the Consiglio di Cento (Council of One Hundred). The council members were drawn mainly from the prosperous merchant class. Agitation among differing factions in the city led to the appointment of a foreign head of state, known as the *podestà*, in 1207.

Highlights

- Gorge yourself on the art treasures of the Uffizi and Bargello
- Climb to the top of the Campanile for wonderful views of the city
- Hang out in the hip Rex Caffè for a cocktail or two
- Take in the views with a drink at Piazzale Michelangelo
- Come to know the work of Brunelleschi, the genius of Renaissance architecture whose work ranges from the dome of the Duomo to the Basilica di San Lorenzo
- Stand slack-jawed before the sublime reality of Michelangelo's David
- Loosen the purse strings and hit the fashion shops around Via de' Tornabuoni

Florence
pp125-135

The first conflicts between the pro-papal Guelphs (Guelfi) and the pro-imperial Ghibellines (Ghibellini) started towards the middle of the 13th century, with power passing from one faction to the other for almost a century. The Guelphs eventually formed a government, known as the Primo Popolo, but in 1260 were ousted after

Florence was defeated by Ghibelline Siena at the Battle of Monteaperti. The Guelphs regained control in 1289.

If you thought that was complicated, it worse in the 1290s as the Guelphs split into two factions: the Neri (Blacks) and Bianchi (Whites). When the latter were defeated in 1302, Dante was among those driven into exile. As the nobility lost ground, the Guelph merchant class took control. But trouble was never far away. The great plague of 1348 halved the city's population and the government was rocked by growing agitation from the lower classes.

During the latter part of the 14th century, Florence was ruled by a caucus of Guelphs under the leadership of the Albizi family. Among the families opposing them were the Medici, whose influence grew as they became the papal bankers.

In the 15th century Cosimo de' Medici emerged as the head of the opposition to the Albizi and eventually became Florence's ruler. His eye for talent and his tact in dealing with artists saw the likes of Alberti, Brunelleschi, Lorenzo Ghiberti, Donatello, Fra Angelico and Fra Filippo Lippi flourish under his patronage. Many of the city's finest buildings are testimony to his tastes.

Cosimo was followed by his grandson, Lorenzo the Magnificent ('il Magnifico'), whose rule (1469–92) ushered in the most glorious period of Florentine civilisation and of the Italian Renaissance. His court fostered a flowering of art, music and poetry, and Florence became the cultural capital of Italy. Lorenzo favoured philosophers, but he maintained family tradition by sponsoring artists such as Botticelli and Domenico Ghirlandaio; he also encouraged Leonardo and the young Michelangelo, who was working under Giovanni di Bertoldo, Donatello's pupil.

Not long before Lorenzo's death in 1492, the Medici bank failed and, two years later, the Medicis were driven out of Florence. The city fell under the control of Girolamo Savonarola, a Dominican monk who led a puritanical republic until he fell from public favour and was fried as a heretic in 1498.

After Florence's defeat by the Spanish in 1512, the Medici returned to the city but were once again expelled, this time by Emperor Charles V, in 1527. Two years later they had made peace, and Charles not only allowed the Medici family to return to Florence (their combined forces besieged the city from 1529 to 1530), but also married his daughter to Lorenzo's great-grandson Alessandro de' Medici, whom he made duke of Florence in 1530. The Medici then ruled for another 200 years, during which time they gained control of all Tuscany.

In 1737 the grand duchy of Tuscany passed to the House of Lorraine (effectively under Austrian control). This situation remained unchanged (apart from a brief interruption under Napoleon from 1799 to 1814) until the duchy was incorporated into the kingdom of Italy in 1860. Florence became the national capital a year later, but Rome assumed the mantle permanently in 1875.

Florence was badly damaged during WWII by the retreating Germans, who blew up all its bridges except the Ponte Vecchio. Devastating floods ravaged the city in 1966, causing inestimable damage to its buildings and artworks. However, the salvage operation led to the widespread use of modern restoration techniques that have saved artworks throughout the country.

ORIENTATION

However you arrive, the central train station, Stazione di Santa Maria Novella, is a good reference point. Budget hotels and *pensioni* are concentrated around Via Nazionale, to the east of the station, and Piazza Santa Maria Novella, to the south. The main route to the city centre is Via de' Panzani and then Via de' Cerretani, about a 10-minute walk. You'll know you've arrived when you first glimpse the Duomo.

Most of the major sights are within easy walking distance – you can stroll from one end of the city centre to the other in about 30 minutes. From Piazza di San Giovanni around the Battistero, Via Roma leads to Piazza della Repubblica and continues as Via Calimala then Via Por Santa Maria to the Ponte Vecchio. Take Via de' Calzaiuoli from Piazza del Duomo for Piazza della Signoria, the historic seat of government. The Uffizi

The Red and the Black

Florence has two street-numbering systems: red or brown numbers indicate commercial premises and black or blue numbers denote a private residence. When written, black or blue addresses are denoted by the number only, while red or brown addresses usually carry an 'r' (for *rosso*, or 'red') after the number. It can be confusing as the black and blue numbers tend to denote whole buildings, while the others may refer to one small part of the same building. When looking for a specific address, keep your eyes on both sets of numbers and accept that backtracking is sometimes inevitable.

is on the piazza's southern edge, near the Arno. Cross the Ponte Vecchio, or the Ponte alle Grazie farther east, and head south-east to Piazzale Michelangelo for a fantastic view over the city.

There is some reasonably priced public parking around the Fortezza da Basso, just north of the train station and a brisk 10-minute walk to the historic centre along Via Faenza.

INFORMATION
Tourist Offices

The main APT (Azienda di Promozione Turistica) office (Map 7; ☎ 055 29 08 32, fax 055 276 03 83, Ⓦ www.firenze.turismo.toscano .it) is just north of the Duomo, at Via Cavour 1r. It opens from 8.15am to 7.15pm Monday to Saturday, and 8.30am to 1.30pm on Sunday, between April and October. It is open until 1.30pm and closed on Sunday the rest of the year. The branch at Amerigo Vespucci Airport (☎ 055 31 58 74) opens 7.30am to 11.30pm daily.

The Comune di Firenze (Florence's city council) operates a tourist office (Map 3; ☎ 055 21 22 45) at Piazza della Stazione 4. It opens 8.45am to 8pm Monday to Saturday in the summer. The hours are cut to 9am to 1.45pm in winter. It has another office (Map 6; ☎ 055 234 04 44) at Borgo Santa Croce 29r, with the same hours.

Inside the train station, you can pick up basic information at the Consorzio ITA (Informazioni Turistiche e Alberghiere) office (Map 3; ☎ 055 28 28 93). Their main role is to book hotels. The office opens 8.45am to 9pm daily.

The police and tourist office combine to operate Tourist Help points for the disoriented at the Ponte Vecchio and Piazza della Repubblica, open 8.30am to 7pm. From April to October, the APT also offers a special service known as Florence SOS Turista (☎ 055 276 03 82). Tourists needing guidance on matters such as disputes over hotel bills can phone from 10am to 1pm and 3pm to 6pm, Monday to Saturday.

One of the handiest commercial maps of the city is the red-covered *Florence* (€5.15), produced by the Touring Club Italiano and scaled at 1:12,500. A cutaway of the centre is scaled at 1:6500.

Money

A number of banks are concentrated around Piazza della Repubblica. Thomas Cook has a bureau de change (Map 7; ☎ 055 28 97 81) at Lungarno Acciaioli 6r, near the Ponte Vecchio. It opens 8.30am to 7.30pm Monday to Saturday, and 9.30am to 5pm on Sunday. American Express (Amex) is at Via Dante Alighieri 22r (Map 7; ☎ 055 5 09 81). It opens 9am to 5.30pm Monday to Friday, and 9.30am to 12.30pm on Saturday.

Post & Communications

The main post office, on Via Pellicceria, off Piazza della Repubblica, opens 8.15am to 7pm weekdays (to 12.30pm on Saturday). Fax and telegram services are available.

Amex customers can have their mail sent to the Amex office (see under Money).

You will find Telecom phones in an unstaffed centre near the ATAF information booth outside the Stazione di Santa Maria Novella (Map 3; open 7am to 10pm). There is an unstaffed phone office (Map 7; open 7am to 11pm) with national phone books at Via Cavour 21r.

Places to get online are mushrooming in Florence. The cheapest deal in town, where, if you go at the right time you can get an hour online for as little as €1.80, is Il Cairo Phone Center (Map 6; ☎ 055 263 83 36) Via de' Macci 90r. The centre opens 9.30am to 9pm daily. Another good choice is Internet Train (W www.internettrain.it/citta.asp), with 15 branches (and growing!), including Via dell' Oriuolo 40r (Map 6; ☎ 055 263 89 68), Via Guelfa 24a (Map 3; ☎ 055 21 47 94), Via Santa Monaca 6/8r (Map 5; ☎ 055 260 88 80) and Borgo San Jacopo 30r (Map 7; ☎ 055 265 79 35). A handy one is in the subterranean pedestrian passage beneath the train station. It costs €6.20 (students €5.15) to hook up for an hour. They open 10am to midnight.

Travel Agencies
At Sestante (Map 7; ☎ 055 29 43 06), Via Cavour 56r, you can book train and air tickets, organise guided tours and so on. A branch of CTS (Map 7; ☎ 055 28 95 70, W www .cts.it), the national youth-travel organisation, is at Via de' Ginori 25r. For discounted international rail tickets (if you are under 26), head for the Wasteels office (Map 3; ☎ 055 28 06 83) next to track 16 at Stazione Santa Maria Novella.

Bookshops
The Paperback Exchange (Map 4; ☎ 055 247 81 54), Via Fiesolana 31r, has a vast selection of new and second-hand books in English. Feltrinelli International (Map 7; ☎ 055 21 95 24), Via Cavour 12r, has a good selection in English, French, German, Spanish, Portuguese and Russian. Internazionale Seeber (Map 7; ☎ 055 21 56 97), Via de' Tornabuoni 70r, also has books in those languages, as well as a fine selection of art books.

Gay & Lesbian Information
Azione Gay e Lesbica Finisterrae (Map 2; ☎/fax 055 67 12 98, W www.agora.stm.it /gaylesbica.fi) is at Via Manara 12.

At the Libreria delle Donne (Map 6; ☎ 055 24 03 84), Via Fiesolana 2b, a bookshop, you can get information to tune you into the lesbian scene in Florence.

Laundry
The Wash & Dry Laundrette chain (☎ 800 23 11 72) has eight branches across the city.

You pay €3.10 for 8kg of washing and the same for drying. They open 8am to 10pm. Addresses include: Via Nazionale 129, Via della Scala 52–54r, and Via dei Servi 105r on Map 3, Via de' Serragli 87r on Map 5 and Via del Sole 29r on Map 7.

Medical Services
The Ospedali Riuniti di Careggi (Map 1; ☎ 055 427 71 11) is the main public hospital and is at Viale Morgagni 85, north of the city centre. The Ospedale di Santa Maria Nuova (Map 3; ☎ 055 2 75 81), Piazza Santa Maria Nuova 1, is just east of the cathedral.

The Tourist Medical Service (Map 3; ☎ 055 47 54 11), Via Lorenzo il Magnifico 59, opens 11am to noon and 5pm to 6pm daily; no appointment is required. Doctors speak English, French and German. The APT office has lists of doctors and dentists who speak various languages.

Twenty-four hour pharmacies include: Farmacia Comunale (Map 3; ☎ 055 21 67 61), inside the Stazione di Santa Maria Novella; Molteni (Map 7; ☎ 055 28 94 90), Via de' Calzaiuoli 7r and All'Insegna del Moro (Map 7; ☎ 055 21 13 43), at Piazza di San Giovanni 28.

The Misericordia di Firenze ambulance station (Map 7; ☎ 055 21 22 22) is at Vicolo degli Adimari 1, just off Piazza del Duomo. They also run a medical attention centre there for tourists, which operates 10am to 7pm, Monday to Friday, and 9am to 2pm on Saturdays. If you need a doctor at night or on a public holiday, call the Guardia Medica on ☎ 055 47 78 91.

Emergency
The *questura* (police station; Map 3; ☎ 055 4 97 71) is at Via Zara 2. You can report thefts at the foreigners office here. The Polizia Assistenza Turistica (Tourist Police; ☎ 055 20 39 11) are at Via Pietrapiana 50r (Map 6; Piazza dei Ciompi). They have interpreters.

Dangers & Annoyances
The most annoying aspect of Florence is the crowds, closely followed by the summer heat. Pickpockets are active in crowds and on buses.

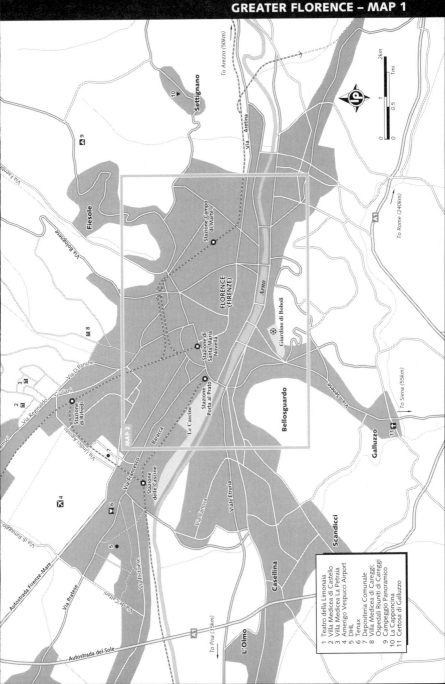

1 Teatro della Limonaia
2 Villa Medicea di Castello
3 Villa Medicea La Petraia
4 Amerigo Vespucci Airport
5 DHL
6 Deposteria Comunale
7 Villa Medicea di Careggi;
  Ospedali Riuniti di Careggi
8 Tenax
9 Campeggio Panoramico
10 La Capponcina
11 Certosa di Galluzzo

FLORENCE
(FIRENZE)

Fiesole

Settignano

Bellosguardo

Galluzzo

Scandicci

Casellina

L'Olmo

Giardino di Boboli

Le Cascine

Stazione Campo di Marte
Stazione di Santa Maria Novella
Stazione Porta al Prato
Stazione di Rifredi
Stazione delle Cascine

Arno

Via Aretina
Via Bolognese
Via Faentina
Via Reginaldo Giuliani
Via D.Pancho
Via Unità d'Apollo
Via Francesco
Baracca
Via Gramsci
Viale Etruria
Via Pistoiese
Via Pratese
Via de' Cattani
Via Cinova
Via di Rimaggio
Viale Etruria

Autostrada Firenze-Mare
Autostrada del Sole

To Arezzo (50km)
To Rome (240km)
To Siena (55km)
To Pisa (35km)

MAP 2

A1

0   0.5   1   2km
0   0.5   1mi

N

MAP 2 – CENTRAL FLORENCE

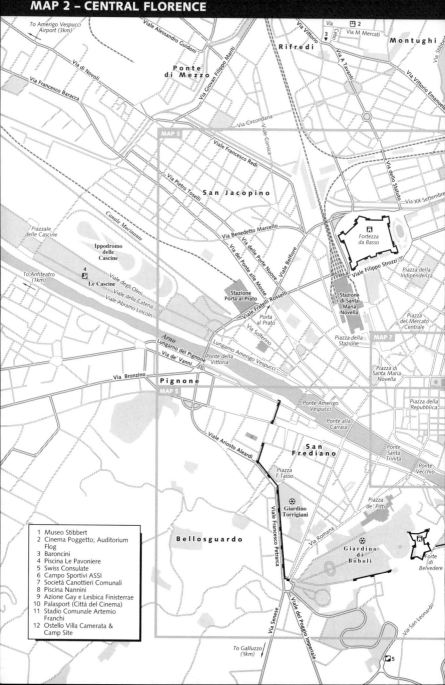

To Amerigo Vespucci Airport (3km)

Viale Alessandro Guidoni

Via di Novoli

Via Francesco Baracca

Via Vittorio

Via M Mercati

Rifredi

Montughi

Via Celso

Via A Tavanti

Via Vittorio Emanuele

Ponte di Mezzo

Via Giovan Filippo Marti

Via Circondaria

MAP 3

Viale Corsica

Via Francesco Redi

Via Pietro Toselli

San Jacopino

Via dello Statuto

Via XX Settembre

Piazzale delle Cascine

Ippodromo delle Cascine

Canale Macinante

Via Benedetto Marcello

Via delle Porte Nuove

Via del Ponte alle Mosse

Viale Belfiore

Fortezza da Basso

Piazza della Indipendenza

To Anfiteatro (1km)

Le Cascine

Viale degli Olmi

Viale della Catena

Viale Abramo Lincoln

Stazione Porta al Prato

Viale Fratelli Rosselli

Porta al Prato

Viale Filippo Strozzi

Stazione di Santa Maria Novella

Piazza del Mercato Centrale

MAP 7

Via Solferino

Piazza della Stazione

Arno

Lungarno del Pignone

Via de' Vanni

Lungarno Amerigo Vespucci

Ponte della Vittoria

Piazza di Santa Maria Novella

Via Bronzino

Pignone

MAP 5

Ponte Amerigo Vespucci

Piazza della Repubblica

Viale Ariosto Aleardi

Ponte alla Carraia

San Frediano

Ponte Santa Trinita

Ponte Vecchio

Piazza T Tasso

Giardino Torrigiani

Piazza de' Pitti

Bellosguardo

Viale Francesco Petrarca

Via Romana

Giardino di Boboli

Forte di Belvedere

Viale del Poggio Imperiale

Via San Leonardo

Via Senese

To Galluzzo (3km)

1 Museo Stibbert
2 Cinema Poggetto; Auditorium Flog
3 Baroncini
4 Piscina Le Pavoniere
5 Swiss Consulate
6 Campo Sportivi ASSI
7 Società Canottieri Comunali
8 Piscina Nannini
9 Azione Gay e Lesbica Finisterrae
10 Palasport (Città del Cinema)
11 Stadio Comunale Artemio Franchi
12 Ostello Villa Camerata & Camp Site

Via Bolognese

Via Faentina

Torrente Mugnone

Via San Domenico

Viale Augusto Righi

■ 12

MAP 4

Via Vittorio Emanuele II

Via C. Landino

Lorenzo il Magnifico

Piazza delle Cure

Viale Alessandro Volta

Ponte Rosso

Viale Don G. Minzoni

Viale Alessandro Volta

Viale dei Mille

Via G Marconi

Via Cairoli

Via A Baldesi

Piazza della Libertà

Viale Spartaco Lavagnini

Piazza Savonarola

Viale Giacomo Matteotti

Gardino dei Semplici

Gardino della Gherardesca

Piazza San Marco

Via Giuseppe La Farina

Campo di Marte

● 11

Viale Pasquale Paoli

● 10

Via Lungo l'Affrico

Via Gabriele d' Annunzio

Stazione Campo di Marte

Via Andrea del Sarto

Via del Mazzetta

Via Antonio Gramsci

Piazza M d'Azeglio

Via Mameli

MAP 6

Via Edmondo de Amicis

● 9

Piazza C Beccaria

Via Vincenzo Giberti

Via Aretina

Chianti

Piazza di Santa Croce

Viale G Amendola

Via Cimabue

Via Piagentina

Via Campofiore

Madonnone Bellariva

8 🏧

Via Arnolfo

Lungarno del Tempio

Lungarno Cristoforo Colombo

Lungarno Aldo Moro

Ponte alle Grazie

Arno

Piazza Giuseppe Poggi

Ponte San Niccolò

Ponte G Da Verrazzano

an Niccolò

Lungarno Francesco Ferrucci

7 ●

Via di Villamagna

Piazzale Michelangelo

Via Coluccio Salutati

Via dell'Erta Canina

Viale Michelangiolo

Via Donato Giannotti

LP

Viale Galileo Galilei

Cemitero Mon della Porte Sante

Monte alle Croci

● 6

| 0 | 250 | 500m |
| 0 | 250 | 500yd |

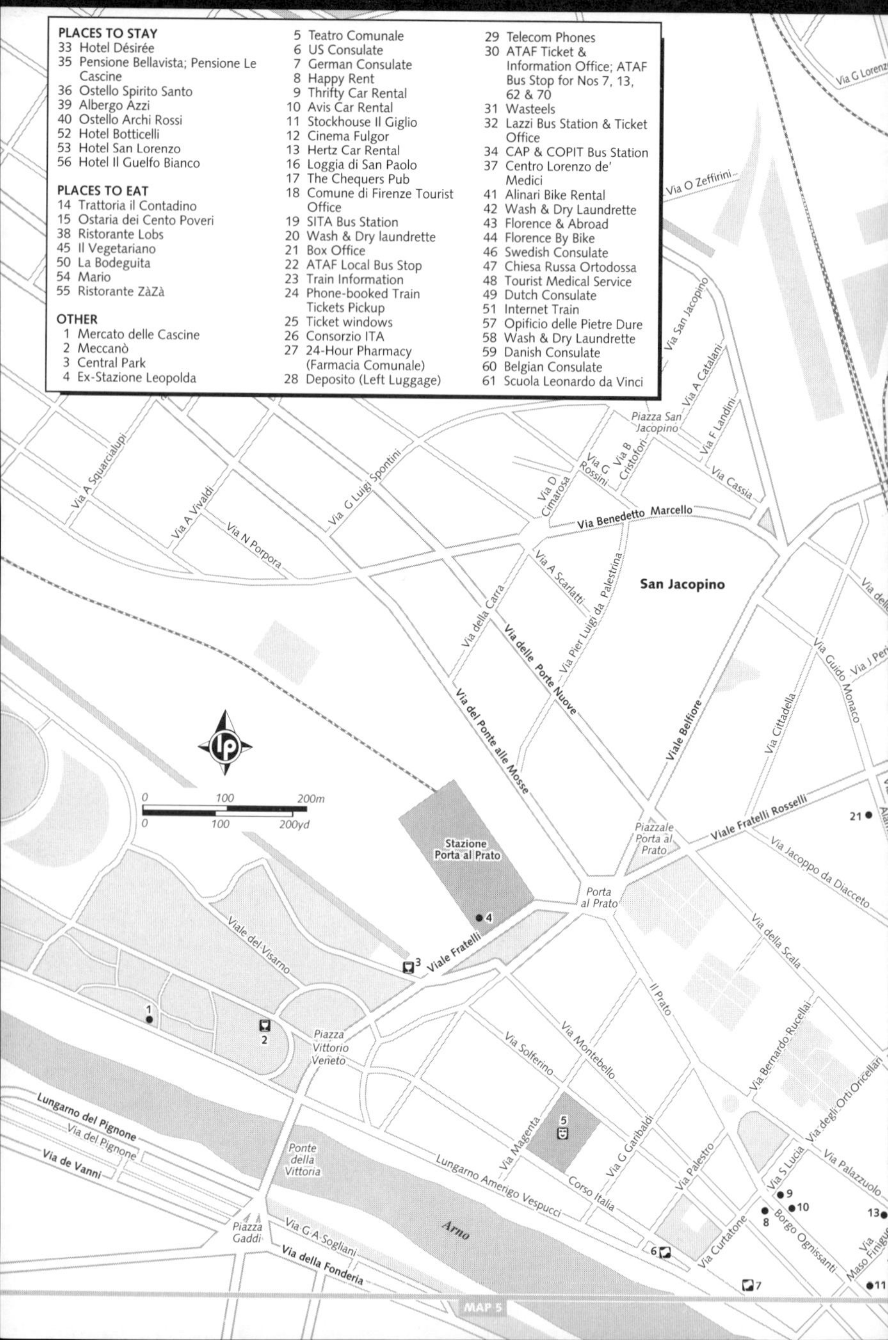

MAP 3

PLACES TO STAY
33 Hotel Désirée
35 Pensione Bellavista; Pensione Le Cascine
36 Ostello Spirito Santo
39 Albergo Azzi
40 Ostello Archi Rossi
52 Hotel Botticelli
53 Hotel San Lorenzo
56 Hotel Il Guelfo Bianco

PLACES TO EAT
14 Trattoria il Contadino
15 Ostaria dei Cento Poveri
38 Ristorante Lobs
45 Il Vegetariano
50 La Bodeguita
54 Mario
55 Ristorante ZàZà

OTHER
1 Mercato delle Cascine
2 Meccanò
3 Central Park
4 Ex-Stazione Leopolda

5 Teatro Comunale
6 US Consulate
7 German Consulate
8 Happy Rent
9 Thrifty Car Rental
10 Avis Car Rental
11 Stockhouse Il Giglio
12 Cinema Fulgor
13 Hertz Car Rental
16 Loggia di San Paolo
17 The Chequers Pub
18 Comune di Firenze Tourist Office
19 SITA Bus Station
20 Wash & Dry laundrette
21 Box Office
22 ATAF Local Bus Stop
23 Train Information
24 Phone-booked Train Tickets Pickup
25 Ticket windows
26 Consorzio ITA
27 24-Hour Pharmacy (Farmacia Comunale)
28 Deposito (Left Luggage)

29 Telecom Phones
30 ATAF Ticket & Information Office; ATAF Bus Stop for Nos 7, 13, 62 & 70
31 Wasteels
32 Lazzi Bus Station & Ticket Office
34 CAP & COPIT Bus Station
37 Centro Lorenzo de' Medici
41 Alinari Bike Rental
42 Wash & Dry Laundrette
43 Florence & Abroad
44 Florence By Bike
46 Swedish Consulate
47 Chiesa Russa Ortodossa
48 Tourist Medical Service
49 Dutch Consulate
51 Internet Train
57 Opificio delle Pietre Dure
58 Wash & Dry Laundrette
59 Danish Consulate
60 Belgian Consulate
61 Scuola Leonardo da Vinci

San Jacopino

Piazza San Jacopino

Via Benedetto Marcello

Via G Lorenzo
Via O Zeffirini

0   100   200m
0   100   200yd

Stazione Porta al Prato

Porta al Prato

Piazzale Porta al Prato

Viale Fratelli Rosselli

Via Jacopoo da Diacceto

21 ●

Piazza Vittorio Veneto

Viale del Visarno

Viale Fratelli

Via della Scala

Il Prato

Via Montebello

Via Bernardo Rucellai

Via degli Orti Oricellari

Lungarno del Pignone
Via del Pignone
Via de Vanni

1 ●
2 ▣
▣ 3

Piazza Gaddi

Via G A Sogliani
Via della Fonderia

Ponte della Vittoria

Lungarno Amerigo Vespucci

Via Solferino
Via Magenta
Via G Garibaldi
Via Palestro
Via S Lucia
Via Palazzuolo

Corso Italia
Borgo Ognissanti

5 ▣

Arno

Ponte alla Vittoria

6 ▣

▣ 7

9 ●
10 ●
13 ●

8

11 ●

MAP 5

MAP 3

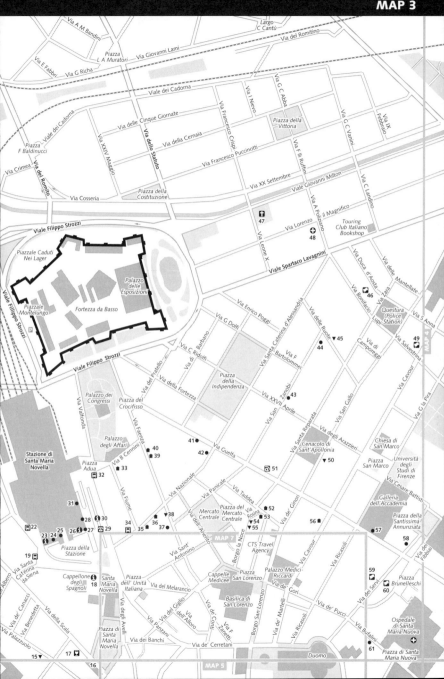

CHRISTOPHER THOMAS

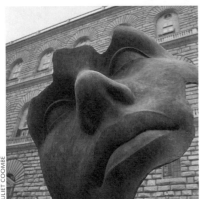

JULIET COOMBE

DAN HERRICK

JULIET COOMBE

Cradle of the Renaissance and sometime home of Machiavelli, Michelangelo and the Medicis,
Florence is a chic centre of art, culture and history.

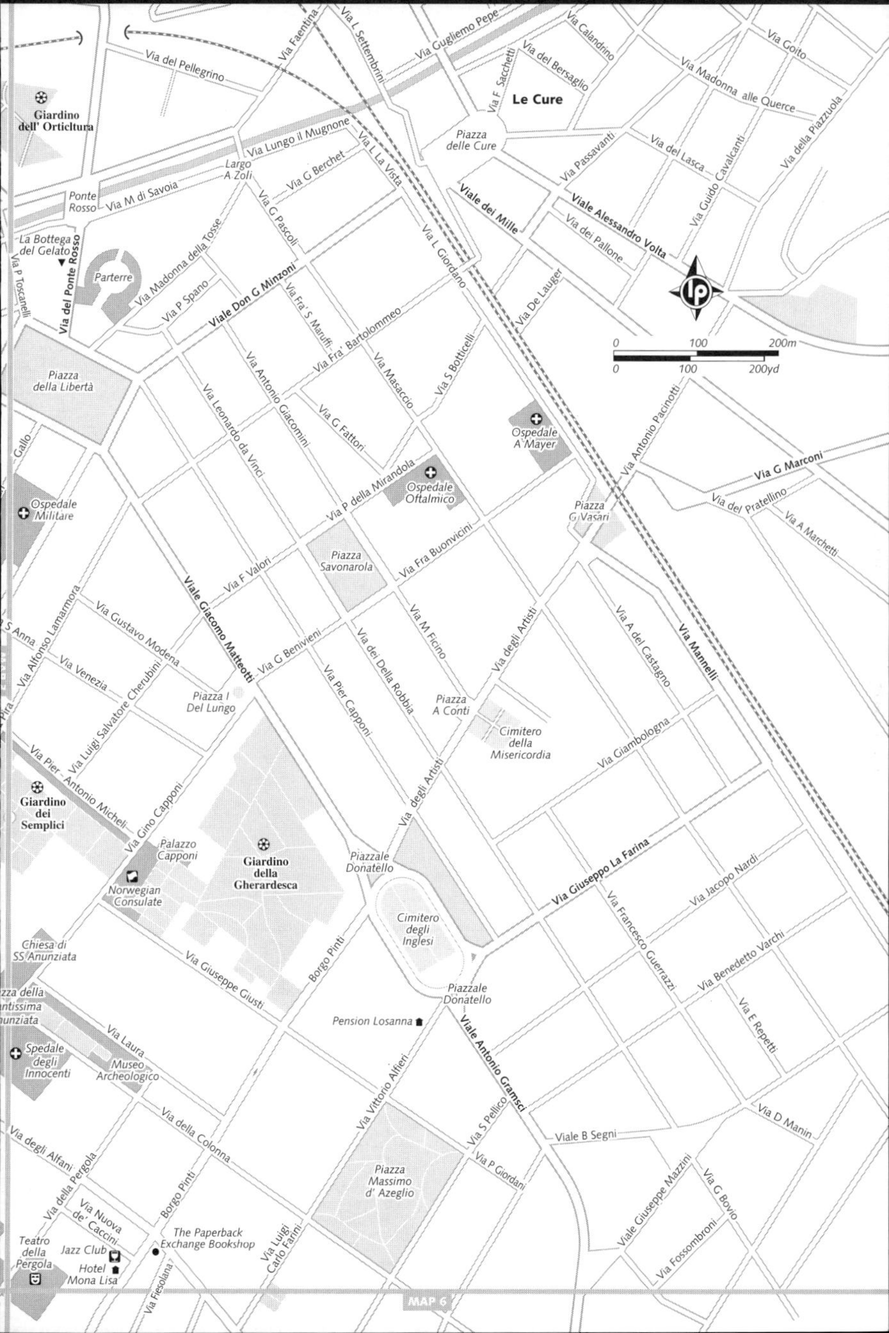

MAP 4

Via L Settembrini

Via Faentina

Via del Pellegrino

Via Guglielmo Pepe

Via Calandrino

Via Golfo

Via del Bersaglio

Via Madonna alle Querce

Via F Sacchetti

Le Cure

Giardino dell' Orticultura

Piazza delle Cure

Via Passavanti

Via del Lasca

Via della Piazzuola

Via Lungo il Mugnone

Via M di Savoia

Largo A Zoli

Via G Berchet

Via La Vista

Ponte Rosso

Viale dei Mille

Via Guido Cavalcanti

Via G Pascoli

Viale Alessandro Volta

La Bottega del Gelato Rosso

Via Madonna della Tosse

Via del Pallone

Via dei Pallone

Via del Ponte Rosso

Parterre

Via P Spano

Viale Don G Minzoni

Via Fra' S Maffei

Via Giordano

Via S Botticelli

Via De Lauger

Via Antonio Pacinotti

Via G Marconi

Piazza della Libertà

Via Antonio Giacomini

Via Fra' Bartolommeo

Via del Pratellino

Via A Marchetti

Gallo

Via Leonardo da Vinci

Via G Fattori

Via Masaccio

Ospedale A Mayer

Ospedale Militare

Via P della Mirandola

Ospedale Oftalmico

Piazza G Vasari

S Anna

Via F Valori

Piazza Savonarola

Via Fra Buonvicini

Via A del Castagno

Via Mannelli

Via Gustavo Modena

Viale Giacomo Matteotti

Via G Benivieni

Via M Ferino

Via degli Artisti

Via Alfonso Lamarmora

Via Venezia

Via I Del Lungo

Via Luigi Salvatore Cherubini

Piazza I Del Lungo

Via Per Capponi

Via della Robbia

Piazza A Conti

Cimitero della Misericordia

Via Giambologna

Via Per

Giardino dei Semplici

Via Gino Capponi

Via Antonio Micheli

Palazzo Capponi

Giardino della Gherardesca

Piazzale Donatello

Via degli Artisti

Via Giuseppe La Farina

Norwegian Consulate

Via Francesco Guerrazzi

Via Jacopo Nardi

Chiesa di SS'Anunziata

Cimitero degli Inglesi

Via Giuseppe Giusti

Borgo Pinti

Via Benedetto Varchi

zza della ntissima nunziata

Piazzale Donatello

Viale Antonio Gramsci

Via E Repetti

Spedale degli Innocenti

Via Laura

Pension Losanna

Museo Archeologico

Via della Colonna

Via Vittorio Alfieri

Via S Pellico

Viale B Segni

Via D Manin

Via degli Affani

Borgo Pinti

Piazza Massimo d' Azeglio

Via P Giordani

Via della Pergola

Via Nuova de Caccini

The Paperback Exchange Bookshop

Via Luigi Carlo Farini

Viale Giuseppe Mazzini

Via G Bovio

Teatro della Pergola

Jazz Club

Hotel Mona Lisa

Via Fiesolana

Via Fossombroni

MAP 6

0   100   200m

0   100   200yd

MAP 5

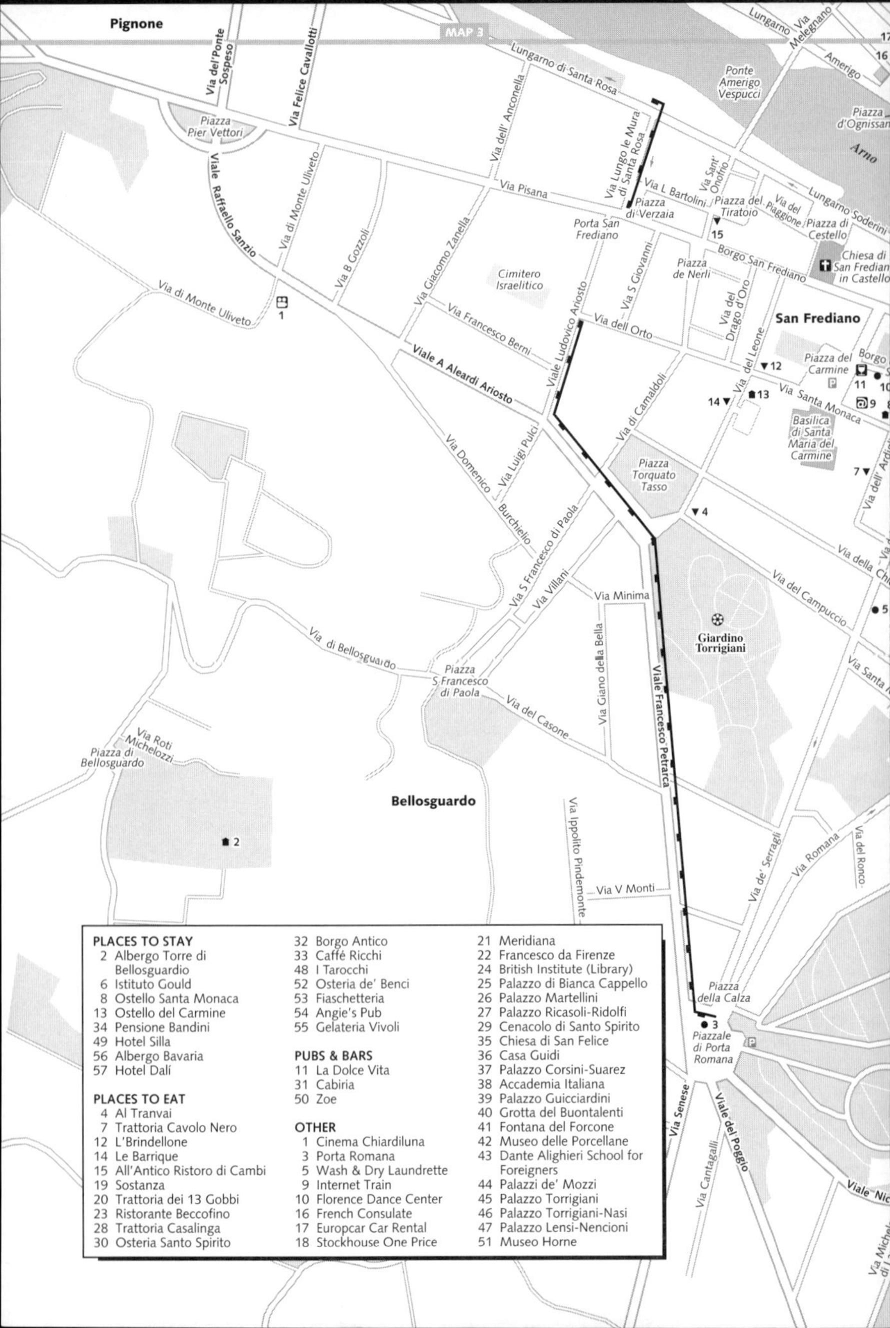

MAP 3
Pignone
Via del Ponte Sospeso
Via Felice Cavallotti
Piazza Pier Vettori
Viale Raffaello Sanzio
Via di Monte Uliveto
Via B Gozzoli
Via Giacomo Zanella
Via dell' Anconella
Lungarno di Santa Rosa
Via Lungo le Mura di Santa Rosa
Via Pisana
Piazza di Verzaia
Porta San Frediano
Cimitero Israelitico
Via Francesco Berni
Viale A Aleardi Ariosto
Viale Ludovico Ariosto
Via S Giovanni
Via dell Orto
Via di Camaldoli
Via Domenico Burchiello
Via Luigi Pulci
Piazza Torquato Tasso
Via S Francesco di Paola
Via Villani
Via Minima
Via di Bellosguardo
Piazza S Francesco di Paola
Via del Casone
Via Giano della Bella
Viale Francesco Petrarca
Via Roti Michelozzi
Piazza di Bellosguardo
Bellosguardo
Via Ippolito Pindemonte
Via V Monti
Lungarno Via Melegnano
Amerigo
Ponte Amerigo Vespucci
Piazza d'Ognissan
Arno
Via Sant' Onofrio
Via L Bartolini
Piazza del Tiratoio
Via del Piaggione
Piazza di Cestello
Lungarno Soderini
Chiesa di San Frediano in Castello
Borgo San Frediano
Piazza de Nerli
Via del Drago d'Oro
San Frediano
Via del Leone
Piazza del Carmine
Borgo
Via Santa Monaca
Basilica di Santa Maria del Carmine
Via dell' Ardiglione
Via della Chiesa
Via del Campuccio
Giardino Torrigiani
Via Santa
Via de' Serragli
Via Romana
Via del Ronco
Piazza della Calza
Piazzale di Porta Romana
Via Senese
Via Cantagalli
Viale del Poggio
Viale Nic
Via Michel
1
2
3
4
5
7
9
10
11
12
13
14
15
16
17
PLACES TO STAY
2 Albergo Torre di Bellosguardio
6 Istituto Gould
8 Ostello Santa Monaca
13 Ostello del Carmine
34 Pensione Bandini
49 Hotel Silla
56 Albergo Bavaria
57 Hotel Dalí
PLACES TO EAT
4 Al Tranvai
7 Trattoria Cavolo Nero
12 L'Brindellone
14 Le Barrique
15 All'Antico Ristoro di Cambi
19 Sostanza
20 Trattoria dei 13 Gobbi
23 Ristorante Beccofino
28 Trattoria Casalinga
30 Osteria Santo Spirito
32 Borgo Antico
33 Caffé Ricchi
48 I Tarocchi
52 Osteria de' Benci
53 Fiaschetteria
54 Angie's Pub
55 Gelateria Vivoli
PUBS & BARS
11 La Dolce Vita
31 Cabiria
50 Zoe
OTHER
1 Cinema Chiardiluna
3 Porta Romana
5 Wash & Dry Laundrette
9 Internet Train
10 Florence Dance Center
16 French Consulate
17 Europcar Car Rental
18 Stockhouse One Price
21 Meridiana
22 Francesco da Firenze
24 British Institute (Library)
25 Palazzo di Bianca Cappello
26 Palazzo Martellini
27 Palazzo Ricasoli-Ridolfi
29 Cenacolo di Santo Spirito
35 Chiesa di San Felice
36 Casa Guidi
37 Palazzo Corsini-Suarez
38 Accademia Italiana
39 Palazzo Guicciardini
40 Grotta del Buontalenti
41 Fontana del Forcone
42 Museo delle Porcellane
43 Dante Alighieri School for Foreigners
44 Palazzi de' Mozzi
45 Palazzo Torrigiani
46 Palazzo Torrigiani-Nasi
47 Palazzo Lensi-Nencioni
51 Museo Horne

MAP 5

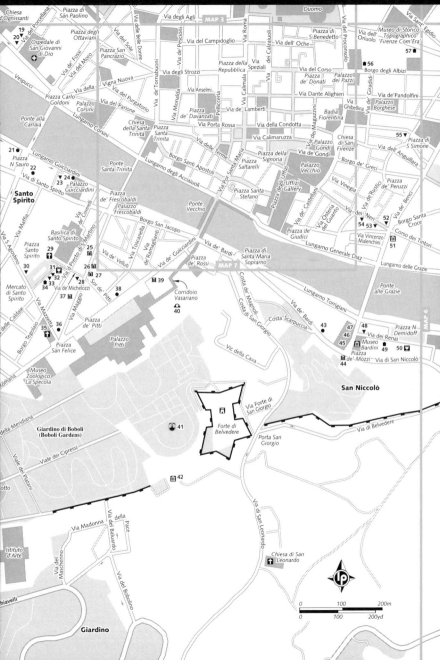

Chiesa d'Ognissanti

Piazza di San Paolino

Via degli Agli — MAP 3

Duomo

Via Sant' Egidio

Via delle Porcellana

19 ▼
20 ▼

Ospedale di San Giovanni di Dio

Via del Moro

Via de' Fossi

Piazza degli Ottaviani

Via del Sole

Via delle Belle Donne

Via de' Pescioni

Via del Campidoglio

Via Roma

Piazza di S Benedetto

Dell' Oche

Via del Procosolino

Via dell' Oriuolo

Museo di Storico Topographico 'Firenze Com'Era'

57 ▮

Vespucci

Via della Spada

Via del Purgatorio

Vigna Nuova

Piazza San Pancrazio

Via de' Tornabuoni

Piazza della Repubblica

Via degli Strozzi

Via Speziali

Via Calimala

Via del Corso

Borgo degli Albizi

56 ▮

Piazza Carlo Goldoni

Palazzo Corsini

Via del Parione

Via Monalda

Via Anselmi

Pellicceria

Piazza de' Donati

Palazzo de' Pazzi

Badia Fiorentina

Via de'Pandolfini

Palazzo Borghese

Via Dante Alighieri

Via Porta Rossa

Via de' Davanzati

Via de' Lamberti

Via Ghibellina

Via de' Gradisti

Ponte alla Carraia

Lungarno Corsini

Chiesa della Santa Trinità

Piazza Santa Trinità

Borgo Santi Apostoli

Via delle Terme

Via Porta Rossa

Via della Condotta

Via Calimaruzza

Palazzo Gondi

Chiesa di San Firenze

Via dell' Anguillara

Piazza di S Simone

55 ▼

21 ●

Piazza N Sauro

Lungarno Guicciardini

22

Via di Santo Spirito

23

Palazzo Guicciardini

Ponte Santa Trinità

Lungarno degli Acciaiuoli

Piazza Saltarelli

Piazza della Signoria

Borgo de' Greci

Piazza de' Peruzzi

Via de' Rustici

Via de' Benci

Santo Spirito

Via Maffia

Via de' Coverelli

Piazza de' Frescobaldi

Palazzo Frescobaldi

Ponte Vecchio

Via Por Santa Maria

Piazza Santa Stefano

Palazzo Vecchio

Uffizi Gallery

Piazza degli Uffizi

Via Vinegia

Via de' Neri

52 ▼

54 53 ▼

Borgo Santa Croce

Corso dei Tintori

Via S. Agostino

Basilica di Santo Spirito

29

Via di Pietro di S. Martino

25

26

Borgo San Jacopo

Via de' Toscanella

Via de' Ramaglianti

Via de' Velluti

Via de' Bardi

Piazza di Santa Maria Sopramo

Via de' Castellani

Via Osteria del Guanto

Piazza de' Giudici

Via dei Neri

Via Vincenzo Malenchini

51

Lungarno Generale Diaz

Lungarno delle Grazie

Piazza Santo Spirito

30 ▼

31

32

33

34

Via de' Michelozzi

Via de' Guicciardini

Piazza de' Rossi

MAP 7

39

Corridoio Vasariano

40

Mercato di Santo Spirito

37

38

Via de' Bardi

Lungarno Torrigiani

Ponte alle Grazie

Via Mazzetta

Via Maggio

Piazza de' Pitti

Costa de' Magnoli

Costa di San Giorgio

43

47 48

46

45

Piazza N Demidoff

Via dei Renai

Museo Bardini

49 50

35

36

Piazza San Felice

Palazzo Pitti

Vic della Cava

Piazza de' Mozzi

44

Via di San Niccolò

San Niccolò

Museo Zoologico La Specola

della Meridiana

Giardino di Boboli (Boboli Gardens)

Viale del Cipressi

41

Forte di Belvedere

Via Forte di San Giorgio

Porta San Giorgio

Via di Belvedere

42

Viale dei Platani

Via Madonna della Pace

Via del Baluardo

Via di San Leonardo

Chiesa di San Leonardo

Istituto d'Arte

Via del Mascherino

chiavelli

Via del Bobolino

Giardino

0   100   200m
0   100   200yd

MAP 6

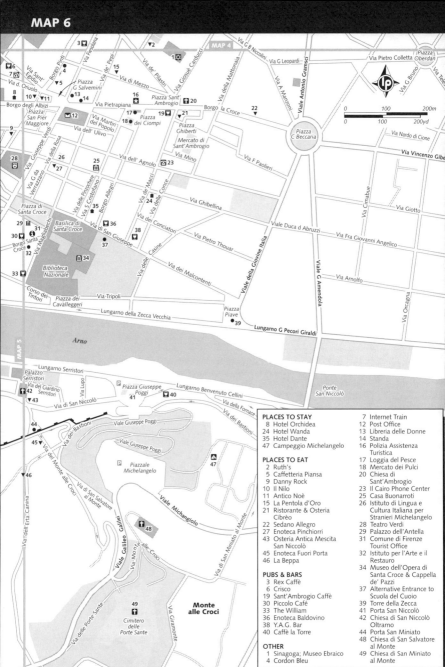

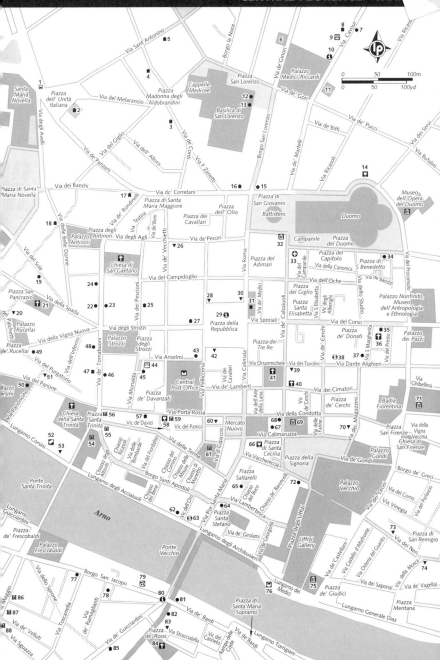

MAP 7 – CENTRAL FLORENCE

BETHUNE CARMICHAEL

The glorious panoramic view over Florence's rooftops

THINGS TO SEE & DO

Florence is the proverbial chocolate box. All cliches apply. Like 'all good things come in small packages'. We won't even try to compete with the battalions of literary greats and other important persons who have spilled rivers of ink in the search for an original superlative. Florence is jammed with monuments and sights, most mercifully confined to a small area.

Opening Times

Museums and monuments tend to be closed on Monday in Italy. Given the hordes of tourists that pour into Florence year-round, quite a few places *do* open here on Monday – you can get a list of them from the APT office.

Opening times vary throughout the year, although many monuments stick to a vague summer/winter timetable. In the case of state museums, summer means 1 May to 31 October. For other sights it can be more like Easter to the end of September. It is impossible to be overly precise, because timetables change from year to year and from summer to winter. Museum staff frequently only find out about changes at the last minute. You should get hold of the latest schedules, especially in winter (when opening times are generally less generous), from the APT as soon as you arrive in Florence.

Warning At most sights the ticket window shuts up to 30 minutes before the advertised closing time. Also, in some of these places (the Uffizi and Cappella Brancacci, to name a couple of the culprits) staff actually shuffle you out at least 15 minutes before closing time. It would seem in such instances that closing time means not when you have to start heading out the door, but when the door has to be bolted shut.

Carnet dei Musei Fiorentini

If you intend to see a good number of the museums in Florence, this carnet (actually a set of 10 vouchers) for €5.15 is worth considering. You get an explanatory booklet and discounts of up to 50% on 10 sights. Some of these are pretty minor, but others you will

probably want to visit. They are (in order of interest): Palazzo Vecchio, Cappella Brancacci; the museum and cloisters in the Basilica di Santa Maria Novella; Museo Stibbert; Museo Bardini (closed at the time of writing); Museo Storico-Topografico 'Firenze Com'Era'; Museo Marino Marini; Fondazione Romano (Cenacolo di Santo Spirito); Raccolta Alberto della Ragione; and Galleria Rinaldo Carnielo. The carnet is valid for a year from the date of purchase.

For information on phone and Internet bookings to major sights, see the 'Queue Jumping' boxed text later in this chapter.

Free Entry

One week of the year (usually in spring but the dates change) entry to *musei statali* (state museums) throughout Italy is made free. Since dates change it is impossible to plan a trip around this, but keep your eyes open.

In addition, admission to all state museums is supposed to be free for EU citizens under 18 and over 65. These include the Uffizi, Palazzo Pitti, Giardino di Boboli, Galleria dell'Accademia, Museo Archeologico, the Bargello, Museo di San Marco, Cappelle Medicee, Opificio and various of the Cenacolos (Last Supper scenes). In some

Queue Jumping

If time is precious and money is not a prime concern, you can skip (or at least shorten) some of the museum queues in Florence by booking ahead. In summer especially, the long and winding queues can mean waits of two to four hours! Watch 'em sweat! For a €1.55 fee, you can book a ticket to the Uffizi by phoning Firenze Musei (☎ 055 29 48 83). You are given a booking number and agree the time you want to visit. When you arrive at the gallery, follow the signs to a separate entrance for those with pre-booked tickets, which you pick up and pay for on the spot without queuing. You can book to any of the *musei statali* (state museums) this way. See also the Free Entry section in this chapter. For the Uffizi, you can also buy the ticket in advance at the gallery itself (the booking fee still applies).

If you prefer the electronic age, Weekend a Firenze (W www.weekendafirenze.com) is an online service for booking museums, galleries, shows and tours. For this you pay €5.70 on top of the normal ticket price. You must book at least three days in advance. You will get an email confirmation that you will have to print out and present at the cashier's desk on the day you go. You can get tickets for the Uffizi, Galleria dell'Accademia, Galleria Palatina, Museo di San Marco, Museo del Bargello, Cappelle Medicee, Museo Archeologico and the Galleria d'Arte Moderna. Many of the bigger hotels will also book these tickets for you.

When you go to the Uffizi or other sights with prepaid tickets, email confirmation or whatever, head for the designated entrance or window for those with booked tickets (where there is one) and smile smugly at the suffering hordes lined up outside the other entrance.

---

other museums EU citizens of differing ages get discounts. There are few discounts for non-EU citizens or nonresidents of Florence. Still, always ask to be sure.

Piazza del Duomo & Around

Duomo (Map 7) When you first come upon the Duomo *(Cathedral; ☎ 055 230 28 85 for the Duomo and all attached sights)* from the crowded streets around the square, you will likely stop momentarily in your tracks, taken aback by the ordered vivacity of its pink, white and green marble facade. You had probably already espied Brunelleschi's sloping, red-tiled dome – the predominant feature of Florence's skyline and at the time a unique stroke of engineering genius.

The great temple's full name is Cattedrale di Santa Maria del Fiore and it is the world's fourth-largest cathedral. Begun in 1296 by Arnolfo di Cambio, it took almost 150 years to complete. It is 153m long and 38m wide, except the transept, which extends 90m.

The present facade was only raised in the late 19th century. Its architect, Emilio de Fabris, was inspired by the design of the cathedral's flanks, which largely date to the 14th century. From the facade, you should do a circuit of the church to take in its splendour before heading inside.

The south flank is the oldest and most clearly Gothic part of the Duomo. The second doorway here, is the **Porta dei Canonici** (Canons' Door); it's a mid-14th-century High Gothic creation (you enter here to climb up inside the dome). Wander around the trio of apses, designed to appear as the flowers on the stem that is the nave of the church (and so reflecting its name – Santa Maria del Fiore, St Mary of the Flower).

The first door you see on the north flank after the apses is the early-15th-century **Porta della Mandorla** (Almond Door), so named because of the relief of the Virgin Mary contained within an almond-shaped frame. Much of the decorative sculpture that graced the flanks of the cathedral has been removed for its own protection to the Museo dell'Opera del Duomo, in some cases to be replaced by copies.

Interior The Duomo's vast and spartan interior *(free; open 10am-5pm Mon-Sat, 10am-3.30pm Thur, 1pm-3pm Sun except during*

Mass) comes as a surprise after the visual assault outside. Down the left aisle you will see two immense frescoes of equestrian statues dedicated to two *condottieri* or mercenaries, who fought in the service of Florence (for lots of dosh of course). The one on the left is Niccolò da Tolentino (by Andrea del Castagno) and the other is Giovanni Acuto, better known to the English as Sir John Hawkwood (by Paolo Uccello).

Although Florence had exiled him (see under Dante in the Facts about Tuscany chapter), Dante and the world he created in the *Divina Commedia* (Divine Comedy) fascinated subsequent generations of Florentines, who revered him. Domenico di Michelino's *Dante e I Suoi Mondi* (Dante and His Worlds), the next painting along the left aisle, is one of the most reproduced images of the poet and his verse masterpiece.

The festival of colour and images that greets you as you arrive beneath Brunelleschi's dome is the work of Giorgio Vasari and Frederico Zuccari. The fresco series depicts the *Giudizio Universale* (Last Judgment). Below the frescoes is the octagonal **coro** (choirstalls). Its low marble 'fence' also encloses the altar, above which hangs a crucifix by Benedetto da Maiano.

From the choirstalls, the two wings of the transept and the rear apse spread out, each containing five chapels. The pillars delimiting the entrance into each wing and the apse are fronted by statues of Apostles, as are the two hefty pillars just west of the choirstalls.

Between the left (north) arm of the transept and the apse is the **Sagrestia delle Messe** (Mass Sacristy), whose panelling is a marvel of inlaid wood created by Benedetto and Giuliano da Maiano. The fine bronze doors were executed by Luca della Robbia, showing he could turn his hand to other material as well as glazed terracotta. That said, the top of the doorway is decorated with one of his 'robbiane', as is the **Sagrestia Nuova** (New Sacristy) by the right transept (no access). By the way, it was through della Robbia's doors that Lorenzo de' Medici fled in the uproar following the assassination by the Pazzi conspirators of his brother Giuliano during Mass in 1478.

Some of the finest stained glass in Italy, by Donatello, Andrea del Castagno, Paolo Uccello and Lorenzo Ghiberti, adorns the windows.

A stairway near the main entrance of the Duomo leads down to the **crypt** *(admission €2.60; open 10am-5pm Mon-Sat, except during Mass)*, actually the site where excavations have unearthed parts of the 5th-century Chiesa di Santa Reparata. Brunelleschi's tomb is also in here. Apart from the remaining floor mosaics, typical of early Christian churches in Italy and recalling their Roman heritage, the spurs and sword of Giovanni de' Medici were dug up in the crypt. Otherwise the remains give only a vague idea of what the Romanesque church was like, and still dimmer a clue of what the church's Roman predecessor might have been.

Dome You can climb up into the dome *(enter by Porta dei Canonici outside south flank of cathedral; admission €5.15; open 8.30am-7pm Mon-Fri, 8.30am-5pm Sat)* to get a closer look at Brunelleschi's engineering feat. The view from the summit over Florence is breathtaking.

On 8 September every year, a walkway that stretches around atop the sides and facade of the dome is opened to the public. You access it by the same entrance as to the dome.

Campanile (Map 7) Giotto designed and began building the graceful and unusual Campanile *(Bell Tower; admission €5.15; open 8.30am-7.30pm Apr-Sept, 9am-5.30pm Oct, 9am-4.30pm Nov-Mar)* next to the Duomo in 1334, but died only three years later. The bell tower is 84.7m high and you can climb its 414 stairs.

Andrea Pisano and Francesco Talenti continued the work on the Campanile. The first tier of bas-reliefs around the base, carved by Pisano but possibly designed by Giotto, depicts the Creation of Man and the *attività umane* (arts and industries). Those on the second tier depict the planets, cardinal virtues, the arts and the seven sacraments. The sculptures of the prophets and sibyls in the niches of the upper storeys are actually copies of works by Donatello and others – the originals are in the Museo dell'Opera del Duomo.

Warning People with heart conditions or who are otherwise unfit should not undertake this climb. There is *no* lift should you get into difficulties.

Museo dell'Opera del Duomo (Map 7)

This **museum** *(Piazza del Duomo 9, admission €5.15; open 9am-7.30pm Mon-Sat, 1pm-5pm Sun)*, behind the cathedral, features many of the sculptural treasures that at one time adorned the Duomo, Baptistry and Campanile.

The first main hall is devoted to statuary that graced Arnolfo di Cambio's original Gothic facade, which was never completed. The pieces include several by Arnolfo himself, among them representations of Pope Boniface VIII, the Virgin and Child and St Reparata. The long flowing beard of Donatello's St John stands out among the four mighty statues of the evangelists.

Out in the courtyard are displayed five of the original 10 panels of Ghiberti's masterpiece, the Porta del Paradiso of the Baptistry (what you see at the Baptistry itself are copies). They were damaged in the 1966 floods and needed urgent restoration. It has taken a while but the end result is definitely worth it.

As you head up the stairs you approach what is the museum's best known piece, Michelangelo's *Pietà*, a late work that he intended for his own tomb. Vasari recorded in his *Lives of the Artists* that, unsatisfied with the quality of the marble or his own work, Michelangelo broke up the unfinished sculpture, destroying the arm and left leg of the figure of Christ. A student of Michelangelo later restored the arm and completed the figure of Mary Magdalene.

Continue upstairs to the next main hall, which is dominated by the two extraordinary *cantorias*, or pulpits (one by Donatello and the other by Luca della Robbia) that once adorned the Sagrestia in the Duomo. In the same hall is Donatello's carving of

the prophet Habakkuk (taken from the Campanile and now under restoration) and, in an adjoining room, his extraordinary wooden impression of Mary Magdalene.

Battistero (Map 7)

The Romanesque **Baptistry** *(admission €2.60; open noon-7pm Mon-Sat, 8.30am-2pm Sun)* may have been built as early as the 5th century on the site of a Roman temple. It is one of the oldest buildings in Florence and dedicated to St John the Baptist (San Giovanni Battista).

The present structure, or at least its facade, dates to about the 11th century. The stripes of white and green marble that bedeck the octagonal structure are typical of Tuscan Romanesque style.

More striking still are the three sets of bronze doors, conceived as a series of panels in which the story of humanity and the Redemption would be told.

The earliest set of doors, which is now on the south side, was completed by Andrea Pisano in 1336.

Lorenzo Ghiberti toiled away for 20 years to get his set of doors, on the north flank, just right. The top 20 panels recount episodes from the New Testament, while the eight lower ones show the four Evangelists and the four fathers of the Church.

Good as this late Gothic effort was, Ghiberti returned almost immediately to his workshops to turn out the east doors. Made of gilded bronze, they took 28 years to complete (1424–52), largely because of Ghiberti's intransigent perfectionism. The bas-reliefs on their 10 panels depict scenes from the Old Testament. So extraordinary were his exertions that, many years later, Michelangelo stood before the doors in awe and declared them fit to be the *Porta del Paradiso* (Gates of Paradise), which is how they remain known to this day.

Most of the doors' panels are copies. The original panels are being restored and five from the Porta del Paradiso are on display in the Museo dell'Opera del Duomo.

Interior Inside is rather reminiscent of the Pantheon in Rome. The two-coloured marble facing on the outside continues within, made more arresting by the geometrical flourishes above the Romanesque windows.

The single most arresting aspect of the decoration is the mosaics. Those in the apse were started in 1225 and are looking a little jaded. The glittering spectacle in the dome is, however, a unique sight in Florence. It was carried out by Venetian experts over 32 years from 1270, to designs by Tuscan artists, including Cimabue.

Donatello carved the tomb of Baldassare Cossa, better known as John XXIII the Antipope, which takes up the wall to the right of the apse.

Loggia del Bigallo (Map 7) This elegant marble loggia was built in the second half of the 14th century for the Compagnia (or Confraternita) di Santa Maria della Misericordia, which had been formed in 1244 to aid the elderly, the sick and orphans. Lost and abandoned children were customarily placed here so that they could be reclaimed by their families or put into the care of foster mothers. Members of the fraternity transported the ill to hospital and buried the dead in times of plague. In 1425, the fraternity was fused with another that had been founded by the same person (San Pietro Martire), the Confraternita del Bigallo. The fusion lasted a century, after which the Misericordia moved to its present position on Piazza del Duomo, from where to this day they continue their ambulance vocation.

The loggia houses a small **museum** *(admission €2.60; open 8.30am-noon Mon, 4pm-6pm Thur)* containing a limited collection of artworks belonging to the two fraternities.

Museo Storico-Topografico 'Firenze Com'Era' (Map 5) This **museum** *(☎ 055 261 65 45, Via dell'Oriuolo 24; admission €2.60; open 9am-2pm Fri-Wed)* is mildly interesting for those who want to get an idea of how the city developed, particularly from the Renaissance to the modern day. Paintings, models, topographical drawings (the earliest dating to 1594) and prints help explain the history of the city.

From the Duomo to Piazza della Signoria (Map 7)

What follows is a rather serpentine meander across the heart of old Florence. You could do it in a million ways, so don't take the following order too much to heart.

Via del Proconsolo Bernardo Buontalenti started work on the **Palazzo Nonfinito**, a residence for members of the Strozzi family, in 1593. Buontalenti and others completed the 1st floor and courtyard, which is Palladian in style, but the upper floors were never completely finished, hence the building's name. The obscure **Museo dell'Antropologia e Etnologia** *(☎ 055 239 64 49, Via del Proconsolo 12; admission €3.10; open 10am-noon Wed-Mon)* is housed here.

Across Borgo degli Albizi stands the equally proud **Palazzo dei Pazzi**, which went up a century earlier and is clearly influenced by the Palazzo Medici-Riccardi. It now houses offices, but you can wander into the courtyard.

Badia Fiorentina The 10th-century Badia Fiorentina *(Florence Abbey; Via del Proconsolo; open 3pm-6pm Mon)* was built on the orders of Willa, who was the mother of one of the early Margraves of Tuscany, Ugo. Willa was inspired to this act by calls for greater piety in the church, which at the time was coming under hefty attack from some quarters for corruption of all kinds. Ugo continued the work of his mother, investing considerably in the Benedictine monastery and church. He was eventually buried here. It is particularly worth a visit to see Filippino Lippi's *Appearance of the Virgin to St Bernard*, to the left as you enter the church through the small (and scaffolding-cluttered) Renaissance cloister. At the left end of the transept is Mino da Fiesole's monument to Margrave Ugo.

Palazzo del Bargello Just across Via del Proconsolo from the Badia is this grand mansion, also known as the Palazzo del Podestà. Started in 1254, the palace was originally the residence of the chief magistrate and was then turned into a police station. During its days as a police complex, many people were tortured near the well in the centre of the medieval courtyard. Indeed for a long time the city's prisons were located here.

It now houses the **Museo del Bargello** (☎ 055 238 86 06, Via del Proconsolo 4; admission €4.15; open 8.30am-1.50pm Tues-Sat & alternating Sun & Mon) and the most comprehensive collection of Tuscan Renaissance sculpture in Italy. The museum is absolutely not to be missed.

You enter the courtyard from Via Ghibellina and turn right into the ticket office. From here you end up in the ground-floor Sala del Cinquecento (16th-Century Room), dominated by early works by Michelangelo. His drunken *Bacco* (Bacchus), executed when the artist was 22, a marble bust of *Brutus* and a tondo of the *Madonna col Bambino* (Madonna and Child) are among his best here. Other works of particular interest are Benvenuto Cellini's rather camp marble *Ganimede* (Ganymede) and *Narciso* (Narcissus), along with Giambologna's *Mercurio Volante* (Winged Mercury).

Upstairs is the majestic Salone del Consiglio Generale (Hall of the General Council). At the far end, housed in a tabernacle, is Donatello's famed *San Giorgio* (St George), which once graced the Orsanmichele. David (as in David and Goliath) was a favourite subject for sculptors. In this hall you can see both a marble version by Donatello and the fabled bronze he did in later years. The latter is extraordinary – more so when you consider it was the first freestanding naked statue done since classical times. This *David* doesn't appear terribly warrior-like.

Up on the 2nd floor you will find a bronze collection that includes two masterpieces: Antonio Pollaiuolo's *Ercole e Anteo* (Hercules and Anteus) as well as Cellini's *Ganimede*.

Chiesa di San Firenze The small medieval parish church of San Firenze is no longer recognisable in this baroque complex *(closed to public)* that is today home to law courts. The original church of San Firenze, on the right, was reduced to an oratory when the church on the left, dedicated

to San Filippo Neri (St Phillip Neri) was built. The late-Baroque facade that unites the buildings was completed in 1775.

Across the piazza (on the western side) is the main facade of **Palazzo Gondi**, once the site of the merchants' tribunal, a court set up to deal with their quarrels.

Casa di Dante & Around 'Dante's House' (☎ 055 21 94 16, Via Santa Margherita 1; admission €2.60; open 10am-6pm Wed-Mon May-Sept, 10am-4pm Wed-Mon Oct-Apr, 10am-2pm Sun & holidays year-round) was built in the early 20th century, so you can be quite sure the claim that Dante lived here is utterly spurious. The display inside could be of mild interest to those with a thing for Dante but it is a bit of a rip-off.

Just up the road is the small **Chiesa di Santa Margherita** *(Via Santa Margherita)*, which dates at least to 1032. Some claim that it was in this small single-nave church with a timber ceiling that Dante met his muse, Beatrice Portinari, although he himself said he bumped into her in the Badia.

Chiesa di Orsanmichele Originally a grain market, this **church** *(Via Arte della Lana; free; open 9am-noon, 4pm-6pm, closed 1st & last Mon of month)* was formed when the arcades of the granary building were walled in during the 14th century and the granary was moved elsewhere. The granary had been built on a spot known as Orsanmichele, a contraction of Orto di San Michele (St Michael's Garden). Under the Lombards, a small church dedicated to St Michael and an adjacent Benedictine convent had indeed been graced with a pleasant garden. The *signoria* (the city's government) cleared the lot to have the granary built. It was destroyed by fire 20 years later and a finer replacement constructed. Considered too good to be a mere granary, this was converted into a church.

The signoria ordered the guilds to finance the decoration of the oddly shaped house of worship, and they proceeded to commission sculptors to erect statues of their patron saints in tabernacles placed around the building's facades.

The statues, commissioned over the 15th and 16th centuries, represent the work of some of the Renaissance's greatest artists. Some of the statues are now in the Museo del Bargello. However, many splendid pieces remain, including Giambologna's *San Luca* (St Luke; third on the right on Via de' Calzaiuoli), a copy of Donatello's *San Giorgio* (St George; last on the right on Via Orsanmichele) and Ghiberti's bronze *San Matteo* (St Matthew; first on the left on Via Arte della Lana).

The main feature of the interior is the splendid Gothic tabernacle, decorated with coloured marble, by Andrea Orcagna. It is an extraordinary item, and to look at the convulsed, twisting columns you could swear you were looking at a scale prototype for the cathedral in Orvieto (Umbria).

Occasionally classical music recitals are held here.

There is also a small museum inside, for which you have to join a guided visit at 9am, 10am or 11am. Admission is free.

Opposite Orsanmichele is the humble little **Chiesa di San Carlo dei Lombardi** *(Via de' Calzaiuoli)*. The church, built in the 14th century, though technically Gothic, still bears Romanesque trademarks in its simple, squat facade.

Piazza della Repubblica Ever since this square was ruthlessly gouged from the city centre in the years following Italian unity in 1861, all and sundry have continued to execrate it.

To create the piazza and restructure the surrounding areas, 26 ancient streets and a further 18 lanes disappeared, along with 341 residential buildings, 451 stores, 173 warehouses and other buildings and services…5822 residents were forcibly relocated to other parts of the city. The entire Mercato Vecchio, which had inherited its function as the central market from the Roman forum, and the nearby lanes of the small Jewish ghetto were simply wiped from the map. Nice one.

If you want to get an idea of what this part of town looked like before the 'squalor' was wiped away, the Museo Storico-Topografico 'Firenze Com'Era' has a model, maps and late-19th-century pictures of the area.

Mercato Nuovo If you stroll south down Via Calimala you arrive at this loggia, built to cover the merchandise (including wool, silk and gold) traded here at the **New Market** *(open daily)* under Cosimo I in the mid-16th century. Nowadays the goods on sale are aimed exclusively at tourists and range from trashy statuettes and other souvenirs to leather goods of mixed quality.

At its southern end is a bronze statue of a boar known as the *fontana del porcellino* (piglet's fountain), an early-17th-century copy of the Greek marble original that is now in the Uffizi. They say that if you chuck a coin into the small basin and rub the critter's snout you will return to Florence.

Palazzo dei Capitani di Parte Guelfa Just off to the south-west of the Mercato Nuovo, this **Palace of the Guelph Faction's Captains** *(closed to public)* was built in the early 13th century and later tinkered with by Brunelleschi and Vasari. The leaders of the Guelph faction raised this fortified building in 1265, taking up land and houses that had been confiscated from the Ghibellines.

Palazzo Davanzati About a block west is this remarkable **14th-century mansion** *(Via Porta Rossa 13)*. One could perhaps be a little put out that it has been closed for restoration since 1995, but sometimes restoration is a good thing.

Indeed, that the building has survived intact in its medieval state is largely due to the intervention of an antiquarian, Elia Volpi, who bought the building in 1904. By that time it had come down in the world, having been divided into small flats and shops and reduced to a pathetic state. Volpi had it restored to its former glory and it eventually became the seat of the **Museo dell'Antica Casa Fiorentina**, which aims to transmit an idea of what life was like in a medieval Florentine mansion.

Ponte Vecchio See the entry later under Oltrarno.

Piazza della Signoria (Map 7)

The hub of the city's political life through the centuries and surrounded by some of its most celebrated buildings, the piazza has the appearance of an outdoor sculpture gallery.

Throughout the centuries, whenever Florence entered one of its innumerable political crises, the people would be called here as a *parlamento* (people's plebiscite) to rubber-stamp decisions that frequently meant ruin for some ruling families and victory for others. Scenes of great pomp and circumstance alternated with others of terrible suffering – here the preacher-leader Savonarola was hanged and fried along with two supporters in 1498. A bronze plaque marks the spot.

Ammannati's huge *Fontana di Nettuno* (Neptune Fountain) sits beside the Palazzo Vecchio. Although the bronze satyrs and divinities frolicking about the edges of the fountain are quite delightful, Il Biancone ('the Big White Thing'), as locals derisively refer to it, is pretty universally considered a bit of a flop.

Flanking the entrance to the palace are copies of Michelangelo's *David* (the original is in the Galleria dell'Accademia) and Donatello's *Marzocco,* the heraldic Florentine lion (the original is in the Museo del Bargello). To the latter's right is a 1980 copy of Donatello's bronze *Giuditta e Oloferne* (Judith Slays Holofernes) – the original is in the Sala dei Gigli inside the palace.

A bronze equestrian statue of Cosimo I de' Medici, created by Giambologna between 1594 and 1598, stands towards the centre of the piazza.

Palazzo Vecchio Formerly known as the Palazzo della Signoria and built by Arnolfo di Cambio between 1298 and 1314, this **palace** (☎ 055 276 82 24, Piazza della Signoria; admission €6.20; open 9am-11pm Mon & Fri, 9am-7pm Tues-Wed & Sat, 9am-2pm Thur, Sun & holidays, mid-June–mid-Sept, 9am-7pm Mon-Wed & Fri, 9am-2pm Thur, Sun & holidays rest of the year) is the traditional seat of Florentine government. Its **Torre d'Arnolfo** is 94m high

and, with its striking crenellations, is as much a symbol of the city as the Duomo.

Built for the *priori* (city government) who ruled Florence (in two-month turns), it came to be known as the Palazzo della Signoria as the government took on this name.

In 1540, Cosimo I de' Medici moved from the Palazzo Medici into this building, making it the ducal residence and centre of government. Cosimo commissioned Vasari to renovate the interior, creating new apartments and decorating the lot. In a sense it was all in vain, because Cosimo's wife, Eleonora de Toledo, was not so keen on it and bought Palazzo Pitti.

The latter took a while to expand and fit out as Eleonora wanted (she died before the work was finished), but the Medici family moved in anyway in 1549. Thus the Palazzo Ducale (or della Signoria for those with a nostalgic bent) came to be called the Palazzo Vecchio (Old Palace) as it still is today. It remains the seat of the city's power, as this is where the mayor does his thing.

Coming in from Piazza della Signoria, you arrive first in the courtyard, reworked in early Renaissance style by Michelozzo in 1453. The decoration came more than a century later when Francesco de' Medici married Joanna of Austria. The cities depicted are jewels in the Austrian imperial crown.

From here you pass into the **Cortile della Dogana** (Customs Courtyard), off which you'll find the ticket office.

A stairway leads up to the magnificent **Salone dei Cinquecento**, also known more simply as the Sala Grande (Big Hall). It was created within the original building in the 1490s to accommodate the Consiglio dei Cinquecento (Council of 500) called into being in the republic under Savonarola. Cosimo I de' Medici later turned the hall into a splendid expression of his own power. The elevated tribune at one end was where Cosimo held audiences. In the 1560s the ceiling was raised 7m and Vasari added the decorations.

From the Salone dei Cinquecento you enter the **Quartiere di Leone X** by another door. The so-called 'Leo X Area' is named after the Medici pope. Upstairs is the

Quartiere degli Elementi (Elements Area), a series of rooms and terraces dedicated to pagan deities. The original *Putto col Delfino* (Cupid with Dolphin) sculpture by Verocchio (a copy graces the courtyard of the building) is in the Sala di Giunone.

From here a walkway takes you across the top of the Salone dei Cinquecento into the **Quartiere di Eleonora**, the apartments of Cosimo I's wife. The room most likely to catch your attention is Eleonora's chapel, just off to the right as you enter the apartments. Il Bronzino's decoration represents the acme of his painting career.

You pass through several more rooms before reaching the **Sala dell'Udienza** (Audience Room), where the priori administered medieval Florentine justice.

The following room is the **Sala dei Gigli**, named after the lilies of the French monarchy that decorate three of the walls (the French were traditionally well disposed to Florence). Domenico Ghirlandaio's fresco on the far wall was supposed to be matched by others. Donatello's restored original bronze of *Giuditta e Oloferne* stands in here. A small, bare study off this hall is the chancery, where Machiavelli worked for a while. The other room off the hall is a wonderful map room. The walls are covered by 16th-century maps of all the known world.

Exiting the Sala dei Gigli you can climb stairs to the **battlements**, from where you have fine views of the city.

By paying a little extra you can join in small guided groups to explore the *percorsi segreti* (secret ways) or head for the **Museo dei Ragazzi** (Children's Museum). The former consist of several options, including the possibility of visiting the Studiolo di Francesco and the nearby treasury of Cosimo I. Another choice takes you into the roof of the Salone dei Cinquecento.

In the Museo dei Ragazzi, you can hang out with actors dressed up as Cosimo I and Eleonora de Toledo – kids are invited to dress up as their kids (Bia and Garcia) and play with the kinds of toys the two grand-ducal imps used to enjoy. Other activities include building and taking apart models of the Palazzo Vecchio, bridges and the like (for

those children with an engineering bent) and peer through a remake of Michelangelo's binoculars.

For any one of these options and the standard visit you pay €7.75. If you want to add on more of the extras, each one costs an additional €1.05. Family tickets for two adults and not more than three kids (€15.50) are also available. Tickets and information on all these extra activities are available in a room just back from the main ticket area.

Loggia della Signoria Built in the late 14th century as a platform for public ceremonies, this loggia eventually became a showcase for sculptures. It also became known as the Loggia dei Lanzi, as Cosimo I used to station his Swiss mercenaries (or *Landsknechte*), armed with lances, in it to remind people who was in charge around here.

To the left of the steps normally stands Benvenuto Cellini's magnificent bronze statue of Perseus holding the head of Medusa, recently unveiled again after more than three years' restoration. To the right is

A triumphant bronze: Cellini's Perseus and Medusa

Giambologna's Mannerist *Ratto delle Sabine* (Rape of a Sabine), his final work (itself now being restored). Inside the loggia proper is another of Giambologna's works, *Ercole col Centauro Nesso* (Hercules with the Centaur Nessus), in which the centaur definitely appears to be coming off second best. The statue originally stood near the southern end of the Ponte Vecchio. Among the other statues (some of which are also being restored) are Roman representations of women.

Raccolta d'Arte Contemporanea Alberto della Ragione

The collection *(☎ 055 28 30 78, Piazza della Signoria 5; admission €2.05; open 9am-1.30pm Wed-Mon)* may awaken mild interest in the art buff with a passion for the Italian 20th-century product. Most of the painters on view worked in the first half of the 20th century. A few Giorgio Morandis in Room IX are worth a quick look. There's even a modest De Chirico in the same room.

The collection was donated to Florence by the Genoese collector Alberto della Ragione on his death in 1970.

Uffizi & Around (Map 7)

Designed and built by Vasari in the second half of the 16th century at the request of Cosimo I de' Medici, the Palazzo degli Uffizi, south of the Palazzo Vecchio, originally housed the city's administrators, judiciary and guilds. It was, in effect, a government office building (*uffizi* means offices).

Vasari also designed the private corridor that links the Palazzo Vecchio and the Palazzo Pitti, through the Uffizi and across the Ponte Vecchio. Known as the **Corridoio Vasariano**, it was long closed to the public but can now be visited occasionally (see Corridoio Vasariano later in this chapter).

Cosimo's successor, Francesco I, commissioned the architect Buontalenti to modify the upper floor of the Palazzo degli Uffizi to house the Medicis' growing art collection. Thus, indirectly, the first steps were taken to turn it into an art gallery.

The Galleria degli Uffizi (Uffizi Gallery) now houses the family's private collection, bequeathed to the city in 1743 by the last of the Medici family, Anna Maria Ludovica, on condition that it never leave the city. Over the years sections of the collection have been moved to the Museo del Bargello and the city's Museo Archeologico. In compensation, other collections, such as the one put together by the Count Augusto Contini-Bonacossi in the 1930s, have joined the core group. Paintings from Florence's churches have also been moved to the gallery. It is by no means the biggest art gallery around (this is no Louvre), but the Uffizi still houses the world's single greatest collection of Italian and Florentine art.

Sadly, several of its artworks were destroyed and others badly damaged when a car bomb planted by the Mafia exploded outside the gallery's west wing in May 1993. Five people died in the explosion. Documents cataloguing the collection were also destroyed. A massive clean-up enabled the gallery to reopen quickly.

Partly in response to the bombing, but even more to the gallery's immense popularity (a staggering 1.4 million visitors marched through in 2000, compared with 100,000 in 1950!), restoration and reorganisation will lead to what promoters once dubbed the 'Grandi Uffizi' and now refer to as the 'Nuovi Uffizi'. The floors below the present gallery have been largely cleared of state archives and in a project estimated to cost €57,000,000, it is hoped to have a much bigger and modernised gallery open by the end of 2004. Many works now in storage, as well as a sizeable archaeological collection and temporary exhibitions, will all be part of the new gallery. Already the occasional temporary exhibit is put on in the lower floors. Visiting is an opportunity to see just how much work is still left to be done!

The gallery as it stands now is arranged to illustrate the evolving story of Italian and, in particular, Florentine art.

It has to be said that, especially when crowded in summer, visiting the Uffizi can be a singularly unpleasant experience. The gallery tends to be hot and stuffy and the crowds render the chances of enjoying anything of what is on display a challenge, to say the least. To queue and then suffer inside seems more like a modern-day act of religious abnegation than a desirable opportunity to contemplate beautiful art. On the other hand, the queuing is in part due to an effort to limit the maximum number inside at any time to 780 people.

To avoid some of the pain, try to arrive in the morning when the gallery first opens, or during lunchtime or the late afternoon. Alternatively, book ahead (see the boxed text 'Queue Jumping' earlier in this chapter). In the high season especially, queuing can mean waits of three or more hours.

The extraordinary wealth of the collection and the sheer number of famous works means one visit is not enough – if you are going to come down with stendhalismo, it might well be here! If you are in Florence for three or four days and can afford the additional cost, try to spend at least two blocks of three or so hours in the gallery, spread over a few days.

Several guidebooks to the gallery are on sale at vendors all over the city, and outside the entrance.

Gallery Visit the restored remains of the 11th-century **Chiesa di San Piero Scheraggio** before heading upstairs to the gallery (☎ 055 238 86 51, Piazza degli Uffizi 6; admission €7.75; open 8.15am-6.50pm Tues-Sun year-round, 8.15am-10pm Sat mid-June–mid-Sept). Ticket office closes 55 mins before gallery). The church's apse was incorporated into the structure of the palace but most of the rest was destroyed. At the time of writing it was closed, but you can get a fractional idea from what remains on the exterior of the northern wall of the palace.

On the 1st floor is a small **Galleria dei Disegni e delle Stampe** (Drawing and Print Gallery), in which sketches and initial drafts by the great masters are often shown. They tend to rotate the display frequently, as prolonged exposure can damage the drawings.

Upstairs in the gallery proper, you pass through two vestibules, the first with busts of several of the Medici clan and other grand dukes, the second with some Roman statuary.

The long corridor has been arranged much as it appeared in the 16th century. Below the

frescoed ceilings is a series of small portraits of great and good men, interspersed with larger portraits, often of Medici family members or intimates. The statuary much of it collected in Rome by the Medicis' agents, is either Roman or at least thought to be. Room 1 (which used to hold archaeological treasures) is closed.

The first accessible rooms feature works by Tuscan masters of the 13th and early 14th centuries. Room 2 is dominated by three paintings of the *Madonna in Maestà* (Madonna in Majesty) by Duccio di Buoninsegna, Cimabue and Giotto. All three were altarpieces in Florentine churches before being placed in the gallery. To look at them in this order is to appreciate the transition from Gothic to the precursor of the Renaissance. In the room also is Giotto's polyptych *Madonna col Bambino Gesù, Santi e Angeli* (Madonna with Baby Jesus, Saints and Angels).

Room 3 traces the Sienese school of the 14th century. Of particular note is Simone Martini's shimmering *Annunciazione,* considered a masterpiece of the school, and Ambrogio Lorenzetti's triptych *Madonna col Bambino e Santi* (Madonna and Child with Saints). Room 4 contains works of the Florentine 14th century.

Rooms 5 and 6 house examples of the International Gothic style, among them Gentile da Fabriano's *Adorazione dei Magi* (Adoration of the Magi).

Room 7 features works by painters of the early-15th-century Florentine school, which pioneered the Renaissance. There is one panel (the other two are in the Louvre and London's National Gallery) from Paolo Uccello's striking *La Battaglia di San Romano* (Battle of San Romano). In his efforts to create perspective he directs the lances, horses and soldiers to a central disappearing point. Other works include Piero della Francesca's portraits of *Battista Sforza* and *Federico da Montefeltro,* and a *Madonna col Bambino* (Madonna with Child) painted jointly by Masaccio and Masolino. In the next room, devoted to a collection of works by Fra Filippo Lippi and Filippino Lippi, is Fra Filippo's delightful *Madonna col Bambino e due Angeli* (Madonna with Child and

FLORENCE

Two Angels). One of those angels has the cheekiest little grin. Have you ever noticed how rarely anyone seems to be smiling in the religious art of this or other periods?

Room 9 is devoted largely to Antonio de Pollaiuolo. His series of six virtues is followed by an addition, *Fortezza* (Strength), by Botticelli. The clarity of line and light, and the humanity in the face set it apart from Pollaiuolo's work and is a taster for the Botticelli Rooms, Nos 10 to 14. They are considered the gallery's most spectacular. Highlights are the *Nascita di Venere* (Birth of Venus) and *Allegoria della Primavera* (Allegory of Spring). *Calunnia* (Calumny) is a disturbing reflection of Botticelli's loss of faith in human potential that came in later life.

Room 15 features Da Vinci's *Annunciazione,* painted when he was a student of Verrocchio. Perhaps more intriguing is his unfinished *Adorazione dei Magi* (now being restored). Room 16 (blocked off, although you can peer in) contains old maps. Room 17, the Sala dell'Ermafrodito, was closed at the time of writing.

Room 18, known as the Tribuna, houses the celebrated *Medici Venus,* a 1st-century BC copy of a 4th-century BC sculpture by the Greek sculptor, Praxiteles. The room also contains portraits of various members of the Medici family.

The great Umbrian painter, Perugino, who studied under Piero della Francesca and later became Raphael's master, is represented in Room 19, as well as Luca Signorelli. Piero di Cosimo's *Perseo Libera Andromeda* (Perseus frees Andromeda) is full of fantastical whimsy with beasts and flying heroes. Room 20 features works from the German Renaissance, including Dürer's (1471–1528) *Adorazione dei Magi.* His depictions of Adam and Eve are mirrored by those of Lucas Cranach. Room 21, with a heavily Venetian leaning, has works by Giovanni Bellini and his pupil, Giorgione, along with a few by Vittorio Carpaccio.

In Room 22, given over to various German and Flemish Renaissance artists, you can see a small self-portrait by Hans Holbein. The following room takes us back to the Veneto region in Italy's north-east with paintings

mainly by Andrea Mantegna and Correggio. Peek through the railings of Room 24 to see the 15th- to 19th-century works in the Miniatures Room and then cross into the west wing, which houses works of Italian masters dating from the 16th century.

The star of Room 25 is Michelangelo's dazzling *Tondo Doni,* which depicts the Holy Family. The composition is highly unusual, with Joseph holding Jesus on Mary's shoulder as she twists around to watch him. The colours are so vibrant, the lines so clear as to seem almost photographic. This masterpiece of the High Renaissance leaps out at you as you enter, demanding attention.

In the next room are works by Raphael (1483–1520), including his *Leo X* and *Madonna del Cardellino* (actually a copy as the original is being restored). The former is remarkable for the richness of colour (especially the reds) and detail. Also on display are some works by Andrea del Sarto. Room 27 is dominated by the sometimes disquieting works of Florence's two main Mannerist masters, Pontormo and Rosso Fiorentino.

Room 28 boasts eight Titians, including *Venere d'Urbino* (Venus of Urbino). His presence signals a shift in the weighting here to representatives of the Venetian school. Rooms 29 and 30 contain works by comparatively minor painters from northern Italy, but Room 31 is dominated above all by Venice's Paolo Veronese, including his *Sacra Famiglia e Santa Barbara* (Holy Family and St Barbara). In Room 32 it is Tintoretto's turn. He is accompanied by a few Jacopo Bassano canvasses. Room 33 is named the Corridor of the 16th Century and contains a mix of lesser-known artists. A couple of pieces by Vasari appear, along with an unexpected foreign contribution, El Greco's *I Santi San Giovanni Evangelista e San Francesco.* The following room is filled mainly with 16th-century works by Lombard painters, although somehow the Venetian Lorenzo Lotto managed to sneak in with three paintings.

Next door comes as a bit of a shock as you are confronted with the enormous, sumptuous canvases of Federico Barocci (1535–1612) of Urbino. Rooms 36 to 37 are part of the exit while the adjoining Room 38 at the moment houses the extraordinary restored *Annunciazione* by Siena's Simone Martini and Lippo Memmi.

For some reason the counting starts at No 41 after this. This room is given over mostly to non-Italian masters such as Flemish painters Rubens and Van Dyck, and Spain's Diego Velázquez. By the former are the two enormous tableaux, sweeping with violence and power, representing the French king Henri IV at the Battle of Ivry and his triumphal march into Paris. The beautifully designed Room 42 (closed at the time of writing), with its exquisite coffered ceiling and splendid dome, is filled with Roman statues.

Caravaggio dominates Room 43 with his play of light and shade (look for *Il Sacrificio d'Isacco*; The Sacrifice of Isaac), while Rembrandt features in Room 44. Room 45 takes us back to Venice, with 18th-century works by Canaletto, Guardi, Tiepolo, the two Longhi and Crespi, along with a couple of stray pieces by the Spaniard Goya.

Between rooms 25 and 34 is an entrance (not usually open to the public) leading down a staircase into the Corridoio Vasariano.

Corridoio Vasariano When Cosimo I de' Medici's wife bought the Palazzo Pitti and the family moved into their new digs, they wanted to maintain their link – literally – with what from then on would be known as the Palazzo Vecchio. And so Cosimo commissioned Vasari to build this enclosed walkway between the two palaces that would allow the Medicis to wander between the two without having to deal with the public.

The corridor, lined with phalanxes of largely minor art works, has changed considerably over the years. Its present aspect dates to 1923, but it is possible that many of the paintings hung here will be moved to the Nuovi Uffizi (see earlier) in the coming years.

Be that as it may, the corridor was opened to the public in a rather limited fashion in 1999. Let's say right away that, given the difficulty and cost of getting in here, many visitors are likely to be disappointed. To appreciate it at all you will want to have a genuine interest in Florentine history and/or a hunger for relatively obscure art. Your average three-day visitor who has done little or no reading on Florence will *not* be interested in this.

In 2001 the opening times were completely unpredictable. Visits are by guided tour (generally in Italian), which lasts a long 2½ hours. Tours tend to take place two or three times on those days when the corridor is open. A maximum of 35 people go through in any one visit, starting in the Corte Dogana in the Palazzo Vecchio and emerging in the Boboli Gardens at Palazzo Pitti. You need to book ahead for this by calling ☎ 055 265 43 21, 8.30am to 1.30pm Monday to Saturday. You pick up your tickets (which cost a whopping €25.80) at the prebooked ticket desk in the Uffizi.

What you can expect is the following. The first part of the tour takes you first to the Salone dei Cinquecento in the Palazzo Vecchio (see earlier in the chapter). From here the tour follows a route upstairs via the Quartiere di Leone X and into the Quartiere di Eleonora. With much unbolting of doors and ceremony you are then ushered in through the first part of the corridor (which houses offices) across to the Uffizi, where you emerge at the beginning of the gallery. Here the tour continues, stopping at certain points of the Uffizi (but without scope for looking at the art) until another door is unlocked to allow you into the main stretch of the corridor. This first part of the tour takes an hour, and for those who have already visited the Palazzo Vecchio and the Uffizi and done some research, you can get the feeling that you'll never get down to business.

What of the corridor? You descend a staircase and follow the corridor's twists and turns along the Arno, over the Ponte Vecchio, around the Torre dei Mannelli (whose owners refused to allow Cosimo I to bulldoze through the medieval tower house), across the road and past the Chiesa di Santa Felicita (where an enclosed balcony allowed the Medici to hear Mass without being seen) and on into the Palazzo Pitti, where you emerge by the Grotta del Buontalenti in the

Giardino di Boboli (which your ticket also allows you to visit). Along the way you can peer out for unusual views of Florence and various paintings are explained. A long corridor of self-portraits of artists starts with one of Leonardo (at least it is believed to be genuine) through to one by Chagall. But for most of us the paintings are a little yawn-inducing.

In September 2001, the corridor also opened on Wednesday and Friday (3pm) for unguided (but accompanied) visits. For this you bought special tickets for the Uffizi that included the corridor (€9.30). At the appointed time, those with tickets (advisable to book well ahead as only limited numbers may enter) were ushered through the door in the Uffizi and downstairs into the corridor, where a custodian would keep an eye on visitors as they wandered around before returning to the Uffizi. This way of doing things has the advantage of being cheaper and mercifully shorter!

Museo di Storia delle Scienze Telescopes that look more like works of art, the most extraordinarily complex-looking instruments for the measurement of distance, time and space, and a room full of wax and plastic cutaway models of the various stages of childbirth are among the highlights in this odd collection in the **Museum of the History of Science** *(☎ 055 239 88 76, Piazza dei Giudici 1; admission €6.20; open 9.30am-5pm Mon & Wed-Fri, 9.30am-1pm Tues & Sat June-Sept, 9.30am-5pm, Mon-Sat (to 1pm Tues, 10am-1pm second Sun of every month Oct-May).*

Given the admission price, you may want to think twice about it. If you have a genuine interest in the history of science, then you will almost certainly find at least some of the exhibits intriguing.

Santa Maria Novella & Around
Basilica di Santa Maria Novella (Map 7)
Just south of Stazione di Santa Maria Novella, this **church** *(☎ 055 21 59 18, Piazza di Santa Maria Novella; admission €2.60; open 9am-5pm Mon-Thur & Sat, 1pm-5pm Fri, Sun & holidays)* was begun in the late

13th century as the Florentine base for the Dominican order. Although mostly completed by around 1360, work on its facade and the embellishment of its interior continued well into the 15th century.

The lower section of the green and white marble facade is transitional from Romanesque to Gothic, while the upper section and the main doorway were designed by Alberti and completed in around 1470. The highlight of the Gothic interior is Masaccio's superb (and recently restored) fresco of the *Trinità* (Trinity; 1428), one of the first artworks to use the then newly discovered techniques of perspective and proportion. It is about halfway along the north aisle.

The first chapel to the right of the choir, the Cappella di Filippo Strozzi, features lively frescoes by Filippino Lippi depicting the lives of St John the Evangelist and St Philip the Apostle. Another important work is Domenico Ghirlandaio's series of frescoes behind the main altar, painted with the help of artists who may have included the young student Michelangelo. Relating the lives of the Virgin Mary, St John the Baptist and others, the frescoes are notable for their depiction of Florentine life during the Renaissance. Brunelleschi's crucifix hangs above the altar in the **Cappella Gondi**, the first chapel on the left of the choir.

To reach the **Chiostro Verde** (Green Cloister), exit the church and follow the signs to the Museo. The portico's arches are propped up by massive octagonal pillars. Three of the four walls are decorated with fading frescoes recounting Genesis. The cloister actually takes its name from the green earth base used for the frescoes. The most interesting artistically, by Paolo Uccello, are those on the party wall with the church. Outstanding is *Il Diluvio Universale* (Great Flood).

Off the next side of the cloister is the **Cappellone degli Spagnoli** (Spanish Chapel; Map 3), which was set aside for the Spanish retinue that accompanied Eleonora de Toledo, Cosimo I's wife, to Florence. It contains some well-preserved frescoes by Andrea di Bonaiuto and his helpers.

On the western side of the cloister is the **museum** *(☎ 055 28 21 87; admission €2.60;*

open 9am-2pm Sat-Thur) itself, which in two rooms that used to be the convent's foyer and refectory contains vestments, relics and some art belonging to the Dominicans.

Chiesa d'Ognissanti (Map 5) This 13th-century **church** *(open 5pm-7.30pm Mon-Tues & Sat only)* was much altered in the 17th century and has a baroque facade, but inside are 15th-century works by Domenico Ghirlandaio and Botticelli. Of interest is Ghirlandaio's fresco above the second altar on the right of the *Madonna della Misericordia,* protector of the Vespucci family. Amerigo Vespucci, who gave his name to the American continent, is supposedly the young boy whose head appears between the Madonna and the old man.

Ghirlandaio's masterpiece, the *Ultima Cena* (Last Supper), covers most of a wall in the former monastery's *cenacolo* or refectory *(closed at the time of writing).*

Cascine (Map 2) Before we turn our steps back to the centre of Florence, you might want to bear in mind that about 10 minutes' walk to the west along Borgo Ognissanti brings you to the **Porta al Prato**, part of the walls that were knocked down in the late 19th century to make way for the ring of boulevards that still surrounds the city.

A short walk south from here towards the Arno brings you to the eastern tip of Florence's great green lung, the Cascine. The Medici dukes made this a private hunting reserve, but Pietro Leopoldo opened it to the public in 1776, with boulevards, fountains and bird sanctuaries (Le Pavoniere, now a swimming pool). In the late 19th century horse racing began here (a British import it seems, since the locals referred to the sport as *le corse inglesi* – the English races). Queen Victoria was a fan of Florence and toddled along to the Cascine during her stays. Nowadays a big market (Mercato delle Cascine) is held in the park on Tuesday mornings.

Palazzo Rucellai (Map 7) Designed by Alberti, the Palazzo Rucellai *(Via della Vigna Nuova; closed at the time of writing)* houses a photographic museum dedicated to

the vast collection compiled by the Alinari brothers. The facade is curious for a few reasons, not least for the seating originally intended for employees of the Rucellai family but now quite handy for anyone passing by. Across the small triangular square is the family loggia, also designed by Alberti and now used for occasional exhibits. Any family worth its salt aimed to have a loggia in addition to the family residence.

Chiesa di San Pancrazio & Museo Marino Marini (Map 7) As early as the 9th century a church stood here. The shabby-looking version you see today is what remains of the building from the 14th and 15th centuries. The church was deconsecrated in the 19th century and now houses the **museum** *(☎ 055 21 94 32, Piazza San Pancrazio; admission €4.15; open 10am-5pm Wed-Mon, to 11pm Thur May-Sept, 10am-1pm Sun & holidays, closed Aug)* donated to the city of Florence by the Pistoia-born sculptor Marino Marini (1901–80). The cost of admission is rather a lot unless you are particularly taken with this guy.

Among the 200 works the artist left behind are sculptures, portraits and drawings. The overwhelmingly recurring theme is man and horse, or rather man on horse. The figures are, in some cases, simple-looking chaps in various poses suggesting rapture or extreme frustration; the horses too seem to express a gamut of emotion. On the other extreme, man and horse seem barely distinguishable from one another.

Via de' Tornabuoni & Around (Map 7) If from Palazzo Rucellai you skittle on down Via del Purgatorio and make a right down the narrow Via Parioncino you reach Lungarno Corsini on the Arno.

For the best view of the Arno-side of the **Palazzo Corsini**, head across the bridge. This grandiose late-Baroque edifice will probably seem a little curious – the u-shaped courtyard isn't in the middle. It would have been had the project been completed. The wing nearest Ponte alla Carraia was originally supposed to mirror the right wing. The building had belonged to the Medici family but they sold it

FLORENCE

in 1640, and from then until 1735 work on the exterior (the mighty facade on Via del Parione is a worthy counterpoint to the Arno frontage) dragged on at a snail's pace. By the time it was completed, the Corsini family was in the ascendant, with Lorenzo Corsini in the driving seat in Rome as Pope Clement XII. The most interesting feature inside the building is the spiral staircase known as the *lumaca* (literally the 'slug'). You can take a look at it by entering the building at Via del Parione 11b (you'll see an Internet point here): turn left and there it is.

Head east for the **Ponte Santa Trinita**, a harmonious and charming river crossing. Cosimo I de' Medici put Vasari in charge of the project and he in turn asked Michelangelo for advice. In the end, the job was handed over to Ammannati, who finished it in 1567. The statues of the seasons are by Pietro Francavilla.

Turning inland, you next arrive at the 13th-century **Chiesa della Santa Trinita** *(Piazza Santa Trinita)*. Although rebuilt in the Gothic style and later graced with a Mannerist facade of indifferent taste, you can still get some idea of what the Romanesque original looked like by looking at the facade wall from the *inside*. Among its more eye-catching art are frescoes depicting the life of St Francis of Assisi by Domenico Ghirlandaio in the Cappella Sassetti (in the right transept).

Across from it is the forbidding **Palazzo Spini-Ferroni** *(Via de' Tornabuoni)*, built in the 14th century with Guelph battlements and now owned by the Ferragamo shoe empire. On the second floor of the building is the **Museo Salvatore Ferragamo** *(Via de' Tornabuoni 2; free; open 9am-1pm & 2pm-6pm Mon-Fri)*. They advise booking by phone at least 10 days ahead, but if you wander in and climb the red-carpeted stairs two floors you may well find you can get in. On display is a wide variety of some of Ferragamo's classic shoes, many worn by princesses and movie stars. The wooden model 'feet' (upon which tailor-made shoes were crafted) of everyone from Katherine Hepburn to Madonna are there to be seen.

The city's most chi-chi street, Via de' Tornabuoni itself, often referred to as the

'Salotto di Firenze' (Florence's Drawing Room), actually follows the original course of the Mugnone tributary into the Arno.

Piazza Santa Trinita is also faced by the **Palazzo Buondelmonti**. The family of the same name was at the heart of the Guelph-Ghibelline feud in Florence. More imposing is the **Palazzo Bartolini-Salimbeni**, an example of High Renaissance with a Roman touch (columns flanking the main door and triangular tympana).

By far the most impressive of the Renaissance mansions is the earthy-coloured **Palazzo Strozzi**, a great colossus of rusticated *pietra forte* (literally 'hard stone') raised by one of the most powerful of the Medici's rival families. It now houses offices and is occasionally used for art exhibitions.

Two blocks north stands the clearly Baroque facade in pietra forte of the **Chiesa di San Gaetano**. The church had been around since the 11th century, but from 1604 it was rebuilt. The facade only went up in 1683. Opposite and a few strides north, the **Palazzo Antinori** was built in the 15th century by Giuliano da Maiano.

San Lorenzo Area
Basilica di San Lorenzo (Map 7) The Medici family commissioned Brunelleschi to rebuild this **church** *(Piazza San Lorenzo; admission €2.60; open 10am-5pm Mon-Sat)* in 1420, on the site of a 4th-century basilica. It is considered one of the most harmonious examples of Renaissance architecture. Michelangelo prepared a design for the facade that was never executed, which is why this, like so many other Florentine churches, appears unfinished from the outside.

It was the Medici parish church; many family members are buried here. It's a masterstroke of Brunelleschi's style. The nave is separated from the two aisles by columns in *pietra serena* (literally 'tranquil stone') and crowned with Corinthian capitals.

Rosso Fiorentino's *Sposalizio della Vergine* (Marriage of the Virgin Mary; 1523) dominates the second chapel on the right aisle after you enter. As you approach the transept, you will see two pulpits or *pergami* (they look like treasure chests on Ionic columns) in dark bronze – or at least what appears to be dark bronze. Some of the panels on each have been attributed to Donatello. Others, added later, are supposedly made of wood (money was obviously running short) made to seem like bronze.

You enter the **Sagrestia Vecchia** (Old Sacristy) to the left of the altar. It was designed by Brunelleschi and mostly decorated by Donatello.

From another entrance off Piazza San Lorenzo you can also enter the peaceful cloisters, off the first of which a staircase leads up to the **Biblioteca Laurenziana Me-dicea** *(admission €2.60; open 8.30am-1.30pm Mon-Sat)*. It was commissioned by Cosimo de' Medici to house the Medici library and contains 10,000 volumes. The real attraction is Michelangelo's magnificent vestibule and staircase. They are executed in grey pietra serena and the curvaceous steps are a sign of the master's move towards Mannerism from the stricter bounds of Renaissance architecture and design.

Cappelle Medicee A separate entrance takes you to the **Medicean Chapels** *(☎ 055 238 86 02, Piazza Madonna degli Aldobrandini; admission €5.70; open 8.15am-5pm Tues-Sun, 8.30am-1.50pm holidays)*. After buying your ticket you first enter a crypt. The stairs from this take you up to the **Cappella dei Principi** (Princes' Chapel), which comes as something similar to a blow over the head with a mallet.

Conceived not as a place of religious reflection, the so-called chapel is rather the triumphalist mausoleum of some (but by no means all) of the Medici rulers.

It is sumptuously decorated top to bottom with various kinds of marble, granite and other stone. Breaking up the colossal splendour of the stone are the decorative tableaux made from painstakingly chosen and cut semi-precious stones, or *pietre dure*. It was for the purpose of decorating the chapel that Ferdinando I ordered the creation of the Opificio delle Pietre Dure, an artists' workshop, which still exists today.

Statues of the grand men were supposed to be placed in the still empty niches, but no one quite got around to finishing the project.

Only the bronze of Ferdinando I and partly gilt bronze of Cosimo II were done.

A corridor leads from the Cappella dei Principi to the **Sagrestia Nuova** (New Sacristy), so called to distinguish it from the Sagrestia Vecchia. It was the Medicis' funeral chapel.

It was here that Michelangelo came nearest to finishing an architectural commission. His haunting sculptures, *Notte e Giorno* (Night and Day), *Aurora e Crepusculo* (Dawn and Dusk) and the *Madonna col Bambino* adorn Medici tombs (1520–34), including that of Lorenzo il Magnifico.

Palazzo Medici-Riccardi (Map 7) When Cosimo de' Medici felt fairly sure of his position in Florence, he decided it was time to move house. He entrusted Michelozzo with the design in 1444. The result is this **palace** *(☎ 055 276 03 40, Via Cavour 3; admission €4.15; open 9am-7pm Thur-Tues)*.

What Michelozzo came up with was ground-breaking and would continue to influence the construction of family residences in Florence for years to come. The fortress town houses with their towers that characterised Gothic Florence were no longer necessary. Cosimo's power was more or less undisputed. Instead Michelozzo created a self-assured, stout but not inelegant pile on three storeys.

The ground floor is characterised by the bulbous, rough surface (known as rustication) in pietra forte. The upper two storeys are less aggressive, maintaining restrained classical lines – already a feature of the emerging Renaissance canon – and topped with a heavy timber roof whose eaves protrude well out over the street below.

The Medicis stayed here until 1540 and the building was finally acquired and somewhat remodelled by the Riccardi family in the 17th century.

You can wander inside to the courtyard and up to some of the rooms upstairs, although much of the building is now given over to public administration offices. The main hall you will want to inspect is the **Galleria** on the 1st floor. It is a rather sumptuous example of late-Baroque designed for the Riccardi family. The room glistens with gold leaf and bursts with curvaceous figures looming out at you, especially from the ceiling frescoes by Luca Giordano. The room is now usually named the **Sala Luca Giordano** after him.

The highlight, however, is the **Cappella dei Magi**, a chapel with striking frescoes (1459) by Benozzo Gozzoli. Buy a ticket first from the office off the second internal courtyard. Staff rotate 15 people through the chapel every 15 minutes as it is rather squeezy inside. Make an effort to see this jewel.

Mercato Centrale (Map 3) Built in 1874, the city's central produce market seems to disappear amid the confusion of makeshift stands of the clothes and leather market that fill the surrounding square and streets during the day. The iron and glass architecture was something of a novelty in Florence when the market was first built.

San Marco Area
Galleria dell'Accademia (Map 3) For many visitors to Florence, this **gallery** *(☎ 055 238 86 09, Via Ricasoli 60; admission €7.75; open 8.15am-6.50pm Tues-Sun (8.15am-10pm Sat mid-June–mid-Sept)* is pretty much unavoidable, if only because it contains the original of one of the greatest (and most trumpeted) masterpieces of the Renaissance, Michelangelo's giant statue of *David*.

After collecting your ticket you enter the grand **Sala del Colosso**, dominated by a plaster model of Giambologna's *Ratto delle Sabine* (Rape of a Sabine) and lined by several interesting paintings. The latter include a fresco of the *Pietà* by Andrea del Sarto, a couple of pieces by Fra Bartolommeo and a *Deposizione* started by Filippino Lippi and finished by Perugino.

Immediately to the left off this first room a doorway leads into a long hall, at the end of which you can make out the *David*. Try to contain the urge to hurtle off in the giant-slayer's general direction and have a look at Michelangelo's four *Prigioni* ('prisoners' or 'slaves') and statue of *San Matteo* (St Matthew) between the two Prigioni on the right. The latter was sculpted about 1506, and

the four others in 1530. All five have in common the feature of not being completed. The experts will tell you completion is in the eye of the beholder. In the case of Michelangelo in particular, it is said he left many works 'unfinished' deliberately. The statues show us a little of how the artist went about extracting such beauty from lumps of marble.

Now, his *David* (1502–04) is finished. Carved from one block of marble and weighing in at 19 tonnes, it's an exquisite, powerful figure that beggars description. While the statue still stood in Piazza della Signoria, the left arm actually fell off and killed a peasant.

In the surrounding rooms there is a mixed collection of paintings and sculpture, including a triptych by Orcagna.

Upstairs is a further collection of 13th- and 14th-century art and Russian icons.

Museo di San Marco (Map 3) Housed in the now deconsecrated Dominican convent and the Chiesa di San Marco is the **museum** *(☎ 055 238 86 08, Piazza San Marco 1; admission €4.15; open 8.30am-1.50pm Tues-Fri, 8.30am-6.50pm Sat, 8.30am-1.50pm every second Mon, 8.30am-6.50pm every second Sun)*. Back in 1481 a rather intense little Dominican friar, Girolamo Savonarola, turned up here as lector and later ended up the de facto head of a short-lived theocracy in Florence before ending up on an Inquisitorial bonfire.

The piazza is the centre of the university area. The church was founded in 1299, rebuilt by Michelozzo in 1437, and again remodelled by Giambologna some years later. It features several paintings, but they pale in comparison with the treasures contained in the adjoining convent.

Famous Florentines who called the convent home include the painters Fra (or Beato) Angelico (c.1400–55) and Fra Bartolommeo (1472–1517). It now serves as a museum of Fra Angelico's works, many of which were moved there in the 1860s, and should be up there on every art lover's top-priority hitlist.

You find yourself in the **Chiostro di Sant' Antonio**, designed by Michelozzo in 1440, when you first enter the museum. Turn immediately to the right and enter the **Sala** dell'Ospizio. Paintings by Fra Angelico that once hung in the Galleria dell'Accademia and the Uffizi have been brought together here. Among the better-known works are the *Deposizione di Cristo* and the *Pala di San Marco,* an altarpiece for the church paid for by the Medici family. It did not fare well as a result of 19th-century restoration.

The eastern wing of the cloister, formerly the monks' rectory, contains works by various artists from the 14th to the 17th centuries. Paintings by Fra Bartolommeo are on display in a small annex off the refectory rooms. Among them is a celebrated portrait of Savonarola.

You reach the upper floor by passing through the bookshop. This is the real treat. Fra Angelico was invited to decorate the monks' cells with devotional frescoes aimed as a guide to the friars' meditation. Some were done by Fra Angelico, others by aides under his supervision. You can peer into them today and wonder what sort of thoughts would swim through the minds of the monks as they prayed before these images.

The true masterpieces up here are, however, on the walls in the corridors. Already at the top of the stairs you climbed to the 1st floor is Fra Angelico's *Annunciazione,* faced on the opposite wall with a *Crocifisso* featuring San Domenico (St Dominic). One of his most famous works is the *Madonna delle Ombre* (Madonna of the Shadows), to the right of cell No 25.

Piazza della Santissima (SS) Annunziata (Map 4)

Giambologna's equestrian statue of the Grand Duke Ferdinando I de' Medici commands the scene from the centre of this square. Some observers find it the city's loveliest square. Certainly part of Florence's junkie community seem to like it in the evening.

Chiesa di SS Annunziata The church *(Piazza della SS Annunziata; free; open 7.30am-12.30pm & 4pm-6.30pm)* that gives the square its name was established in 1250 by the founders of the Servite order and rebuilt by Michelozzo and others in the mid-15th century. It is dedicated to the Virgin Mary and

in the ornate tabernacle, to your left as you enter the church from the atrium, is a so-called miraculous painting of the Virgin.

The painting, no longer on public view, is attributed to a 14th-century friar, and legend says an angel completed it. Also of note are frescoes by Andrea del Castagno in the first two chapels on the left of the church, a fresco by Perugino in the fifth chapel and the frescoes in Michelozzo's atrium, particularly the *Nascita della Vergine* (Birth of the Virgin), by Andrea del Sarto, and the *Visitazione,* by Jacopo Pontormo.

Spedale degli Innocenti This 'hospital of the innocents' was founded on the southeastern side of the piazza in 1421 as Europe's first orphanage.

Brunelleschi designed the portico, which Andrea della Robbia then decorated with terracotta medallions of a baby in swaddling clothes. Under the portico to the left of the entrance is the small revolving door where unwanted children were left. A good number of people in Florence with surnames such as degli Innocenti, Innocenti and Nocentini, can trace their family tree only as far back as the orphanage. Orphans were no novelty but the growing number of foundlings made a more systematic approach to the problem necessary. Undoubtedly life inside was no picnic, but the Spedale's avowed aim was to care for and educate its wards until they turned 18.

A small **gallery** *(☎ 055 249 17 08, Piazza della SS Annunziata 12; admission €2.60; open 8.30am-2pm Thur-Tues)* on the 2nd floor features works by Florentine artists. If you are already overdosing on the seemingly endless diet of art in Florence, you could skip this stop. Those truly interested will find it worthwhile. The most striking piece is Domenico Ghirlandaio's *Adorazione dei Magi* (1488) at the right end of the hall.

Museo Archeologico (Map 4) About 200m south-east of the piazza is the Museo Archeologico *(☎ 055 2 35 75, Via Colonna 38; admission €4.15; open 2pm-7pm Mon, 8.30am-7pm Tues & Thur, 8.30am-2pm Wed, Fri-Sun)*, considered one of Italy's best. A great deal of the Medici family's horde of antiquities ended up here. Further collections have been added in the centuries since.

For those interested in antiquity, this museum offers a surprisingly rich collection of finds. Many items were damaged in the floods of 1966 and even today parts of the museum are still being worked on. But it's well worth the effort.

On the 1st floor you can either head left into the ancient Egyptian collection, or right into the section on Etruscan and Greco-Roman art.

The former is an impressive collection of tablets inscribed with hieroglyphics, statues and other sculpture, various coffins and a remarkable array of everyday objects – it is extraordinary to ponder on how sandals, baskets and all sorts of other odds and ends have survived to this day.

In the Etruscan section you pass first through two rooms dominated by funeral urns. Particularly noteworthy is the marble *Sarcofago delle Amazzoni* (Amazons' Sarcophagus) from Tarquinia and the alabaster *Sarcofago dell'Obeso* (Sarcophagus of the Fat Man) from Chiusi.

From the funerary urns you pass into a hall dedicated to bronze sculptures, ranging from miniatures depicting mythical beasts through to the life-size *Arringatore* (Orator). Dating from the 1st century BC, the figure, draped in clearly Roman garb, illustrates the extent to which Rome had come to dominate the Etruscans at this point. By the time the statue was made, Etruria had been under the Roman thumb for a good 200 years. Other outstanding works include the statue of *Minerva* from Arezzo, a Roman copy of a Greek original, and the *Chimera,* a beast of classical mythology.

From this display you enter an enclosed corridor lined on one side by ancient rings, pendants and amulets, many made of chalcedony (a type of quartz). When you reach the end you swing left and walk back along another corridor with windows overlooking the museum's gardens. Here you can admire a selection of the museum's treasure of ancient gold jewellery.

The museum's 2nd floor is taken up with an extensive collection of Greek pottery from various epoques. Again it is surprising for its sheer extent.

Santa Croce Area

Piazza di Santa Croce (Map 6) The Franciscan Basilica di Santa Croce stands haughty watch over the piazza of the same name. The square was initially cleared in the Middle Ages primarily to allow hordes of the faithful to gather when the church itself was full (Mass must have been quite an event in those days). On a more sober religious note, the piazza was used in Savonarola's day for the execution of heretics.

Such an open space inevitably found other uses and from the 14th century on it was often the colourful scene of jousts, festivals and *calcio storico* matches. The latter was like a combination of football (soccer) and rugby with no rules. They still play it today (see Special Events in the Facts for the Visitor chapter). Below the gaily frescoed facade of the **Palazzo dell'Antella**, on the south side of the piazza, is a marble stone embedded in the wall – it marks the halfway line on this, one of the oldest football pitches in the world. Today the square is lined with the inevitable souvenir shops.

Curiously enough, the Romans used to have fun in much the same area centuries before. The city's 2nd-century amphitheatre took up the area facing the western end of Piazza di Santa Croce. To this day, Piazza de' Peruzzi, Via Bentaccordi and Via Torta mark the oval outline of the north, west and south sides of the theatre.

Basilica di Santa Croce (Map 6) Attributed to Arnolfo di Cambio, Santa Croce *(free; open 9.30am-5.30pm Mon-Sat, 3pm-5.30pm Sun Mar-Oct, 9.30am-12.30pm & 3pm-5.30pm Mon-Sat, 3pm-5.30pm Sun Nov-Apr)* was started in 1294 on the site of a Franciscan chapel but not completed until 1385. The name stems from a splinter of the Holy Cross donated to the Franciscans by King Louis of France in 1258. Today the church is known as much for the celebrities buried here as its captivating artistic treasures.

The magnificent facade is actually a 19th-century neo-Gothic addition, as indeed is the bell tower. Rather austere compared with the contemporary job done on the Duomo, the main source of jollity is the variety of colour in the different types of marble used. The statue in front of the left end of the facade is of Dante.

The church's massive interior is divided into a nave and two aisles by solid octagonal pillars. The ceiling is a fine example of the timber A-frame style used occasionally in Italy's Gothic churches.

Heading down the right aisle you see first, between the first and second altar, Michelangelo's tomb, designed by Vasari (1570). The three muses below it represent his three principal gifts – sculpting, painting and architecture. Next up is a cenotaph to the memory of Dante, followed by a tomb sculpted by Antonio Canova in 1810. After the fourth altar is Machiavelli's tomb.

Beyond the next altar is an extraordinary piece of sculpture of the *Annunciazione* (1430–35) by Donatello. You won't see many other sculptures in grey pietra serena, brightened here by some gilding. Between the sixth and seventh altars you can peer out the doorway into the cloister and get a look at Brunelleschi's Cappella de' Pazzi (see later in this chapter).

Dogleg round to the right as you approach the transept and you find yourself before the delightful frescoes by Agnolo Gaddi in the **Cappella Castellani** (1385). By the way, the church is covered in more than 2500 square metres of frescoes. Taddeo Gaddi did the frescoes, depicting the life of the Virgin, and the stained-glass window in the adjacent **Cappella Baroncelli** (1332–38). Next a doorway designed by Michelozzo leads into a corridor off which is the **Sagrestia**, an enchanting 14th-century room dominated on the right by Taddeo Gaddi's fresco of the *Crocifissione*.

Through the next room, which now serves as a bookshop, you can get to the **Scuola del Cuoio**, a leather school where you can see things being made and also buy finished goods. At the end of the Michelozzo corridor is a Medici chapel, which features a large altarpiece by Andrea della Robbia.

Back in the church, the transept is lined by five minor chapels on either side of the **Cappella Maggiore**. The two chapels nearest the right side of the Cappella Maggiore are decorated by partly fragmented frescoes by Giotto. In the ninth chapel along, you can see a glazed terracotta altarpiece by Giovanni della Robbia, while the final chapel (Bardi di Vernio; c.1340) is frescoed by Maso di Banco. These frescoes depict scenes from the life of St Sylvester, among them the *Miracolo del Santo che Chiude le Fauci del Drago e Risuscita due Maghi Uccisi Dall'Alito del Mostro* (Miracle of the Saint who Shuts the Dragon's Jaws and Brings Back to Life the Magi Killed by the Monster's Breath – how's that for a title), and burst with life.

From the entrance, the first tomb in the left aisle is Galileo Galilei's. You will also have noticed by now that the floor is paved with the tombstones of famous Florentines of the past 500 years. Monuments to the particularly notable were added along the walls from the mid-16th century.

Cloisters & Cappella de' Pazzi Brunelleschi designed the serene **cloisters** just before his death in 1446. Brunelleschi's **Cappella de' Pazzi**, at the end of the first cloister, is a masterpiece of Renaissance architecture. The **Museo dell'Opera di Santa Croce** (☎ 055 24 46 19, Piazza di Santa Croce 16; admission €4.15; open 10am-7pm Thur-Tues Mar-Oct, 10am-6pm Thur-Tues Nov-Apr), off the first cloister, features a partially restored crucifix by Cimabue, which was badly damaged during the disastrous 1966 flood, when the Santa Croce area was inundated. Donatello's gilded bronze statue of *San Ludovico di Tolosa* (St Ludovic of Toulouse; 1413) was originally placed in a tabernacle on the Orsanmichele facade.

Museo Horne (Map 5) Herbert Percy Horne was one of those eccentric Brits abroad with cash. He bought this building in the early 1900s and installed his eclectic collection of 14th- and 15th-century Italian paintings, sculptures, ceramics, coins and other odds and sods, creating this **museum** (☎ 055 24 46 61, Via de' Benci 6; admission

€5.15; open 9am-1pm Mon-Sat). Horne renovated the house in an effort to recreate a Renaissance ambience. Although the occasional big name pops up among the artworks, such as Giotto, Luca Signorelli and Giambologna, most of the stuff is minor. Perhaps more interesting than many of the paintings is the furniture, some of which is exquisite. On the top floor is the original kitchen; kitchens tended to be on the top floor to reduce the risk of fire.

Ponte alle Grazie (Map 5) In 1237, Messer Rubaconte da Mandella, a Milanese then serving as a *podestà* (external martial in Florence), had this bridge built – or so Giovanni Villani tells us (c.1276–1348; author of the *Florentine Chronicle*, a 12-volume history of the city). It was swept away in 1333 and on its replacement were raised chapels, one of them dubbed Madonna alle Grazie, from which the bridge then took its name. The Germans blew up the bridge in 1944, and the present version went up in 1957.

Teatro Verdi (Map 6) Rather than cross the bridge at this point, we will head back north along Via de' Benci (which becomes Via Giuseppe Verdi after Piazza Santa Croce). At the intersection with Via Ghibellina stands this 19th-century theatre on the site of the 14th-century prison, Le Stinche, which had also been used as a horse-riding school. The theatre was built in 1838. We now head east along Via Ghibellina.

Casa Buonarotti (Map 6) Three blocks from the Teatro Verdi at No 70 is the Casa Buonarroti *(Via Ghibellina 70; admission €6.20; open 9.30am-1.30pm Wed-Mon)*, which Michelangelo owned but never inhabited. Upon his death, the house went to his nephew and eventually became a museum in the mid-1850s.

Although not uninteresting, the collections are a little disappointing given what you pay to get in. On the ground floor is a series of rooms on the left used for temporary exhibitions, usually held annually from May to September. To the right of the ticket window is a small archaeological display. The Buonarroti family collected about 150 pieces over the

years, many of which were for a long time in the Museo Archeologico (see San Marco Area earlier in the chapter). The last of them were returned to this house in 1996.

Beyond this room are some paintings done in imitation of Michelangelo's style, along with some fine glazed terracotta pieces by the della Robbia family.

Upstairs you can admire a detailed model of Michelangelo's design for the facade of the Basilica di San Lorenzo – as close as the church came to getting one. By Michelangelo also are a couple of marble bas-reliefs and a crucifix. Of the reliefs, *Madonna della Scala* (Madonna of the Steps) is thought to be his earliest work.

Otherwise, a series of rooms designed by Michelangelo Il Giovane, the genius' grandnephew, are intriguing. The first is full of paintings and frescoes that together amount to a kind of apotheosis of the great man. Portraits of Michelangelo meeting VIPs of his time predominate.

Piazza Sant'Ambrogio & Around (Maps 4 & 6) From the Casa Buonarroti, turn northwards up Via Michelangelo Buonarroti and proceed to **Piazza dei Ciompi**. The piazza was cleared in the 1930s and named after the textile workers who used to meet in secret in the Santa Croce area and whose 14th-century revolt, which had seemed so full of promise, came to nothing. Nowadays it is the scene of a busy flea market.

The **Loggia del Pesce** *(Fish Market; Via Pietrapana)* was designed by Vasari, on the orders of Cosimo I de' Medici, for the Mercato Vecchio (Old Market), which was at the heart of what is now Piazza della Repubblica. The loggia was moved to the Convento di San Marco when the Mercato Vecchio and the surrounding area were wiped out towards the end of the 19th century to make way for Piazza della Repubblica. Then in 1955 it was set up here.

A block east, the plain **Chiesa di Sant' Ambrogio** *(Via Pietrapiana)* presents an inconspicuous 18th-century facade on the square of the same name. The first church here was raised in the 10th century, but what you see inside is a mix of 13th-century Gothic and 15th-century refurbishment. The name comes from Sant'Ambrogio (St Ambrose), the powerful 4th-century archbishop of Milan who stayed in an earlier convent on this site when he visited Florence. The church is something of an artists' graveyard too. Among those who rest in peace here are Mino da Fiesole, Il Verrocchio and Il Cronaca.

Nearby is the local produce market, the **Mercato Sant'Ambrogio** *(Piazza Ghiberti)*.

A quick nip up Via de' Pilastri off Piazza Sant'Ambrogio and right up Via Luigi Carlo Farini brings us to the late-19th-century synagogue, the **Sinagoga** *(☎ 055 234 66 54, Via Farini 4; admission to synagogue & museum €3.10; open 10am-5pm Sun-Thur, 10am-1pm Fri Apr-Sept, 10am-1pm & 2pm-4pm Sun-Thur, 10am-1pm Fri Oct-Apr)*. It is a fanciful structure with playful Moorish and even Byzantine elements. In the **Museo Ebraico** you can see Jewish ceremonial objects and some old codices.

Oltrarno

Ponte Vecchio (Map 7) The first documentation of a stone bridge here, at the narrowest crossing point along the entire length of the Arno, dates to 972. The Arno looks placid enough, but when it gets mean, it gets very mean. Floods in 1177 and 1333 destroyed the bridge, and in 1966 it came close again. Many of the jewellers with shops on the bridge were convinced the floodwaters would sweep away their livelihoods but this time the bridge held.

The jewellers are still here. Their trade has been passed down from generation to generation since Grand Duke Ferdinando I de' Medici ordered them here in the 16th century to replace the rather malodorous presence of the town butchers. The latter tended to jettison unwanted leftovers into the river.

The bridge as it stands was built in 1345 and those of us who get the chance to admire it can thank...well, someone...that it wasn't blown to smithereens in August 1944. The retreating German forces blew all the other bridges on the Arno, but someone (some say Hitler himself) among them decided blowing the Ponte Vecchio would have been a bridge too far. Instead they mined the areas on either side of the bridge. As you reach the southern bank, this becomes pretty obvious. Take a halfway careful look at the buildings around Lungarno Guicciardini and Borgo San Jacopo – they ain't exactly ancient heritage sites.

Two medieval towers survived the Nazi mines. The first, **Torre dei Mannelli**, just on the southern end of the bridge, looks very odd, as the Corridoio Vasariano was built *around* it, not simply straight through it as the Medici would have preferred. Across Via de' Bardi as your eye follows the Corridoio, you can espy **Torre degli Ubriachi**, the Drunks' Tower. Nice surname!

Chiesa di Santa Felicita (Map 7) The most captivating thing about the facade of this 18th-century remake of what had been Florence's oldest (4th century) **church** *(Lungarno Guicciardini; free; open 9am-noon & 3pm-6pm Mon-Fri, 9am-1pm Sun & holidays)* is the fact that the Corridoio Vasariano passes right across it. The Medicis could

Ponte Vecchio remains cluttered with higgledy-piggledy shops, as it has been for centuries

FLORENCE

stop by and hear Mass without being seen by anyone!

Inside, the main interest is in Brunell-eschi's small **Cappella Barbadori**, on the right as you enter. Here Jacopo Pontormo (1494–1557) left his disquieting mark with a fresco of the Annunciation and a *Deposizione*. The latter depicts the taking down of Christ from the Cross in disturbingly surreal colours. The people engaged in this operation look almost as if they've been given a fright by the prying eyes of the onlooker.

Palazzo Pitti (Map 5) When the Pitti family, wealthy merchants, asked Brunell-eschi to design the family home, they did not have modesty in mind. Great rivals of the Medicis, there is not a little irony in the fact that their grandiloquence would one day be sacrificed to the bank account.

Begun in 1458, the original nucleus of the **palace** (☎ 055 238 86 14, Piazza de' Pitti; biglietto cumulativo – combined ticket €10.35, €7.75 after 4pm. For individual admission fees and timetables see each item later) took up the space encompassing the seven sets of windows on the second and third storeys. The combined ticket only makes sense if you plan to see the lot on one day. Watch the time, as you may be too late for some of the museums.

In 1549 Eleonora de Toledo, wife of Cosimo I de' Medici, finding Palazzo Vecchio too claustrophobic, acquired the palace from a by-now rather skint Pitti family. She launched the extension work, which ended up crawling along until 1839! Through all that time the original design was respected and today you would be hard-pressed to distinguish the various phases of construction.

After the demise of the Medici dynasty, the palace remained the residence of the city's rulers, the dukes of Lorraine and their Austrian and (briefly) Napoleonic successors.

When Florence was made capital of the nascent kingdom of Italy in 1865, it became a residence of the Savoy royal family, who graciously presented it to the state in 1919.

Museums The palace houses five museums. First, the **Galleria Palatina** *(Palatine Gallery;* admission €6.20, includes Appartamenti Reali; open 8.15am-6.50pm, Tues-Sun) houses paintings from the 16th to 18th centuries, which are hung in lavishly decorated rooms. The works were collected mostly by the Medicis and their grand ducal successors.

After getting your ticket you head up a grand staircase to the gallery floor. The first rooms you pass through are a seemingly haphazard mix of the odd painting and period furniture.

The gallery proper starts after the **Sala della Musica** (Music Room). The paintings hung in the succeeding rooms are not in any particular order. Among Tuscan masters you can see work by Fra Filippo Lippi, Sandro Botticelli, Giorgio Vasari and Andrea del Sarto. The collection also boasts some important works by other Italian and foreign painters. Foremost among them are those by Raphael, especially in the Sala di Saturnio. A close second is Titian, one of the greatest of the Venetian school. Other important artists represented include Tintoretto, Paolo Veronese, Ribera, Rubens and Van Dyck. Caravaggio is represented with the striking *Amore Dormiente* (Love Sleeping) in the **Sala dell'Educazione di Giove**.

From the gallery you can pass into the **Appartamenti Reali** (Royal Apartments), a series of rather sickeningly furnished and decorated rooms, where the Medicis and their successors slept, received guests and generally hung about. The style and division of tasks assigned to each room is reminiscent of Spanish royal palaces.

The other galleries are worth a look if you have plenty of time. The **Galleria d'Arte Moderna** *(Modern Art Gallery; admission €4.15; open 8.15am-1.50pm Tues-Sat & alternating Sun & Mon)* covers mostly Tuscan works from the 18th until the mid-20th century, and the **Museo degli Argenti** *(Silver Museum; admission €2; open 8.15am 1.50pm Tues-Sat & alternating Sun & Mon)*, entered from the garden courtyard, has a collection of glassware, silver and semi-precious stones from the Medici collections. The **Galleria del Costume** *(Costume Gallery; admission €4.15, open 8.30am-1.50pm Tues-Sat & alternating Sun & Mon)* has high-class clothing from the 18th and 19th centuries, while the **Museo delle Carrozze** *(closed at the time of writing)* contains ducal coaches and the like.

Giardino di Boboli (Map 5) Take a break in the palace's Renaissance **Boboli Gardens** *(admission €2; open 8.15am-8pm June-Aug, 8.15am-7pm Apr-May & Sept, 8.15am-6pm Mar & Oct, 8.15am-5pm Nov-Feb)*, which were laid out in the mid-16th century and based on a design by the architect known as Il Tribolo. Buontalenti's noted artificial grotto (Grotta del Buontalenti), with a Venere (Venus) by Giambologna, is interesting.

Within the garden is the **Museo delle Porcellane** *(Porcelain Museum; admission included in garden entrance fee; closed at the time of writing)*, which houses a varied collection of the fine porcelain collected over the centuries by the illustrious tenants of Palazzo Pitti, from Cosimo I de' Medici and Eleonora of Toledo on. The exhibits include some exquisite Sèvres and Vincennes pieces. You could skip the museum if the tupperware of the rich and famous leaves you cold. On the other hand, since you have already paid to get into the garden, it can't hurt to get a glimpse of how the other half must have lived in this town.

You can get into the **Forte di Belvedere** (see later in this chapter) from the south-eastern end of the garden.

Chiesa di San Felice (Map 5) This unprepossessing church has been made over several times since the Romanesque original went up in 1066. The simple Renaissance facade was done by Michelozzo. Inside you can admire an early-14th-century crucifix by Giotto's workshop.

At No 8 on this square is Casa Guidi, where the Brownings lived.

Museo Zoologico La Specola (Map 5) A little farther down Via Romana from Piazza San Felice, this rather fusty **zoological museum** *(☎ 055 228 82 51, Via Romana 17; admission €3.10; open 9am-1pm Thur-Tues)* offers for your delectation, the stuffed animal collection apart, a collection of wax models of various bits of human anatomy in varying states of bad health. An offbeat change from all that art and history anyway!

To Porta Romana (Map 5) Pilgrims to Rome headed down Via Romana as they left Florence behind them. The end of the road is marked by the Porta Romana, an imposing city gate that was part of the outer circle of city walls knocked down in the 19th century. A strip of this wall still stretches to the north from the gate. If you head along the inside of this wall (the area is now a car park) you will soon come across an entrance that allows you to get to the top of Porta Romana.

Via Maggio (Maps 5 & 7) No it doesn't mean May St, but rather Via Maggiore (Main St). In the 16th century this was a rather posh address, as the line-up of fine Renaissance mansions duly attests. The following are all on Map 5 unless otherwise noted. **Palazzo di Bianca Cappello**, at No 26, has the most eye-catching facade, covered as it is in *graffiti* designs. Bianca Cappello was Francesco I de' Medici's lover and eventual wife. Across the street, a series of imposing mansions more or less following the same Renaissance or Renaissance-inspired style include the **Palazzo Ricasoli-Ridolfi** at No 7, **Palazzo Martellini** at No 9, **Palazzo Michelozzi (Map 7)** at No 11, **Palazzo Zanchini (Map 7)** at No 13 and **Palazzo di Cosimo Ridolfi (Map 7)** at No 15. All were built and fiddled around with over the 14th, 15th and 16th centuries. Another impressive one is **Palazzo Corsini-Suarez** at No 42.

Piazza Santo Spirito (Map 5) From Via Maggio you can turn into Via de' Michelozzi to reach the lively Piazza Santo Spirito. At its northern end, the square is fronted by the flaking facade of the **Basilica di Santo Spirito** *(free; open 8am-noon & 4pm-6pm Mon, Tues, Thur & Fri, 4pm-6pm Sat-Sun)*, designed by Brunelleschi. It's a shame that it wasn't provided with a dignified front, but don't let this put you off. The inside is a masterpiece of Florentine Renaissance design.

The church was one of Brunelleschi's last commissions. The entire length of the church inside is lined by a series of 40 semicircular chapels. Unfortunately the architects who succeeded the master were not entirely faithful to his design. He wanted the chapels to form a shell of little apses right around the church, which clearly would have been a revolutionary step. Instead they chose to hide them behind a rather ad-hoc-looking wall, flattening off the flanks of the church in an unsatisfying and untidy fashion.

More than the chapels, the colonnade of 35 columns in pietra serena is particularly striking inside. Not only do they separate the aisles from the nave, they continue around into the transept, creating the optical impression of a grey stone forest.

One of the most noteworthy works of art is Filippino Lippi's *Madonna col Bambino e Santi* (c.1457–1504) in one of the chapels in the right transept. The main altar, beneath the central dome, is a voluptuous Baroque flourish rather out of place in the spare setting of Brunelleschi's church. The *sagrestia* (sacristy) on the left side of the church is worth a look, particularly for its barrel-vaulted vestibule.

Next door to the church is the refectory, **Cenacolo di Santo Spirito** *(admission €2; open 9am-2pm Tues-Sun)*, which is home to the Fondazione Romano. Andrea Orcagna decorated the refectory with a grand fresco depicting the Last Supper and the Crucifixion (c.1370). In 1946 the Neapolitan collector Salvatore Romano left his sculpture collection to Florence's council, the Comune di Firenze. Among the most intriguing pieces are rare pre-Romanesque sculptures and other works by Jacopo della Quercia and Donatello. Only those with a genuine interest in pre-Romanesque and Romanesque sculptures need enter.

Basilica di Santa Maria del Carmine (Map 5) West of Piazza Santo Spirito, Piazza del Carmine is an unkempt square used as a car park. On its southern flank stands the Basilica di Santa Maria del Carmine, high on many art lovers' list of must-sees because of the **Cappella Brancacci** *(☎ 055 238 21 95;* admission €3.10; open 10am-4.45pm Wed-Mon, 1pm-4.45pm Sun & holidays).

This chapel is a treasure of paintings by Masolino da Panicale, Masaccio and Filippino Lippi. Above all, the frescoes by Masaccio are considered among his greatest works, representing a definitive break with Gothic art and a plunge into new worlds of expression in the early stages of the Renaissance. His *Cacciata dei Progenitori* (Expulsion of Adam and Eve), on the left side of the chapel, is his best-known work. His depiction of Eve's anguish in particular lends the image a human touch hitherto little seen in European painting. In times gone by prudish church authorities had Adam and Eve's privates covered up. Masaccio painted these frescoes in his early 20s and interrupted the task to go to Rome, where he died aged only 28. The cycle was completed some 60 years later by Filippino Lippi.

That you can even see these frescoes today is little short of miraculous. The 13th-century church was nearly destroyed by a fire in the late 18th century. About the only thing the fire spared was the chapel.

The church interior is something of a saccharine Baroque bomb. Look up at the barrel-vaulted ceiling above the single nave. It fairly drips with excessive architectural trompe l'oeil fresco painting, with arches, pillars, columns and tympana (decorative parts above the door – often triangular) all colliding into one another in a frenzy of movement. Opposite the Cappella Brancacci is the **Cappella Corsini**, one of the first (and few) examples of the extremes of Roman Baroque executed in Florence. The billowy statuary is all a bit much.

Should you arrive too late for the chapel but find the church still open, you can wander in and get a distant look at the chapel from behind barriers – but the close-up inspection is what you need to appreciate the staggering detail.

Borgo San Frediano (Map 5) Heading northwards from Piazza del Carmine you reach Borgo San Frediano. The street and surrounding area retain something of the feel of what they have always been, a working-class quarter where artisans have been beavering away for centuries.

At the western end of the street stands the lonely **Porta San Frediano**, one of the old city gates left in place when the walls were demolished in the 19th century. Before you reach the gate, you'll notice the unpolished feel of the area neatly reflected in the unadorned brick walls of the **Chiesa di San Frediano in Cestello** *(free; open 9am-11.30am & 5pm-6pm Mon-Fri, 5pm-6pm Sun & holidays)*, whose incomplete facade hides within a fairly bland, restrained version of a Baroque church interior.

The western side of Piazza di Cestello is occupied by granaries built under Cosimo III de' Medici.

Back to Ponte Vecchio (Maps 5 & 7)
From the front of Chiesa di San Frediano in Cestello you can wander along the river back towards the Ponte Vecchio. Along the way you pass several grand family mansions, including **Palazzo Guicciardini (Map 5)** at Lungarno Guicciardini 7 – another of their mansions can be seen at Via de' Guicciardini 15 – and the 13th-century **Palazzo Frescobaldi (Map 7)** on the square of the same name. Round this palazzo you continue east along Borgo San Jacopo, on which still stand two 12th-century towers, the **Torre dei Marsili** and **Torre de' Belfredelli**. On Via de' Ramaglianti once stood the old synagogue.

Ponte Vecchio to Porta San Niccolò (Maps 5, 6 & 7) Continuing east away from the Ponte Vecchio, the first stretch of Via de' Bardi shows clear signs of its recent history. This entire area was flattened by German mines in 1944 and hastily rebuilt in questionable taste after the war.

The street spills into **Piazza di Santa Maria Soprarno (Map 7)**, which takes its name from a church that has long ceased to exist. Follow the narrow Via de' Bardi (the right fork) away from the square and you enter a pleasantly quieter corner of Florence. The powerful Bardi family once owned all the houses along this street, but by the time chubby Cosimo de' Medici married Contessina de' Bardi in 1415, the latter's family was well on the decline.

Via de' Bardi expires in **Piazza de' Mozzi (Map 5)**, which is also surrounded by the sturdy facades of grand residences belonging to the high and mighty. No 2, the southern flank of the piazza, is occupied by the **Palazzi de' Mozzi**, where Pope Gregory X stayed when brokering peace between the Guelphs and Ghibellines. The western side is lined by the 15th-century **Palazzo Lensi-Nencioni, Pala-zzo Torrigiani-Nasi** (with the graffiti ornamentation) and the **Palazzo Torrigiani**.

Across the square, the long facade of the **Museo Bardini** *(☎ 055 234 24 27; admission €3.10; open Thur-Tues, closed for refurbishment at the time of writing)* is the result of an eclectic 19th-century building project by its owner, the collector Stefano Bardini. The collection is a broad mix ranging from Persian carpets to Etruscan carvings, from paintings by many lesser- and occasionally well-known artists through to sculptures in stone and wood from a wide variety of artists and periods.

Next, turn east down Via dei Renai past the leafy **Piazza Nicola Demidoff (Map 5)**, dedicated to Nicola Demidoff, a 19th-century Russian philanthropist who lived nearby in Via San Niccolò. The 16th-century **Pala-zzo Serristori (Map 6)**, at the end of Via dei Renai was home to Joseph Bonaparte in the last years of his life (he died in 1844). At the height of his career he had been made king of Spain under his brother Napoleon.

Turn right and you end up in Via San Niccolò. The bland-looking **Chiesa di San Niccolò Oltrarno (Map 6)** is interesting if for nothing else than the little plaque indicating how high the 1966 flood waters reached – about 4m. If you head east along Via San Niccolò you emerge at the tower marking the **Porta San Niccolò (Map 6)**, all that is left of the city walls here.

To get an idea of what the walls were like, walk south from the Chiesa di San Niccolò Oltrarno through **Porta San Miniato (Map 6)**. The wall extends a short way to the east and quite a deal farther west up a steep hill that leads you to the Forte di Belvedere.

Forte di Belvedere (Map 5) Bernardo Buontalenti helped design the rambling fortifications *(free; open 9am-dusk, closed for repairs at the time of writing)* here for Grand Duke Ferdinando I towards the end of the 16th century. From this massive bulwark soldiers could keep watch on four fronts, and indeed it was designed with internal security in mind as much as foreign attack. The views are excellent.

The main entrance is near Porta San Giorgio, and you can approach, as we have, from the east along the walls or by taking Costa di San Giorgio from up near the Ponte Vecchio. You can also visit the fort from the Boboli Gardens, which is what most people do (see Giardino di Boboli earlier in this section).

Piazzale Michelangelo (Map 6) From Porta San Miniato you could turn east instead of following the climb up to the Forte di Belvedere. A few twists and turns and you find yourself looking over Ponte San Niccolò. Several paths and stairways lead up from here to Piazzale Michelangelo, a favoured spot for viewing the city.

Local bus No 13, which leaves from Stazione di Santa Maria Novella and crosses Ponte alle Grazie, stops at the piazzale.

Chiesa di San Salvatore al Monte (Map 6) A short steep climb up from the piazzale brings you to this spartan church, which you will most probably find closed. That is no great disaster as this early-16th-century structure ain't that fascinating inside either.

Chiesa di San Miniato al Monte (Map 6) The real point of your exertions is about five minutes farther up, at this wonderful **Romanesque church** *(free; open 8am-7pm May-Oct, 8am-12.30pm & 2.30pm-7.30pm Nov-Apr)*, surely the best surviving example of the genre in Florence. The church is dedicated to St Minius (San Miniato), an early Christian martyr in Florence who is said to have flown to this spot after his death down in the town.

The church was started in the early 11th century; the typically Tuscan marble facade features a mosaic depicting Christ between the Virgin and St Minius, that was added 200 years later.

Inside you will see 13th- to 15th-century frescoes on the right wall, intricate inlaid marble designs down the length of the nave and a fine Romanesque crypt at the back, below the unusual raised *presbiterio* (presbytery). The latter boasts a fine marble pulpit replete with intriguing geometrical designs. The sacristy, to the right of the church (they suggest you donate €0.50 to get in), features marvellously bright frescoes. The four figures in the cross vault are the Evangelists. The **Cappella del Cardinale del Portogallo** to the left side of the church features a tomb by Antonio Rossellino and a ceiling decorated in terracotta by Luca della Robbia.

It is possible to wander through the cemetery outside. Michelangelo made use of the church during the Medici siege of 1529 to 1530, and some of his battlements remain standing around here.

Bus No 13 stops nearby.

North of the Old City

Fortezza da Basso (Map 3) Alessandro de' Medici ordered this huge defensive fortress built in 1534 and the task went to a Florentine living in Rome, Antonio da Sangallo il Giovane. The Medici family and Alessandro in particular were not flavour of the month in Florence at the time and construction of the fortress was an ominous sign of oppression. It was not designed to protect the city from invasion – Alessandro had recently been put back in the saddle after a siege by papal-imperial forces. The idea of this fort was to keep a watchful eye over the Florentines themselves. Nowadays it is sometimes used for exhibitions and cultural events.

Chiesa Russa Ortodossa (Map 3) A couple of blocks east of the fortress, the onion-shaped domes are a bit of a giveaway on this Russian Orthodox church. Built in 1902 for the Russian populace resident here, it was designed in the northern Russian style, with two interior levels decorated in part by Florentine artists but mostly by Russians expert in iconography.

Museo Stibbert (Map 2) Frederick Stibbert was one of the grand wheeler-dealers on the European antiquities market in the 19th century and unsurprisingly had quite a collection himself. He bought the Villa di Montughi with the intention of creating a **museum** (☎ 055 47 55 20, Via Federico Stibbert 26, W www.vps.it/propart/stibbert.htm; admission €4.15; open 10am-2pm Mon-Wed, 10am-6pm Fri-Sun) exuding the atmosphere of the various countries and periods covered by his collections. The result is certainly an intriguing mix.

An eye-opener is his collection of armour and arms. In one room, the **Sala della Cavalcata** (Parade Room), are life-size figures of horses and their soldierly riders in all manner of suits of armour from Europe and the Middle East. The exhibits also include clothes, furnishings, tapestries and paintings from the 16th to the 19th centuries.

The museum is north of the Fortezza da Basso. The No 4 bus from Stazione di Santa Maria Novella takes you as close as Via Vittorio Emanuele II, from where you have a fairly short walk.

South Of the Old City

Bellosguardo (Map 5) A favourite spot for 19th-century landscape painters was the hill of Bellosguardo (Beautiful View) south-west of the city centre. A narrow winding road leads up past a couple of villas from Piazza Torquato Tasso to Piazza Bellosguardo. You can't see anything from here, but if you wander along Via Roti Michelozzi into the grounds of the Albergo Torre di Bellosguardo, you'll see what the fuss was about. The hotel is the latest guise of what was once a 14th-century castle.

Try to get a look at things before you are not so kindly requested to be on your way. The hotel is great if you are staying there (see Oltrarno under Places to Stay – Top End in the Places to Stay section later in this chapter) but otherwise they won't even let you spend money at the bar. No buses run here.

Certosa di Galluzzo (Map 1) About 3km south of Porta Romana, along Via Senese, is Galluzzo, which is home to a remarkable

14th-century monastery, the Certosa (☎ 055 204 92 26; admission by donation; open 9am-midday & 3pm-6pm Tues-Sun May-Oct, 9am-midday & 3pm-5pm Tues-Sun Nov-Apr). Its great cloister is decorated with busts from the della Robbia workshop and there are frescoes by Pontormo in the Gothic hall of the Palazzo degli Studi.

The Certosa can only be visited with a guide. Try not to be overly stingy with your donation. To get there catch bus No 37 from Stazione di Santa Maria Novella.

ACTIVITIES
Rowing
It may be possible to sign up for one of the two rowing clubs in Florence, although beginners are unlikely to find much favour. Handier for the centre is **Società Canottieri Firenze (Map 7)** (☎ 055 28 21 30, Lungarno dei Medici 8). Farther out is the **Società Canottieri Comunali (Map 2)** (☎ 055 681 21 51, Lungarno Ferrucci 6). You are more likely to have luck getting in at the latter. Non-residents can take out a three-month membership for €129.10 (renewable once). Courses in rowing for beginners are available.

Swimming
The **Piscina Nannini (Map 2)** (☎ 055 67 75 21, Lungarno Aldo Moro 6; adult €5.70, carnet of 10 tickets €44, membership €5.15 plus carnet €42; open 10am-6.30pm, 8pm-11.30pm June-Sept) is 3.5km east of the Ponte Vecchio along Lungarno Aldo Moro in Bellariva (bus No 14 from Piazza dell'Unità and the Duomo takes you closest to the pool). In summer, when they pull back the movable roof over the Olympic-size pool, it becomes a watery haven on those torrid Florentine days. Opening times tend to change from month to month; it's a good idea to ring up and check.

The **Piscina Le Pavoniere (Map 2)** (☎ 055 36 22 33, Viale della Catena 2; admission €5.70, €6.20 Sun & holidays; open 10am-6pm June–mid-Sept) opens late into the night on some evenings and has a pizzeria and bar.

From mid-September to June is winter for Florentine pools and it all becomes much more complicated. You have to take out one-month (or longer) subscriptions and access is restricted to certain times on no more than four days a week. Pathetic, as most Florentines would agree.

Tennis

You can book courts (€11.35 per hour) at the **Campo Sportivo ASSI (Map 2)** (☎ *055 68 78 58, Viale Michelangelo 64*).

COURSES

Florence has more than 30 schools offering courses in Italian language and culture. Numerous other schools offer courses in art, including painting, drawing, sculpture and art history, and several offer cooking courses. See also under Courses in the Facts for the Visitor chapter.

While Florence is one of the most attractive cities in which to study Italian language or art, it is also one of the more expensive. You may want to check out the options in places like Siena, Perugia and Urbino. Also, as far as learning the language is concerned, Florence is a poor choice – for English speakers at any rate – as most Anglo students find themselves hanging out with other Anglos and never speaking a word of the language. If you are serious about learning Italian, you may want to think about picking a less touristed town.

Brochures detailing courses and prices are available at Italian cultural institutes throughout the world (see Cultural Centres in the Facts for the Visitor chapter). Florence's APT also has lists of schools and courses, which it will mail on request. You can write in English to request information and enrolment forms – letters should be addressed to the *segretaria* (secretary).

Non-EU citizens who want to study at a university or language school in Italy must have a study visa. See Study Visas under Visas & Documents in the Facts for the Visitor chapter for details.

Language Courses

The cost of language courses in Florence depends on the school, the length of the course (one month is usually the minimum duration) and its intensity. Local authorities

sometimes run irregular courses, generally for free and aimed at impecunious immigrants, for a couple of hours a week – enquire at the tourist office. The APT in Via Cavour has long lists of schools running language courses. Among them are:

Istituto Europeo (☎ *055 238 10 71, Piazzale delle Pallottole 1, 50122)* **Map 7**. Courses here start at €201 for 20 hours (one week). A much better deal is to hang around for four weeks (€460).

Istituto di Lingua e Cultura Italiana per Stranieri Michelangelo (☎ *055 24 09 75, Via Ghibellina 88, 50122)* **Map 6**. At this institute you will pay €475 for four weeks' tuition, but the school will also organise private one-on-one courses, starting at €2190 for two weeks (six hours a day Mon-Fri and lunch with the teacher – so you'd better like your teacher!).

Dante Alighieri School for Foreigners (☎ *055 234 29 84, Via de' Bardi 12, 50125)* **Map 5**. Another well-known school for language and culture classes. Course fees range from €360 to €750 for four weeks; long courses are available too.

Scuola Leonardo da Vinci (☎ *055 29 44 20,* W *www.scuolaleonardo.com, Via Bufalini 3, 50122)* **Map 3**. Courses offered range from two to 24 weeks, usually averaging four hours' class a day. Basic course costs start at €465 for four weeks.

Centro Lorenzo de' Medici (☎ *055 28 31 42, Via Faenza 43, 50122)* **Map 3**. This school is popular with American students. Four hours a day for a month costs €490. They offer many levels and a variety of courses in art, cooking, history and the like.

Other Courses

Several of the schools already listed also offer courses on art history, cooking, art, music and the like.

Some schools specialise in these sorts of courses. Art courses range from one-month summer workshops (costing from €260 to more than €520) to longer-term professional diploma courses. These can be expensive; some cost more than €3360 per year. Schools will organise accommodation for students, on request and at added cost, either in private apartments or with Italian families. As well as the following taster, many schools offer courses in applied arts, ceramics, gold work, leather, cinema studies, theatre and fashion. The APT office in Via Cavour has exhaustive lists.

***Istituto per l'Arte e il Restauro** (☎ 055 24 60 01, Palazzo Spinelli, Borgo Santa Croce 10, 50122)* **Map 6**. Here you can learn to restore anything from paintings to ceramics, interior and graphic design, gilding and marquetry.

***Accademia Italiana** (☎ 055 28 46 16, Piazza de' Pitti 15, 50125)* **Map 5**. This school offers a wide range of design programmes. They include one-month courses for dilettantes and more rigorous semester courses in painting, graphic arts, fashion design and related fields.

***Cordon Bleu** (☎ 055 234 54 68, W www.cordonbleu-it.com, Via di Mezzo 55r, 50123)* **Map 6**. This is the place to go to learn some stylish cooking methods.

***Florence Dance Center** (☎ 055 28 92 76, W www.florencedance.org, Borgo della Stella 23r)* **Map 5**. This centre offers a range of courses in classical, jazz and modern dance.

ORGANISED TOURS

***Walking Tours of Florence** (☎ 055 264 50 33, W www.artviva.com, Piazza Santo Stefano 2)* **Map 7** organises walks of the city led by historians (or at least graduates in art history). It does several three-hour walks for €21 per person. In addition you can organise all sorts of specific walks to suit your own needs and tastes – at a price.

SPECIAL EVENTS

Major festivals include: the Scoppio del Carro (Explosion of the Cart), when a cart full of fireworks is exploded in front of the cathedral at noon on Easter Saturday; the Festa di San Giovanni (St John is Florence's patron saint) on 24 June, celebrated with the lively Calcio Storico medieval football matches played on Piazza Santa Croce and ending with a fireworks display over Piazzale Michelangelo; Festa delle Rificolone (Festival of the Paper Lanterns), during which a procession of drummers, *sbandieratori* (flag-throwers), musicians and others in medieval dress winds its way from Piazza Santa Croce to Piazza SS Annunziata to celebrate the eve of Our Lady's supposed birthday on 7 September.

Every two years Florence hosts the Internazionale Antiquariato, an antiques fair attracting exhibitors from across Europe, held at the Palazzo Strozzi, Via de' Tornabuoni. The next fair will be in September/October 2003.

Further Florentine special events are listed in that section of the Facts for the Visitor chapter.

PLACES TO STAY

The city has hundreds of hotels in all categories and a good range of alternatives, including hostels and private rooms. There are more than 200 one- and two-star hotels in Florence, so even in the peak season it is generally possible – although not always easy – to find a room.

You are advised to book ahead in summer (from mid-April to October) and for the Easter and Christmas to New Year holiday periods. Frankly, it's not a bad idea at any time.

In addition to the hotels, about 175 houses have been registered as *affittacamere* – basically offering beds in private houses. The authorities are taking it a step further, inviting Florentines looking to make a few euros on the side to enter the 'bed & breakfast' game.

Hotels and pensiones are concentrated in three main areas: near Stazione di Santa Maria Novella, near Piazza Santa Maria Novella and in the old city between the cathedral and the Arno.

If you arrive at Stazione di Santa Maria Novella without a hotel booking head for the Consorzio ITA office there (☎ 055 28 28 93, fax 055 247 82 32). Using a computer network, the office, open 8.45am to 9pm daily, can check room availability and make a booking for a small fee, ranging from €2.30 to €7.75 (for one- to five-star places).

You can also contact the APT for a list of affittacamere (private rooms), where you can sometimes find rooms for about €21 to €26. Most fill with students during the school year (from October to June), but are a good option if you are staying for a week or longer.

When you arrive at a hotel, always ask for the full price of a room before putting your bags down. Florentine hotels and pensiones are notorious for their bill-padding, particularly in summer. Some may require up to €5.15 extra for compulsory breakfast and others will charge €1.50 or more for a shower. Contact the APT's SOS Turista (see earlier) if you have any problems.

Prices listed here are for the high season. Many places, especially at the lower end, offer triples and quads as well as the standard *singola/matrimoniale* (single/double) arrangement. If you are travelling in a group of three or four, these bigger rooms are generally the best value.

High season for those hotels that lift their prices starts on 15 April and fizzles out by mid-October (some dip a little in the hot months of July and August). Some hotels have an intermediate stage starting on 1 March. The Christmas and New Year period also signals price hikes. Others don't bother changing prices much at any time of the year.

It follows that the low season (from mid-October to the end of February, and for some places also March) is the thinnest time for tourists and so the best for getting the cheapest hotel rates.

See the Facts for the Visitor chapter for more information on accommodation.

Hotel Associations

The following organisations can book you into member hotels. They usually offer a fair range of possibilities, but rarely drop below two stars.

Associazione Gestori Alloggi Privati (AGAP; ☎/fax 055 28 41 00, W www.agap.it) Piazza San Marco 7. This organisation can get you a room in an affittacamere.

Florence Promhotels (☎ 055 57 04 81 or ☎ 800 86 60 22, fax 055 58 71 89, W www.promhotels .it) Viale Volta 72

Top Quark (incorporating Family Hotels and Sun Ray Hotels; ☎ 199 18 99 99 or ☎ 055 33 40 41, fax 055 324 70 58, W www.familyhotels .com) Viale Fratelli Rossi 39r

Inphonline (☎ 800 00 87 77 or ☎ 02 272 01 330 (Milan), fax 02 256 40 30, W www.initalia.it). This phone and online booking service operates Italy-wide and is free. You can book hotels, rent cars and organise conferences.

Places to Stay – Budget

Camping *Campeggio Michelangelo* (☎ 055 681 19 77, fax 055 68 93 48, Viale Michelangelo 80) **Map 6** Person/tent/car €7/5/5. Open Apr-end Oct. This is the closest camping ground to the city centre, just off Piazzale Michelangelo, south of the Arno. Take bus No 13 from Stazione Santa Maria Novella. It's a big and comparatively leafy location and makes a lovely starting point for wanders down into the city (but a little painful getting back!).

Villa Camerata (☎ 055 61 03 00, Viale Augusto Righi 2-4) **Map 2** Person/tent €5.15/4.65. This camping ground is next to the HI hostel of the same name (see under Hostels for more details). It has space for 220 people and is well equipped in a congenial, verdant setting, but it is inconvenient for the city centre. But one advantage is that it opens year-round, which the others do not.

Campeggio Panoramico (☎ 055 59 90 69, fax 055 5 91 86, Via Peramonda 1) Person/car & tent €7.75/13. To get to this camping ground at Fiesole, take bus No 7 from the Stazione di Santa Maria Novella. It is a big rambling site and in the hot Tuscan summer has the advantage of being just a little cooler and more airy than down in Florence itself.

Hostels *Ostello Villa Camerata* (☎ 055 60 14 51, fax 055 61 03 00, Viale Augusto Righi 2-4) **Map 2** Dorm beds €14.50. Open 7am-9am, 2pm-midnight. This Hostelling International (HI) hostel is considered one of the most beautiful in Europe. Only members are accepted and the hostel is part of the International Booking Network (IBN), the online booking system for HI (see W www.iyhf.org for more details). Breakfast is included, while dinner costs €7.75, and there is a bar. Take bus No 17B, which leaves from the right side of Stazione Santa Maria Novella as you leave the platforms. The trip takes 30 minutes.

Ostello del Carmine (☎ 055 29 19 74, fax 055 61 03 00, Via del Leone 35) **Map 3** €11.90. Open 7am-midnight, 15 Mar-31 Oct. HI's other Florence rep is much closer to the action in a fairly soulless new building. But the location in a comparatively untouristed corner of the Oltrarno lends it a lot of contextual charm.

Ostello Archi Rossi *(☎ 055 29 08 04, fax 055 230 26 01, Via Faenza 94r)* **Map 3** Dorm beds/small singles €15/21. This private hostel, particularly popular with a young American set, is close to the train station and a reasonable option. It is generally full to the gills.

Ostello Santa Monaca *(☎ 055 26 83 38, fax 055 239 67 04,* **W** *www.ostello.it, Via Santa Monaca 6)* **Map 5** Dorm beds €15.50. This hostel is a 15- to 20-minute walk south from the train station in the Oltrarno area. You sleep in bunk-bed dorms and it is fine if you like this lifestyle! The price includes the rental of sheets.

Ostello Spirito Santo *(☎ 055 239 82 02, fax 055 239 81 29, Via Nazionale 8)* **Map 3** Beds €23. Open July-Oct. This is a religious institution near the train station, which offers beds to women and families only. The nuns seem cagey about accepting bookings over the phone – but try in any case. Rooms come with two or three beds so you avoid the dorm situation. The place is predictably quiet.

Istituto Gould *(☎ 055 21 25 76, fax 055 28 02 74, Via de' Serragli 49)* **Map 5** Dorm beds around €20. The bunk beds in rooms of three or four are small but comfortable enough. Some of the rooms look out over a pleasant garden.

Hotels – East of Stazione di Santa Maria Novella

Many of the hotels in this area are well-run, clean and safe, but there are also a fair number of seedy establishments. The area includes the streets around Piazza della Stazione and east to Via Cavour. If you have nothing booked and don't wish to tramp around town, the area has the advantage of being close to Stazione Santa Maria Novella.

Pensione Bellavista *(☎ 055 28 45 28, fax 055 28 48 74, Largo Alinari 15)* **Map 3** Singles/doubles €52/72. Rooms in this hotel at the start of Via Nazionale are small, but a bargain if you can manage to book one

of the two doubles with balconies that overlook the Duomo and Palazzo Vecchio. Breakfast costs €5.15 per head.

Albergo Azzi *(☎/fax 055 21 38 06, Via Faenza 56)* Singles €31-46.50, doubles with shared/private bath €62/72. Rooms here are simple and comfortable – ask for one away from the noisy Via Faenza and enjoy breakfast on the hotel's terrace. The helpful management will arrange accommodation for you in other Italian cities as well.

Hotel Globus *(☎ 055 21 10 62, fax 055 239 62 25,* **W** *www.hotelglobus.com, Via Sant'Antonino 24)* **Map 7** Singles/doubles €43.90/69.70, €56.80/85.50 with bathroom. You can snag a single for €33.50 in the low season, which is about as cheap as this kind of place gets around here. This is a handy little place with reasonable if unspectacular rooms; everything is kept spotlessly clean.

Hotels – Around Piazza di Santa Maria Novella

This area is just south of the Stazione di Santa Maria Novella and includes Piazza di Santa Maria Novella, the streets running south to the Arno and east to Via de' Tornabuoni.

Via della Scala, which runs north-west off the piazza, is lined with pensiones. It is not the most salubrious part of town, but if you want to find a place to put your head down quickly after arriving, at least you have plenty of choice.

Pensione Ferretti *(☎ 055 238 13 28, fax 055 21 92 88,* **W** *www.emmeti.it/Hferretti, Via delle Belle Donne 17)* **Map 7** Singles/doubles with bathroom up to €52/83. Hidden away on a tiny, quiet intersection, this modest hotel has simple but quiet rooms. Frequently prices are lower than the maximum rates and they have some rooms without private bath that are a little cheaper still.

Hotel Abaco *(☎/fax 055 238 19 19, Via dei Banchi 1)* **Map 7** Doubles with bathroom €72.30/77.50. This is a simple but well-maintained establishment with no singles, although in the low season they will rent a double out for €39.

Albergo Scoti (☎/*fax 055 29 21 28, Via de' Tornabuoni 7)* **Map 7** Singles/doubles €39/57. This hotel, on Florence's posh shopping strip, has a handful of perfectly good rooms, none of which have private bathroom.

Hotels – Between the Duomo & the Arno

This area is a 15-minute walk south from Stazione di Santa Maria Novella in the heart of old Florence, and so is a convenient place to stay.

Hotel San Giovanni (☎ *055 28 83 85, fax 055 21 35 80,* W *www.hotelsangiovanni .com, Via de' Cerretani 2)* **Map 7** Singles/doubles/triples €46.50/62.60/83, doubles/triples with bathroom €72.30/87.80. Although the stairwell up to the 2nd floor isn't promising, the charming and often spacious rooms in this hotel, many with views of the Duomo, are well worth seeking out.

Pensione Maria Luisa de' Medici (☎/*fax 055 28 00 48, Via del Corso 1)* **Map 7** Doubles €59, triples with bathroom €74, all with breakfast. This hotel is in a mansion dating from the 17th century. The rooms are enormous and cater for families. Indeed some of the bigger rooms can easily sleep four or five people.

Albergo Bavaria (☎/*fax 055 234 03 13, Borgo degli Albizi 26)* **Map 5** Singles/doubles €57/72, doubles with bathroom €88. This hotel is housed in the fine Palazzo di Ramirez di Montalvo, built around a peaceful courtyard by Amannati. It is a good bet if you can get a room.

Hotel Orchidea (☎/*fax 055 248 03 46, Borgo degli Albizi 11)* **Map 6** Singles/doubles €39/72.30. This is a fine, homey, old-fashioned pensione in a grand mansion. Rooms are simple but well maintained and it is one of the better deals at this price range.

Hotel Dalí (☎/*fax 055 234 07 06,* W *www .hoteldali.com, Via dell'Oriuolo 17)* **Map 5** Singles/doubles €31/51.60, doubles with bathroom €67. The young couple, Marco and Samantha, recently took over this place and have injected a fresh new spark into what is a simple and pleasant hotel. Try for a room overlooking the serene inner court-

yard. The managers are helpful and there is parking.

Hotels – Santa Croce & East of the Centre

Hotel Wanda (☎ *055 234 44 84, fax 055 24 21 06,* W *www.hotelwanda.it, Via Ghibellina 51)* **Map 7** Singles/doubles range from €52 to €104. A somewhat higgledy-piggledy spot close to Piazza Santa Croce, this hotel has large rooms, many with ceiling frescoes.

Hotels – Elsewhere

Pensione Losanna (☎/*fax 055 24 58 40, Via Vittorio Alfieri 9)* **Map 4** Singles/doubles €31/49, doubles with bathroom €64.50. This well-run establishment lies a few blocks east of the Museo Archeologico as the crow flies. The lady here runs a tight, if small, ship and the place is frequently full. A couple of rooms can be made up as triples.

Places To Stay – Mid-Range

East of Stazione di Santa Maria Novella *Pensione Le Cascine* (☎ *055 21 10 66, fax 055 21 07 69,* W *www.hotellecascine .com, Largo Alinari 15)* **Map 3** Singles/doubles with bathroom €93/144.60, breakfast included. Near the train station, this two-star hotel is one of the better choices in an area overburdened with hotels. Its rooms are attractively furnished and some of them have balconies.

Via Fiume is stacked with hotels. It is the slightly upmarket hotel flank of the station. The bulk of the cheaper but frequently not so savoury options is over on the Via della Scala side.

Hotel Désirée (☎ *055 238 23 82, fax 055 29 14 39,* e *hoteldesiree@tin.it, Via Fiume 20)* **Map 3** Singles/doubles €72.30/104. Breakfast €5.15 per person. This is a very personable hotel that offers fine rooms, many of which overlook a tranquil, leafy courtyard out the back. The spick and span high-ceilinged rooms are simply but tastefully furnished, with their own bathrooms.

Pensione Accademia (☎ *055 29 34 51, fax 055 21 97 71,* W *www.accademiahotel .net, Via Faenza 7)* **Map 7** Single (one only) €77.50, doubles with bathroom €129, all

FLORENCE

with breakfast. This attractive hotel has pleasant rooms with television and incorporates an 18th-century mansion with magnificent stained-glass doors and carved wooden ceilings.

Hotel Bellettini (*☎ 055 21 35 61, fax 055 28 35 51,* W *www.firenze.net/hotelbellettini, Via de' Conti 7)* **Map 7** Singles/doubles with bathroom €82.65/108.50. This is a delightful small hotel with well-furnished rooms – try for one with a view of the Basilica di San Lorenzo. They also have a couple of triples and quads and some slightly cheaper rooms with bathroom in the corridor.

Hotel San Lorenzo (*☎/fax 055 28 49 25,* W *www.fionline.it/sanlorenzo, Via Rosina 4)* **Map 3** Singles/doubles €72.30/104. This is one of the many small family pensions that dot the city. It has just eight rooms, including one single with shower but the loo in the corridor. Two of the doubles are likewise appointed and cost €93. The five remaining rooms, some of which are big enough to turn into triples or, at a pinch, quads, come with full bathrooms. In the low season a double normally costing €104 can come down to €62.

Hotel Casci (*☎ 055 21 16 86, fax 055 239 64 61,* W *www.hotelcasci.com, Via Cavour 13)* Singles/doubles €93/124. The charm of this lower mid-range hotel is the chance to stay in a 15th-century mansion on one of the city's main streets. The rooms are a little fusty and musty but come equipped with satellite TV, phone, heating and air-con. Look up at the fresco as you quaff your buffet breakfast.

Between the Duomo & the Arno *Pendini* (*☎ 055 21 11 70, fax 055 28 18 07, Via degli Strozzi 2)* **Map 7** Singles/doubles with bathroom €104/144.60. Another excellent choice; its rooms are furnished with antiques and reproductions. In low season they're willing to come down in price too.

Hotel Porta Rossa (*☎ 055 28 75 51, fax 055 28 21 79, Via Porta Rossa 19)* **Map 7** Singles €93-124, doubles €134-165. At the time of writing the building was getting some restoration work but it was still in operation. The sizeable price differences reflect variations in room size. This is a bit of an old workhorse in central Florence but the rooms are not bad in their class.

Santa Croce & East of the Centre *Hotel Dante* (*☎ 055 24 17 72, fax 055 234 58 19,* W *www.hoteldante.it, Via San S Cristofano 2)* **Map 6** Singles/doubles €76/112. Tucked away in a quiet street right by the Basilica di Santa Croce, the rooms are fine without being spectacular. They all have smallish bathrooms but the real distinguishing feature is that three out of the four rooms on each floor have kitchens.

Oltrarno *Pensione la Scaletta* (*☎ 055 28 30 28, fax 055 28 95 62,* W *www.lascaletta .com, Lungarno Guicciardini 13)* **Map 7** Singles/doubles with private bathroom & breakfast €87.80/124. A good choice if you want to stay south of the river, this hotel has a terrace with great views. Some of the rooms looking onto the street cost a little bit less.

Pensione Bandini (*☎ 055 21 53 08, fax 055 28 27 61, Piazza Santo Spirito 9)* **Map 7** Doubles/doubles with bathroom €96/115.70. This is a rattling old pension overlooking the hippest square in Florence. The rooms are not world class in comfort but the position and old world atmosphere of the place more than make up for any lack in the mod cons department.

Hotel Silla (*☎ 055 234 28 88, fax 055 234 14 37,* W *www.hotelsilla.it, Via dei Renai 5)* Singles/doubles €108.50/150. Set in a charming old palazzo in one of the most attractive and leafy parts of Florence, this hotel offers pleasant and impeccably maintained rooms that are a stone's throw from the centre.

Places to Stay – Top End
East of Stazione di Santa Maria Novella *Hotel Monna Lisa* (*☎ 055 247 97 51, fax 055 247 97 55,* W *www.monnalisa.it, Borgo Pinti 27)* **Map 4** Singles/doubles/superior doubles €180/274/310. This hotel is tucked away in a fine Renaissance palazzo. The best rooms are good value; some overlook the private garden where you can enjoy a buffet breakfast in summer.

Hotel Botticelli (☎ *055 29 09 05, fax 055 29 43 22, Via Tadea 8,* **W** *www.panorama hotelsitaly.com*) **Map 3** Singles/doubles €119/191. This charming bijou hotel near the San Lorenzo market is an attractive deal. Rooms are very elegantly appointed with all the mod cons.

Hotel Il Guelfo Bianco (☎ *055 28 83 30, fax 055 29 52 03,* **W** *www.ilguelfobianco .it, Via Cavour 57r*) Singles/doubles €119/165. This hotel's 29 rooms are attractively laid out and comfortable. If you are alone, see if you can get the charming single with its own private terrace. A handful of doubles of 'superior' quality go for €199 and they have still better rooftop views than the others.

Around Piazza di Santa Maria Novella
Grand Hotel Baglioni (☎ *055 2 35 80, fax 055 235 88 95,* **W** *www.hotelbaglioni.it, Piazza dell'Unità Italiana 6*) **Map 7** Singles/doubles €196/248. Some rooms fall into the 'superior' category and cost an extra €21 to €26 per person. All rooms have TV, phone, air-con and heating. The rooftop terrace dining area affords some really fine views over the city.

Between the Duomo & the Arno
Hotel Helvetia & Bristol (☎ *055 28 78 14, fax 055 234 67 35,* **W** *www.charminghotels.it, Via dei Pescioni 2*) **Map 7** Singles/doubles €217/408. The web address hints at it. One of Florence's most inviting top-level hotels, oozing charm and elegance from another era without being haughty. Prices come down considerably in the low season and the 37 well-appointed rooms are all worthy choices.

Savoy (☎ *055 2 73 51, fax 055 27 35 88,* **W** *www.rfhotels.com, Piazza della Repubblica 7*) **Map 7** Singles/doubles €387.50/329. Recently reopened and completely refurbished and modernised, this stylish jewel in the Forte chain offers spacious living in rooms with a fresh, contemporary feel. Suites come in at €599.

Oltrarno
Albergo Torre di Bellosguardo (☎ *055 229 81 45, fax 055 22 90 08, Via Roti Michelozzi 2,* **e** *torredibellosguardo@dada .it*) **Map 5** Singles/doubles/suites €150/253/305. This is worth considering if only for its position. Long appreciated as a bucolic escape from the simmering heat of summertime Florence, the Bellosguardo hill to the south-west of the city centre offers not only enchanting views, but also enticing accommodation in what started life as a small castle in the 14th century.

Rental Accommodation
If you want an apartment in Florence, save your pennies and start looking well before you arrive, as apartments are difficult to come by and can be very expensive. A one-room apartment with kitchenette in the city centre will cost around €516 per month (minimum six months), more for short-term rental. *Florence & Abroad* (*Map 3;* ☎ *055 48 70 04, fax 055 49 01 43, Via San Zanobi 58*) specialises in short- and medium-term rental accommodation in Florence and the Fiesole area for those with a fairly liberal budget.

PLACES TO EAT
There is no shortage of places to eat in Florence, and although Florentines have largely abandoned the city centre to the foreigners, you can still dig up quite a few fine little eateries dotted about the place. Of course, there is room for big spenders too.

Places to Eat – Budget
Eating at a good trattoria can be surprisingly economical – a virtue of the competition for customers' attention. The definition of budget eating is as solid as a bowl of soup, so what follows is an arbitrary division. Anywhere you can fairly safely assume you will pay below about €26 for a full meal has been classed as 'budget' – ranging from sandwich joints (where you might pay around €2.60 for a filling roll) through trattorie serving respectable and good-value set meals *(menù del giorno* or *menù turistico)* and upwards into the modest categories of restaurant. Anything from around €26 up to €52 is classed here as mid-range, and everything beyond that as top end. Obviously in that category the sky's the limit.

Fast Food Florence-Style

Some habits die hard. When Florentines feel like a fast snack instead of a sit-down lunch, they might well stop by a *trippaio* (often just a mobile stand) for a nice tripe burger (well, tripe on a bread roll). It may sound a little nauseating to the uninitiated but it's really not that bad. McDonald's has very definitely arrived in Florence, but the American giant fronted by the silly-looking clown has yet to snuff out local preferences. But then, who knows what a generation fed on the Big Mac might think of tripe rolls in years to come?

Savouring fine wines is one of the great pleasures of the palate in Florence, and for many there is nothing better than a couple of glasses of a good drop accompanied by simple local snacks – sausage meats, cheeses, *ribollita* (vegetable stew) and the like. And the good news is that the tradition of the *vinaio* has won new life in the past few years in Florence. You may never see the word 'vinaio' on the doorway, but the idea remains the same. The old traditional places still exist – often dark little grog shops where you can get a bite to eat too. Look out for the sign 'Mescita di Vini' (roughly 'wine outlet').

Enoteca Fuori Porta (☎ 055 234 24 83, *Via Monte alle Croci 10r*) **Map 6** Dishes €4.15-6.20. Open Mon-Sat. In this fine old *enoteca* the wine list comprises hundreds of different drops (and an impressive roll-call of Scotch whiskies and other liquors). You can order from a limited list of *primi* ('first courses') for a pleasant evening meal. The desserts are also good.

Le Barrique (☎ 055 22 41 92, *Via del Leone 40r*) **Map 5** Full meal with wine €31. Open Tues-Sun. Hidden deep in the San Frediano area this charming little spot offers a limited *menù del giorno* (menu of the day) or, for those just stopping in for a quick drink or two, snacks at the bar. Again the emphasis is on wine, although the pasta dishes are good. It also offers a selection of Tuscan and French cheeses.

Fiaschetteria (☎ 055 21 74 11, *Via dei Neri 17r*) **Map 5** Dishes €4.15-6.20. Open Tues-Sun. You can drop by this, one of the few remaining *fiaschetterias* (wine shops) dedicated to producing quality snacks and dishes at affordable prices, for an excellent ribollita (€5.70), accompanied by a few glasses of wine.

It seems barely conceivable that within about 10 seconds' walk off Piazza della Signoria, which is lined with tourist rip-off restaurants, one of the city centre's last surviving, more or less genuine, osterie should remain. **Vini e Vecchi Sapori** (☎ 055 29 30 45, *Via dei Magazzini 3r*) **Map 7** €15.50-18. Open 1pm-11pm. Inside this little den of 'wines and old tastes' there is barely room to swing a Florentine rat, but you can eat decently and taste some solid local wines at low prices. They also import *fragolino*, a strawberry-flavoured wine made in the north-east of Italy.

Le Volpi e l'Uva (☎ 055 239 81 32, *Piazza dei Rossi 1r*) **Map 7** Open 11.30am-8pm Mon-Sat. Hidden away off the Oltrarno end of the Ponte Vecchio, at 'the Foxes and the Grape' you can sample cheeses, have a *tramezzino* (sandwich) and try out new wines. It's a bit of a gourmet's corner.

Enoteca Baldovino (☎ 055 234 72 00, *Via di San Giuseppe 18r*) **Map 6**. A recent addition to the wine-sampling scene in Florence, the Enoteca Baldovino is a pleasant location, with footpath seating and in the shadow of Santa Croce. You can taste fine wines accompanied by sophisticated snacks and salads.

East of Stazione di Santa Maria Novella

Mario (☎ 055 21 85 50, *Via Rosina 2r*) **Map 3** Mains €3.60-4.65, pasta €3.10-4.15. Open Mon-Sat lunch only. This small bar and trattoria is usually heaving with people and attracts an interesting, eclectic mix of various foreign strays and local workers.

Ristorante ZàZà (☎ 055 21 54 11, *Piazza del Mercato Centrale 20*) **Map 3** Set lunch menu €12.90. Open Mon-Sat. A few doors down from Mario, this place is so popular that it has spread out into the open. It is the best place on the square for outdoor dining. The menu changes regularly and often sparkles with imaginative dishes.

International Cuisine La Bodeguita (☎ 055 21 78 82, Via San Gallo 16r) **Map 3** Mains around €10.35. Open Mon-Sat. If meat is OK with you, get yourself down to this place. Although the people running it aren't Cuban, they put on tasty versions of *picadillo* (a spicy minced meat with vegetables and rice) and some good chicken dishes. The mojitos are mean.

Vegetarian Il Vegetariano (☎ 055 47 50 30, Via delle Ruote 30r) **Map 3** Meal with wine €15.50. Open Tues-Sat (dinner only Sat & Sun). One of the few veggie options in town, this is an unassuming *locale* with a limited (but changing) menu.

Around Piazza di Santa Maria Novella
Trattoria il Contadino (☎ 055 238 26 73, Via Palazzuolo 71r) **Map 3** Set menu with wine €8.25. Open Mon-Sat. The set menu price says it all. Don't expect marvellous food, but if you need to fill up on edible combustibles without inflicting fiscal damage, this is one place to do it.

Between the Duomo & the Arno The streets between the Duomo and the Arno harbour many pizzerias where you can buy takeaway pizza by the slice for around €1.50, depending on the weight.
Ristorante Self-Service Leonardo (☎ 055 28 44 46, Via de' Pecori 35r) **Map 7** Mains €3.85. Open 11.45am-2.45pm & 6.45pm-9.45pm Sun-Fri. When it comes to eating a full meal while you pinch pennies, it's hard to beat this refectory-style spot for simply filling an empty tum.
Trattoria Pasquini (☎ 055 21 89 95, Via Val di Lamona 2r) **Map 7** Full meal with wine €25.80. Open Thur-Tues. In this tiny corner they offer a varied menu that includes Tuscan meals such as tripe or *bistecca alla fiorentina,* and a mix of other national dishes. The *gnocchi al pomodoro* (€6.20) are good. Great wreaths of garlic and tomato grace the little bar, while the simple timber furnishing and dimly lit, vaulted ceiling all help to create a cosy atmosphere.
Trattoria da Benvenuto (☎ 055 21 48 33, Via della Mosca 16r) **Map 7** Full meal €23.25. Open Mon-Sat. Eating here, on the corner of Via dei Neri, is hardly an ambient dining experience, but the food is reliable and modestly priced. Mains include several Florentine favourites, including *lampredotto* and bistecca, while the pasta dishes are an interesting mix, including a decent *rigatoni alla siciliana.*
Angie's Pub (☎ 055 239 82 45, Via dei Neri 35r) **Map 5** Snacks from €2. Open 11am-1am (3am Fri & Sat) Mon-Sat. Among the great little treasures of Florence is this place, east of the Palazzo Vecchio. It offers a vast array of panini and focaccia, as well as hamburgers Italian-style with mozzarella and spinach, and real bagels.

Around Ognissanti Da il Latini (☎ 055 21 09 16, Via dei Palchetti 4) **Map 5** Mains from €10.35, pasta from €5.15. Open Tues-Sat. This is an attractive trattoria just off Via del Moro and something of a classic for Florentines. The food is largely Tuscan but the dining area has a singularly Spanish touch – all those legs of ham dangling off the ceiling!
Trattoria dei 13 Gobbi (☎ 055 21 32 04, Via del Porcellana 9r) **Map 5** Pasta from €5.15, mains from €10.35. Open Tues-Sat. There is a somewhat artificially bucolic scene set inside this trattoria, but it's tastefully done. The courtyard out the back and the low ceilings all add atmosphere.
Sostanza (☎ 055 21 26 91, Via del Porcellana 25r) **Map 5** Mains from €7.25. Open noon-2pm & 7pm-9.45pm Mon-Fri. This traditional Tuscan eatery is a good spot for bistecca alla fiorentina if you're not fussy about your surrounds. A no-nonsense approach dominates. The minestrone (€5.15) is also good.

Santa Croce & East of the Centre Caffetteria Piansa (☎ 055 234 23 62, Borgo Pinti 18r) **Map 6** Set lunch €8. Open Mon-Sat for lunch only. At this vaulted restaurant, you point and choose from a limited number of cheap and tasty dishes. Get in early, as by 2pm it's all over.
Osteria de' Benci (☎ 055 234 49 23, Via de'Benci 13r) **Map 5** Full meal €23. Open Mon-Sat. This is a consistently good bet.

They change their menu often and serve up honest slabs of bistecca alla fiorentina. The food is well prepared, the atmosphere cosy and prices moderate.

***Antico Noè** (☎ 055 234 08 38, Arco di San Piero 6r)* **Map 7** Panini €3.10, full meal €23. Open Tues-Sun. This legendary sandwich bar, just off Piazza San Pier Maggiore, is another option for a light lunch. They have two sections. The sandwich bar is takeaway only, but next door they run a cosy restaurant where you can enjoy fine cooking to slow jazz and blues tunes.

***Danny Rock** (☎ 055 234 03 07, Via Pandolfini 13r)* **Map 7** Meals around €10. Open 7pm-3am. This place does not sound promising, but inside is an immensely popular place for pizza, pasta and, perhaps best of all their *insalatoni* (huge salads for €6.20).

***Sant'Ambrogio Caffè** (☎ 055 24 10 35, Piazza Sant'Ambrogio 7)* **Map 7** Sandwiches from €2, pasta from €4.65. Open Mon-Sat. St Ambrose's cafe is really not a cafe at all. It plays two roles, the senior of them without doubt as hip evening cocktail bar. But you can combine this with a little food, which is average in terms of quality but allows you to eat and sip hip at the same time.

***Osteria Cibrèo** (☎ 055 234 11 00, Via de' Macci 114r)* **Map 6** Meals around €21. Open Tues-Sat. This is a true delight to the palate, next door to the much more expensive restaurant of the same name (see below). They offer no pasta at all, but some enticing first courses such as *ricotta al ragù* (ricotta cheese in a meat sauce). There follows a variety of seafood and meat options for the main course.

International Cuisine *Il Nilo (Arco di San Piero 9r)* **Map 7** Shawarma & falafel sandwiches to €3.10. Open 8am-midnight Mon-Sat. Revellers, dropouts and a host of other weird and wonderful beings wander in here during the course of the evening for a takeaway falafel. Some hang about and eat it here, although there's nowhere to sit.

***Ruth's** (☎ 055 248 08 88, Via Farini 2a)* **Map 6** Meals around €10. Open 12.30pm-2.30pm & 8pm-10.30pm Sun-Fri. For something a little different, try out this place by the synagogue. They serve tasty kosher Jewish food – it bears a strong resemblance to other Middle Eastern cuisine and makes a good choice for vegetarians.

Vegetarian *Sedano Allegro (☎ 055 234 55 05, Borgo della Croce 20r)* **Map 6** Dishes €5.15-7.25. Open Tues-Sun. For *scaloppina di seitan* or a *bavette al gorgonzola*, this is the place to come. In the warmer months they open up a garden at the rear.

Oltrarno *Borgo Antico (☎ 055 21 04 37, Piazza Santo Spirito 6r)* **Map 5** Mains €6.20-11.35. This pizzeria and restaurant is a great location in summer, when you can sit at an outside table and enjoy the atmosphere in the piazza. Try the big salads for €6.20.

***Caffè La Torre** (☎ 055 68 06 43, Lungarno Benvenuto Cellini 65r)* **Map 6** Dishes around €5.15. Open 8.30am-4am. If you are in need of food of indifferent quality in the wee hours of the morning, this is about the only choice you have. It is a busy late-night bar and a great deal of fun. It's also about the only place to get a meal as late as 3am.

***All'Antico Ristoro di Cambi** (☎ 055 21 71 34, Via Sant'Onofrio 1)* **Map 5** Full meals up to €23.25. Open Mon-Sat. The food here is traditional Tuscan and the bistecca alla fiorentina is succulent. You can eat inside or out on the square.

***Al Tranvai** (☎ 055 22 51 97, Piazza Tasso 14r)* **Map 5** Full meals up to €18. Open Mon-Fri. If you don't mind eating elbow to elbow with complete (local) strangers, this is a wonderful rustic Tuscan eatery. They serve up a limited range of pastas as primi and specialise in offal, including *trippa alla fiorentina* (tripe).

***Trattoria Casalinga** (☎ 055 21 86 24, Via de' Michelozzi 9r)* **Map 5** Meals around €15.50. Open Mon-Sat. This is a bustling, popular eating place. The food is great and a filling meal of pasta, meat or vegetables plus wine will come in at bargain basement prices. Don't expect to linger over a meal, as there is usually a queue of people waiting for your table.

***L'Brindellone** (☎ 055 21 78 79, Piazza Piattellina 10/11r)* **Map 5** Full meal with wine €10. Open for dinner only Thur-Tues. Surrounded by dangling garlic strands and old Chianti bottles, this is a truly Tuscan spot with a slightly vegetarian bent too. Alongside such classics as *vitello tonnato* (veal in a tuna sauce) you can get vegetable cous cous.

I Tarocchi (☎ *055 234 39 12, Via dei Renai 12-14r*) **Map 5** Pizzas, first & second courses around €5.15. Open Tues-Sat. This is a popular pizzeria/trattoria serving excellent pizzas. The first courses alone are substantial enough to satisfy most people's hunger.

Osteria Antica Mescita San Niccolò (☎ *055 234 28 36, Via San Niccolò 60r*) **Map 6** Full meal with wine €20.65. Open 7pm-11pm Mon-Sat. This is a fine little eating hideaway where the food is tasty and authentic. Throw in a good bottle from their impressive wine collection and the equation is good.

Places to Eat – Mid-Range

East of Stazione di Santa Maria Novella *Ristorante Lobs* (☎ *055 21 24 78, Via Faenza 75*) **Map 3** Set menu €33.50, mains around €18. Open until 12.30am. This excellent fish restaurant offers a seafood menu including oysters and Norwegian salmon, and Soave wine from the country's northeast. Round off with *sorbetto al vodka.*

Around Piazza di Santa Maria Novella *Ostaria dei Cento Poveri* (☎ *055 21 88 46, Via del Palazzuolo 31r*) **Map 3** Open 6.30pm-midnight Wed-Mon. Full meal from €25.80. A congenial little spot in a not so congenial part of town, the 'hostel of the hundred poor people' sits apart from most other places around here as a quality dining option. Tuck in to creative Tuscan food in a down-to-earth setting.

Between the Duomo & the Arno *Trattoria Coco Lezzone* (☎ *055 28 71 78, Via Parioncino 26r*) **Map 7** Full meal with wine up to €41.30. Open Mon-Sat. Ribollita is the house speciality here, but they will do you a genuine bistecca alla fiorentina for €31 (enough for two in most cases) if you

book it ahead. One oddity is that they do not serve coffee.

International Cuisine *Eito* (☎ *055 21 09 40, Via dei Neri 72r*) **Map 7** Sushi & sashimi €18-26. Open Tues-Sun. A reasonable representative of the Japanese genre can be found here. Wednesday is 'sushi' day, when you are offered the choice of two set menus, one with 12 pieces of sushi and six of sashimi and one the other way around.

Santa Croce & East of the Centre *La Pentola d'Oro* (☎ *055 24 18 08, Via di Mezzo 24r*) **Map 6** Full meal up to €52. Open Mon-Sat. Long a jealously guarded secret among Florentine gourmands, this place is a one off that in the past few years has started to advertise itself. Signor Alessi is a man of encyclopaedic learning, who spends much of his time studying medieval recipes and transforming them into the most remarkable meals. The menu is largely up to his whim, and can involve all sorts of mixes, such as beef prepared with a black pepper and pear sauce.

Oltrarno *Osteria Santo Spirito* (☎ *055 238 23 83, Piazza Santo Spirito 16r*) **Map 5** Full meal €31. If you prefer a slightly higher quality meal than in the bustling locales across the square, this cosy restaurant is the place. Try the *ravioli burro e salvia,* large ravioli prepared in butter and sage, a Tuscan classic (€7.75).

Trattoria Cavolo Nero (☎ *055 29 47 44, Via dell'Ardiglione 22*) **Map 5** Meals up to €31. Open noon-3pm & 7pm-1am Tues-Sat. This place is hidden away in a back street. Try the entrecote of Angus steak prepared with herbs (€13.40).

La Beppa (☎ *055 234 76 81, Via all'Erta Canina 6r*) **Map 6** Full meal with wine €31. Open Wed-Mon. In new hands and with a new name, this spot remains a delightful location. For an almost sweet and sour effect, try the *spaghetti alle acciughe e pomodorini* (spaghetti with anchovies and baby tomatoes; €7.75) followed by *coniglio agli agrumi* (rabbit in a citrus sauce; €10.35). After your meal you could take a stroll along this back lane through vineyards guarded by retiring villas.

Ristorante Beccofino *(☎ 055 29 00 76, Piazza degli Scarlatti)* **Map 5** First courses up to €9.30, seconds up to €19.60. Open Tues-Sun. This place is one of a rare breed in this town. The grub is pricey and the surroundings contemporary chic – no traditional bucolics in here thank you (and check out the stainless steel, floor-lit loos!).

Outside Florence *La Capponcina (☎ 055 69 70 37, Via San Romano 17r, Settignano)* Full meals around €31.15. Open 7.30pm-midnight Tues-Sun. Up in the hills overlooking Florence from the north-east, this is one of the city's better-known restaurants. The kitchen is known in particular for its *tagliata di manzo*, succulent beef fillets sliced up and served on a bed of lettuce. Sitting in the garden is a true pleasure in summer. You can get bus No 10 from the train station, or Piazza San Marco. This service is replaced from 9pm by the No 67. The restaurant is a few steps off the central Piazza San Tommaseo, where the bus terminates. Book ahead.

Places to Eat – Top End
Between the Duomo & the Arno *Gilli (☎ 055 21 38 96, Piazza della Repubblica 39r)* **Map 7** Coffee at the bar €0.75, at a table outside €3.10. Open 8am-1am Wed-Sun. This is one of the city's finest cafes and it's reasonably priced if you stand at the bar.

The square is actually host to a series of fine historic cafes.

Café Concerto Paskowski *(☎ 055 21 02 36, Piazza della Repubblica 31-35r)* **Map 7** Open 7am-2am Tues-Sun. With more than 150 years of history, this is one of the class cafe acts of the city. Prices are similar to those in Gilli and the interior is worth making the trip to the square for, even if it's a little out of your way. It makes a stylish way to start the day.

Giubbe Rosse *(☎ 055 21 22 80, Piazza della Repubblica 13-14r)* **Map 7** Cappuccino outside €4.15. Open 8am-2am. The early-20th-century Futurist artistic movement, although it didn't make as big an impact in Florence as elsewhere in Italy,

nevertheless had its following – and this is where its die-hard members used to drink and debate. Inside, long vaulted halls lined with old photos, sketches and artwork make a great place for coffee over a paper – there are some hanging up for the customers' use.

Santa Croce & East of the Centre The restaurants mentioned in this section can be found on Map 6.

Ristorante Cibrèo *(☎ 055 234 11 00, Via de' Macci 118r)* Full meal up to €77.45. Open Tues-Sat. Next door to the fine osteria of the same name, this is the place to come for a special splurge. The decor is much the same as in the osteria, although the table settings are suitably several notches up in elegance.

Enoteca Pinchiorri *(☎ 055 24 27 77, Via Ghibellina 87)* Meals €93. Open Tues-Sat. This is one of the city's finest restaurants, noted for its Italian-style nouvelle cuisine.

Gelato
Gelato can cost anything from €2 for a *coppetta* (small cup) to around €5 for a *cono* (massive cone).

Gelateria Vivoli *(☎ 055 29 23 34, Via dell'Isola delle Stinche 7)* **Map 5** Open 9am-1am Tues-Sat. People queue outside this place, near Via Ghibellina, to delight in the gelati widely considered to be the city's best.

Perchè No? *(☎ 055 239 89 69, Via dei Tavolini 19r)* **Map 7** Open Wed-Sun. This gelateria, off Via de' Calzaiuoli, is excellent.

Caffè Ricchi *(☎ 055 21 58 64, Piazza Santo Spirito 8-9r)* **Map 5** Open 7am-1pm Mon-Sat. Although you can get meals here, the main reason to stop by is for a tasty gelato – there are plenty of flavours to choose from. They have tables outside. If you choose to lunch here, do so inside – they have a lovely little garden.

La Bottega del Gelato *(☎ 055 47 67 76, Via del Ponte Rosso 57r)* **Map 4** Open Mon-Sat. Just off Piazza della Libertà, this place does a particularly enticing range of fruit-flavoured gelato.

Baroncini *(☎ 055 48 91 85, Via Celso 3r)* **Map 2** Open Thur-Tues. If you happen to be in the area, drop in to one of the best-known gelaterie in town.

Self-Catering

You can save money by getting your own groceries from small shops, produce markets and small supermarkets and throwing your own sandwiches and the like together.

Standa (☎ 055 234 78 56, Via Pietrapiana 42) **Map 6**. This is a handy central supermarket open from 8.30am to 9pm daily except Sunday.

ENTERTAINMENT

Several publications list the theatrical and musical events and festivals held in the city and surrounding areas. The free, bimonthly *Florence Today*, the monthly *Firenze Information* and *Firenze Avvenimenti*, a monthly brochure distributed by the council, are all available (haphazardly) at the tourist offices. *Firenze Spettacolo*, the city's definitive entertainment publication, is available monthly for €1.55 at newsstands.

A handy centralised ticket outlet is Box Office (Map 3; ☎ 055 21 08 04), Via Luigi Alamanni 39. A Web ticket service, Ticket One (**W** www.ticketone.it – Italian only) allows you to book tickets for theatre, football and other events on the Internet.

Pubs & Bars

The Chequers Pub (☎ 055 28 75 88, Via della Scala 7-9r) **Map 3** Foreigners hang about here, one of a huge swag of UK/Irish-style pubs in Florence.

Astor Caffè (☎ 055 239 90 00, Piazza del Duomo 5r) **Map 7** Open 10am-3am. You can take breakfast here if you will but the nocturnal folk gather around for loud music and cocktails both inside and out, right by the solemn walls of the Duomo.

Capocaccia (☎ 055 21 07 51, Lungarno Corsini 12/14r) **Map 7** Open midday-1am Tues-Sun. The beautiful people of Florence gather here, especially on balmy spring and summer evenings, for a riverside nibble and cocktail before heading on to dinner and clubs.

Loonees (☎ 055 21 22 49, Via Porta Rossa 15) **Map 7** Open 8pm-3am. You wouldn't

know this place existed if you hadn't been told. Walk into the building and the door is to the left of the staircase. It's a fairly small 'club' – basically just a bar with an expat bent and occasional live music of dubious taste.

The William (☎ 055 246 98 00, Via Magliabechi 7r) **Map 6** Open 6pm-2am. This is a loud English-style pub but it has found quite a following among young Florentines in search of a pint of ale rather than Anglos in search of six.

Sant'Ambrogio Caffè (☎ 055 24 10 35, Piazza Sant'Ambrogio 7r) **Map 6** Cocktails €5.15. Open 9am-2am Mon-Sat. As well as being a place to get snacks, Sant'Ambrogio Caffè is especially dedicated to the sipping of cocktails. On summer nights they set up tables outside.

Rex Caffè (☎ 055 248 03 31, Via Fiesolana 25r) **Map 6** Open 5pm-3am (happy hour 5pm-9.30pm). Another stop on the cocktail circuit, this is a hip place to sip your favourite mixed concoction. Take a martini at the luridly lit central bar or a quiet beer sitting at one of the penumbral metallic tables.

Cabiria (☎ 055 21 57 32, Piazza Santo Spirito 4r) **Map 5** Open 11am-2am, closed Tues. This popular cafe by day converts into a busy music bar by night. In summer the buzz extends on to Piazza Santo Spirito, which itself becomes a stage for an outdoor bar and regular free concerts.

La Dolce Vita (☎ 055 28 45 95, Piazza del Carmine 6r) **Map 5** Open until 1am Mon-Thur, until 3am Fri-Sun. Just a piazza away from Santo Spirito, this place attracts a rather more self-consciously select crowd of self-appointed beautiful types.

Zoe (☎ 055 24 31 11, Via dei Renai 13r) **Map 5** Open 3pm-2am Mon-Sat. This deep-blue lit bar heaves with young locals as its squadrons of punters end up spilling out onto the street.

Caffè La Torre (☎ 055 68 06 43, Lungarno Benvenuto Cellini 65r) **Map 6** Mixed drinks around €5.15. Open 8.30am-4am. Hang out drinking until the wee hours and listening to all kinds of music from jazz to Latin rhythms.

Live Music

Some of the bigger venues are well outside the town centre. Depending on who is playing at these venues, admission costs from nothing to €10. Then the drinks will cost you on top of that – at least €5.15 for a beer.

Jazz Club (☎ 055 247 97 00, Via Nuova de' Caccini 3) **Map 4** Admission €5.15 (for a year's membership), drinks around €6.20. Open 9.30pm-1am, to 2am Fri-Sat. This is one of Florence's top jazz venues.

Tenax (☎ 055 30 81 60, Via Pratese 46) **Map 1** Bus No 29 or 30 from Stazione di Santa Maria Novella. Free-€10, mixed drinks around €5.15. Open 10pm-4am Tues-Sun. One of the city's more popular clubs, this place is well out to the north-west of town. It is one of Florence's biggest venues for Italian and international acts. You'll be looking at a taxi to get home.

Auditorium Flog (☎ 055 49 04 37, Via M Mercati 24b) **Map 2** Bus No 8 or 14 from the train station. Free-€10, mixed drinks around €5.15. Open 10pm-4am. Another venue for bands, this place is in the Rifredi area, also north of the centre but a little closer than Tenax. It's not as big (in any sense) as Tenax but has a reasonable stage and dance area.

Discos/Clubs

Central Park (☎ 055 35 35 05, Via Fosso Macinante 2) **Map 3** Drinks around €7.75. Open 10pm-6am Tues-Sun. This is one of the city's most popular clubs. What music you hear will depend partly on the night, although as you wander from one dance area to another (there are four) you can expect a general range from Latin and pop through to house.

Meccanò (☎ 055 331 33 71, Viale degli Olmi) Admission €7.75-10. Open 10pm-5am, Tues-Sat. Three dance spaces offer house, funk and mainstream commercial music to appeal to a fairly broad range of tastes. Occasionally they put on special theme nights.

Gay & Lesbian Venues

Florence ain't memorable for gay nightlife and the following four options are about the extent of it. See also the Gay & Lesbian Travellers section in the Facts for the Visitor chapter.

Bars *Piccolo Café (☎ 055 24 17 04, Borgo Santa Croce 23r)* **Map 6** Open 5pm-1am. This is a relaxed little place to hang out and get acquainted with the remainder of the scene. You should probably make this your first stop if you are a gay male, although the bar is relaxed and by no means gay male exclusive.

Y.A.G. Bar (☎ 055 246 90 22, Via de' Macci 8r) **Map 6** Open 5pm-2am. Barely a stone's throw away from the Piccolo Café, this recently opened gay bar is another relaxed and mixed location. It claims to be the largest gay bar in Florence. Well, that's not too hard given the scant competition. Still, it is much more up front about its identity. If you don't want to chat there are some computer terminals for going online and video games.

Crisco (☎ 055 248 05 80, Via Sant' Egidio 43r) **Map 6** Open 8pm-4am Mon-Thur, to 6am Fri & Sat. This is a strictly men-only club with dark rooms and a somewhat furtive air about it.

Discos/Clubs *Tabasco (☎ 055 21 30 00, Piazza di Santa Cecilia 3r)* **Map 7** Free, drinks €6.20. Open 8pm-4am; disco until 6am Tues, Fri & Sat. Florence has only one serious gay club where you can dance through the wee hours and then some. This place boasts a disco, cocktail bar and dark room. Wednesday is leather night. You are obliged to have at least one drink.

Classical Music & Opera

Teatro Comunale (☎ 055 2 77 91, Corso Italia 12) **Map 3** Concerts, opera and dance are performed at various times of the year here, on the northern bank of the Arno. In May and June the theatre hosts Maggio Musicale Fiorentina, an international concert festival. Contact the theatre's box office.

Teatro Verdi (☎ 055 21 23 20, Via Ghibellina 101) **Map 6** There are seasons of drama, opera, concerts and dance here from January to April and October to December.

Teatro della Pergola (☎ *055 247 96 51, Via della Pergola 18)* **Map 4** The Amici della Musica (☎ 055 60 84 20) organise concerts here from January to April and October to December.

In summer especially, concerts of chamber music are held in churches across the city. Keep an eye out for programmes of the Orchestra da Camera Fiorentina (Florentine Chamber Orchestra), whose performance season runs from March to October.

Cinemas

You have a few venue choices for seeing movies in the *versione originale* (original language). This generally means movies in English with Italian subtitles. At most cinemas there are three or four sessions a day; the latest starts between 10pm and 10.45pm. Wednesday is cheap day, when tickets cost €4.15. Normally they go for around €6.70.

Odeon Cinehall (☎ *055 21 40 68, Piazza Strozzi)* **Map 7** This is the main location for seeing subtitled movies, screened on Monday and Tuesday.

Cinema Fulgor (☎ *055 238 18 81, Via Maso Finiguerra 22r)* **Map 3** Here they screen movies in English on Thursday nights.

The British Institute also puts on English-language movies at 6pm on various days of the week at its **library** (☎ *055 26 77 82, Lungarno Guicciardini 9)*. Admission costs €7.75 for nonmembers.

From mid-June to September, several places open up outdoor cinemas (programmes available from tourist offices). Among them are: **Chiardiluna** (☎ *055 233 70 42, Via Monte Uliveto 1)* **Map 5**; **Cinema Poggetto** (☎ *055 48 12 85, Via M Mercati 24b)* **Map 2**; **Città del Cinema** in Palasport at the Campo di Marte (☎ *055 67 88 41, Viale Paoli)* **Map 2**; **Raggio Verde** at the Palazzo dei Congressi (☎ *055 260 26 09, Viale Filippo Strozzi)* **Map 3**.

Theatre & Dance

The theatre season kicks off in October and continues into April/May. Which is not to say Florence comes to a standstill then but many of the main stages stay quiet while more festive cultural events take centre billing.

Ex-Stazione Leopolda (☎ *055 247 83 32, Viale Fratelli Rosselli 5)* **Map 3** One of the council's smarter ideas some years back was to convert this former train station (near the Cascine) into a performance space – in fact several spaces. Theatre, most of it of an avant-garde nature, is frequently the star, although occasionally concerts are put on here too. For programmes and tickets it is easiest to go to Box Office (see the beginning of this section) or any of the tourist offices in Florence.

The theatres mentioned earlier under Classical Music & Opera also frequently stage drama. You will find productions at these and several other smaller theatres dotted about town advertised in *Firenze Spettacolo*. Clearly, most theatre is in Italian.

Teatro della Limonaia (☎ *055 44 08 52, Via Gramsci 426, Sesto Fiorentino)* **Map 1** One of the leading avant-garde theatres in Italy is this place well beyond the centre of Florence (bus 28A or 28C).

Spectator Sports

Football (Soccer) Your average Florentine is as passionate about football as the next Italian, but their side, AC Fiorentina, has never quite been one of the creme de la creme of the Italian premier league.

If you want to see a match, tickets, which start at around €18 and can easily rise beyond €104, are available at **Stadio Comunale Artemio Franchi** (☎ *055 58 78 58 or* ☎ *055 262 55 37, Campo di Marte)* **Map 2** or at **Chiosco degli Sportivi** ticket outlet (☎ *055 29 23 63, Via Anselmi, just off Piazza della Repubblica; open 9am-1pm & 3pm-6pm Mon-Tues & Thur, 9am-7.30pm Wed, 9am-7pm Fri, 9am-1pm & 3pm-8pm Sat, 10am-12.30pm Sun)* **Map 7**. While you're at it you can have a flutter on the Totocalcio, or football pools.

You can also book tickets through the Box Office ticket outlet or Ticket One (see the introduction to the Entertainment section for details).

SHOPPING

It is said that Milan has the best clothes and Rome the best shoes, but Florence without doubt has the greatest variety of goods. The main shopping area is between the Duomo and the Arno, with boutiques concentrated along Via Roma, Via de' Calzaiuoli and Via Por Santa Maria, leading to the goldsmiths lining the Ponte Vecchio. Window-shop along Via de' Tornabuoni, where the top designers, including Gucci, Saint-Laurent and Pucci, sell their wares.

By the way, Gucci and Prada each have massive wholesale stores in the Tuscan countryside. The savings, especially compared with, for example, London and Paris prices, can be considerable. Some Japanese tour companies organise trips that have these stores as their prime objective!

Gucci (☎ 055 865 77 75, Via Aretino 63) Open 9am-6pm Mon-Sat. This enormous outlet is on the SS67 highway at the northern edge of Leccio, about 30 to 40 minutes south-east of Florence on the road to Arezzo.

Prada (☎ 055 919 05 80) Open 9.30am-12.30pm & 1.30pm-6pm Mon-Fri, 9.30am-7pm Sat, 4pm-7pm, Sun. This outlet, which has the elegance of a high-street store with a cafe and taxis waiting, is just outside the village of Levanella, about another 30 minutes' drive down the same road from Leccio towards Arezzo. The quickest way from Florence by car is to take the A1 motorway, leave at the Valdarno exit and follow the signs for Montevarchi.

Should you prefer to shop for fashion without leaving Florence, a few classic starting points include:

Gucci (☎ 055 26 40 11, Via de' Tornabuoni 73r) **Map 7** One of the most successful families in Florentine-born fashion. Of course the soap opera family saga has put a lot of spice into the name, but the fashion-conscious take little notice and keep on buying. The Japanese especially can be seen lining up to pay homage.

Ferragamo (☎ 055 29 21 23, Via de' Tornabuoni 16r) **Map 7** Another grand Florentine name, the one-time shoe specialists now turn out a range of clothes and accessories for the serious fashion aficionado. They also have a curious shoe museum – see the Things to See & Do section earlier in this chapter.

House of Florence (☎ 055 28 81 62, Via de' Tornabuoni 6) **Map 7** Here you can spend €60 on a leather belt or silk tie. Conservative handmade clothes and accessories for the well-lined.

In fact you are warned of this as you reach the heart of the shop by a little sign reminding you that one never forgets quality but soon forgets the price paid for it. That might be open to debate.

Neuber (☎ 055 21 57 63, Via de' Tornabuoni 17) **Map 7** Here is another mecca of Florentine class for men and women who want to cut an elegant swathe through life.

Loretta Caponi (☎ 055 21 36 68, Piazza Antinori 4r) If nothing is too good for your infant or small child, particularly girls, this store sells exquisite small persons' clothing (and a few things for big people too), some of it finely embroidered. Your three-year-old may not fully appreciate it, but will be dressed to impress.

If you are looking for labels without the snobbery, hunt around the so-called 'stockhouses' where designer wear is often on sale for affordable prices – if you cast around a little you will frequently find bargains. Try:

Stockhouse Il Giglio (☎ 055 21 75 96, Borgo Ognissanti 86r) **Map 3** Cheap is a relative term in Florence, but you can pick up some interesting men's and women's fashion items here and occasionally turn up some genuine bargains. Name labels can come in at a considerable discount. Florentines consider it one of the best 'stockhouses' for picking up labelled items at back-of-truck rates.

Stockhouse One Price (☎ 055 28 46 74, Borgo Ognissanti 74r) **Map 5** Although more densely stocked (in a smaller space) this place is along similar lines to Stockhouse Il Giglio.

Leather and shoes are worth hunting out in Florence. You can try the markets (see later) or some of the speciality stores. For instance:

Francesco da Firenze (☎ 055 21 24 28, Via di Santo Spirito 62r) **Map 5** If only every shoemaker made shoes this way. Hand-stitched leather is the key to this tiny family business. Expect to pay a fair amount for your footwear, but the investment will pay off. You can have shoes and sandals made to specification.

Scuola del Cuoio (☎ 055 24 45 33, Piazza di Santa Croce 16) **Map 7** If you get lucky you will see apprentices beavering away at some hide. Otherwise it is not a bad place to get some measure of quality-price ratios. Access is either through the Basilica di Santa Croce or through an entrance behind the basilica at Via San Giuseppe 5r.

FLORENCE

Il Bisonte (☎ 055 21 57 22, Via del Parione 31r) **Map 7** Here they concentrate on accessories, ranging from elegant bags in natural leather through to distinguished desktop items, leather-bound notebooks, briefcases and the like.

Florence is famous for its beautifully patterned paper, which is stocked in the many stationery and speciality shops throughout the city and at the markets.

Pineider (☎ 055 28 46 55, Piazza della Signoria 13r) **Map 7** These purveyors of paper and related products have been in business since 1774. If you want to make a gift of stationery, this is the city's class act.

Open-air Market (near Piazza del Mercato Centrale) **Map 3** Open Mon-Sat. This market offers leather goods, clothing and jewellery at low prices, but quality varies greatly. You could pick up the bargain of a lifetime, but check the item carefully before paying. It is possible to bargain, but not if you want to use a credit card.

Mercato dei Pulci (flea market; off Borgo Allegri near Piazza dei Ciompi) **Map 7** Open Mon-Sat. Antiques and bric-a-brac are the speciality at this market.

GETTING THERE & AWAY
Air
Florence is served by two airports: Amerigo Vespucci (Map 1; ☎ 055 37 34 98), 5km north-west of the city centre at Via del Termine 11; and Galileo Galilei (☎ 050 50 07 07; W www.pisa-airport.com), near Pisa and about an hour by train or car from Florence. Amerigo Vespucci caters for domestic and a handful of European flights. Galileo Galilei is one of northern Italy's main international and domestic airports and has regular connections to London, Paris, Munich and major Italian cities.

Bus
The SITA bus station (Map 3; ☎ 800 37 37 60 or ☎ 055 21 47 21, W www.sita-on-line .it), Via Santa Caterina da Siena 15, is just to the west of Piazza della Stazione. There is a direct, rapid service to/from Siena (€5.70, 1¼ hours) and buses leave here for Poggibonsi, where there are connecting buses for San Gimignano (€5.15, 1½ hours)

and Colle di Val d'Elsa, where you change for Volterra (€6.20, 1¼ hours). Direct buses serve Arezzo, Castellina in Chianti, Faenza, Grosseto and other smaller cities throughout Tuscany.

Several bus companies, including CAP (Map 3; ☎ 055 21 46 37, W www.capauto linee.it) and COPIT (same tel), operate from Largo Alinari, at the southern end of Via Nazionale, with services to nearby towns including Prato (€1.80, 45 minutes) and Pistoia (€2.60, 50 minutes).

Lazzi (Map 3; ☎ 055 35 10 61, W www .lazzi.it), Piazza Adua 1, next to the Stazione Santa Maria Novella, runs services to Rome, Pistoia and Lucca. Lazzi forms part of the Eurolines network of international bus services. You can, for instance, catch a bus to/from Barcelona, Paris, Prague or London.

Train
Florence is on the Rome-Milan line, which means that most of the trains to/from Rome (€21.95, two hours), Bologna (€8.75, one hour) and Milan (€21.70, three hours 20 minutes) are Intercities or Eurostar Italia, for which you have to pay a supplement.

There are also regular trains to and from Venice (€18.75, three hours) and Trieste. For Verona you will generally need to change at Bologna. To get to Genoa and Turin, a change at Pisa is necessary.

The train information office (open 7am to 9pm) is in the main foyer at Stazione di Santa Maria Novella.

Car & Motorcycle
Florence is connected by the A1 to Bologna and Milan in the north and Rome and Naples in the south. The Autostrada del Mare (A11) connects Florence with Prato, Lucca, Pisa and the coast and a superstrada (no tolls) joins the city to Siena. From the north on the A1, exit at Firenze Nord and then simply follow the bulls-eye 'centro' signs. If approaching from Rome, exit at Firenze Sud.

The more picturesque SS67 connects the city with Pisa to the west and Forlì and Ravenna to the east.

GETTING AROUND
To/From the Airports

There are no trains to Amerigo airport. SITA (☎ 800 37 37 60) and ATAF (☎ 800 42 45 00) run the 'Volainbus' shuttle bus service between Amerigo Vespucci airport and Florence city centre. The bus runs every 30 minutes from outside Stazione di Santa Maria Novella to/from Amerigo Vespucci airport. The service from the airport runs from 6.00am to 11.30pm daily; from the train station the service runs from 5.30am to 11.00pm daily. The trip takes about 20 minutes (sometimes more in heavy traffic). Tickets, which cost €4.15 for a single, can be purchased on board or at the airport.

Regular trains leave from platform 5 at the stazione for Galileo Galilei Airport near Pisa. Check in your luggage 15 minutes before the train departs. Services are roughly hourly from 6.46am to 5pm, with a final service leaving at 11.07pm, from Florence and from 8.49am to 6.50pm (7.09pm on Sundays and holidays) from the airport. The trip takes one and a half hours and costs €4.70.

Bus

Azienda Trasporti Area Fiorentina (ATAF) buses service the city centre, Fiesole and other areas in the city's periphery. For information, call ☎ 800 42 45 00.

You'll find several main bus stops for most routes around the Stazione di Santa Maria Novella. Some of the most useful lines operate from a stop just outside the southeastern exit of the train station below Piazza Adua. Buses leaving from here include:

No 7, for Fiesole
No 13, for Piazzale Michelangelo
No 70 (night bus), for the Duomo and Uffizi

A network of dinky little *bussini* (electric minibuses) operates around the centre of town. They can be handy for those getting tired of walking around or needing to backtrack right across town. Only Linea D operates 8am to 9.20pm daily. The others run 8am to 8.20pm Monday to Saturday. You can get a map of the routes published by ATAF from tourist offices.

Tickets cost €0.75 for one hour and €1.30 for three hours. A 24-hour ticket costs €3.10. A *biglietto multiplo* (four-ticket set) for night buses (valid for one hour each) costs €3. You are supposed to stamp these in the machine when you get on your first bus. If you are hanging around Florence longer, you might want to invest in a *mensile* (monthly ticket) at €28.40 (€18.60 for students). *Annuale* (annual) tickets are also available. If you just hop on the bus without a ticket between 9pm and 6am, you can get one for €1.55 (double the normal price).

There is a special 30-day ticket for using the bussini (lines A to D) only. It costs €12.90.

Car & Motorcycle

Traffic is restricted in the city centre. A no-parking regime (except for residents) rules 7.30am to 6.30pm Monday to Friday. Non-residents may only stop in the centre to drop off or pick up luggage from hotels or park in hotel or public garages (the latter will cost you a fortune).

There are several major car parks and numerous smaller parking areas around the fringes of the city centre. If you are planning to spend the day in Florence, your best option is to park at the Fortezza da Basso, which costs €1 per hour.

If your car is towed away, call ☎ 055 41 57 81 for the Depositeria Comunale (car pound) at Via Olmatello, which is way out on the city limits. You will have to pay around €46.50 to recover it, plus whatever fine you are charged. Fines vary depending on the offence.

Rental A bunch of car-rental agencies cluster together in the Borgo Ognissanti area, all of which are on Map 3. Among the biggies, Avis (☎ 199 10 01 33) is at Borgo Ognissanti 128r, Europcar (☎ 800 82 80 50) at Borgo Ognissanti 53r and Hertz (☎ 199 11 22 11) at Via Maso Finiguerra 33r. Thrifty Car Rental (☎ 055 28 71 61), Borgo Ognissanti 134r, and Happy Rent (☎ 055 239 96 96), Borgo Ognissanti 153r, are two local competitors. Their rates are similar, with small cars starting at €62 per day.

Happy Rent also rents out motorbikes and scooters.

Alinari (☎ 055 28 05 00), Via Guelfa 85r, rents out motorcycles for up to €93 per day and scooters for up to €41 per day. In summer it also sets up shop at several camping grounds – check at the APT for details.

Taxi

Taxis can be found outside Stazione di Santa Maria Novella and several other ranks around town. Or call ☎ 055 42 42, ☎ 055 47 98, ☎ 055 44 99 or ☎ 055 43 90. The flagfall is €2.30, on top of which you pay €0.75 per kilometre within the city limits (€1.35 per kilometre beyond). You are charged at the rate of €0.10 every 20 seconds while stationary. There is a night-time surcharge (10pm to 6am) of €0.10. On public holidays you pay an extra €1.65 (not if you are already paying the night surcharge). Each piece of luggage costs €0.55.

Bicycle

Cycling around Florence is one way to beat the traffic – though the cobbles may rattle your bones. Alinari hires out scooters, motorbikes (see under Car & Motorcycle earlier) and bicycles. You can rent a bicycle for €6 for five hours, €10 per day or €18 per weekend. A mountain bike costs €10 for five hours, €15.50 per day or €20 for a weekend.

Florence by Bike (Map 3; ☎ 055 48 89 92, Ⓦ www.florencebybike.it) is at Via San Zanobi 120/122r. You can hire anything from a standard bicycle for getting around town (up to €10 per day) to a scooter (€62 per day).

Around Florence

One of the beauties of Florence, believe it or not, is leaving it behind. Whether it's just to check out less-visited towns to the north and west, to make a delicious lunchtime assault on the nearby towns of Fiesole and Settignano, or explore the hilly wine region of the Chianti to the south, there's no shortage of things to do. Public transport, while often slow, enables you to get to most places listed in this chapter without excessive difficulty, although you shouldn't be overly ambitious about how much you try to get done. With your own motor, the world, as they say, is your oyster (which is fine if you like oysters).

PISTOIA
postcode 51100 • pop 90,200
A pleasant city at the foot of the Apennines and a half-hour west of Florence by train, Pistoia has grown beyond its well-preserved medieval ramparts and is today a world centre for the manufacture of trains. In the 16th century the city's metalworkers created the pistol, named after the city.

Orientation & Information
Although spread out, the old city centre is easy to negotiate. From the train station in Piazza Dante Alighieri, head north along Via XX Settembre, through Piazza Treviso, and continue heading north to turn right into Via Cavour. Via Roma, branching off the northern side of Via Cavour, takes you to Piazza del Duomo and the APT office (☎ 0573 2 16 22), which opens 9am to 1pm and 3pm to 6pm Monday to Saturday year-round (also Sunday from April to September).

The main post office is at Via Roma 5, and an unstaffed Telecom phone booth is at Corso Antonio Gramsci 96, near Via della Madonna.

The *questura* (police station; ☎ 0573 2 67 05) is out of the centre at Via Macallè 23. The public hospital (Ospedale Riuniti; ☎ 0573 35 21) is off Viale Giacomo Matteotti, behind the old Ospedale del Ceppo.

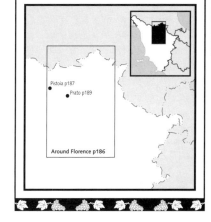

Pistoia p187
Prato p189
Around Florence p186

Piazza del Duomo
Much of Pistoia's visual wealth is concentrated on this central square. The Pisan-Romanesque facade of the **Cattedrale di San Zeno** (☎ 0573 2 50 95, Piazza del Duomo; free; open 8.30am-12.30pm & 3.30pm-7pm) boasts a lunette of the *Madonna col Bambino fra due Angeli* (Madonna and Child with two Angels) by Andrea della Robbia, who also made the terracotta tiles that line the barrel vault of the main porch. Inside, in the Cappella di San Jacopo, is the remarkable silver **Dossale di San Jacopo** *(Altarpiece of St*

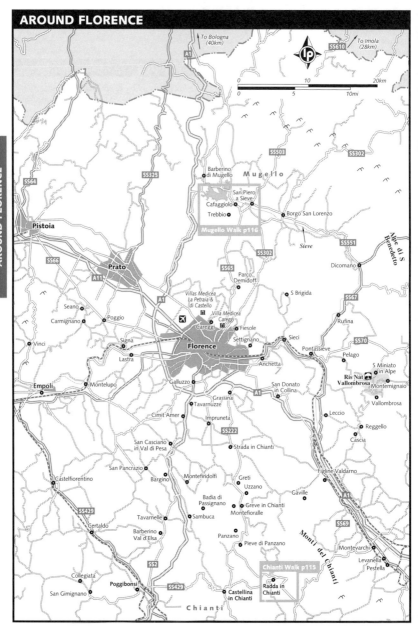

AROUND FLORENCE

James; admission €1.55; open 10am-noon & 4pm-7.30pm). Begun in the 13th century, artisans added to it over the ensuing two centuries until Brunelleschi contributed the final touch, the two half-figures on the left side. You can also climb the cathedral's **bell tower** *(€5.15; open 10am-1pm & 3pm-6pm)* for splendid views of the town. It's by guided tour only and reservations must be made at the tourist office.

The venerable building between the cathedral and Via Roma is the **Antico Palazzo dei Vescovi** *(☎ 0573 36 92 16, Piazza del Duomo; admission €3.60; open 10am-1pm*

& 3pm-5pm Tues, Thur & Fri). Guided tours four times a day take you through what little remains of an original Roman-era structure on this site as well as displays of artefacts dating as far back as Etruscan times, which were discovered during restoration work.

Across Via Roma is the striking **baptistry** (battistero). Elegantly banded in green-and-white marble, it was started in 1337 to a design by Andrea Pisano.

Dominating the eastern flank of the piazza, the Gothic Palazzo del Comune houses the **Museo Civico** *(☎ 0573 37 12 96, Piazza del Duomo 1; adult/child €3.10/1.55, free Sat*

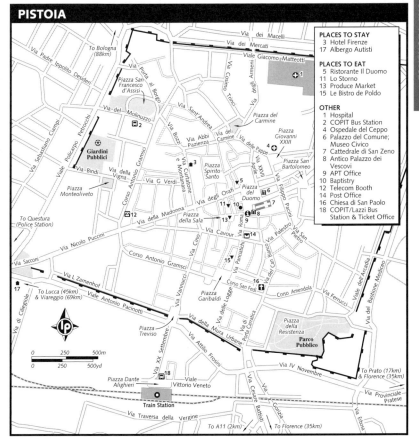

PISTOIA

PLACES TO STAY
3 Hotel Firenze
17 Albergo Autisti

PLACES TO EAT
5 Ristorante Il Duomo
11 Lo Storno
13 Produce Market
15 Le Bistro de Poldo

OTHER
1 Hospital
2 COPIT Bus Station
4 Ospedale del Ceppo
6 Palazzo del Comune;
   Museo Civico
7 Cattedrale di San Zeno
8 Antico Palazzo dei
   Vescovi
9 APT Office
10 Baptistry
12 Telecom Booth
14 Post Office
16 Chiesa di San Paolo
18 COPIT/Lazzi Bus
   Station & Ticket Office

afternoon; open 10am-7pm Tues-Sat, 9am-12.30pm Sun & holidays), with works by Tuscan artists from the 13th to 19th centuries.

The portico of the nearby **Ospedale del Ceppo** will stop even the more monument-weary in their tracks, for the incredibly detailed terracotta frieze by Giovanni della Robbia is quite unique. It depicts the *Virtù Teologali* (Theological Virtues) and the *Sette Opere di Misericordia* (Seven Works of Mercy) and is one of the best examples to come from the della Robbia family workshops.

Special Events
For a weekend in mid-July Pistoia hosts Pistoia Blues, one of Italy's bigger music events. Van Morrison, David Byrne and Jeff Beck performed in 2001. Tickets range from €20.65 for one night to €51.65 for all three.

On 25 July Pistoia is the site of the so-called Joust of the Bear – Giostro dell'Orso.

Places to Stay
Albergo Autisti (☎ 0573 2 17 71, Via Antonio Pacinotti 89) Singles/doubles €15.50/31, doubles with bathroom €36.15. This hotel is generally full with permanent residents so it's advisable to call ahead. Rooms are rather small.

Hotel Firenze (☎ 0573 2 31 41, Via Curtatone e Montanara 42) Singles/doubles €31/51.65, with bathroom €41.30/62. At the time of writing this pleasant hotel was about to change hands. Call ahead to check prices haven't changed as well.

Places to Eat
Ristorante Il Duomo (☎ 0573 3 19 48, Via Bracciolini 5) Dishes €3.60/5.15. Open lunch only noon-3pm Mon-Sat. Try this cheap, self-service buffet place for quick, filling meals.

Il Sipario (☎ 0573 3 33 30, Corso Antonio Gramsci 159) Meals from €12.90. Open Tues-Sun. On Friday nights this agreeable restaurant has specials on fish.

Le Bistro de Poldo (☎ 0573 2 92 30, Via Panciatichi 4) Pasta from €5.15. Open Mon-Sat. This place is situated on a quiet

street and is a classier affair but slightly more expensive.

Lo Storno (☎ 0573 2 61 93, Via del Lastrone 8) Full meals €31. Open Mon-Sat. If you are looking for something a little special but still affordable, try your luck here. An *osteria* of one sort or another has been documented on this site for the past 600 years! Today the chef prepares a continually changing array of dishes.

A **produce market** is open Monday to Saturday in Piazza della Sala, west of the cathedral.

Getting There & Around
Buses connect Pistoia with most towns in Tuscany. The main ticket office and bus station for COPIT and Lazzi buses is on the corner of Viale Vittorio Veneto and Via XX Settembre, near the train station. Buses for Florence (€2.60, 50 minutes) depart from Piazza Treviso, at the other end of Via XX Settembre. Other COPIT buses leave from Via del Molinuzzo, off Piazza San Francesco d'Assisi.

Trains connect Pistoia with Florence (€2.50, 40 minutes), Bologna, Lucca and Viareggio. By car, the city is on the A11, as well as the SS64 and SS66, which head north-east for Bologna and north-west for Parma, respectively. Bus Nos 1, 3, 4 and 10 connect the train station with the town centre, although the city is easily explored on foot.

PRATO
postcode 59100 • pop 167,000
Virtually enclosed in the urban and industrial sprawl of Florence, Prato is one of Italy's main centres for textile production. Founded by the Ligurians, the city fell to the Etruscans and later the Romans, and by the 11th century was an important centre for wool production. Unlike some towns in Tuscany, Prato has a vibrant, lively feel to it and seems to cater to locals first, tourists second. It is well worth visiting.

Orientation & Information
The old centre is small and is surrounded by the city wall. The main train station, on

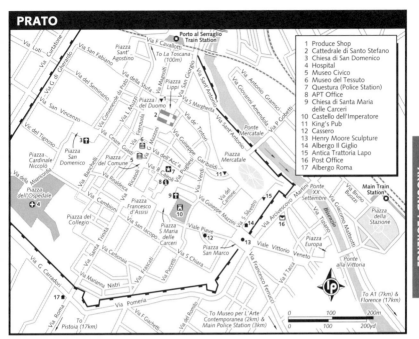

PRATO

1 Produce Shop
2 Cattedrale di Santo Stefano
3 Chiesa di San Domenico
4 Hospital
5 Museo Civico
6 Museo del Tessuto
7 Questura (Police Station)
8 APT Office
9 Chiesa di Santa Maria delle Carceri
10 Castello dell'Imperatore
11 King's Pub
12 Cassero
13 Henry Moore Sculpture
14 Albergo Il Giglio
15 Antica Trattoria Lapo
16 Post Office
17 Albergo Roma

Piazza della Stazione, is to the east of the city centre.

The APT office (☎ 0574 2 41 12) is at Piazza Santa Maria delle Carceri 15, two blocks east of the central Piazza del Comune, and opens 9am to 1.30pm and 2pm to 7pm (to 6.30pm October to March) Monday to Saturday.

The main post office is at Via Arcivescovo Martini 8.

The police station (☎ 0574 55 55) is well out of the centre at Via Cino 10, but operates a small station at Via B Cairoli 29. For medical emergencies, the hospital (Ospedale Misericordia e Dolce; ☎ 0574 43 41) is in Piazza dell'Ospedale, south-west of Piazza del Comune.

Museo Civico

This **museum** *(Piazza del Comune; currently closed for restoration)*, with its small but impressive collection of largely Tuscan paintings, is housed in the imposing medieval Palazzo Pretorio. During the museum's restoration, part of its collection is on show at the Museo di Pittura Murale.

Museo del Tessuto

Opposite Museo Civico, this **museum** *(☎ 05 74 61 15 03, Piazza del Commune; admission €2.60, free Sun; open 10.30am-6.30pm Mon & Wed-Fri, 10.30am-2.30pm Sat, 4pm-7pm Sun)* devotes itself to textiles through the ages. Unsurprisingly, the museum is slanted towards production and innovation aspects of local industry, but you'll also find examples of textiles (dating from as early as the 3rd century) from around Italy, Europe, and as far afield as India and the Americas.

Cattedrale di Santo Stefano

Head along Via Mazzoni from Piazza del Comune to the 12th-century Cattedrale di Santo Stefano *(☎ 0574 2 62 34, Piazza del Duomo; free; open 7am-12.30pm & 3.30pm-7pm)*. The rather simple Pisan-Romanesque facade

The Merchant of Prato

'Fate has so willed that, from the day of my birth, I should never know a whole happy day…' So wrote one of Prato's most celebrated sons, Francesco di Marco Datini, in the 1390s.

Datini, to whom a statue was erected in the shadow of the Palazzo Pretorio after his death in August 1410, was neither a hero of the battlefield nor a great statesman. Nor was he a man of learning or an inventor. Born in 1335 to a poor innkeeper, Datini grew up to become a highly successful international merchant.

Although he never reached the dizzy heights of the great Florentine trading families, Datini carved out for himself a respectable business empire that stretched from Prato and Florence to Avignon, Barcelona and the Balearic Islands. Not bad for a 15-year-old boy who arrived in Avignon, then a thriving political and trading centre by virtue of the Pope's presence, with 150 florins from a small land sale.

Prato was (and remains) a town of shopkeepers and small businesses. Datini rose above

Datini's letters were solemnly headed: 'In the name of God and Profit.'

this and, by the time of his return from Avignon 33 years later, was the richest man in town. For the people of Prato, this made him something of a hero. In the following years he put his wealth to work in the creation of, well, more wealth. Basing himself principally in Florence, he traded in just about anything that looked likely to turn a profit. Indeed, in those years he and most other traders frequently headed up their letters and business papers with the pious exclamation: 'In the name of God and Profit.' At one stage he ran what was considered one of the most modern banking houses in Europe.

Through his branches in Italy, France and Spain, and agents in London, Flanders and elsewhere, he moved cloth, raw materials, arms, slaves, primary produce – you name it, he had an interest in it.

Datini knew how to have fun, and the stories of his banquets, luxury possessions and womanising demonstrate he was no aesthete. On the other hand, he worked like a slave himself, often sleeping no more than four hours a night. Only at the end of his life did he seem to give thought to things other than the accumulation of money. In his will he left all his wealth (after bequests) to a new charitable foundation established in his name in his fine house on Via Rinaldesca.

It is not so much Datini's financial exploits that make him interesting today. Something of a control freak, he spent long hours every day writing correspondence, not only to his branches but to his wife Margherita and friends too. He was meticulous about keeping all mail that came to him and ordered his branch managers to do the same. His charity, the Ceppo di Francesco di Marco (housed in his former home), has kept the archive of this correspondence in one piece for more than 500 years. It provides a rare glimpse not only into the business life of a late medieval trader, but also into the daily life of middle-class Tuscans, especially in Prato and Florence.

Iris Origo distilled this wealth of material into a fascinating account of medieval life, predictably entitled *The Merchant of Prato* (1957).

features a lunette by Andrea della Robbia and the white-and-green marble banding you will find elsewhere in Tuscany (Siena, Pistoia, Lucca). The most extraordinary element, however, is the oddly protruding **Pulpito della Sacra Cintola** jutting out over the piazza on the right-hand side of the main entrance. The eroded panels of the pulpit, designed by Donatello and Michelozzo in the 1430s, are housed next door in the **Museo dell'Opera del Duomo** (☎ 0574 2 93 39, Piazza del Duomo; adult/child €5.15/3.10, combined ticket €5.15 includes Castello dell'Imperatore, Cassero & Museo di Pittura Murale; open 9.30am-12.30pm & 3pm-6.30pm Wed-Mon, except Sun afternoon). The pulpit was expressly added on so that the sacra cintola (sacred girdle) could be displayed to the people five times a year (Easter, 1 May, 15 August, 8 September and 25 December). It is believed the girdle (or belt) was given to St Thomas by the Virgin, and brought to the city from Jerusalem after the Second Crusade.

In medieval times great importance was attached to such holy relics, but just how many girdles did Mary have? Another, declared the real thing in 1953 by the Orthodox Patriarch of Antioch, is stored in the Syrian city of Homs.

Among the magnificent frescoes inside the church look for those behind the high altar by Filippo Lippi, depicting the martyrdoms of John the Baptist and St Stephen, and Agnolo Gaddi's Legend of the Holy Girdle in the chapel to the left of the entrance.

Chiesa di Santa Maria delle Carceri

Built by Giuliano da Sangallo towards the end of the 15th century, the interior of this church (☎ 0574 2 79 33, Piazza Santa Maria delle Carceri; free; open 7am-noon & 4pm-7pm) is considered a Renaissance masterpiece, with a frieze and medallions of the Evangelists by the workshop of Andrea della Robbia.

Also here is the **Castello dell'Imperatore** (☎ 0574 3 82 07; Piazza Santa Maria delle Carceri; admission €2.05, combined ticket €5.15 includes Museo dell'Opera del Duomo & Museo di Pittura Murale; open 10am-

7pm Wed-Mon May-Sept, 10am-5pm Mar & Apr, 10am-4pm Nov-Feb). It was built in the 13th century by the Holy Roman Emperor Frederick II. Included in the ticket price is the **Cassero** (Viale Piave; open 10am-1pm & 4pm-7pm Wed-Mon), a much-restored covered passageway that originally allowed access from the castle to the city walls.

Chiesa di San Domenico

The main reason for dropping into this church is to have a look at the **Museo di Pittura Murale** (☎ 0574 44 05 01, Piazza San Domenico; adult/child €5.15/3.10, combined ticket €5.15 includes Museo dell'Opera del Duomo, Castello dell'Imperatore & Cassero; open 10am-6pm Mon & Wed-Sat, 10am-1pm Sun). A collection of 14th- to 17th-century frescoes and graffiti, it is reached through the church's cloister. It also houses a number of paintings normally on display at the Museo Civico.

Contemporary Art

Prato has more than its fair share of contemporary art. The most striking piece is Henry Moore's **sculpture** Forma squadrata con taglio, a great white monolith smack bang in the middle of Piazza San Marco. South of the city walls is the **Museo per l'Arte Contemporanea** (☎ 0574 53 17, Viale della Repubblica 277; adult/child €6.20/4.15; open 10am-6pm Mon-Fri by reservation only, 10am-7pm Sat & Sun). Part of a centre devoted to contemporary art, its permanent collection of mainly paintings and sculptures is complemented by temporary exhibitions and performances throughout the year.

Special Events

Outside town in Poggio a Caiano and in various locations around Prato they have been celebrating the Festival delle Colline (hill festival) since 1979. The concert series brings together class acts of world music from late June to late July. In 2001 they included acts from as far afield as Mali and Romania.

Places to Stay

Albergo Roma (☎ 0574 3 17 77, fax 0574 60 43 51, Via G Carradori 1) Singles/doubles

€46.50/55. This is your cheapest hotel option in town. The rooms are clean but could do with a bit of modernising.

Albergo Il Giglio (☎ *0574 3 70 49, fax 0574 60 43 51, Piazza San Marco 14)* Singles/doubles €38.75/54, with bathroom €54.25/67.15. The same people run this place, of similar standard.

La Toscana (☎ *0574 2 80 96, fax 0574 2 51 63, Piazza Ciardi 3)* Singles/doubles €41.30/56.80. Another cheapie (for Prato) is La Toscana, just north of the city walls.

Places to Eat
Piazza Mercatale, with its popular restaurants and lively atmosphere, is a good place to eat out.

Antica Trattoria Lapo (☎ *0574 2 37 45, Piazza Mercatale 141)* Meals from €18. For a relaxed, informal atmosphere and service with a personal touch, head here. The menu has plenty of Tuscan dishes and if you turn up too late, you'll probably have to queue.

King's Pub (☎ *0574 2 86 41, Via Garibaldi 148)* Pizzas & mains €4.15-6.70. Open Thur-Tues. Don't be put off by the name, or some of the menu items (hamburgers and wurstels in Tuscany?!). The large pizzas and salads are particularly inviting, and you have the choice between the dark-wood interior and the outdoor umbrella-covered seating.

There's an excellent ***produce shop*** on the corner of Via Cironi and Via Magnolfi.

Getting There & Around
CAP and Lazzi buses operate regular services to Florence and Pistoia from in front of the train station, on Piazza della Stazione. Prato is on the Florence-Bologna and Florence-Lucca lines. It's quicker and cheaper to Florence (€1.40, 25 minutes) by train. By car, take the A1 from Florence and exit at Calenzano, or the A11 and exit at Prato Est or Ovest. The SS325 connects Prato with Bologna. Several buses connect the train station with the town centre, generally terminating at Piazza San Domenico.

FIESOLE
Perched in hills about 8km north-east of Florence, between the valleys of the Arno and Mugnone rivers, Fiesole has attracted the likes of Boccaccio, Carducci, Giovanni Dupré, Marcel Proust, Gertrude Stein and Frank Lloyd Wright, all drawn by the lush olive groves and valleys – not to mention the spectacular view of Florence. Fiesole was founded in the 7th century BC by the Etruscans and remained the most important city in northern Etruria. The views and fresh air alone make it worth your trouble to come up. It makes a fabulous spot for a picnic and a short walk, and there's even a little sightseeing to be done.

The APT office (☎ 055 59 87 20), at Via Portigiani 3/5, can assist with information about the town, accommodation, walks and other activities. Most other services – including a bank, an ATM and a post office – are located on the main square, Piazza Mino da Fiesole.

Things to See & Do
Overlooking the main square is the **cathedral** (☎ *055 59 95 66, Piazza della Cattedrale 1; free; open 7.30am-noon & 3pm-6pm daily May-Oct, 7.30am-noon & 3pm-5pm daily Nov-Apr)*. It was started in the 11th century and altered in the 13th century, although a 19th-century renovation has eradicated many earlier features. Behind the cathedral is the **Museo Bandini** (☎ *055 5 94 77, Via Duprè; admission €6.20 includes Zona Archeologica; open 10am-7pm daily May-Oct, 9am-5pm Wed-Mon Nov-Apr)*, featuring an impressive collection of early Tuscan Renaissance works, including Taddeo Gaddi's *Annunciazione* (Annunciation) and Petrarch's beautifully illustrated *Trionfi* (Triumphs).

Opposite the entrance to the museum, the **Zona Archeologica** (☎ *055 5 94 77, Via Portigiana; admission €6.20 includes Museo Bandini; open 9.30am-7pm Wed-Mon May-Oct, 9.30am-5pm Wed-Mon Nov-Apr)* features a 1st-century-BC Roman theatre that is used from June to August for the Estate Fiesolana, a series of concerts and performances. Also in the complex are a small Etruscan temple and Roman baths, which date from the same period. The small archaeological museum is worth a look, as

Michelangelo's *David* guards Palazzo Vecchio.

Ponte Vecchio has vaulted the Arno since 1345.

The orderly vivacity of Florence's Duomo

Graceful buildings lining the Arno and peaceful Ponte Santa Trinita, viewed from Oltrarno

Cypresses were introduced to the Chianti region in the Roman era for their decorative qualities.

Another low-key Tuscan harvest

Romanesque Abbazia di Sant'Antimo

Forests and farmland cover the central hills.

it includes exhibits from the Bronze Age to the Roman period.

For some of the best views of Florence take Via di San Francesco west from Piazza Mino da Fiesole. After a few hundred metres you'll come across a small park and the fantastic views.

Places to Stay & Eat
Campeggio Panoramico (☎ 055 59 90 69, fax 055 5 91 85, Via Peramonda 1) Adult/car & tent €7.75/12.90. Bus No 70 from Piazza Mino da Fiesole. The camping ground at Fiesole also has bungalows for hire.

Bencistà (☎/fax 055 5 91 63, Via Benedetto da Maiano 4) Doubles only from €154.95 with half board. About 1km short of Fiesole just off the road from Florence, this is an old villa and from its terrace there is a magnificent view of Florence. It might bust the budget, but for one or two days it's well worth it. Ask for a room with a view (couldn't resist it).

Trattoria Cave di Maiano (☎ 055 5 91 33, Via Cave di Maiano 16) Meals €36.15. Open daily except Mon lunch. This is one of the best places in Fiesole for good Florentine cooking. In the summer you can sit in the pleasant garden. Getting here without a car is a little tricky as the restaurant is actually in Maiano, a short distance from Fiesole, and off the bus routes. You could try getting a taxi from central Fiesole.

Otherwise, there are several restaurants of varying quality around Piazza Mino da Fiesole.

Getting There & Away
Fiesole is easily reached from Florence. ATAF bus No 7 from the Stazione di Santa Maria Novella in Florence connects with Piazza Mino da Fiesole, the centre of this small town. If you are driving, find your way to Piazza della Libertà, north of the cathedral, and then follow the signs to Fiesole.

SETTIGNANO
Just 6km south-east of Fiesole, along a delightful back-country lane, Settignano offers even more splendid views of Florence than Fiesole (come in the morning, as by early afternoon all you can see is glare). It is a pleasant little *borgo* (ancient town) worth visiting for the dining opportunity alone.

La Capponcina (☎ 055 69 70 37, Via San Romano 17r) Full meals about €36. Open Tues-Sun. This is one of the city's better-known restaurants, up in the hills overlooking Florence to the north-east. The kitchen is known in particular for its *tagliata di manzo*, succulent beef fillets sliced up and served on a bed of rocket. Sitting in the garden is a true pleasure in summer. You are sure of being several degrees cooler than down in Florence.

You can get bus No 10 from the Stazione di Santa Maria Novella or Piazza San Marco in Florence (this service is replaced from 9pm by bus No 67). The restaurant is a few steps off the central Piazza San Tommaseo, where the bus terminates.

THE MEDICI VILLAS
The Medicis built several opulent villas in the countryside around Florence as their wealth and prosperity grew during the 15th and 16th centuries. Most of the villas are now enclosed by the city's suburbs and industrial sprawl, and are easily reached by taking ATAF buses from the train station. Ask at the APT office in Florence for details of bus numbers and opening times.

One of the finest is the **Villa Medicea La Petraia** (☎ 055 45 26 91, Via della Petraia 40; admission €2, includes Villa Medicea di Castello; open 8.15am-8pm daily June-Aug, closes earlier in other months & 2nd & 3rd Mon of the month year-round). Commissioned by Cardinal Ferdinando de' Medici in 1576, this former castle, about 3.5km north of the city, was converted by Buontalenti and features a magnificent garden.

Farther north of the city is the **Villa Medicea di Castello** (☎ 055 45 47 91, Via di Castello 47; admission €2, includes Villa Medicea La Petraia; open 8.15am-8pm daily June-Aug, closes earlier in other months & 2nd & 3rd Mon of the month year-round). It was the summer home of Lorenzo the Magnificent. You may only visit the park.

The **Villa Medicea di Careggi** (☎ 055 427 97 55, Viale Pieraccini 17; free; open 9am-6pm Mon-Fri, 9am-noon Sat, groups must *book ahead)* is where Lorenzo the Magnificent breathed his last in 1492. Access is limited as it is used as administration offices for the local hospital.

Another Medici getaway was the **Villa di Poggio a Caiano** *(☎ 055 87 70 12, Piazza Medici 14; admission €2, grounds free; open 9am-6.30pm June-Aug, 9am-5.30pm Apr, May & Sept, 9am-4.30pm Mar & Oct, 9am-3.30pm Nov-Feb, closed 2nd & 3rd Mon of the month).* About 15km from Florence on the old road to Pistoia, and set in magnificent sprawling gardens, the interior of the villa is sumptuously decorated with frescoes and furnished much as it was early in the 20th century as a royal residence of the Savoys. Visits inside are permitted every hour. The easiest way here without your own transport is with the COPIT bus service running between Florence and Pistoia – there is a bus stop right outside the villa.

THE MUGELLO

The area north-east of Florence leading up to Firenzuola, near the border with Emilia-Romagna, is known as the Mugello and features some of the most traditional villages in Tuscany. The Sieve River winds through the area and its valley is one of Tuscany's premier wine areas. It's also a great area for walks (for more information see the Tuscany on Foot chapter).

For information on the area contact the Comunità Montana del Mugello (☎ 055 849 53 46), Via P Togliatti 45, or Borgo Informa (☎/fax 055 845 62 30, e infoborgo@tin.it), Villa Pecori Giraldi, both in Borgo San Lorenzo.

The Medicis originated from the Mugello and held extensive property in the area. Some of their family castles, villas and palaces are open to the public, while others can be visited with a guide.

Just outside Pratolino, the **Parco della Villa Medici-Demidoff** *(☎ 055 276 04 19; adult/child €2.60/1.55; open 10am-8.30pm Thur-Sun May-July, 10am-8pm Thur-Sun Aug-Oct)* was the focal point of one of the Medici family's villas, which was demolished in 1824. The Demidoff family acquired the land and transformed the property

into a fine romantic garden. If you keep following the SS65 for another 13km you will reach a turn-off (east) for **Trebbio** and, a few kilometres farther on, another for **Cafaggiolo**, both sites of Medici villas. Visits are by appointment only; contact the Associazione Turismo Ambiente (☎ 055 845 87 93), Piazza Dante 29, Borgo San Lorenzo.

If you're interested in a wineries tour, there is a *strada del vino* (wine road) mapped out. For more details see the special section 'The Tuscan Table'.

EAST OF FLORENCE
Vallombrosa

An interesting little excursion, most easily accomplished with your own transport, has as its prime objective the cool forest of Vallombrosa and the *abbazia* (abbey) of the same name. Although you can get to many of these spots by bus, doing things this way could turn the following enterprise into a project of several days!

Exiting Florence eastwards along the SS67 (follow the blue signs for Arezzo), you first strike a **Commonwealth war cemetery** *(open 8am-4.30pm daily)* half a kilometre short of **Anchetta**. It is sobering to stop here and think of the soldiers who died in and around Florence in 1944.

You follow the road to **Sieci**, whose Romanesque church is accompanied by a graceful, slender bell tower. A detour 6km north (signposted) would take you up to the one-time Pazzi family's **Castello del Trebbio** *(☎ 055 830 49 00, Via Montetrini 10),* a typical 12th-century fortified rural outpost that now operates as an *agriturismo*. You can go horse riding here and/or stock up on wine.

Back on the SS67, you next pass through **Pontassieve**, a busy little town that is picturesquely set on the Sieve River. Shortly after, take the SS70 for a short distance, turning off for **Pelago**, which is perched high on a ledge overlooking farming valleys. From here it's another 12km to **Vallombrosa**. As you wind higher, the forest thickens with the fir trees planted over the centuries by the Vallombrosan monks and the air freshens noticeably (it's a great little escape in summer).

The **abbey** *(☎ 055 86 20 74; free; open 9am-noon & 3pm-6pm)* is almost 1000m above sea level. Back in the 11th century, San Giovanni Gualberto formed this branch of the Benedictine order in the midst of what no doubt was an even more impressive forest. The monks set themselves the task of wiping out simony and corruption in the Church in Florence and eventually the abbey came to play an important role in the city's politics. The monks were booted out by Napoleon and only since the 1950s have they returned to get the monastery back into working order. You can wander into the grounds at any time or join a guided tour at 10.30am Tuesday and Friday in July and August. And like many monasteries in Tuscany, you can purchase ointments and elixirs produced within the monastery at their Antica Farmacia.

The surrounding area is great for picnics and walks, including one up to **Monte Secchieta** (1449m). At the abbey and in **Saltino**, 2km farther down the road, you will find a few restaurants and places to stay. The tourist office in Saltino (☎ 055 86 20 03, Piazzale Roma), open 9.30am to 12.30pm and 4pm to 7pm daily mid-June to mid-September, has maps and information on walks in the area.

From here we follow the road south to **Reggello** and **Cascia** (which has a small Romanesque church) and finally on to **Figline Valdarno**. The centre of this town, once known as Florence's granary, has a few interesting buildings, including the 14th-century Palazzo Pretorio, the seat of local power. Much of the city wall and its towers still stand.

Another detour here would see you heading 6km south-west to **Gaville** (you could catch the local Maddii bus) to see the 11th-century Romanesque Pieve di San Romolo, set in olive groves.

Back in Figline Valdarno, you can follow the SS69 back up to Florence.

THE CHIANTI REGION

When most people think of classic Tuscan countryside, the hills and valleys spreading out between Florence and Siena, known as 'Il Chianti', usually spring to mind. The region is also known as Chiantishire, and in some of the small-town tourist offices they just assume everyone who wanders in speaks English! The area is split between the provinces of Florence and Siena, and conveniently named Chianti Fiorentino and Chianti Senese. Apart from gentle countryside, Chianti is home to some of the country's best-marketed wines. Of the wines, Chianti Classico is the most well known. It is a blend of white and red grapes and sold under the Gallo Nero (Black Cockerel) symbol.

Chianti is indeed very pleasant – lots of rolling hills, olive groves and vineyards dotted with castles and Romanesque churches known as *pievi*. But perhaps the hype has been just a trifle overdone. In other areas of Tuscany there's plenty of more spectacular country to be seen (around Pitigliano, for instance, or up in the Apuane Alps). Not that we want to put you off, but the Tuscan countryside by no means begins and ends in the Chianti.

It's possible to catch buses around the Chianti countryside, but the best way to explore the area is by car. However, you might also like to do it by bicycle, or even on foot. You could take a few days to travel along the state road SS222, known as the Strada Chiantigiana, which runs between Florence and Siena.

Budget accommodation is not the area's strong point, and you'll need to book well ahead, since it is a popular area for tourists year-round. However, if you have some extra funds and you're in search of a romantic spot, you shouldn't pass Chianti by.

Getting information about the area is easy. Virtually every tourist office in Tuscany has good information, but the best is at Radda in Chianti. For information online check out **W** www.chiantionline.com. For more details about Chianti wines, and Tuscan wines in general, see the special section 'The Tuscan Table'.

Chianti Fiorentino

South of Florence If you are heading down from Florence under your own steam, you might want to call in at the **Castello di Verrazzano** *(☎ 055 85 42 43, Greti; free; ring ahead to check opening hours)* along the way. It's about 1.5km west of the Strada

Chiantigiana, just before Greti. The word 'castle', as often in this area, is a little overplayed – these places tend to be fortified manors. This one is well known for its wine. You can drop by to taste and buy and even have a meal on the terrace, from where you have fine views across the valleys. Another castle, **Uzzano**, lies a little farther south. Follow the signs east of the Strada Chiantigiana.

Greve in Chianti About 20km south of Florence on the Strada Chiantigiana is Greve in Chianti, a good base for exploring the area. You can get there easily from Florence on a SITA bus. The unusual triangular 'square', Piazza Matteotti, is the old centre of the town. An interesting provincial version of a Florentine piazza, it is surrounded by porticoes.

The tourist office (☎ 055 854 62 87) at Via L Cini 1, 500m east of the piazza, opens 10am to 1pm and generally 2.30pm to 5pm in summer. It can provide maps and information in several languages, including English.

Giovanni da Verrazzano (☎ 055 85 31 89, fax 055 85 36 48, Piazza Matteotti 28) Singles/doubles from €56.80/72.30. If you're looking for accommodation in Greve, try here. Some rooms overlook the main square.

For a quick snack try the small *bakery* at Piazza Matteotti 87. The queues out the door are a sure indication of how good the pastries and buns are.

Montefioralle This ancient castle-village, only 2km west of Greve, is worth the walk, particularly to see its church of Santo Stefano, which contains precious medieval paintings. From Montefioralle, follow the dirt road for a few hundred metres, then turn off to the right to reach the simple **Pieve di San Cresci**. From here you can descend directly to Greve.

Badia di Passignano About 7km west, in a magnificent setting of olive groves and vineyards, is the mighty Badia di Passignano, founded in 1049 by Benedictine monks of the Vallombrosan order. The abbey is a massive towered castle encircled by cypresses.

The abbey church of **San Michele** *(☎ 055 807 16 22; free; open 3pm-5pm Sat & Sun)* has early-17th-century frescoes by Passignano (so called because he was born here). In the refectory there's an *Ultima Cena* (Last Supper) done by Domenico and Davide Ghirlandaio in 1476. Take a look at the huge medieval chimney in the kitchen. You can try to persuade the monks to let you in at other times. Food and drinks are available in the tiny village surrounding the abbey.

Panzano Travelling south along the Chiantigiana you will pass the medieval village of Panzano; after about 1km, turn off for the Chiesa di San Leolino at **Pieve di Panzano**. Built in the 10th century, it was rebuilt in the Romanesque style in the 13th century. From here you can continue on to Chianti Senese.

Chianti Senese

With lots of hotels and restaurants, **Castellina in Chianti** is one of the best-organised Chianti towns for tourists. Its information office (☎ 0577 74 23 11) is at the central Piazza del Comune 1 and opens 10am to 1pm and 3.30pm to 7.30pm daily (morning only Sunday).

More charming is **Radda in Chianti**, which is east of Castellina in Chianti. It makes a handy springboard to many of Chianti's most beautiful spots. The excellent information office (☎/fax 0577 73 84 94, W www.chiantinet.it), at Piazza Ferrucci 1, has enthusiastic and helpful staff. It opens 10am to 1pm and 3pm to 7pm daily (morning only Sunday) March to October, and 10am to 1pm Monday to Friday, November to March. The staff have loads of information about places to stay and eat in Chianti, as well as things to see and do, including suggestions for independent walking or organised tours to wineries (around €154.95 per person), where you can try the local wines before enjoying a traditional lunch.

For cooking courses in this area, you could consider trying **Podere le Rose** *(☎ 055 29 45 11; 1-week course €671 excluding accommodation)*, in the village of Poggio San Polo, about 10km from Radda.

One of the cheapest forms of accommodation is a room in a private house. The Radda tourist office can provide details about the apartments and the numerous farms and wineries offering accommodation. Prices start at around €67.15 for a double room and it's usually three-night minimum stay.

Da Giovannino (☎/fax 0577 73 80 56, Via Roma 6-8) Single/doubles €41.30/51.65. This is a real family house in the centre of Radda, complete with wood-beamed ceilings and views of the countryside.

Getting There & Away Buses connect Florence (€3.20, 1¾ hours) and Siena (€2.40), passing through Castellina and Radda, as well as other small towns. Chianti Senese is an easier destination to get to from Siena than from Florence.

Florence to the Val d'Elsa

Another route south from Florence could start from the Certosa di Galluzzo (see the Florence chapter). You could take the SS2 *superstrada* that connects Florence with Siena, or the more tortuous and windy road that runs alongside it. Follow the latter to **Tavarnuzze**, where you could make a detour for **Impruneta**, about 8km south-east.

Impruneta is famed for its production of terracotta – from roof tiles to more imaginative garden decorations. The centre of town is Piazza Buondelmonti. Not the most fascinating of Chianti towns by any stretch, it has been around since the 8th century. Its importance historically was due above all to an image of the Madonna dell'Impruneta, supposedly miraculous, now housed in the Basilica di Santa Maria, which looks onto the piazza.

Back at Tavarnuzze, you head south towards **San Casciano in Val di Pesa**. An important wine centre, the town came under Florentine control in the 13th century and was later equipped with a defensive wall, parts of which remain intact. The town centre itself is not overly interesting, however, so you could drink in the views and hit the road again. Before reaching San Casciano, you pass the **US war cemetery** *(☎ 055 20 20 020; free; open 8am-6pm mid-Apr–Sept, 8am-5pm Oct–mid-Apr)*, where the clean rows of white crosses are a powerful reminder of the carnage of WWII.

Just before Bargino, take the side road east for **Montefiridolfi**. It's one of those charming little detours that takes you winding up onto a high ridge through vineyards and olive groves. Along the way you pass the **Castello di Bibbione** *(☎/fax 0545 824 92 31, Ⓦ www.castellodibibbione.com)*, a picturesque stone manor house, once owned by Niccolò Machiavelli. A week's accommodation for two here will set you back €655.50 in the high season. Another 1.5km brings you to a large Etruscan tomb. You can keep going until you hit a crossroads. From there turn west for **Tavarnelle Val di Pesa**, from where you can reach the charming little medieval borgo of **Barberino Val d'Elsa**, which is worth a stop for a brief stroll along the main street.

Ostello del Chianti (☎/fax 055 80 50 265, Via Roma 137) Dorm beds €15.50 including breakfast. Open March-end Oct. At Tavarnelle you have the option of staying in this youth hostel, though the building is a rather characterless modern job. It also has family rooms, and you can get main meals for €7.75.

Heading directly south from Barberino would take you to Poggibonsi, from where you can make bus connections for San Gimignano (see the Central Tuscany chapter). Some of the spots indicated above can be reached by bus (especially with the SITA company) from Florence, but progress can be painfully slow this way.

Certaldo

About 15km west of Barberino lies this pretty hilltop town, well worth the effort of a detour, although this move takes you out of Chianti territory. The upper town (Certaldo Alto) has Etruscan origins, while the lower town in the valley sprang up in the 13th century – by which time both had been absorbed into the Florentine republic.

The upper town was the seat of the Boccaccio family. Giovanni Boccaccio died and was buried here in 1375. Along the main street you can visit the largely reconstructed version of **Boccaccio's house** *(☎ 0571 66 42 08, Via Boccaccio; admission €3.10 includes audio guide of Certaldo Alto; open 10am-7pm Wed-Mon, 10.30am-4.30pm Tues*

May-Sept, 10.30am-4.30pm Mon-Fri, 10am-7pm Sat & Sun Apr & Oct, 10.30am-4.30pm Wed-Mon Nov-Mar). It was severely damaged in WWII. The library inside contains several precious copies of Boccaccio's *Decameron.* A couple of doors up, the Chiesa di SS Jacopo e Filippo houses a cenotaph to the writer.

The whole of the upper, walled borgo is commanded by the stout figure of the **Palazzo Pretorio** *(☎ 0571 66 12 19; adult/child €2.60/1.30; open 10am-1pm & 2pm-7.30pm),* the seat of power whose 14th-century facade is very richly decorated with family coats of arms. Frescoed halls lead off the Renaissance courtyard.

The steep climb to the upper town can easily be avoided using the *funicolare* (funicular railway; one-way/return €0.75/1), departing from Piazza Boccaccio in the new town.

Fattoria Bassetto *(☎/fax 0571 66 83 42,* [W] *www.bassettobackpack.com, Via Avanella 42)* Beds in dorm or room €20, private singles/doubles €52/70. 2-night minimum stay. This place, 2km east of Certaldo on the road to Siena, is a real find if you need a place to stay. A 14th-century Benedictine convent, it was transformed into a farm by the Guicciardini counts. It is surrounded by a garden complete with swimming pool, and romantic rooms with antique furniture are available in the adjacent 19th-century manor house. Wine tasting, barbecues, and sunset walks are organised by the staff. You can reach Bassetto by foot from the train station, or if you ask nicely they might pick you up. It's best to book five days in advance.

See Lonely Planet's *Walking in Italy* for details of a three-day walk from Certaldo to San Gimignano and on to Volterra.

WEST OF FLORENCE

West of Florence and south of Pistoia (see earlier in this chapter) lie several towns of secondary interest. If time is on your side you could include them in a trip between Pistoia and Florence. There is little reason to stay in any of these places, but all have hotels if you get stuck.

If you plan to visit a few museums in the area consider buying a joint €4.15 ticket that allows entry to Museo Leonardiano in Vinci, Museo della Collegiata di Empoli and Museo Archeologico e della Ceramica in Montelupo.

Vinci & Around

From Pistoia a small country road (the SP13) leads south towards Empoli. After a long series of winding curves through the forested high country of the Monte Albano, you come across a sign pointing left to the **Casa di Leonardo** *(Leonardo's House; Via di Anchiano 36; free; open 9.30am-7pm Mar-Oct, 9.30am-6pm Nov-Feb)* in **Anchiano**. It's about 1km up the hill. Here, it is believed, Leonardo da Vinci was born the bastard child of a Florentine solicitor, Piero. You can poke your nose around inside but there isn't a whole lot to see.

Back down on the SP13, you are about 1.5km short of arriving in Vinci itself. The helpful tourist office (☎ 0571 56 80 12), at Via della Torre 11, opens 10am to 7pm daily. The town is dominated by the **Castello dei Guidi**, named after the feudal family that lorded it over this town and the surrounding area until Florence took control in the 13th century. Inside the castle is the **Museo Leonardiano** *(☎ 0571 5 60 55; admission €3.60; open 9.30am-7pm Mar-Oct, 9.30am-6pm Nov-Feb)*, which contains an intriguing set of more than 50 models based on Leonardo's far-sighted designs. Down below the castle is the **Museo Ideale Leonardo da Vinci** *(☎ 0571 5 62 96, Via Montalbano 2; adult/child €4.15/2.60; open 10am-1pm & 3pm-7pm)*, a private competitor to the museum listed earlier; it's a little on the silly side and not really worth it.

COPIT buses run regularly between Empoli and Vinci (€1.50, 25 minutes). To get to/from Pistoia you need to change at Crocifisso for the Pistoia-Lamporecchio bus. The drive from Pistoia is lovely, as indeed is the ride between Poggio a Caiano (see the Medici Villas section earlier) and Vinci via the wine centre of **Carmignano**, famous for its DOCG wines. The Carmignano wine was first documented in 1396, so unsurprisingly the area reeks of history. One winery worth stopping at is Tenuta di Capezzana (☎ 055 870 60 05, Via di Capezzana 100, Seano),

3km north-east of Carmignano. The regal winery produces some of the finest wine in the area and organises tours and tastings for €12.90 per person. The tourist office in Prato has information and maps pinpointing other wineries in the area.

Empoli

From Vinci you can head south to Empoli. It's a fairly nondescript sort of a place, but the small centre is pleasant to wander around. The Romanesque white-and-green-marble facade (reminiscent of what you can see at the Battistero in Florence) of the **Collegiata di Sant'Andrea** in Piazza Uberti is testimony that the medieval settlement that emerged from a place called Emporium must have been of some importance. Next door is the **Museo della Collegiata di Empoli** (☎ *0571 7 62 84, Piazza Uberti; admission €2.60; open 9am-noon & 4pm-7pm Tues-Sun*), which houses religious works by Tuscan artists dating from the 14th to the 16th centuries.

On the western edge of town rises the somewhat worn profile of the 12th-century **Chiesa di Santa Maria a Ripa**. The original town, documented in the 8th century, lay here.

A regular COPIT bus connects Vinci and Empoli. From Florence take the train (€4.50, 40 minutes), which is quicker and cheaper than the bus.

Montelupo

A short hop from Empoli by train (in the direction of Florence) is Montelupo, a market town on the confluence of the Arno and Pesa. The town has been a well-known centre of Tuscan ceramics production since medieval times and there is no shortage of shops here in which to browse or part with money.

Before you do buy anything, you might want to inspect the **Museo Archeologico e della Ceramica** (☎ *0571 5 13 52, Via Baccio da Montelupo 43; admission €2.60; open 9am-noon & 2.30pm-7pm Tues-Sun*), housed in the 14th-century Palazzo del Podestà opposite the tourist office. Examples of pottery from prehistoric times right up to the 18th century are displayed.

Across the Pesa stream, the Medici villa known as the **Ambrogiana**, and built for Ferdinando I, is now a psychiatric hospital.

In the third week of every month a pottery market is held in an exposition centre in Corso Garibaldi. In the last week of June Montelupo hosts an international pottery fair, which might be a good time for ceramics fans to turn up for a day. If you want to visit ceramics workshops, you may need to make an appointment. Call ☎ 0571 91 75 27 for more information.

To get to Florence (or head west towards Pisa) the easiest bet is the train (€1.90, 25 minutes).

North-Western Tuscany

While the bulk of tourists in Tuscany battle their way through hordes of their confreres in Florence, Siena and the hill towns of the Chianti region and around, considerably fewer bother with the north-west.

Admittedly, a good number of day-trippers pour into Pisa (usually from Florence or en route to or from the nearby international airport) to get the obligatory look at the Leaning Tower but they tend to ignore the rest of the city. Lucca, a gracious medieval enclave sheltered behind impressive bulwarks, has certainly not been left untouched by the busloads, but the numbers remain manageable.

The curious wanderer aspiring to taste lesser known parts of the 'real Tuscany' has no shortage of options here. Walkers can get serious in the Apuane Alps, known to Italians but largely ignored by foreigners.

Need to fit a spot of skiing in during a winter sojourn in Tuscany? Head for Abetone. It's not quite the Dolomites, but then the Dolomites are a mighty way off, aren't they?

In the rural Garfagnana and more rugged Lunigiana territories you can be pretty sure not to stumble across too many Hawaiian shirts and tour leaders waving little flags.

And this is marble territory. The business is centred above all on the town of Carrara, whose name is synonymous throughout the world with the best in exquisite white stone. To this day sculptors from all over the world (among many other less artistically inclined customers) seek their raw materials here, just as Michelangelo did four centuries ago.

You can even have a dip in the sea if you're in the area in summer. The seaside resorts are not terribly exciting (except when Viareggio puts on its party clothes for *carnevale* in February), but quite acceptable. Locals clearly love 'em, to judge by the summertime crowds.

LUCCA
postcode 55100 • pop 87,000
Hidden behind imposing Renaissance walls, Lucca is a pretty base from which to explore

Highlights

- Take a hike in the Apuane Alps
- Relax in the walled town of Lucca, one of the most attractive in northern Tuscany
- Scratch your head in bewilderment at Pisa's Leaning Tower – will it stay up?
- Party at Viareggio's *carnevale* in February and March
- Look around at the most famous marble quarries in the world – Carrara
- Explore the rural Garfagnana region and its northern neighbour, Lunigiana

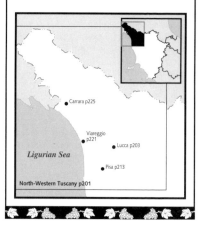

Carrara p225

Viareggio p221

Lucca p203

Ligurian Sea

Pisa p213

North-Western Tuscany p201

the Apuane Alps and the Garfagnana, and is well worth a visit in its own right.

Founded by the Etruscans, Lucca became a Roman colony in 180 BC and a free commune during the 12th century, initiating a period of prosperity based on the silk trade. In 1314 it fell to Pisa but, under the leadership of local adventurer Castruccio Castracani degli Anterminelli, the city regained its independence and began to amass territories in western Tuscany. Carrara was among these acquisitions, and the monopoly of control over its marble trade was a

200

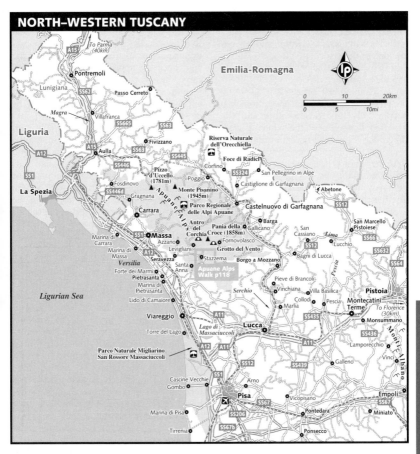

NORTH-WESTERN TUSCANY

powerful element in the prosperity of the city and the maintenance of its independence. Castruccio died in 1325, but Lucca remained an independent republic for almost 500 years.

Napoleon ended all this in 1805 when he created the principality of Lucca. Unswerving in his democratic values, he placed one of the seemingly countless members of his family in need of an Italian fiefdom (this time his sister Elisa, who in 1809 was entrusted with all of Tuscany) in control. Twelve years later the city became a Bourbon duchy before being incorporated first into the grand duchy of Tuscany in 1847 and subsequently into the Kingdom of Italy.

The long periods of peace it enjoyed explain the almost perfect preservation of the city walls: they were rarely put to the test.

Orientation

From the train station in Piazza Ricasoli, just outside the city walls to the south, walk north-westwards to Piazza Risorgimento and through Porta San Pietro. Head northwards along Via Vittorio Veneto to the immense Piazza Napoleone and on to Piazza San Michele – the centre of town.

Information

Tourist Offices Lucca's APT office (☎ 0583 44 29 44) is in Piazzale G Verdi, on the western edge of the walled city. It opens 9am to 7pm daily June to September and 9am to 3pm the rest of the year.

The regional APT office (☎ 0583 91 99 31), on Piazza Santa Maria, opens from 9am to 7pm daily July to September, and you may find it open over the winter period. They also do accommodation bookings from 3pm to 7pm (no phone reservations).

At the main office you can pick up an audio-tour of the city. The gizmo looks like a clumsy mobile phone and the commentary, which you listen to as you follow its directions around the town (this works here since the old centre is so compact), lasts two hours. You hire it for the day (thus giving you time to interrupt the thing and go and get a coffee or lunch) for €7.75 (€5.15 per person for two or more people).

Money The Deutsche Bank at Via Fillungo 76 has a user-friendly ATM, or you can change money over the counter. Several other banks with ATMs are scattered about town. Both the train station and tourist offices have exchange counters.

Post & Communications The main post office is in Via Vallisneri 2, just north of the cathedral, and unstaffed Telecom phone centres are at Via Cenami 19 and Via del Gonfalone 5.

Rinascimento (☎ 0583 46 98 73), Via C Battisti 58/60, is your best bet for logging onto the Net. The charge is €1.55 for 30 minutes and €2.60 for an hour online.

Medical Services & Emergency The main hospital (☎ 0583 97 01) is on Via dell' Ospedale, beyond the city walls to the north-east. The *questura* (police station; ☎ 0583 45 51) is at Viale Cavour 38, near the train station.

Cathedral

Lucca's Romanesque cathedral *(☎ 0583 49 05 30, Piazza San Martino; free; open 7am-7pm Apr-Oct, 7am-5pm Nov-Mar)*, dedicated to St Martin, dates from the 11th century. The exquisite facade, built in the Lucca-Pisan style, was designed to accommodate the pre-existing *campanile* (bell tower). Each of the columns in the upper part of the facade was carved by a local artisan and all are quite different from one another. The reliefs over the left doorway of the portico are believed to be by Nicola Pisano.

The interior was rebuilt in the 14th and 15th centuries with a Gothic flourish. Matteo Civitali designed the pulpit and, in the north aisle, the 15th-century *tempietto* (small temple) containing the **Volto Santo**, an image of Christ on a wooden crucifix said to have been carved by Nicodemus, who witnessed the crucifixion. It is a major object of pilgrimage and each year on 13 September is carried through the streets in a procession at dusk.

In the sacristy the **tomb of Ilaria del Carretto** *(admission €1.55, €5.15 combined ticket includes Museo della Cattedrale & Chiesa di SS Giovanni; open 9.30am-5.45pm Mon-Fri, 9.30am-6.45pm Sat, 9.30am-5pm Sat Nov-Mar, 9am-9.50am, 11.20am-11.50am, 1pm-6.15pm Sun, 1pm-5pm Sun Nov-Mar)* is a masterpiece of funerary sculpture, for the wife of the 15th-century lord of Lucca, Paolo Guinigi, executed (if you'll forgive the expression) by Jacopo della Quercia. The church contains numerous other artworks, including a magnificent *Ultima Cena* (Last Supper) by Tintoretto, over the third altar of the south aisle.

Next to the cathedral is the **Museo della Cattedrale** *(☎ 0583 49 05 30, Via Arcivescovato; admission €3.10 includes audio guide, €5.15 combined ticket includes the tomb of Ilaria del Carretto & Chiesa di SS Giovanni; open 10am-6pm daily Apr-Oct, 10am-2pm Mon-Fri, 10am-6pm Sat & Sun Nov-Mar)*, which houses religious art mainly of the 15th and 16th centuries, sculpture from the cathedral and illuminated manuscripts.

Chiesa di SS Giovanni e Reparata

The 17th-century facade of this one-time **Lucca cathedral** *(☎ 0583 49 05 30, Piazza San Martino; admission €2, €5.15 combined ticket includes the tomb of Ilaria del*

LUCCA

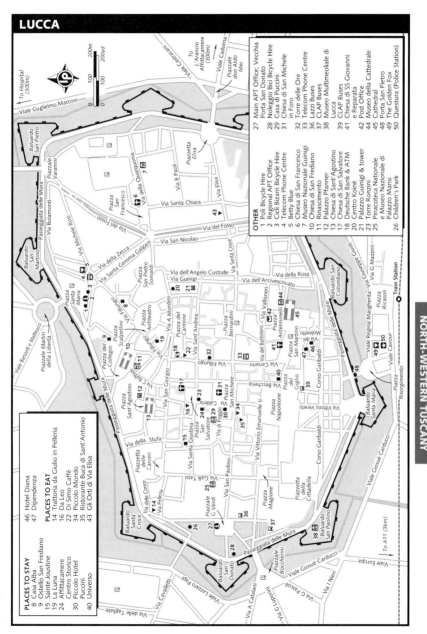

NORTH-WESTERN TUSCANY

PLACES TO STAY
1 Casa Alba
9 Ostello San Frediano
15 Sainte Joustine
19 La Luna
24 Affittacamere Centro Storico
30 Piccolo Hotel Puccini
40 Universo
46 Hotel Diana
47 Dipendenza

PLACES TO EAT
14 Trattoria da Giulio in Pelleria
16 Da Leo
22 Di Simo Caffè
34 Piccolo Mondo
35 Ristorante Buca di Sant'Antonio
43 Gli Orti di Via Elisa

OTHER
1 Poli Bicycle Hire
2 Regional APT Office
3 Cicli Bizarri Bicycle Hire
4 Telecom Phone Centre
5 Betty Blue
6 Chiesa di San Francesco
7 Museo Nazionale Guinigi
10 Chiesa di San Frediano
11 Rinascimento
12 Palazzo Pfanner
13 Chiesa di Sant'Agostino
17 Chiesa di San Salvatore
18 Deutsche Bank & ATM
20 Centro Koinè
21 Palazzo Guinigi & tower
23 Torre Ronzini
25 Pinacoteca Nazionale e Museo Nazionale di Palazzo Mansi
26 Children's Park
27 Main APT Office; Vecchia Porta San Donato
28 Noleggio Bici Bicycle Hire
29 Casa di Puccini
31 Chiesa di San Michele in Foro
32 Torre delle Ore
33 Telecom Phone Centre
36 Lazzi Buses
37 CLAP Buses
38 Museo Multimeolale di Lucca
39 CLAP Buses
41 Chiesa di SS Giovanni e Reparata
42 Post Office
44 Museo della Cattedrale
45 Cathedral
48 Porta San Pietro
49 The Golden Fox
50 Questura (Police Station)

Carretto & the Museo della Cattedrale; open 10am-6pm, 10am-2pm Mon-Fri, 10am-6pm Sat & Sun Nov-Mar) hides more than 1000 years of history. Parts of its *area archeologica* have even been dated to the 2nd century BC. Remains of the original early-Christian church and baptistry, built in the 5th century, are visible in the present Gothic baptistry. Remains of Roman buildings have been revealed below floor level and can be viewed. The church as you see it today is largely the 12th-century remodelling of its 5th-century predecessor, although some restructuring took place in later centuries.

Chiesa di San Michele in Foro

As dazzling as the cathedral is this **Romanesque church** *(Piazza San Michele; free; open 8am-noon & 3pm-6pm)*, built on the site of its 8th-century precursor over a period of nearly 300 years from the 11th century. The exquisite wedding-cake facade is topped by a figure of the Archangel Michael slaying a dragon. Look for Andrea della Robbia's *Madonna e Bambino* (Madonna and Child) to your right as you enter.

Near the church, off Via di Poggio, is the **Casa di Puccini** *(☎ 0583 58 40 28, Corte San Lorenzo 9; adult/child €2.60/1.55; open 10am-6pm daily June-Sept, 10am-1pm & 3pm-6pm Tues-Sun mid-Mar–May, Oct-Dec)*, where the composer was born in 1858. It houses a small museum dedicated to his life.

Via Fillungo

Lucca's busiest street, Via Fillungo, threads its way through the medieval heart of the old city and is lined with fascinating, centuries-old buildings. The **Torre delle Ore** *(city clock tower; Via Fillungo; admission €3.10; open 10.30am-6.30pm Mon-Fri, 10.30am-7.30pm Sat & Sun Mar-Sept, 10am-6pm daily Oct, 10am-4.30pm daily Nov-Feb)*, is about halfway along. Ascend the tower's 207 steps for sweeping views of the city.

East of Via Fillungo

You would never know it by simply parading northwards along Via Fillungo, but just off to the east (accessed from Piazza Scalpellini) is

the place where local Thespians regularly gathered in Roman days for a spot of outdoor theatre. Centuries later the unique oval-shaped theatre became **Piazza Anfiteatro** as houses were built on the foundations of the imperial amphitheatre. In some respects it's a bit of a theatre even today. Arty shops and cool cafes jostle to accommodate one another around the edges of the one-time stage.

Due south-east of Piazza Anfiteatro is Palazzo Guinigi and its **torre** *(tower; ☎ 0583 4 85 24, Via Sant'Andrea; adult/child €3.10/2; open 9am-7.30pm Mar-Sept, 10am-6pm Oct, 10am-4.30pm Nov-Feb)*. An oak tree, having managed to take root at the top of the tower, is an intriguing sight, and after mounting 230 steps, its shade is very welcome on a hot day.

A short walk farther east you enter **Piazza San Francesco** and the attractive 13th-century church of the same name. Farther eastwards still is the Villa Guinigi, which houses the **Museo Nazionale Guinigi** *(☎ 0583 49 60 33, Via della Quarquonia; adult/child €4.15/free, combined €6.20 ticket includes Museo Nazionale Mansi; open 8.30am-7.30pm Tues-Sat, 8.30am-1pm Sun & holidays)*, and the city's art collection, consisting of paintings, sculptures and archaeological finds.

West of Via Fillungo

Another example of Lucca's adaptation of Pisan Romanesque, the facade of the **Chiesa di San Frediano** *(Piazza San Frediano; free; open 8.30am-noon & 3pm-5pm daily)* features a unique (and much-restored) 13th-century mosaic. The main feature of the beautiful basilica's interior is the **Fontana Lustrale**, a 12th-century baptismal font decorated with sculpted reliefs. Behind it is an *Annunciazione* by Andrea della Robbia.

Of some interest are the interior and artworks of the **Museo Nazionale di Palazzo Mansi** *(☎ 0583 5 55 70, Via Galli Tassi 43; adult/child €4.15/free, combined €6.20 ticket includes Museo Nazionale Guinigi; open 8.30am-7pm Tues-Sat, 8.30am-1pm Sun & holidays)*.

Located within the city walls is the **Museo Multimeoliale di Lucca** *(Baluardo*

San Paolino), a museum with visual displays and videos on Lucca and its province. Whether it will reopen next year is up for debate, so check with the tourist office for news and prices.

Palazzo Pfanner

Erected in the late 17th century, the palazzo *(Via degli Asili 33; adult/child €3.60/2 garden & palace; €2/1 garden or palace; open 10am-6pm 1 Mar-15 Nov)* is a fine example of how the other half lived in Lucca. A sweeping flight of stairs leads up to the Baroque residence, adorned with frescoes and furniture from the 18th and 19th centuries, or you can head straight for the ornate 18th-century garden.

City Walls

If you have the time, do the 4km walk, jog or cycle along the top of the city walls. These ramparts were raised in the 16th and 17th centuries and are similar to the defensive systems later developed by the French military engineer Vauban. When you have finished torturing any kids you may have with churches and high culture you could take them to the swings and things near the Vecchia Porta San Donato.

Courses

Centro Koinè (☎ 0583 49 30 40, e koinelu@ tin.it, Via A Mordini 60; 2-week summer course €346, month-long year-round course €488) offers Italian courses for foreigners. The school can also arrange accommodation.

Special Events

Lucca has hosted the Summer Festival since 1998, and each year the series attracts top international acts. Neil Young & Crazy Horse, George Benson and the Eagles (resurrected from the dead) were among the performers in action in the city's Piazza Anfiteatro and Piazza Napoleone in 2001. It is held in July and tickets cost from €23.25 to €36.15 for the whole festival. An information and ticket office can be found at Piazza Napoleone from June onwards, otherwise check out the Web site at w www.summer-festival.com, or ask at the main APT office for further details.

On the third Sunday in July there is a torchlit procession and crossbow competition at Festa di San Paolino. On 14 September, Luminaria di Santa Croce sees another torchlit procession.

Places to Stay

The tourist offices can book accommodation for you, but you need to turn up in person after 3pm.

Hotel options within the walls of the old city are rather limited, and but they are complemented by *affittacamere* (rooms to rent) and a youth hostel. It really makes a difference to stay within the old city if possible, although some of the extramural options are admittedly only a quick stroll away.

Ostello San Frediano (☎ 0583 46 99 57, fax 0583 46 10 07, Via della Cavallerizza 12) Dorm beds from €15. This new HI hostel, near Chiesa di San Frediano, is by far the cheapest accommodation inside the city walls, and its small garden backs right onto them.

Sainte Joustine (☎ 0583 58 79 64, Via Santa Giustina 30) Singles/doubles up to €36/46.50. Sainte Joustine is a perfectly acceptable place to bed down. When business is slow they may rent out doubles to lone travellers for the same price.

Casa Alba (☎ 0583 49 53 61, fax 0583 49 53 61, e casaalba@info.it, Via Fillungo 142) Singles/doubles up to €36/51.65. This affittacamere has good, clean rooms.

Affittacamere Centro Storico (☎/fax 0583 49 07 48, Corte Portici 16) Doubles €56.80, with bathroom €82.65. Simple, stylish decor and stone floors make this is a good option in the heart of town. Reception closes at 8pm.

Hotel Diana (☎ 0583 49 22 02, fax 0583 46 77 95, e info@albergodiana.com, Via del Molinetto 11) Singles €46.50, doubles with bathroom up to €67.15, singles/doubles at *dipendenza* (annexe) €67.15/113.60. This small, modern hotel also runs a dipendenza at Via della Dogana 18, where the rooms have the advantage of air conditioning.

Piccolo Hotel Puccini (☎ 0583 5 54 21, fax 0583 5 34 87, e info@hotelpuccini.com Via di Poggio 9) Singles/doubles €55/80. If you can afford the extra, this friendly three-star hotel is a good bet.

La Luna (☎ *0583 49 36 34, fax 0583 49 00 21,* e *laluna@onenet.it, Corte Compagni 12)* Singles/doubles €61.95/93. Another welcoming hotel with all mod-cons, this place has the advantage of a private garage (but you need to reserve a space).

Universo (☎ *0583 49 36 78, fax 0583 95 48 54, Piazza del Giglio 1)* Singles/doubles €93/134.30. Another three-star place within the city walls, this is on a charming square. Prices drop slightly in the low season.

If you're stuck for accommodation and don't mind staying outside the city walls, there are a number of hotels and affitta-camere on and around Via Romana, just east of the centre.

L'Arancio Affittacamere (☎ *0583 49 65 17, fax 0583 24 03 43, Via Romana 57)* Doubles €46.50. This is one of the better places. The bathrooms are exceptionally large and there are cooking facilities and a fridge in each room.

Places to Eat
Lucca boasts a good selection of relatively reasonable trattorias and several reasonably priced restaurants and pizza joints.

Piccolo Mondo (☎ *0583 5 52 65, Piazza dei Cocomeri 5)* Set lunch menu €7.75. Open Sat-Wed. This is a good spot for a cheap meal – the set menu is filling if bland.

Ristorante Buca Sant'Antonio (☎ *0583 5 58 81, Via della Cervia 3)* Full meal €31. Open Tues–midday-Sun. Just around the corner, this is a rather classier affair and well recommended.

Gli Orti di Via Elisa (☎ *0583 49 12 41, Via Elisa 17)* Pizzas €4.15-6.20, mains around €4.65. Open Thur-Tues. This trattoria serves some of the biggest pizzas in town, and there's a wide range to choose from to boot. They also have a good salad bar you can help yourself to.

Trattoria da Giulio in Pelleria (☎ *0583 5 59 48, Via delle Conce 47)* Mains €4.15-8.25. Open Tues-Sat. Giulio in Pelleria is one of the best compromises in town. A somewhat impersonal barn of a place, they serve up high quality food at very affordable prices, so it's generally packed with

tourists and locals alike. Service is efficient and just for once you should not let the multilingual menu put you off.

Da Leo (☎ *0583 49 22 36, Via Tegrimi 1)* Mains €7.25-10.35. Open Mon-Sat. Tucked away off Piazza del Salvatore, this lovely little restaurant has a traditional feel to it and intimate outdoor seating.

Di Simo Caffè (☎ *0583 49 62 34, Via Fillungo 58)* Snacks & *gelati* €1.30-2.60. Open Tues-Sun. This is a grand bar and *gelateria* (ice-cream parlour) serving local specialities such as *buccellato*, a kind of sweet bun typical of Lucca. Occasionally, tinkling piano can be heard in the evenings.

Entertainment
Unless you arrive when the summer festival is on, Lucca is not exactly a jumping joint.

Betty Blue (☎ *0583 49 21 66, Via del Gonfalone 16/18)*. Open to 1am. This lively spot is a local mecca and is by far the best place to hang out.

The Golden Fox (☎ *0583 49 16 19, Viale Regina Margherita 207)* Open Tues-Sun. You can down a pint in pseudo-pub surroundings at this place near the train station.

Getting There & Away
CLAP buses (☎ 0583 58 78 97) serve the region, including the Garfagnana. Lazzi (☎ 0583 58 48 76) operates buses to Florence (€4.45, 1¼ hours), La Spezia, Carrara and Pisa (€1.85, one hour). Both companies operate from near Piazzale G Verdi.

Lucca is on the train line between Florence (€4.30, 1½ hours) and Viareggio, and there are also services into the Garfagnana. By car, the A11 passes to the south of the city, connecting it with Pisa and Viareggio. The SS12, which becomes the SS445 at Barga, connects the city with the Garfagnana.

Getting Around
Most cars are banned from the city centre, although tourists are allowed to drive into the walled city and park in the residents' spaces (yellow lines) if they have a permit from one of the hotels. There are parking areas (€1 per hour) in piazzas Bernardini, San Martino, Santa Maria and Boccherini. At some points

along the road running the length of the walls you will find free parking spaces.

CLAP bus No 3 connects the train station, Piazza Napoleone and Piazzale G Verdi, but it is just as easy, and more pleasurable, to walk.

You can hire bicycles from several outlets. There is one near the local APT office (look for the **Noleggio Bici** sign). Others, including **Poli** and **Cicli Bizarri**, are huddled together on Piazza Santa Maria. Rates are similar wherever you go. A normal bicycle costs €2 per hour or €3.10 for a mountain bike (which you don't need in town). Additional hours are cheaper and day rates are around €12.90. You can hire tandems too (but do you really want to?).

For a taxi, call ☎ 0583 49 49 89.

EAST OF LUCCA
Villas
From the 16th to the 19th centuries, Luccan businessmen who had finally arrived built themselves country residences – some 300 of them all told. Today most have gone, have been abandoned or are inaccessible, but a dozen fine examples still dot the countryside to the north-east of Lucca.

Villa Reale *(☎ 0583 3 00 09, Via Fraga Alta; admission €4.65; gardens open Tues-Sun Mar-Nov)* at Marlia, about 7km from Lucca, is the most striking. Much of its present look, and that of the meticulously planned gardens, is owed to the tastes of Elisa Baciocchi, Napoleon's sister and short-lived ruler of Tuscany. You can only visit the villa on a guided tour (there are six from 10am to 6pm).

Not far off to the east but less engaging is the **Villa Mansi** *(☎ 0583 92 02 34, Via delle Selvette 257; admission €6.20; open 10am-12.30pm & 3pm-5pm, to 7pm in summer, Tues-Sun)*, at Segromigno in Monte. The gardens are a not entirely happy mix of rigid French design and the intentionally haphazard English style.

A couple of kilometres farther on is the **Villa Torrigiani** *(☎ 0583 92 80 41, Via Gomberaio 3; adult/child for park & villa €8/6.20, park only €5.20/4.20; open 10am-noon & 3pm-7pm Apr-Oct, 10am-noon*

Mar & Nov, Wed-Mon only in Mar) in Camigliano, whose gardens stick more to the English taste. Some of the *giochi d'acqua* (water games) still work. Guests would be sprayed when they least suspected it by a series of water-spurting mechanisms. The house is fronted by a Baroque facade, said to be among the best examples of the style in all of Tuscany. You can join a guided tour of the villa, which lasts about 20 minutes.

To get to the villas, take the SS435 towards Pescia then turn northwards for Marlia (signposted 7km east of Lucca). It's slow but possible with public transport (CLAP buses) and the Lucca APT office can help you with timetables. If you have your own wheels (even of the hired bicycle variety), so much the better.

Collodi
If you stick to the SS435 you will, after another 8km, reach a turn-off north to this town. Alternatively, while heading south towards the SS435 from Villa Torrigiani, you could take a left-hand turn at the signpost for the village of **Petrognano**. This road winds its way uphill through olive groves and affords fantastic views of the valley below. In Petrognano, follow the signs to **San Gennaro** where the road starts its decent into Collodi. It is moderately interesting in its own right, if only for the **Villa Garzoni** *(☎ 0572 42 95 90. Piazza della Vittoria; adult/child €5.15/3.10; open 9am-sunset)*, whose majestic gardens rise away from the entrance on the town's main road. The Baroque building, richly frescoed inside, is quite impressive, but the gardens are more absorbing.

The **Parco di Pinocchio** *(☎ 0572 42 93 42; adult/child €6.70/4.15; open 8.30am-sunset)* might be one for the kids. Pinocchio is quite a phenomenon in Italian literature (and considerably more meaningful than the Disney version – see the boxed text 'The Real Adventures of Pinocchio'). The Florentine Carlo Lorenzini, who spent some time when he was a child in Collodi, took the hamlet's name for a pseudonym, so the town felt it should repay the compliment with the park. It started off in 1956 as a monument to the writer and his

The Real Adventures of Pinocchio

No, the story of Pinocchio, the wooden pup-pet that eventually turns into a boy, is not a Walt Disney invention. It is, rather, one of the most widely read and internationally popu-lar pieces of literature ever to emerge from Italy.

Back in the early 1880s Carlo Collodi, a Florentine journalist, could hardly have guessed that the series he was writing for one of united Italy's first children's periodicals, *Storia di un Burattino* (Story of a Puppet), would become an international classic.

Later collated under the title of *Le Avventure di Pinocchio* (The Adventures of Pinocchio), the tale would have made Collodi (a pseudo-nym taken from a town north-west of Florence where Carlo's family spent some time when he was a child) a multi-millionaire had he lived to exploit film and translation rights!

Collodi (his real name was Lorenzini) did not merely intend to pen an amusing child's tale. Literary critics have been trawling the text for the past century in search of ever more evidence to show that it was as much aimed at adult readers as kiddies.

The character of Pinocchio is a frustrating mix of the likeable and the odious. At his worst he is a wilful, obnoxious and deceitful little devil who

JANE SMITH

deserves just about everything he gets. Humble and blubbering when things go wrong, he has the oh-so-human tendency to return to his dismissive ways when he thinks he's in the clear. The wooden puppet is a prime example of flesh-and-blood failings. You thought Jiminy Cricket was cute? Pinoc-chio thought him such a pain he splattered him against the wall (in the real, not the Disney, version).

Pinocchio spends a good deal of the tale playing truant and one of Collodi's central messages seems to be that only good, diligent schoolchildren have a hope of getting anywhere (or in this case of turning into a fine human lad). But Collodi was not merely taking a middle-class swipe at naughty-boyish behaviour. He was convinced that the recently united Italy was in urgent need of a decent education system to help the country out of its poverty and lethargy. His text can be read in part as criticism of a society as yet incapable of meeting that need.

Indeed the tale, weaving between fantasy and reality, is a mine of references, some more veiled than others, to the society of late-19th-century Italy – a troubled country with enormous socio-economic problems and little apparent will to do much about them. Pinocchio waits the length of the story to become a real boy. But while his persona might provoke laughter, his encounters with poverty, petty crime, skewed justice and just plain bad luck constitute a painful education in the machinations of the 'real' world.

For those English-speaking adults curious enough to rediscover this little classic, the bilingual edi-tion translated and prefaced by Nicolas J Perella and published by the University of California Press is a handsome tool for better understanding and enjoying the tale.

creation and consisted of a bronze statue symbolising the moment when Pinocchio becomes a boy and a set of mosaics recounting the main episodes of the puppet's adventures. Later other elements were added, including Il Paese dei Balocchi (Toyland), with bronze statues of characters out of the book.

Getting here can be a bit of a pain without your own car, as buses between Lucca and Montecatini Terme don't stop that often in Collodi. If you happen to have your own wheels, head northwards about 5km until you strike a sharp turn-off to the left for **Villa Basilica**, a high mountain town with a remarkable Romanesque church.

Pescia

Pescia is the self-proclaimed Tuscan flower capital. Three-quarters of all Tuscany's floriculture businesses operate in and around here and the flower trade, including national and international exports, is worth some €130 million annually. Every second September (even-numbered years) a flower fair is held in Pescia. The town, split by the north-south flow of the Pescia river, is quite an interesting place for a bit of a wander too.

The medieval heart of town is the unusually long and uneven Piazza Mazzini, which gets busy on Saturday with the weekly market. The northern end is capped by the Palazzo Comunale and the Palazzo del Vicario – the latter dates back to the 13th century. A couple of streets to the west is the Chiesa di SS Stefano e Niccolao, dating partly to the 14th century. A couple of other fine palazzi around the church complete the picture on the western bank. The eastern bank is dominated above all by the Gothic Chiesa di San Francesco and the less interesting Baroque cathedral. There's no real need to stay overnight.

Boutique del Cibo (☎ 0572 47 61 76, Via Libria Andreotti 6). Pizzas €1.50-7.75, full meals €21 including wine. Open Fri-Wed. On the eating front, head here for home-cooked meals and pizzas.

CLAP buses connect Pescia with Lucca (€2.30, 45 minutes). Plenty of buses head east to Montecatini Terme too (€1.20, 20 minutes). You can also make connections for Collodi (but rarely).

Montecatini Terme & Around

If you are in need of spa baths, mud packs and other related activities for beauty or health reasons, Montecatini Terme is ready for you. It is, however, overrun with throngs of people after the same thing, and isn't the most exciting place around.

The APT office (☎ 0572 77 22 44), Viale Verdi 66, opens 9am to 12.30pm and 3pm to 6pm Monday to Saturday and 9am to noon on Sunday (closed Sunday in winter). For more specifics on the *terme* (hot spring centres) and the various treatments available, try the Terme di Montecatini information office (☎ 0572 77 81, Ⓦ www.termemontecatini.it), at Viale Verdi 41. It opens 8am to noon and 4pm to 6pm Monday to Friday and mornings only on Saturday.

Nine separate *terme* operate, many of them encased in grand late-19th-century buildings ranging from the moderately ornate to the rather silly. They work from May to October, although some services in some of the baths go on longer.

Excelsior's Centro di Benessere *(Thermal Well-Being Centre; ☎ 0572 77 85 11, Viale Verdi)* is the only one open year-round. The range of services, treatments and medical tests available is staggering – you could go for an afternoon swim (€3.60), or go all out and have a body and facial with mud and bath (€93).

A pleasant distraction is the late-19th-century **funicolare** *(funicular railway; every 30 mins; open 10am-1pm & 3pm-midnight daily, to 7.30pm Mon May-Sept, 10am-7.30pm daily Mar-Apr & Oct; €2.30/4.15 one way/return)* uphill to Montecatini Alto. This small, quiet borgo has inevitably ceded to temptation and the pretty central square is given over to cafes that probably could not exist without the passing thermal tourist trade. Aficionados of Montecatini's waters, such as Giuseppe Verdi, have been keeping those very cafes in business for quite some time. Such visitors are considerably more benign than was Cosimo I de' Medici, who had the medieval town largely destroyed and its walls pulled down after it had been taken and used by Henri II of France in his campaign against Medici Florence.

Montecatini is swamped with hotels – over 200 at last count.

L'Etrusco (*☎ 0572 7 96 45, Via Talenti 2*) Full board €51.65. If you do decide to stay, try to get into this place up in Montecatini Alto. In the high season you will probably be obliged to pay full board, but at other times you should be able to negotiate for a room alone. It also has a good, mid-priced restaurant (closed Wednesday).

Montecatini Terme is on the train line between Lucca and Florence. Regular buses, running from the station next to the train station, service Florence (€3.10, 50 minutes), Pistoia, Lucca, Pescia, Monsummano (€0.80) and other nearby locations.

Monsummano

Diehard lovers of spa complexes could also wander over to Monsummano, a few kilometres away from Montecatini Terme by bus (€4.65). There's really nothing much here apart from the **Grotta Giusti Terme** (*☎ 0572 9 07 71, Via Grotta Giusti; open 9am-1pm & 3pm-7pm Mon-Sat 21 Mar-8 Jan*), just outside town. The bus goes right to the complex.

THE GARFAGNANA

The heart of the Garfagnana is in the valley formed by the Serchio River and its tributaries. This is a good area for trekking, horse riding and a host of other outdoor pursuits, and the region is well geared to tourism. The tourist offices in Lucca or Pisa can advise, or you can approach the tourist offices in Castelnuovo di Garfagnana. Pro Loco tourist offices in several smaller villages can help with details on hotels and *rifugi*. Many use this area as a launch pad for treks into the Apuane Alps (see the Tuscany on Foot chapter).

The SS12 sneaks away from the north walls of Lucca (follow the signs for Abetone) and proceeds to follow the Serchio river valley northwards. It is a fairly uneventful route but hides a few surprises off to the sides. If you turn east at **Vinchiana** and follow the

narrow winding road a few kilometres you will arrive at the **Pieve di Brancoli**, a fine 12th-century Romanesque church.

Farther upstream you hit **Borgo a Mozzano**, where you cannot fail to see the extraordinary medieval Ponte della Maddalena (also known as Ponte del Diavolo, or Devil's Bridge). Each of its five arches is different, and the engineer must have been on interesting drugs. Typical of the era, the bridge rises to a midpoint and then descends to the other side of the Serchio – only the 'midpoint' here is well off centre!

Bagni di Lucca

A few kilometres farther on, as the SS12 curves east and just past the turn-off north for Barga (where we return shortly), is Bagni di Lucca. Since Roman days the thermal waters have been much appreciated and an 11th-century document contains instructions on how best to use the waters for cures. In the early 19th century the place became particularly well known, both to the gentry of Lucca and to an international set. Byron, Shelley, Heinrich Heine and Giacomo Puccini were among the celebrity guests to take the waters. The dignified neoclassical buildings are a distinct, atmospheric reminder of the town's former splendour and status.

The town straggles along the Lima River and seems to have two focal points. The following two hotels and restaurant listed are in the more easterly part, as is the small tourist office (*☎ 0583 80 57 45*) at Via Angelina Wipple.

Hotel Roma (*☎/fax 0583 8 72 78, Viale Umberto I 110*) Singles/doubles €33.55/43.90. This hotel on Bagni's main street has good-sized rooms and a large, private garden.

Hotel Svizzero (*☎/fax 0583 80 53 15, Via Casalini 30*) Singles/doubles €36.15/49. Svizzero is slightly more upmarket and about a five-minute walk away.

Circolo dei Forestieri (*☎ 0583 8 60 38, Viale Umberto I*) Set menu €10.35. Open Tues evening-Sun. This 'Foreigners Club' seems straight out of Victorian times, complete with high ceilings and chandeliers.

You can dine exceedingly well here for a steal.

Lazzi buses from Lucca run here on a regular basis (€2.25, 50 minutes).

The Lima Valley & Abetone

The SS12 proceeds in a north-easterly direction away from the Garfagnana into Pistoia province. If you felt the urge to do some skiing, then this would be the way to go.

En route, those with vehicles could take a couple of small detours. **San Cassiano**, 10km from Bagni di Lucca, boasts a 12th-century church, while **Lucchio**, another 10km farther on, is spectacular for its position on the north-eastern slope of a wooded ridge.

Back down to earth, the SS12 passes through **San Marcello Pistoiese**. From here the road banks north and quickly gains altitude through a series of sharp s-bends on its picturesque way up to **Abetone**.

This latter is the centre of Tuscany's main skiing resort. It's not the Alps, but it's not bad. About 30 pistes, ranging from barely 500m to 3km, will keep you amused enough, with 28 lifts and tow-ropes to get you around. You can obtain tickets at the **Ufficio Centrale Biglietti** (☎ 0573 6 05 56, Piazza Piramidi, Abetone; 1-day weekday/weekend €21.75/25.80, 3-day weekdays €56.80, 7 days €101; open 8am-1pm, 3pm-7pm) You can also sign up for lessons with a couple of ski schools.

Ostello Renzo Bizzarri (☎ 0573 6 01 17, fax 0573 60 66 56, Via Brennero 157) Dorm bed €10.35 with breakfast, full board €25.80. This large HI hostel is well equipped for skiers, nicely secluded and is the cheapest place to stay by far.

Otherwise the town has 14 hotels in which the cheapest rates for a single/double hover around the €41/67 mark. Bear in mind that at the height of the ski season the hotels tend to prefer bookings of at least three days and may also make half board obligatory. Another dozen or so hotels are strung out in nearby towns. For those without their own transport, the easiest way up is to catch a bus from Pistoia (see Around Florence chapter).

Barga

The high point of the steep old town of Barga is quite literally the high point. Climb to the top of town for panoramic views and take a look inside the cathedral, built between the 10th and 14th centuries. The pulpit is the prime object of curiosity, exquisitely carved and resting on four red marble pillars. Look at them more closely. The two front ones rest on lions dominating a dragon and a heretic. One of the back pillars rests on an unhappy-looking dwarf!

Albergo Alpino (☎ 0583 72 33 36, fax 0583 72 37 92, e alpino@bargaholiday.com, Via Pascoli 41) Singles/doubles €33.55/56.80. This is a fairly decent lower mid-range hotel, with its own restaurant, about five minutes' walk to the old town.

La Pergola (☎ 0583 71 12 39, fax 0583 71 04 33, Via San Antonio 1) Singles/doubles €40.80/53.70. Another good option with its own restaurant closer to the old town is this place.

CLAP buses from Lucca run up to 10 times daily, but there are only three on Sunday (€2.75, 1¼ hours). The buses stop in Piazzale del Fosso by Porta Mancianella, the main gate into the old city. Other buses run to Bagni di Lucca twice daily.

Castelnuovo di Garfagnana

Apart from the formidable 14th-century **Rocca**, a castle built for the Este dukes of Ferrara, there is not an awful lot to see here. This is, however, one of the best centres to get information on walking in the Apuane Alps (for more information see the Tuscany on Foot chapter).

The Pro Loco tourist office (☎ 0583 64 10 07), at Via Covalieri di Vittorio Veneto, opens 9.30am to 12.30pm and 3.30pm to 7pm Monday to Saturday. A second tourist office (☎ 0583 6 51 69), at Piazza delle Erbe 1, has similar opening hours and concentrates on walking information. You can stock up on maps and get information on rifugi, walking trails and other tips.

Walkers should pick up a copy of *Garfagnana Trekking* (€6.70), which details a specific signposted and well-maintained 10-day walk around the area and extending into the western Apuane Alps. A less detailed brochure, *Hiking in Garfagnana* (free) is also available. Another booklet, *Ippovie della Garfagnana* (free), details guided horse treks that cost around €12.90 to €15.50 per hour, or €72.30 per day.

Da Carlino (☎ 0583 64 42 70, fax 0583 6 26 16, Via Garibaldi 15). Singles/doubles €36.15/62. This hotel is a good option. The rooms at the back with views are the best, and there's a decent restaurant attached.

There are up to 11 CLAP buses from Lucca on weekdays (€3.10, 1½ hours).

Around Castelnuovo di Garfagnana

Several scenic roads fan out from Castelnuovo, so if you have your own transport plenty of options open themselves up to you. If you are relying on public transport things get considerably slower and sometimes impossible, but you can still enjoy the area.

One option is to follow the concertina of hair-pin bends that constitute the road leading, via Castiglione, to the Foce di Radici pass across the Apennines into Emilia-Romagna. The scenery in parts is splendid. Occasional buses run this route. With your own car you may want to take the minor parallel road to the south that leads you to **San Pellegrino in Alpe**, site of a fine monastery. A few places to stay at San Pellegrino and along the main road give you the option of overnighting if need be.

Walkers will want to head for the small **Riserva Naturale dell'Orecchiella** park on the narrow road via **Corfino**, itself a pleasant village with four hotels. Seven kilometres farther north is the park's visitor centre (☎ 0583 61 90 98), open daily June to September. Here you can pick up information and maps for walks inside the reserve. To take one of the most scenic routes to get here, start on the main road that takes you through Castiglione. Shortly after, a tiny road leads off to the west (left) to Villa Collemandine, after which you turn right along the road for Corfino.

The SS445 road follows the Serchio valley to the east of the Apuane Alps and into the Lunigiana region that occupies the northern end of Tuscany (for more on the

Lunigiana see that section later in this chapter). The road is scenic and windy, and takes you through lush, green countryside. About 8km north along this road from Castelnuovo at Poggio is a pretty turn-off to the artificial Lago Vagli along the Torrente Edron stream. You can undertake some pleasant little walks in the area, or simply some circular driving routes that can lead you back to Castelnuovo.

PISA
postcode 56100 • pop 98,000

Once, if briefly, a maritime power to rival Genoa (Genova) and Venice (Venezia), Pisa now draws its fame from an architectural project gone terribly wrong: its Leaning Tower. But the city offers quite a deal more. Indeed, the tower is only one element of the trio of Romanesque beauties around the green carpet of the Campo dei Miracoli – along with Piazza San Marco in Venice, one of Italy's most memorable squares.

Pisa has a centuries-old tradition as a university town and even today is full of young students. A perhaps unexpectedly beautiful city, it really deserves more than the usual one-day stopover planned by the average tourist.

History

Possibly of Greek origin, Pisa became an important naval base during the Roman Empire and remained a significant port for many centuries. The city's so-called Golden Days began late in the 11th century when it became an independent maritime republic and a rival of Genoa and Venice. The good times rolled on into the 13th century, by which time Pisa controlled Corsica, Sardinia and all of the Tuscan coast. The majority of the city's finest buildings date from this period, as does the distinctive Pisan-Romanesque architectural style.

Pisa's support for the Ghibellines during the tussles between the Holy Roman Emperor and the pope brought the city into conflict with its mostly Guelph Tuscan neighbours, in particular Florence but also Lucca. The real blow, however, came when Genoa's fleet inflicted a devastating defeat

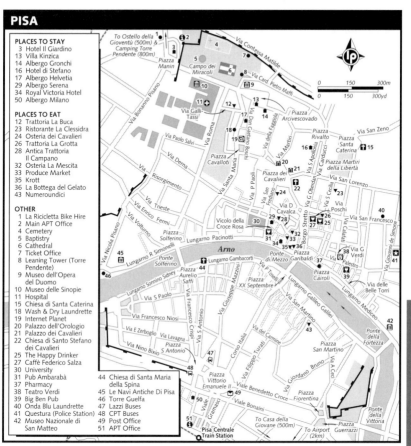

PISA

PLACES TO STAY
3 Hotel Il Giardino
13 Villa Kinzica
14 Albergo Gronchi
16 Hotel di Stefano
17 Albergo Helvetia
29 Albergo Serena
34 Royal Victoria Hotel
50 Albergo Milano

PLACES TO EAT
12 Trattoria La Buca
23 Ristorante La Clessidra
24 Osteria dei Cavalieri
26 Trattoria La Grotta
28 Antica Trattoria
   Il Campano
32 Osteria La Mescita
33 Produce Market
35 Krott
36 La Bottega del Gelato
43 Numeroundici

OTHER
1 La Ricicletta Bike Hire
2 Main APT Office
4 Cemetery
5 Baptistry
6 Cathedral
7 Ticket Office
8 Leaning Tower (Torre
   Pendente)
9 Museo dell'Opera
   del Duomo
10 Museo delle Sinopie
11 Hospital
15 Chiesa di Santa Caterina
18 Wash & Dry Laundrette
19 Internet Planet
20 Palazzo dell'Orologio
21 Palazzo dei Cavalieri
22 Chiesa di Santo Stefano
   dei Cavalieri
25 The Happy Drinker
27 Caffè Federico Salza
30 University
31 Pub Ambarabà
37 Pharmacy
38 Teatro Verdi
39 Big Ben Pub
40 Onda Blu Laundrette
41 Questura (Police Station)
42 Museo Nazionale di
   San Matteo
44 Chiesa di Santa Maria
   della Spina
45 Le Navi Antiche Di Pisa
46 Torre Guelfa
47 Lazzi Buses
48 CPT Buses
49 Post Office
51 APT Office

NORTH-WESTERN TUSCANY

on Pisa in the Battle of Meloria in 1284. The city fell to Florence in 1406 and, as if by way of compensation, the Medici encouraged artistic, literary and scientific endeavour and re-established Pisa's university. The city's most famous son, Galileo Galilei, later taught at the university.

The medieval city underwent profound change under the grand dukes of Tuscany, who began a process of demolition to make way for wider boulevards and so ease traffic. The single heaviest blow came in WWII, during the course of which about 50% of old Pisa was destroyed.

Orientation

By train you'll arrive at Pisa Centrale train station, which is at the southern edge of the old city centre. The main intercity bus terminus is Piazza Vittorio Emanuele II, a short walk northwards along Viale Gramsci.

The medieval centre is about a 15-minute walk northwards, across the Arno river, and Campo dei Miracoli (also known as Piazza del Duomo) is about another 10-minute walk north-westwards. It is quicker to catch a city bus from outside the train station (see Getting Around later in this section).

Information

Tourist Offices The main APT office (☎ 050 56 04 64, W www.pisa.turismo.toscana.it) is at Via Cammeo 2, just outside the city walls. It opens 9am to 7pm Monday to Saturday (to 6pm in the low season) and 10.30am to 4.30pm on Sunday. The office at the train station (☎ 050 4 22 91) opens 9am to 7pm Monday to Saturday and 9.30am to 3.30pm on Sunday, but has little more than a map and a list of hotels.

Money Avoid the exchange booths near the cathedral. Change money at banks along Corso Italia, or at the train station.

Post & Communications The main post office is on Piazza Vittorio Emanuele II. You'll find phones scattered about all over town. The best place to get online is Internet Planet (☎ 050 83 07 02), at Piazza Cavallotti 3/4. It opens 10am to 12.30am Monday to Saturday and 3pm to midnight on Sunday, and charges €3 for an hour's access.

Laundry There's an Onda Blu self-service laundrette at Via San Francesco 8a (€5.40 for wash and dry) and a Wash & Dry laundrette is at Via Santa Maria 105 (€6.20 for wash and dry).

Medical Services & Emergency The Ospedali Riuniti di Santa Chiara (☎ 050 99 21 11) is a hospital complex at Via Roma 67. The Farmacia Nuova Fantoni (pharmacy), Lungarno Mediceo 51, is open 24 hours. The questura (☎ 050 58 35 11) is on Via Mario Lalli.

Campo dei Miracoli

The Pisans can justly claim that the Campo dei Miracoli is one of the most beautiful squares in the world. Set among its sprawling lawns is surely one of the most extraordinary concentrations of Romanesque splendour – the cathedral, the baptistry *(battistero)* and the Leaning Tower. On any day the piazza is teeming with people – students studying or at play, tourists having their photos taken holding up the tower, and local workers eating lunch.

A staggered pricing system operates for tickets to enter one or more of the monuments in and around the square. €4.65 gets you admission to one monument, €6.20 to two, and €8.25 to four – the two museums, baptistry and cemetery *(cimitero)*. The cathedral is not included in the joint tickets. Tickets are available from an office (☎ 050 56 05 47) behind the tower.

Cathedral The majesty of Pisa's cathedral *(admission €1.55; open from 10am-7.40pm Mon-Sat, 1pm-7.40pm Sun Apr-Oct; 10am-12.45pm & 3pm-4.45pm Mon-Sat, 3pm-4.45pm Sun Oct-Mar)* made it a model for Romanesque churches throughout Tuscany and even in Sardinia. Begun in 1064, it is covered inside and out with the alternating bands of (now somewhat faded) dark green and cream marble that were to become characteristic of the Pisan-Romanesque style.

The main facade is a sight to behold, adorned as it is with four tiers of columns. The bronze doors of the transept, facing the Leaning Tower, are by Bonanno Pisano. The 16th-century bronze doors of the main entrance were designed by the school of Giambologna to replace the wooden originals, destroyed in a fire in 1596.

The huge interior is lined with 68 columns in classical style. This unusual feature is a remarkable reminder of the fact that among the many artisans at work on this church were also Arabs. The forest of columns is reminiscent of many a great Middle Eastern mosque.

After the 1596 fire, much of the inside was redecorated. Important works to survive the blaze include Giovanni Pisano's early 14th-century pulpit and an apse mosaic of *Il Redentore fra la Vergine e San Giovanni Evangelista* (Christ between the Virgin Mary and St John the Evangelist) completed by Cimabue in 1302.

Leaning Tower No matter how many postcards and holiday snaps of the Leaning Tower *(Torre Pendente; admission around €10.35, groups of around 30 people only at one time, advance bookings essential)* you've seen, nothing prepares you for the

Brace, Brace, Brace

When architect Bonanno Pisano undertook construction work on the *campanile*, or bell tower, for the Romanesque cathedral in 1173, he was on shaky ground. Barely 2m above sea level, what lies below the deep green lawns of the Campo dei Miracoli is hardly ideal for major building. A treacherous sand and clay mix sits atop a series of alternate strata of clay and sand to a depth of more than 40m – not exactly rock solid.

Pisano had barely begun to build when the earth below the southern foundations started to give. By the time construction ground to a halt five years later, with only three storeys completed, Pisano's stump of a tower already had a noticeable lean.

A new band of artisans and masons set to work on it again almost 100 years later – in 1272. They attempted to bolster the foundations, but could not right the tower. Their solution was to keep going, compensating for the lean by gradually building straight up from the lower storeys, creating a slight but definite banana curve. The bell chamber at the top was built in 1370. At some point the process came to a halt and until the 18th century the lean remained stable.

Over the following centuries, the banana solution showed it was no solution, as the tower continued to lean a further 1mm each year. By 1993 it was 4.47m out of plumb, more than five degrees from the vertical.

In addition to the problems down on the ground floor, the structure is itself a little on the dodgy side. The tower is basically a pretty but hollow cylinder, cased on the inside and out with layers of marble. Between those layers is a loosely packed mix of rubble and mortar, very unevenly distributed. The stresses caused by the lean have led some observers to fear they might be too much and simply cause the casing to crack and crumble.

In 1990 the tower was closed to the public. Two years later the government in Rome assembled a panel of experts to debate a solution. In 1993 engineers placed 1000 tonnes of lead ingots on the northern side in a bid to counteract the subsidence on the southern side. Steel bands were wrapped around the 2nd storey to try to keep it all together. For a while it seemed to have worked, until in 1995 it slipped a whole 2.5mm.

In 1999, a new solution was tried which consisted of slinging steel braces around the 3rd storey and attaching them to heavy hydraulic A-frame anchors some way from the northern side. These frames were later replaced by steel cables attached to neighbouring buildings. The tower thus held in place, engineers gingerly removed soil from below the northern foundations. After extracting some 70 tonnes of earth from the northern side the tower had sunk to where it was in the 18th century, rectifying the lean by 43.8cm. This, say the experts, guarantees the tower's future (and the tourist dollar) for the next three centuries.

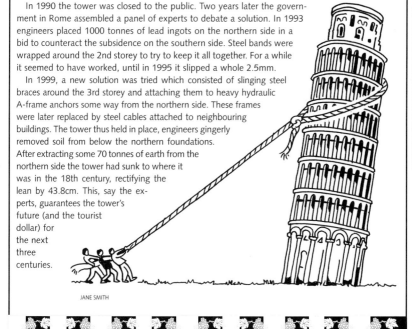

JANE SMITH

real thing. It's, well, gravity defying. The cathedral's bell tower was in trouble from the start: its architect, Bonanno Pisano, managed to complete only three tiers before the tower started to lean on the south side. The problem is generally believed to have been caused by shifting soil, and the 'Leaning Tower' continued to lean by an average of 1mm per year. Galileo supposedly took advantage of the tower's unique lean and climbed its 294 steps to experiment with gravity. Several solutions were tried and failed and the tower was closed in 1990 while the experts struggled to try to work out how to stop its inexorable lean towards the ground.

Fortunately for Pisa's tourism board and the houses directly in the towers shadow, the unstoppable tilting has been slowed, for the time being. A group of scientists have managed to rectify the lean by 43.8cm, bringing it back where it was 300 years ago (for more on successful and unsuccessful solutions see the boxed text 'Brace, Brace, Brace'). So in theory, locals can breath easy for another 300 years. The key to the tower was handed back to the city in June 2001, and it reopened with great fanfare to the public in December 2001.

Baptistry The unusual, round baptistry *(battistero; open 8am-7.40pm Apr-Oct, 9am-4.40pm Nov-Mar)* was started in 1153 by Diotisalvi, remodelled and continued by Nicola and Giovanni Pisano more than a century later, and finally completed in the 14th century – which explains the mix of architectural styles. The lower level of arcades is in the Pisan-Romanesque style and the pinnacled upper section and dome are a Gothic add-on. Inside, the beautiful pulpit was carved by Nicola Pisano and signed in 1260, and the white marble font was carved by Guido da Como in 1246. The acoustics beneath the dome are quite remarkable too.

Cemetery Located behind the white wall to the north of the cathedral, this exquisite cemetery, also known as the **Camposanto** *(same hours as baptistry),* is said to contain soil shipped across from Calvary during the Crusades. Many precious frescoes in the cloisters were badly damaged or destroyed during WWII Allied bombing raids. Among those saved were the *Trionfo della Morte* (Triumph of Death) and *Giudizio Universale* (Last Judgment), attributed to an anonymous 14th-century painter known as 'The Master of the Triumph of Death'.

Museo delle Sinopie Directly south of the baptistry, this **museum** *(same hours as baptistry)* houses some reddish-brown sketches drawn onto walls as the base for frescoes, discovered in the cemetery after the WWII bombing raids. The *sinopie* have been restored and provide a fascinating insight into the process of creating a fresco, although they are really only worth visiting if you have a particular interest in the subject.

Museo dell'Opera del Duomo In the line of fire if the tower should ever fall, this **museum** *(Arcivescovado 8; same hours as baptistry)* features many artworks from the tower, cathedral and baptistry, including a magnificent ivory carving of the *Madonna e Crocifisso* by Giovanni Pisano. Another highlight is the bust known as the *Madonna del Colloquio*, by the same artist, taken from the exterior of the baptistry.

The City

Once you've had your fill of the splendour and majesty of Campo dei Miracoli, a good thing to do is leave it behind. South of the Campo, the swarms of tourists are exchanged for quiet back alleys and vibrant shopping streets filled with locals going about their daily business.

Head southwards on Via Santa Maria and turn left at Piazza Cavallotti for the splendid **Piazza dei Cavalieri**, the centre of temporal power in the city remodelled by Vasari in the 16th century. The **Palazzo dell'Orologio**, on the northern side of the piazza, occupies the site of a tower where, in 1288, Count Ugolino della Gherardesca, his sons and grandsons, were starved to death on suspicion of having helped the Genoese enemy at the Battle of Meloria. The incident was recorded in Dante's *Inferno*.

The **Palazzo dei Cavalieri**, on the north-eastern side of the piazza, was redesigned by Vasari and features remarkable graffiti decoration. The piazza and palace are named after the Knights of St Stephen, a religious and military order founded by Cosimo I de' Medici. Their church, **Chiesa di Santo Stefano dei Cavalieri**, was also designed by Vasari.

The **Chiesa di Santa Caterina** *(Piazza Martiri della Libertà; free; open 9am-noon & 3pm-7pm)*, on Piazza Santa Caterina, is a fine example of Pisan Gothic architecture and contains works by Nino Pisano.

Wander southwards to the area around **Borgo Stretto**, the city's medieval heart. East along the waterfront boulevard, the Lungarno Mediceo, is the **Museo Nazionale di San Matteo** *(☎ 050 54 18 65, Lungarno Mediceo; adult/child €4.15/free; open 9am-7pm Tues-Sat, 9am-2pm Sun)*, an interesting enough art gallery housing mostly religious art, particularly from the 14th century. It features works by Giovanni and Nicola Pisano, Masaccio and Donatello.

The following joint tickets apply to the next three attractions: a combined €4.15 ticket gets you entry to all three, a €3.10 ticket combines entry to Le Navi and Santa Maria, while a €2 ticket admits you to the Torre and Sant Maria.

Cross the Arno and head westwards to reach the **Chiesa di Santa Maria della Spina** *(☎ 050 2 14 41, Lungarno Gambacorti; adult/child €1/0.50; open 11am-1.30pm & 2.30pm-6pm Tues-Fri, to 8pm Sat & Sun Jun-Aug, 10am-1.30pm & 2.30pm-5pm Tues-Fri, to 7pm Sat & Sun Apr, May & Sept, 10am-2pm Tues-Sun Oct-Mar)*, oddly perched on the road along the Arno and built in the early 14th century to house a thorn purportedly from Christ's crown.

Cross to the northern bank of the Arno and continue westwards to **Le Navi Antiche Di Pisa** *(Ancient Navy of Pisa; ☎ 050 2 14 41, Lungarno Simonelli 'Arsenali Medicei';*

Low & Dry

In the 19th century, the arrival of the railway in Pisa represented the death blow to river transport along the Arno. It will strike some as a little ironic that the State Railways (FS) should stumble across one of the greatest archaeological finds of the 20th century – a veritable port of ancient Roman shipwrecks.

While digging on a building site near the San Rossore train station, a couple of kilometres west of Campo dei Miracoli, in 1998, FS contractors came across the vessels. Six months later excavators, whose work is partly subsidised by the FS, had uncovered 10 boats, eight of which are currently being excavated.

Archaeologists could hardly believe their eyes. From a small warship through to cargo vessels of various kinds, a squadron of ships wrecked in storms at ancient Pisa's port had come to light. Up to 700 years of ancient maritime history was unveiled, as the wrecks clearly date to different epochs between the 3rd century BC and the 4th century AD.

On board some of the vessels rigging and sailing instruments were discovered, which will doubtless shed light on Roman-era seafaring. Just as important were the goods being transported. Hundreds of amphorae used to carry wine, fish, cherries, chestnuts, walnuts, olives and so on have been discovered, some actually containing remains of their contents.

Ceramics and other materials found on board these ships will provide clues to trade routes and communications in the ancient Mediterranean world. Many of the finds are on display at Le Navi Antiche Di Pisa (The Ancient Navy of Pisa) museum.

How was all this preserved? It appears that, after sinking, the vessels were slowly buried deep in an airtight sepulchre of mud. That very mud preserved this precious archaeological treasure for around 2000 years.

adult/child €2.60/free; open 10am-1pm & 2pm-6pm Tues-Fri, 11am-1pm & 2pm-9pm Sat & Sun May-Sept, 10am-1pm & 2pm-6pm Tues-Sun Oct-Apr). This small museum is devoted to the Roman Empire ships uncovered at San Rossore (for more information on the discovery see the boxed text 'Low & Dry') and their cargo. On display is a plethora of jugs, bowls and amphoras from the archaeological site, some of which have remained sealed and contained liquid residue thought to be wine or fruit. Alongside the pottery are animal bones, including the tooth from a lion thought to be taken from Africa for gladiator matches. The boats themselves are also well represented; small models and computer-generated 3D images give you a good idea of what condition they were in when discovered.

A few paces west again is the **Torre Guelfa** *(☎ 050 2 14 41, Lungarno Simonelli; adult/child €1.50/1; same opening times as Chiesa di Santa Maria della Spina),* where you can climb 200 steps for views over the city's rooftops.

Special Events

On 16 and 17 June, the Arno River comes to life with the Regata di San Ranieri, a rowing competition commemorating the city's patron saint. It is preceded by the Luminaria, a torchlit procession. On the third Sunday of the month is the Gioco del Ponte (Game of the Bridge), when two groups dressed in medieval costume battle over the Ponte di Mezzo, a bridge over the Arno.

Rotating between Pisa, Venice, Amalfi and Genoa is an annual race between the four – Palio delle Quattro Antiche Repubbliche Marinare (Historical Regatta of the Four Ancient Maritime Republics). It takes place in mid-June, in Pisa in 2002.

Places to Stay

Pisa has a reasonable number of budget hotels for a small town, but many double as residences for students during the school year so it can be difficult to find a cheap room. A booking service (☎ 050 83 02 53, fax 050 83 02 43, **e** pisa.turismo@traveleurope.it), open 9am to 1pm and 2pm to 5pm Monday to Saturday, in the main tourist office can help you out if you're stuck.

Camping Torre Pendente *(☎ 050 56 17 04, fax 050 56 17 34, Via delle Cascine 86)* Person/tent €6.45/5.65, cabins from €31. Less than 1km from the cathedral, this is Pisa's closest campsite. It's not the most attractive campsite in Tuscany, but its pool is welcome relief in summer.

Ostello della Gioventù *(☎ 050 89 06 22, Via Pietrasantina 15)* Bed in quad €11.90. This non-HI hostel is a long hike north-west of the cathedral. Take bus No 3 from the train station (walking it from Campo dei Miracoli is a huge pain).

Casa della Giovane *(☎/fax 050 4 30 61, Via Corridoni 29)* Singles/doubles €25.80/31. This woman-only hostel is 500m east of the train station. The rooms are simple and clean, and guests have the use of a small kitchen and garden.

Albergo Gronchi *(☎ 050 56 18 23, Piazza Arcivescovado 1)* Singles/doubles €17.05/32. This 'no-frills' kind of place is an absolute bargain for its position alone.

Albergo Serena *(☎/fax 050 58 08 09, **e** serena.pisa@csinfo.it, Via D Cavalca 45)* Singles/doubles up to €25.80/36.15. Another basic hotel, Serena is just off Piazza Dante Alighieri.

Albergo Helvetia *(☎ 050 55 30 84, Via Don Gaetano Boschi 31)* Singles/doubles €31/41.30, doubles with bathroom €56.80. Just south of the cathedral, this place offers pleasant rooms on a quiet street. Doors are locked at midnight.

Hotel di Stefano *(☎ 050 55 35 59, fax 050 55 60 38, **e** hds@csinfo.it, Via Sant'Apollonia 35)* Singles/doubles €36.15/56.80, with bathroom €49.05/64.55. You'll find good-sized rooms here, and a private terrace for guests.

Hotel Il Giardino *(☎ 050 56 21 01, fax 050 83 10 392, **e** giardino@csinfo.it, Piazza Manin 1)* Singles/doubles €62/93. This place, just west of Campo dei Miracoli, has sparkling rooms, all with air-con.

Villa Kinzica *(☎ 050 56 04 19, fax 050 55 12 04, Piazza Arcivescovado 2)* Singles/doubles €67.15/93. More upmarket is this place with views of the Leaning Tower.

Albergo Milano (☎ *050 2 31 62, fax 050 4 42 37,* e *hotelmilano@csinfo.it, Via Mascagni 14)* Singles/doubles €33.55/43.90, doubles with bathroom €62. Stumbling distance from the train station, this place is clean, friendly and rooms have air-con.

Royal Victoria Hotel (☎ *050 94 01 11, fax 050 94 01 80,* e *mail@royalvictoria.it, Lungarno Pacinotti 12)* Singles/doubles €80/95.55. For a little old-world luxury by the river, this is the only choice. Rooms are attractively maintained, and it goes without saying that rooms with river views are sought after.

Places to Eat

Being a university town, Pisa has a good range of cheap eating spots. Head for the area north of the river around Borgo Stretto and the university.

Antica Trattoria il Campano (☎ *050 58 05 85, Via Cavalca 44)* Full meal €25.80. Open Thur-Tues. This trattoria, in an old tower, is full of atmosphere. The menu sports a good selection of vegetarian pizzas.

Osteria la Mescita (☎ *050 54 42 94, Via Cavalca 2)* Mains €6.70-12.90. Open Tues-Sun. This charming place is a modest little eatery where the food is good and well worth a look. A one-time *mescita* (wine purveyor), the tiny eatery still has its 15th-century brick vaulted ceilings.

Trattoria la Grotta (☎ *050 57 81 05, Via San Francesco 103)* Mains €5.15-13.65. Open Mon-Sat. La Grotta is another good choice and similarly priced. It is, as the name suggests, suitably cavern-like.

Ristorante la Clessidra (☎ *050 54 01 60, Via Santa Cecilia 34)* Set meals €15.50 (meat), €18.10 (seafood). Open Mon-Sat. This is a great place to come for the choice of meat and fish dishes.

Osteria dei Cavalieri (☎ *050 58 08 58, Via San Frediano 16)* Dishes less than €11.40. Open Mon-Fri. Here you can opt for a *piatto unico* (single dish) or choose from a mouth-watering menu.

Trattoria la Buca (☎ *050 56 06 60, Via Galli Tassi 6b)* Pizzas from €4.15, set menu €15.50. Open Sat-Thur. This is not a bad choice near the Campo. The seafood

selection is quite extensive, but the only drawback is the pale green lighting – it makes everyone look slightly ill.

Numeroundici (☎ *050 2 72 82, Via San Martino 47)* Dishes €3.60-6.20. Open noon-10pm Mon-Sat (closed Sat lunch). The low prices and relaxed self-service alone make this place worth knowing. They serve up great salads, *focaccine* (a kind of filled bread) and a superb vegetarian lasagne.

Krott (☎ *050 58 05 80, Lungarno Pacinotti 1)* Gelati €1-2. This is a wonderfully exuberant spot for coffee, gelato, a cocktail or some fine focaccia.

La Bottega del Gelato (☎ *050 57 54 67, Piazza Garibaldi 11)* Gelati €1-2. Open Thur-Tues. For great gelato, head for this place just north of the river.

There is an open-air *produce market* in Piazza delle Vettovaglie, off Borgo Stretto.

Entertainment

Pisa can hardly be described as a club mecca, in spite of the student population. Still, a few watering holes in the centre suggest themselves. The tourist office may be able to make suggestions on the club front farther out of town, although (relatively) nearby Viareggio is a better option.

Caffè Federico Salza (☎ *050 58 01 44, Borgo Stretto 46)* Open Tues-Sun. This is one of the city's finest bars and a popular hangout for Pisa's young crowd. The cakes, gelati and chocolates are worth stopping for too.

Big Ben Pub (☎ *050 58 11 85, Via Palestro 11)* This place makes a decent attempt at impersonating a UK-style pub and has the advantage of Guinness on tap.

The Happy Drinker (☎ *050 57 85 55, Vicolo del Poschi 5/7)* Open Wed-Mon. This is another bar/pub trying hard to pass as a pub. It doesn't get going till late.

Pub Ambarabà (☎ *050 57 67 97, Vicolo della Croce Rossa 5)* Open Wed-Mon. For a somewhat more refined atmosphere try this place.

Teatro Verdi (☎ *050 94 11 11, Via Palestro 40)* Opera and ballet are staged here. Cultural and historic events include the Gioco del Ponte, a festival of traditional costume held on the last Sunday in June.

Getting There & Away

Air The city's Galileo Galilei Airport (☎ 050 50 07 07), about 2km south of the city centre, is Tuscany's main international airport and handles flights to major cities in Europe. Alitalia (☎ 8488 6 46 41) and other major airlines are based at the airport.

Bus Lazzi (☎ 050 4 62 88), Piazza Vittorio Emanuele II, operates regular services to Lucca (€1.85, 45 minutes), Florence (€5.80, three hours) and Viareggio. Less frequent services run to Prato, Pistoia, Massa and Carrara.

CPT (☎ 050 50 55 11), Piazza Sant'Antonio, also near the train station, serves Volterra, Livorno (Leghorn), Marina di Pisa and Tirrenia.

Train The train station, Stazione Pisa Centrale, is on Piazza della Stazione at the southern edge of town. The city is connected to Florence (via Empoli; €4.70, one hour) and is also on the Rome–La Spezia line, with frequent services in all directions.

Car & Motorcycle Pisa is close to the A12, which connects Genoa to Livorno and is being extended south to Rome, although that may yet take some years to complete. The city is also close to the A11 (tollway) and SS67 to Florence, while the north-south SS1, the Via Aurelia, connects the city with La Spezia and Rome.

Large car parks abound in Pisa. The one just north of the cathedral is perfect for day-trippers.

Getting Around

To get to the airport, take a train (€0.95) from the main station for the four-minute journey to Stazione FS Pisa Aeroporto, or the more frequent CPT city bus No 3 (€0.75), which passes through the city centre and past the train station on its way to the airport (it also goes to the Ostello della Gioventù).

To get from the train station to the cathedral, take CPT bus No 3 or 4 or walk 1.5km. Bus tickets cost €0.75 for an hour, €1 for two hours or €7 for a book of 10 one-hour tickets (you can change as often as you like within the validity of the ticket).

An excellent way to see Pisa is by bicycle. You can rent one at **La Ricicletta** (☎ 050 83 00 49, Via Cammeo 51) for €2.60 a day.

For a taxi, call ☎ 050 54 16 00.

VIAREGGIO

postcode 55049 • pop 60,000

Funny that Italy's second carnevale capital after Venice should also begin with 'v'. That's about where the comparisons between the two cities end, however. Viareggio is the not unpleasant leading resort town on the northern Tuscan coast, an area known as La Versilia. The town's architectural wonders are limited to some pleasing Liberty (Art Nouveau) edifices, mostly on or a block or two back from the palm-lined Passeggiata, the (almost) waterfront boulevard.

Orientation

It's a 10-minute walk (if that) from the train station to the waterfront and the main APT office. The city is ranged roughly north to south on a grid pattern. South from the pleasure-boat-lined Canale Burlamacca stretch the enticing woods of the Pineta di Levante. Another smaller wood, the Pineta di Ponente, occupies a large chunk of the northern end of town. Beyond it Viareggio blends seamlessly into the next beach resort of Lido di Camaiore.

Information

Tourist Offices The APT office (☎ 0584 96 22 33, fax 0584 4 73 36, e viareggio@versilia.turismo.toscana.it) is at Viale Carducci 10. There's an abundance of info on the town and surrounding area and staff speak several languages, but they do not make hotel bookings. The office opens 9am to 1pm and 4pm to 7pm Monday to Saturday (9am to 1pm only Sunday) June to mid-September. For the rest of the year (except the excitable time of carnevale – see under Special Events later in this section) it opens 9am to 1pm and 3pm to 6pm Monday to Saturday. A smaller office also operates at

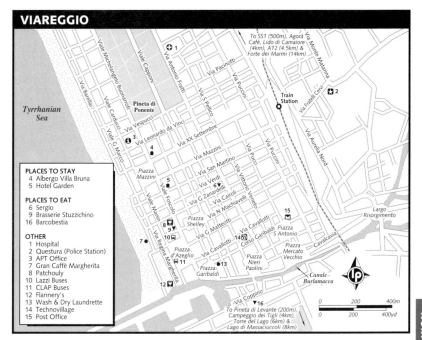

VIAREGGIO

Tyrrhanian Sea

To SS1 (500m), Agorà
Café, Lido di Camaiore
(4km), A12 (4.5km) &
Forte dei Marmi (14km)

Train Station

Pineta di Ponente

Piazza Mazzini

Piazza Shelley

Piazza d'Azeglio

Piazza Garibaldi

Piazza Nieri Paolini

Piazza Mercato Vecchio

Piazza S Antonio

Largo Risorgimento

Canale Burlamacca

To Pineta di Levante (200m),
Campeggio dei Tigli (4km),
Torre del Lago (6km) &
Lago di Massaciuccoli (8km)

0   200   400m
0   200   400yd

PLACES TO STAY
4 Albergo Villa Bruna
5 Hotel Garden

PLACES TO EAT
6 Sergio
9 Brasserie Stuzzichino
16 Barcobestia

OTHER
1 Hospital
2 Questura (Police Station)
3 APT Office
7 Gran Caffè Margherita
8 Patchouly
10 Lazzi Buses
11 CLAP Buses
12 Flannery's
13 Wash & Dry Laundrette
14 Technovillage
15 Post Office

the train station 9am to 12.30pm daily from June to mid-September.

Money You can change money at the main post office and most banks, of which plenty are scattered about town.

Post & Communications The main post office is on Corso Garibaldi. For a Web fix, try Technovillage at Corso Garibaldi 126. It opens 9am to 2.30am. Surfing costs €4.15 per hour. You can quickly check your email account at the main tourist office for free.

Laundry There's a Wash & Dry laundrette at Corso Garibaldi 5. A full load costs at least €2.60.

Medical Services & Emergency The main hospital (☎ 0584 94 91, accident & emergency ☎ 0584 94 92 80) is at Via Antonio Fratti 530. The questura (☎ 0584 4 27 41) is at Via Fratelli Cervi 32.

Things to See & Do
Apart from strolling along the tracks in the Pineta di Levante, around the Canale Burlamacca and along Via Regina Margherita, there's not much to occupy your time but the beach.

A good deal of the waterfront as it is now went up in the 1920s and '30s, and some of the buildings, such as Puccini's favourite, the Gran Caffè Margherita, retain something of their Liberty stylishness.

The beach costs. It has been divided up into *stabilimenti,* individual lots where you can hire change cabins, umbrellas, recliners and the like. Two recliners will set you back about €12.90 to €15.50. To get to free beaches you have to leave town.

Special Events
Viareggio's moment of glory comes for about three weeks in (usually) February and March when the city lets its hair down for carnevale – a festival of floats (usually with

giant and rarely flattering effigies of political and other topical figures), fireworks and fun. They have been doing this here since 1873 (from 15 February to 9 March in 2003).

Places to Stay

Camping You have a choice of about half a dozen camping grounds spread out between Viareggio and Torre del Lago in the Pineta di Levante woods. Most open from April to September.

Campeggio dei Tigli (☎/fax 0584 34 12 78, Viale dei Tigli) Adult/tent €7.25/10.35. This is one of the biggest sites, and includes a restaurant and disco. Without a car from Viareggio, take CLAP bus No 1 or 2 from Piazza d'Azeglio.

Hotels Viareggio boasts more than 120 hotels of all classes, along with affittacamere, villas and the like. They mostly jostle for space on, or a couple of blocks in from, the waterfront and it seems unfair to single any out, as they are invariably much of a muchness. In high summer, especially July, many hotels charge at least *mezza pensione* (half board) and often *pensione completa* (full board).

Albergo Villa Bruna (☎ 0584 3 10 38, Via Michelangelo Buonarroti 10) Rooms/full board €20.65/41.30 per person. This quiet little place has straightforward, clean rooms, and a lovely dated feel.

Hotel Garden (☎ 0584 4 40 25, fax 0584 4 54 45, Viale Foscolo 70) Singles/doubles €98.15/139.50, full board €113.60. You can be confident of the quality here. In high summer they like you to take full board, but won't necessarily insist on it.

Places to Eat

If you dodge full board in the hotels, there are plenty of restaurant options around town. The waterfront places tend to be expensive and uninspiring.

Brasserie Stuzzichino (☎ 0584 4 50 85, Viale Foscolo 3) Salads €4.65-8.25. Open Thur-Tues. For all sorts of snacks, salads and full meals if you are so inclined, try this simply decorated eatery. The speciality of the house is the amazing range of salads.

Sergio (☎ 0584 96 37 50, Piazza del Mercato 130) Meals around €7.75. Open Tues-Sun. This fantastic place is Viareggio's favourite roast chicken joint, but you can also get other meals and they offer a decent selection of wines to try. It's more of a takeaway, but there are a few tables both inside and out.

Barcobestia (☎ 0584 38 44 16, Via Copponi 201) Full meals €31. Open Tues-Sun. For fish specialities, head here. The decor is modern seafarer (with portholes and the like) but the food is very good. Book ahead.

Entertainment

Viareggio is one of Tuscany's better places for a night out on the tiles. Which is not necessarily saying an awful lot, but you can find a few bars and clubs to keep you occupied. To get started pick up a copy of *Note* or the more comprehensive *Il Mangiarbere,* both monthly events listing brochures, from the tourist office.

Patchouly (☎ 0368 353 99 00, Viale Foscolo 17) For cocktails and New Age music, float into this ambient cafe.

Flannery's (☎ 0584 4 58 46, Del Greco Lungomolo) Another attempt at an Irish pub, this is a lively place with a huge rooftop patio and live bands from midnight Thursday to Sunday.

Agorà Café (☎ 0584 61 04 88, Viale Colombo 666, Lido di Camaiore) Catch live music of varying types at this place. Later in the evening it converts into a disco – the standard musical fare is house and its relatives.

Getting There & Around

Bus Lazzi (☎ 0584 4 62 34) and CLAP (☎ 0584 3 09 96) buses run from Piazza d'Azeglio to destinations around of Tuscany, such as Florence (€6.50, 1½ hours).

CLAP has fairly regular buses up the coast to Pietrasanta and Forte dei Marmi, as well as up to 12 daily to Lucca and from three to six a day to Massa. CLAP also runs the town's local buses.

June to September long-distance buses run to such destinations as Milan (€21.75).

Train Local trains run to Livorno (€3, one hour), Pisa (€1.90, 20 minutes), and to La

Spezia (€3.45, one hour) via Massa and Carrara. Regular Florence-bound trains run via Lucca. A couple of Eurostar Italia trains bound for Rome, Genoa and Turin stop here.

Taxi Several taxi companies operate in Viareggio. You can order one on ☎ 0584 4 54 54, operating 24 hours.

Boat June to September Navigazione Golfo dei Poeti (☎ 0187 73 29 87), based at Via Minzoni 13 in La Spezia in the region of Liguria, puts on boats connecting Viareggio (along with Forte dei Marmi, Marina di Carrara and Marina di Massa) with coastal destinations in Liguria such as the Cinque Terre and Portofino. Call the boat company or inquire at the tourist office for more information. The same company also operates day excursions from Viareggio to the islands of Capraia (see the Central Coast chapter) and Elba (mid-July to August only). Boats leave for both at 9am and return at 6.15pm. Round trips cost €33.50.

SOUTH OF VIAREGGIO
Torre del Lago
A couple of kilometres south of Viareggio on the other side of the Pineta di Levante, Torre del Lago is a quiet continuation of the seaside theme. With one important difference. The **Lago di Massaciuccoli** spreads out a couple of kilometres inland, a shallow lagoon forming part of the **Parco Naturale Migliarino San Rossore Massaciuccoli** (see the following section). The lagoon hosts more than 100 species of permanent, migratory and nesting birds, including heron, egret, wild duck and moor buzzard. Eco-Idea (☎ 0584 35 02 52) run boat excursions across the lagoon for about an hour from Villa Puccini which cost €4.65 per person (minimum 20 people).

The composer Puccini had a **villa** *(adult/child €3.60/1.55, open 10am-12.30pm & 3pm-6.30pm Tues-Sun, to 5.30pm in winter)* built here by the lake, where he hammered out some of his operas. In July and August the open-air theatre by the lagoon is one of the stages for the Festival Pucciniano in July and August, in which his operas are performed (contact the Viareggio APT for details or

check out the festival Web site at Ⓦ www .puccinifestival.com).

A couple of modest hotels here could make a nice calming base to stay – although you'd really want wheels to get around unless you want to rely on CLAP bus No 4 to get into central Viareggio.

Parco Naturale Migliarino San Rossore Massaciuccoli
Covering 24,000 hectares and stretching from Viareggio in the north to Livorno in the south, this park is one of the rare stretches of protected coastline in Tuscany.

Part swamp, part pine forest, the park plays host to particularly diverse birdlife, especially during the migratory periods. Several species of falcon, duck, heron, cormorant and a series of other waterbirds call the area home for some or part of the year. Deer, wild boar and goats constitute the bulk of the land-going critter contingent.

You can get more information at the Centro Visite in Cascine Vecchie, a cluster of buildings dating to the first half of the 19th century. To get to it, take the road westwards from Pisa off the SS1, which ends on the coast at Gombo. The centre is open 8am to 7.30pm (to 5.30pm in winter) at weekends only. You can also call ☎ 050 53 01 01 or ☎ 050 52 30 19.

A sliver of coast between the Arno River and Livorno is not part of the park, and for Pisans the small seaside towns of **Marina di Pisa** and **Tirrenia** are the hub of the weekend beach-going experience. Of the two, Tirrenia is marginally more attractive. Regular CPT buses run to both towns from Pisa en route for Livorno.

Beyond the park, the next stop south on the coast is the sprawling port town of Livorno (covered in the Central Coast chapter).

LA VERSILIA
The coastal area from Viareggio north to the regional border with Liguria is known as La Versilia. Although popular with local holiday-makers in the summer and, surprisingly, with a good number of foreigners (Germans, French and Brits), it is hardly the Mediterranean's premier beach resort. Strip

development is fronted by sandy beaches, many of them in private hands (which means you have to pay to use them).

It does however make a good gateway to the Apuane Alps (see the Apuane Alps section later in this chapter), with roads from the coastal towns snaking their way deep into the heart of the mountains, connecting to small villages and walking tracks.

Pietrasanta & Around

Pressing up the coast from Viareggio you cross a municipal boundary into **Lido di Camaiore**. The development becomes sparser as you head northwards, and on slower days at least the beaches are a little less crowded.

When you reach **Marina di Pietrasanta** turn inland 3.5km for the town of **Pietrasanta** itself. The centre of the old town is Piazza Duomo, which represents the sum total of this town's attractions. If it's open, pop into the Chiesa di Sant'Agostino. Its rather stark, Gothic facade won't necessarily appeal, but the cloister inside is pleasant. Other structures of note on the square are the cathedral (13th century) and the Palazzo Moroni, which houses a modest archaeological museum.

With a car (or indeed a circle line CLAP bus from Piazza Matteotti) you could push farther inland to **Seravezza**, since the 16th century an important centre for marble extraction (Michelangelo spent some time here looking for raw materials) and now a gateway to the Parco delle Alpi Apuane. The Parco delle Alpi Apuane information centre (☎ 05 84 75 73 25), at Via Corrado del Greco 11, can supply you with maps and booklets on walks in the Alps. It opens 9am to 1pm and 4pm to 8pm daily June to September, and 9am to 1pm and 2.30pm to 4.30pm Monday to Saturday October to May. Set on the confluence of the rivers Serra and Vezza into La Versilia, and with the Apuane Alps rising behind it, Seravezza is a pleasant little spot. You could have a look at the cathedral and, about 4.5km north, the Pieve della Cappella (parish church) in Azzano. Also worth a look is the Palazzo Mediceo, built by Cosimo I de' Medici as a summer getaway.

While in this area you could proceed south-eastwards along the Vezza River (also by CLAP bus from Piazza Matteotti) to the picturesque *frazione* (hamlet) of **Stazzema** high in the hills. The village entrance is marked by the Romanesque Chiesa di Santa Maria Assunta, and it makes a great base for walks in the Apuane Alps. For more information see the Tuscany on Foot chapter.

Procinto (☎ *0584 77 70 04, Via Novembre 21).* Singles/doubles from €24.80/41.80. This rural hotel in the heart of Stazzema is full of rustic charm and the owners serve up huge meals for a very reasonable price.

If you feel like a dip in the briny, you could return to Seravezza and then take a direct road to **Forte dei Marmi**. It's in much the same league as Viareggio, with plenty of places to eat and drink scattered along and just in behind the waterfront. Oh, and if you feel the urge to stay, some 70 hotels offer their services. Ask for a list at the APT office (☎ 0584 8 00 91), Via Franceschi 8b.

Between Forte dei Marmi and the regional border with Liguria the seaside becomes less attractive. Indeed, if you are moving around under your own steam you would be better off heading straight into Liguria in search of coastal delights.

Massa

Inland, the next town of note is Massa, the administrative centre of the province of the same name (the province is also known as Massa Carrara).

The main tourist office (☎ 0585 24 00 63), at Viale Vespucci 24, is on the coast in Marina di Massa. There is precious little reason for calling in to Massa, where hardly anything remains of the old core of the town apart from the cathedral, itself of slight interest. Dominating the town and quite a sight from a distance is the **Castello Malaspina** (☎ *0585 4 47 74; admission €3.60; open 9.30am-12.30pm & 5.30pm-8pm Tues-Sun mid-June–mid-Sept, Sat & Sun only mid-Sept–end Sept).* The Malaspina family was in charge here for hundreds of years from the mid-15th century onwards. From this high point they could keep a watch on the surrounding territory.

There are only two hotels in Massa itself, should you for some strange reason want to stay. You are better off trying your luck on the

A different slant – *that* Pisan tower

Porto Ercole sits between two Spanish forts.

On track to Pizzo d'Uccello in the Apuane Alps

Pointy Pinocchio was created in 1880s' Florence.

Piombino's old quarter on the waterfront provides a glimpse of its 15th-century glory.

Medici-built walls back Portoferraio port, Elba.

Etruscan burial sites surround Sorano.

coast at Marina di Massa – again if you really feel the need.

Ostello della Gioventù (*☎ 0585 78 00 34, fax 0585 77 42 66, Via delle Pinete 237)* Beds €7.75. Open mid-Mar–Sept. The youth hostel is on the seafront north of Marina di Massa and is the cheapest place for miles around.

About 60 hotels of all categories compete for business down here too. Buses for a good number of destinations around the north-west of Tuscany leave from the train station, which is in Massa itself. Buses to Lucca run five times daily (€2.90, 1½ hours).

Carrara

Carrara, about 8km north-west of Massa, is a more attractive spot. And if your idea of a good time is staring at marble quarries perhaps you should hang out here for a wee while.

Indeed, Carrara is thought of as the world capital of both the extraction and working of white marble. Michelangelo made frequent trips to Carrara and other marble-producing centres in the area to select the best-quality material for his commissions. Watching the trucks rumble down from the quarries today makes you wonder just how back-breaking and treacherous a business the extraction and transport of marble must have been in Michelangelo's day. No doubt the concept of danger money had not yet occurred to anyone.

The marble quarries up in the hills behind Carrara were already being worked during the Roman Empire, so the tradition is a long one. In 1442 the town came under the control of the Malaspina family, and shared the fate of Massa farther south. Apart from a couple of Napoleonic interludes, the town remained in the Malaspinas' control until it was handed over to the Estense family in the early 19th century. Quarrying marble is no child's game, and a monument to workers who have lost their lives in the quarries can be seen in Piazza XXVII Aprile. The tough men who worked these stone faces formed the backbone of a strong leftist and anarchist tradition in Carrara, something that won them no friends among the Fascists or, later, the occupying German forces.

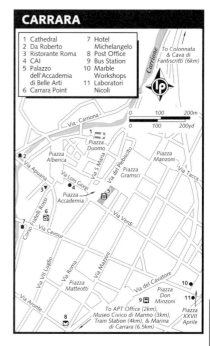

CARRARA

1 Cathedral
2 Da Roberto
3 Ristorante Roma
4 CAI
5 Palazzo dell'Accademia di Belle Arti
6 Carrara Point
7 Hotel Michelangelo
8 Post Office
9 Bus Station
10 Marble Workshops
11 Laboratori Nicoli

The gracious little old centre of Carrara is tucked away in the north-western corner of the town, almost 10km inland from its coastal counterpart, Marina di Carrara, and nuzzling up the first hills of the Apuane Alps, some of them visibly scarred by years of marble extraction.

Information The APT office (*☎ 0585 84 44 03*), Via Settembre XX, is about 2km south of the town centre on the way to the coast. It opens 9.30am to 7pm daily June to September and 10am to 1pm and 2pm to 5pm Monday to Saturday the rest of the year. If you are interested in visiting the *laboratori,* or marble workshops, ask them for the relevant map. As you will see from this, they are spread out between Carrara and Marina di Carrara.

The main post office is on the corner of Via Mazzini and Via Aronte. Carrara Point (*☎ 0585 77 96 36*), at Ulivi 19, provides Internet access for €5.15 an hour.

Things to See The **cathedral** (☎ *0585 7 19 42. Piazza Duomo; free; open 7am-noon & 3.30pm-7pm)*, at the heart of the old town, is one of the earliest medieval buildings to have been constructed entirely of Apuane marble. Building began in the 11th century, but it dragged on for two centuries. The facade, a mix of Romanesque (the lower half) and Gothic, was largely inspired by Pisan models. The rose window is especially noteworthy.

The prettiest square in the town, with its festively painted houses, is without doubt **Piazza Alberica**, created in the 15th century.

The 'castle' on Piazza Gramsci started life as a fortified residence of the Malaspina clan and is now the **Palazzo dell'Accademia di Belle Arti** (☎ *0585 7 16 58, Via Roma 1; free; open 9am-1pm Tues-Sat)*. Inside you can cast a glance at a collection of Roman sculptural fragments and other odds and ends.

South of the centre towards Marina di Carrara is the **Museo Civico di Marmo** (☎ *0585 84 57 46, Via Settembre XX; adult/child €3.10/1.55; open 10am-8pm Mon-Sat July-Aug, 10am-6pm Mon-Sat May, June & Sept; 8.30am-1.30pm Oct-Apr)*. Here you can find out everything you wanted to know about marble and were afraid to ask. On display are examples of no less than 310 types of marble, granite and other decorative stones found in Italy and a modest modern sculpture collection. Buses running between Marina di Carrara and Carrara will drop you off – it's near the *stadio* (stadium).

Many visitors feel drawn to marble quarries; here you can get a look at several. Roads run northwards into the hills to **Colonnata** and the **Cava di Fantiscritti**, among others. If you are driving, follow the yellow signs for the *cava* (quarry). Local buses make regular runs to Colonnata (€1.30, ½ hour). It appears this latter town was home to Roman slaves used to extract marble down below. Nowadays they use mechanical saws to carve out great blocks of the white stone. At the Cava di Fantiscritti, a chap called Walter Danesi has installed a private **museum** (☎ *0585 7 09 81; free; open 9am-7pm daily Easter-Nov)*, where you can see the kinds of tools with which quarriers used to struggle. To get to this spot you cross the Ponti di Vara, a viaduct

built in the 19th century for the railways. At the time it was considered one of the great feats of modern engineering.

If you've still not had enough, you could consider visiting some of the marble *laboratori* where the stuff is worked into all sorts of shapes. The commissions can range from the banal to the bizarre. Artists frequently instruct the workshops on how they want a piece executed, or at least begun – thus cleverly avoiding the hard and dusty work themselves. A handy one is **Laboratori Nicoli** on Piazza XXVII Aprile. If nothing else you could poke your nose into the dust-filled air of the workshops on either side of the square.

CAT buses provide a hop-on hop-off service over the summer that passes many of the laboratori, the museum and Colonnata. Tickets cost €7.75; pick up information at the tourist office.

Places to Stay & Eat There are a couple of places worth considering.

Da Roberto (☎ *0585 7 06 34, Via Apuana 3f)* Singles/doubles up to €31/46.50. This fairly basic place is at the junction of two busy roads.

Hotel Michelangelo (☎ *0585 77 71 61, fax 0585 7 45 45, Corso Fratelli Rossi 3)* Singles/doubles with phone & TV up to €56.80/87.80. This hotel has past its best but the rooms are still comfortable and filled with some lovely old furniture.

Ristorante Roma (☎ *0585 7 06 32, Piazza Cesare Battisti 1)* Full meal from €18. Open Sun-Fri. The decor here may be a little dated but the food makes up for it and the service is quick and friendly. Their vanilla gelato is particularly good.

Getting There & Away The bus station is on Piazza Don Minzoni. CAT buses (☎ *0585 8 53 11)* serve the surrounding area, including Massa (€0.75, ½ hour) to the south and, in the Lunigiana area, Fivizzano (€3.10, two hours), Aulla (€2.60, one hour) and Pontremoli (€3.50, two hours).

Trains along the coastal line (from Genoa, Rome, Viareggio and so on) stop nearer Marina di Carrara, from where local buses shuttle into Carrara itself (€0.75).

LUNIGIANA

Now we proceed farther northwards into one of the least explored pockets of Tuscany. The Lunigiana, a landlocked enclave of Tuscan territory bordered to the north and east by Emilia-Romagna, to the west by Liguria and the south by the Apuane Alps, caters little to tourism. Its main towns, with the exception of Pontremoli, are scarcely inviting.

The pleasure of the area comes from pottering about the back roads and small villages, using a combination of motorised propulsion and walking. The rugged territory abutting the mountains in Parma province to the north is great to explore. The medieval Via Francigena, a vital route connecting northern and central Italy in Roman days and again a key to armies and Rome-bound pilgrims alike, roughly follows the modern A15 autostrada from the Cisa pass south to Sarzana (in Liguria) on the coast.

Our route is one of several you could take. From Carrara take the provincial SP446d road northwards and follow the signs to **Fosdinovo**.

The only reason for calling in here is to take a closer look at the formidable **castle** (☎ 0187 6 88 91; admission €3.10; open from 10am-11am & 3.30pm-5pm Tues-Sun). Owned by the Malaspina clan since 1340 (it still belongs to a branch of the family), its defensive walls and towers were gradually modified from the 16th century on as the family converted it into a residence. Legend has it that a young princess died of a broken heart within the castle walls, and at full moon her shadow can be seen drifting from window to window. There are hourly guided visits; call for the latest information on times and prices.

From Fosdinovo you can follow the SS446 to a T-junction with the SS63. Heading right (eastwards) will bring you to **Fivizzano** (buses serve this route). You could stop for a food break in this largely modern farming centre before proceeding up to the border with Emilia-Romagna and the Apennines. Apart from the vaguely charming Piazza Medicea there is precious little to keep you here. On or near the square are clustered a few bars and restaurants, and a hostel.

CAT buses run regularly to Aulla and less so to Massa, Carrara, Fosdinovo and Passo Cerreto (the pass over the Apennines into Emilia). Indeed, beyond Fivizzano the mountain road offers wonderfully pretty country deep into Emilia-Romagna.

Heading in the opposite direction, south-westwards from Fivizzano, you would hit **Aulla**, a rather uninviting town with a 16th-century *fortezza* as its only drawcard.

Proceeding northwards from Aulla, you arrive in **Villafranca**, a one-time way station on the Via Francigena and, according to the stories, something of a medieval tourist trap, where the difference between local tax collectors and plain old thieves was vague to say the least. The northern end of what is essentially a one-street medieval settlement is dominated by a mill (now housing a local ethnographic museum) and bridge over the Magra River.

Albergo Manganelli (☎/fax 0187 49 30 62, Piazza San Nicolò 5) Singles/doubles €31/36.15, with bathroom €36.15/41.30. This inviting place is at the southern end of the old village. The rooms are big and airy, and there's a decent restaurant attached (set menu €12.90).

Pontremoli

This is the most winsome of the Lunigiana's main towns. A primary halting place along the Via Francigena, the original old town is a long sliver of a place stretched north to south between the Magra and Verde Rivers. These watercourses served as natural defensive barriers in this, a key position for the control of traffic between northern and central Italy. After it was absorbed into the grand duchy of Tuscany in the 17th century, the town enjoyed a boom. Much of the grace of Pontremoli dates to the fine residences built in those times.

The Pro Loco tourist office (☎ 0187 83 32 78), in the Palazzo Comunale in a courtyard off Piazza della Repubblica, opens 9am to 1pm and 3.30pm to 6.30pm Monday to Friday, and 9.30am to 12.30pm on Saturday. Pick up copies of *Trekking in Lunigiana* from the office, which maps out routes and accommodation in the area.

From the central Piazza della Repubblica and Piazza del Duomo (the latter is flanked by the 17th-century cathedral with its neo-classical facade) a steep and winding way takes you to the **Castello del Piagnaro** *(☎ 0187 83 14 39; admission €3.10; open 9am-noon & 3pm-6pm Tues-Sun, 9am-noon & 2pm-5pm Tues-Sun Oct-Mar)*. Although originally raised in the 9th century, what you see today is largely the result of 14th- and 15th-century reconstruction. The views across the town are enchanting and inside you can visit the museum, which houses a number of striking prehistoric menhirs (carved standing stones) found in the area, ranging in age from 3000 BC to 200 BC.

There are only two not overly cheap hotel options here. You are actually better off staying down the road at Villafranca (see earlier in this chapter).

Hotel Napoleon (☎/fax 0187 83 05 44, Piazza Italia 2b) Singles/doubles €46.50/ 69.70. This modern place is nothing special, but it's tucked away on a quiet street.

Trattoria Da Bussè (☎ 0187 83 13 71, Piazza Duomo 31) Full meals €25.80. Open Sat-Thur. In the shadow of the cathedral is this place, where you can dine on excellent local specialities. It is well worth stopping for.

CAT buses run regularly south to Aulla and other destinations around the Lunigiana. You can also get to La Spezia (an important coastal town in Liguria). Pontremoli is also on the Parma–La Spezia train line.

APUANE ALPS

This mountain range is bordered on one side by the Versilia coastline and on the other by the vast valley of the Garfagnana. Altitudes are relatively low (the highest peak, Monte Pisanino, is 1945m high) in comparison with the Alps farther north, but the Apuane Alps are certainly not lacking in great walking possibilities: some trails afford spectacular views to the coast and the Ligurian Sea.

The landscape in some areas has been utterly destroyed by marble mining, an industry that has exploited these mountains since Roman times. No environmental laws have been in place to prevent mining companies from literally removing entire peaks in some places. But, in the end, the extent of interference in the natural landscape has created a new environment that has a certain slightly bizarre aesthetic appeal.

The heartland of the mountains was constituted as the 543 sq km Parco Regionale delle Alpi Apuane in 1985. Some 22,000 people live within its boundaries.

There is a good network of marked trails, as well as several rifugi in the Apuane Alps, making walking in the region a popular choice. For further details of walking in this region, see the Tuscany on Foot chapter.

Apart from the walking opportunities, the main attractions in the area are underground caves. **Grotta del Vento** *(☎ 0583 72 20 24, W www.grottadelvento.com; tours €6.20-14.50)* is a series of caves with stalagmites, stalactites and crystal-encrusted lakes. The caves are open year-round, and three possible guided itineraries are offered (ranging in length from one to three hours). The first groups start at 10am. From November to March only the one-hour walk is available Monday to Saturday. Most visitors arrive by car. Barga, to the east, and Castelnuovo di Garfagnana, to the north, make possible bases. Lucca, to the south, is about an hour away by car. By bus it's more of an ordeal. From Lucca you take a bus for Gallicano, where you have to change and wait for one of the not-too-frequent connections to Fornovalasco, from where you have another 1km on foot, on the road northwards towards Trimpello.

Antro del Corchia *(☎ 0584 77 84 05; adult/child €10.35/7.75)*, to the north of Seravezza near the small mountain village of Levigliani, is a newly opened cave that is part of the deepest and longest cave in Italy. The first tours leave at 10am and last two hours. Bring something warm to wear as the caves maintain a chilly 7.6°C year-round. Buses do run from Pietrasanta via Seravezza (€1.45, 40 minutes), but there are no return services in the evening so you'd have to stay in Levigliani overnight.

Central Coast

The Medici grand dukes first gave life to the little town of Livorno on the central Tuscan coast, and it remains a busy port to this day. Eager for a little naval grandeur, the masters of Florence chose Livorno because it is close to Pisa, but also because it was one of the few handy coastal positions not surrounded by malarial swamps.

Much of the coast south of Livorno as far as Piombino, known as the Maremma Pisana, was indeed unpleasantly damp and mosquito-infested. Although initial attempts to dry out these swamps were carried out in the 18th century, it was really only under Leopoldo II that serious land reclamation took place. As a result, agricultural and industrial activity grew, old roads were rebuilt and new ones laid out. The Maremma Pisana only formally became a part of Livorno province in 1925.

Although some of the inland mountain towns are definitely worth some exploration and the occasional beach (especially on the southern Golfo di Baratti) is pleasant enough, this is not the most riveting part of Tuscany. For those into searching out remnants of Etruscan civilisation, Populonia and its medieval twin, Populonia Alta, make interesting diversions. Livorno and Piombino are also departure points for ferries to the Tuscan islands and points beyond (such as Corsica), so you may well find yourself passing through the area anyway. If so, and you have time to spare, a few of the options below will make your travels here more enjoyable.

LIVORNO (LEGHORN)
postcode 57100 • pop 173,000

Tuscany's second-largest city, Livorno is not really worth a visit unless you are catching a ferry to Sardinia or Corsica. This modern port and industrial centre was heavily bombed during WWII (it was one of Fascist Italy's main naval bases) and there is something unnervingly melancholy about the centre of town. The postwar rebuilding programme may be charitably described as unimaginative.

Highlights

- Chow down to a generous helping of *cacciucco*, a kind of seafood hotpot
- Sail out to the charming island of Capraia from Livorno
- Visit the historic towns of Campiglia Marittima and Suvereto
- Combine a rest on the beach of the Golfo di Baratti with an exploration of the Etruscan and medieval settlements of Populonia

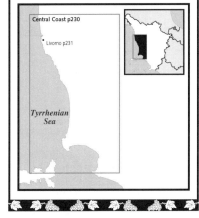

Central Coast p230

Livorno p231

Tyrrhenian Sea

Earliest references to the town date to 1017 and the port was in the hands of Pisa and then Genoa for centuries. Florence, in need of an opening onto the sea, bought it in 1421. It was still tiny – by the 1550s it boasted a grand total of 480 permanent residents! All that changed under Cosimo I de' Medici, who converted the scrawny settlement into a heavily fortified coastal bastion. It is quite extraordinary that by the end of the 18th century 80,000 people lived in Livorno, a busy port that had become one of the main staging posts for British and Dutch merchants operating between Western Europe and the Middle East. In the following century it was

CENTRAL COAST

Tyrrhenian Sea

declared a free port, no doubt stimulating further growth and prosperity.

Livornese cuisine is, as you might expect, seafood-based. If you find yourself here (or in any of the middling beach 'resorts' farther down the coast), try to tuck into a *cacciucco*, a quite remarkable mixed seafood stew (see the special section 'The Tuscan Table' for the recipe).

Orientation & Information

From the train station in Piazza Dante, east of the city centre, walk west along Viale G Carducci and then Via Grande into the central Piazza Grande. The main APT tourist office (☎ 0586 89 81 11, ⓔ info@livorno .turismo.toscana.it) is at Piazza Cavour 6 (2nd floor) to the south. From Piazza Grande, head north to Piazza del Municipio and a second small APT. A third APT (☎ 0586 89 53 20) is near the main ferry terminal, known as Calata Carrara, near Stazione Marittima. The main office opens

9am to 1pm and 3pm to 5pm Monday to Friday. The other two open 8am to 1pm and 2pm to 8pm daily (from 4pm Monday and Wednesday), but the Calata Carrara APT only operates June to September.

The main post office is at Via Cairoli 46, and there's an unstaffed Telecom office at Largo Duomo 14. The latter has a full complement of Italian phonebooks.

The *questura* (police station; ☎ 0586 23 51 11) is in the Palazzo del Governo, Piazza Unità d'Italia. The hospital (Ospedale Civile; ☎ 0586 22 31 11) is at Viale Alfieri 36, between the centre and the main train station.

Things to See

The city does have a few worthy sights. The **Fortezza Nuova** (New Fort), in the area known as Piccola Venezia (oh please) because of its small canals, was built for the Medici in the late 16th century and is now a pleasant public park. The resemblance to Venice is notable by its absence – why is it that whenever someone builds a canal or two in a city they are inevitably drawn to call it Little Venice? In this case there is some small excuse – the methods used to reclaim the land from the sea to extend the city northwards in the 17th century were based on the tried and tested practice of the Venetians.

Close to the waterfront is the city's other fort, the **Fortezza Vecchia** (Old Fort), built 60 years earlier on the site of an 11th-century building. It is in pretty bad shape – some amazing subsidence must be happening judging by the yawning chasms that some might politely call cracks in the wall.

Livorno has a couple of extremely modest museums. Perhaps the only one worth your time (if you have some of the latter to kill) is the **Museo Civico Giovanni Fattori** (☎ 0586 80 80 01, Via San Jacopo 65; admission €4.15; open 9am-1pm Tues-Sun). It's located in a villa in a pretty park south of the centre, and features works by the 19th-century Macchiaioli movement led by the artist Giovanni Fattori. Temporary exhibitions are also occasionally held in the gallery.

If you still need a museum fix try the **Museo di Storia Naturale del Mediterraneo** (☎ 0586 80 22 94, Via Roma 234; admission

€2.60; open 9am-1pm & 3pm-6pm Tues-Sun), where you'll find a range of botanical and sea-faring creatures (specimens only) from the Mediterranean, including 'Annie', a common whale skeleton.

The city's unspectacular **cathedral** is just off Piazza Grande.

South of town what's known as the Etruscan Coast (Costa degli Etruschi) begins. The town beaches stretch for some way south, but they are pebbly and generally nothing special. The grand old seaside villas are worth seeing. The No 1 bus from the main train station heads down the coast

road passing via the town centre and Porto Mediceo.

Places to Stay & Eat

Finding accommodation shouldn't be a problem.

Villa Morazzana (☎ *0586 50 0076, fax 0586 50 24 26, Via di Collinet 68)* Dorm beds €12.90, rooms €25.80, with bathroom €41.30. This hostel has a pleasant spot in the hills, only a couple of kilometres south-east of the town centre. The rooms are spacious and bright, and the hallways attractively decked in artwork.

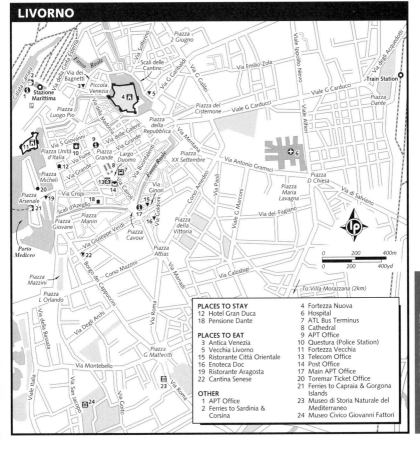

LIVORNO

PLACES TO STAY	OTHER
12 Hotel Gran Duca	1 APT Office
18 Pensione Dante	2 Ferries to Sardinia & Corsina
	4 Fortezza Nuova
PLACES TO EAT	6 Hospital
3 Antica Venezia	7 ATL Bus Terminus
5 Vecchia Livorno	8 Cathedral
15 Ristorante Città Orientale	9 APT Office
16 Enoteca Doc	10 Questura (Police Station)
19 Ristorante Aragosta	11 Fortezza Vecchia
22 Cantina Senese	13 Telecom Office
	14 Post Office
	17 Main APT Office
	20 Toremar Ticket Office
	21 Ferries to Capraia & Gorgona Islands
	23 Museo di Storia Naturale del Mediterraneo
	24 Museo Civico Giovanni Fattori

CENTRAL COAST

Amedeo Does Paris

Among the most striking nudes painted in the 20th century have to be those by Amedeo Modigliani. Born in Livorno in 1884, he showed talent as an artist at an early age and trained under the influence of the former Macchiaioli artists who had shaken up the Florentine, and indeed Italian, art scene in the years before and after Italian Unity. Livorno's own Giovanni Fattori had been a leading light among the Macchiaioli.

Modigliani was soon drawn away from his home town. He headed first to Florence, where he studied in 1902, but this was not enough. A year in Venice, where he became more closely acquainted with Austrian painters such as Gustav Klimt and the Jugendstil, was followed finally by a move to Paris in 1906.

Fauvism and cubism were taking off and Paris was the epicentre of the art world. It was here that Modigliani's particular style, marked but not swamped by the exciting new influences with which he now surrounded himself, came to life.

JANE SMITH

Modigliani returned to Italy briefly in 1909, but from then until the end of his life in 1920 remained in Montparnasse in Paris. For the next five years he turned to sculpture, rapidly accelerating the process of simplification – seeking to emphasise the contours. This period was then reflected in his subsequent paintings – the long faces typical of his later work are a result of his venture into sculpture. In 1914 and 1915 he concentrated on portraiture and then, in the last years of his life, produced the series of nudes that figure among his best-known works. These nudes ooze a sultry, voluptuous sensuality, bursting with rich, warm colour. Yet they are painted with remarkable simplicity. His figures are infused with a touching, imperfect humanity.

Predictably, his work really only began to receive critical acclaim after his death, particularly in the wake of an exhibition of his paintings at the Venice Biennale in 1930. The bulk of his work has been scattered across art galleries in various parts of Italy and from Switzerland to France, Britain, the USA and beyond.

Breakfast and a garden are thrown in with the price. To get here, take bus No 3 from Piazza Grande.

Pensione Dante (☎ 0586 89 34 61, Scali d'Azeglio 28) Singles/doubles €20.65/41.30. Near the waterfront, this place has modest rooms and a friendly welcome.

Hotel Gran Duca (☎ 0586 89 10 24, fax 0586 89 11 53, **e** grandduca@sysnet .it, Piazza Micheli) Singles/doubles €83/118.80. For greater comfort you could try this hotel, where rooms have all mod cons.

For produce, the *market* is on Via Buontalenti, and the area around Piazza XX Settembre is encouraging for *bars* and *cafes*.

Ristorante Aragosta (☎ 0586 89 53 95, Piazza Arsenale 6) Fish mains €7.25-12.90. Open Mon-Sat. For seafood try this reputable place right on the waterfront.

Cantina Senese (☎ 0586 89 02 39, Borgo dei Cappuccini 95) Meals from €10.35. Open Mon-Sat. This is a popular local eatery with a relaxed atmosphere and a pleasantly inexpensive menu.

Enoteca Doc (☎ 0586 88 75 83, Via Goldoni 40-44) Meals from €18. Open Tues-Sun. The menu changes weekly at this *enoteca* (wine bar), and you can enjoy fresh pasta dishes and good *carpaccio* (dish of fine slices of usually meat or fish), as well as snacks. As with any enoteca, the main attraction is the wine, of which there is a broad selection, along with grappas and whiskies.

Vecchia Livorno (☎ 0586 88 40 48, Scali delle Cantine 34) Full meal with wine €25.80. Open Wed-Mon. Fronting the Fortezza Nuova, this is a family-run place of disarming simplicity. When you are quite comfortably seated at your wooden table, go for the seafood dishes.

Antica Venezia (☎ 0586 88 73 53, Via dei Bagnetti 1) 1st course €5.15, fish mains €41.30 per kg. Open Mon-Sat. Not far off, in the heart of the so-called Venice quarter, is another good local seafood eatery.

Ristorante Città Orientale (☎ 0586 88 82 66, Via Ginori 23) Dishes €3.10-6.20. For a change from Italian come to this Chinese restaurant which offers a wide selection of dishes.

Getting There & Away

Bus ATL buses (☎ 0586 88 42 62) depart from Largo Duomo for Cecina (€2.60, one hour), Piombino (€5.65, 2¼ hours) and Pisa (€2, ¾ hour).

Train The main train station in Piazza Dante is on the Rome–La Spezia line and the city is also connected to Florence (€5.40, 1½ hours) and Pisa (€1.35, 15 minutes). Trains are less frequent to Stazione Marittima, the second station near the main port. It's easier to catch a train to the main train station and then a bus to the ports.

Car & Motorbike The A12 runs past the city and the SS1 connects Livorno with Rome. There are several car parks near the waterfront.

Boat Livorno is a major west-coast port. Regular departures for Sardinia and Corsica leave from the area called Calata Carrara, just north of Fortezza Vecchia. In addition, ferries depart from a smaller terminal known as Porto Mediceo, near Piazza Arsenale, and occasionally from the Porto Nuovo. The first two can be easily reached by bus from the main train station. There's a Toremar ticket office, for ferries to the islands of Capraia and Gorgona, on the opposite side of Piazza Arsenale to the ferry terminal.

Ferry services from Livorno include:

Stazione Marittima
Corsica Ferries (☎ 0586 88 13 80, W www. corsicaferries.com) Regular services to Corsica (return daytime deck-class fares to Bastia range from €21.40 to €34.30 plus €2 taxes).

Corsica Marittima (☎ 0586 21 05 46, W www .corsica-marittima.com) Services to Corsica (to Bastia and Porto Vecchio costs €18 to €31).

Sardinia Ferries (☎ 0586 88 13 80, W www .sardiniaferries.com) Regular services to Sardinia (return deck-class fares to Golfo Aranci, near Olbia, range from €31 to €47.50 – the higher fares on summer weekends only).

Moby Lines (☎ 0586 82 68 23/4/5, W www .mobylines.it) Services to Corsica (one-way deck-class fares to Bastia range from €14.95 to €27.35 depending on the season) and Sardinia (one-way deck-class fares to Olbia range from €21.15 to €46.50).

Porto Mediceo
Toremar (☎ 0586 89 61 13, W www.toremar.it) Services to Gorgona and Capraia.

Porto Nuovo
Lloyd Sardegna Compagnia di Navigazione Marittima (☎ 0586 22 23 00) At Varco Galvani, Calata Tripoli, with ferries to Olbia (Sardinia).

Grandi Navi Veloci (☎ 0586 40 98 04) At Varco Galvani, Calata Tripoli, Darsena 1, with boats to Palermo in Sicily (one-way seats range from €54.25 to €85.25).

Getting Around

To get from the train station to Piazza Arsenale and the Porto Mediceo, take ATL bus No 1. To reach the Stazione Marittima take bus No 7. Both these and several others pass through Piazza Grande in the centre. Tickets cost €0.75.

AROUND LIVORNO
Capraia & Gorgona

As you will have noticed earlier, Toremar operates boats to the islands of Capraia and Gorgona from Livorno. Along with their big sister to the south, Elba, and four others farther south still (Pianosa, Montecristo, Giglio and Giannutri), they form the Parco Nazionale dell'Arcipelago Toscano.

The tiny island of **Gorgona** is the greenest and northernmost of the islands. At just 2.23 sq km in area, there's not much to it. The two towers were built respectively by the Pisans and Medicis of Florence. Part of the island is off limits as a low-security prison farm. You can effectively only visit the island on Tuesday, when the 8.30am Toremar ferry from Livorno stops there on the way to and from Capraia, giving you about five hours from the arrival time at 10am. Other days of the week, some ferries stop on the way out to Capraia, but none stops on the way back, which would leave you in a pickle.

The elliptical, volcanic island of **Capraia** lies 65km from Livorno. It is hilly (the highest point is Monte Castello at 447m) and covered mainly in *macchia*, various types of Mediterranean scrub. It has changed hands several times over the course of its history, belonging to Genoa, Sardinia, the Saracens from North Africa and Napoleon.

You can join boat trips around the 30km coastline of the island (for which you will pay around €10.35 per person) or trek across the island. The most popular walk is to the Stagnone, a small lake in the south. There are also a couple of dive sites off the coast (for more information check out the Web site at [W] www.capraiadiving.it). The only beach worthy of the name is **Cala della Mortola**, a few kilometres north of the island's town, **Capraia Isola**. The town is a 1km walk from the little port.

Accommodation on the island is tight; make reservations in advance.

Le Sughere (☎/fax 0586 90 50 66, Via delle Sughere) Adult/tent €10.35/9.30 in the high season. Open May–end Sept. The one camping ground on the island is a popular spot and has a small restaurant on site.

Il Saracino (☎ 0586 90 50 18, fax 0586 90 50 62, Via Cibo 30) Singles/doubles €101/170.40 in the high season. Il Saracino has all the luxury you would expect of a four-star hotel.

Da Beppone (☎/fax 0586 90 50 01, Via della Assunzione 78) Singles/doubles €51.65/67.15. This hotel is not as flash but its *restaurant* is a good place to eat.

A daily boat to Capraia with Toremar sails from Livorno. On most days there is also a return trip, but triple check before you go. The one-way trip costs €10.35, whether you go to Capraia or Gorgona. In summer, excursions from Elba to Capraia are also organised.

THE ETRUSCAN COAST

The province of Livorno stretches down the coast to a little way beyond Piombino, from where you catch the ferry to the island of Elba (see the Elba chapter for more details on this island).

Tuscany is never going to win any prizes as great beach territory, but if you are trundling around in the area and fancy a dip in the briny, some of the beaches are OK.

A handful of little towns of some interest are scattered about in the hilly hinterland of this slender province. A couple of archaeological parks and the possibility of discovering some of Tuscany's lesser-known, but often very good, wines complete the picture.

Livorno to Cecina

You can chug down the coast from Livorno by train, bus or car, but your own transport makes life a lot easier.

There's a cute little beach a couple of kilometres short of **Quercianella**, but describing how to find it ain't easy. Keep a watch out for a tower and castle atop a promontory before you (assuming you are heading south from Livorno). The inlet directly north of that promontory is where the beach is. As you round a curve into the inlet there is a small sign for a path down to the beach. Limited parking is available in a lay-by just to the right of the road a little farther on.

In Quercianella itself you'll find a couple of little grey stone beaches. At the northern end of the town surfers gather even when an adverse wind is up. It's a leafy, sleepy little place. Another 5km or so down the road you will see a sign for the **Parco Comunale di Fortullino**. If you can find a place to leave your vehicle and walk down to the water's edge, the park is pleasant and a bar operates in summer. But again, the beach is a disappointing rocky affair.

Comparatively cute is the high northern end of **Castiglioncello**, which sits on a small promontory a few kilometres farther on from Fortullino. The small sandy beaches (for a spot on which you will have to fork out around €7.75 to €10.35) on the north side of the town are the nicest and sheltered. On the south side the backdrop is flat and dominated by the smokestacks of the industrial plant at Rosignano Solvay just beyond.

You could do worse than stay in the high part of Castiglioncello. It's a pleasant, leafy spot with a few restaurants scattered about to keep your jaws happy.

Pensione Bartoli *(☎ 0586 75 20 51, Via Martelli 9)* Singles/doubles €33.55/41.30, with bathroom €38.75/49, full board up to €56.80 July & Aug. This is not a bad little choice just off the main square. Some rooms have views along the coast.

Inland from Rosignano Solvay, perched on a hill, is **Rosignano Marittimo**. Already a small settlement in Lombard times, Rosignano was one of Lorenzo the Magnificent's preferred bases for hunting. Although there has been a castle here since the 8th century, the fortifications you see today date to the times of Cosimo I de' Medici.

Back down on the coast, **Vada** is a typically characterless seaside spot. At least the beaches have sand. Another 8km and you reach **Marina di Cecina**, where the story is much the same, although being a bigger place there is a little life. About halfway between the sea and the modern centre of **Cecina** you can visit the **Parco Archeologico** *(☎ 0568 26 08 37, Via Ginori; admission €4.15, combined ticket €6.20 includes museum; open 5pm-8.30pm Tues-Fri, 9am-noon & 5pm-9pm Sat & Sun July-Sept)*, which preserves Etruscan remains. To muse over an assortment of ancient artefacts dug up in these parts you could pop into the **Museo Archeologico** *(☎ 0586 66 04 11, Villa Cinquatina, Via Guerrazzi; admission €4.15, combined ticket €6.20 includes park; open same hours as park)*.

Places to stay (some open only in summer) abound here and in places such as Vada. Cecina is encircled by a total of five camping grounds.

Le Tamerici *(☎ 0586 62 06 29, fax 0586 62 24 92, Località Il Paiolo)* Adult/tent €7.75/15. This place, at the southern end of Marina di Cecina, has all the facilities you are likely to need.

You can train or bus it to Cecina from Livorno. The train (€4.50, 30 minutes) is a better deal, being cheaper and quicker.

Cecina to Piombino

From Cecina you could follow the SS1 or minor coast roads south, but even the latter aren't too loaded with excitement. A more enticing idea is to head inland. Livorno's tourist office has come up with a *Strada del Vino* (wine route), with a map and comprehensive list of outlets (also available at tourist offices in the small towns along the way), that moves inland from Cecina to **Montescudaio**. This is a pretty drive and as good as any for moving away from the relatively drab coastal flats. Along the following route towards Piombino you will pass the odd vineyard where you can taste and purchase local wines. There is a particular concentration of them around Castagneto Carducci (see later in this section).

Head south from Montescudaio and you soon reach **Bibbona**, a medieval hill town that dominates the plain running below to the coast. A little farther south and on the coast is **Marina di Bibbona**, south of which stretches a narrow strip of sandy beach backed by macchia and pine woods. A couple of accommodation options present themselves.

Hotel Paradiso Verde *(☎/fax 0586 60 00 22, Via del Forte 9)* Doubles up to €67.15. This is the cheapest place you'll find here. It's about a 100m stumble from the front door to the beach.

A short way south of Marina di Bibbona is the small but important **Rifugio Palustre di Bolgheri** *(☎ 0565 22 43 61, entrance just west off the SS1; adult/child €5.15/2.60; open 2pm-4.30pm 1st & 3rd Sat of each month and Tues & Fri Apr-Nov)*. This nature reserve is a key stop for migratory birds. The number of birds is greatest from November to March, and the best time for seeing them is from December to January. Visits are severely limited and you need to arrange it beforehand. The entrance to the park is a short way south of the cypress-lined, arrow-straight road that leads eastwards to the pretty little settlement of **Bolgheri**. The castle that takes in the city gate and Romanesque Chiesa di SS Giacomo e Cristoro, and so serves as the village entrance, was restructured towards the end of the 19th century. You can get a bite to eat or do a little low-key tourist shopping for local food products and wine.

CENTRAL COAST

So far we have assumed you will have some form of transport of your own, as getting about here with buses is extremely tedious. That also goes for the next stretch of the Strada del Vino, which takes you initially through dense woodland along a minor road due south of Bolgheri. The route becomes less interesting towards the end until you climb up into the hills to reach **Castagneto Carducci**.

Behind the town walls here lies a web of steep narrow lanes crowded in by brooding houses and dominated by the castle (turned into a mansion in the 18th century) of the Gherardesca clan that once controlled the surrounding area. The 19th-century poet Giosuè Carducci spent much of his childhood here.

Unfortunately there's nowhere to stay in town; *agriturismi* scattered around the countryside are your only bet.

Ristorante Glorione *(☎ 0565 76 33 22, Via Carducci 6)* 1st course €5.15-7.75, 2nd course €10.85-14.50. Open Wed-Mon. This is a pleasing little restaurant with a shaded garden.

L'Elixir *(☎ 0565 76 60 17, Via Garibaldi 7)* To pick up some local liqueurs and other drinks, try this 100-year-old shop. By the way, some of the country's finest olive oil is said to come from here.

Next stop on the winding forested hill road is the tiny hamlet of **Sassetta**. Coming at it from Castagneto, its houses seem to be hanging on to their perches for dear life. There's not an awful lot to it, but it's pleasant enough.

Albergo La Selva *(☎/fax 0565 79 42 39,* e *hotel.selva@tiscallinet.it, Via Fornaci 32)* Singles/doubles €43.90/62. This place has seen better days, but it's comfortable enough and accommodation is rare enough in these parts not to be picky. It's just outside the town on the road to Castagneto Carducci.

Suvereto This next stop is a surprise packet. The tortuous streets and steep stairways of Suvereto have constituted a busy little centre since well before the year 1000. For a while it was even the seat of a bishopric and was only incorporated into the Tuscan grand duchy in 1815. The town has maintained much of its Gothic feel and would make a great base for exploring this area for a day or two. A tourist office (☎/fax 0565 82 93 04), on Piazza Gramsci, opens 10am to 12.30pm and 5pm to 10pm daily (evening session only on Sunday) June to September. It also opens during the Sagra del Cinghiale (see later). The staff can provide info on walking in the surrounding hills.

Apart from a handful of *affittacamere* and *agriturismo* options scattered in the vicinity, the accommodation options are scarce.

Casa per le Ferie La Rocca *(☎ 0565 82 98 82, Via della Rocca)* Doubles €41.30. This place is right up at the top of the town near the Rocca, the old (and now largely ruined) fort. In the low season you can probably bargain them down a little for single occupancy.

Il Chiostro *(☎ 0565 82 87 11, fax 82 87 44,* e *ilchiostro@valdicornia.it, Via del Crocifisso 14)* Apartments per week from €196.20-€826.50 plus electricity used. This is a good choice if you plan to stay for a week. The apartments vary in size and quality, but even the smallest is lovely, complete with kitchen, wood-beamed ceilings and stone walls. Call ahead as they often offer stays of less than a week.

Enoteca dei Difficili *(☎ 0565 82 80 18, Via San Leonardo)* Salads €4.15, cold dishes €5.15-7.75. Open Tues-Sun. This is an atmospheric spot for a meal and, more critically, a drink. Alongside an array of delightful snacks and a limited serving of salads and main courses, you can take a pick from the huge selection of wines.

If you are here in mid-August, you may catch the traditional Corsa delle Botte, when townsfolk race each other to push huge tumbling wine barrels along the cobbled lanes of the town. In December the people of Suvereto tuck into their Sagra del Cinghiale (Wild Boar Festival), which happily involves plenty of eating, drinking, and a show of crossbow skills.

Campiglia Marittima to the Coast From Suvereto you drop down onto the plains along the SS398 road to Piombino for about 5km before turning off right to head back into the hills, in which nestle the dun-coloured stone houses of **Campiglia Marittima**, another surprisingly intact medieval town.

The other principal hue, spattered about across the town, is the fern green of the doors and shutters, which appears to be standard issue. From the central Piazza della Repubblica, fronted by centuries-old mansions, you walk up to the Palazzo Pretorio, long the seat of government. Its main facade, covered in an assortment of coats of arms, is akin to the bulky bemedalled chest of many a modern-day general. Campiglia belonged to the Pisan republic and then, from 1406, to Florence, but the location has been inhabited since Etruscan times. Accommodation options consist of a camp site close by and several affittacamere and agriturismi located in the immediately surrounding area.

A few kilometres north-west of Campiglia on the road to San Vincenzo is the **Parco Archeominerario di San Silvestro** (*☎ 0565 83 86 80, Via di San Vincenzo 34b; adult/child €10.35/7.25 for both tours, one tour €6.20/ 3.60, family ticket €25.80; open 9.30am-sunset Tues-Sun June-Sept, Sat & Sun only Oct-May)*. Just before you reach the turn-off (on the right) you pass the church of Madonna di Fucinaia, right by which you can inspect Etruscan smelting ovens which were used for copper production.

The park is dedicated to the 3000-year mining history of the area. The highlight for most is Rocca di San Silvestro, a medieval mining town abandoned in the 14th century. The Temperino mines around it produced copper and lead, some used for the mints of Lucca and later Pisa.

You can make two guided tours, one of Rocca di San Silvestro and the other of part of the Temperino mine and museum. The mine and museum (the latter is in the same building as the ticket office) are near the entrance, while Rocca di San Silvestro is about a half-hour walk away (or take the park shuttle). Tours of each location take place every hour or so (timetables vary throughout the year).

The occasional bus runs to the park from San Vincenzo, about 6km down the road.

If you get back on the road leading away from Campiglia, you would end up on the coast at the rather bland but popular seaside town of **San Vincenzo**. Yachties can park their vessels here, but there's not much to do after that. Sandy beaches stretch to the north and south of the town. Those to the south are the more tempting, backed by macchia and pine plantations. Although there are quite a few hotels, getting a room in summer is challenging. And so are the prices. There is only one camping ground.

Ristorante La Barcaccina *(☎ 0565 70 19 11, Via Tridentina)* Fish mains €12.90-15.50. Open Thur-Tues. If you get hungry while on the beach to the south of town, head here. Fine seafood matches the restaurant's good location – right on the beach. From the coast road (not the SS1), follow the signs to the parking area near Parco Comunale.

Golfo di Baratti & Populonia Twenty-three kilometres south of San Vincenzo along the coast road, a minor road leads off to the south-west and the Golfo di Baratti. This must be one of the mainland Tuscan coast's prettiest beaches, although as the weird and wonderful postures of the trees attest, it is often a touch windy – handy for windsurfers and surfers though.

Inland from the gulf is the **Parco Archeologico di Baratti e Populonia** *(☎ 0565 2 90 02, Populonia; adult/child €10.35/7.25 for whole park, €6.20/3.60 for set areas, family ticket €25.80; open 9am-8pm daily July & Aug, 9am-sunset Tues-Sun Apr-June, 9am-2pm Tues-Fri & 9am-sunset Sat & Sun Sept-Mar)*, where Etruscan tombs of varying interest have been unearthed. The most interesting are the circular ones in the Necropoli di San Cerbone, between the coast road and the visitors centre. You have several choices when you enter. You can get a ticket that permits you to walk all over the park (an exercise that will take several hours at a leisurely pace). Otherwise you can visit one of the two set areas. The first is the Necropoli di San Cerbone. The second includes quarries and underground tombs along the so-called Via delle Cave. Both are worth the time and effort.

You probably have already espied the crenellations of a castle and town walls up among the woods farther down the road. Your curiosity is worth following as medieval

Populonia Alta is a rather fetching little three-street hamlet, walled in and protected by the castle. Built in the 15th century, the hamlet grew up on the site of a Pisan watchtower. You can visit the small **Etruscan Museum** *(adult/child €1.30/0.75; opening times irregular)* for an inspection of a few local finds. Opening times seem flexible – to wit: '*Il brutto tempo, l'umore e la fame potrebbero influenzare l'orario di apertura e chiusura*' ('Bad weather, mood and hunger could affect opening and closing times'). For superb views south along the coast climb the **Torre di Populonia** *(adult/child €1.55/0.75; open 9am-12.30pm & 2pm-7pm)* north of the museum.

Virtually across the road from the car park is the **Etruscan acropolis** of ancient Populonia *(admission free; open 9am-7pm)*, Popluna to the Etruscans, which was excavated from 1980 to 1990. If your Italian is up to it, join a short guided visit (every half-hour). In a nutshell, the digs have revealed the foundations of an Etruscan temple dating to the 2nd century BC, along with its adjacent buildings.

There's an expensive restaurant and an inordinate number of souvenir-shopping options, but no place to stay in Populonia. It appears the only way up here from the Golfo di Baratti (which can be reached by ATM buses from Piombino and San Vincenzo) is under your own steam (parking costs €0.75 for two hours).

Piombino Poor old Piombino, it really gets a lot of lousy press. Unfortunately it is largely true for the busy visitor that the best thing to come out of Piombino is the Elba ferry. The smoke stacks to the south of the town are a rather disconcerting sight and only urge you to hop on the next ferry. A Roman-era port and from the late-19th century a centre of steel production, the city was heavily damaged during WWII and thus sadly precious little remains of the walled historical centre.

The more indulgent out there might want to give it a quick shufti. The centre, whose focal point is the 15th-century **Torrione Rivellino**, and fishing port are not without a little charm. Those with wheels might want to follow the signs just out of town for the scruffy **Parco di Punta Alcone**. You can follow a couple of brief trails to wartime German bunkers and gun emplacements and gaze out across to Elba.

Farther to the north (along the coast in the direction of Populonia) are a couple of modest beaches (don't bother if you are going to Elba).

Hotel Roma (☎ 0565 3 43 41, fax 0565 3 43 48, Via San Francesco 43) Singles/doubles with bathroom up to €41.30/56.80. Should you need, for whatever emergency, to stay, this is a reasonable, central choice two minutes' walk from the ATM bus stop.

Piombino is on the Rome-Genoa train line. There are fairly regular connections to Florence too. ATM buses *(☎ 0565 26 01 80)* leave from the centre of town at Via Leonardo da Vinci 13.

For Elba ferry information see the Elba chapter.

Getting Around

With enormous reserves of patience you can get pretty much anywhere mentioned earlier by bus. Piombino-based ATM buses running between Piombino and Cecina (€2.60, 1½ hours), for instance, stop (in some cases – ask before boarding) at Castagneto Carducci (€2.40, one hour), Sassetta (€2.75, 1¼ hours), San Vincenzo (€1.85, 40 minutes) and Golfo di Baratti (€1, 15 minutes). Another line serves Suvereto (€1.85, 40 minutes) on a regular basis on its way to Monterotondo. Yet another connects Piombino with Campiglia Marittima. ATM buses also run to Massa Marittima (€3.40, 1½ hours; see the Southern Tuscany chapter). For coastal stops, such as San Vincenzo, the train is probably a better bet, but the hill towns are generally a long distance from the nearest train station in the plains below. Remember also that ATL buses from Livorno make quite a few stops along the coast on their way south to Piombino.

Elba

postcode 57307 • pop 29,400

Napoleon should have considered himself lucky to be shunted off to such a pretty spot. He arrived in May 1814 and lasted a year – he just had to have another shot at imperial greatness. Well, he met his Waterloo and the rest is histrionics.

Nowadays people would willingly be exiled here, and the island attracts more than a million tourists per year. They come to swim in its glorious blue waters, lie on the beaches, eat fine (if often pricey) food and generally loll about. Some combine sun-worshipping with a bit of walking, as the island's mountainous terrain can provide some tough treks.

Just 28km long and 19km across at its widest point, Elba is well equipped for tourists, with plenty of hotels and camping grounds. The main towns are Portoferraio on the northern side and Marina di Campo on the southern.

Don't come in August (the best thing anyone can do in August anywhere in Europe is leave altogether or stay at home and wait for better days), as it gets unpleasantly crowded and everything costs even more than usual.

History

Elba has been inhabited since the Iron Age. Funny we should mention that, because the extraction of iron ore and metallurgy were, until the second half of the 20th century, the island's principal sources of economic well-being (the last of the mines closed in 1981). Elba is something of a geologist's dream. It fairly reeks of mineral wealth – so much so that you can fossick around to your heart's content in museums dedicated to rocks.

Ligurian tribespeople were the island's first inhabitants, followed later by Etruscans and Greeks from Magna Graecia. The iron business was well established by this point and no doubt made the island doubly attractive to the Romans, the richer of whom took to building holiday villas on the island.

Centuries of peace under the Pax Romana gave way to more uncertain times during

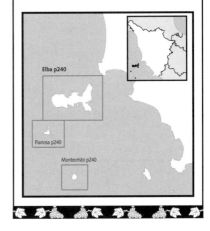

Highlights

- Relax on some of the little beaches and coves in the north-west and south of the island
- Indulge in good food and late-night drinks in the island's prettiest town, Capoliveri
- Put on your walking boots or saddle up on a mountain bike to explore the western heights of the island around Monte Capanne

Elba p240

Pianosa p240

Montecristo p240

the barbarian invasions, when Elba and the other Tuscan islands became refuges for those fleeing mainland marauders. By the 11th century, Pisa (and later Piombino) was in control and built fortresses to help ward off attacks by Muslim raiders and pirates operating out of North Africa.

In the 16th century, Cosimo I de' Medici obtained territory in the north of the island, where he founded the port town of Cosmopolis (today Portoferraio). At the same time, the Spanish acquired control of the south-eastern strip of the island.

Grand Duke Pietro Leopoldo II encouraged land reform, the drainage of swamps

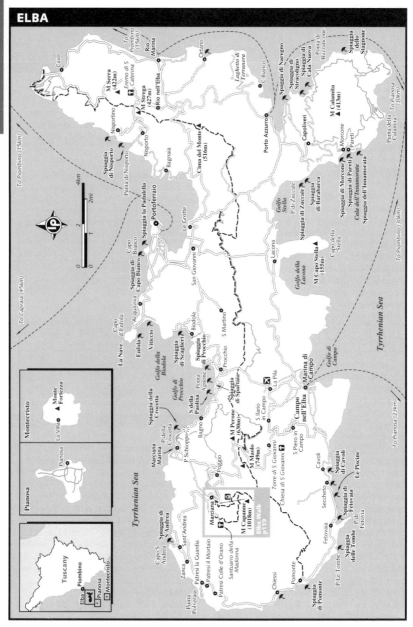

and greater agricultural production on the island in the 18th century. Nevertheless, iron remained the major industry. In 1917 some 840,000 tonnes were produced, but during WWII the industry was hit hard by the Allies and by the beginning of the 1980s production was down to 100,000 tonnes. The writing was on the wall, but tourism had arrived to take the place of mining and smelting.

Orientation & Information

Most ferries arrive at Portoferraio, Elba's capital and its main transport hub. There are also less frequent ferries that call at Rio Marina, Marina di Campo and Porto Azzurro.

The APT office staff (☎ 0565 91 46 71 Ⓦ www.aptelba.it), Calata Italia 35, Portoferraio, are helpful and speak a number of languages. The office opens 8am to 8pm daily April to October and 8am to 6pm Monday to Saturday November to March. If you plan to visit in summer, book ahead – the Associazione Albergatori Isola d'Elba (☎ 0565 91 55 55, ⓔ agenziailva@elbalink.it), Calata Italia 20, will find you a room. Should you choose to roam around the island without booking rooms ahead, look out for 'camere' or 'affittacamere' signs, which indicate rooms for rent in private houses. They often represent reasonable value for money. Generally prices quoted for places to stay are for the high season.

A tourist medical service operates during summer at: Portoferraio (☎ 0565 91 42 12) at the public hospital, Località San Rocco; Marina di Campo (☎ 0565 97 60 61), Piazza Dante Alighieri 3; Rio Marina (☎ 0565 96 24 07), Via Principe Amadeo; Marciana Marina (☎ 0565 90 44 36), Viale Regina Margherita; and Capoliveri (☎ 0565 96 89 95), Via Soprana. The questura (police station; ☎ 0565 91 95 11) is in Palazzo Comune, Via Garibaldi, Portoferraio.

Onda Blu, a self-service laundrette, is at Viale Elba 51, Portoferraio. A wash and dry costs €6.20 per load. Quite a few bars scattered around the island have Internet points, generally charging an exorbitant €5.15 per half hour.

Activities

Elba's popularity with walkers is steadily growing. For further information on walks, see the Tuscany on Foot chapter.

Other popular activities on the island include mountain biking, windsurfing, diving and sailing. Schools offering courses or hiring out equipment abound in the main coastal resorts on the island, particularly in Portoferraio, Marina di Campo and Porto Azzurro. Generally, open-water diving courses and six-day sailing courses cost from €232.50, and six-day windsurfing courses from €129.10. The tourist office in Portoferraio has an extensive list of operators.

Getting There & Away

In the summer months Lufthansa and several minor airlines operate regular flights from Vienna, Altenrhein, Zürich, Berne, Brescia, Parma and Milan to Elba's tiny aerodrome at La Pila. Charter flights also operate to the island. Prices from mainland Italy start at €217.50 and around €360 from farther afield in Europe.

Ferries sail from Piombino to Elba. If you arrive in Piombino by train, get a connecting train to the port. Moby Lines and Toremar operate ferries and have offices in Piombino and Portoferraio. Unless it is the middle of August, you shouldn't have any trouble buying a ticket at the port. Prices (including port tax) start at around €6.20 per person or €26.75 for a small car plus driver (other passengers extra). Both lines offer a special deal on certain runs (indicated in timetables). The ferry trip takes an hour.

Toremar also operates a hovercraft service (€9.80, ½ hour) for passengers only throughout the year, and a fast vehicle and passenger service in the summer (passenger/car from €6.70/26.75, ½ hour).

Getting Around

Bus The island's bus company, ATL (☎ 0565 91 43 92), runs regular services across the island. From Portoferraio, for instance, you can reach all of the main towns, including Marciana Marina, Marina di Campo, Capoliveri and Porto Azzurro (all €1.80, ½ hour), as well as smaller resorts and beaches such as Bagnaia (€2, ½ hour), Cavo (€2.60, 1¼ hours) and Fetovaia (€2.20, one hour). ATL also make the return trip from Portoferraio around the western end of the island (€5.70, 2½ hours) calling at the likes of Seccheto, Cavoli and Le Piscine. Timetables are available from the main ATL office at Viale Elba, Portoferraio, or the tourist office.

Car, Motorcycle & Bicycle The best way to get around Elba is to rent a mountain bike (be aware that the island is hilly – some would say mountainous – and cycling can be a real pain in the legs), scooter or motorcycle. In the high season mountain bikes start at €10.35 per day and €51.65 for one week, mopeds (50cc) cost from €18.10 to €25.80 per day, and motorbikes start at about €51.65 per day. TWN (Two Wheels Network; ☎ 0565 91 46 66, **W** www.twn-rent.it), Viale Elba 32, Portoferraio (branches at Marciana Marina, Marina di Campo, Porto Azzurro and several other locations) is one of several car/bike/motorbike rental outlets. Happy Rent (☎ 0565 91 46 65), Viale Elba 5, is another, although there are plenty of others.

PORTOFERRAIO
Known to the Romans as Fabricia and later Ferraia (on account of its use as a port for iron exports), this small port was acquired by Cosimo I de' Medici in the mid-16th century. It was from this time that the fortifications and town you see today took shape. The walls link two forts (Stella and Falcone) on high points and a third tower closing the port (Linguella). In 1814 Napoleon took up residence here as he began his exile on Elba, which his enemies had generously turned into a Napoleonic statelet (see the boxed text 'Napoleon in Early Retirement'). Steelworks began operating in 1902 but were destroyed by the Allies in 1943.

The new part of Portoferraio encompasses the modern ferry port, but otherwise is of little interest, so head around to the old town, gathered picturesquely around the fishing and pleasure port built under Cosimo I de' Medici and enclosed by the above-mentioned walls. You can wander around the forts, **Falcone** (*Via del Falcone; admission €2; open*

9am-7pm daily Sept-June, 9am-8pm Jul & Aug) and **Stella** *(Via della Stella; admission €1.30; open 9am-7pm daily)*. Down from the walls leading to Forte Falcone is a narrow but rather fetching little sliver of beach.

In the old town, up on the bastions between the two forts, you'll also encounter the **Villa dei Mulini** *(☎ 0565 91 58 46, Piazzale Napoleone; admission €4.65, €7.75 includes Villa Napoleonica di San Martino; open 9am-7pm Mon-Sat, 9am-1pm Sun)*, one of the residences where Napoleon mooched about. It features a splendid terraced garden and his library.

The **Villa Napoleonica di San Martino** *(☎ 0565 91 46 88, Località San Martino; admission €4.65, €7.75 ticket includes Villa dei Mulini, parking €1.30; open 9am-7pm Tues-Sat, 9am-1pm Sun)*, Napoleon's summer residence, is set in hills about 5km south-west of the town. The villa houses a modest collection of Napoleonic paraphernalia and also hosts an annual exhibition based on a Napoleonic theme.

The Linguella fortifications down by the port house the modest **Museo Civico Archeologico** *(☎ 0565 93 73 70, La Linguella; admission €2; open 9.30am-2.30pm & 5pm-midnight mid-June–mid-Sept, 10.30am-1.30pm & 4pm-8pm Wed-Mon mid-Sept–mid-June)*. The museum's collection generally focuses on ancient seafarers.

For information on hiking around Elba`, visit Il Genio del Bosco – Centro Trekking Isola d'Elba (☎ 0565 93 08 37).

Places to Stay & Eat
The closest camping grounds are about 4km west of Portoferraio towards Viticcio.

Campeggio La Sorgente (☎/fax 0565 91 71 39, Località Acquaviva) Adult/tent/car €11.40/9.30/2.60. This quiet camping ground has plenty of sites with shade.

Acquaviva (☎/fax 0565 91 55 92, Località Acquaviva) Adult/tent/car €10.35/9.30/2.30. Acquaviva occupies a great spot right near the beach.

*Albergo Ape Elbana (☎/fax 0565 91 42 45, **e** apelbana@elba2000.it, Salita de' Medici 2)* Singles/doubles up to €51.65/92.30. Many of the bright rooms at this

Napoleon in Early Retirement

At 6pm on 3 May 1814, the English frigate *Undaunted* dropped anchor in the Medici harbour of Portoferraio. The cargo was unusual to say the least. Under the Treaty of Fontainebleau, the emperor who since the beginning of the century had held all Europe in his thrall, campaigning with superhuman energy from Spain to Russia, was exiled to the island of Elba.

It could have been a lot worse for the emperor, but the Allies decided on a soft option, partly to short-circuit any possible adverse reaction in France. Napoleon was awarded the island as his private fiefdom, to hold until the end of his days.

His arrival was greeted with considerable pomp. The guns of Portoferraio shot off a 100-round salute, to which the English frigate replied. That at least is Alexandre Dumas' version. Others say the guns were actually firing *at* the frigate.

Whatever may have been the case, Elba would never be quite the same again. Although no doubt watching the situation in Europe with a hawk's eye, Napoleon threw himself into frenetic activity in his new, somewhat humbler domain.

After touring the island and making all the right noises to its inhabitants, he undertook a long series of public works. They included improving operations in the island's iron-ore mines (whose revenue now went to Napoleon), boosting agriculture, initiating a road-building programme, draining marshes, overhauling the legal and education systems and so on. On some of the programmes he often set members of his faithful 500 guardsmen to work.

A great deal of ink has been spilled over the Corsican's dictatorial style and seemingly impossible ambitions, but he can't have been all bad. To this day they still say a Mass for his soul at the Chiesa della Misericordia in May!

Napoleon had by now installed himself in the bastions of the city wall, in what became known as the Residenza dei Mulini. His so-called country or summer home, outside town in San Martino, he used as an occasional stopover on excursions – he never slept there. Some weeks after his arrival Napoleon was joined by his mother Letizia and sister Paolina. But he remained separated from his wife Maria Luisa and was visited for just two days by his lover Maria Walewska.

On the Continent, things were hotting up. Rumours were rife that Napoleon's really rather comfortable exile might be curtailed. At the Congress of Vienna, France called for Napoleon's removal to a more distant location. Austria, too, was nervous. Some suggested Malta, but Britain objected. London then suggested the South Atlantic islet of St Helena.

Napoleon could not be sure which rumours to believe. According to some he would sooner or later be moved. Others suggested such reports were designed to induce him to some rash act in breach of the Treaty of Fontainebleau that would provide the Allies with the excuse they needed to get rid of him, for they were not keen to be seen to break what they could claim had been the generous terms of the treaty. The congress broke up with no official decision, although the Allies were well aware that Napoleon still had many supporters in and beyond France and could easily raise a new army should he be of a mind to try.

He was. Under no circumstances was he going to allow himself to be meekly shipped off to some rocky speck in the middle of the Atlantic. A lifelong risk-taker, he decided to have another roll of the dice. Perhaps, during his time on Elba, he always knew he would. For months he had sent out a couple of vessels flying his Elban flag on 'routine' trips around the Mediterranean. When one of them, the *Incostante*, set sail early in the morning of 26 February 1815 (a Sunday), no-one suspected he might be hidden on board. Sir Neil Campbell, his English jail warden, had only returned to Livorno the previous day under the impression that Napoleon was, as ever, fully immersed in the business of the island.

Elba lost its emperor and Napoleon his gilded cage. He had embarked on the Hundred Days that would culminate in defeat at Waterloo – he got the Atlantic exile after all, but at least he had tried.

place in the old town overlook Piazza della Repubblica.

Villa Ombrosa *(☎ 0565 91 43 63, fax 0565 91 56 72,* **e** *info@villaombrosa.it, Via De Gasperi 3)* Singles/doubles with bathroom up to €85.20/134.30. This hotel has fine views of Portoferraio's northern beach. They may insist that you take half board, which is OK as their restaurant, ***Ristorante Villa Ombrosa***, is good. It serves tasty Tuscan dishes and a full meal costs around €23.25.

Trattoria da Zucchetta *(☎ 0565 91 53 31, Piazza della Repubblica 40)* Full meal around €25.80. Open Wed-Mon. In the old town, you could do worse than this Neapolitan eatery, which has been in business since 1891. It could be a little too full of other foreigners for your tastes though.

Stella Marina *(☎ 0565 91 59 83, Banchina Alto Fondale)* Mains around €7.75. Open Thur-Tues. Nearer the ferry terminal on the waterfront, this place ain't cheap, but the loud and contrary (with each other!) staff serve some good local dishes. Seafood takes centre stage.

Entertainment
Sir William's Irish Bar *(☎ 0565 91 92 88, Via Manganaro 28)* Pints around €5.15. Open 6pm-6am daily. For a wee dram o' whiskey or a pint of bitter, head here. It generally doesn't start jumping till at least midnight.

AROUND PORTOFERRAIO
West to Capo d'Enfola
Several modest little beaches spread west from Portoferraio. Quite nice, although narrow and shelly, are **Spiaggia La Padulella** and its counterpart just west of Capo Bianco, **Spiaggia di Capo Bianco**. A couple of similar beaches dot the coast along the 7km stretch out to **Capo d'Enfola**. You can have a dip here or head south down the coast a few kilometres to **Viticcio**, a more pleasant little place. The area is quieter than much of the rest of the island and is served by ATL buses. It is possible to walk around from Viticcio to the beaches of the **Golfo della Biodola**.

At Viticcio you could stay in one of a couple of places.

Hotel Scoglio Bianco *(☎ 0565 93 90 36, fax 0565 93 90 31, Località Viticcio)* Half board €41.30-77.50. The rooms here are generally spacious and bright, and its restaurant is perfect for sunset watching.

Emanuel *(☎ 0565 93 90 03, Località Enfola) Menù di degustazione* €23.25. Open daily in summer, Thur-Tues the rest of the year. This great place has been serving up consistently good Elban dishes for years – probably the best way to go is the *menù di degustazione*, which gives you a rounded experience of the local cuisine.

WEST TO MARCIANA MARINA
From Portoferraio, a provincial road heads south and then forks westwards along the coast to Marciana Marina, via Procchio.

The pick of the beaches are the sandy strands lining the **Golfo della Biodola**. When the Hermitage opened its doors in 1951, there were only five small *pensioni* scattered elsewhere on the island. Since then a succession of other hotels and camping grounds has followed on this little gulf.

Hermitage *(☎ 0565 93 69 11, fax 0565 96 99 84,* **e** *hermitage@elbalink.it, Località Biodola)* Singles/doubles up to €181/444. It's reasonably low key, tasteful, supplies everything you need and most of the beach is for hotel guests only.

Procchio, a little farther on, is an unlovely road junction, but the beaches are still sandy and at least you can get on to them!

Osteria del Piano *(☎ 0565 90 72 92, Via Provinciale 24)* Full meal around €23.25. Open Thur-Tues. This unassuming restaurant is on the road just outside Procchio heading towards Marciana Marina. Looks aren't everything. Here they make all their own pasta and serve up some astonishing concoctions, such as black-and-white spaghetti in a crab sauce. They also have a good selection of wine and a large outdoor seating area.

West from Procchio, the road hugs the cliffs, presenting you with an endless parade of fine views along the winding coast. If you can tie up your steed somewhere, **Spiaggia di Spartaia** and **Spiaggia della Paolina** are part of a series of beautiful little beaches (all requiring a steep walk down from the highway).

MARCIANA MARINA & THE WEST

Almost 20km west of Portoferraio, Marciana Marina is slightly less crowded with tourists and is fronted by some pleasant pebble beaches. It makes a fine base for some of the island's best walking trails too.

Casa Lupi (☎/fax 0565 9 91 43, Località Ontanelli 35) Singles/doubles €41.30/67.15. This cheap hotel occupies a quiet spot about half a kilometre inland on the road to Marciana. There's also a lovely garden in which to sun yourself.

Poggio & the Interior

Following the inland road up into the mountains is especially advisable for those who are getting a little sick of sweating on the coast. The first town you reach is Poggio, an enchanting little place with a medieval core and winding cobblestone streets that is famed for its spring water.

Albergo Monte Capanne (☎/fax 0565 9 90 83, Via dei Pini 13) Singles/doubles €25.80/51.65, half board €46.50 per person. Chill out a little at this place, with great views of Marciana Marina. They may insist on half board.

Publius (☎ 0565 9 92 08) Full meals around €36.15. Open Tues-Sun. If you want to spill money on a great meal, try this place, at the entrance to the village. The breathtaking views down to the coast (you feel as if you are suspended in mid-air) should keep your mind off the high prices.

From Poggio you have two choices. You can proceed west to Marciana and then head around the coast (see the next section), or opt for the narrow SP37 road that winds up into some of the highest and most densely wooded country on the island. This latter option is comparatively neglected by most sun-and-sand-obsessed tourists.

The vegetation is so dense in parts you could be forgiven for thinking you are about to enter rainforest. Stop at the picnic site at the foot of Monte Perone (you can't miss it). If you have a car, this is the best place to park it. Mountain bikers should proceed with caution. To the left (east) you can wander up to **Monte Perone** (630m), which

offers spectacular views across much of the island. To the right (west) you can scramble fairly quickly to a height that affords broad vistas down to Poggio, Marciana and Marciana Marina. From there you could press on to **Monte Maolo** (749m).

The road descends from this location into the southern flank of the island. On the way you will notice the granite shell of the Romanesque **Chiesa di San Giovanni** and, shortly after, the ruined **tower** named after the same saint.

Those with their own transport should give a little time to two small hamlets here, **Sant'Ilario in Campo** and **San Piero in Campo**. Short on sights, they are pleasant enough and little affected by tourism. The latter is a little larger and boasts a few *osterie* and snack bars, although you can pick up a quick pizza at the former.

Albergo La Rosa (☎ 0565 98 31 91, Piazza Maggiore Gadani 17) Singles/doubles up to €46.50/56.80. The comfortable rooms at this pink hotel overlook the main square of San Piero.

The hamlets lie on separate routes that lead around to Marina di Campo (see later in this chapter) and for those with their own transport they are easily reached. Up to eight buses a day link both with Marina di Campo, where you can connect with most spots on the island.

MARCIANA & THE WEST COAST

From Poggio, the other possibility is to continue west to Marciana (355m), the most engaging of the western interior towns. Once an important defensive position under Pisan rule, it subsequently passed to Piombino, the French and finally to the grand duchy of Tuscany.

The **Fortezza Pisana** *(closed)* is a reminder of the town's medieval days while about a 40-minute walk west out of town is the **Santuario della Madonna**, the most important object of pilgrimage on the island. A much-altered 11th-century church houses a stone upon which a divine hand is said to have painted an image of the Virgin. The path to the church is known as the *Via Crucis*, because of 14 stations spaced along it.

Each station represents a pause Jesus took while carrying the cross. The town also houses the small **Antiquarium Archeologico** (☎ *0565 90 12 15, Via del Pretorio; closed for refurbishment)* behind the fortezza.

From near Marciana a **cable car** (☎ *0565 90 10 20; one-way/return €7.25/11.40)* runs to the summit of **Monte Capanne** (1018m), the island's highest point. From here you can see across Elba and as far as Corsica to the west. Alternatively you can walk up (for more information see the Tuscany on Foot chapter).

The road west out of Marciana pursues a course around the island, maintaining a prudent distance and altitude from the often precipitous coastline.

A popular coastal hangout is **Sant' Andrea**, which now has an astounding concentration of 11 hotels and other assorted accommodation options winding back up the hill to the main road.

Bambù (☎ *0565 90 80 12, Sant'Andrea)* Singles/doubles €41.30/51.65. Obligatory half board in Aug €56.80. This is one of the cheapest hotels in the area and a spit from the tiny beach.

A series of small beaches appear as you follow the road round to the south side of the island. **Chiessi** and **Pomonte** have pebbly beaches, but the water is beautiful. The sandy **Spiaggia delle Tombe** is one of the few spots on the island where nude bathing is OK.

At **Fetovaia**, **Seccheto** and **Cavoli** you will find further protected sandy beaches, accommodation and restaurants. West of Seccheto, **Le Piscine** is another mostly nudist stretch.

MARINA DI CAMPO

Elba's second-largest town, Marina di Campo, is on Golfo di Campo to the island's south. The beaches are not bad at all and popular (although if you venture farther west you will find a few less crowded ones). Many camping grounds are located around the town and along the coastline. The place gets ridiculously packed in high summer, but this is where some of the island's action can be found too – a few bars and discos keep young holiday-makers happy through the hot months.

Albergo Thomas (☎ *0565 97 77 32, fax 0565 97 68 70, Viale degli Etruschi 32)* Doubles €67.15, half board €64.50 per person. This is one of the cheapest hotels, about a two-minute walk to the beach. Like most places around here, obligatory half or full board is a standard story during the summer.

CAPOLIVERI & THE SOUTH-EAST

This town, high up on a majestic ridgeback in the south-eastern pocket of the island, is an enchanting village, all steep, narrow alleys and interlocking houses. At the height of the season it is jammed with tourists (at least one Italian newspaper writer has remarked tartly that one may as well hoist the German flag at Capoliveri). Come out of season and you can rediscover some of the peace of this hamlet, which used to live off iron-ore mining in the Punta della Calamita area.

There's nowhere to stay in the town itself, although several possibilities suggest themselves around the coast to either side of the town. The tourists have brought an eating-and-drinking culture to Capoliveri, however, and it's quite astounding just how many eateries and the like have been crammed in.

Il Chiasso (☎ *0565 96 87 09, Via Cavour 32)* Meals around €41.30. Open Wed-Mon. This is one of the best restaurants in town. Even though some seating consists of simple wooden tables and benches, the place still retains a touch of class.

Summertime (☎ *0565 93 51 80, Via Roma 56)* Full meals around €25.80, including local wine. This is another good place, where fine local dishes such as *guazzetto all'Elbana* (soup with mixed seafood) are served.

Fandango (☎ *0565 93 54 24, Via Cardenti 1)* Drinks from €4.15. Open Tues-Sun. Here you can taste fine Tuscan wines and snacks, located downstairs just below the main square.

Velvet Underground (*Vicolo Lungo 14)* Another entertainment spot just off the main square is this pub-style establishment.

Sugar Reef (☎ *0338 917 90 26, Località La Trappola)* This is *the* place on the island for Latin music, both live and DJ-mixed. It's about a kilometre south of Capoliveri on the road to Morcone.

Around Capoliveri

If you have your own transport you can visit a series of pleasant little beaches. By bus it's possible, but not easy. Directly west of Capoliveri (take the Portoferraio road and watch for the signs) are the beaches of **Zuccale** and **Barabarca**. You end up on a dirt track – leave your vehicle in the car park and walk the final stretch.

If you take the road heading south from Capoliveri, another three charming sandy little coves come in quick succession: **Morcone**, **Pareti** and **Spiaggia dell'Innamorata**. The *innamorata* ('woman in love') of the last of these was apparently an orphan girl of Capoliveri in love with a young man of means. When the latter's parents finally consented to marriage, they went down to the seaside to give vent to their joy. Pirates spoiled the party and captured the man, killing him. The girl, beside herself with sorrow and having managed to escape, threw herself off the cliffs.

There are several hotel options at these beaches and some simple restaurants keep people's tummies from rumbling too hard.

East of Capoliveri you have two choices. One road takes you to the comparatively long (for this part of the island) stretch of beach at **Naregno**, fronted by a series of discreet hotels.

The more adventurous will follow the signs for **Stracoligno**. This is one of the first in a series of beaches down the east coast here. The road at this point becomes a dirt track and if you don't mind dusting up your vehicle somewhat, you can push on to a couple of less-frequented beaches. **Cala Nuova** is a nice enough little beach with a good restaurant.

Ristorante Calanova (☎ 0565 96 89 58) 1st course €7.75-10.35, 2nd course €15.50-18. Open Wed-Mon Easter–early Sept. As it's the only building here, this place is perfect for a secluded evening. Unsurprisingly, seafood dishes are the ones to go for.

Another 4km or 5km and you reach a path down to the **Spiaggia dello Stagnone**,

which even in summer you should not find too crowded, if only because of the effort required to rattle down this far.

PORTO AZZURRO

Dominated by its fort, which was built in 1603 by Philip III of Spain and is now used as a prison, Porto Azzurro is a pleasant resort town, close to some good beaches.

Albergo Villa Italia (☎/fax 0565 9 51 19, e villaitalia@infoelba.it, Viale Italia 41) Singles/doubles €36.15/92.30. Open Mar-Nov. The small but adequate rooms here are about the cheapest in the town.

Hotel Belmare (☎ 0565 9 50 12, fax 0565 95 82 45, Banchina IV Novembre) Singles/doubles €56.80/82.65. This hotel is nicely located right on the waterfront. It was undergoing renovation at the time of writing so prices may increase.

Ristorante Cutty Sark (☎ 0565 95 78 21, Piazza del Mercato 25) Full meals €36.15. Open Wed-Mon. If you can loosen the purse strings a little around dinner time, pull up a pew here. The *ravioloni alla Cutty Sark* are big ravioli filled with zucchini and shrimp meat and layered in a shrimp and tomato sauce.

Otherwise, portside restaurants are good options.

La Lanterna Magica (☎ 0565 95 83 94, Lungomare Vitaliani 5) Full meals €32.50. Open Tues-Sun. This place has a great spot right on the waterfront with views of the marina. Typical Elban cuisine is the mainstay of the menu.

THE NORTH-EAST

If, on leaving Portoferraio, you were to swing around to the east and head for Rio nell'Elba and beyond, you would be opting to explore the least-touristed part of the island. There is a simple enough reason for this – the beaches are generally not so hot. Although in some cases the locations are pretty, sand tends to contend with pebbles, shingle and shells. If you don't mind that, it can be quite an intriguing corner to poke around in for a couple of days.

The road out of Portoferraio hugs the coast on its way around to **Bagnaia**, the first worthwhile stop. En route you will scoot by **San Giovanni**, home to a rather expensive and dull mud spa and **Le Grotte**, where a few stones still managing to stand one on top of the other are all that remain of a Roman villa. At the fork in the road for Porto Azzurro and Bagnaia is a possible last resort for the kids to run riot for a while. Yes, it's **Elbaland** *(☎ 0335 819 46 80, Località Fonte Murato; adults/children aged under 12 €6.20/3.60; open noon-7pm Tues-Sun)*, a rather low-key amusement park, more like an outsize park with swings and other such attractions.

From Elbaland swing northwards to Bagnaia. The beach is attractive but accommodation possibilities are nothing special.

Pizzeria Sunset (☎ 0565 93 07 86, Bagnaia) Pizzas €5.15/7.75. Open May–mid-Oct. Eat here, where the views across the gulf to Portoferraio are wonderful, the sunset especially.

From Bagnaia you have the option of following the partly dirt road to **Nisporto**, and then on farther up the coast to **Nisportino**. The views along the way are quite spectacular in parts and in each of the settlements you will find a small beach and, in summer, snack stands and one or two restaurants. From Nisportino you head back down a few kilometres to the junction with the road that links Nisporto and Rio nell'Elba. About halfway along this road you can stop to take a short stroll to what little is left of the **Eremo di Santa Caterina**, a tiny stone hermitage. There are sweeping views from around here.

The road plunges down to the inland bastion of **Rio nell'Elba**, which lay at the heart of the island's iron-mining operations. It's a little gloomy, but the simple fact that it caters little to tourism is almost attractive. Actually, it's not quite accurate to say that. Rio nell'Elba ignores tourism altogether. However,

The Count of Montecristo

Alexandre Dumas could hardly have known when he penned the swashbuckling adventures of the much wronged Edmond Dantès in the mid-19th century just how much success his character would have.

The dashing officer of the French merchant marine, incarcerated for 'Bonapartism' in the Château d'If, near Marseilles, had been set up and wasn't very happy about it. But life is a funny thing, as they say, and never funnier than in a good read. So it is that Abbot Faria clues the seething Dantès in to the existence of a fabulous treasure in the caves of the little island of Montecristo.

Itching to get rich and revenge, Dantès manages the daring escape from the castle and heads off for Italy. As his boat glides past Elba Dantès can see Pianosa before him and, in the distance, his burning objective – the island of Montecristo.

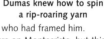

JANE SMITH

Dumas knew how to spin a rip-roaring yarn

Well, following much adventure and jolly japes, our man wins all the prizes really – getting rich, becoming the Count of Montecristo and exacting a full measure of revenge on those who had framed him.

Of course, it's all a tall tale. No-one has ever found any treasure on Montecristo, but this particular yarn has made a lot of loot for a lot of people. At least 25 film and TV versions of the story were made in the 20th century, with greater or lesser skill. Among the better ones are the oldies. Rowland Lee's 1935 film and the 1943 flick by Robert Vernay were equally good tales in the spirit of Dumas' writing. In Italy, Andrea Giordana had women swooning at their TV sets in the 1966 series by Edmo Fenoglio. Richard Chamberlain had a go at the lead role in David Greene's 1975 *The Count of Montecristo*, as did Gérard Depardieu in *Montecristo* (1997).

there is the **Museo di Minerali Elbani** (☎ *0565 93 92 94, Passo della Pietá; admission* €*2.60; open 10am-1pm, 4pm-7.30pm Tues-Sun mid-Apr–Sept)*, with 700 rare mineral specimens from the east of the island and also Monte Capanne. Amateur geologists should have a field day. You are unlikely to want to hang around too long, but you can get lunch at one of a handful of restaurants on and around the central Piazza del Popolo.

You could take another road back north from Rio nell'Elba to **Cavo** on the northeastern coast, but no obvious reasons spring to mind for making the effort. Easier is the short run downhill to Rio nell'Elba's coastal outlet, **Rio Marina**. Oh goody, there's yet another mineral museum here! Apart from that, not a lot will hold you up here either.

Hotel Rio *(☎ 0565 92 42 25, fax 0565 92 41 62,* **W** *www.elbahotelrio.it, Via Palestro 31)* Singles/doubles €98.15/134.30. Open Mar–mid-Oct. If you feel the need to stay over, you could stay here, one block back from the waterfront.

Da Oreste La Strega *(☎ 0565 96 22 11, Via Vittorio Emanuele 6)* Meals around €36.15. Open Wed-Mon. Lunch might be an idea at this rather distinguished seafood restaurant.

The best beach choice around here is a little way south at **Ortano**. To get there you need to head back a couple of kilometres towards Rio nell'Elba and then swing south. It's a nice location, but again the beach is that far-from-ideal part-sand part-pebble mix. If you want to stay, the choice is between camping or a sprawling hotel complex.

Campeggio Canapei *(☎/fax 0565 93 91 65, Localitá Ortano)* Adult/tent/car up to €11.40/12.40/3.10. This camp site occupies a quiet, tree-lined valley 15 minutes' walk from the beach.

MINOR ISLANDS

Elba is part of what is now called the Parco Nazionale dell'Arcipelago Toscano. Two of the seven islands, Capraia and Gorgona, are dealt with in the section on Livorno in the Central Coast chapter (note that in the summer you can join boat excursions to Capraia from Elba) and the islands of Giglio and Giannutri are discussed in the Southern Tuscany chapter. That leaves Elba, Pianosa and Montecristo.

Pianosa, 14km west of Elba, is a remarkably flat, triangular affair measuring about 5.8km by 4.6km. From 1858 until the mid-1990s it was a penal colony, but it is now part of the national park. ***Trips*** *(adult/child* €*61.95/31; maximum of 110 people per day)* to the island leave from Marina di Campo during summer at 9am and 11am, returning eight hours later. Most travel agencies around Elba make bookings. The island can also be reached on Tuesday only by Toremar ferry from Porto Azzurro. Unless you want to be stranded for a week, you have about two hours to poke around before heading back! And if you go this way, you are not allowed into the grounds of the former prison (so the two hours will probably be more than sufficient).

There are no ferry services to Montecristo, 40km south of Elba. Montecristo was also at one stage a prison island, but that role was short-lived. Since 1979 it has been a marine biological reserve and can be seen only as part of an organised visit. You need special permission from the Ufficio Forestale in Follonica (on the Italian mainland). Call ☎ 0566 4 06 11 if you're interested.

Southern Tuscany

The area known as the Maremma (really just an extension of the Maremma Pisana) stretches southwards from Piombino and its flat hinterland until Tuscany's border with Lazio.

As in the Maremma Pisana (see the Central Coast chapter), serious land reclamation and the drying out of the extensive swamps that characterised the whole area only began at the end of the 18th and start of the 19th centuries under the direction of the Lorraine grand dukes. This went hand in hand with a series of reforms aimed at loosening the grip of the feudal-style landholders on the bulk of this previously unproductive land. Roads were built and canals dug, agriculture was stimulated and dairy production encouraged – in a region as hilly and mountainous as Tuscany, the plains of the newly 'cleansed' Maremma were ideal for grazing. Today, agriculture still plays a big part in this once mosquito-infested land, but industry (and an increasing amount of tourist dollars) has come to the table to boost the economy.

Several of Tuscany's most important Etruscan sites (and a host of minor ones too) can be found in this area. Touring the wild high country towns of Vetulonia, Sovana, Sorano and Pitigliano allows you to combine the hunt for Etruscan sites with some spectacular medieval towns neglected by the majority of tourists swanning about farther north in Tuscany. Lovers of hot water should make for the springs and thermal baths at Saturnia, once also an Etruscan settlement. Massa Marittima is one of the more interesting towns in the area, with a rich mining history dating back to the Etruscans.

Along the coast, the highlights are the Parco Regionale della Maremma and the Monte Argentario peninsula. Otherwise, several acceptable beaches allow for some relief from the summertime heat.

For the sake of simplicity, the area covered in this chapter roughly corresponds to Grosseto, the southernmost of the Tuscan provinces.

Highlights

- Explore the extraordinary town of Pitigliano, rising dramatically from a rocky outcrop
- Follow in the footsteps of the Etruscans in the necropolises around Sovana and their *via cave* (sunken roads)
- Bathe in the natural hot springs of Saturnia
- Join a guided walk in the unspoiled Parco Regionale della Maremma
- Take a boat trip to the island of Giglio

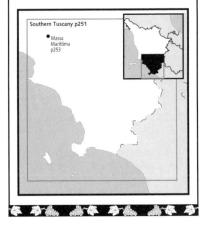

GROSSETO

postcode 58100 • pop 71,600

Precious little about this place – provincial capital and the biggest town in the Maremma – draws attention to it. If for whatever reason you wind up here (and it will almost always be because you are waiting for a transport connection), you could kill a couple of hours in what's left of the old walled town.

Information

The APT office (☎ 0564 41 43 03) is at Via Fucini 43c, a block from the train station.

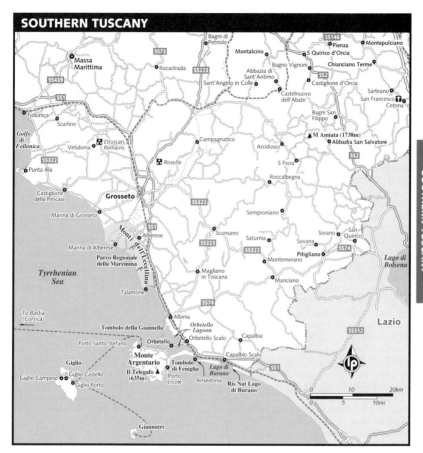

SOUTHERN TUSCANY

Bagni di Petriolo
Montalcino
S Quirico d'Orcia
Montepulciano
Pienza
SS146
SS73
Rocastrada
SS223
Bagno Vignoni
Chianciano Terme
SS2
Abbazia di Sant'Antimo
Sant'Angelo in Colle
Castiglione d'Orcia
Sarteano
San Francesco
Cetona
Castelnuovo dell'Abate
Massa Marittima
SS439
SS1
Follonica
Scarlino
Golfo di Follonica
Vetulonia
Etruscan Remains
Roselle
Campagnatico
Arcidosso
M Amiata (1738m)
Abbadia San Salvatore
Bagni San Filippo
SS2
SS322
Punta Ala
S Fiora
Castiglione della Pescaia
Grosseto
SS322
Roccalbegna
Marina di Grosseto
Semproniano
Monti dell'Uccellina
Alberese
Scansano
SS1
Saturnia
Sorano
San Quirico
Marina di Alberese
Parco Regionale della Maremma
SS223
SS322
Sovana
Pitigliano
SS574
Lago di Bolsena
Tyrrhenian Sea
Magliano in Toscana
Montemerano
Manciano
Talamone
SS574
To Bastia (Corsica)
Albinia
Orbetello Lagoon
Tombolo della Giannella
Orbetello Scalo
Capalbia
Lazio
SS312
Porto Santo Stefano
Orbetello
Capalbio Scalo
SS1
Giglio
Monte Argentario
Tombolo di Feniglia
Lago di Burano
Il Telegafo (635m)
Porto Ercole
Ansedonia
Ris Nat Lago di Burano
Giglio Campese
Giglio Castello
Giglio Porto
0   10   20km
0   5   10mi
Giannutri

SOUTHERN TUSCANY

Information about the Parco Regionale della Maremma can be obtained here or at Alberese (see later in this chapter). Plans are afoot to move the tourist office in the near future, so it's prudent to call ahead to check.

Things to See

Grosseto was the last of the Siena-dominated towns to fall into Medici hands, in 1559. The walls, bastions and fortress that you see today were built on the orders of Florence to protect what was then an important grain and salt depot for the grand duchy.

Within the city walls, Grosseto's **cathedral** (☎ 0564 42 01 43, Chiasso degli Zuavi 6; free; open 8am-1pm & 3pm-7pm) was begun in the late 13th century and has a distinctive Sienese touch. It has been added to, however, and much of the facade was renewed along neo-Romanesque lines in the 19th century and the bell tower dates from the early 1900s. The other interesting-looking building on the not at all unpleasant Piazza Dante, is the Palazzo della Provincia. It appears to be Sienese Gothic, which is exactly what its early-20th-century architects hoped you might think.

Places to Stay & Eat

Albergo Appennino (☎ *0564 2 30 09, fax 0564 2 32 92, Via Mameli 1)* Singles/doubles €25.80/41.30. If you are stranded for the night, this cheap hotel has the advantage of being handy for the train station and old centre.

Il Canto del Gallo (☎ *0564 41 45 89, Via Mazzini 29)* Full meal €23.25-28.40. Open Mon-Sat. This restaurant in the old town presents all sorts of options on the menu and comes with plenty of local recommendations. Try the gnocchi, which are home-made and very good.

Getting There & Away

Bus Rama buses (☎ 0564 2 52 15), Piazza Marconi, leave for points throughout the province. Most of the buses depart from in front of the train station. There are fairly regular buses for Siena (mainly during the morning), where you can connect with either Tra-in or SITA buses to Florence. Direct services to Florence are less frequent – no more than two a day. Strangely there is only one direct bus a day to Massa Marittima (€2.85, none on Sunday). Other destinations include: Piombino (€4.15), Magliano in Toscana (€1.95), Follonica (€2.85), Castiglione della Pescaia (€1.70), Porto San Stefano (€2.85) and Pitigliano (€4.80).

Train Grosseto is on the main coastal train line between Rome and Livorno. For places such as Pisa (€7.30, two hours), Florence (€9.35, three hours) or Siena (€5.50, 1½ hours), train is probably a smarter bet.

AROUND GROSSETO
Roselle

Populated as early as the 7th century BC, Roselle was a middle-ranking Etruscan town which came under Roman control in the 3rd century BC.

Although no great monuments are left standing, the extensive **historic site** (☎ *05 64 40 24 03; admission €4.15; open 9am-sunset)* retains defensive walls, an oddly elliptical amphitheatre, traces of houses, the forum and streets. Much of it is attributable to periods after the arrival of the Romans, but you'll also find traces of an abandoned medieval village as well. It is of course no match for Pompei and other more famous Italian archaeological sights, but its scattered ruins and high position in a seemingly hidden basin afford wonderful views down to the plains and out to sea.

Getting there is easiest by private means. Otherwise get the bus driver to let you off at the appropriate spot on the Siena-Grosseto run and walk a few kilometres.

Vetulonia

This windswept mountain town seems to rise out of nothing from the surrounding plains. You can see the sea from here, but it seems to belong to another time dimension. A pleasing enough distraction for a brief stroll, most of Vetulonia's visitors come in search of Etruscan remains, but the views are just as magnificent and make it quite obvious why the Etruscans set up shop here. The town sports what are purported to be some blocks from the ancient Etruscan town's wall, and a small **Museo Archeologico** (☎ *0564 94 80 58, Via Garibaldi; €4.15; open 10am-2pm & 4pm-8pm)* is dedicated to the Vetulonia sites. Just outside are two separate **sites** (☎ *0564 94 95 87; free; open 9am-dusk)* where excavations have revealed bits and bobs of the Etruscan settlement. The more extensive site, known as *Scavi Citta* (town excavations), is just below the town as you leave by the only road.

More interesting are four unearthed **Etruscan tombs** *(Via dei Sepolcri; free; open 9am-dusk)*, a couple of kilometres farther downhill and along a turn-off to the right. The most interesting of these is the last, which is about 1km down a rough dirt track.

Taverna Etrusca (☎/fax *0564 94 98 02, Piazza Stefani 12)* Doubles €41.30. If you get stuck, this place, on the central square, is accommodating.

A couple of *restaurants* on the square will keep you fed at lunchtime.

Buses run twice daily from Grosseto and once from Castiglione della Pescaia.

MASSA MARITTIMA
postcode 58024 • pop 9500

Without doubt this is about the most interesting town in the Maremma. Its proximity

MASSA MARITTIMA

PLACES TO STAY
3 Hotel Il Sole
17 Ostello Le Clarisse
19 Ostello Sant' Anna

PLACES TO EAT
2 Osteria da Tronca
7 Trattoria Vecchio Borgo
11 Ristoro Il Gatto e La Volpe

OTHER
1 Chiesa di San Francesco
4 Palazzo Comunale
5 Ufficio Turistico
6 Palazzo del Podestà & Museo Archeologico
8 Pub dei Fantasmi
9 Cathedral
10 Banca Toscana & ATM
12 Torre del Candeliere & Arco Senese
13 Museo di Arte e Storia delle Miniere
14 Chiesa di Sant'Agostino
15 Post Office
16 Bus Terminal
18 Museo della Miniera

to the sea and pretty medieval centre makes it a good base. Dating back to the 8th century, the walled nucleus of the old town was already in place by the 12th. For a while under Pisan domination, the medieval town thrived on the local metal mining industry. In 1225 it became an independent commune but was swallowed up by Siena a century later. The plague in 1348 and the end of mining 50 years later reduced the city almost to extinction. Only in the 18th century, with the draining of marshes and re-establishment of mining, did Massa Marittima finally come back to life.

Information

The Ufficio Turistico (☎ 0566 90 27 56), Via Norma Parenti 22, opens 9.30am to 1pm and 3.30pm to 7pm Monday to Saturday (9.30am to 1pm Sunday) April to October, and 10am to 12.30pm Tuesday to Sunday the rest of the year. *Strada del Vino* maps are available from the office.

The post office is at Corso Diaz 28, and the Banca Toscana at Piazza Garibaldi 17 has an ATM.

Things to See

The heart of medieval Massa is Piazza Garibaldi, dominated by the imposing bulk of the **cathedral** (*Piazza Garibaldi; free; open 8am-noon & 3.30pm-7pm*), in Pisan Romanesque style. It is thought Giovanni Pisano designed the church, although much of the work may have been carried out by Sienese workmen. The inside is graced with substantial remnants of frescoes and several paintings, including a *Madonna delle Grazie* by the workshop of Siena's Duccio di Buoninsegna.

Opposite is the **Palazzo Comunale**, the city's historic seat of government. The proud coat of arms of Florence's Medicis doesn't quite distract attention from the earlier symbol of rival Siena's one-time ascendancy here – the wolf with Romulus and Remus.

The 13th-century **Palazzo del Podestà** nowadays houses the **Museo Archeologico** (☎ *0566 90 22 89, Piazza Garibaldi 1; admission €2.60; open 10am-12.30pm & 3.30pm-7pm Tues-Sun Apr-Oct, 10am-12.30pm & 3pm-5pm Tues-Sun Nov-Mar)*, visited above all for Ambrogio Lorenzetti's magnificent *Maestà* (Majesty). Paling into comparative insignificance is a modest collection of ancient Roman and Etruscan artefacts that were dug up in the area around Massa.

The Città Nuova (New Town) is dominated by the **Torre del Candeliere** *(Piazza Matteotti; admission €1.55; open 11am-1pm & 3.30pm-7.30pm daily July & Aug, 10am-1pm & 3pm-6pm Tues-Sun Apr-June & Sept, 10am-1pm & 2.30pm-5.30pm Tues-Sun Oct-Mar)*. The tower is in turn joined to defensive bastions in the wall by the so-called **Arco Senese** (Sienese Arch). You can enter the tower and bestride the arch – the views over the Città Vecchia (Old Town) are stupendous; they are at their very best in the early morning.

At the **Museo della Miniera** *(Via Corridoni; adult/child €5.15/2.60; open 10.15am-5.45pm Tues-Sun)* you can examine the city's mining history. The display includes a replica of a length of mine. Guided tours (1½ hours) go through up to seven times daily. The **Museo di Arte e Storia delle Miniere** *(Piazza Matteotti 4; admission €1.50; open 10am-11.30am & 3.30pm-7pm Tues-Sun Apr-Oct)* has more mining material, such as art by the miners, but also concentrates on the area's mining history.

Places to Stay

Overnight options are rather scarce. If you find them all full, the tourist office may be able to help organise something else in the surrounding area.

***Ostello Le Clarisse** (☎ 0566 90 11 15, fax 0566 94 05 15, ⓔ leclarisse@libero.it, Piazza XXIV Maggio)* Dorm beds €12.40. Housed in an old monastery, this newcomer is situated in a quiet area of town. Rooms are particularly large and the colourful interior and friendly staff make the place instantly relaxing.

***Ostello Sant'Anna** (☎ 0566 90 46 11, fax 0566 90 46 00, Via Gramsci 7)* Dorm beds €20.65. This hostel, in the new part of town, isn't as chilled out as Le Clarisse but is still a good bet.

***Hotel Il Sole** (☎ 0566 90 19 71, fax 0566 90 19 59, Corso della Libertà 43)* Singles/doubles €46.50/64.50. In Massa itself this is your only choice of hotel. Some rooms have views and there is garage parking as well (extra €12.90).

Places to Eat

As surprising as the lack of accommodation is the concentration of above-average restaurants. Even the touristy places on Piazza Garibaldi aren't bad.

***Trattoria Vecchio Borgo** (☎ 0566 90 39 50, Via Norma Parenti 12)* Mains €7.75-9.30. Open Tues-Sun. This is a good spot for carnivores and the cavernous interior has a medieval feel about it.

***Ristoro Il Gatto e La Volpe** (☎ 0566 90 35 75, Vicolo Ciambellano 12)* Mains around €7.75. Open Tues-Sun. Tucked away on a side street, this fine restaurant serves up quality fodder. Try the divine *filetto tartufato* (fillet steak prepared with truffles).

***Osteria da Tronca** (☎ 0566 90 19 91, Vicolo Porte 5)* Full meals €26-31. Open Thur-Tues. The food at this split-level restaurant is fantastic (try anything with *cinghiale* – wild boar), along with the stone walls and arches of the interior.

Entertainment

***Pub dei Fantasmi** (☎ 0566 94 02 74, Via Norma Parenti 2/4)* Open until 3am Thur-Tues. If you are feeling a little frisky after dinner, this is about the only place big enough to hold a crowd.

On the first Sunday after 19 May a crossbow competition – the Balestro del Girifalco – takes place here.

Getting There & Away

Getting in and out of Massa requires some patience. Irregular bus services connect Massa with Siena and Volterra to the north. For Grosseto, you're better off taking a bus to Follonica train station (€1.55) and then taking a train rather than relying on the meagre bus service to the town. The bus terminal is south of the new town on Via Valle Aspra.

The nearest train station is at Follonica on the coastal Rome-Livorno line. Up to 20 FMF buses connect Massa with the train station each weekday.

THE COAST

Don't get your hopes too high when cruising the coast from Piombino south. Occasional stretches of pine-backed beach are pleasant without being breathtaking. The best that this southern stretch of mainland Tuscan coast has to offer is down in the Parco Regionale della Maremma.

Golfo di Follonica

Picture yourself in your car or on a bike disembarking in Piombino from Elba. Take in the reassuring picture of chimney stacks and industry at work. All quite necessary, to be sure, but no reason to hang about. Hit the road and head south. The first town of note you will reach is **Follonica**. It is interesting if only because it leaves you wondering what kind of town-planning rules they have that allow all that cheap and tacky high-rise building. Right up on the beach too. Unless you need a dip in the sea right now, don't even bother entering town. On a slightly less nasty note, the beach improves, with a pleasant pinewood backdrop, if you proceed a few kilometres farther around the gulf – about where you see the turn-off signs inland for **Scarlino**.

You will find a couple of camping grounds in the same vicinity. If you are obliged by fate to spend a night in Follonica, there is no shortage of hotels and eateries to keep your spirits up.

A very annoying committee must have been hard at work in **Punta Ala** to devise the most Kafkaesque road system imaginable when it set to designing this leafy but rather fake getaway for the filthy rich. On the plus side, the promontory is green and rather sparingly brutalised by building development. Along the north flank and hidden

from view by the serried ranks of inevitable pines is a long if narrow stretch of sandy beach, quite a lot of it open to the public. On the down side, most of the accommodation is in the interstellar price range. The best way to get wet is to ditch the car while still on the straight stretch of road (or jump off the bus) just before entering the labyrinth of roundabouts in Punta Ala proper, and follow your nose through the pinewoods. The odd bus dares to make an appearance here from Grosseto, but the obvious way in is with your own wheels.

Castiglione della Pescaia

At last, something seriously worth stopping for on the mad rush southwards. The modern sprawl around the feet of the hill on which this medieval stone village sits is surprisingly not too disturbing. In fact, the point where old meets new is quite contagious with its bustle, and is still lively as late as mid-October.

The walled old town, brooding in its stoney quiet, has no specific monuments of interest, but the views out to sea are majestic and a wander is as pleasing as tends to be the case in such places.

The tourist office (☎ 0564 93 36 78, Piazza Garibaldi) opens 9am to 1pm and 4pm to 8pm Monday to Saturday, and 10am to 1pm Sunday.

Places to Stay & Eat Castiglione has the advantage that it is fairly liberally blessed with hotels and other sleeping options. Hotels average around €52 or €72 for a single or double room respectively.

Camping Etruria (☎ 0564 93 34 83, fax 0564 93 82 47, Le Marze) Adult/tent €6.20/10.35. Of the half-dozen camping grounds around the town (four of which are actually near Le Rocchette, itself closer to Punta Ala than Castiglione), this is a reasonable choice. The site is a few kilometres south of town off the road to Marina di Grosseto.

Hotel Bologna (☎/fax 0564 93 37 46, Piaza Garibaldi 8) Singles/doubles €23.25/43.90. If you are looking for a cheap doss, this is nothing special but it is in the heart of the action next to the tourist office and rather a steal (by local standards) for the fairly basic rooms on offer.

Whether or not you want to stay, Castiglione does boast some rather recommendable places to eat in the old town.

Osteria nel Buco (☎ *0564 93 44 60, Via del Recinto 11)* Mains €8.25-11.40. Open Tues-Sun. This is a lively little hole in the wall (as its name and position just inside the old town walls suggest). They serve up typical dishes of the Maremma, and have an excellent range of soups.

Ristorante La Fortezza (☎ *0564 93 61 00, Via del Recinto 1/3)* Mains €8.80-15.50. Open Tues-Sun. If Osteria nel Buco is packed, or you want to sit outside, try this more ample spot that also serves good local cuisine.

Getting There & Away Rama buses frequently run to/from Grosseto (€2.85) and connect with other places on the coast, such as Castiglione della Pescaia (€1.70). Up to five buses a day in the height of summer connect with Follonica train station, one of the main stops around here.

Marina di Grosseto

Yes, by Tuscan standards the beach is broad and sandy, but it's nothing to write home about. Luckily the grid-like town with its thoughtlessly slapped-together housing is rendered less of an eyesore by the fact that it is spread out and low, and well camouflaged by the umbrella pines typical of the Maremma coast. It's a nice spot for locals to come and splash in the sea, but there are more interesting places close by (see the entries on Castiglione della Pescaia and Parco Regionale della Maremma either side of this section).

If for whatever reason you get stuck or actually like the place, there is a fair range of places to stay and you won't go hungry.

Tre Stelle (☎ *0564 3 45 38, fax 0564 3 41 53, Via dei Platani 15)* Singles/doubles €38.75/49. This is about the most economical of digs, so book ahead in summer.

The marina is a short and comparatively regular bus ride away from Grosseto.

Parco Regionale della Maremma

Along the entire coastline from Piombino to Rome, this is arguably the main attraction. The park incorporates the Monti dell' Uccellina and a magnificent stretch of unspoiled coastline. Many native animals call this home, including deer, wild boar, foxes, wild cats, porcupines and hawks.

The main **Centro Visite del Parco** (visitors centre) is at Alberese *(☎ 0564 40 70 98; open 7am-6pm mid-June–Sept, 8am-2pm Oct–mid-June)*. There's a small office (same contact details and opening hours) located at the southern extremity of the park. A turn-off 1km before Talamone leads directly to it. **Talamone** itself is a fetching little fortress village with a camping ground and several hotel and restaurant options.

Entry to the park is limited and cars must be left in designated parking areas. Walking is the best way to explore the park, and nine trails have been marked out within its borders. For more information see the Tuscany on Foot chapter.

Other options for exploring the park present themselves. A number of companies run canoeing and horse-riding tours in certain areas, costing around €18 and €21 respectively. It's also possible to ride with the legendary *butteri*, cowboys who still work the area in and around the park. Contact Azienda Agricola la Apergolaia (☎ 0564 40 71 80) for more details – this is only for people who can ride well. Cycling options are also available. The visitor centre in Alberese has a full list of places to contact.

There are no shelters or bars (with the exception of a couple at Marina di Alberese) within the park, so make sure you carry water and are properly dressed. The Marina gets crowded in summer, especially at the weekend.

It's impossible to stay in the park. The nearest you will get is a few *agriturismi* scattered around the flatlands between the park and the SS1.

Trattoria Romoli (☎ *0564 40 50 33, Via Provinciale Alberese)* Full meal from €21. Open Wed-Mon. This fantastic place is just outside Santa Maria di Rispescia on the road to Alberese. Specialities include home-made tiramisu, *cinghiale* (wild boar) in a red-wine sauce and anything fresh from the sea.

MONTE ARGENTARIO

Once an island, this promontory came to be linked to the mainland by an accumulation of sand that is now the isthmus of Orbetello. Further sandy bulwarks form the Tombolo della Giannella and the Tombolo di Feniglia to the north and south. They enclose a lagoon that is now a protected nature reserve. Intense building has spoiled the northern side of the promontory, but the south and centre have been left in peace (forest fires aside). It is something of a weekend getaway fave with Romans in summer and is inevitably packed to the gunwales.

Orbetello

Orbetello's main attraction is its **cathedral**, which has retained its 14th-century Gothic facade despite being remodelled in the Spanish style in the 16th century. Other reminders of the Spanish garrison that was stationed in the city include the fort and city wall. Parts of the latter belong to the original Etruscan wall.

The best place for observing the birdlife (as many as 140 species have been identified) on Orbetello's lagoon is out along the **Tombolo della Feniglia**, the southern strip of land linking Monte Argentario to the mainland. It is blocked to traffic – you can park your car near the camping ground and proceed on foot or bicycle (see Getting There & Around later). The beach on the seaward side is quite popular too (indeed it is about the nicest on the peninsula).

Around the Peninsula

Monte Argentario is popular with Romans, and tourists are slowly joining them in ever-increasing numbers. **Porto Santo Stefano** and **Porto Ercole** are resort towns for the wealthy, but Porto Ercole, in a picturesque position between two Spanish forts, retains some of its fishing village character. The main tourist office (☎ 0564 81 42 08) is in Porto Santo Stefano, in the Monte dei Paschi di Siena building, at Corso Umberto I 55. It opens 9am to 1pm and 4pm to 6pm

(5pm to 7pm July and August), Monday to Saturday.

The new **Acquario Mediterraneo** *(☎ 0564 81 59 33, Lungomare dei Navigatori 44/48; admission €4.15; open 5pm-midnight daily)*, on the waterfront in Porto Santo Stefano, has a small but interesting collection of marine life plucked from the Mediterranean. **Fortezza Spagnola** *(☎ 0564 81 06 81, Piazza del Governatore; admission €4.15; open 6pm-midnight daily June-Sept, Sat & Sun only Oct-May)* is a little overpriced for the underwater archaeological finds it houses, but the breathtaking views of Porto Santo Stefano are worth the dosh.

For a pleasant drive, follow the signs to Il Telegrafo, one of the highest mountains in the region, and turn off at the **Convento dei Frati Passionisti**, a church and convent with sensational views across to the mainland. Another good drive is the Via Panoramica, a circuit running out from Porto Santo Stefano.

There are several good beaches, mainly of the pebbly or rocky (rather than sandy) variety. Near Porto Ercole the beach is serviced, which means it's clean but cluttered with deck chairs and umbrellas for hire. As you move farther away the beach becomes less crowded but, as with most public beaches in Italy, it also gets dirtier.

Places to Stay

Accommodation on the peninsula is generally expensive and sought after over the summer months. Breakfast is usually included in the price.

Orbetello On the way onto the peninsula, this village is a possibility.

Albergo La Perla *(☎ 0564 86 35 46, fax 0564 86 52 10, Via Volontari del Sangue 10)* Singles €25.80-36.15, doubles with bathroom €62. If it's no-frills cheap you are looking for, this place, just outside the old town on the road back to the mainland, has pokey singles.

Porto Santo Stefano This resort town has a few more options.

Pensione Weekend *(☎/fax 0564 81 25 80, Via Martiri d'Ungheria 3)* Doubles with bathroom from €51.65. This fine hotel is recommended by readers and is one of your best bets on the peninsula. The rooms don't exactly sparkle but they are airy, comfortable and have a lot of character. The owner is warm, welcoming and speaks enough languages to satisfy most people.

Albergo Belvedere (☎ 0564 81 26 34, Via del Fortino 51) High-season singles/doubles €67.15/87.80. This luxurious complex overlooks the water shortly before you enter the town proper. It also has a private beach.

Torre di Cala Piccola (☎ 0564 82 51 11, fax 0564 82 53 25, W www.torredicalapiccola .com, Località Cala Piccola) Singles/doubles €170.40/284. For splendid isolation and good views over the sea, open your wallet and head for this place, out on the Via Panoramica.

Porto Ercole If you want to camp, this is the best choice.

Feniglia (☎ 0564 83 10 90, fax 0564 86 71 75, on the northern fringe at the Feniglia beach) Adult/tent €7.75/10.35. This camping ground has all the amenities you need, including a restaurant and laundry facilities.

Places to Eat

The peninsula is full of its fair share of restaurants and, unsurprisingly, seafood rules OK. Remember, however, that at the weekend freshly caught fish is hard to come by – there are simply too many people eating their way through the peninsula at that time!

Orbetello There are a couple of top choices here.

Osteria del Lupacante (☎ 0564 86 76 18, Corso Italia 103) Mains €8.25-12.90. Open Wed-Mon. While in Tuscany, why not eat Sicilian? If you haven't had the chance to tuck into true Sicilian cooking, justifiably known for its imaginativeness, and often quite spicy (an Arab legacy), you will be pleased you sauntered into this place. The *spaghetti alla messinese* (Messina style) comes with swordfish meat, tomato, peppers, sunflower seeds and spices.

Osteria il Nocchino (☎ 0564 86 03 29, Via dei Mille 64) Meals from €23.25. Open

Thur-Tues. This place is another excellent choice, albeit with about as much seating capacity as a glorified matchbox (in summer there's also outdoor seating though). Prices are moderate and the food is like mamma used to make.

Porto Santo Stefano You'll find plenty of seafood options in this resort.

Il Veliero (☎ 0564 81 22 26, Via Panoramica 149) Meals around €31. Open Tues-Sun. Expect to find fresh fish on the menu every day here – the owner's father runs a local fish shop. If that doesn't tempt you to tackle the steep climb to Via Panoramica, then the restaurant's outdoor seating with views should.

Trattoria da Siro (☎ 0564 81 25 38, Corso Umberto I 100) Meals around €31. Open Tues-Sun. This trattoria, just off the waterfront, is another good bet for fine seafood.

Lo Sfizio (☎ 0564 81 99 52, Corso Umberto I 26) Meals from €20.65. Open Wed-Mon. A cheaper bet on the waterfront is this restaurant. You can have *bruschette*, pizza or seafood, such as *sauté di cozze e vongole veraci* (sautéed mussels and clams).

Porto Ercole Among others, you could try the following for a good meal.

El Pirata (☎ 0564 83 11 78, Lungomare Andrea Doria 24) Meals from €25.80. Open Thur-Tues. For good pizza try this place, right on the marina.

Getting There & Around

Rama buses connect most towns on the Monte Argentario with Orbetello Scalo (coinciding with train arrivals) and Grosseto. By car, follow the signs to Monte Argentario from the SS1, which connects Grosseto to Rome. Some shacks near the Feniglia camp site rent bicycles for €2.60 a day.

THE ISLANDS

More than a few locals skip Monte Argentario altogether and choose to head off on excursions to one of two islands off the coast. The islands of Giglio and Giannutri are both part of the Parco Nazionale dell' Arcipelago Toscano.

Giglio

The hilly island of Giglio lies 14km off Monte Argentario. Regular boat services from Porto Santo Stefano make getting to this pretty little spot easy. You arrive at Giglio Porto, once a Roman port and now the best spot to find a room. A local bus service will take you 6km to the inland fastness of Giglio Castello, dominated by a Pisan castle.

The only beaches are on the western side of the island, and the best of them is fronted by the modern resort of Giglio Campese. It's relatively low key and the beach is protected.

A dozen hotels, a sprinkling of *affitta-camere* and a camp site total the accommodation options. If you don't have a list from the tourist office, get a morning boat over and do the rounds. That way if you are out of luck (probable on summer weekends) you can always get back to the mainland.

Toremar (☎ 0564 81 08 03) and Mare-giglio (☎ 0564 81 29 20) run boats to the island. Toremar has three or four a day year-round, while Maregiglio runs three or four in summer, but drops its service to three or so per day at weekends and on Monday out of season. The one-way trip costs €5.15 weekdays and €6.20 weekends.

Giannutri This tiny islet is the southern-most of the archipelago and is a flat and rel-atively lacklustre affair with just two tiny beaches barely worthy of the name. Still, the curious can get over on a day tour from Porto Santo Stefano from May to September. Ask at the Maregiglio office for times and prices. It may run at weekends out of season too.

THE ROAD TO ROME
Lago di Burano

Little more than 10km farther east along the coast, and about 5km short of the regional frontier with Lazio, this saltwater flat has since 1980 been a WWF-run nature reserve – the **Riserva Naturale Lago di Burano** (☎ 0564 89 88 29, Capalbio Scalo; admis-sion €5.15; guided visits 10am & 2.30pm Sun Sept-Apr). Covering 410 hectares, it is typical of the Maremma in its flora, but in-teresting above all for its migratory bird life. Tens of thousands of birds of many

species winter here, including several kinds of duck and even falcons. Among the ani-mals, the most precious is the beaver. A path dotted with seven observation points winds its way through the park.

To get there you take the Capalbio Scalo exit from the SS1 (the odd train stops at the station here too).

INLAND & ETRUSCAN SITES

The relatively untouristed 'deep south' of Tuscany, home to thermal springs, a plethora of medieval hill towns and Etruscan archae-ological finds, is more than worthy of a few days' exploration. And if you're into ruins, rubble and ancient villages you might end up skipping the coast altogether and heading straight for the hills. The following route passes through the hot spots of the area.

Magliano & Scansano

From **Albinia**, at the northern tip of the Or-betello lagoon, take the SS74 in the direction of Manciano (where we will arrive a little later on) and make a detour up the SS323.

First stop is **Magliano in Toscana**, impres-sive above all for its largely intact city walls. Some date from the 14th century, while the bulk were raised by Siena in the 16th century. The town is a little scrappy on the inside.

Antica Trattoria Aurora (☎ 0564 59 20 30, Via Chiasso Lavagnini 12/14) Meals around €31. Open Thur-Tues. Lunch here is a good idea, but its inviting garden is only open for dinner.

A few buses connect with Grosseto, Scansano and Orbetello. Next proceed up to **Scansano**. Although there are no monu-ments of great importance, the old centre is a pleasure to wander around, all narrow lanes and archways, with some great views over the surrounding country.

A couple of Rama buses from Grosseto trundle through Scansano on their way to Manciano via Montemerano.

Montemerano, Manciano & Saturnia

Heading towards Manciano, you first hit the small walled medieval town of **Monte-merano**, where you can buy outstanding

Tuscan olive oil at *La Piaggia (☎ 0564 60 29 09, Via Fermi 21)*, an *agriturismo* establishment. Visit the town's Chiesa di San Giorgio, which is decorated with 15th-century frescoes of the Sienese school.

From here it is a 6km hike or occasional bus or car ride to **Saturnia** and its sulphur spring and thermal baths at **Terme di Saturnia**, just outside the village. Bring along a bathing costume and towel for a restorative dip. You have two options here. You can fork out for the hi-tech private spa with all the services typical of such establishments (from €12.40 for the privilege), or go for a free hot shower under the sulphurous waterfall and a dip in its hot pools. A small lane leads off to the waterfall, a pleasantly secluded spot often jammed with an international crew of hippies and all sorts.

Saturnia's Etruscan remains, including part of the town wall, are worth a diversion if you are into that sort of thing. A tomb at **Sede di Carlo**, just north-east of the town, is one of the area's best preserved.

Getting here by bus is a real hassle and virtually impossible on our route, as about the only service is by the odd bus running between Grosseto and Pitigliano. Many hitchhike from Montemerano.

Another former Sienese fortress, **Manciano** could end up being a compulsory transport stop on your travels around here. Apart from the much interfered with Rocca (the fortress) there is not an awful lot to hold you up.

Pitigliano

From Manciano head east along the SS74 for Pitigliano. The visual impact of this town is hard to forget. It seems to grow organically out of a high volcanic rocky outcrop that towers over the surrounding country. The gorges that surround the town on three sides constitute a natural bastion, completed to the east by the man-made fort.

Originally built by the Etruscans, the town remained beyond the orbit of the great Tuscan city states, such as Florence and Siena, until it was finally absorbed into the grand duchy under Cosimo I de' Medici.

In the course of the 15th century a Jewish community began to grow here, a tendency that accelerated when Pope Pius IV banned Jews from Rome in 1569. Perhaps they felt themselves still too close to the cockpit of Catholicism, for in subsequent years they began to move away, to Livorno, Florence and often farther afield still, such as to Venice. Maybe it was just that there was no room, for in 1622 the Jews of Pitigliano were obliged to move into a tiny ghetto, where they remained until 1772. From then until well into the following century, the local community of 400 flourished and Pitigliano was dubbed Little Jerusalem. By the time the Fascists introduced their race laws in 1938, most Jews had moved away (only 80 or so were left, precious few of whom survived the war).

Information The tourist information office (☎ 0564 61 70 81) is at Via Roma 4, just off Piazza della Repubblica, and opens 10.20am to 1pm and 3pm to 7pm Wednesday to Monday June to September. There's talk of keeping it open till December, but don't rely on it. The office produces an excellent map of the surrounding area, showing the *via cave* (the so-called Etruscan 'sunken roads' – for more information, see the boxed text 'Via Cave' later) and other attractions.

Things to See Apart from the spectacle of viewing the town from the Manciano approach road (arrive at night and you see it all lit up – quite breathtaking), it is a joy to wander around its narrow little lanes. Perched as it is on a sharp outcrop surrounded by gorges, the place seems like it could have inspired Escher. Twisting stairways disappear around corners, cobbled alleys bend out of sight beneath arches and the stone houses seem to have been piled up one on top of the other by a giant drunk playing with building blocks.

As you enter the town, the first intriguing sight is the aqueduct, built in the 16th century. Keeping watch over the interlocking Piazza Garibaldi and Piazza Petruccioli is the 13th-century **Palazzo Orsini** *(☎ 0564 61 44 19; admission €2.60; open 10am-1pm & 5pm-7pm (8pm Aug) Tues-Sun Apr-Sept, 10am-1pm &*

3pm-5pm Tues-Sun Oct-Mar). Eighteen of its rooms are open to the public, decked out with sacred art, including two works by Francesco Zuccarelli, who was born here. Much of what you see was built over the following centuries. Now seat of the local bishopric, it is a true citadel, a city within a city – fortress, residence and supply dump. In a separate area of the palace you'll find the **Museo Archeologico** *(☎ 0564 63 37 67, Piazza della Fortezza; adult/child €2.60/1.55; open 10am-1pm & 4pm-7pm Tues-Sun Apr-Sept, 10am-1pm & 3pm-6pm Tues-Sun Oct-Mar)*, with an instructive display rather than just the usual glass containers full of all sorts of unexplained ancient odds and sods. In the cellars of the palace is the **Museo della Civiltà Giubonnai**, dedicated to agricultural equipment specific to the Maremma. It was closed at the time of writing; check with the tourist office for opening times and prices.

If you wander down Via Zuccarelli deep into the town, after a few minutes you will see a sign pointing left off to the **synagogue** *(☎ 0347 78 92 033, Vicolo Manin 30; free; open 10am-noon & 4pm-7pm Sun-Fri June-Sept, 10am-noon & 3pm-5pm Sun-Fri Oct-May)*, at the heart of the town's once busy little ghetto. It had largely gone to seed until 1995, when it was restored using old photos and other material to reconstruct it. A museum dedicated to Jewish culture is due to be opened within the synagogue by summer 2002.

The town's **cathedral** dates back to the Middle Ages, but its facade is Baroque and its interior has been modernised. Older is the oddly shaped **Chiesa di Santa Maria**.

The local drop, Bianco di Pitigliano, is a lively dry white wine of DOC calibre. The shops lining Via San Chiara, just off Piazza Petruccioli, are good places to procure a bottle or two of this fine wine.

Places to Stay & Eat Several affitta-camere operate in and about the town. You'll see the occasional sign or you can get information from the tourist office.

La Casa dei Carrai (☎ 0338 677 32 42, Viale San Francesco 68b) Singles/doubles €20.65/41.30. This place is a good, cheap option, with decent-sized rooms and a small garden. It's about 500m outside town, heading towards Sorano.

Hotel Valle Orientina (☎ 0564 61 66 11, fax 0564 61 77 28, e orientina@ laltramaremma.it, Località Valle Orientina) Singles €25.80-35.60, doubles €46.50-60.95. This secluded hotel is 3km outside town, on the road to Orvieto. It's great for a bit of peace and quiet and you can rent bicycles for €7.75 per day.

Osteria Il Tufo Allegro (☎ 0564 61 61 92, Vico della Costituzione 2, just off Via Zuccarelli) Full meal around €28.40. Open Wed-Mon. This is definitely *the* place to eat. The service and food are superb but the seating limited, so it would be wise to book.

Jerry Lee Bar (☎ 0564 61 60 66, Via Roma 28) Open Tues-Sun. This is the best place to catch any nightlife in town. There's a young vibe, occasional live music and an Internet point.

Getting There & Away Rama buses stop just outside Piazza Petruccioli, on Via San Chiara. Up to five buses a day Monday to Saturday run to Grosseto via Manciano, but drop off to nothing on Sunday. Quite a few buses run to Sorano, while only two go to Sovana (none on Sunday). To get to Saturnia you need to go to Manciano and connect. Enquire at the terminus in advance to make sure of the connections.

Sovana

This pretty little town has more than its fair share of important Etruscan sites and historical monuments. The information office (☎ 0564 61 40 74), in the Palazzo Pretorio on Piazza del Pretorio, opens 9am to 1pm and 3pm to 8pm daily in July and August, and till 7pm the rest of the year (Friday to Sunday only from November to February). Palazzo Pretorio also houses a small **archaeological museum** *(admission €2; open same times as the tourist office)*.

If you plan to visit all the archaeological sites in and around Sovana and Sorano (see later in this chapter), it's well worth purchasing a combined €6.20 ticket. This allows entry to the archaeological museum in

Via Cave

Via cave, sunken roads carved into the rock in this area by the Etruscans, are a mystery to one and all, and speculation as to why they bothered to create these artificial pedestrian gorges still goes on today. Some suggest they were used as sacred routes for ritual processions or funeral ceremonies (since many link *necropoli* to other religious sites), while others believe they were used to move livestock or as some kind of defence, allowing people to move from village to village unseen. Whatever the reason, the Etruscans sure put in a lot of effort carving the cave: they average 20m in height, 3m in width and around half a kilometre in length.

The countryside around Pitigliano, Sovana and Sorano is riddled with via cave, and they make great excursions from any of the towns. Two particularly good examples, half a kilometre west of Pitigliano on the road to Sovana, are Via Cava di Fratenuti, with high vertical walls and Etruscan inscriptions, and Via Cava di San Giuseppe, which passes the Fontana dell'Olmo, a fountain of Etruscan origins. Via Cava San Rocco is another fine example, near Sorano. It winds its way through the hills for 2km between the town and the Necropoli di San Rocco.

Sovana, the Tomba della Sirena and Tomba di Ildebranda, the Fortezza Orsini in Sorano, the Necropoli di San Rocco, and the Vitozza rock caves outside San Quirico. Tickets can be purchased at any of the sites.

Pope Gregory VII was born here. Medieval mansions and the remains of a fortress belonging to his family are at the eastern end of the town, where you enter. Proceed west along the main street (this is essentially a one-street town) and you emerge in the broad Piazza del Pretorio. Here the **Chiesa di Santa Maria** *(Piazza del Pretorio; free; open 10am-1pm & 2.30pm-7pm May-Sept, to 6pm Oct-Apr, Sat & Sun only Jan)* is a starkly simple Romanesque church (although interfered with in parts in later centuries) featuring a magnificent 9th-century ciborium in white marble, one of the last remaining pre-Romanesque works left in Tuscany. It is a highly curious piece of work placed over the altar. The church also contains some early-16th-century frescoes.

Walk along the Via del Duomo to reach the imposing Gothic-Romanesque **cathedral** *(☎ 0564 61 65 32; free; same opening times as Chiesa di Santa Maria)*, at the far western end of the town. The original construction dates back to the 9th century, although it was largely rebuilt in the 12th and 13th centuries. Of particular note are the cathedral's marble portal and the capitals of the columns that divide the interior into three naves. Several of the capitals feature biblical scenes and are thought to be the work of the Lombard school, dating from the 11th century. The small crypt to the rear of the cathedral contains seven simple but elegant columns.

A couple of kilometres out of town proceeding west along the road to Saturnia (if you have no vehicle, walking is the only real option) you will come to a series of **archaeological sites** *(admission €5.15 to both sites, guided tours at 10.30am & 4pm €10.35; open 9am-7pm daily Mar-Oct, 9am-6pm Fri-Sun Nov-Feb)*. They harbour the most significant Etruscan tombs in Tuscany. Look for the yellow sign on the left for the **Tomba della Sirena**. At the first site you can follow a trail running alongside a series of monumental tomb facades cut from the rock face, as well as walk along a *via cava*.

The second site, 300m farther west along the same road, is dominated by the **Tomba di Ildebranda**, by far the grandest of Etruscan tombs, and still preserving traces of the columns and stairs that made up this majestic resting place.

You could easily devote a good day to exploring these sites and/or other less obvious ones in the area. It makes for some pleasant walking.

Places to Stay & Eat Sovana has a couple of good places to stay, which also have restaurants.

Taverna Etrusca (☎ 0564 61 61 83, fax 0564 61 41 93, Piazza Pretorio 16) Singles/doubles €46.50/72.30. If you'd like to stay in Sovana, try this place. Its fine *restaurant* (open Tues-Sun) serves typical Maremma cuisine; you're looking at a bill of €31 a head.

Scilla (☎ 0564 61 65 31, fax 0564 61 43 29, [e] scilla@l'altramaremma.it, Via Siviero 1/3) Singles/doubles €62/93. All eight rooms (recently renovated) at this hotel have a touch of class about them. In summer book ahead. Scilla also boasts a classy glassed-in *restaurant* (open Wed-Mon), well worth the €36 you are likely to spend.

Sorano

From Sovana we turn back down the road we arrived on and past the turn-off for Pitigliano to proceed north-east to Sorano. Two kilometres before Sorano is the **Necropoli di San Rocco** *(admission €2; open 9am-7pm Mar-Oct, Fri-Sun only Nov-Feb)*, another Etruscan burial site. From here you can proceed on foot to Sorano via one of the via cave.

High on a rocky spur, the small medieval town of Sorano has largely retained its original form. Its houses seem to huddle together in an effort not to shove one another off their precarious perch. Many of the back streets in the town's medieval heart are rather forlorn

and only inhabited by our feline friends. There's a small tourist information office (☎ 0546 63 30 99) on Piazza Busati.

The town's main attraction is the partly renovated **Fortezza Orsini** *(☎ 0564 63 37 67; admission €2; open 9am-1pm & 3pm-7pm daily Mar-Oct, Fri-Sun only Nov-Feb)*, which houses a small museum devoted to the medieval era. Guided visits to the underground cellars and quarters of the castle cost €2.60 and leave at 11am and 4pm.

You could also climb up **Masso Leopoldino** *(admission €2; open 10am-2.45pm & 3.45pm-7.15pm daily Apr-Nov)*, a large platform at the top of the village, for absolutely spectacular views of the surrounding countryside.

Hotel della Fortezza (☎ 0564 63 20 10, fax 0564 63 32 09, Piazza Cairoli) Singles/doubles €56.80/93. If you like the fortress so much that you want to stay there, you can do. The rooms have a lovely rustic feel to them (wood-beamed ceilings etc), and some also have fantastic views.

Talismano (☎ 0564 63 32 81, Via San Marco 29) Pizza €4.15-6.20, mains €4.40-9.30. Open Wed-Mon. This cavernous place comes highly recommended by locals. The menu is filled with an excellent selection of pizzas and plenty of Tuscan dishes, so you'll be hard pressed not to find something to your liking.

Central Tuscany

The hottest frontier in medieval Tuscany was the demarcation line that separated Florence and its possessions from the county of Siena. This proud Gothic hilltop city, although long ago swallowed up by Florence into what became the grand duchy of Tuscany, even today maintains a separate identity. In some respects the Sienese have neither forgiven nor forgotten.

Siena province and the rest of central Tuscany is predominantly hill country, its peaks and ridges dotted with some of the most enchanting towns and villages in the region. From steep, straggling Montepulciano to the one-time defensive bulwark of Monteriggioni, the traveller with time to explore will stumble across numerous gems.

Moving westwards, the pilgrim-route bastion of San Gimignano, with its ranks of medieval towers, gives us insight into the pomp and circumstance even relatively small towns enjoyed in the Middle Ages. Volterra, the brooding medieval successor to an Etruscan settlement, stands aloof watch over lunar expanses to the south.

Within the patchwork quilt of countryside stretching from Chianti Senese (see the Around Florence chapter) in the north to Montalcino and Montepulciano in the south you will find yourself continually reminded of two of the principal vocations of the area – wine and olive oil. Here you will have the chance to try some of Tuscany's most prized drops, such as Brunello, on their home turf.

South of Siena hot springs bubble forth in various spots. A hot outdoor bath in the depths of winter is a unique experience.

For the energetic, central Tuscany offers plenty of walking options. Indeed, the most satisfying way to discover its small medieval towns and Romanesque *pievi* (parish churches) is by following the country lanes.

SIENA
postcode 53100 • pop 59,200
Siena is without doubt one of Italy's most enchanting cities. Its medieval centre bristles

Highlights

- Visit the great Gothic feast that is Siena's cathedral
- Climb the Torre del Mangia for glorious views and follow up with a coffee in the unique Piazza del Campo, the heart of medieval Siena
- Tour around the Crete and visit the imposing monasteries of Sant'Antimo and the Abbazia di Monte Oliveto Maggiore
- Marvel at the 'medieval Manhattan' formed by the towers of the town of San Gimignano
- Sip on a glass of Brunello in its home, Montalcino
- Wander the streets of Montepulciano, one of the prettiest of the area's hill towns
- Seek out of the captivating walled hamlet of Monteriggioni

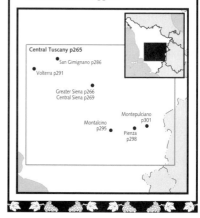

with majestic Gothic buildings, such as the Palazzo Pubblico on the main square, Piazza del Campo, while the churches, museums and public buildings are home to an extraordinary treasure-trove of art.

264

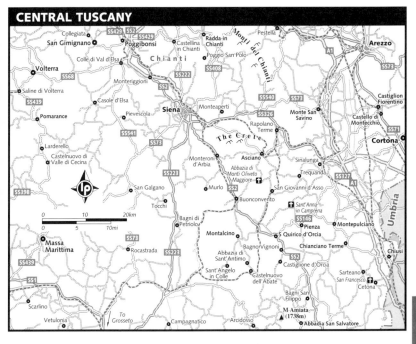

CENTRAL TUSCANY

Like Florence, Siena offers an incredible concentration of things to see, which simply can't be appreciated in a day trip. Try to plan at least one night's stay, or better still allow yourself a few days to take in properly the richness of the city's Gothic architecture and the art of the Sienese school.

Siena actually makes a good base from which to explore central Tuscany, in particular the medieval towns of San Gimignano and Volterra (see later in the chapter). Note, however, that it can be difficult to find budget accommodation in Siena unless you book ahead.

History

According to legend Siena was founded by Senius, son of Remus, and the symbol of the wolf feeding the twins Romulus and Remus is as ubiquitous in Siena as it is in Rome. In reality the city was probably of Etruscan origin, although it wasn't until the 1st century BC, when the Romans established a military colony called Saena Julia, that it began to grow into a proper town.

It remained a minor outpost until the arrival of the Lombards in the 6th century AD. Under them Siena became a key point along the main route from northern Italy to Rome, the Via Francigena. The medieval town was an amalgamation of three areas (Città, Camollia and San Martino) that would come to be known as the *terzi* (thirds). From Lombard hands the city passed under the control of local bishops and then to a first line of locally elected administrators, the *consoli* (consuls).

By the 13th century, Siena had become a wealthy trading city, the pillars of whose riches lay in the production of textiles, saffron, wine, spices and wax. International traders and bankers (the Piccolomini, Chigi, Malavolti and Buonsignori families to name a few) were increasingly active.

The parallel with Florence is hard to miss and it is hardly surprising that their rivalry grew. Both cities were also bent on occupying more and more Tuscan territory, so war between the two was inevitable. Ghibelline Siena defeated Guelph Florence at the Battle of Monteaperti in 1260, but it was a short-lived victory. Only nine years later the Tuscan Ghibellines were defeated by Charles of Anjou, and for almost a century Siena was obliged to toe the Florentine line in international affairs, becoming a member of the Tuscan Guelph League (supporters of the pope).

During this period Siena reached its peak under the republican rule of the Consiglio dei Nove (Council of Nine), an elected executive

dominated by the rising mercantile class. Many of the finest buildings in the Sienese Gothic style, which give the city its striking appearance, were constructed under the direction of the Consiglio, including the cathedral, the Palazzo Pubblico and the Piazza del Campo. The Sienese school of painting had its beginnings at this time with Guido da Siena and reached its peak in the early 14th century with the works of artists including Duccio di Buoninsegna, Simone Martini and Pietro and Ambrogio Lorenzetti.

A plague outbreak in 1348 killed two-thirds of the city's 100,000 inhabitants and led to a period of decline for Siena.

CENTRAL TUSCANY

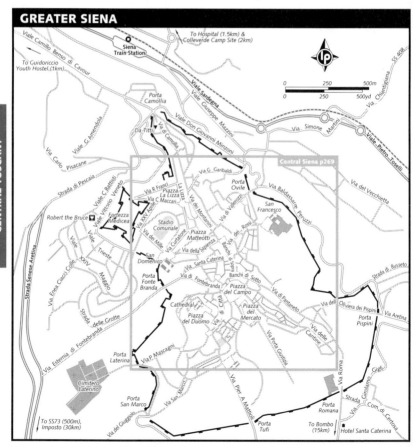

GREATER SIENA

At the end of the 14th century, Siena came under the control of Milan's Visconti family, followed the century after by the autocratic patrician Pandolfo Petrucci. Under the power of Petrucci, the city's fortunes improved, but the Holy Roman Emperor Charles V conquered Siena in 1555 after a two-year siege that left thousands dead. Consequently, the city was handed over to Cosimo I de' Medici, who for a while even barred the inhabitants from operating banks and thus curtailed Siena's power for good.

Siena was home to St Catherine (Santa Caterina), one of Italy's most venerated saints. But saints don't make money. Siena today relies for its prosperity on tourism and the success of its Monte dei Paschi di Siena bank, founded in 1472 and now one of the city's largest employers.

That Siena has remained largely intact as a Gothic city is the silver lining in what was for the people of this city a particularly dark cloud. Its decline in the wake of the Medici takeover was so complete that no-one gave thought to demolition and/or new construction. As the population again finally grew in the years after WWII (it had dropped to 16,000 in the latter half of the 18th century), the city became the first in Italy (in 1965) to ban motorised traffic in the old centre.

Orientation

Historic Siena, still largely surrounded by its medieval walls, is small and easily tackled on foot, although the way in which streets swirl in semicircles around the city's heart, Piazza del Campo (also known as 'Il Campo'), may confuse you.

That the city once thrived on banking is evident by the name of two of its main central streets, the Banchi di Sopra and Banchi di Sotto. Together they form part of the medieval Via Francigena pilgrims road from the north to Rome. Another artery is the Via di Città, which joins the others just behind Piazza del Campo.

By bus you will arrive at Piazza Gramsci, north of the cathedral and Piazza del Campo. Walk south along Via dei Montanini, which turns into Banchi di Sopra which in turn leads to Piazza del Campo.

Tickets Please

If you plan to visit a number of monuments, you should consider one of the following combination tickets, or *biglietto unico*. A €7.25 ticket (valid three days) allows entrance to the Museo dell' Opera, Libreria Piccolomini, Battistero di San Giovanni and Oratorio di San Bernardino. For €8.80 (valid two days) you gain access to the Museo Civico, Santa Maria della Scala and Palazzo delle Papesse. The Grand-Daddy €15.50 ticket (valid one week) covers the Museo Civico, Santa Maria della Scala, Palazzo delle Papesse, Museo dell' Opera, Libreria Piccolomini, Battistero di San Giovanni, Chiesa di Sant'Agostino and the Oratorio di San Bernardino. From November to mid-March it costs €3.10 less as the last two of these monuments are shut.

There's even a combination ticket for audio guides for the cathedral, Libreria Piccolomini and Museo dell' Opera (each normally €2.60). A €5.15 ticket covers all three, €3.60 the cathedral and Libreria Piccolomini, and €4.15 the cathedral and Museo dell' Opera.

From the train station you will need to catch a bus to Piazza Gramsci.

Drivers note that streets within the walls are blocked to normal traffic – even if you are staying at a hotel in the centre of town you will be required to leave your car in a car park after dropping off your bags.

You can enter Siena through any of eight city gates. Porta Romana, south of the centre, is a good option; it's a relatively flat 10-minute walk to Piazza del Campo and there's parking. See Getting There & Away later in the chapter for details.

Information

Tourist Offices The APT office (☎ 0577 28 05 51, fax 0577 27 06 76, W www .siena.turismo.toscana.it) is at Piazza del Campo 56 and opens 8.30am to 7.30pm Monday to Saturday and 9am to 3pm on Sunday, April to October. For the rest of the year it opens 8.30am to 1pm and 3.30pm to

CENTRAL TUSCANY

6.30pm Monday to Friday (to midday on Saturday).

Money Several banks ply their trade near Piazza del Campo in Piazza Tolomei, Banchi di Sopra, Banchi di Sotto and Via di Città. The main branch of the Monte dei Paschi di Siena bank is in Piazza Salimbeni. It offers an automatic exchange service at Via dei Montanini 2, and ATMs at Banchi di Sopra 74.

The Exact Change exchange bureau (☎ 0577 28 81 15) is at Via di Città 80–82. There's another branch (☎ 0577 22 61 33) at Via Banchi di Sopra 33.

Post & Communications The main post office is at Piazza Matteotti 1. Unstaffed Telecom phone offices are at Via dei Rossi 86, Via di Città 113 and Via di Pantaneto 44.

A branch of Internet Train (☎ 0577 24 74 60, W www.sienaweb.com), at Via di Pantaneto 54, opens Sunday to Friday. An hour online costs €6.20 (€5.15 for students), but they usually have deals running. Another option is E-Geko (☎ 0577 23 60 33), at Via Di Salicotto 130, where an hour online costs €4.15. It's open 10am to 1pm and 3.30pm to 8pm Monday to Saturday, and from 4pm to 8pm on Sunday.

Laundry At the self-service laundrette Onda Blu, Via del Casato di Sotto 17, you can wash and dry 6.5kg for €5.15.

Medical Services The public hospital (☎ 0577 58 51 11) is in Viale Bracci, just north of Siena at Le Scotte.

Police The *questura* (police station; ☎ 0577 20 11 11) is at Via del Castoro (open 24 hours a day), between the cathedral and Via di Città. The Foreigners Office *(Ufficio Stranieri)* is in Piazza Jacopo della Quercia, facing the cathedral. It opens 8.30am to 10.30am daily except Thursday and Sunday for everyone, and noon to 1pm for EU citizens only.

Piazza del Campo

This shell-shaped, slanting square has been the city's civic centre since it was laid out by the Council of Nine in the mid-14th

century. Siena's republican government intended that the public life of the city should run its course on this spot, which was once the Roman market place.

Today tourists and locals alike gather in the square to take a break from the day's errands or sightseeing – backpackers and students lounge on the pavement in the square's centre, while the more well-heeled drink expensive coffee or beer at the outdoor cafes around the periphery.

The square's paving is divided into nine sectors, representing the number of members of the ruling council. In 1346 water first bubbled forth from the **Fonte Gaia** (Happy Fountain) in the upper part of the square – it took its name from the evident pleasure of locals at this new source of water. The fountain's panels are reproductions of those done by Jacopo della Quercia in the early 15th century. The much-worn originals are on display in the Complesso Museale di Santa Maria della Scala (see later in this section).

Palazzo Pubblico At the lowest point of the square, the impressive Palazzo Pubblico *(☎ 0577 29 22 63; adult/student €6.20/ €3.60, combined ticket for Palazzo & tower €9.30; open 10am-11pm July & Aug, 10am-7pm mid-Mar–Jun & Sept-Oct, 10am-4pm Nov–mid-Mar)* is also known as the Palazzo Comunale (town hall). Its 102m bell tower, the **Torre del Mangia**, was built in 1344. You can hire an audio guide to lead you around the palazzo for €3.60.

Dating from 1297, the palazzo itself is one of the most graceful Gothic buildings in Italy. Its construction as the nerve centre of republican government was planned as an integral part of the project for the piazza before it – the whole creates the effect of an amphitheatre with the Palazzo Pubblico as central stage.

The Council of Nine wanted to unite the offices of government and the courts in one central building, thus further removing the instruments of power, symbolically and actually, from the hands of the feudal nobles who had once called the shots here.

Inside is the **Museo Civico**, a series of rooms on an upper floor of the palazzo with

CENTRAL SIENA

PLACES TO STAY
1 Piccolo Hotel il Palio
16 Albergo Cannon d'Oro
20 Chiusarelli
23 Albergo Bernini
27 Albergo La Perla
31 Albergo La Toscana
32 Hotel Le Tre Donzelle
33 Piccolo Hotel Etruria
53 Locanda Garibaldi
69 Miniresidence il Casato

PLACES TO EAT
10 Supermarket
12 Trattoria Tullio
(Tre Cristi)
24 La Chiacchiera
30 Nannini
41 Grotta del Gallo Nero
44 Spizzico-Ciao
47 Ristorante da Mugolone
55 Hostaria il Carroccio
61 Taverna del Capitano

62 Al Marsili
66 Supermarket
67 Osteria del Castelvecchio

CHURCHES & MUSEUMS
7 Chiesa di San Francesco
9 Oratorio di San Bernardino
13 Palazzo Salimbeni
22 Chiesa di San Domenico
25 Casa di Santa Caterina
35 Palazzo Piccolomini
42 Chiesa di San Martino
48 Battistero di San
Giovanni (Baptistry)
49 Cathedral
50 Museo dell'Opera
Metropolitana
52 Palazzo Pubblico;
Torre del Mangia
58 Duomo Nuovo
60 Complesso Museale di
Santa Maria della Scala;
Museo Archeologico

63 Palazzo delle Papesse
64 Palazzo Chigi-Saracini;
Accademia Musicale
Chigiana
68 Pinacoteca Nazionale;
Palazzo Buonsignori
70 Chiesa di Sant'Agostino
72 Basilica di Santa Maria dei
Servi

OTHER
2 Società Dante Alighieri
3 Enoteca Italiana
4 Local Bus Terminus
5 The Dublin Post
6 Associazione Siena Jazz
8 Economics Faculty Library
11 Telecom Office
14 ATMs
15 Monte dei Paschi
di Siena Bank
17 Post Office
18 Vigili Urbani (Police Station)

19 Scuola Leonarda da Vinci
21 Siena Hotels Promotion;
Ecco Siena
26 Feltrinelli Bookshop
28 Exact Change
29 Caffè del Corso
34 APT Office
36 Logge del Papa
37 Università per Stranieri
38 Telecom Office
39 Al Cambio
40 Internet Train
43 Synagogue
45 Fonte Gaia
46 Loggia dei Mercanti
51 Exact Change
54 Onda Blu Laundrette
56 Siena Ricama
57 Questura
(Police Station)
59 Foreigners Office
65 Telecom Office
71 E-Geko

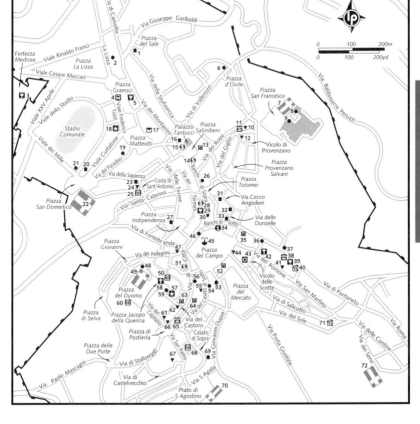

CENTRAL TUSCANY

frescoes by artists of the Sienese school. As you will soon come to notice, the Sienese penchant for frescoes is unique. Here, as in other great buildings of Siena, and indeed elsewhere in the province (the Palazzo del Popolo and Collegiata in San Gimignano are sufficient confirmation), the decoration, often with a foundation of deep-blue hues on the ceiling, tends to be rich and full, leaving scarcely a millimetre uncovered.

After buying your ticket, head up two flights of stairs to have your ticket stamped. Here you are in the first of five rather nondescript rooms filled with equally unarresting paintings, mostly by Sienese artists of the 16th to the 18th centuries. Do the anticlockwise circuit or turn immediately left into the **Sala del Risorgimento**, which is bedecked by a series of late-19th-century frescoes serialising key events in the campaign to unite Italy.

A door from this room crosses the central corridor into the **Sala di Balìa** (or Sala dei Priori). The 15 scenes depicted in frescoes around the walls recount episodes in the life of Pope Alexander III (the Sienese Rolando Bandinelli), including his clashes with the Holy Roman Emperor Frederick Barbarossa. Much renovation was underway at the time of writing.

You then pass into the **Anticamera del Concistoro**, remarkable above all for the fresco (moved here in the 19th century) of *Santi Caterina d'Alessandria, Giovanni e Agostino*, executed by Ambrogio Lorenzetti.

The following hall, the **Sala del Concistoro**, is dominated by the allegorical ceiling frescoes by the Mannerist Domenico Beccafumi.

Back in the Anticamera del Concistoro, you pass to your right into the **Vestibolo** (Vestibule), whose star attraction is a bronze wolf, symbol of the city. Above the doorway is a Lorenzetti fresco of the *Madonna col Bambino* (Madonna with Child). Next door in the **Anticappella** are frescoes of scenes from Greco-Roman mythology and history, while the **Cappella** (Chapel), with its heavy wrought-iron screen, contains a fine *Sacra Famiglia e San Leonardo* (Holy Family and St

Leonardo) by Sodoma and intricately carved wooden choir stalls.

The best is saved till last. From the Cappella you emerge in the **Sala del Mappamondo**, so-called because it was once adorned with a circular map fresco, in which you can admire the masterpiece of the building, the *Maestà* (Majesty) by Simone Martini. The striking fresco is his earliest-known work and depicts the Virgin Mary enthroned with the Christ child, surrounded by angels, saints and other figures. It is one of the most important works of the Sienese school.

On the opposite wall, the equestrian fresco of *Guidoriccio da Fogliano* has also long been attributed to Martini, although there is some doubt about it now. Other large frescoes along the inside long wall depict famous Sienese victories.

The next room, the **Sala dei Nove** (or Sala della Pace) is dominated by Ambrogio Lorenzetti's fresco series depicting the *Effetti del Buon e del Cattivo Governo* (Allegories of Good and Bad Government), which are among the most significant to survive from the Middle Ages. On the party wall with the Sala del Mappamondo are scenes of a charming serenity that happen to lend a little insight into everyday life in medieval Siena and its countryside. This sunlit idyll is the result of good and wise government, symbolised by the figures on the narrow inner wall. Turning to the next long wall you see the symbolic figures of all the nasty vices that can come to rule the hearts of princes and lead to the misery depicted next to them. Unfortunately, this fresco has been much damaged.

You can wind up the visit by leaping up the stairs to the **loggia** which looks out north over Piazza del Mercato and the countryside.

Torre del Mangia Climb this graceful bell tower *(admission €5.15, joint ticket for tower & Palazzo €9.30; open same hours as Palazzo)* for splendid views across the city. Note that the ticket office closes 45 minutes before the tower shuts and only 30 people are allowed up at any time. You may find yourself queuing at a wooden door waiting for people to come down. On rainy days you're not allowed to climb the 400 steps (there is no lift) at all.

Cathedral

Despite the retention of some Romanesque elements, Siena's cathedral *(Piazza del Duomo; free; open 7.30am-7.30pm mid-Mar–Oct, 7.30am-1pm & 2.30pm-5pm Nov–mid-Mar)* is one of Italy's great Gothic churches. Begun in 1196, it was largely completed by 1215, although work continued on features such as the apse and dome well into the 13th century.

Exterior After the cathedral's completion, work then began on changing, enlarging and embellishing the structure. The magnificent facade of white, green and red polychrome marble was begun by Giovanni Pisano, who completed only the lower section, and was finished towards the end of the 14th century. The mosaics in the gables were added in the 19th century. The statues of philosophers and prophets by Giovanni Pisano, above the lower section, are copies, the originals being preserved in the adjacent Museo dell'Opera Metropolitana. The bell tower is Romanesque, although the exact date of its completion is uncertain.

In 1339, the city's leaders launched a plan to enlarge the cathedral and create one of Italy's largest churches. Known as the Duomo Nuovo (New Cathedral), the remains of this unrealised project can be seen in Piazza Jacopo della Quercia, on the eastern side of the main cathedral. According to the ambitious plan, an immense new nave would be built and the present church would have become the transept. The plague of 1348, which devastated the city, put a stop to this formidable scheme. The main facade is interesting as it clearly combines elements of Gothic and Renaissance (look at the top central arch). You can climb to the top for great views from the Museo dell'Opera Metropolitana (see later in this section).

Interior The cathedral's interior is rich with artworks and warrants an hour or more of your time. Walls and pillars continue the black-and-white-stripe theme of the exterior,

while the vaults are painted blue with gold stars (a common device in Sienese territory). High along the walls of the nave is a long series of papal busts.

After looking up, look down... and you'll see the cathedral's most precious feature – the inlaid-marble floor, which is decorated with 56 panels depicting historical and biblical subjects. The earliest panels are graffiti designs in simple black-and-white marble, dating from the mid-14th century. The latest panels were completed in the 16th century. Many of them are kept covered throughout the year, but a select few are uncovered and fenced off, allowing you a glimpse of these glorious panels. Between late August and September all the panels are revealed – in 2001 the period ran from 23 August to 3 October. Check with the APT or at the cathedral itself for the latest dates. You can inspect the 19th-century drawings in the Museo dell'Opera del Duomo (see the following section), if you need another fix.

After the floor, the most exquisite item in the church is, however, the beautiful octagonal pulpit carved in marble and porphyry by Nicola Pisano in the 13th century. Often compared with Pisano's hexagonal pulpit in the Baptistry in Pisa, this is, if anything, better still and is one of the outstanding masterpieces of Gothic sculpture. The more you behold the seven panels, laden with crowd scenes of remarkable reality, the more they seem to come to life. Unfortunately you can't inch as close as you might like as barriers keep you at a respectful distance. To shed a little light on the subject, stick coins into the machine (€0.25 gets you a generous one minute of illumination).

Other significant artworks include a bronze statue of St John the Baptist by Donatello, in the north transept.

Libreria Piccolomini Through a door off the north aisle, the Libreria Piccolomini *(admission €1.55; open 9am-7.30pm mid-Mar–Oct, 10am-1pm & 2.30pm-5pm Nov–mid-Mar)* is another of the cathedral's great treasures. Pope Pius III (pope in 1503) built this compact hall to house the books of his uncle, Enea Silvio Piccolomini, who was

Pope Pius II. Of the books, only a series of huge choral tomes belonging to the cathedral remains on display.

You are not here for the books, however, but for the walls. They are covered by an impressive series of richly coloured frescoes by Bernardino Pinturicchio. They depict events in the life of Piccolomini, starting from his early career days as a secretary to an Italian bishop on a mission to Basle, through to his ordination as pope and eventually his death in Ancona while trying to get a crusade against the Turks off the ground.

In the centre of the hall is a group of statues known as the *Tre Grazie* (Three Graces), a 3rd-century-AD Roman copy of an earlier Hellenistic work.

Museo dell'Opera Metropolitana

The Museo dell'Opera del Duomo *(☎ 0577 4 23 09, Piazza del Duomo 8; admission €5.15; open 9am-7.30pm mid-Mar–Sept, 9am-6pm Oct, 9am-1.30pm Nov–mid-Mar)* is next to the cathedral, in what would have been the south aisle of the nave of the new cathedral. Its great artworks formerly adorned the cathedral, including the 12 statues of prophets and philosophers by Giovanni Pisano that decorated the facade. These stand on the ground floor. Their creator designed them to be viewed from ground level, which is why they look so distorted (they all crane uncomfortably forward).

However, the museum's main draw card, on the first floor, is Duccio di Buoninsegna's striking early-14th-century *Maestà*, painted on both sides as a screen for the cathedral's high altar. The front and back have now been separated and the panels depicting the *Passione* (Story of Christ's Passion) hang opposite the *Maestà*. It is interesting to compare Buoninsegna's work with Martini's slightly later *Maestà* in the Palazzo Pubblico. The closer you look at the Passion scenes, the more you are absorbed into the story. It is important to remember that this kind of art was above all didactic. The 'pretty pictures' tell the story of the Scriptures, which the largely illiterate masses could not read. Duccio's narrative genius is impressive. Take the

lower half of the bottom big middle panel. In one 'shot' three scenes take place: Christ preaches to the Apostles in the Garden of Gethsemane; he then asks them to wait up for him; and then is portrayed while in prayer. In the half panel above, he is kissed by Judas while Peter lops off a soldier's ear and the remaining Apostles flee.

To the right of the *Maestà* a door leads into a back room with statues by Jacopo della Quercia, while the door to the left leads to a room with 19th-century illustrations of the entire collection of marble floor panels in the cathedral.

On the upper floors other artists represented in the museum are Ambrogio Lorenzetti, Simone Martini and Taddeo di Bartolo. The collection also includes tapestries and manuscripts.

Follow the signs to the **Panorama del Facciatone** (which involves a claustrophobic climb up winding stairs) to come out on top of the facade of what would have been the huge extension of the cathedral. The views over all Siena are marvellous.

Battistero di San Giovanni

Behind the cathedral and down a flight of stairs is the Battistero di San Giovanni *(Baptistry of St John; Piazza San Giovanni; admission €2.05; open 9am-7.30pm mid-Mar–Sept, 9am-6pm Oct, 10am-1pm & 2.30pm-5pm Nov–mid-Mar)*. Its Gothic facade is unfinished at the upper levels but is nonetheless a quite remarkable extravagance in marble.

Inside, the ceiling and vaults are bedecked with predictable lavishness in frescoes depicting the Apostles, sibyls, and a series devoted to the articles of the creed. The life of Jesus is portrayed in frescoes in the apse of this oddly shaped rectangular baptistry. The lower illustrations are by Il Vecchietta – the one on the right showing Christ carrying the Cross is of particular interest. If you look at the city from which it appears he and the crowd have come, it is hard to escape the feeling that among the imaginary buildings have been illustrated Brunelleschi's dome and Giotto's Campanile in Florence. Is this a nasty little

Sienese terracotta pots

Piazza del Campo and the 102m-tall Torre del Mangia

Siena cat in search of a saucer

Glorious Gothic with Renaissance touches – cathedral facade, Siena

Local district flags in Siena

Late-afternoon sun on the medieval highrise of San Gimignano: 14 towers protect the hill-top town.

San Gimignano's Piazza della Cisterna is flanked by 13th- and 14th-century houses and towers.

Viareggio's vibrant three-week *carnevale* – an annual riot of colour and music since 1873

A light supper in Siena cathedral

Second only to Venice – *carnevale* in Viareggio

Not much beats touring Tuscany on a motorcycle: *motorini* await their next outing.

Spreading the word in San Gimignano

Instantly recognisable – a rural post box

San Gimignano elders set the world to rights.

Summer poppies splash colour across Chianti.

anti-Florentine dig suggesting Siena's rival as the source of Christ's tribulations?

The real attraction is, however, a marble font by Jacopo della Quercia, decorated with bronze panels in relief depicting the life of St John the Baptist. The panels were carried out by several top-notch artists and include Lorenzo Ghiberti's *Battesimo di Gesù* (Baptism of Christ) and *Cattura del Battista* (St John in Prison), and Donatello's *Banchetto di Erode* (Herod's Feast).

Complesso Museale di Santa Maria della Scala

Until a few years ago a working hospital with almost a millennium of history, this immense space is being transformed into a major **arts centre** (☎ *0577 22 48 11, Piazza del Duomo 2; adult/child €5.15/3.10, €4.65/2.60 with booking; open 10am-7pm mid-Mar–Oct, 10.30am-4.30pm Nov–mid-Mar)*. Located on the south-west side of Piazza del Duomo, the main attraction remains the extraordinary series of frescoes by Domenico di Bartolo in what was the main ward.

First references to the hospital date to the 11th century. It appears it was initially more of a hospice for pilgrims on the Via Francigena. The medical aspects of the work done here by sisters, and later doctors, only became paramount some time further on.

Before entering the hospital proper, enter the **Chiesa della Santissima Annunziata** (free) to the left of the ticket booth. This is a church built into the complex in the 13th century and remodelled two centuries later.

From the ticket office turn right into the **Cappella del Manto**, decorated with frescoes, of which the most striking is that by Beccafumi (done in 1514) portraying the *Incontro di San Gioacchino con Santa Anna* (Meeting of St Joaquim and St Anna), the supposed parents of the Virgin Mary.

Next you pass into a long hall and turn left into the room of principal interest in the complex, the remarkable 14th-century **Sala del Pellegrinaio**. As its name suggests, it was initially more like a dorm for tired pilgrims. With time it became the hospital's main ward.

One can only wonder whether patients were uplifted by the frescoes celebrating the charitable nature of bringing succour to the ill and needy. The bulk of the series was carried out by Domenico di Bartolo in the 1440s. The first panel, by Il Vecchietta, depicts *gettatelli* (orphans) ascending to heaven. Taking in orphans was frequently one of the routine tasks of hospitals throughout Tuscany. Later panels show *balie* (wet-nurses) suckling orphans and other needy children – for which they were either paid in kind or hard cash. Panels on the opposite wall depict the tending of the sick, distribution of alms and other charitable deeds.

As you pass out of the ward you are directed to the **Sagrestia Vecchia** (Old Sacristy), which is decorated with complex frescoes explaining the articles of the creed. Next door is the little Baroque **Cappella della Madonna**.

Backtrack to the Cappella del Manto, where you'll find an entrance leading downstairs to the **Fienile**, once storage space for the hospital. The original panelling of the Fonte Gaia (and a few replicas) is now housed here. Through the Fienile is the **Oratorio di Santa Caterina della Notte** (Oratory of St Catherine of the Night), a gloomy little chapel for sending up a prayer or two for the unwell upstairs.

Museo Archeologico After you've had enough of gloomy chapels, follow the signs to this museum housed in the Il Labirinti di Santa Maria (labyrinth of Santa Maria). Much of the collection consists of pieces found in the region surrounding Siena, mostly in the 19th century. Objects on show range from elaborate Etruscan alabaster funerary urns to gold Roman coins. In between you'll see some statuary (much of it Etruscan and dating from several centuries BC), a variety of household items, votive statuettes in bronze and even a pair of playing dice. The collection is well presented, and the surroundings – twisting, arched tunnels – perfectly compliment it, and are a cool blessing on stifling-hot summer days.

Admission is included in the price for Santa Maria; it also has the same opening hours as Santa Maria except that it opens 10am to 1pm only on the 2nd and 4th Sunday of the month and is closed on the 1st, 3rd & 5th Sunday of the month.

Palazzo delle Papesse

Head to this contemporary **art gallery** (☎ 0577 2 20 71, Via di Città 126; adult/child €4.65/3.10; open noon-7pm) if you've had your fill of medieval religious art. The gallery houses a number of permanent pieces from the likes of Micha Ullman and Botto & Bruno, mixed in with ever-changing exhibitions. The top floor is given over to a rooftop terrace with views over Siena.

Palazzo Chigo-Saracini

The magnificent curving Gothic facade of this palazzo on Via di Città is in part a travesty, the result of 'restoration' in the 18th and 19th centuries to re-create the medieval feel. From the tower, which is the genuine article, they say a young boy with particularly good eyesight watched the Battle of Monteaperti in 1260 and shouted down details of the home side's progress against the Florentines to eager crowds in the streets below (as you may remember, the home side won this time round).

The palazzo is now home to the Accademia Musicale Chigiana and is not generally open to the public. You can, however, arrange to visit by calling the Monte dei Paschi di Siena bank on ☎ 0577 29 47 87. Inside you can see sumptuously furnished rooms and an interesting collection of principally Sienese art.

Pinacoteca Nazionale

This **gallery** (☎ 0577 28 11 61, Via San Pietro 29; adult/child €4/2; open 8.15am-7.15pm Tues-Sat, 8.15am-1.15pm Sun, 8.30am-1.30pm Mon), located in the 15th-century Palazzo Buonsignori, constitutes the greatest concentration of Sienese art in the city. This means, in particular, an excursion into the Gothic masterpieces of the Sienese school. As you progress through the collection, you can only marvel at the gulf that lay between artistic life in Siena and Florence in the 15th century. While the Renaissance flourished 70km to the north, Siena's masters and their patrons remained firmly rooted in the Byzan-

tine and Gothic precepts that had stood them in such good stead from the early 13th century. Stock religious images and episodes predominate, typically lavishly filled with gold and generally lacking any of the advances in painting (such as perspective, emotion or movement) that artists in Florence were indulging in.

Follow the gallery's advice and start your tour on the 2nd floor, which is where the Sienese masters from the early 13th to the 15th century are on show.

In the first two rooms you can see some of the earliest surviving pre-Gothic works of the Sienese school, including pieces by Guida da Siena. Rooms 3 and 4 are given over to a few works by Duccio di Buoninsegna (to see him at his best you need to go to the Museo dell'Opera del Duomo) and his followers. The most striking exhibit in Room 6 is Simone Martini's *Madonna della Misericordia*, in which the Virgin Mary seems to take the whole of society protectively under her wings.

The brothers Pietro and Ambrogio Lorenzetti dominate Rooms 7 and 8, while the following three rooms contain works by several early-15th-century artists, including Taddeo di Bartolo, who is responsible for a massive *Crocifisso*.

Giovanni di Paolo dominates most of Rooms 12 and 13, and a couple of his paintings show refreshing signs of a break from strict tradition. His two versions of the *Presentazione nel Tempio* (the Presentation of Jesus in the Temple) introduce new architectural themes, a hint of perspective, virtually no gold and a discernible trace of human emotion in the characters depicted. A few of the radical ideas unleashed in Florence were clearly filtering through. From here to the end of the floor, however, the themes and styles remain remarkably faithful to the old formulae.

The small **Collezione Spannochi** (closed at the time of writing) on the 3rd floor is a rather motley group of paintings with a few highlights, including a Dürer, and a striking nativity scene by Lorenzo Lotto in which all the light emanates from the Christ child.

Walking Tours from Piazza del Campo

Walk One

This walk takes you from the centre of Siena to the city's south-eastern gate, Porta Romana.

Start at the **Loggia dei Mercanti**, finished in the early 15th century and designed to give merchants a central place to do their deals. It is inserted among the row of palazzi that form the backdrop to Piazza del Campo.

From here take Banchi di Sotto to the east for the **Palazzo Piccolomini** (☎ 0577 24 71 45, Via Banchi di Sotto 52; free; open 9am-1pm Mon-Sat), Siena's finest Renaissance palace built by Pope Pius II, the leading figure of the Piccolomini family. It houses the city's archives and a small museum that was closed at the time of writing.

A block east are the **Logge del Papa**, another of Pius II's Renaissance contributions to the city. On the same intersection you see the Mannerist facade of the **Chiesa di San Martino**, a makeover that disguises the fact that this is one of the oldest churches in Siena. The original building went up here in the 8th century. Siena's only **synagogue** (Vicolo delle Scotte 14; admission €2.60; open 10am-1pm & 2pm-4pm Sun only) is just near here.

Proceed east along Via del Porrione (which becomes Via San Martino) and you will run into the 13th-century **Basilica di Santa Maria dei Servi**. Inside you can see Pietro Lorenzetti's depiction of the Strage degli Innocenti (Massacre of the Innocents) and a painting of the Madonna del Bordone by Coppo di Marcovaldo, done after the Florentine artist was captured during the Battle of Monteaperti in 1260.

A short stroll south of the church is the massive 14th-century **Porta Romana**, one of the city's main gates. As the name suggests, the road to Rome once went directly from this gate.

Walk Two

This short walk winds its way from Piazza del Campo north-east to the busy square of Piazza San Francesco.

Once again starting from Loggia dei Mercanti, head north along Banchi di Sopra and past Piazza Tolomei, dominated by the 13th-century **Palazzo Tolomei**. Farther along there's the Piazza Salimbeni, featuring the **Palazzo Tantucci** to the north, the Gothic **Palazzo Salimbeni** to the east, the head office of the Monte dei Paschi di Siena bank and the Renaissance **Palazzo Spannocchi**.

Backtrack a few metres and turn left into Via dei Rossi, which heads north-east to Piazza San Francesco. Directly in front of you is the **Chiesa di San Francesco**, which is every bit as big and bare as its Dominican rival. The two orders had a habit of competing in the construction of gargantuan Gothic churches (see Santa Croce and Santa Maria Novella in Florence) but in Siena they seemed to outdo themselves in the creation of unadorned empty space. The cloister next door is now part of the Universitàdi Siena.

Also facing Piazza San Francesco is the **Oratorio di San Bernardino** (☎ 0577 28 30 48, Piazza San Francesco 9; admission €2; open 10.30am-1.30pm & 3pm-5.30pm daily mid-March–end October), notable for its frescoes, particularly those by Sodoma, and a small museum of religious art.

Down on the 1st floor, the Sienese roll call continues, and although there are some exceptions, the interest starts to fade. The best rooms include Nos 27 to 32 and 37, which are dominated by works of the Mannerist Domenico Beccafumi and Il Sodoma. Of all these, Sodoma's *Cristo alla Colonna* (Christ Tied to the Pillar) in Room 31 is the most disturbing. Christ's tears are a heart-rending human touch. Beccafumi's *Discesa di Cristo al Limbo* (Christ's Descent into Limbo) in Room 37 is also worth close inspection.

Chiesa di San Agostino

A few streets south of Pinacoteca Nazionale is this **church** (☎ 0577 38 57 86; Prato di San Agostino; admission €1.55; open 10.30am-1.30pm & 3pm-5.30pm mid-Mar–Oct). It was built in the second half of the 13th century; however its interior dates from the 18th century after it was gutted by fire.

Chiesa di San Domenico

This imposing Gothic **church** (Piazza San Domenico; free; open 7.30am-1pm & 3pm-6.30pm) was started in the early 13th century, but has been much altered over the centuries.

The bare, barn-like interior surprises by its sheer emptiness, although this was in keeping with the Dominican order's spartan outlook. At the bottom end of the church (near the door where you enter) is the raised **Cappella delle Volte**, where St Catherine took her vows as a Dominican and supposedly performed some of her miracles. In the chapel is a portrait of the saint painted during her lifetime.

In the **Cappella di Santa Caterina**, on the south side of the church, are frescoes by Sodoma depicting events in the saint's life. St Catherine died in Rome and most of her body is preserved there in the Chiesa di Santa Maria Sopra Minerva. In line with the bizarre practice of collecting relics of dead saints, her head was given back to Siena. It is contained in a tabernacle on the altar of the Cappella di Santa Caterina.

Another bit of her that managed to find its way here is a thumb, on display in a small window box to the right of the chapel. Also on show is a rather nasty-looking chain whip with which she used to apply a good flogging to herself every now and then for the well-being of the souls of the faithful.

Fortezza Medicea

A short walk west of the Chiesa di San Domenico, this fortress is typical of those built in major cities in the early years of the grand duchy. Also known as the Forte di Santa Barbara, the Sienese could have been given little more obvious a reminder of who was in charge than this huge Medici bastion, raised on the orders of Cosimo I de' Medici in 1560.

Casa di Santa Caterina

This is the **house** (☎ 0577 4 41 77, Costa di Sant'Antonio 6; free; open 9am-12.30pm & 2.30pm-6pm) where St Catherine was born. The rooms inside the house were converted into small chapels in the 15th century and are decorated with frescoes and paintings by Sienese artists, including Sodoma. The frescoes within L'Oratorio della Cucina (on your left once you enter the house grounds) tell the story of the saint's life.

Courses

Language Siena's **Università per Stranieri** (University for Foreigners; ☎ 0577 24 01 15, fax 0577 28 10 30, W www.unistrasi.it, Via di Pantaneto 45; 10-week course €620) is open year-round and the only requirement for enrolment is a high-school graduation or pass certificate. (The four-week summer courses have no prerequisites.) Brochures can be obtained by making a request to the secretary of the university, or from the Istituto Italiano di Cultura in your own country (for more information see Useful Organisations in the Facts for the Visitor chapter).

The **Scuola Leonardo da Vinci** (☎ 0577 24 90 97, fax 0577 24 90 96, W www.scuolaleonardo.com, Via del Paradiso 16; 24-week courses €232.40-465) has courses varying from one-to-one tutorials to 12 per class. They also run culture, wine and cookery courses.

Another option is the **Società Dante Alighieri** (☎ 0577 4 95 33, fax 0577 27 06 46, W www.dantealighieri.com, Piazza La Lizza 10; 2- to 4-week courses €335.70-542.30). Like da Vinci, this place also runs culture and cookery courses.

See Study Visas under Visas & Documents in the Facts for the Visitor chapter for details of necessary visas.

Music The **Accademia Musicale Chigiana** (☎ 0577 4 61 52, fax 0577 28 81 24, Via di Città 89, W www.chigiana.it, courses €93-439) offers classical-music classes every summer, as well as seminars and concerts performed by visiting musicians, teachers and students as part of the ettimana Musicale

Il Palio

This spectacular event, held twice yearly on 2 July and 16 August in honour of the Virgin Mary, dates back to the Middle Ages and features a series of colourful pageants, a wild horse race around Piazza del Campo and much eating, drinking and celebrating in the streets.

Il Palio is probably one of the only major medieval spectacles of its type in Italy that has survived through the sheer tenacity of Sienese traditionalism. Most of the other charming displays of medieval nostalgia, although doubtless pleasing, have in fact been brought back to life in the 20th century out of a combination of nostalgia and the desire to earn a few more tourist bucks.

Ten of Siena's 17 town districts, or *contrade*, compete for the coveted *palio*, a silk banner. Each of the contrade has its own traditions, symbol and colours, and its own church and palio museum. The centuries-old local rivalries make the festival very much an event for the Sienese, although the horse race and pageantry predictably attract larger crowds of tourists.

Local allegiance to the contrade is much in evidence year-round. As you wander the streets you will be hard-pressed to miss the various flags and plaques delineating these quarters, each with a name and symbol related to an animal.

The contrade were first noted unofficially in the 14th century but it was only in 1729 that they were given judicial recognition as tiny units of local administration.

On festival days Piazza del Campo becomes a racetrack, with a ring of packed dirt around its perimeter serving as the course. From about 5pm representatives of each *contrada* parade in historical costume, each bearing their individual banners.

The race is run at 7.45pm in July and 7pm in August. For not much more than one exhilarating minute, the 10 horses and their bareback riders tear three times around Piazza del Campo with a speed and violence that makes your hair stand on end.

Even if a horse loses its rider it is still eligible to win, and since many riders fall each year, it is the horses in the end who are the focus of the event. There is only one rule: riders are not to interfere with the reins of other horses. The Sienese place incredible demands on the national TV network, RAI, for rights to televise the event.

Book well in advance if you want to stay in Siena at this time, and join the crowds in the centre of Piazza del Campo at least four hours before the start, or even earlier if you want a place on the barrier lining the track. Streets leading to the Piazza are closed off well before the race begins, except for Via Giovanni Dupré, which stays open right up until the flag drops. So if you arrive late you can try your luck reaching the Piazza via this street, but don't count on it as everyone else has the same idea. If you'd prefer a more comfortable seat overlooking the race from one of the buildings lining the Piazza, ask around in the cafes and shops. They're as rare as hen's teeth, but if you do manage to find one expect to pay around €205 for the privilege. If you can't find a good vantage point, don't despair – the race is televised live and then repeated throughout the evening on TV.

If you happen to be in town in the few days immediately preceding the race, you may get to see the jockeys and horses trying out in Piazza del Campo – almost as good as the real thing.

JANE SMITH

Senese. The school offers classes in most classical instruments.

The **Associazione Siena Jazz** (☎ *0577 27 14 01, fax 0577 28 14 04, Via di Vallerozzi 77; courses from €196)*, which offers courses in jazz, is one of Europe's foremost institutions of its type.

Organised Tours

The Treno Natura is a great way to see the stunning scenery of the Crete, south of Siena. The train line extends in a ring from Siena, through Asciano, across to the Val d'Orcia and the Monte Antico station, before heading back towards Siena. The line, which opened in the early 1800s, was closed in 1994 and trains now run exclusively for tourists.

Trains run on some Sundays during May, June, September and October (and rarely in November and December). There are usually three per day (8.12am, 11.14am and 3.40pm), stopping at Asciano and Monte Antico, and they are generally met by connecting trains from Florence. Tickets cost €12.90. Check at the Siena APT or at Siena's train station for precise details, or call ☎ 0577 20 74 13.

Ecco Siena (☎ 0577 4 34 97, W www .guidedisiena.it, located at Siena Hotels Promotion; see Places to Stay) currently operates tours of the city for groups only, but plans to cater for individuals by summer 2002. It's expected to cost around €15.50 per person.

Special Events

The Accademia Musicale Chigiana holds the Settimana Musicale Senese each July, as well as the Estate Musicale Chigiana (☎ 0577 2 20 91) in July and August. Tickets cost €4.15 to €31. Concerts in these series are often held at the Abbazia di San Galgano (a former abbey about 20km south-west of the city and regarded as one of Italy's finest Gothic buildings) and at Sant'Antimo, near Montalcino (see Abbazia di San Galgano and Abbazia di Sant'Antimo later in the chapter). Concerts are also held throughout the year.

The city hosts Siena Jazz (☎ 0577 27 14 01, W www.sienajazz.it), an international festival each July and August, with concerts at the Fortezza Medicea as well as various sites throughout the city.

In November, concerts and exhibitions take place to honour the patron saint of musicians in the Festa di Santa Cecilia.

Places to Stay

Siena offers a good range of accommodation but budget hotels generally fill quickly, so it is advisable to book in advance year-round if you want to pay less than about €70 per double. Forget about finding a room during the Palio unless you have a booking. For assistance in finding a room, contact the APT or Siena Hotels Promotion (☎ 0577 28 80 84, fax 0577 28 02 90, W www.hotelsiena.com, Piazza San Domenico). The latter opens 9am to 8pm Monday to Saturday in summer and 9am to 7pm in winter.

If you are having trouble in finding a hotel, don't despair. The tourist office has a list of about 120 *affittacamere* (rooms to rent) in town, which are private households letting out rooms. *Agriturismo* (accommodation on farms) is well organised around Siena, and the tourist office has a list of various rural establishments that rent rooms by the week or month.

Colleverde (☎ *0577 28 00 44, fax 0577 33 32 98, Strada di Scacciapensieri 47)* Site per adult/child €7.75/5.15. Opens late Mar–early Nov. Bus No 3 from Piazza Gramsci. This camping ground, north of the historical centre, is situated in a quiet, tree-filled valley.

Guidoriccio (☎ *0577 5 22 12, W www .alfaweb.it/franchostel, Via Fiorentina 89, Località Stellino)* B&B €13. Bus No 15 from Piazza Gramsci. This non-HI youth hostel is about 2km north-west of the city centre. It's a little awkwardly placed and not the best of the Italian hostel crop – you are better off with a pensione room in town. If you want to stay here anyway, and you're driving, leave the city by Via Vittorio Emanuele II, which is an extension of Via di Camollia. It also offers meals for €8.80.

Hotel Le Tre Donzelle (☎ *0577 28 03 58, fax 0577 22 39 33, Via delle Donzelle 5)* Singles/doubles €31/44, double with bathroom €56.80. In town, try this place off Banchi di Sotto north of Piazza del Campo. It has clean, simple rooms.

Piccolo Hotel Etruria (☎ *0577 28 80 88, fax 0577 28 84 61,* **e** *hetruriqa@tin.it, Via delle Donzelle 3)* Singles/doubles with bathroom €41.30/67.15. For a friendly welcome and pleasant rooms head here.

Locanda Garibaldi (☎ *0577 28 42 04, fax 0577 28 42 04, Via Giovanni Duprè 18)* Doubles €62. Locanda Garibaldi is brilliantly located just south of Piazza del Campo. The rooms are big, bright and modern, and the whole place has an individual, funky feel.

Albergo Bernini (☎/*fax 0577 28 90 47,* **W** *www.albergobernini.com, Via della Sapienza 15)* Doubles €62, singles/doubles with bathroom €52/77.50. The nine rooms here are nothing special but the terrace, with views of the cathedral, make the stay well worth it.

Albergo La Perla (☎ *0577 4 71 44, Via delle Terme 25)* Singles/doubles with bathroom €50/65. This place is a short walk north-west of Piazza del Campo, with small but clean rooms.

Albergo La Toscana (☎ *0577 4 60 97, fax 0577 27 06 34, Via Cecco Angioleri 12)* Singles/doubles €52/72.30. This place has a variety of rooms. The singles are large but nothing to write home about, and the doubles are fine.

Piccolo Hotel il Palio (☎ *0577 28 11 31, fax 0577 28 11 42, Piazza del Sale 19)* Singles/doubles with bathroom €67.15/83. Il Palio is a good 15-minute walk north of Piazza del Campo. The rooms are clean but comfortable and cosy.

Albergo Cannon d'Oro (☎ *0577 4 43 21, fax 0577 28 08 68, Via dei Montanini 28)* Singles/doubles with bathroom €67.15/80. This place is handy if you're arriving by bus. The rooms are clean; only one has views.

Miniresidence il Casato (☎ *0577 23 60 01, fax 0577 22 69 97, Via Casato di Sopra 33)* Singles/doubles with bathroom €67.15/93. This is a nice option south of the action. The rooms are large and have rustic charm. There's a small, secluded garden, usually bathed in sunlight, and a kitchen you can use for €5.15 per day.

Chiusarelli (☎ *0577 28 05 62, fax 0577 27 11 77, Viale Curtatone 15)* Singles/doubles

with bathroom €72.30/109. Just off Piazza San Domenico, this place is in a handy location if you have a car (it also has a small garage). The rooms have all mod cons and breakfast is included.

Hotel Santa Caterina (☎ *0577 22 11 05, fax 0577 27 10 87,* **e** *hsc@sienanet.it, Via Enea Silvio Piccolomini 7)* Singles/doubles €98.15/144.60. This is another good option if you have a car. It's a friendly place with good service and a lovely, secluded garden.

If you are thinking about hanging around long-term and want to share a flat with students, check out the noticeboards at the university (such as the one at the economics faculty library in the cloister of the Chiesa di San Francesco).

Places to Eat

Local Cuisine The Sienese claim that most Tuscan cuisine has its origins in Siena, where the locals still use methods introduced to the area by the Etruscans.

Tuscans elsewhere may well dispute such claims, but the Sienese maintain that such dishes as *ribollita*, *panzanella* and *pappardelle al sugo di lepre* (hare sauce) are their own. *Pici*, a kind of bloated rough spaghetti, is also claimed by the Sienese, but also by Montalcino (see later in this chapter). *Panforte*, a rich cake of almonds, honey and candied melon or citrus fruit, has its origins in the city. Loosely translated, panforte is 'strong bread', and it was created as sustenance for the crusaders to the Holy Land.

Restaurants *Spizzico-Ciao* (☎ *0577 4 01 87, Piazza del Campo 77-81)* Meals up to €10.35. Open Wed-Mon. You can eat solidly at this cheap self-service place, right on Il Campo.

Hostaria Il Carroccio (☎ *0577 4 11 65, Via Casato di Sotto 32)* Pasta €5.20-6.20. Open Thur-Tues. The pasta at this place, off Piazza del Campo, is excellent. Try the pici followed by the *friselle di pollo ai zucchini* (bite-sized juicy chicken bits with a courgette side).

Taverna del Capitano (☎ *0577 28 80 94, Via del Capitano 8)* Full meals around €18. Open Wed-Mon. This little spot, with a small but reliable menu, is good for local cuisine.

Osteria del Castelvecchio *(☎ 0577 4 95 86, Via di Castelvecchio 65)* Mains €5.15-9.30. Open Wed-Mon. More expensive, but highly regarded by locals is this osteria nearby. The menu changes regularly and it's advisable to book ahead.

La Chiacchiera *(☎ 0577 28 06 31, Costa di Sant'Antonio 4)* Pasta from €4.15, mains €4.15-5.70. Open Wed-Mon. This tiny place, off Via Santa Caterina, has a good menu with local specialities.

Al Marsili *(☎ 0577 4 71 54, Via del Castoro 3)* Mains from €9.30. Open Tues-Sun. This is one of the city's better-known restaurants, but it is a bit on the expensive side. Traditional Sienese dishes are a good option here, such as *pici alla casareccia* (pici with a meat and mushroom sauce). It's good for a blow-out.

Ristorante da Mugolone *(☎ 0577 28 32 35, Via dei Pellegrini 8)* Pasta from €6.20, mains €9.30-15.50. Open Fri-Wed. This is another excellent restaurant, with local specialities. The setting is a little on the starched-collar side, with besuited waiters gliding noiselessly about the tables and the well-dressed customers.

Da Titti *(☎ 0577 4 80 87, Via di Camollia 193)* Mains around €6.70. Open Sun-Fri. This no-frills establishment with big wooden benches is close to Porta Camollia, about 10 to 15 minutes' walk north of Piazza del Campo.

Grotta del Gallo Nero *(☎ 0577 28 43 56, Via del Porrione 67)* Banquets €21-31. Open Tues-Sun. Here you can feast at a medieval banquet. It appears some research has gone into the meals, so your five or six courses will be a departure from the average Italian fare. The musical accompaniment may not be to everyone's taste.

Trattoria Tullio (Tre Cristi) *(☎ 0577 28 06 08, Vicolo di Provenzano 1)* Full meals around €25.80. Open Wed-Mon. Returning to modern times, this place is tucked away on a small lane not far from the Chiesa di San Francesco. Beneath its historic brick vaults, this place has been operating in one way or another since the early 19th century.

Self Catering There are a number of small supermarkets scattered around the town centre, including one at Via di Città 152–156 and at Via Dei Rossi, 88.

Nannini *(☎ 0577 74 15 91, Banchi di Sopra 22 & 95)* Pastries from €0.75. This is one of the city's finest cafes and *pasticcerie* (cake and pastry shops).

Entertainment

Enoteca Italiana *(☎ 0577 28 84 97, Fortezza Medicea)* Open Mon-Sat (closed Mon evening). Although a little too much publicised, this is an interesting place to taste a wide range of fine Tuscan wines.

The Dublin Post *(☎ 0577 28 90 89, Piazza Gramsci 20-21)* Open to 1am. This is one of the more popular joints in town, especially in summer when the small outdoor-seating area is full to overflowing. It has a pseudo-Irish lilt, and you can get cold dishes.

Robert the Bruce *(Via Monte Santo 1)* Open to 2am Thur-Tues. If you feel in need of a British ale, you could always pop over to this wee place, but it's only heaving in winter.

Caffé del Corso *(Bianchi di Sopra 25)* Right in the heart of the action, this bar is popular with young, trendy Italians and is generally a place to see and be seen.

Al Cambio *(☎ 0577 22 05 81, Via di Pantaneto 48)* Open 7pm-3am Tues-Sun. This is one of the few dance spots in Siena keeping young students busy.

As elsewhere in Italy, the big dance venues are generally well outside town. You should check ads for these places, for instance at the uni noticeboard in the cloister of the Chiesa di San Francesco, for details of what is happening – often one or more bars in Siena are selected as meeting points. The following two places only operate over summer.

Bombo *(☎ 0577 37 50 21, Via Roma)* Entrance around €15.15, including one drink. This popular place is in Monteroni d'Arbia, about 15km south-east of Siena on the SS2.

Imposto *(Località I'Imposto)* Entrance around €5.15-7.75. This open-air club is about 30km south of Siena on the SS223, just north of Bagni di Petriolo (see later in this chapter). It also hosts the occasional concert.

Shopping

Via di Città is a chic shopping street (with a clear leaning to selling products to tourists) where you can buy ceramics, food items, antiques, jewellery and so on. For clothes there are more shops on Banchi di Sopra.

Siena Ricama (☎ 0577 28 83 38 Via di Città 61) This shop promotes the crafts of Siena, in particular embroidery, and is worth a visit.

Feltrinelli (☎ 0577 27 11 04, Banchi di Sopra 54) This bookshop has a good stock of English books and a vast range of Italian titles.

Getting There & Away

Bus From Siena, bus is generally the way to go. The hub for buses is Piazza Gramsci, where up to seven SENA buses leave for Rome (€13.95, three hours, about every two hours).

Regular Tra-in buses race up the superstrada to Florence (€4.15, 2¼ hours; *rapido* service €6.20, 1¼ hours) while LFI buses (as many as eight a day in summer) connect to Arezzo (€4.15).

Tra-in buses connect Siena with destinations around its province. Connections to San Gimignano (€4.45, one hour, half hourly, change at Poggibonsi) and Colle di Val d'Elsa (€2.15, half an hour, half hourly, change for Volterra) are frequent. Regular buses run to Montalcino (€2.85, 1¼ hours) and Montepulciano (€4.15, 1½ hours). Other destinations include Monterrigioni, Chianciano, Pienza, Radda in Chianti, Rapolano, San Quirico d'Orcia and Grosseto.

At Piazza Gramsci, Tra-in and SENA operate an underground ticket sales and information service, along with left luggage (half/full-day €1.55/2.60) and even public showers (€2.60). Several sets of signposted stairs lead you to the office.

Train Siena is not on a major train line, so from Rome it is necessary to change at Chiusi, and from Florence at Empoli, making buses a better alternative. Trains arrive at Piazza F Rosselli, north of the city centre.

Car & Motorcycle Take the SS2 which connects Florence and Siena. Alternatively, take the SS222 ('la Chiantigiana'), which meanders its way through the Chianti hills. From the Florence-Siena superstrada, follow the signs for Porta Romana, which offers the most gentle walk to Piazza del Campo.

Getting Around

Bus Tra-in operates city bus services from a base in Piazza Gramsci. From the train station (€0.75), catch bus No 3, 9 or 10 to Piazza Gramsci.

Car & Motorcycle No cars, apart from those of residents, are allowed in the city centre. There are large car parks at the Stadio Comunale and around the Fortezza Medicea; both are just north of Piazza San Domenico. Technically, even to just drop off your luggage at your hotel it is necessary to get a special permit to enter the city by car. This can be obtained from the *vigili urbani* in Viale Federico Tozzi, but only if you have a hotel booking. Otherwise, phone your hotel for advice. Don't park illegally inside the city or around the city gates; you'll be towed quicker than you can yell 'where the *&@! is my car?'

Taxi For a taxi, call ☎ 0577 4 92 22. A taxi from the train station to the city centre is around €7.75.

AROUND SIENA
The Crete

Just south-east of Siena, this area of rolling clay hills is a feast of classic Tuscan images – bare ridges topped by a solitary cypress tree flanking a medieval farmhouse, four hills silhouetted one against the other as they fade off into the misty distance. The area of the Crete changes colour according to the season – from the creamy violet of the ploughed clay to the green of the young wheat, which then turns to gold. If you have the funds to spare, hire a car in Florence or Siena and spend a few days exploring the Crete. Another option is the Treno Natura, a tourist train which runs from Siena through Asciano and along the Val d'Orcia (see Organised Tours under Siena earlier in the chapter).

Rapolano Terme This is a relatively modern spa town that holds little interest for anyone not intent on taking an old-fashioned cure in the hot bubbling waters here. One of the two bathing establishments operates year-round. There are more interesting places to take a sulphur bath elsewhere in central and southern Tuscany (such as Bagni di San Filippo, Bagno Vignoni and Saturnia – for the latter see the Southern Tuscany chapter).

Asciano This pretty little hamlet is home to a trio of small museums dedicated to Sienese art and Etruscan finds in the area. It is most easily reached along the scenic SP438 road running south-east from Siena. The occasional slow local train passes through the town from Siena. While the town and its museums are interesting enough, the travelling is more rewarding than the arriving. Asciano is at the heart of the Crete, so the trip there and beyond (such as south to the Abbazia di Monte Oliveto Maggiore) is a real treat. The small tourist office (☎ 0577 71 95 10), at Corso Matteotti 18, has information on the town and its surrounding area.

Abbazia di Monte Oliveto Maggiore

This 14th-century **Olivetan monastery** *(☎ 0577 70 70 61; free; open 9.15am-noon & 3.15pm-6pm Apr-Oct; 9.15am-noon & 3.15pm to 5pm Nov-Mar)* is famous for the frescoes by Signorelli and Sodoma that decorate its **Choistro Grande** (Great Cloister). They illustrate events in the life of St Benedict. About 40 monks still live in the monastery.

The fresco cycle begins with Sodoma's work on the east wall (immediately to the right of the entrance into the church from the cloisters), and continues along the south wall of the cloisters. The nine frescoes by Signorelli line the west side of the cloisters, and Sodoma picks up again on the north wall. Sodoma's frescoes offer some ambiguous food for thought. Just why this artist was known as 'the Sodomite' has never been confirmed, although it is not too hard to

guess that it may have been a reference to his sexual preferences. At any rate, careful inspection of his frescoes reveals rather effeminate traits in many of the male figures represented. Part of the second fresco along the east wall (on the bulging column), in which a potential new acolyte kneels before the severe St Benedict, who is holding up part of his habit, has a suspect air about it. Even if the sexual allusion is imaginary, it seems odd that the monastery's abbot should not have objected to the image. Farther around on the south wall, St Benedict is depicted giving a fellow friar a sound thrashing to exorcise a demon – again a rather kinky image.

Note the decorations on the pillars between some of Sodoma's frescoes – they are among the earliest examples of 'grotesque' art, copied from decorations found in the then newly excavated Domus Aurea of Nero, in Rome.

After the frescoes you can wander into the **church** off the cloister. The baroque interior is a pleasingly sober play of perspective and shape. You can also see further works by Sodoma here. Off the cloister is a staircase leading up to the Renaissance **library**, which you are allowed to view only through small windows in the door.

It is possible to stay at the monastery *(☎ 0577 70 76 52, fax 0577 70 76 70)* for €21 from December to October, although as a rule this possibility is reserved for priests, families and laypersons intending to remain for spiritual purposes. It fills up quickly, so it's best to book one month ahead.

From the monastery, if you have your own transport, head for **San Giovanni d'Asso**, where there's an interesting 11th-century church with a Lombard-Tuscan facade, and a picturesque *borghetto* with the remains of a castle. Continue on to Montisi and Castelmuzio. Along a side road just outside Castelmuzio is the **Pieve di Santo Stefano in Cennano**, which is an abandoned 13th-century church. Ask for the key at the adjacent farm buildings if it's not open.

On the road to Pienza, around 2km past Castelmuzio, is the 14th-century Olivetan monastery of **Sant'Anna in Camprena**

(☎ 0578 74 80 37; free; open 3.30pm-7.30pm Tues-Sun). In the refectory there are frescoes by Sodoma.

The route from Monte Oliveto Maggiore to Pienza runs almost entirely along a high ridge, with great views of the Crete.

Buonconvento On first approaching Buonconvento down the SS2 highway, you could almost be forgiven for thinking it a large roadside rest stop. Lying perfectly flat in a rare stretch of plain, the low-slung fortified walls of this farming centre hide from view a quiet little town of medieval origins. One of its biggest moments in history came when the Holy Roman Emperor Henry VII, having shortly before captured it, expired here in August 1313 and so put an end to any hopes the Empire might have had of reasserting direct control over Tuscany. About the only sight is the local **Museo d'Arte Sacra** *(☎ 0577 80 71 81, Via Soccini 18; admission €3.10; open 10.30am-1pm & 3pm-7pm Tues-Sat Mar-Oct, 10am-1pm & 3pm-5pm Sat & Sun Nov-Feb)* in the main street. It contains religious art collected in the town and from neighbouring churches and hamlets.

Handy as it is for the highway, Buonconvento makes an easy stop for a cup of coffee or stretch of the legs while touring the area. It is also on the Siena-Grosseto bus route. If you are looking for a place to stay, San Quirico d'Orcia, just down the road, is a prettier location.

San Galgano & Around

Abbazia di San Galgano About 20km south-west of Siena, just off the SS73, is the ruined 13th-century San Galgano abbey *(free; open sunrise-sunset)*, one of the country's finest Gothic buildings in its day and now an atmospheric ruin.

A former Cistercian abbey, its monks were among Tuscany's most powerful, forming the judiciary and acting as accountants for the *comuni* (councils) of Volterra and Siena. They presided over disputes between the cities, played a significant role in the construction of the cathedral in Siena and built for themselves an opulent church.

As early as the 14th century Sir John Hawkwood, the feared English mercenary, sacked the abbey on at least two occasions. Things went from bad to worse and by the 16th century the monks' wealth and importance had declined and the church had deteriorated to the point of ruin. An attempt at restoration was made towards the end of the 16th century, but the rot had set in. In 1786 the bell tower simply collapsed, followed by the vaults of the ceiling a few years later.

The great, roofless stone and brick monolith stands silent in the fields. Come on a rainy winter's day and you feel more like you are in France or England, surrounded by glistening green fields and confronted by this classic grey Gothic ruin. The French reference is no coincidence, since the style of building is reminiscent of French Gothic.

Next door to the church are what remain of the monastery buildings, as well as a brief stretch of cloister housing a small tourist office (☎ 0577 75 67 38).

The abbey is definitely worth a diversion if you are driving, but visiting by public transport is quite difficult. The only option is the bus service between Siena and Massa Marittima, a little farther south-west.

The Accademia Musicale Chigiana in Siena sponsors concerts at the abbey during summer. See Special Events under Siena earlier in the chapter.

On a hill overlooking the abbey is the tiny, round Romanesque **Cappella di Monte Siepi**. This is where the original Cistercian settlement lived – from it came the impulse to build the great abbey below. Inside the chapel are badly preserved frescoes by Ambrogio Lorenzetti depicting the life of St Galgano, a local soldier who had a vision of St Michael on this site. A real-life 'sword in the stone' is under glass in the floor of the chapel, put there, legend has it, by San Galgano.

Murlo You could continue across the valley towards this interesting medieval fortified village. This was once an important Etruscan settlement and experts claim that DNA tests show the locals are close relatives of these ancient people. There's not much to see but it's a quaint spot with a few walks branching out into the surrounding hills.

Bagni di Petrioli About halfway down the SS223 highway between Siena and Grosseto, a side road leads down to the hot sulphur springs of Bagni di Petrioli. Scorching-hot spring water cascades into a few small natural basins. Anyone can come and sit in them, and there's usually a motley assortment of permanent campers making use of the natural shower.

About the only way to get here is with your own transport, since the 9km walk from the highway (along which run several buses between Siena and Grosseto) won't appeal to everyone.

Val d'Elsa

Monteriggioni This captivating walled medieval stronghold is just off the SS2 about 12km north of Siena.

Established in 1203 as a forward defensive position against Florence, the walls and towers today constitute one of the most complete examples of such a fortified bastion in Tuscany. The walls were rebuilt in the 1260s and seven of the 14 towers were reconstructed in the 20th century. It appears from Dante's descriptions that they were considerably higher when the Florentines had reason to fear them and their Sienese defenders.

Once inside the small town, there is really precious little to it. Should the quiet of the place appeal, you could opt to stay a while, or perhaps you'd prefer just to hang about for a meal.

Hotel Monteriggioni (☎ 0577 30 50 09, fax 0577 30 50 11, Via Primo Maggio 4) Singles/doubles €103/196.25. This rather expensive hotel has enticing rooms, a pool and a garden and comes highly recommended by readers.

Ristorante Il Pozzo (☎ 0577 30 41 27, Piazza Roma 20) Full meals around €3. Open Tues–noon Sun. If you can loosen the purse strings a little, you will be pleased you sat down at this place for its delicious meals, often with a game base.

Regular buses run to Monteriggioni from Siena (€1.35).

Colle di Val d'Elsa All most 'visitors' do here is change buses for Volterra. That's a shame, because the town is definitely worth a little exploration time. Florentine forces won a telling victory over the Sienese in 1269 in the plains below the town. The great medieval architect Arnolfo di Cambio was born here. From the Middle Ages on Colle was a bustling little town and had long been an important centre of Italian crystal production.

The most engaging part of town is **Colle Alta**, the old centre perched up on a ridge. From Piazza Arnolfo, where you will arrive by bus, it is about a 10-minute climb up along Via San Sebastiano. By car, park near Porta Nova at the western end of town. It's still a 10-minute walk but there's no climb involved.

Eventually you will find yourself walking along Via Castello, the main drag through Colle Alta. At its eastern end is a medieval *casa-torre* (tower house) where they say Arnolfo di Cambio was born. About halfway along the road is Piazza del Duomo, dominated by the rather unprepossessing neoclassical facade of the cathedral itself.

Three little museums cluster around the cathedral. The **Museo Civico** and **Museo d'Arte Sacra** (☎ 0577 92 38 88, Via del Castello 31; admission €2.60 for both; open 10am-noon & 4pm-7pm Tues-Sun Apr-Oct, 10am-noon & 3.30pm-6.30pm Sat, Sun & hols only Nov-Mar) are housed together, while the **Museo Archeologico** (☎ 0577 92 29 54, Piazza Duomo 42; admission €1.55; open 10am-noon & 5pm-7pm Tues-Sun May-Sept, 3.30pm-5.30pm Tues-Fri, 10am-noon & 3.30pm-6.30pm Sat & Sun Oct-Apr) is right on Piazza del Duomo. The most interesting is the Museo d'Arte Sacra, with some good paintings by Sienese masters.

You have a choice of three hotels, two in the lower part of town (Colle Bassa).

Hotel Arnolfo (☎ 0577 92 20 20, fax 0577 92 23 24, Via Campana 8) Singles/doubles

€52/72.30. This one, in Colle Alta, is the pick of the bunch.

Regular buses run here from Siena (€2.15). Up to four connecting buses with the CPT company head west to Volterra.

Casole d'Elsa & Around South-west of Colle di Val d'Elsa, this quiet fortified backwater was once a key part of Siena's western defences. In the course of the Middle Ages, Sienese troops found themselves squaring off on several occasions with enemy units from rivals Volterra and Florence. Little remains to detain you for more than a cursory inspection, but those with romantic tastes and a Swiss bank account could stick to the tiny road that winds south out of town to **Mensano** (a pretty little borgo) and swing east to **Pievescola**.

Relais La Suvera (☎ 0577 96 03 00, fax 0577 96 02 20, Pievescola) Doubles €258, Villa Pontificia €620. Here is an exquisite former castle and Renaissance villa. Aside from centuries of now well-manicured charm, rooms here offer all the comforts you could want, along with a heated pool and plenty of privacy.

Poggibonsi WWII managed to take care of what little was interesting about Poggibonsi, which takes line honours as one of the ugliest places in central Tuscany. If you are travelling by bus between Florence or Siena and San Gimignano you will pass through the town.

Albergo Italia (☎ 0577 93 61 42, fax 05 77 93 99 70, Via Trento 36) Singles/doubles €38.75/54.25. Should you get stuck, this is the cheapest hotel.

You will have no trouble finding places to eat or have a coffee.

SAN GIMIGNANO
postcode 53037 • pop 7100

As you crest the hill coming from the east, the 14 towers of this medieval walled town look in the distance for all the world like some medieval Manhattan. And when you arrive you might feel half of Manhattan's population has moved in – San Gimignano (San Jimmy to some of the Anglos who have opted to live in the area) is quite a tourist magnet. Come in the dead of winter, preferably when it's raining, to indulge your imagination a little. In summer most of your attention will probably be focused on dodging fellow visitors!

There is a reason for all this, of course. The towers were symbols of the power and wealth of the city's medieval families, and once numbered 72. San Gimignano delle Belle Torri ('of the Fine Towers') is surrounded by lush and productive land and the setting is altogether enchanting.

Originally an Etruscan village, the town later took its name from the bishop of Modena, St Gimignano, who is said to have saved the city from a barbarian assault. It became a comune in 1199, but fought frequently with neighbouring Volterra and the internal battles between the Ardinghelli family (Guelph) and the Salvucci family (Ghibelline) over the next two centuries caused deep divisions. Most towers were built during this period – in the 13th century one *podestà* (town chief) forbade the building of towers higher than his (51m).

In 1348, plague decimated the town's population and weakened the power of its nobles, leading to the town's submission to Florence in 1353. Today, not even the plague would dent the summer swarms!

Orientation
The manicured gardens of Piazzale dei Martiri di Montemaggio, at the southern end of the town, lie just outside the medieval wall and next to the main gate, the Porta San Giovanni. From the gate, Via San Giovanni heads northwards to Piazza della Cisterna and the connecting Piazza del Duomo, in the city centre. The other major thoroughfare, Via San Matteo, leaves Piazza del Duomo for the main northern gate, Porta San Matteo.

Information
Tourist Offices The Associazione Pro Loco (☎ 0577 94 00 08, fax 0577 94 09 03, W www.sangimignano.com), at Piazza del Duomo 1, opens 9am to 1pm and 3pm to 7pm daily (closing at 6pm November to March).

If you're enthusiastic about Tuscany's only white DOCG wine, Vernaccia di San

SAN GIMIGNANO

To Certaldo (10km), Pisa (60km) & Livorno (68km)

To Hotel La Collegiata (50m)

Via Ghiacciaia

Piazza S Agostino

Via XX Settembre

Via Folgore da San Gimignano

Porta San Jacopo

Porta San Matteo

Via delle Romite

Via delle Fonti

Porta delle Fonti

Via San Matteo

Via Mainardi

Piazza delle Erbe

Piazza del Duomo

Piazza della Cisterna

Via Santo Stefano

Via del Castello

Viale dei Fossi

Piazza Pecori

Via Quercecchio

Via Piandornella

Via di Bonda

Porta Quercecchio

Via Berignano

Via San Giovanni

Viale dei Fossi

Porta San Giovanni

Piazzale dei Martiri di Montemaggio

Via Roma

To Il Boschetto di Piemma Camp Site (2km)

To Poggibonsi (8km), Colle di Val d'Elsa (8km), SS68 (9.5km), Siena (40km) & Florence (62km)

0   100   200m
0   100   200yd

PLACES TO STAY
4 Foresteria Monastereo di San Girolamo
8 Hotel L'Antico Pozzo
15 Hotel Leon Bianco
27 Hotel La Cisterna
30 Hotel Bel Soggiorno

PLACES TO EAT
2 Locanda di Sant'Agostino
6 Osteria Le Catene
7 Trattoria La Mangiatoia
11 Il Castello
12 Osteria al Carcere
18 Enoteca Gustavo
26 Gelateria di Piazza
28 Le Vecchie Mura

OTHER
1 Chiesa di Sant'Agostino
3 Museo Archeologico; Speziera di Santa Fina
5 Tam Tam
9 Fonti Medievali
10 Vigili Urbani
13 Museo della Tortura
14 Exact Change
16 Palazzo del Podestà; Torre della Rognosa
17 Telephones
19 Post Office
20 Rocca
21 Collegiata
22 Museo d'Arte Sacra
23 Palazzo del Popolo; Museo Civico
24 Associazione Pro Loco
25 Associazione Strutture Extralberghiere
29 Collezione Ornitologico
31 Siena Hotels Promotion
32 Bus Terminus
33 Carabinieri
34 Bruno Bellini Bike Hire

Gimignano, you can take the opportunity to join a tour of vineyards in the surrounding area organised by the tourist office. Tours leave at 10.30am on Tuesday and 5pm on Thursday during summer, and cost €25.80 per person. Reservations one day in advance are essential.

For more information on walking in the area, see the Tuscany on Foot chapter.

Money Exact Change (☎ 0577 94 32 38) operates a change office at Piazza della Cisterna 16. A couple of banks also operate in the town centre.

Post & Communications The post office is in Piazza delle Erbe 8, on the northern side of the cathedral. You can make telephone calls from an unstaffed office at Via San Matteo 3.

For Internet access try Tam Tam (☎ 0577 90 71 00) at Via XX Settembre 4b. It opens 10am to 7pm and charges €6.20 for an hour online.

Police The *carabinieri* (☎ 0577 94 03 13) are behind the bus stop in Piazzale dei Martiri di Montemaggio. The *vigili urbani* (☎ 0577 94 03 46) are on Via Santo Stefano.

Things to See

If you're intent on visiting everything, buy the €10.35 ticket, which allows admission into most of San Gimignano's museums, from the ticket offices of any of the city's sights. If you only want to see a selection of the museums, consider one of the following: the €5.15 ticket, which allows entry to the Collegiata and Museo d'Arte Sacra, or the €7.75 ticket, which gains access to the Museo Civico, Torre Grossa, Museo Archeologico & Speziera di Santa Fina and Collezione Ornitologico.

Start in the triangular Piazza della Cisterna, named after the 13th-century cistern in its centre. The square is lined with houses and towers dating from the 13th and 14th centuries. In the adjoining Piazza del Duomo, the Collegiata (cathedral) looks across to the late-13th-century **Palazzo del Podestà** and its tower, known as the **Torre della Rognosa**. The Palazzo del Popolo, left of the cathedral, still operates as the town hall.

Collegiata Up a flight of steps from the square is the town's Romanesque **cathedral** (☎ 0577 94 22 26, Piazza Luigi Pecozi 4; adult/child €3.10/1.55; open 9.30am-7.30pm Mon-Fri, 9.30am-5pm Sat & 1pm-5pm Sun Apr-Oct, 9.30am-5pm Mon-Sat & 1pm-5pm Sun Nov-Mar), its simple facade belying the remarkable frescoes covering the walls of its interior. There are three main cycles.

You get your ticket at an office in the little square (Piazza Pecori) off the southern flank of the church, which you are then obliged to enter via a turnstile. You thus enter the church by the southern (left) flank and near the transept. The first look at this feast of (much restored) frescoes amid the black-and-white striped arches and columns separating three naves is likely to be a bit of a shock.

Pull yourself together and head to the end of the church to the main entrance (where visitors now exit through another turnstile). The fresco by Taddeo di Bartolo covering the top half of the rear wall depicts the Last Judgment, while below Benozzo Gozzoli's rendering of the martyrdom of St Sebastian dominates. From either side of these frescoes walls extend into the interior of the church. On the right side are frescoes depicting *Paradiso* (Heaven) and on the left *Inferno* (Hell). Both are by Taddeo di Bartolo, who seems to have taken particular delight in presenting the horrors of the underworld – remember that many of the faithful in these times would have taken such images pretty much at face value.

Along the left (southern) wall are scenes from Genesis and the Old Testament by Bartolo di Fredi, dating from around 1367. The top row runs from the creation of the world through to forbidden fruit, the eating of which leads to the first scene of the following level – the expulsion of Adam and Eve from Heaven. Further scenes on this level include Cain killing Abel, the story of Noah's ark, and Joseph's coat. The last level picks up this story, the tale of Moses leading the Jews out of Egypt and the story of Job.

On the right (northern) wall are scenes from the New Testament by Barna da Siena, completed in 1381. Again, the frescoes are spread over three levels, starting in the six lunettes at the top. Commencing with the Annunciation, the panels proceed through episodes such as the Epiphany, the presentation of Christ in the temple and the massacre of the innocents on Herod's orders. The subsequent panels on the lower levels summarise the life and death of Christ, the Resurrection and so on. Some are in poor condition.

One of the delights of the church is the **Cappella di Santa Fina**, a Renaissance chapel off to the right. Apart from Benedetto da Maiano's tomb-altar to the saint, two beautiful frescoes by Domenico Ghirlandaio depicting events in her life stand out.

Museo d'Arte Sacra An interesting collection of religious art, including sculpture and an assortment of paintings by lesser-known artists, can be seen in this **museum** (☎ 0577 94 03 16, Piazza Pecori 1; adult/child €2.60/1.55; open 9.30am-7.30pm, 9.30am-5pm Nov-Mar). More curious than anything else is Sabastiano Mainardi's *Il Volto Santo Adorato*, on the ground floor. Two hooded figures, looking suspiciously like KKK members, kneel at the feet of an incredibly well-dressed Jesus on the cross.

Palazzo del Popolo To balance the religious, the other principal sight in San Gimignano is this seat of secular power. Since 1288 the comune has sat here, although the present building is the result of expansion in the 14th century. The neo-Gothic facade was actually added late in the 19th century.

From the internal courtyard, which contains frescoes and heralds, climb the stairs to the **Museo Civico** (☎ 0577 94 00 08, Piazza del Duomo; adult/child museum & tower €6.20/4.65, museum only €3.60/2.60, tower only €4.15/3.10; open 9.30am 7.30pm, 10am-5.30pm Sat-Thur Nov-Feb).

After purchasing your ticket, follow the signs into the museum, whose main room is known as the **Sala di Dante**. The great poet is said to have addressed the town's council here, imploring it to join a Florentine-led Guelph League. Your attention is captured above all by the Maestà, a masterful fresco by Lippo Memmi dating from 1317 and depicting the enthroned Virgin Mary and Christ child with angels and saints. Other frescoes portray jousts, hunting scenes, castles and other medieval goings-on.

Upstairs to the right is the small **Pinacoteca**, where you can admire a limited collection of medieval religious works, including a Crocifisso by Coppo di Marcovaldo and a pair of remarkable tondi by Filippino Lippi, the Angelo Annunciante (Angel Gabriel) and Vergine Annunciata, which depicts the Virgin receiving Gabriel's news.

Opposite the Pinacoteca is a small frescoed room. Opinion on what these frescoes showing wedding scenes are all about is divided. It all looks like great fun, with the newly weds taking a bath together and then hopping into the sack.

When you have had enough of the art you can climb the stairs to the top of the **Torre Grossa** for a spectacular view of the town and surrounding countryside.

Museo Archeologico & Speziera di Santa Fina This new museum (☎ 0577 94 03 48, Via Fologore da San Gimignano 11;

adult/child €4.15/3.10 for both; open 11am-6pm daily Mar–mid-Jan, Fri-Mon mid-Jan–Feb) is in fact two museums. The first room you enter holds a plethora of ceramic and glass storage vessels from the original pharmacy of the Speziera di Santa Fina (Hospital of Santa Fina), begun in the early 16th century. Many are beautifully painted and still contain concoctions used as cures for ailments in the Middle Ages. Follow your nose to the second room, called 'the kitchen', which is filled with herbs and spices used for elixirs.

Past 'the kitchen' is a small archaeological museum. It's divided into Etruscan/Roman and Medieval sections, and consists of pieces that were generally found in the surrounding area.

Upstairs you'll find galleries devoted to temporary exhibitions of modern art.

Museo della Tortura Sadomasochists in need of a few new ideas should pop along to this rather gruesome little **museum** (☎ 0577 94 22 43, Via del Castello 1-3; admission €7.75 (not included in combined ticket); open 10am-7pm Nov–mid-July, 10am-8pm mid-Sept–Oct, 10am-midnight mid-July–mid-Sept). It's all here, from gibbets to thumbscrews – over 100 ways to inflict unspeakable pain on your neighbour. There is no doubt that people really knew how to live in the Middle Ages!

Other Sights The **Rocca**, a short walk to the west of Piazza del Duomo, is the atmospheric ruin of the town's fortress from where you have great views across the valley. There's little left but the crumbling shell, and at the foot of it on the southern side are a few swings for the kids.

Just south of the Rocca is the **Collezione Ornitologica** (Via Quercecchio; adult/child €2/1.50; open 11am-6pm Apr-Sept), whose collection of stuffed birds dates right back to 1886.

At the northern end of the town is the **Chiesa di Sant'Agostino**, whose main attraction is the fresco cycle by Benozzo Gozzoli in the apse, depicting the life of St Augustine.

If you head out of the town walls to the east you will be guided by signs to the **Fonti Medievali**, ruined arches around one-time springs.

Places to Stay
Inside the walls of San Gimignano you will find only a handful of hotels, all with eye-popping prices. Coming to the rescue are, apart from the foresteria and a camp site, numerous affittacamere at reasonable prices. The tourist office can make bookings for you.

The Siena Hotels Promotion (☎ 0577 94 08 09, fax 0577 94 01 13, W www .sangimignano.com, Via San Giovanni 125) can place you in a hotel. It will make arrangements months in advance and charges a €1.55 fee.

Il Boschetto di Piemma (☎ 0577 94 03 52, e bpiemma@tiscalinet.it) Sites per adult /child/tent €4.65/3.60/4.65. Open Apr–mid-Oct. This is the closest camp site to town – it's at Santa Lucia, a couple of kilometres south of the Porta San Giovanni. Buses leave from Piazzale dei Martiri di Montemaggio.

Foresteria Monastero di San Girolamo (☎ 0577 94 05 73, Via Fologore da San Gimignano 32) Dorm beds €20.65. Accommodation doesn't come much cheaper than this inside the walls of a Tuscan hilltop town. The rooms are basic but spotless, roomy and comfortable, and the Benedictine nuns are incredibly friendly and welcoming to people of any religious denomination. Breakfast is included and there's free parking.

While on cheaper options, there were 20 *affittacamere* within the town walls at last count. You can pretty safely assume the cheapest it will get is €36.15 for rooms with use of a shared bathroom in the corridor. In that case you need your own wheels and should consider instead the agriturismo option. Get lists from the Associazione Pro Loco. Alternatively, for any of these non-hotel options contact the Associazione Strutture Extralberghiere (☎/fax 0577 94 31 90), at Piazza della Cisterna 6.

Hotel Leon Bianco (☎ 0577 94 12 94, fax 0577 94 21 23, Piazza della Cisterna 13)

Singles/doubles €56.80/87.80. This place, right in the heart of the old town, is comfortable and well kept. Rooms on the inner courtyard come cheaper than those with views.

Hotel La Cisterna (☎ 0577 94 03 28, fax 0577 94 20 80, e lacisterna@iol.it, Piazza della Cisterna 24) Singles/doubles €64.50/95.50. Across the square, La Cisterna is marginally more expensive and offers much the same standards. Again, rooms with views are slightly more expensive.

Hotel L'Antico Pozzo (☎ 0577 94 20 14, fax 0577 94 21 17, W www.anticopozzo.com, Via San Matteo 87) Singles/doubles from €87.80/95.50. Rooms in this 15th-century town house, with their high ceilings and wrought-iron beds, have a real touch of class.

Hotel Bel Soggiorno (☎ 0577 94 03 76, fax 0577 90 75 21, W www.hotelbelsog giorno.it, Via San Giovanni 91) Rooms from €98.15. At the opposite end of town is this hotel. Many of the rooms have great views of the countryside.

Hotel La Collegiata (☎ 0577 94 32 01, fax 0577 94 05 66, e collegia@tin.it, Località Strada 27) Singles/doubles €258/335.70. If the bank has given you a generous overdraft you may be tempted to stay here, outside the town. The assumption is you will have a car to get to and from this magnificent old country residence. Elegantly appointed rooms have all the mod cons and outside you can splash about in the pool. They have a fine restaurant too.

Places to Eat
Enoteca Gustavo (☎ 0577 94 00 57, Via San Matteo 29) Snacks and wine from €2.05. Open Sat-Thur. This is an excellent place to sip wines with snack food.

Il Castello (☎ 0577 94 08 78, Via del Castello 20) Pasta from €5.70. Open until midnight. This wine bar and restaurant has a lovely patio, perfect for sipping your glass of Vernaccia di San Gimignano.

Trattoria La Mangiatoia (☎ 0577 94 15 28, Via Mainardi 5) Mains around €12.90. Open Wed-Mon. This is one of the city's better restaurants, a romantic spot where you eat to the accompaniment of slow, classical music.

CENTRAL TUSCANY

Osteria Le Catene (☎ *0577 94 19 66, Via Mainardi 18)* Mains €11.35-12.90. Open Thur-Tues. Virtually across the road, this is an interesting option. Alongside many Tuscan stalwarts they also experiment a little, for instance using saffron, a standard spice in medieval cooking, in dishes such as *zuppa medievale.*

Le Vecchie Mura (☎ *0577 94 02 70, Via Piandornella 15)* Mains €7.75-15.50. Open Wed-Mon evenings only. The terrace at this popular restaurant, with splendid views of the countryside to the south, is worth the visit alone. The food is also above average, so you should book ahead if you want a table on the terrace.

Osteria al Carcere (☎ *0577 94 19 05, Via Castello 5)* Soup €6.20. Open Thur-Tues. This fine osteria offers great food at moderate prices. They have an original menu including a half-dozen soups.

Locanda di Sant'Agostino (☎ *0577 94 31 41, Piazza Sant'Agostino) Bruschette* from €5.15. This place is good for a relatively quiet drink and a sampling of one or two of 49 bruschette – they are a tad overpriced but quite delicious and filling, and they make a rather palatable light lunch option.

Gelateria di Piazza (☎ *0577 94 22 44, Piazza della Cisterna 4)* Gelato from €1.30. This great place turns the local wine, Vernaccia, into a delicious ice cream.

For your self-catering needs, a ***produce market*** is held on Thursday mornings in Piazza della Cisterna and Piazza del Duomo. The ***alimentari*** on Via Cellolese makes good *panini* (€1.30).

Getting There & Around

Bus San Gimignano is accessible from Florence and Siena by regular buses, but you need to change at Poggibonsi. For Volterra you need to change in Colle di Val d'Elsa, but there's a direct bus to Certaldo. Buses arrive in Piazzale dei Martiri di Montemaggio at Porta San Giovanni. Remember that Sunday is a bad day for doing this trip, in that connections are reduced.

The closest train station to San Gimignano is in Poggibonsi.

Car & Motorcycle From Florence, it's easiest is to take the SS2 to Poggibonsi and follow the signs. You could also approach by taking the SS68 from Colle di Val d'Elsa. From Volterra, take the SS68 east and follow the turn-off signs north to San Gimignano.

When you arrive, signs direct you to various car parks where you pay €1.50 an hour. Some car parks are for residents only. It is possible to find free parking in the new parts of town that sprawl north-west of the old centre.

Bicycle It's possible to hire mountain bikes at Bruno Bellini (☎ 0577 94 02 01, Via Roma 41) for €7.75 an hour, or €15.50 a day. They also rent scooters (€15.50 per hour, €31 per day) and motorcycles (€25.80 per hour, €52 per day).

VOLTERRA
postcode 56048 • pop 13,400

Straggling high on a rocky plateau, Volterra's well-preserved medieval ramparts give the windswept ridge town a proud and forbidding air.

The Etruscan settlement of Velathri was an important trading centre and senior partner of the Dodecapolis. It is believed as many as 25,000 people lived here in its Etruscan heyday. Partly because of the difficult terrain of which it was master, the city was one of the last to succumb to Rome – it was absorbed into the Roman confederation around 260 BC and renamed Volaterrae.

The bulk of the old city as it stands today was raised in the 12th and 13th centuries under a fiercely independent free comune. The city first entered into Florence's orbit in 1361, but it was some time before it took full control. When this was threatened in 1472, Lorenzo the Magnificent made one of his few big mistakes and lasting enemies of the people of Volterra when he marched in and ruthlessly snuffed out every vestige of potential opposition to direct Florentine rule.

Since Etruscan times Volterra has been a centre of alabaster extraction and workmanship. The quarries lay fallow for several centuries until the Renaissance brought renewed interest in the material for sculpture. To this day, the traditions have been maintained and passed from generation to generation.

Orientation & Information

Driving and parking inside the walled town are more or less prohibited. Park in one of the designated parking areas and enter the nearest city gate – all the main streets lead to the central Piazza dei Priori.

The tourist office (☎ 0588 8 72 57, W www.volterratur.it), at Piazza dei Priori 20, opens 10am to 1pm and 2pm to 7pm April to October; to 6pm Monday to Saturday and mornings only on Sunday November to March (closed last three weeks of November). Here you can hire an audio guide for €7.75, which provides detailed information of the town and its history.

Exchange money at the Cassa di Risparmio di Firenze bank on the corner of Via dei Marchesi and Via Giacoma Matteotti, or at Exact Change (☎ 0588 8 89 99) on Piazza Martiri della Libertà (the latter

shuts down in December and January due to lack of tourist interest). The post office and telecom office face the tourist office on the northern side of Piazza dei Priori. Next door to them is the police station in the Palazzo Pretorio. Internet access for €6.20 per hour is available at SESHA Computers (☎ 0588 8 40 92, Piazza XX Settembre 10).

Things to See

A €6.70 ticket, valid for a year, covers visits to the Museo Etrusco Guarnacci, the Pinacoteca Comunale and Museo Diocesano di Arte Sacra. Access to the Roman theatre and Parco Archeologico is free.

Piazza dei Priori & Around Piazza dei Priori is surrounded by austere medieval mansions. The 13th-century **Palazzo dei Priori** (admission €1; open 10am-1pm & 2pm-6pm Sat and Sun) is the oldest seat of local government in Tuscany and is believed to have been a model for Florence's Palazzo

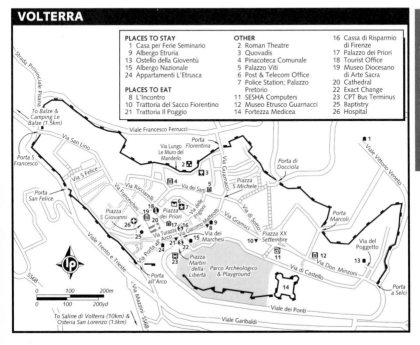

VOLTERRA

PLACES TO STAY
1 Casa per Ferie Seminario
9 Albergo Etruria
13 Ostello della Gioventù
15 Albergo Nazionale
24 Appartamenti L'Etrusca

PLACES TO EAT
8 L'Incontro
10 Trattoria del Sacco Fiorentino
21 Trattoria Il Poggio

OTHER
2 Roman Theatre
3 Quovadis
4 Pinacoteca Comunale
5 Palazzo Viti
6 Post & Telecom Office
7 Police Station; Palazzo Pretorio
11 SESHA Computers
12 Museo Etrusco Guarnacci
14 Fortezza Medicea

16 Cassa di Risparmio di Firenze
17 Palazzo dei Priori
18 Tourist Office
19 Museo Diocesano di Arte Sacra
20 Cathedral
22 Exact Change
23 CPT Bus Terminus
25 Baptistry
26 Hospital

CENTRAL TUSCANY

Vecchio. The **Palazzo Pretorio**, also dating from the 13th century, is dominated by the Piglet's Tower, so named because of the wild boar sculpted on its upper section.

Behind the Palazzo dei Priori is the **cathedral** (☎ 0588 8 76 54, Via Turazza; free; open 8am-12.30pm & 3pm-6pm), built in the 12th and 13th centuries. Inside, highlights include a small fresco by Benozzo Gozzoli, the *Adorazione dei Magi*, behind a nativity group in the oratory at the beginning of the left aisle. The 15th-century tabernacle on the high altar is by Mino da Fiesole. The black-and-white marble banding on the inside and the Renaissance coffered ceiling are unusual touches.

Facing the cathedral is the 13th-century **baptistry** (battistero) which features a font by Andrea Sansovino. On the western side of the square you can tell the porticoed **Ospedale di Santa Maria Maddalena** was once a foundlings hospital by the robbiane depicting infants in swaddling clothes. Next to the cathedral you can see works of religious art, sculpture in particular, collected in the **Museo Diocesano di Arte Sacra** (☎ 0588 8 62 90, Via Roma 13; admission €6.70 combined ticket; open 9am-1pm & 3pm-6pm mid-Mar–Oct, 9am-1pm Nov–mid-Mar).

The **Pinacoteca Comunale** (☎ 0588 8 75 80, Via dei Sarti 1; admission €6.70 combined ticket; open 9am-7pm mid-Mar–Oct, 9am-2pm Nov–mid-Mar), in the Palazzo Minucci Solaini, houses a modest collection of local, Sienese and Florentine art, including some works by Rosso Fiorentino and Luca Signorelli.

Museo Etrusco Guarnacci All the exhibits in this fascinating **Etruscan museum** (☎ 0588 8 63 47, Via Don Minzoni 15; admission €6.70 combined ticket; open 9am-7pm mid-Mar–Oct, 9am-2pm Nov–mid-Mar) were unearthed locally, including a vast collection of some 600 funerary urns carved from alabaster, tufa and other materials.

The urns are displayed according to the subjects depicted in their bas-reliefs and the period from which they date. Be selective, as they all start to look the same after a while. The best examples – those dating from later periods – are on the 2nd and 3rd floors.

Most significant are the *Ombra della Sera* sculpture, a strange, elongated nude figure that would fit in well in any museum of modern art, and the urn of the *Sposi*, featuring an elderly couple, their faces depicted in portrait fashion rather than the stylised method usually employed.

Fortezza Medicea & Parco Archeologico Farther along Via Don Minzoni is the entrance to the **Fortezza Medicea**, built in the 14th century and altered by Lorenzo the Magnificent, and now used as a prison (you cannot enter unless you would like to stay for a while).

Near the fort is the pleasant Parco Archeologico (free; open 8.30am-8pm summer, 8.30pm-5pm winter), whose archaeological remains have suffered with the passage of time. This is where the heart of the ancient city, the Acropolis, was located. Little has survived, but the park has swings and things for kids to burn up all their excess energy on, and is a good place for a picnic.

Palazzo Viti Built at the end of the 16th century and completely renovated by a successful alabaster merchant, Benedetto Viti, in the 1850s, Palazzo Viti (☎ 0588 8 40 47, Via dei Sarti 41; admission €3.60; open 10am-1pm & 2.30pm-6.30pm daily, appointment only Dec-Feb) affords you a glance into the luxury enjoyed by the wealthy business class in Tuscany. The great halls are richly decorated, sometimes too much so (the impression of parvenu wealth seeps through the place).

Other Sights On the city's northern edge is a **Roman theatre** (free; open 11am-5pm), a well-preserved complex that includes a Roman bath.

The **Balze**, a deep ravine created by erosion, about a 20-minute walk north-west of the city centre, has claimed several churches since the Middle Ages, the buildings having fallen into its huge gullies. A 14th-century monastery is perched close to the precipice and is in danger of toppling into the ravine. To get there, head out of the north-west end of the city along Via San Lino and follow its continuation, Borgo Santo Stefano and then Borgo San Giusto.

Places to Stay

The tourist office makes accommodation bookings, and has lists of affittacamere and agriturismo.

Camping Le Balze (☎ 0588 8 78 80, Via di Mandringa 15) Sites per adult/child/tent €5.70/3.10/3.60. This is the closest camp site to town. It has a pool and sits right on the Balze.

Ostello della Gioventù (☎/fax 0588 8 55 77, Via del Poggetto 3) Beds from €10.35. The cheapest deal is at this non-HI hostel near the Museo Etrusco Guarnacci. It's clean and comfortable but rather characterless.

Casa per Ferie Seminario (☎ 0588 8 60 28, fax 0588 9 07 91, Viale Vittorio Veneto 2) Singles €13.95, with bathroom €17.55. This place, in the Monastero di Sant'Andrea, is an excellent deal. Rooms are large and clean.

Albergo Etruria (☎ /fax 0588 8 73 77, Via Giacomo Matteotti 32) Singles/doubles with bathroom €13.95/17.55. This is the cheapest hotel within the town walls. The rooms are average but clean and quiet.

Albergo Nazionale (☎ 0588 8 62 84, fax 05 88 8 40 97, W www.albergonazio nalevolterra.it, Via dei Marchesi 11) Singles/doubles from €46.50/67.15. Nazionale is handy for parking and boasts its own restaurant.

Appartamenti L'Etrusca (☎/fax 0588 8 40 73, Via Porta all'Arco 37-41) Single/double/triple self-contained apartments €36.15/62/67.15. If you would prefer to have an apartment, this is a good option. The rates come down marginally if you rent for a week or more.

Places to Eat

L'Incontro (☎ 0588 8 05 00, Via Giacoma Matteotti 18) Open Thur-Tues. This is a cheerful and rather cavernous place for breakfast, a coffee during the day or even a drink or two in the evening.

Trattoria del Sacco Fiorentino (☎ 0588 8 85 37, Piazza XX Settembre 18) Full meal from €18.10. Open Sat-Thur. This is a nice little eatery serving up fine food with a happy selection of local wines. Try the *coniglio in salsa di aglio e Vin Santo*, rabbit cooked in a garlic dessert-wine sauce.

Trattoria Il Poggio (☎ 0588 8 52 57, Via Porta all'Arco 7). Pizza up to €18.10. Open Wed-Mon. This place is not quite as good, but pleasant enough, with fine pizzas.

Osteria San Lorenzo (☎ 0588 4 41 60, Via Massetana) Full meals with wine around €18.10. Open Wed-Mon. If you have wheels and would like to venture out of town a little, drive down to Saline di Volterra and then take the SS439 road south heading to Pomarance. About 3km out of Saline di Volterra you enter the tiny settlement of San Lorenzo, home to this place where you can get superb, home-style cooking.

Entertainment

Quovadis (☎ 0588 8 00 33, Via Lungo Le Mura del Mandorlo 18) This is about the only place in town where you can get a lager or Guinness seven days a week. The garden bar is pleasant on hot summer nights.

Getting There & Away

Bus Volterra is a little bit of a pain to get to. If you are coming from Florence (€6.30, two hours), Siena (€4.25, 1½ hours) or San Gimignano (€4.15, 1½ hours), you need to reach Colle di Val d'Elsa first and change buses. From Monday to Saturday CPT has four connections Monday to Saturday between Volterra (Piazza Martiri della Libertà) and Colle di Val d'Elsa (€2.15, 50 minutes).

Up to nine buses a day run to Pisa (€4.90, two hours) via Pontedera. Other buses head south in the direction of Massa Marittima, but only go as far as Pomarance and Castelnuovo di Val di Cecina.

Train From the small train station in Saline di Volterra, 9km to the south-west of Volterra, you can get a train to Cecina on the coast (see the Central Coast chapter), from where you can catch trains on the Rome-Pisa line. Up to five CPT buses a day run between Volterra and the train station.

Car & Motorcycle By car, take the SS68, which runs between Cecina and Colle di

Val d'Elsa. A couple of back routes to San Gimignano are signposted north off the SS68.

SOUTH OF VOLTERRA

If you have a car and want to head for Massa Marittima (a worthwhile objective – see the Southern Tuscany chapter), the ride south from Volterra is interesting enough.

The SS68 drops away to the south-west from Volterra towards Cecina. At Saline di Volterra (where you'll find the nearest train station for Volterra), the SS439 intersects the SS68 on its way from Lucca, south towards Massa Marittima. **Saline di Volterra** takes its name from the nearby saltmines, which were the source of its wealth in the 19th century.

The lunar-landscape ride south is engaging in its own way. You can pass straight through **Pomarance**, a largely industrial town. To the south, take the hilly road for **Larderello**, which has the strange honour of being Italy's most important boric acid producer. The road out of here keeps winding its way south to Massa.

SOUTHERN SIENA PROVINCE

You may already have had a taste of the strange undulating countryside of the Crete (see earlier in the chapter). For a while similar countryside persists as you roam south, and it's here you'll find what you've seen on postcards and calendars all over Tuscany – rolling hills of hay topped with a huddle of cypress trees. Gradually the landscape gives away to more unruly territory as you get farther away from the more touristed centres. This part of the province offers everything: the haughty hilltop medieval wine centres of Montalcino and Montepulciano, hot sulphurous baths in spots such as Bagno Vignoni, Romanesque splendours of the Abbazia di Sant'Antimo, or the renaissance grace of Pienza, an early example of idealised town planning.

Montalcino

postcode 53024 • pop 5100

A pretty town perched high above the Orcia valley, Montalcino is best known for its wine, the Brunello. Produced only in the vineyards surrounding the town, it is said to be one of Italy's best reds and has gained considerable international fame.

Plenty of *enoteche* (wine bars) around town provide you with the chance to taste and buy Brunello, as well as the other main local wine, the Rosso di Montalcino, although you'll pay a minimum of €12.90 for a Brunello. Top names in excellent years can come with price tags heading up to the €103 mark (or break the bank with a bottle from 1945 – a mere €4648.50). Price alone is not necessarily an indication of the wine's quality. Bear in mind that all Brunello is made to strict regulations so that, in some respects, price differences are often as much a matter of marketing as of drinking quality.

A helpful Pro Loco tourist office (☎ 0577 84 93 31, ⓦ www.prolocomontalcino.it – Italian only) is at Costa Municipio 1, just off Piazza del Popolo, the town's main square. It opens 10am to 1pm and 2pm to 5.40pm daily April to October and Tuesday to Sunday November to March.

Things to See & Do The **Fortezza** (*☎ 0577 84 92 11, Piazzale Fortezza; admission to courtyard free, ramparts €2.60, combined €5.15 ticket includes Museo Civico; open 9am-8pm Apr-Oct, 9am-6pm Tues-Sun Nov-Mar*), an impressive 14th-century fortress that was later expanded under the Medici dukes, dominates the town from a high point at its southern end. You can sample and buy local wines in the *enoteca* inside, from where you can also climb up to the fort's ramparts.

The **Museo Civico e Diocesano d'Arte Sacra** (*☎ 0577 84 60 14, Via Ricasoli; adult/child €4.15/2.60, combined €5.15 ticket includes Fortezza; open 10am-6pm Tues-Sun Apr-Oct, 10am-1pm & 2pm-6pm Tues-Sun Nov-Dec, 10am-1pm & 2pm-5pm Jan-Mar*), housed in the former convent of the neighbouring **Chiesa di Sant'Agostino**, contains an important collection of religious art from the town and surrounding region. Among the items on show are a triptych by Duccio di Buoninsegna and a *Madonna col Bambino* by Simone Martini. Other artists represented include the Lorenzetti brothers,

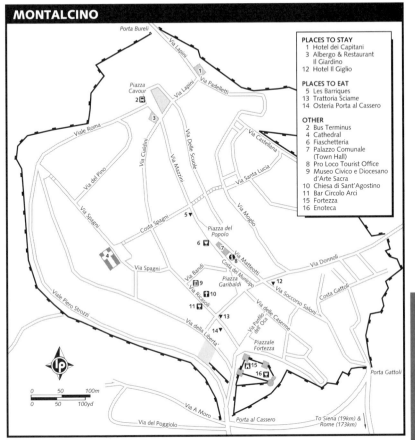

MONTALCINO

PLACES TO STAY
1 Hotel dei Capitani
3 Albergo & Restaurant
    Il Giardino
12 Hotel Il Giglio

PLACES TO EAT
5 Les Barriques
13 Trattoria Sciame
14 Osteria Porta al Cassero

OTHER
2 Bus Terminus
4 Cathedral
6 Fiaschetteria
7 Palazzo Comunale
    (Town Hall)
8 Pro Loco Tourist Office
9 Museo Civico e Diocesano
    d'Arte Sacra
10 Chiesa di Sant'Agostino
11 Bar Circolo Arci
15 Fortezza
16 Enoteca

CENTRAL TUSCANY

Giovanni di Paolo, Bartolo di Fredi and Sano di Pietro.

Several churches dot the town, but none are of especial interest. The **cathedral** in particular is a rather awful 19th-century neoclassical travesty of what was probably once a fine Romanesque church.

If you want to visit vineyards in the Montalcino area, start by getting a list of those generally open to visitors from the tourist office. Normally it's best to visit during the week and you may have to book. The office can also provide a full list of the 141 Brunello producers (many smaller ones have

little more than a hectare or two of land) and information on good and mediocre years.

Montalcino hosts a week of 'Jazz and Wine' in mid-July, which attracts both national and international acts. Ask the tourist office for more details.

Places to Stay The hotel front in Montalcino is limited, so try not to arrive at night when everything is taken. If you have no luck with the hotels get a list of affittacamere (10 in town) or agriturismo dotted around the countryside from the tourist office (they can make a booking for you).

Il Giardino (☎/fax 0577 84 82 57, Piazza Cavour 4) Singles/doubles €41.30/52. This is your cheapest option, and rests above an excellent restaurant (see Places to Eat later).

Hotel Il Giglio (☎/fax 0577 84 81 67, e hotelgiglio@tin.it, Via Soccorso Saloni 5) Singles/doubles €46.50/67.15. This place, with comfortable rooms, is probably the pick of the crop. The hotel also runs a nearby dependence where rooms are slightly cheaper.

Hotel dei Capitani (☎ 0577 84 72 27, fax 0577 84 72 39, e deicapitani@tin.it, Via Lapini 6) Singles/doubles €82.65/98.15. Another option in town, this hotel is also perfectly comfortable, if lacking a little atmosphere. It has a pool to splash around in.

Places to Eat There are several good options to try in town.

Ristorante Il Giardino (☎ 0577 84 90 76, Piazza Cavour 1) Mains €6.20-10.35. Open Thur-Tues. This restaurant, in the hotel of the same name, has a good selection of traditional dishes, including the *coniglio alla paesana* (rabbit prepared in a Brunello sauce).

Trattoria Sciame (☎ 0577 84 80 17, Via Ricasoli 9) Mains €5.15-9.30. Open Wed-Mon. This is an unassuming place where you can eat fairly straightforward but well-prepared meals at surprisingly low prices.

Osteria Porta al Cassero (☎ 0577 84 71 96, Via Ricasoli 29) Mains around €7.75. Open Thur-Tues. For home-made pasta at reasonable prices, you should make a beeline for this place.

Les Barriques (☎ 0577 84 84 11, Piazza del Popolo 20-22) Mains €5.15-12.90. This is a particularly attractive bar, where you can also dine.

Entertainment Several bars around town are perfectly good for trying out the local wines.

Enoteca (☎ 0577 84 92 11, Piazza Fortezza) Wine by the glass €2.60-6.20. Open 9am-8pm daily Apr-Oct, 9am-6pm Tues-Sun Nov-Mar. This place, in the Fortezza, is perfect for trying out one of countless varieties of Brunello, buying a bottle and/or climbing up onto the ramparts. They also organise tasting-evenings for €5.15 to €7.75 per person (bookings essential).

Bar Circolo Arci (Via Ricasoli 2) The courtyard of this popular bar is a perfect spot for wasting a few hours over a bottle of wine.

Fiaschetteria (☎ 0577 84 90 43, Piazza del Popolo 6) Open Fri-Wed. This is a fine old cafe where you can get yourself a glass of wine or pot of tea and read the paper.

Getting There & Away Montalcino is accessible from Siena by up to nine buses (€2.85) a day. Buses leave from Piazza Cavour for the return journey. By car, follow the SS2 south from Siena, and take the turnoff for Montalcino, about 8km after Buonconvento.

Abbazia di Sant'Antimo

It is best to visit this superb Romanesque church (☎ 0577 83 56 59, Castelnuovo dell' Abate; free; open 10.30am-12.30pm & 3pm-6.30pm Mon-Sat, 9am-10.30pm & 3pm-6pm Sun & hols) in the morning, when the sun shines through the east windows to create an almost surreal atmosphere. At night, it is lit up impressively and shines like a beacon into the darkness. Actually, it's an arresting sight any time of the day or night. Set in a broad valley, just below the village of **Castelnuovo dell' Abate**, the 12th-century church in pale travertine stone is notable for its simplicity and unusual grandeur – the style is clearly influenced by northern European versions of Romanesque, especially that of the Cistercians.

It's thought Charlemagne founded the original monastery here in 781. In subsequent centuries the Benedictine monks became among the most powerful feudal landlords in southern Tuscany, until they came into conflict with Siena in the 13th century, when the monastery went into decline. Until the mid-1990s, the church and abbey lay pretty much abandoned. Then seven monks moved in at the local bishop's wish. They have supervised restoration work and hold daily prayers (7pm) and Masses in the church, which anyone is welcome to attend. This is a worthwhile exercise as the monks sing Gregorian chants. If you can't make any of the services, they have some CDs on sale in the church.

Among the decorative features note the stone carvings of the bell tower and the apse windows, which include a *Madonna col Bambino* and the various fantastic animals typical of the Romanesque style. Inside, take the time to study the capitals of the columns lining the nave, including one representing Daniel in the lion's den (second on the right as you enter).

If you're lucky the attendant may let you into the **sacristy**, where there are monochrome frescoes depicting the life of St Benedict. They probably date to the 15th century. The 11th-century crypt beneath the chapel is closed to the public, but you can get a murky glimpse of it through the small round window at the base of the exterior of the chapel's apse.

Concerts are sometimes held here as part of Siena's Estate Musicale Chigiana (see Special Events under Siena earlier in the chapter).

Osteria Bassomondo (☎ 0577 83 56 19, Via Bassomondo 7) Full meals around €18. Open Tues-Sun. If you're planning a visit to Sant'Antimo, stop for lunch at this place, which is less than 1km away at Castelnuovo dell'Abate.

Three buses a day run from Montalcino (€1) to Castelnuovo dell'Abate, from where you can walk to the church.

If you have your own transport, you may want to consider an alternative lunch or dinner excursion west along a dirt road to **Sant'Angelo in Colle**. The views from the little settlement are wonderful. Those without a car can get here by bus (three or four times a day Monday to Saturday; nothing on Sunday) from Montalcino.

Trattoria Il Pozzo (☎ 0577 84 40 15) Full meal from €15.50. Open Wed-Mon. You can eat excellent home-cooked food at this place in the middle of the village, just off the square.

San Quirico d'Orcia

This fortified medieval town on the Via Cassia (SS2) is well worth a stopover. Its Romanesque **Collegiata**, dating from the 12th century, is notable for its unusual three

doorways, decorated with extraordinary stone carvings. Inside is a triptych by Sano di Pietro. Wander through the **Horti Leononi**, a lovely Italian Renaissance garden at the other end of town. This is a pleasant little town and doesn't make a bad base for exploring the area, sitting just off the highway and at a crossroads between Montalcino and Pienza.

Places to Stay & Eat Several possibilities present themselves here.

Agriturismo Aiole (☎ 0577 88 74 54, Strada Provinciale 22 della Grossola) B&B €41.30. If you're interested in some seclusion, try this place about 8km south-east of Sant'Antimo. It's very comfortable and has a pool. You must book ahead.

Affittacamere L'Orcia (☎ 0577 89 76 77, Via Dante Alighieri 49) Singles/doubles with bathroom €25.80/41.30. Right in the centre of town, this is a fine little affittacamere with immaculately kept rooms.

Trattoria Al Vecchio Forno (☎ 0577 89 73 80, Via Piazzola 8) Full meals around €28.40. Open Thur-Tues. You will eat well indeed at this place, a few steps away from Via Dante Alighieri. Local dishes such as *Il pollo al Brunello* (chicken cooked in Brunello wine) are particularly good.

Getting There & Away San Quirico is accessible by bus from Siena (€2.85), Buonconvento, Pienza and Montepulciano.

Bagno Vignoni

About 5km from San Quirico along the SS2 towards Rome, this tiny spa town dates back to Roman times. The hot sulphurous water bubbles up into a picturesque pool, built by the Medici in the town's main square. Some 36 springs cook at up to 51°C and collect in the pool, although in winter the water is considerably cooler.

Unfortunately you are not allowed to bathe in the pool, but it is such a picturesque sight that it merits a quick stop regardless. If you do wish to take the waters you can go to the open-air Piscina del Sole at the **Hotel Posta Marcucci** (☎ 0577 88 71 12, fax 0577 88 71 19, Via Ara Urcea 43a; day ticket May-Sept/Oct-Apr €10.35/9.30, afternoon *session €7.25/6.20; open 9am-1pm & 2.30pm-6pm).*

Hotel Le Terme *(☎ 0577 88 71 50, fax 0577 88 74 97, ⓦ www.albergoleterme.it – Italian only)* Singles/doubles from €41.30/ 72.30. If you want to stay, this is the cheapest hotel. Ask for rooms at the front, with views of the pool.

Osteria del Leone *(☎ 0577 88 73 00, Piazza del Moretto 28)* Meals around €25.80. Just back a block from the pool, this is a fine choice for a lunch or dinner, whether you choose to stay or not. In a pleasantly lit rustic building with a heavy-beamed ceiling, you can eat solid Tuscan country fare, such as *faraona al vinsanto* (pheasant cooked in sweet white wine).

Buses serving the Siena-Grosseto route call in here.

Bagni San Filippo

While on the subject of baths, those who prefer not to pay for their hot-water frolics could press on about 15km south along the SS2 highway to Bagni San Filippo (which lies a couple of kilometres west of the SS2). Most Siena-Grosseto buses call in here too. A park is signposted off the village's only

road, just a little uphill from the hotel and paying baths. A short stroll down the lane brings you to a set of hot little tumbling cascades where you can plant yourself for a relaxing soak. It is best in winter, which is off-season for the hotel and is when the water pressure is greatest.

Pienza

postcode 53026 • pop 2400

A superb example of Renaissance architecture, this town was designed and built in the mid-15th century by the Florentine architect Bernardo Rossellino on the orders of Pope Pius II, Aeneas Silvius Piccolomini, who was born there in 1405. The pope even had the town's name changed from Corsignano. The town had been a modest medieval village since the 8th century, but was transformed by the pope's projects. Inspired in part by Leon Battista Alberti, who was busy elaborating a whole philosophy of the ideal city, Pius II entrusted Rossellino with the experimental project.

Information The tourist information office (☎/fax 0578 74 90 71) is in the Palazzo Pubblico, on the town's main square, Piazza

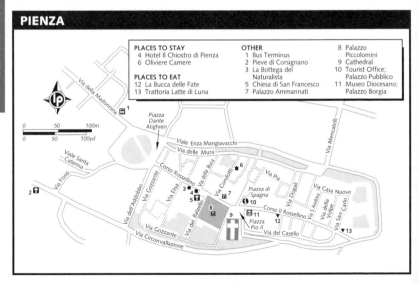

PIENZA

PLACES TO STAY
4 Hotel Il Chiostro di Pienza
6 Oliviere Camere

PLACES TO EAT
12 La Bucca delle Fate
13 Trattoria Latte di Luna

OTHER
1 Bus Terminus
2 Pieve di Corsignano
3 La Bottega del Naturalista
5 Chiesa di San Francesco
7 Palazzo Ammannati
8 Palazzo Piccolomini
9 Cathedral
10 Tourist Office; Palazzo Pubblico
11 Museo Diocesano; Palazzo Borgia

Pio II. It opens 9.30am to 1pm and 3pm to 6.30pm daily. You can pick up an audio guide of the town here for €5.15, which lasts 50 minutes.

Things to See The most important buildings are grouped around Piazza Pio II, a short walk from the town's entrance along Corso Rossellino. The square was designed by Rossellino, who left nothing to chance. The available space was limited, so to increase the sense of perspective and dignity of the great edifices that would grace the square, Rossellino set the Palazzo Borgia and Palazzo Piccolomini off at angles to the cathedral.

The **cathedral** *(Piazza Pio II; free; open 7am-1pm & 2pm-6pm)* was built on the site of the Romanesque Chiesa di Santa Maria, of which little remains. The Renaissance facade, in travertine stone, is of clear Albertian inspiration.

The interior of the building is itself a strange mix of Gothic and Renaissance, and contains a collection of five altarpieces painted by Sienese artists of the period, as well as a superb marble tabernacle by Rossellino.

Perhaps the most bizarre aspect of the building is the state of collapse of the transept and apse. Built on dodgy ground, the top end of the church seems to be breaking off. The huge cracks in the wall and floor are matched by the crazy downward slant of this part of the church floor. Various attempts to prop it all up have failed to solve the problem, as is quite clear from the major cracking in the walls and floor.

The **Palazzo Piccolomini** *(☎ 0578 74 85 03, Piazza Pio II; adult/child (with guide only) €3.10/2; open 10am-12.30pm & 3pm-6pm Tues-Sun)*, to your right as you face the cathedral, was the pope's residence and is considered Rossellino's masterpiece. Built on the site of former Piccolomini family houses, the building demonstrates some indebtedness on Rossellino's part to Alberti, whose Palazzo Rucellai in Florence it appears in part to emulate.

Inside you enter a fine courtyard, from where stairs lead you up into the papal apartments, now filled with an assortment of period furnishings, minor art and the like. To the rear, a three-level loggia facing out over the countryside afforded Pius II and his guests splendid views.

To the left of the cathedral is the **Palazzo Borgia**, built by Cardinal Borgia, later Pope Alexander VI. The building is now more commonly known as the Palazzo Vescovile and contains the **Museo Diocesano** *(☎ 0578 74 99 05, Corso Il Rossellino 30; adult/child €4.15/2.60; open 10am-1pm & 3pm-6.30pm Wed-Mon mid-Mar–Oct, Sat & Sun only Nov–mid-Mar)*. The museum contains an intriguing miscellany of art works, illuminated manuscripts, tapestries and miniatures.

Make time to visit the Romanesque **Pieve di Corsignano**, half a kilometre out of town along Via Fonti from Piazza Dante Alighieri. This church dates from the 10th century and boasts a strange circular bell tower. Ask at the tourist office in town where you can get hold of the key.

Places to Stay & Eat There are a couple of good places to stay overnight here and others to sample something delicious.

Oliviere Camere *(☎ 0578 74 82 74, Via Condotti 4)* Rooms €31/46.50. This place is a good option in town. The rooms are modern and attractive, if a little small.

Albergo Il Chiostro di Pienza *(☎ 0578 74 84 00, fax 0578 74 84 40, Corso Rossellino 26)* Singles/doubles up to €103/155. If you want a bit of luxury try this hotel, in the former convent and cloister of the adjacent Chiesa di San Francesco.

La Bucca delle Fate *(☎ 0578 74 84 48, Corso Il Rossellino 38)* Mains €5.15-7.25. Open Tues-Sun. This rather large establishment has a simple menu but everything on it is a joy to the taste buds.

Trattoria Latte di Luna *(☎ 0578 74 86 06, Via San Carlo 6)* Mains €6.20-12.90. Open Wed-Mon. This restaurant, on a kind of squarette where the street splits off from Corso Rossellino, is a charming little spot to eat outside. Try the *anatra arrosto alle olive* (roast duck with olives).

La Bottega del Naturalista *(☎ 0578 74 80 81, Corso Rossellino 16)* Pienza is renowned

CENTRAL TUSCANY

as a centre for that ever-so-Tuscan cheese, *pecorino*. If you want to get an idea of all the varieties available (from fresh to well-aged and smelly, from the classic pecorino to ones lightly infused with peppers or truffles), pop into this shop. They have a truly mouth-watering choice of cheeses (if you can stand the smell), but you should possibly use it as a learning experience and do your actual shopping elsewhere, as the products are all a little expensive.

Getting There & Away Up to five buses run on weekdays from Siena to Pienza (€3.05, 1¼ hours). You can also make connections to San Quirico d'Orcia and Montepulciano. The buses stop just a short way off Piazza Dante Alighieri.

Montepulciano
postcode 53045 • pop 14,000
Set atop a narrow ridge of volcanic rock, Montepulciano combines Tuscany's superb countryside with some of the region's finest wines. This medieval town is the perfect place to spend a few quiet days. Be sure to stop by the various enoteche to sample the local wines.

A late Etruscan castrum was the first in a series of settlements here. During the Middle Ages it was a constant bone of contention between Florence and Siena, until in 1404 the city finally passed under the permanent jurisdiction of the former. And so the Marzocco, or lion of Florence, came to replace the she-wolf of Siena as the city's symbol, on a column just off Piazza Savonarola. The new administration brought a new wind of construction taste as Michelozzo, Sangallo il Vecchio and others were invited in to do some innovative spring cleaning, lending this Gothic stronghold a fresh wind of Renaissance vigour. That mix alone makes the town an intriguing place for a stopover.

Orientation & Information However you arrive, you will probably end up at the Porta al Prato (also known as the Porta al Bacco) on the town's northern edge. From here, buses take you through the town to Piazza Grande. Alternatively, the 15-minute walk is mostly uphill but well worth the effort.

The Pro Loco tourist office (☎ 0578 75 73 41), at Via di Gracciano nel Corso 59a, is next door to the Chiesa di Sant'Agostino at the lower end of town. It opens 9am to 12.30pm and 3pm to 8pm Monday to Saturday (to 6pm October to March), and mornings only on Sunday and holidays.

The Strada del Vino Nobile di Montepulciano information office (☎ 0578 71 74 84), at Piazza Grande 7, has everything you need to know about the local drop. They also organise wine tours, which cost €18.10 per person.

The post office is at Via dell' Erbe 12 and you'll find a couple of banks with ATMs scattered about the town. A reliable one is the Banca Nazionale di Lavoro at Piazza Savonarola 14.

The *polizia municipale* (police station; ☎ 0578 75 74 52) is in the Palazzo Comunale.

Things to See & Do Most of the main sights are clustered around Piazza Grande, although the town's streets boast a wealth of palazzi and other fine buildings.

On the assumption you arrive by bus or park your car near Porta al Prato, you'll see the bee-like banding that is the facade of the Chiesa di Sant'Agnese. The original church was built in the early 14th century, but this version was the result of a remake by Antonio da Sangallo il Vecchio in 1511. He may also have restructured the medieval gate leading into the city proper, the Porta al Prato.

To the left shortly after you enter the gate, you'll see the 18th-century Chiesa di San Bernardo. Nearby is the late-Renaissance Palazzo Avignonesi by Giacomo da Vignola. Several other mansions line Via di Gracciano nel Corso, including the Palazzo di Bucelli at No 73, whose facade features Etruscan and Latin inscriptions. Sangallo also designed Palazzo Cocconi at No 70.

Piazza Michelozzo is dominated by the striking Renaissance facade of Michelozzo's Chiesa di Sant'Agostino. Directly in front is a medieval tower-house, Torre di Pulcinella, topped by the town clock and the bizarre figure Pulcinella (Punch of Punch & Judy fame), who strikes the hours.

Continue up the hill and take the first left past the **Loggia di Mercato** for Via del Poggiolo, which eventually becomes Via Ricci. In the Renaissance **Palazzo Ricci** is one of the town's wine *cantine* (wine cellars), the Cantina Redi. The town's **Museo Civico** (☎ 0578 71 73 00, Via Ricci 10; adult/child €4.15/2.60; open 10am-7pm Tues-Sun in summer, 10am-1pm & 3pm-6pm Tues-Sun in winter) is opposite in the Gothic Palazzo Neri-Orselli. The small collection features terracotta reliefs by the della Robbia family and some Gothic and Renaissance paintings.

Piazza Grande marks the highest point of the town and features the austere **Palazzo Comunale** (☎ 0578 75 74 52, Piazza Grande 1; free; open 9am-1.30pm Mon-Sat), a 13th-century Gothic building remodelled in the 15th century by Michelozzo (the comparison with the Palazzo Vecchio in Florence, in form if not in colour, is hard to avoid). From the top of the 14th-century tower, on a clear day, you can see the Monti Sibillini to the east and, they say, Siena to the north-west.

The other palaces in the piazza are the **Palazzo Contucci**, now a wine cellar, and the **Palazzo Tarugi**, attributed to Giacomo da Vignola, near the fountain. The **cathedral** (Piazza Grande; free; open 9.30am-1pm & 3pm-7pm), whose facade is noticeable by its absence, dates from the 16th century. Inside there is a lovely triptych above the high altar, depicting the Assumption, by Taddeo da Bartolo.

If from Piazza Michelozzi you were to take the low road and follow Via di Voltaia nel Corso, you would pass first, on your left, the Renaissance **Palazzo Cervini**, built for Cardinal Marcello Cervini, the future Pope Marcellus II. The unusual – most palazzi have austere, straight fronts – U-shape at the front, including a courtyard into the facade design, appears to have been another Sangallo creation. A few blocks farther along you reach, again on the left, the **Chiesa del Gesù**, an elaborate Baroque job.

Outside the town wall, about 1km from the Porta della Grassa, stands the **Chiesa di**

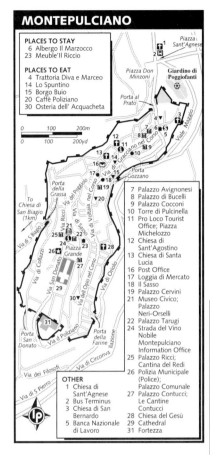

MONTEPULCIANO

PLACES TO STAY
6 Albergo Il Marzocco
23 Meuble'Il Riccio

PLACES TO EAT
4 Trattoria Diva e Marceo
14 Lo Spuntino
15 Borgo Buio
20 Caffè Poliziano
30 Osteria dell' Acquacheta

7 Palazzo Avignonesi
8 Palazzo di Bucelli
9 Palazzo Cocconi
10 Torre di Pulcinella
11 Pro Loco Tourist Office; Piazza Michelozzo
12 Chiesa di Sant'Agostino
13 Chiesa di Santa Lucia
16 Post Office
17 Loggia di Mercato
18 Il Sasso
19 Palazzo Cervini
21 Museo Civico; Palazzo Neri-Orselli
22 Palazzo Tarugi
24 Strada del Vino Nobile Montepulciano Information Office
25 Palazzo Ricci; Cantina del Redi
26 Polizia Municipale (Police); Palazzo Comunale
27 Palazzo Contucci; Le Cantine Contucci
28 Chiesa del Gesù
29 Cathedral
31 Fortezza

OTHER
1 Chiesa di Sant'Agnese
2 Bus Terminus
3 Chiesa di San Bernardo
5 Banca Nazionale di Lavoro

San Biagio, a fine Renaissance church built by (yet again) Antonio da Sangallo il Vecchio and consecrated in 1529 by the Medici Pope Clement VII.

Bravio delle Botti takes place on the last Sunday in August, when the streets are given over to barrel races.

Courses *Il Sasso* (☎ 0578 75 83 11, fax 0578 75 75 47, Via di Gracciano nel Corso 2) can organise language courses for you. One-hour lessons cost from €26; four hours a day for two weeks costs €310. The same place can also organise mosaic- and gold-jewellery-making classes. By happy coincidence, the organisation doubles as an estate agency specialising in the rental of apartments, villas and the like to foreigners.

Places to Stay You might consider visiting Montepulciano on a day trip when you discover the hotel prices. Several affittacamere are scattered about town. Get a list of them from the tourist office and expect to pay anything up to €77.45 for a double.

Meuble'll Riccio (☎/fax 0578 75 77 13, Via Talosa 21) Singles/doubles €56.80/77.50. This place has a lot going for it. Along with your spacious room, you can enjoy a rooftop terrace with fantastic views, and enjoy a glass of vino on the bar's balcony. Breakfast is included.

Albergo Il Marzocco (☎ 0578 75 72 62, fax 0578 75 75 30, Piazza Savonarola 18) Singles/doubles from €62/87.80. The rooms at this 16th-century building are large and comfortable; be sure to ask for one with terrace and views (no extra cost).

Places to Eat There are numerous places to sample Tuscan food and wine in Montepulciano.

Lo Spuntino (☎ 0578 75 77 68, Via Gracciano nel Corso 25) Pizza slices €0.90-1.50. Open Wed-Mon. You can buy filling pizza slices here.

Osteria dell' Acquacheta (☎ 0578 75 84 43, Via del Teatro 22) Mains around €6.20-7.75. Open Wed-Mon. This small eatery has the look and feel of a country trattoria. The food is excellent, and ranges from huge steaks to *zucchine con tonne* (tuna-stuffed courgettes).

Trattoria Diva e Marceo (☎ 0578 71 65 91, Via di Gracciano nel Corso 92) Mains up to €10. Open Wed-Mon. You can feast on Tuscan cuisine in simple surroundings at this place.

Borgo Buio (☎ 0578 71 74 97, Via Borgo Buio 10) Mains €7.75-12.90. Open Fri-Wed. This is a rustic, low-lit sort of a place where you can enjoy good Tuscan meals at reasonable prices. In addition, it functions as an enoteca (you can tipple from 10.30am to midnight) with a good selection of wines.

Other places to get your palate wet on the local red, Vino Nobile, include the several long-established cantinas around town.

Cantina del Redi (Via Ricci 13) Open 10.30am-1pm & 3pm-7pm Apr-Sept. This place doubles as a wine cellar, which you can wander around at will. It's downhill from Piazza Grande along Via Ricci.

Le Cantine Contucci (☎ 0578 75 70 06, Palazzo Contucci, Piazza Grande) This is another active wine cellar where you can sample a drop of the local wine.

Caffè Poliziano (☎ 0578 75 86 15, Via di Voltaia nel Corso 27) Mains €6.20-7.75. If you just want a good old-fashioned coffee, this is a fine place to procure one. The views are magnificent and the interior a pleasure. You can also eat here should the fancy take you.

Getting There & Around Tra-in operates five bus services daily between Montepulciano and Siena (€4.15; 1½ hours), via Pienza. Regular LFI buses connect with Chiusi (€1.90, 50 minutes, half hourly). One direct LFI bus goes to Siena (at 6.25am), while two travel to Florence. Two buses make the run to Arezzo (change at Bettolle). It is possible to pick up the occasional bus to Rome here too. Buses leave from Piazza Sant'Agnese, outside the Porta al Prato at the northern end of town.

The most convenient train station is at Chiusi-Chianciano Terme, 10km south-east, on the main Rome-Florence line. Buses for Montepulciano (€1.95) meet each train, so it's the best route from Florence or Rome. Stazione di Montepulciano, about 5km to the north-east, has less frequent local services.

By car, if you are not coming from Pienza, take the Chianciano Terme exit off the A1 and follow the SS166 for the 18km trip to Montepulciano.

Most cars are banned from the town centre and there are car parks near the Porta al Prato. Small town buses weave their way from here to Piazza Grande (€0.70).

Chianciano Terme

This place is a short trip south from Montepulciano by bus or car, but you could skip

Chianciano Terme unless you think a local spa-water treatment for your liver is in order. The town is blessed with a small conical medieval core, which seems to recoil at all the surrounding development. Given its proximity to Montepulciano, it does make an alternative accommodation possibility if you really can't find a thing in Montepulciano. Some 200 hotels cater to spa guests, so finding a room shouldn't be that difficult.

Chiusi
postcode 53043 • pop 9000
One of the most important of the 12 cities of the Etruscan League, Chiusi was once powerful enough to attack Rome, under the leadership of the Etruscan king Porsenna. These days it is a fairly sleepy country town, but is highly recommended as a stopover. There is a Pro Loco information office (☎ 0578 22 76 67) at Via Porsenna 67, on the corner of the main square. It opens 9.30am to 12.30pm daily (plus 3.30pm to 6.30pm in summer).

Things to See Chiusi's main attractions are the **Etruscan tombs** that dot the countryside around the town. Chiusi is noted as having the most painted tombs after Tarquinia (Lazio) – unfortunately, almost all are in a serious state of disrepair and are closed to the public. Visits to the three accessible tombs, Tomba della Scimmia (by far the best), Tomba del Colle Casuccini and Tomba del Leone, are with a guide only, and leave from the **Museo Archeologico Nazionale** *(☎ 0578 2 01 77, Via Porsenna 93; admission €4.15 including tomb guided tour; open 9am-8pm)*. Tours leave at 11am, noon, 4pm and 5pm Tuesday, Thursday and Saturday. Reservations are essential. The museum itself has a reasonably interesting collection of artefacts found in the local tombs.

Also take a look at the Romanesque **cathedral** and the adjacent **Museo della Cattedrale** *(☎ 0578 22 64 90, Piazza Duomo; adult/child €1.55/free; open 9.30am-12.45pm & 4.30pm-7pm Jun–mid-Oct; 9.30am-12.45pm Mon-Sat, 9.30am-12.45pm & 4.30pm-7pm Sun & hols mid-Oct–May)*, which has an important collection of 22 illustrated antiphonals (psalm books).

The **Labirinto di Porsenna** is a series of tunnels underneath the Piazza del Duomo which date back to Etruscan times and formed part of the town's water-supply system. Since ancient times, legend has associated the labyrinth with the Etruscan king Porsenna – it supposedly hid his grand tomb. A section of the labyrinth was excavated in the 1980s and can be visited with a guide (€2.60). Tickets can be bought at the Museo della Cattedrale.

It's also possible to visit a number of Christian **catacombs** *(€3.10; guided tours 11am & 5pm Jun–mid-Oct; 11am Mon-Sat, 11am & 4pm Sun mid-Oct–May)* 2km from Chiusi. Tours leave from the Museo della Cattedrale, where you buy your ticket.

Places to Stay & Eat There are several agriturismo establishments in the countryside near Chiusi; contact the Pro Loco office for details.

Albergo La Sfinge (☎/fax 0578 2 01 57, W *www.albergolasfinge.com, Via Marconi 2)* Singles/doubles with bathroom €36.15/52. Just within the confines of Chiusi's historical centre, this hotel has large rooms, some with views. Rooms with air-con cost a little more.

La Solita Zuppa (☎ 0578 2 10 06, Via Porsenna 21) Meals with wine around €25.80. Open Wed-Mon. This is arguably one of the better places to eat in Tuscany. The menu is heavily Tuscan based and sports a wide range of soup options, which is the restaurant's forte. The food is wholesome and cooked to perfection, and the owners make you feel like a long-lost friend.

Getting There & Away Chiusi is easily accessible by public transport. Its train station, in the valley below the town, is on the main Rome-Florence line. The town is just off the Autostrada del Sole (A1).

Sarteano & Cetona
Heading into this part of the province, you definitely feel you have left the last of the tour buses well and truly behind you. This quiet rural territory is best explored with your own wheels. Both Sarteano and Cetona are curious little medieval settlements,

the former topped by a brooding castle. No specific outstanding sights present themselves, but they are both fun to wander around for a little while. At the camp site at Via Campo dei Fiori 30 in Sarteano, you can luxuriate in the warm waters of the Piscina Bagno Santo. Near Cetona is the modest mountain of the same name, which invites some vigorous meanderings in the clean country air.

Frateria di San Francesco (☎ 0578 23 82 61, fax 0578 23 92 20, e *frateria@ftbcc.it, Via di San Francesco)* Doubles €196.25-258. Restaurant open Wed-Mon, meals €82.65 excluding wine; closed Jan-Feb. Those with wads of money and a desire for a special retreat might like to consider staying or eating at this place. A couple of kilometres along a side road (which leads up to Monte Cetona) outside the northern entrance to Cetona, this former convent has been lovingly restored and converted into a top-class restaurant with seven rooms added. You can expect a five-course dining experience of world-class standing. Look for the Mondo X signs when driving up.

Up to five buses a day (Monday to Saturday) head down to both towns from Montepulciano (some involve a change at Chianciano Terme).

Abbadia San Salvatore & Around

On your travels in this part of Tuscany you'd have to be rather shortsighted not to notice the village of **Radicofani**, or more precisely, its **Rocca** *(☎ 0578 5 57 00; admission €2.60; open 9.30am-4pm Tues-Sun Jun-Mar).* Built high on a basalt hill, it's an impressive sight from any approach, and the views from its ramparts are stunning. It now houses a small museum devoted to the Medieval Age. Radicofani itself is a pleasant village worth a stroll, and is 17km south-west of Sarteano on the SS478.

Eighteen kilometres farther west is Abbadia San Salvatore, a largely rather ugly mining town that grew rapidly and tastelessly

from the late 19th century. It does have a couple of saving graces however. The old town, a sombre stone affair entered off the main Piazzale XX Settembre, is curious enough although perhaps not really worth an excursion on its own. A small APT office (☎ 0577 77 58 11) operates from Via Adua 25. It opens 9am to 1pm and 4pm to 7pm daily (closed on Sunday, September to June).

The **Abbazia di San Salvatore** *(☎ 0577 77 80 83, Piazzale Michelangelo 8; free; open 7am-6pm Mon-Sat, 10.30am-6pm Sun summer, 7am-5pm Mon-Sat, 10.30am-5pm Sun winter)* was founded in 743 by the Lombard Erfo. It eventually passed into the hands of Cistercian monks, who still occupy it today. Of the monastery little remains, but the church is extremely interesting (for people into churches and architecture, at any rate). Built in the 11th century and Romanesque in style, it was reconstructed in a curious manner in the late 16th century, when the whole area from the transept to the apse was raised and adorned with broad, frescoed arches. Best of all, however, is the Lombard crypt, a remarkable stone forest of 36 columns. No-one is sure what purpose this hall served.

The town lies in the shadow of **Monte Amiata** (1738m) and serves as a base for local holidaymakers getting in a little skiing on one run on the peak (snow permitting) in winter or some walking in summer. You can, for instance, walk right around the mountain following a 30km trail known as the Anello della Montagna. The path is signposted and maps are available from the tourist office (these also cover walks in the surrounding area). For this reason there are plenty of hotels in Abbadia San Salvatore and several others in towns dotted about the broad expanse of the mountain, so you should not have too much trouble finding a place to sleep should the need arise.

A handful of RAMA buses running between Grosseto and Bagni San Filippo call in at Abbadia San Salvatore (€4.15, 2 hours 20 minutes). It is also possible to get down from Siena (€4.15, 1¾ hours, two daily).

Eastern Tuscany

An easy train ride from Florence puts the capital of this region, Arezzo, within tempting reach even of many fleeting tourists in Tuscany, but relatively few get beyond this former Etruscan city. The old centre, dominated by one of the most inspiring examples of Tuscan Romanesque construction, certainly makes the trip worth every euro, even if much of the rest of the town is a little scrappy. The only other seriously sought-out destination is Cortona, the spectacularly located hilltop eyrie that looks out over the surrounding Tuscan and Umbrian plains.

Art lovers will no doubt be attracted by what could be called the Piero della Francesca trail. Starting with his fresco cycles in Arezzo itself, you can head out into the country in search of other of his masterpieces in towns such as Monterchi and Sansepolcro.

Beyond the towns, one of the least visited corners of Tuscany is the forests and hill country of the Casentino farther east en route for the Apennine frontier with the region of Emilia-Romagna.

AREZZO
postcode 52100 • pop 91,700

Heavily bombed during WWII, Arezzo is not the prettiest city in Tuscany. That said, the small medieval centre retains some inspiring highlights. The sloping Piazza Grande and the Romanesque jewel that is the Pieve di Santa Maria are less known perhaps than the fresco cycle by Piero della Francesca in the Chiesa di San Francesco. In all, though, it is well worth a visit, easily accomplished as a day trip from Florence.

An important Etruscan town, Arezzo was later absorbed into the Roman Empire, remaining an important and flourishing centre. It became a free republic from the 10th century and supported the Ghibelline cause in the awful battles between pope and emperor. Arezzo was eventually subjugated by Guelph Florence in 1384, when Florence effectively bought the place. Conquering should be achieved like that more often.

Highlights

- Follow the Piero della Francesca trail from Arezzo to Sansepolcro
- Take a load off your feet and enjoy a drink on Arezzo's Piazza Grande while you admire the Romanesque Pieve di Santa Maria
- Turn up for the monthly antiques market in Arezzo
- Embark on a back road journey through the little-visited Casentino region
- Walk in the footsteps of St Francis of Assisi at the Santuario di San Francesco
- Wander the steep medieval streets of Cortona and soak up the splendid views across the Tuscan and Umbrian countryside

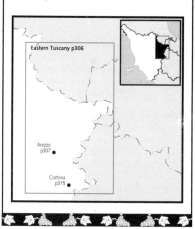

Eastern Tuscany p306

Arezzo p307

Cortona p315

Sons of whom Arezzo can be justly proud include the poet Petrarch, the writer Pietro Aretino, the artist Vasari, most famous for his book *Lives of the Artists*, and comic actor and producer Roberto Benigni, who created and starred in the Oscar-winning *Life is Beautiful*.

A renowned antiques fair is held in Piazza Grande and the surrounding streets on the

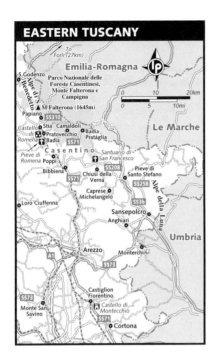

EASTERN TUSCANY

To Forlì (27km)
Emilia-Romagna
S.Godenzo
Parco Nazionale delle
Foreste Casentinesi,
Monte Falterona e
Campigna
Monte Falterona (1645m)
Papiano
SS310
Castello
di
Romena
Stia Camaldoli
Pratovecchio
Badia
Prátaglia
Badia
SS71
Le Marche
Pieve di
Romena
Poppi
Casentino
Santuario di
San Francesco
Bibbiena
SS71
Chiusi della
Verna
SS208
Pieve di
Santo Stefano
SS258
Caprese
Michelangelo
Loro Ciuffenna
Sansepolcro
Anghiari
SS3b
Umbria
Arezzo
Monterchi
A1
SS73
Castiglion
Fiorentino
SS573
Monte San
Savino
Castello di
Montecchio
SS71
Cortona

first Sunday of every month, which means accommodation can be difficult to find unless you book well ahead.

Orientation & Information

From the train station on the southern edge of the walled city, walk north-eastwards along Via Guido Monaco to the garden piazza of the same name. The old city is to the north-east and the modern part to the south-east along Via Roma.

The APT office (☎ 0575 37 76 78), near the train station at Piazza della Repubblica 28, opens 9am to 1pm and 3pm to 7pm Monday to Saturday, and 9am to 1pm on Sunday, April to October, and to 6.30pm (Monday to Saturday) November to March. The post office is at Via Guido Monaco 34.

The Nuovo Ospedale San Donato (hospital; ☎ 0575 30 51) is located west of the train tracks on Via Paolo Toscanelli. The *questura* (police station; ☎ 0575 31 81) is at Via Fra Guittone 3.

Chiesa di San Francesco

The apse of this 14th-century Gothic **church** (☎ 0575 35 27 27, Piazza San Francesco; free; open 8.30am-noon & 2.30pm-6.30pm) houses one of the greatest works of Italian art, Piero della Francesca's fresco cycle of the *Leggenda della Vera Croce* (Legend of the True Cross). This masterpiece, painted between 1452 and 1456, relates in 10 episodes the story of Christ's death, and its restoration has recently finished (after 15 years' work).

This Renaissance 'cartoon strip' brings an uncommonly human element to the medieval tale, which involves characters from the Old and New Testaments. The illustration starts in the top right-hand corner with Adam announcing his death to his son Seth, and follows the story of the tree Seth plants on Adam's grave from which, eventually, the cross on which Christ is crucified is made.

The chapel of the cross is cordoned off so if you need to get up-close-and-personal you need to purchase a ticket, which costs €5.15. Viewing times are 9am to 7pm Monday to Friday, 9am to 6pm on Saturday and 1pm to 6pm on Sunday. A half-hour audioguide tour is included in the price. The ticket office is right (west) of the main entrance to the church. Otherwise simply take a pew and view from afar. The rest of the church is richly decorated in frescoes by lesser mortals.

Pieve di Santa Maria

This 12th-century **church** (☎ 0575 2 26 29, Corso Italia; free; open 8am-12.30pm & 3pm-6.30pm) has a magnificent Romanesque arcaded facade reminiscent of the cathedral at Pisa (but without the glorious marble facing). Each column is of a different design. Over the central doorway are carved reliefs representing the months. The 14th-century bell tower, with its 40 windows, is something of an emblem for the city. The stark, monochrome interior of the church shows a Gothic influence, with the only colour coming from the polyptych by Pietro Lorenzetti on the raised sanctuary at the rear of the church.

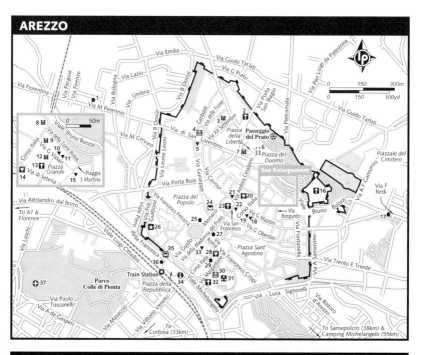

AREZZO

Piazza Grande & Around

This lumpy sloping piazza, featured in Roberto Benigni's *Life is Beautiful*, is lined at its upper end by the porticoes of the **Palazzo delle Logge Vasariane**, completed in 1573. The **Palazzo della Fraternità dei Laici** on the western flank dates from 1375.

It was started in the Gothic style and finished after the onset of the Renaissance. The south-east flank of the square is lined by a huddle of medieval houses.

Via dei Pileati leads to **Casa di Petrarca**, the former home of the poet, which contains a small museum and the Accademia Petrarca.

Visits are by appointment and really only for serious Petrarch fans. Enquire at the tourist office for further details.

Cathedral & Around

At the top of the hill is the cathedral (☎ 0575 2 39 91, Via Ricasoli; free; open 7am-12.30pm & 3pm-6.30pm), started in the 13th century and not completed until the 15th century. The Gothic interior houses several artworks of note, the most important of which is easily the fresco of the *Maddalena* (Mary Magdalene) by Piero della Francesca. The church has a rather gaunt feel about it.

Virtually in front of the cathedral is the seat of the city's secular power, the **Palazzo dei Priori** on Piazza della Libertà. It retains relatively little of its original 14th-century grandeur. To the south-east of the cathedral, across the peaceful gardens of the **Passeggio del Prato** lies the hulk of the **Fortezza Medicea** (free; open 7am-8pm Apr-Oct, 7.30am-6pm Nov-Mar), built in 1538. The grand views of the town and surrounding countryside are best at sunset.

Chiesa di San Domenico & Around

It is worth the walk to the rather odd-looking Gothic Chiesa di San Domenico (☎ 0575 2 29 06, Piazza di San Domenico; free; open 9am-7pm) to see the crucifix painted by Cimabue (unveiled in January 2002 after restoration), which hangs above the main altar. Tickets to view the crucifix cost €4.15.

West of San Domenico, the **Casa di Vasari** (☎ 0575 40 90 40, Via XX Settembre 55; free; open 8.30am-7.30pm Mon-Sat, 8.30am-1pm Sun) was built and sumptuously decorated by the architect himself.

Farther west again, the **Museo Statale d'Arte Medioevale e Moderna** (☎ 0575 40 90 50, Via di San Lorentino 8; admission €4.15; open 8.30am-7.30pm Tues-Sun, 8.30am-11pm Sat July-Sept) houses works by local artists, including Luca Signorelli and Vasari, spanning the 13th to 18th centuries. A small sculpture gallery (mostly containing pieces from churches in the surrounding area) occupies the ground floor. The first floor is taken up with paintings from the 13th to 15th cen-

turies. There is also an extensive porcelain collection. Upstairs the art continues into the 19th century.

Museo Archeologico & Roman Amphitheatre

Not far from the train station, the **museum** (☎ 0575 2 08 82, Via Margaritone 10; admission €4.15; open 8.30am-7.30pm) is in a convent overlooking the remains of the Roman amphitheatre (anfiteatro Romano). It houses a healthy-sized collection of Etruscan and Roman artefacts, including locally produced ceramics, bronzeware and the like. The highlight is the *Cratere di Euphronios*, a striking ceramic vase dating from around 500BC.

Special Events

Over four or five days in late June/early July the town hosts Arezzo Wave (free), a music festival featuring named artists and bands from Italy and abroad and a range of new and emerging bands. Nick Cave and Living Colour were among the international artists at the 2001 festival.

JANE SMITH

Modern medieval knights parade the streets prior to Arezzo's Joust of the Saracen.

Good old medieval jousting fun happens on the second to last Sunday of June and again on the first Sunday of September. For the Giostro del Saracino (Joust of the Saracen), the four medieval quarters of the city present teams of knights, who aim to score as many points as they can by charging with their lances at an effigy of a Saracen warrior in Piazza Grande. The jousts are preceded by parades in period costume, accompanied by lots of trumpet blowing and general clamour.

The first Sunday of every month sees the centre of Arezzo converted into one of Tuscany's biggest antique fairs, which is well worth checking out.

Places to Stay

Villa Severi (☎ /fax 0575 29 90 47, Via F Redi 13) B&B up to €15.15. This non-HI youth hostel is in a wonderfully restored villa overlooking the countryside.

La Toscana (☎/fax 0575 2 16 92, Via M Perennio 56) Singles/doubles from €23.25/36.15. La Toscana has clean, comfortable rooms, and a small garden to relax in.

Astoria (☎ 0575 2 43 61, fax 0575 2 43 62, Via Guido Monaco 54) Singles/doubles from €28.40/43.90. The rooms here aren't particularly inspiring but the place is nice and central. It's best to try to get one of the rooms on the inner courtyard; they're a great deal quieter.

Cecco (☎ 0575 2 09 86, fax 0575 35 67 30, Corso Italia 215) Singles/doubles €25.80/36.15, with bathroom & TV €36.15/52. This Soviet-style edifice near the train station has soulless but clean rooms.

Cavaliere Palace Hotel (☎ 0575 2 68 36, fax 0575 2 19 25, Via della Madonna del Prato 83) Singles/doubles €82.60/124. This place is the top dog in town, but the adequate and accommodating rooms are nothing special. Breakfast is included.

Places to Eat

Piazza Sant'Agostino comes to life each Tuesday, Thursday and Saturday with the city's *produce market*.

Antica Trattoria da Guido (☎ 0575 2 37 60, Via della Madonna del Prato 85) Meals around €18. This unassuming place next to the Cavaliere Palace Hotel (see Places to Stay) is one of the best-value trattorias in town, with excellent, homely food.

La Buca di San Francesco (☎ 0575 2 32 71, Via San Francesco 1) Meals up to €31. Open Wed-noon Mon. This, near the eponymous church, is one of the city's better restaurants and is generally packed.

La Torre di Gnicche (☎ 0575 35 20 35, Piaggia San Martino 8) Mains around €5.15. Open Thur-Tues. Not far off the Piazza Grande is this fine old osteria, with fine outdoor seating and a superb wine selection. Try the *insalata di farro*, which is particularly good.

Trattoria Lancia dell'Oro (☎ 0575 2 10 33, Logge Vasariane 18/19) Mains €10.35-15.50. Open Tues-Sun. The food here is not quite as good, but the commanding position over Piazza Grande almost makes up for it.

Restorante Vasari (☎ 0575 2 19 45, Logge Vasariane) Mains €10.35-18.10. Open Mon-Sat. This place, a couple of doors up, is just as fine for either a meal or a relaxing drink.

A few places further downhill on Via G Mazzini will tickle your fancy.

Trattoria Il Saraceno (☎ 0575 2 76 44, Via G Mazzini 6) Mains €5.15-7.75. Open Thur-Tues. This place is recommended by locals for no-nonsense Tuscan food at moderate prices.

Osteria L'Agania (☎ 0575 2 53 81, Via G Mazzini 10) Mains €5.15-7.75. Open Tues-Sun. This is another reliable choice. The cooking is earthy and solid and much appreciated by locals, and the decor is bright and simple.

Afroteranga (☎ 0575 35 53 93, Via di San Lorentino 9-13) Mains €8.25-9.30. Open Thur-Tues. This is an overpriced 'African' restaurant where you can indulge in a range of dishes of more or less African origin. You can snack on things such as samosas (which are pretty good) instead of having a full meal. The food's main virtue is that it makes a change if, for whatever reason, you are a little tired of the local stuff.

Caffè dei Costanti (☎ 0575 2 16 60, Piazza di San Francesco 19) Drinks €1.80-9.30. Open Tues-Sun. This is one of Arezzo's finest cafes.

Entertainment

Crispi's Pub *(☎ 0575 2 28 73, Via Francesco Crispi 112)* For an evening tipple with a young crowd, try this place. It's not very pub-like but it's big and open.

Brocante *(Corso Italia 9).* For a more chilled-out evening, this bar, with its ambient music and relaxed staff, is a good bet.

Enoteca Vinodivino *(Via Andrea Cesalpino 10)* Open to midnight Tues-Sat. And if you're looking for something a little more refined, drop in here where you can try out a nice range of drinks. There is seating out the back and snacks are served.

Getting There & Away

Buses depart from and arrive at Piazza della Repubblica, serving Cortona (€2.30, one hour), Sansepolcro, Monterchi, Siena (€4.15, 1½ hours), San Giovanni Valdarno, Florence (€5.10, 2½ hours) and other local towns. The city is on the Florence (€4.45, 1½ hours) to Rome train line. Arezzo is a few kilometres east of the A1, and the SS73 heads east to Sansepolcro.

NORTH-EAST OF AREZZO

The art lovers' trail in search of masterpieces by Piero della Francesca leads away north-east of Arezzo to the towns of Monterchi and Sansepolcro, both easy day trips from Arezzo.

Monterchi & Anghiari

Visit **Monterchi** to see Piero della Francesca's fresco **Madonna del Parto** *(Pregnant Madonna; ☎ 0575 7 07 13, Via Reglia 1; adult/child €2.60/1.05; open 9am-1pm & 2pm-7pm Tues-Sun Apr-Sept, to 5pm Oct-Mar).* The *Pregnant Madonna* is considered one of the key works of 15th-century Italian art. It was removed from its original home in the local cemetery for restoration and is currently on display in a former primary school; there are no plans to move the fresco back to the cemetery in the near future. A second room in the schoolhouse contains information and displays on the restoration process of the fresco.

A few kilometres north of Monterchi along the way to Sansepolcro lies the still-compact preserved medieval centre of **Anghiari**, which is worth a brief stop-off just to meander along its narrow twisting lanes. A local bus occasionally runs the 17km north to **Caprese Michelangelo**, birthplace of the painter of the Sistine Chapel. The town's castle plays host to the **Museo Michelangelo** *(☎ 0575 79 37 76, Via Capoluogo 1; adult/child €2.10/1; open 9.30am-6.30pm Tues-Sun mid-June–Oct, 10am-5pm Nov–mid-June),* a rather lacklustre affair devoted to the great man and his works.

There are a couple of bargain-basement accommodation options in the area.

Camping Michelangelo *(☎ 0575 79 38 86, fax 0575 79 11 83)* €3.60 per person. Open Mar-Oct. This camp site, on the outskirts of Caprese Michelangelo, has plenty of tree-shade.

Ostello Michelangelo *(☎ 0575 79 20 92, fax 0575 79 39 94, Località Fragaiola)* Dorm beds €10.35, singles/doubles €15.15/25.80. Open May-Sept. This fairly basic non-HI youth hostel is about 3km west of Caprese Michelangelo.

Sansepolcro

Piero della Francesca (c.1420–92) was born in Sansepolcro. He left the town when he was quite young and returned when he was in his 70s to work on his treatises, which included *On Perspective in Painting.* Although most visitors give little thought to the town itself, Sansepolcro as it stands now dates largely to the 15th century, although it is thought possible that an earlier medieval settlement grew up where once there had been a Roman *castrum* (camp). Today it is a centre of light industry whose sprawl can hardly be said to enhance the upper Tiber valley countryside in which it is located. The town's heart is pleasant enough for a stroll, however.

The small tourist office (☎ 0575 74 05 36), at Piazza Garibaldi 2, can assist with some local information. Following the trail of della Francesca's work will take you to other towns in Tuscany and Le Marche, including Rimini, Urbino, Perugia and Florence.

In the former town hall, just outside the main city gate, is the **Museo Civico** *(☎ 05 75 73 22 18, Via Aggiunti 65; adult/child*

€5.15/2.60; open 9am-1.30pm & 2.30pm-7.30pm June-Sept, 9.30am-1pm & 2.30pm-6pm Oct-May). It's the pride of Sansepolcro and features a couple of Piero della Francesca's masterpieces. The most celebrated of them is doubtless the *Risurrezione* (Resurrection), but other important works by the master include the *Misericordia*, an impressive polyptych.

Beyond the museum, the cathedral and a handful of other churches are scattered about Sansepolcro, while just beyond the city walls looms the great forbidding hulk of the inevitable 16th-century Fortezza Medicea.

On the second Sunday in September there is a rematch of the Palio della Balestra, a crossbow contest between the men of Gubbio and Sansepolcro. The men dress in medieval costume and use antique weapons.

If you need to stay in the town, there are several hotels.

Orfeo (☎ 0575 74 20 61, Viale A Diaz 12) Singles/doubles €25.80/46.50. This decent budget option is just outside the old town's western gate.

Albergo Fiorentino (☎ 0575 74 03 50, fax 0575 74 03 70, Via Luca Pacioli 60) Singles/doubles €31/41.30, with bathroom €41.30/62. This is easily the pick of the crop within the town's walls, and boasts an atmospheric *restaurant* (open Sat-Thur) up on the first floor. Meals are taken in a spacious dining area, all heavy exposed beams and chunky tables, and prices are moderate.

SITA buses connect Arezzo with Sansepolcro (€2.75, one hour, hourly), and the town is on the Terni-Perugia train line.

THE CASENTINO REGION

A driving tour through the remote forest and farming region of Casentino will take you through a little-visited area boasting two of Tuscany's most important monasteries and some wonderful walking in the Parco Nazionale delle Foreste Casentinesi, Monte Falterona e Campigna.

We start this route as though you were coming from Florence, but it (or variations on it) could just as easily be accomplished from Arezzo, making your initial stops in Monterchi, Anghiari and Sansepolcro (see the previous sections).

Buses and a private train line from Arezzo make it possible to get around the Casentino region slowly, but ideally you would have your own transport.

Pratovecchio & Around

From Florence, follow the Arezzo road (SS67) east along the northern bank of the Arno (see the Vallombrosa section of the Around Florence chapter for directions to the village). From Vallombrosa you could head north to the SS70 highway via San Miniato in Alpe or take another route through **Montemignaio**, a pretty country town. Either way, it is worth getting to the SS70 (which you can follow all the way from Pontassieve rather than making the Vallombrosa detour if you so wish). The point is that, as you climb across the Pratomagno range and head east, you have wonderful views of the sparsely populated countryside to the north and south of this winding hill road.

Once over the Consuma pass, you could follow the road to Poppi and beyond (it becomes the SS71) down to Arezzo, but about 10km short of Poppi we detour off to the north along the SS310 to Stia. Follow the brown signs for the **Castello di Romena** and the Romanesque **Pieve di Romena**. Both are well worth the visit (the only way here is by car or your own two feet – a Club Alpino Italiano (CAI) walking trail meanders through the area).

The **castle** (☎ 0575 58 25 20, Via Romena 12a), still in private hands and housing a small archaeological and arms museum, is a shadow of its former self. Erected around the year 1000 on the site of an Etruscan settlement, the castle in its heyday was an enormous complex surrounded by three sets of defensive walls. Supposedly Dante got his inspiration for the Circles of Hell from observing the castle's prison tower. The Guidi counts were the local feudal lords until Florence took over. All around it slope green fields of such peacefulness it is hard to imagine the chaos and carnage that medieval armies might have wrought while fighting over the stronghold. It was closed at the time of writing – check at the tourist office in Arezzo or call ahead.

About 1km downhill on a side road that eventually slithers into Pratovecchio stands one of the mightiest examples of Romanesque church-building in the Casentino. The dark (and now much weather-beaten) stone of the church, with its heavy triple apse, has been here since the 12th century.

Pratovecchio itself is of minimal interest. The spacious porticoed Piazza Garibaldi is about all there is to it. However, La Ferroviaria Italiana (LFI) private train line runs through here with regular trains that connect Arezzo (via Bibbiena and Poppi) with Stia. The trip between Arezzo and Stia takes just over an hour. If you are approaching this way, you can stock up on supplies and then walk out to the Romena castle and church.

There's an information office (☎ 0575 5 03 01, fax 0575 50 44 97), at Via Brochi 7, for the Parco Nazionale delle Foreste Casentinesi, Monte Falterona e Campigna in Pratovecchio. It's in the centre of the town and opens 9am to 1pm Monday to Friday (also 3pm to 5pm Tuesday and Thursday) year-round.

Stia, a couple of kilometres up the road, marks the end of the train line. Like Pratovecchio, there is nothing of extraordinary interest here, although the porticoed central square is pretty.

Parco Nazionale delle Foreste Casentinesi, Monte Falterona e Campigna

This national park, instituted in 1993, spreads over both sides of the frontier between Tuscany and Emilia-Romagna, taking in some of the most scenic stretches of the Apennines. If you have a few days to spend in this part of Tuscany you should get information on all of the park. The Tuscan half is gentler territory than on the Emilian side.

One of the highest peaks, Monte Falterona (1654m) marks the source of the Arno river. The park authorities have laid out nine easy-to-cover short *sentieri natura* (nature walks). Apart from the human population, which includes the inhabitants of two monasteries (see the following sections), the park is also home

to some 160 species of animal, from squirrel and fox to wolves, deer and wild boar. They are accompanied by about 80 bird species and some 30 kinds of fish and reptiles. The dense forests are a cool summer refuge, ideal for walking and also escaping the hordes of tourists that invade much of Tuscany. The Grande Escursione Appenninica (GEA) passes through here, and several other walking paths (such as those marked by the CAI) criss-cross the park area. Approach the park office in Pratovecchio (see under Pratovecchio & Around earlier) for more details.

Camaldoli

A winding hill road sneaks westwards out of Pratovecchio (crossing the train line on the north side of the station) towards Camaldoli. The drive itself is a pleasure; the lush forest and superb views easily make up for energy exerted coping with the corners. Where it emerges at a crossroads you are pointed left to the **Eremo di Camaldoli** and right to the **Monastero di Camaldoli**. The distance between the two is 3km.

According to the story, Conte Maldolo handed the land for this isolated retreat to St Romualdo in 1012. From the name of the count came that of the location, and Romualdo set about building the monastery. He founded the hermitage *(eremo)* around 1023. The Camaldolesi, a branch of the Benedictines, came to be one of the most powerful forces in medieval Tuscany. What you can see today is the result of a mix of developments. The Baroque church stands on the same spot as the original (built in 1027). Through a fence you can see 20 small tiled houses – they are the cells of the monks who still live here to this day. Free guided tours of the hermitage leave at 3pm, 4pm and 5pm daily, and also at 10am and 11am on Saturday.

Follow the road the 3km downhill and you come to the monastery. Originally designed as a *hospitium* for passing pilgrims, it evolved into a fully fledged monastery and centre of learning. The monks cultivated the forests that still stand around the monastery and developed all sorts of medicinal and herbal products. You're free to wander about the place, and be sure to take a look inside the *Antica Farmacia (open 9am-12.30pm & 2.30pm-6pm)*. As you can see, the monks still make all sorts of liqueurs, honey, chocolate, essences and (if you'll pardon the expression) God knows what else. If it is closed, the bar in the Albergo Camaldoli has some of their products for sale, and they're also available in Cortona (see Shopping under Cortona later in this chapter).

On the subject of hotels, there are three around here. Two serene places stand right opposite the monastery, both with decent restaurants.

La Foresta (☎/fax 0575 55 60 15, Via Camaldoli 5) Singles/doubles €18.10/31, with bathroom €23.25/36.15. The rooms here are quite spartan, but they are large, clean, free of modern appliances and altogether pleasant.

Albergo Camaldoli (☎ 0575 55 60 19, fax 0575 55 60 73, Via Camaldoli 13) Singles/doubles €25.80/38.75. Again, this hotel isn't the Ritz but it's comfortable, quiet and a place to relax.

See Bibbiena for transport details.

Poppi & Bibbiena

Easily the most striking town of the Casentino region is Poppi, perched up on a hill in the Arno plain and topped by the brooding hulk of the **Castello dei Conti Guidi** *(☎ 0575 52 05 16, Piazza Repubblica 1; adult/child €4.15/2.60; open 10am-7pm mid-Jun–Oct)*. It was built by the same counts who raised the Romena castle. The castle's library and frescoed walls (on the second floor) are some of the highlights. Speculation surrounds the origins of this fortified medieval residence. Vasari attributes it to the father of Arnolfo di Cambio, who subsequently used it as a model for the Palazzo Vecchio in Florence. Others claim Arnolfo built this one here and modelled it on his own work in Florence. A hard one to call.

Hotel Casentino (☎ 0575 52 90 90, fax 0575 52 90 67, e info@albergocasentino.it, Piazza Repubblica 6) Singles/doubles up to €46.50/56.80. You can stay in pleasant rooms within sight of the castle here. There's also a *restaurant* with a shaded garden.

Poppi is on the LFI train line between Arezzo and Stia. LFI buses also connect with several destinations throughout the province.

The attraction of **Bibbiena** is its transport links to the national park. Frequent buses to both Camaldoli and Verna (45 minutes, both up to six buses daily) generally leave a few minutes after trains pull into the town's station.

Santuario di San Francesco (Verna)

Of more interest than the Camaldoli monastery to many modern pilgrims is this Franciscan monastic complex 23km east of Bibbiena. It marks the southern edge of the national park, 5km uphill from Chiusi della Verna at a spot called Verna. Its serene location (it would be a lot more serene if the throng of visitors respected the 'silence, please' signs throughout the monastery), perched on a rocky outcrop, makes it a popular destination for pilgrims and non-pilgrims alike. This is where St Francis of Assisi is said to have received the stigmata and lived other key episodes in his life. In a sense, this place is closer to the essence of the saint than Assisi itself.

When you enter the dark stone complex follow the signs around to the **sanctuary** *(santuario; free; open 6am-9.30pm)*. You will find yourself first at the Chiesa Maggiore (also known as the Basilica), decorated with some remarkable enamelled ceramics by Andrea della Robbia. Also on display are various reliquaries containing items associated with the saint, including his walking stick, clothing stained with blood from stigmatic wounds and a discipline (scourge of knotted cords) for castigating himself (self-flagellation and the like played a large part in the religiosity of many in the Middle Ages).

By the entrance to the basilica is the Cappella della Pietà (another ceramic from the della Robbia family), off which the Corridoio dell Stimmate (with frescoes recounting the saint's life) leads you to the core of the sanctuary – a series of chapels associated with St Francis' life. The masterpiece is the Cappella delle Stimmate, beautifully decorated with ceramic works by Luca and Andrea della Robbia. In the older church, or Chiesa di Santa Maria degli Angeli, adjacent to the basilica (which was mostly built in the 15th century), is a further masterpiece by Andrea della Robbia.

Pilgrims can stay in the Foresteria of the monastery. For more information either call ☎ 0575 53 42 11, fax 0575 599 93 20, or write to Santuario della Verna, 52010 Chiusi della Verna (Arezzo). There's also a restaurant on site.

See Bibbiena for transport details.

SOUTH OF AREZZO
Castiglion Fiorentino
Most visitors to the area make a beeline from Arezzo to Cortona or vice versa, scarcely giving this steep hillside town a thought. It deserves better attention than that and, given the frequent bus service that connects south to Cortona and north to Arezzo, is an easy stop-off.

A fortified settlement has existed here since Etruscan times. In the Middle Ages it changed owners several times, belonging at one time or another to, among others, Arezzo and Perugia. It finally fell under Florence's sway in 1384. The old town has changed little since that day.

A stroll up through the steep streets brings you to the central square, whose main feature is a stylish *loggia* supposedly by Vasari. Just up the hill behind the Palazzo Comunale (town hall) is the **Pinacoteca** *(☎ 0575 65 74 66, Via del Tribunale 8; adult/child €2.60/ 0.50; open 10am-12.30pm & 3.30pm-6pm Tues-Sun)*. It is housed in the town fortifications, or Cassero, along with the Chiesa di Sant'Angelo. The Pinacoteca contains mostly paintings from the 13th to the 15th centuries. Nearby you'll find the **Museo Archeologico** *(☎ 0575 65 94 57, Biblioteca Comunale; adult/child €2.60/0.50, €4.15 including Pinacoteca; open 10am-12.30pm & 4pm-6.30pm Tues-Sun)*, filled with a small collection of local finds. Several churches dotted about the town are worth poking your nose into if you have time to kill.

There is no reason to stay, since the bus connections on to Arezzo and Cortona are frequent. The only hotel is a fairly sad option

by the highway, and the town isn't exactly overloaded with quality eateries either. But the main square does have a couple of pleasant cafes where you can rest your feet.

A few kilometres farther south along the road to Cortona, you will hardly fail to notice rising proudly on the left the **Castello di Montecchio Vesponi**, a formidable redoubt that a somewhat intimidated Florence gave to the English mercenary John Hawkwood (c.1320–94) in return for his military services. The castle walls date from the 13th century.

Cortona
postcode 52044 • pop 22,500
Set into the side of a hill covered with olive groves, Cortona offers stunning views across the Tuscan countryside and has changed little since the Middle Ages. It was a small settlement when the Etruscans moved in during the 8th century BC and it later became a Roman town. In the late 14th century, it attracted the likes of Fra Angelico, who lived and worked in the city for about 10 years. Luca Signorelli and the artist known as Pietro da Cortona were born here. The city is small, easily seen in a couple of hours, and well worth visiting for the sensational view alone. Even better, spend a night and soak up the charming atmosphere as well.

Orientation Buses arrive at Piazzale Garibaldi, on the south-eastern edge of the walled city, after a long winding climb out of the valley. The square has a large car park, and also offers some of the best views from the city over the surrounding Tuscan and Umbrian countryside. From the piazza, walk straight up Via Nazionale to Piazza della Repubblica, the centre of town.

Information The APT office (☎ 0575 63 03 52), Via Nazionale 42, can assist with a hotel list and the useful *Cortona* brochure, a complete guide to tourist essentials. It opens 9am to 1pm and 3pm to 7pm Monday to Saturday, and mornings only on Sunday, from May to September. The rest of the year it shuts on Saturday afternoon as well, and at 6pm during the week.

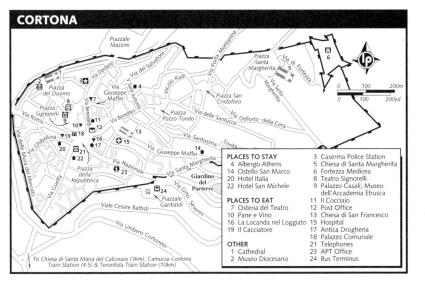

CORTONA

PLACES TO STAY
4 Albergo Athens
14 Ostello San Marco
20 Hotel Italia
22 Hotel San Michele

PLACES TO EAT
7 Osteria del Teatro
10 Pane e Vino
16 La Locanda nel Loggiato
19 Il Cacciatore

OTHER
1 Cathedral
2 Museo Diocesano

3 Caserma Police Station
5 Chiesa di Santa Margherita
6 Fortezza Medicea
8 Teatro Signorelli
9 Palazzo Casali; Museo dell'Accademia Etrusca
11 Il Cocciaio
12 Post Office
13 Chiesa di San Francesco
15 Hospital
17 Antica Drogheria
18 Palazzo Comunale
21 Telephones
23 APT Office
24 Bus Terminus

To Chiesa di Santa Maria del Calcinaio (3km), Camucia-Cortona Train Station (4.5) & Terontola Train Station (10km)

The post office is on the corner of Via Benedetti and Piazza Pescheria. You can find some phones in a little office just off Piazza della Repubblica on Via Guelfa.

The Ospedale Civico (hospital; ☎ 0575 63 91) is high up in the old town on Via Giuseppe Maffei. For a night locum you can call ☎ 0575 6 28 93. The *caserma* (police station; ☎ 0575 60 36 90) is on the corner of Via Dardano and Piazza Tommasi.

Things to See Start in Piazza della Repubblica with the crenellated **Palazzo Comunale**, which was renovated in the 16th century and again, unhappily, in the 19th.

To the north is Piazza Signorelli, named after the artist and dominated by the 13th-century **Palazzo Casali** (which in medieval times was known as the Palazzo Pretorio). Any hint of its medieval grandeur has been obscured by the rather unimaginative facade that was added in the 17th century. Inside is the **Museo dell'Accademia Etrusca** *(☎ 0575 63 04 15, Piazza Signorelli 9; admission €4.15; open 10am-7pm Tues-Sun Apr-Oct, 10am-5pm Tues-Sun Nov-Mar)*, which over about a dozen rooms displays a substantial haul of Etruscan artefacts dug up in the area

around Cortona. One of the single most intriguing pieces is an elaborate 5th-century-BC oil lamp. The collection also includes jewellery, funerary urns, some ancient Egyptian artefacts, bronzeware and household implements. Guided tours (€6.70 including admission) of the museum leave from the ticket booth at 10.30am, or you can opt for a guided tour (€10.35, reserve a day in advance) of three Etruscan tombs in the surrounding countryside.

Little is left of the Romanesque character of the **cathedral** in Piazza Duomo, northwest of Piazza Signorelli. It was completely rebuilt late in the Renaissance and again in the 18th century. The result can most tactfully be described as indifferent. Opposite, in the former church of Gesù, is the **Museo Diocesano** *(☎ 0575 6 28 30, Piazza Duomo 1; adult/child €4.15/1.05; open 9.30am-1.30pm & 3.30pm-7pm Tues-Sun Apr-Sept; 10am-1pm & 3pm-5pm Tues-Sun Oct-Mar)*. It contains a fine, if fairly limited, collection of artworks. Room 1 houses a remarkable Roman-era sarcophagus made of Carrara marble, along with a series of paintings by Luca Signorelli and his workshop. This series continues into the adjoining Room 4.

EASTERN TUSCANY

Of Signorelli's personal contributions, *Compianto sul Cristo Morto* (Grief at Christ's Death) is possibly the most interesting. Easily the star work of the collection is to be found in Room 3. Fra Angelico's *Annunciazione* is a triumph and by its sheer luminosity leaves all the surrounding works in the shade. Downstairs in the Oratorio del Gesù you can see frescoes that were carried out by Vasari.

The eastern part of town is in stark contrast to the busy west end around Piazza della Repubblica. Here you'll find quiet cobblestone streets slowly winding their way uphill to meadows and small orchards. Close to the eastern edge of the city centre is the **Chiesa di Santa Margherita**, which features the Gothic tomb of St Margaret. Farther up the hill is the imposing 16th-century **Fortezza Medicea** (☎ *0575 60 37 93, Via di Fortezza; adult/child €2.60/1.55; open 10am-6pm Tues-Sun Apr-Sept)*, built for the Medicis by Laparelli, who designed the fortress city of Valletta in Malta.

If you care for a walk of a few kilometres south out of the old town, you could inspect the rather weather-beaten **Chiesa di Santa Maria del Calcinaio**. Francesco di Giorgio's original approach to Renaissance architecture will intrigue students of the subject. Note how the main body of the church is free of columns and is basically a two-storey structure topped with tabernacle windows – all unusual elements. If it's open you can just push the door and wander inside.

Special Events Every year for about a week from late August into the first days of September, Cortona becomes a big Mostra Antiquaria, which is one of Italy's main antique fairs. If you are interested in antique furniture, this will interest you. Of course getting a room in Cortona around then is virtually impossible without a reservation. The Sagra della Bistecca (steak festival), held on the 14th and 15th of August, will interest meat lovers and appal vegetarians. On these two days Giardino del Parterre becomes an open-air grill where people celebrate steak, by stuffing themselves full of the stuff.

Places to Stay The city has several cheap hotels and a hostel, and finding a room shouldn't be a problem.

Ostello San Marco (☎ */fax 0575 60 13 92, Via Giuseppe Maffei 57)* B&B €10.35. Open mid-Mar–mid-Oct. This attractive HI hostel is a short, but uphill, walk east of Piazzale Garibaldi, and has decent-sized rooms holding between four and six beds. The hostel also puts on a filling dinner for €7.75.

Albergo Athens (☎ *0575 63 05 08, fax 0575 60 44 57, Via Sant'Antonio 12)* Singles/doubles €23.25/36.15. About the next cheapest option is a further stretch in the uphill luggage-lugging stakes, with smallish, straightforward rooms, some with commanding views.

Hotel Italia (☎ *0575 63 02 54, fax 0575 63 05 64,* e *hotel.italia@technet.it, Via Ghibellina 5)* Singles/doubles up to €59.75/88.15 high season. Rooms at this old mansion, just off Piazza della Repubblica, include TV and phone.

Hotel San Michele (☎ *0575 60 43 48, fax 0575 63 01 47,* e *sanmichele@ats.it, Via Guelfa 15)* Singles/doubles €82.65/129.10. This is the luxury option in town, with comfortable rooms and guest parking.

Places to Eat Piazza del Duomo hosts a *produce market* each Saturday and several grocery shops dot the area.

Il Cacciatore (☎ *0575 63 05 52, Via Roma 11)* Pasta dishes €6.20-7.75. Open Thur-Tues. This is one of the city's better restaurants and offers local specialities. The restaurant is on the first floor.

La Locanda nel Loggiato (☎ *0575 63 05 75, Piazza Pescheria 3)*. Mains €5.15-12.90. Open Tues-Sun. The outdoor seating of this restaurant, with views over Piazza della Repubblica, is a great complement to the food.

Pane e Vino (☎ *0575 63 10 10, Piazza Signorelli 27)* Meals around €18.10 excluding wine. This is a huge and hugely popular dining hall in the heart of Cortona. The *lambatine di cinghiale brasato* (cured wild boar) is an excellent choice.

Osteria del Teatro (☎ *0575 63 05 56, Via Giuseppe Maffei 5)* Meals around €23.25. Open Thur-Tues. The nicest of the crop is probably this place, the latest incarnation of what was perhaps the last genuine osteria in Cortona. Your meal could include *ravioli ai fiori di zucca* (pumpkin-flower ravioli).

Shopping *Il Cocciaio* (☎ *0575 60 12 46*, **W** *www.toscumbria.com/cocciaio, Via Benedetti 24)* Tucked away from the madding crowds is this friendly little store that's absolutely crammed full of ceramics. Not for small children or bulls.

Antica Drogheria (Via Nazionale 1) If you want specialist and handmade food products from around the province, try this place. Among other comestibles, the owner brings stuff down from the Antica Farmacia at the Camaldoli monastery in the north of the province (see Camaldoli earlier). This street, Via Nazionale, is lined with all sorts of shops, from antiques to tacky souvenirs.

Getting There & Around LFI buses connect Cortona frequently (at least 12 a day on work days) with Arezzo (via Castiglion Fiorentino) from Piazzale Garibaldi.

Two train stations serve the town. Trains from Arezzo stop at the Camucia-Cortona station, which is around 5km away in the valley below Cortona, and trains for Rome stop at Terontola, which is located about 10km to the south of town. Shuttle buses connect Camucia (€1, 10 minutes) and Terontola (€1.50, 25 minutes) with Piazzale Garibaldi. A board in a shop window on the north side of Via Nazionale, about 50m in from Piazzale Garibaldi, details schedules.

By car, the city is on the north-south SS71, which runs to Arezzo, and it is also close to the *superstrada* that connects Perugia to the A1.

Language

Italian is a Romance language related to French, Spanish, Portuguese and Romanian. The Romance languages belong to the Indo-European group of languages, which includes English. Indeed, as English and Italian share common roots in Latin, you will recognise many Italian words.

Modern literary Italian began to develop in the 13th and 14th centuries, predominantly through the works of Dante, Petrarch and Boccaccio, who wrote chiefly in the Florentine dialect. The language drew on its Latin heritage and many dialects to develop into the standard Italian of today. Although many dialects are spoken in everyday conversation, standard Italian is the national language of schools, media and literature and is understood throughout the country.

The cant is that Florentine *is* standard Italian, but anyone who has learned Italian sufficiently well will find many Florentines surprisingly hard to understand, at least at first. Whether or not they have their own non-standard vocabulary you could argue about at length. No one can deny the peculiarity of the local accent. Here and in other parts of Tuscany you are bound to hear the hard 'c' pronounced as a heavily aspirated 'h'. *Voglio una cannuccia per la Coca Cola* (I want a straw for my Coca Cola) in Florence sounds more like *voglio una hannuccia per la Hoha Hola*!

There are 58 million speakers of Italian in Italy; 500,000 in Switzerland, where Italian is one of the official languages; and 1.5 million speakers in France, Slovenia and Croatia. As a result of migration, Italian is also spoken in the USA, Argentina, Brazil and Australia.

Visitors to Italy with more than the most fundamental grasp of the language need to be aware that many older Italians still expect to be addressed by the third person formal, that is, *lei* instead of *tu*. Also, it is not considered polite to use the greeting *ciao* when addressing strangers, unless they use it first; it's better to say *buon giorno* (or *buona sera*,

as the case may be) and *arrivederci* (or the more polite form, *arrivederla)*. We have used the formal address for most of the phrases in this guide. Use of the informal address is indicated by (inf). Italian also has both masculine and feminine forms (they usually ending in 'o' and 'a' respectively). Where both forms are given in this guide, they are separated by a slash, the masculine form first.

If you'd like a more comprehensive guide to the language, get a copy of Lonely Planet's *Italian phrasebook*.

Pronunciation

Italian pronunciation isn't very difficult to master once you learn a few easy rules. Although some of the more clipped vowels and stress on double letters require careful practice for English speakers, it is easy enough to make yourself understood.

Vowels

Vowels are generally more clipped than in English:

a	as in 'art', eg, *caro* (dear); sometimes short, eg, *amico/a* (friend)
e	as in 'tell', eg, *mettere* (to put)
i	as in 'inn', eg, *inizio* (start)
o	as in 'dot', eg, *donna* (woman); as in 'port', eg, *dormire* (to sleep)
u	as the 'oo' in 'book', eg, *puro* (pure)

Consonants

The pronunciation of many Italian consonants is similar to that of their English counterparts. Pronunciation of some consonants depends on certain rules:

c	as the 'k' in 'kit' before **a**, **o** and **u**; as the 'ch' in 'choose' before **e** and **i**
ch	as the 'k' in 'kit'
g	as the 'g' in 'get' before **a**, **o**, **u** and **h**; as the 'j' in 'jet' before **e** and **i**
gli	as the 'lli' in 'million'
gn	as the 'ny' in 'canyon'

h	always silent
r	a rolled 'rr' sound
sc	as 'sk' before **a**, **o**, **u** and **h**; as the 'sh' in 'sheep' before **e** and **i**
z	as the 'ts' in 'lights', except at the beginning of a word, when it's as the 'ds' in 'suds'

Note that when **ci**, **gi** and **sci** are followed by **a**, **o** or **u**, the 'i' is not pronounced unless the accent falls on the 'i'. Thus the name 'Giovanni' is pronounced 'joh-**vahn**-nee'.

Word Stress
A double consonant is pronounced as a longer, more forceful sound than a single consonant.

Stress generally falls on the second-last syllable, as in *spa-**ghet**-ti*. When a word has an accent, the stress falls on that syllable, as in *cit-**tà*** (city).

Greetings & Civilities
Hello.	*Buongiorno.*
	Ciao. (inf)
Goodbye.	*Arrivederci.*
	Ciao. (inf)
Yes.	*Sì.*
No.	*No.*
Please.	*Per favore/Per piacere.*
Thank you.	*Grazie.*
That's fine/ You're welcome.	*Prego.*
Excuse me.	*Mi scusi.*
Sorry. (forgive me)	*Mi scusi/Mi perdoni.*

Small Talk
What's your name?	*Come si chiama?*
	Come ti chiami? (inf)
My name is ...	*Mi chiamo ...*
Where are you from?	*Di dov'è?*
	Di dove sei? (inf)
I'm from ...	*Sono di ...*
I (don't) like ...	*(Non) Mi piace ...*
Just a minute.	*Un momento.*

Language Difficulties
Please write it down.	*Può scriverlo, per favore?*
Can you show me (on the map)?	*Può mostrarmelo (sulla carta/pianta)?*
I understand.	*Capisco.*

I don't understand.	*Non capisco.*
Do you speak English?	*Parla inglese?*
	Parli inglese? (inf)
Does anyone here speak English?	*C'è qualcuno che parla inglese?*
How do you say ... in Italian?	*Come si dice ... in italiano?*
What does ... mean?	*Che vuole dire ...?*

Paperwork
name	*nome*
nationality	*nazionalità*
date of birth	*data di nascita*
place of birth	*luogo di nascita*
sex (gender)	*sesso*
passport	*passaporto*
visa	*visto*

Getting Around
What time does the ... leave/arrive?	*A che ora parte/ arriva ...?*
(city) bus	*l'autobus*
(intercity) bus	*il pullman*
plane	*l'aereo*
train	*il treno*

I'd like a ... ticket.	*Vorrei un biglietto ...*
one-way	*di solo andata*
return	*di andata e ritorno*
1st class	*di prima classe*
2nd class	*di seconda classe*

I want to go to ...	*Voglio andare a ...*
The train has been cancelled/delayed.	*Il treno è soppresso/ in ritardo.*

the first	*il primo*
the last	*l'ultimo*
platform number	*binario numero*
ticket office	*biglietteria*
timetable	*orario*
train station	*stazione*

I'd like to hire a ...	*Vorrei noleggiare ...*
bicycle	*una bicicletta*
car	*una macchina*
motorcycle	*una motocicletta*

Directions
Where is ...?	*Dov'è ...?*
Go straight ahead.	*Si va sempre diritto.*
	Vai sempre diritto. (inf)

LANGUAGE

Signs

Ingresso/Entrata	Entrance
Uscita	Exit
Informazione	Information
Aperto	Open
Chiuso	Closed
Proibito/Vietato	Prohibited
Camere Libere	Rooms Available
Completo	Full/No Vacancies
Polizia/ Carabinieri	Police
Questura	Police Station
Gabinetti/Bagni	Toilets
Uomini	Men
Donne	Women

Turn left.	*Giri a sinistra.*
Turn right.	*Giri a destra.*
at the next corner	*al prossimo angolo*
at the traffic lights	*al semaforo*
behind	*dietro*
in front of	*davanti*
far	*lontano*
near	*vicino*
opposite	*di fronte a*

Around Town

I'm looking for ...	*Cerco ...*
a bank	*un banco*
the church	*la chiesa*
the city centre	*il centro (città)*
the ... embassy	*l'ambasciata di ...*
my hotel	*il mio albergo*
the market	*il mercato*
the museum	*il museo*
the post office	*la posta*
a public toilet	*un gabinetto/ bagno pubblico*
the telephone centre	*il centro telefonico*
the tourist office	*l'ufficio di turismo/ d'informazione*

I want to change ...	*Voglio cambiare ...*
money	*del denaro*
travellers cheques	*degli assegni per viaggiatori*

beach	*la spiaggia*
bridge	*il ponte*

castle	*il castello*
cathedral	*il duomo/la cattedrale*
church	*la chiesa*
island	*l'isola*
main square	*la piazza principale*
market	*il mercato*
old city	*il centro storico*
palace	*il palazzo*
ruins	*le rovine*
sea	*il mare*
square	*la piazza*
tower	*la torre*

Accommodation

I'm looking for a ...	*Cerco ...*
guesthouse	*una pensione*
hotel	*un albergo*
youth hostel	*un ostello per la gioventù*

Where is a cheap hotel?	*Dov'è un albergo che costa poco?*
What is the address?	*Cos'è l'indirizzo?*
Could you write the address, please?	*Può scrivere l'indirizzo, per favore?*
Do you have any rooms available?	*Ha camere libere?*

I'd like (a) ...	*Vorrei ...*
bed	*un letto*
single room	*una camera singola*
double room	*una camera matrimoniale*
twin room (room with two beds)	*una camera doppia*
room with a bathroom	*una camera con bagno*
to share a dorm	*un letto in dormitorio*

How much is it ...?	*Quanto costa ...?*
per night	*per la notte*
per person	*per ciascuno*

May I see it?	*Posso vederla?*
Where is the bathroom?	*Dov'è il bagno?*
I'm/We're leaving today.	*Parto/Partiamo oggi.*

Shopping

I'd like to buy ...	*Vorrei comprare ...*
How much is it?	*Quanto costa?*
I don't like it.	*Non mi piace.*
May I look at it?	*Posso dare un'occhiata?*
I'm just looking.	*Sto solo guardando.*
It's cheap.	*Non è caro/a.*
It's too expensive.	*È troppo caro/a.*
I'll take it.	*Lo/La compro.*
Do you accept ...?	*Accettate ...?*
credit cards	*carte di credito*
travellers cheques	*assegni per viaggiatori*
more	*più*
less	*meno*
smaller	*più piccolo/a* (m/f)
bigger	*più grande*

Time & Dates

What time is it?	*Che ore sono?*
It's (8 o'clock).	*Sono (le otto).*
in the morning	*di mattina*
in the afternoon	*di pomeriggio*
in the evening	*di sera*
When?	*Quando?*
today	*oggi*
tomorrow	*domani*
yesterday	*ieri*
Monday	*lunedì*
Tuesday	*martedì*
Wednesday	*mercoledì*
Thursday	*giovedì*
Friday	*venerdì*
Saturday	*sabato*
Sunday	*domenica*
January	*gennaio*
February	*febbraio*
March	*marzo*
April	*aprile*
May	*maggio*
June	*giugno*
July	*luglio*
August	*agosto*
September	*settembre*
October	*ottobre*
November	*novembre*
December	*dicembre*

Emergencies

Help!	*Aiuto!*
There's been an accident!	*C'è stato un incidente!*
I'm lost.	*Mi sono perso/a.*
Go away!	*Lasciami in pace!*
	Vai via! (inf)
Call ...!	*Chiami ...!*
	Chiama ...! (inf)
a doctor	*un dottore/ un medico*
the police	*la polizia*

Numbers

0	*zero*
1	*uno*
2	*due*
3	*tre*
4	*quattro*
5	*cinque*
6	*sei*
7	*sette*
8	*otto*
9	*nove*
10	*dieci*
11	*undici*
12	*dodici*
13	*tredici*
14	*quattordici*
15	*quindici*
16	*sedici*
17	*diciassette*
18	*diciotto*
19	*diciannove*
20	*venti*
21	*ventuno*
22	*ventidue*
30	*trenta*
40	*quaranta*
50	*cinquanta*
60	*sessanta*
70	*settanta*
80	*ottanta*
90	*novanta*
100	*cento*
1000	*mille*
2000	*due mila*
one million	*un milione*

Health

I'm ill.	*Mi sento male.*
It hurts here.	*Mi fa male qui.*

I'm ...	*Sono ...*
asthmatic	*asmatico/a*
diabetic	*diabetico/a*
epileptic	*epilettico/a*

I'm allergic ...	*Sono allergico/a ...*
to antibiotics	*agli antibiotici*
to penicillin	*alla penicillina*
to nuts	*alle noci*

antiseptic	*antisettico*
aspirin	*aspirina*
condoms	*preservativi*
contraceptive	*anticoncezionale*
diarrhoea	*diarrea*
medicine	*medicina*
sunblock cream	*crema/latte solare (per protezione)*
tampons	*tamponi*

FOOD
Basics

breakfast	*prima colazione*
lunch	*pranzo*
dinner	*cena*
restaurant	*ristorante*
grocery store	*un alimentari*

I'd like the set lunch.	*Vorrei il menù turistico.*
Is service included in the bill?	*È compreso il servizio?*
I'm a vegetarian.	*Sono vegetariano/a.*
What is this?	*(Che) cos'è questo?*

bill/check	*conto*
menu	*menù*
waiter/waitress	*cameriere/a*
fork	*forchetta*
knife	*coltello*
plate	*piatto*
spoon	*cucchiaio*
teaspoon	*cucchiaino*

On the Menu

This glossary is intended as a brief guide to some of the basics and by no means covers all of the dishes you're likely to encounter in Italy. Names and ingredients of dishes often vary from region to region, and even pizza toppings can change. Most travellers to Italy will already be well acquainted with the various Italian pastas, which include spaghetti, fettucine, penne, rigatoni, gnocchi, lasagne, tortellini and ravioli. The names are the same in Italy and no further definitions are given here.

Cooking Methods

affumicato	smoked
al dente	firm (as all good pasta should be!)
alla brace	cooked over hot coals
alla griglia	grilled
arrosto	roasted
ben cotto	well done (cooked)
bollito	boiled
cotto	cooked
crudo	raw
fritto	fried

Staples & Condiments

aceto	vinegar
burro	butter
formaggio	cheese
marmellata	jam
miele	honey
olio	oil
olive	olives
pane	bread
pane integrale	wholemeal bread
panna	cream
pepe	pepper
peperoncino	chilli
polenta	cooked cornmeal
riso	rice
risotto	rice cooked with wine and stock
sale	salt
uovo/uova	egg/eggs
zucchero	sugar

Meat & Fish

acciughe	anchovies
agnello	lamb
aragosta	lobster
bistecca	steak
calamari	squid

capretto	kid (goat)
coniglio	rabbit
cotoletta	cutlet or thin cut of meat, usually crumbed and fried
cozze	mussels
dentice	dentex (type of fish)
fegato	liver
gamberi	prawns
granchio	crab
lumaca	snail
manzo	beef
merluzzo	cod
ostriche	oysters
pesce spada	swordfish
pollo	chicken
polpo	octopus
salsiccia	sausage
sarde	sardines
seppia	cuttlefish
sgombro	mackerel
sogliola	sole
tacchino	turkey
tonno	tuna
trippa	tripe
vitello	veal
vongole	clams

Vegetables

asparagi	asparagus
carciofi	artichokes
carote	carrots
cavolo/verza	cabbage
cicoria	chicory
cipolla	onion
fagiolini	string beans
melanzane	aubergines
patate	potatoes
peperoni	peppers
piselli	peas
spinaci	spinach

Fruit

arance	oranges
banane	bananas
ciliegie	cherries
fragole	strawberries
limone	lemon
mele	apples
pere	pears
pesche	peaches
uva	grapes

Soups & Antipasti

brodo – broth

carpaccio – very fine slices of raw meat or fish

insalata caprese – sliced tomatoes with mozzarella and basil

insalata di mare – seafood, generally crustaceans

minestrina in brodo – pasta in broth

minestrone – vegetable and pasta soup

olive ascolane – stuffed, deep-fried olives

prosciutto e melone – cured ham with melon

stracciatella – egg in broth

Pasta Sauces

alla matriciana – tomato and bacon

al ragù – meat sauce (bolognese)

arrabbiata – tomato and chilli

carbonara – egg, bacon, cheese and black pepper

napoletana – tomato and basil

panna – cream, prosciutto and sometimes peas

pesto – basil, garlic and oil, often with pine nuts

vongole – clams, garlic, oil and sometimes with tomato

Pizzas

All pizzas listed have a tomato (and sometimes mozzarella) base.

capricciosa – olives, prosciutto, mushrooms and artichokes

frutti di mare – seafood

funghi – mushrooms

margherita – oregano

napoletana – anchovies

pugliese – tomato, mozzarella and onions

quattro formaggi – with four types of cheese

quattro stagioni – like a capricciosa, but sometimes with egg

verdura – mixed vegetables; usually courgette (zucchini) and aubergine (eggplant), sometimes carrot and spinach

Glossary

abbazia – abbey
ACI – Automobile Club Italiano, the Italian automobile club
aereo – aeroplane
affittacamere – rooms for rent (cheaper than a *pensione*, and not part of the classification system)
affresco – fresco; the painting method in which watercolour paint is applied to wet plaster
agriturismo – tourist accommodation on farms
AIG – Associazione Italiana Alberghi per la Gioventù, Italy's youth hostel association
albergo – hotel (up to five stars)
alimentaro – grocery shop
aliscafo – hydrofoil
alloggio – lodging (cheaper than a *pensione*, and not part of the classification system)
alto – high
ambulanza – ambulance
anfiteatro – amphitheatre
antipasto – starter, appetiser
appartamento – apartment, flat
APT – Azienda di Promozione Turistica, the provincial tourist office
arco – arch
assicurato/a – insured
autobus – local bus
autostazione – bus station/terminal
autostop – hitchhiking
autostrada – motorway, highway

bagno – bathroom; toilet
baldacchino – canopy supported by columns over the altar in a church
bancomat – ATM (Automated Teller Machine), cashpoint
basilica – in ancient Rome, a building used for public administration, with a rectangular hall flanked by aisles and an apse at the end; later, a Christian church built in the same style
battistero – baptistry
benzina – petrol
bicicletta – bicycle
biglietteria – ticket office

biglietto – ticket
binario – platform
bivacco – unattended hut
borgo – ancient town or village
bruschetta – toasted bread with various toppings
busta – envelope

cabinovia – two-seater cable car
CAI – Club Alpino Italiano, for information on hiking and mountain refuges
cambio – exchange office
camera – room
camera doppia – double room with twin beds
camera matrimoniale – double room with a double bed
camera singola – single room
campanile – bell tower
campeggio – camping
campo – field
cappella – chapel
carabinieri – military police (see *polizia*)
carnevale – carnival period between Epiphany and Lent
carta telefonica – phonecard (also *scheda telefonica*)
cartoleria – stationery shop
cartolina (postale) – postcard
castello – castle
cattedrale – cathedral
cava – quarry (as in the marble quarries around Carrara)
cena – evening meal
centro – city centre
centro storico – (literally, historical centre) old town
chiesa church
chilo – kilo
chiostro – cloister; covered walkway, usually enclosed by columns, around a quadrangle
cin cin – cheers (a drinking toast)
(il) Cinquecento – (the) 16th century
circo – oval or circular arena
CIT – Compagnia Italiana di Turismo, the Italian national travel agency

codice fiscale – tax number
colazione – breakfast
colonna – column
comune – equivalent to a municipality or county; town or city council; historically, a commune (self-governing town or city)
contado – district around a major town (historically the area immediately surrounding Florence was known as the *contado di Firenze*
contorno – vegetable side dish
contrada – town district
convalida – ticket stamping machine
coperto – cover charge
corso – main street, avenue
cortile – courtyard
CTS – Centro Turistico Studentesco e Giovanile, the student/youth travel agency
cupola – dome

deposito bagagli – left luggage
digestivo – after-dinner liqueur
distributore di benzina – petrol pump (see *stazione di servizio*)
duomo – cathedral

ENIT – Ente Nazionale Italiano per il Turismo, the Italian tourist board
espresso express mail; express train; short black coffee
etto – 100g

farmacia (di turno) – pharmacy (open late)
ferrovia – train station
festa – festival
fiume – river
fontana – fountain
foro – forum
francobollo – postage stamp
fresco – see *affresco*
FS Ferrovie dello Stato, the Italian state railways
funghi – mushrooms
funicolare – funicular railway
funivia – cable car

gabinetto – toilet, WC
gelato – ice cream
gelateria – ice-cream parlour
golfo – gulf

granita – drink of crushed ice flavoured with lemon, strawberry, coffee and so on
grotta cave

HI – Hostelling International

IC – Intercity; fast train
intarsia – inlaid wood, marble or metal
isola – island

lago – lake
largo – (small) square
lavanderia – laundrette
lavasecco – dry-cleaning
lettera – letter
lettera raccomandata – registered letter
locanda – inn, small hotel (cheaper than a *pensione*)
loggia – covered area on the side of a building; porch
lungomare – seafront road; promenade

macchia – Mediterranean scrub
mare – sea
mercato – market
monte – mountain, mount
motorino – moped
municipio – town hall

navata centrale – nave; central part of a church
navata laterale – aisle of a church
nave – ship
necropoli – (ancient) cemetery, burial site

oggetti smarriti – lost property
ospedale – hospital
ostello per la gioventù – youth hostel
osteria – snack bar, cheap restaurant

pacco – package, parcel
palazzo – palace; a large building of any type, including an apartment block
panetteria – bakery
panino – bread roll with filling
parco – park
passaggio ponte – deck class
passeggiata – traditional evening stroll
pasta – cake; pasta; pastry or dough
pasticceria – shop selling cakes, pastries and biscuits

pensione – small hotel, often with board
permesso di lavoro – work permit
permesso di soggiorno – residence permit
piazza – square
piazzale – (large) open square
pietà – (literally, pity or compassion) sculpture, drawing or painting of the dead Christ supported by the Madonna
polizia – police
poltrona – (literally, armchair) airline-type chair on a ferry
polyptych – altarpiece consisting of more than three panels (see *triptych*)
ponte – bridge
portico – covered walkway, usually attached to the outside of buildings
porto – port
posta aerea – air mail
presepio – nativity scene
primo – first; starter (meal)
pronto soccorso – first aid; casualty ward
pullman – long distance bus

(il) Quattrocento – (the) 15th century
questura – police station

raccomandata – registered mail
rifugio – mountain hut, Alpine refuge
rocca – fortress

sagra – festival (usually dedicated to one culinary item or theme, such as *funghi, vino* etc)
salumeria – delicatessen that sells mainly cheeses and sausage meats
santuario – sanctuary
scalinata – stairway
scavi – excavations
scheda telefonica – see *carta telefonica*
sci di fondo – cross-country skiing
sci alpinismo – ski mountaineering
(il) Seicento – (the) 17th century
servizio – service fee

spiaggia – beach
spiaggia libera – public beach
stazione – station
stazione di servizio – service/petrol station
stazione marittima – ferry terminal
strada – street, road
superstrada – expressway; highway with divided lanes (but no tolls)

teatro – theatre
telamoni – large statues of men, used as columns in temples
telegramma – telegram
tempio – temple
terme – thermal baths
tesoro – treasury
torre – tower
torrente – stream
torrone – nougat
traghetto – ferry
tramezzino – sandwich
trattoria – cheap restaurant
treno – train
triptych – painting or carving on three panels, hinged so that the outer panels fold over the middle one, often used as an altarpiece (see *polyptych*)

ufficio postale – post office
ufficio stranieri – (police) foreigners' bureau
uffizi – offices

via – street, road
via ferrata – climbing trail with permanent steel cables to aid walkers
villa country house or detached town house
vino bianco/rosso/rosato – white/red/rosé wine
vinsanto – type of sweet white wine, often used in Mass

Zona Rimozione – vehicle removal zone

LONELY PLANET

You already know that Lonely Planet produces more than this one guidebook, but you might not be aware of the other products we have on this region. Here is a selection of titles that you may want to check out as well:

Europe on a shoestring
ISBN 1 86450 150 2
US$24.99 • UK£14.99

Mediterrean Europe
ISBN 1 86450 154 5
US$27.99 • UK£15.99

Read This First: Europe
ISBN 1 86450 136 7
US$14.99 • UK£8.99

Italy
ISBN 1 86450 352 1
US$24.99 • UK£14.99

Milan, Turin & Genoa
ISBN 1 86450 362 9
US$14.99 • UK£8.99

Italian phrasebook
ISBN 0 86442 456 6
US$5.95 • UK£3.99

Rome
ISBN 1 86450 311 4
US$15.99 • UK£9.99

Venice
ISBN 1 86450 321 1
US$15.99 • UK£8.99

Florence
ISBN 1 74059 030 9
US$17.99 • UK£8.99

Walking in Italy
ISBN 0 86442 542 2
US$17.95 • UK£11.99

World Food Italy
ISBN 1 86450 022 0
US$12.95 • UK£7.99

Rome Condensed
ISBN 1 86450 360 2
US$11.99 • UK£5.99

Available wherever books are sold

LONELY PLANET

ON THE ROAD

Travel Guides explore cities, regions and countries, and supply information on transport, restaurants and accommodation, covering all budgets. They come with reliable, easy-to-use maps, practical advice, cultural and historical facts and a rundown on attractions both on and off the beaten track. There are over 200 titles in this classic series, covering nearly every country in the world.

 Lonely Planet Upgrades extend the shelf life of existing travel guides by detailing any changes that may affect travel in a region since a book has been published. Upgrades can be downloaded for free from **www.lonelyplanet.com/upgrades**

For travellers with more time than money, **Shoestring** guides offer dependable, first-hand information with hundreds of detailed maps, plus insider tips for stretching money as far as possible. Covering entire continents in most cases, the six-volume shoestring guides are known around the world as 'backpackers bibles'.

For the discerning short-term visitor, **Condensed** guides highlight the best a destination has to offer in a full-colour, pocket-sized format designed for quick access. They include everything from top sights and walking tours to opinionated reviews of where to eat, stay, shop and have fun.

CitySync lets travellers use their Palm™ or Visor™ hand-held computers to guide them through a city with handy tips on transport, history, cultural life, major sights, and shopping and entertainment options. It can also quickly search and sort hundreds of reviews of hotels, restaurants and attractions, and pinpoint their location on scrollable street maps. CitySync can be downloaded from **www.citysync.com**

MAPS & ATLASES

Lonely Planet's **City Maps** feature downtown and metropolitan maps, as well as transit routes and walking tours. The maps come complete with an index of streets, a listing of sights and a plastic coat for extra durability.

Road Atlases are an essential navigation tool for serious travellers. Cross-referenced with the guidebooks, they also feature distance and climate charts and a complete site index.

ESSENTIALS

Read This First books help new travellers to hit the road with confidence. These invaluable predeparture guides give step-by-step advice on preparing for a trip, budgeting, arranging a visa, planning an itinerary and staying safe while still getting off the beaten track.

Healthy Travel pocket guides offer a regional rundown on disease hot spots and practical advice on predeparture health measures, staying well on the road and what to do in emergencies. The guides come with a user-friendly design and helpful diagrams and tables.

Lonely Planet's **Phrasebooks** cover the essential words and phrases travellers need when they're strangers in a strange land. They come in a pocket-sized format with colour tabs for quick reference, extensive vocabulary lists, easy-to-follow pronunciation keys and two-way dictionaries.

Miffed by blurry photos of the Taj Mahal? Tired of the classic 'top of the head cut off' shot? **Travel Photography: A Guide to Taking Better Pictures** will help you turn ordinary holiday snaps into striking images and give you the know-how to capture every scene, from frenetic festivals to peaceful beach sunrises.

Lonely Planet's **Travel Journal** is a lightweight but sturdy travel diary for jotting down all those on-the-road observations and significant travel moments. It comes with a handy time-zone wheel, a world map and useful travel information.

Lonely Planet's eKno is an all-in-one communication service developed especially for travellers. It offers low-cost international calls and free email and voicemail so that you can keep in touch while on the road. Check it out on **www.ekno.lonelyplanet.com**

FOOD & RESTAURANT GUIDES

Lonely Planet's **Out to Eat** guides recommend the brightest and best places to eat and drink in top international cities. These gourmet companions are arranged by neighbourhood, packed with dependable maps, garnished with scene-setting photos and served with quirky features.

For people who live to eat, drink and travel, **World Food** guides explore the culinary culture of each country. Entertaining and adventurous, each guide is packed with detail on staples and specialities, regional cuisine and local markets, as well as sumptuous recipes, comprehensive culinary dictionaries and lavish photos good enough to eat.

Lonely Planet Guides by Region

onely Planet is known worldwide for publishing practical, reliable and no-nonsense travel information in our guides and on our Web site. The Lonely Planet list covers just about every accessible part of the world. Currently there are 16 series: Travel guides, Shoestring guides, Condensed guides, Phrasebooks, Read This First, Healthy Travel, Walking guides, Cycling guides, Watching Wildlife guides, Pisces Diving & Snorkeling guides, City Maps, Road Atlases, Out to Eat, World Food, Journeys travel literature and Pictorials.

AFRICA Africa on a shoestring • Botswana • Cairo • Cairo City Map • Cape Town • Cape Town City Map • East Africa • Egypt • Egyptian Arabic phrasebook • Ethiopia, Eritrea & Djibouti • Ethiopian Amharic phrasebook • The Gambia & Senegal • Healthy Travel Africa • Kenya • Malawi • Morocco • Moroccan Arabic phrasebook • Mozambique • Namibia • Read This First: Africa • South Africa, Lesotho & Swaziland • Southern Africa • Southern Africa Road Atlas • Swahili phrasebook • Tanzania, Zanzibar & Pemba • Trekking in East Africa • Tunisia • Watching Wildlife East Africa • Watching Wildlife Southern Africa • West Africa • World Food Morocco • Zambia • Zimbabwe, Botswana & Namibia
Travel Literature: Mali Blues: Traveling to an African Beat • The Rainbird: A Central African Journey • Songs to an African Sunset: A Zimbabwean Story

AUSTRALIA & THE PACIFIC Aboriginal Australia & the Torres Strait Islands •Auckland • Australia • Australian phrasebook • Australia Road Atlas • Cycling Australia • Cycling New Zealand • Fiji • Fijian phrasebook • Healthy Travel Australia, NZ & the Pacific • Islands of Australia's Great Barrier Reef • Melbourne • Melbourne City Map • Micronesia • New Caledonia • New South Wales • New Zealand • Northern Territory • Outback Australia • Out to Eat – Melbourne • Out to Eat – Sydney • Papua New Guinea • Pidgin phrasebook • Queensland • Rarotonga & the Cook Islands • Samoa • Solomon Islands • South Australia • South Pacific • South Pacific phrasebook • Sydney • Sydney City Map • Sydney Condensed • Tahiti & French Polynesia • Tasmania • Tonga • Tramping in New Zealand • Vanuatu • Victoria • Walking in Australia • Watching Wildlife Australia • Western Australia
Travel Literature: Islands in the Clouds: Travels in the Highlands of New Guinea • Kiwi Tracks: A New Zealand Journey • Sean & David's Long Drive

CENTRAL AMERICA & THE CARIBBEAN Bahamas, Turks & Caicos • Baja California • Belize, Guatemala & Yucatán • Bermuda • Central America on a shoestring • Costa Rica • Costa Rica Spanish phrasebook • Cuba • Cycling Cuba • Dominican Republic & Haiti • Eastern Caribbean • Guatemala • Havana • Healthy Travel Central & South America • Jamaica • Mexico • Mexico City • Panama • Puerto Rico • Read This First: Central & South America • Virgin Islands • World Food Caribbean • World Food Mexico • Yucatán
Travel Literature: Green Dreams: Travels in Central America

EUROPE Amsterdam • Amsterdam City Map • Amsterdam Condensed • Andalucía • Athens • Austria • Baltic States phrasebook • Barcelona • Barcelona City Map • Belgium & Luxembourg • Berlin • Berlin City Map • Britain • British phrasebook • Brussels, Bruges & Antwerp • Brussels City Map • Budapest • Budapest City Map • Canary Islands • Catalunya & the Costa Brava • Central Europe • Central Europe phrasebook • Copenhagen • Corfu & the Ionians • Corsica • Crete • Crete Condensed • Croatia • Cycling Britain • Cycling France • Cyprus • Czech & Slovak Republics • Czech phrasebook • Denmark • Dublin • Dublin City Map • Dublin Condensed • Eastern Europe • Eastern Europe phrasebook • Edinburgh • Edinburgh City Map • England • Estonia, Latvia & Lithuania • Europe on a shoestring • Europe phrasebook • Finland • Florence • Florence City Map • France • Frankfurt City Map • Frankfurt Condensed • French phrasebook • Georgia, Armenia & Azerbaijan • Germany • German phrasebook • Greece • Greek Islands • Greek phrasebook • Hungary • Iceland, Greenland & the Faroe Islands • Ireland • Italian phrasebook • Italy • Kraków • Lisbon • The Loire • London • London City Map • London Condensed • Madrid • Madrid City Map • Malta • Mediterranean Europe • Milan, Turin & Genoa • Moscow • Munich • Netherlands • Normandy • Norway • Out to Eat – London • Out to Eat – Paris • Paris • Paris City Map • Paris Condensed • Poland • Polish phrasebook • Portugal • Portuguese phrasebook • Prague • Prague City Map • Provence & the Côte d'Azur • Read This First: Europe • Rhodes & the Dodecanese • Romania & Moldova • Rome • Rome City Map • Rome Condensed • Russia, Ukraine & Belarus • Russian phrasebook • Scandinavian & Baltic Europe • Scandinavian phrasebook • Scotland • Sicily • Slovenia • South-West France • Spain • Spanish phrasebook • Stockholm • St Petersburg • St Petersburg City Map • Sweden • Switzerland • Tuscany • Ukrainian phrasebook • Venice • Vienna • Wales • Walking in Britain • Walking in France • Walking in Ireland • Walking in Italy • Walking in Scotland • Walking in Spain • Walking in Switzerland • Western Europe • World Food France • World Food Greece • World Food Ireland • World Food Italy • World Food Spain **Travel Literature:** After Yugoslavia • Love and War in the Apennines • The Olive Grove: Travels in Greece • On the Shores of the Mediterranean • Round Ireland in Low Gear • A Small Place in Italy

Lonely Planet Mail Order

onely Planet products are distributed worldwide. They are also available by mail order from Lonely Planet, so if you have difficulty finding a title please write to us. North and South American residents should write to 150 Linden St, Oakland, CA 94607, USA; European and African residents should write to 10a Spring Place, London NW5 3BH, UK; and residents of other countries to Locked Bag 1, Footscray, Victoria 3011, Australia.

INDIAN SUBCONTINENT & THE INDIAN OCEAN Bangladesh • Bengali phrasebook • Bhutan • Delhi • Goa • Healthy Travel Asia & India • Hindi & Urdu phrasebook • India • India & Bangladesh City Map • Indian Himalaya • Karakoram Highway • Kathmandu City Map • Kerala • Madagascar • Maldives • Mauritius, Réunion & Seychelles • Mumbai (Bombay) • Nepal • Nepali phrasebook • North India • Pakistan • Rajasthan • Read This First: Asia & India • South India • Sri Lanka • Sri Lanka phrasebook • Tibet • Tibetan phrasebook • Trekking in the Indian Himalaya • Trekking in the Karakoram & Hindukush • Trekking in the Nepal Himalaya • World Food India **Travel Literature:** The Age of Kali: Indian Travels and Encounters • Hello Goodnight: A Life of Goa • In Rajasthan • Maverick in Madagascar • A Season in Heaven: True Tales from the Road to Kathmandu • Shopping for Buddhas • A Short Walk in the Hindu Kush • Slowly Down the Ganges

MIDDLE EAST & CENTRAL ASIA Bahrain, Kuwait & Qatar • Central Asia • Central Asia phrasebook • Dubai • Farsi (Persian) phrasebook • Hebrew phrasebook • Iran • Israel & the Palestinian Territories • Istanbul • Istanbul City Map • Istanbul to Cairo • Istanbul to Kathmandu • Jerusalem • Jerusalem City Map • Jordan • Lebanon • Middle East • Oman & the United Arab Emirates • Syria • Turkey • Turkish phrasebook • World Food Turkey • Yemen **Travel Literature:** Black on Black: Iran Revisited • Breaking Ranks: Turbulent Travels in the Promised Land • The Gates of Damascus • Kingdom of the Film Stars: Journey into Jordan

NORTH AMERICA Alaska • Boston • Boston City Map • Boston Condensed • British Columbia • California & Nevada • California Condensed • Canada • Chicago • Chicago City Map • Chicago Condensed • Florida • Georgia & the Carolinas • Great Lakes • Hawaii • Hiking in Alaska • Hiking in the USA • Honolulu & Oahu City Map • Las Vegas • Los Angeles • Los Angeles City Map • Louisiana & the Deep South • Miami • Miami City Map • Montreal • New England • New Orleans • New Orleans City Map • New York City • New York City City Map • New York City Condensed • New York, New Jersey & Pennsylvania • Oahu • Out to Eat – San Francisco • Pacific Northwest • Rocky Mountains • San Diego & Tijuana • San Francisco • San Francisco City Map • Seattle • Seattle City Map • Southwest • Texas • Toronto • USA • USA phrasebook • Vancouver • Vancouver City Map • Virginia & the Capital Region • Washington, DC • Washington, DC City Map • World Food New Orleans **Travel Literature**: Caught Inside: A Surfer's Year on the California Coast • Drive Thru America

NORTH-EAST ASIA Beijing • Beijing City Map • Cantonese phrasebook • China • Hiking in Japan • Hong Kong & Macau • Hong Kong City Map • Hong Kong Condensed • Japan • Japanese phrasebook • Korea • Korean phrasebook • Kyoto • Mandarin phrasebook • Mongolia • Mongolian phrasebook • Seoul • Shanghai • South-West China • Taiwan • Tokyo • Tokyo Condensed • World Food Hong Kong • World Food Japan **Travel Literature:** In Xanadu: A Quest • Lost Japan

SOUTH AMERICA Argentina, Uruguay & Paraguay • Bolivia • Brazil • Brazilian phrasebook • Buenos Aires • Buenos Aires City Map • Chile & Easter Island • Colombia • Ecuador & the Galapagos Islands • Healthy Travel Central & South America • Latin American Spanish phrasebook • Peru • Quechua phrasebook • Read This First: Central & South America • Rio de Janeiro • Rio de Janeiro City Map • Santiago de Chile • South America on a shoestring • Trekking in the Patagonian Andes • Venezuela **Travel Literature**: Full Circle: A South American Journey

SOUTH-EAST ASIA Bali & Lombok • Bangkok • Bangkok City Map • Burmese phrasebook • Cambodia • Cycling Vietnam, Laos & Cambodia • East Timor phrasebook • Hanoi • Healthy Travel Asia & India • Hill Tribes phrasebook • Ho Chi Minh City (Saigon) • Indonesia • Indonesian phrasebook • Indonesia's Eastern Islands • Java • Lao phrasebook • Laos • Malay phrasebook • Malaysia, Singapore & Brunei • Myanmar (Burma) • Philippines • Pilipino (Tagalog) phrasebook • Read This First: Asia & India • Singapore • Singapore City Map • South-East Asia on a shoestring • South-East Asia phrasebook • Thailand • Thailand's Islands & Beaches • Thailand, Vietnam, Laos & Cambodia Road Atlas • Thai phrasebook • Vietnam • Vietnamese phrasebook • World Food Indonesia • World Food Thailand • World Food Vietnam

ALSO AVAILABLE: Antarctica • The Arctic • The Blue Man: Tales of Travel, Love and Coffee • Brief Encounters: Stories of Love, Sex & Travel • Buddhist Stupas in Asia: The Shape of Perfection • Chasing Rickshaws • The Last Grain Race • Lonely Planet ... On the Edge: Adventurous Escapades from Around the World • Lonely Planet Unpacked • Lonely Planet Unpacked Again • Not the Only Planet: Science Fiction Travel Stories • Ports of Call: A Journey by Sea • Sacred India • Travel Photography: A Guide to Taking Better Pictures • Travel with Children • Tuvalu: Portrait of an Island Nation

Index

Text

Bold indicates maps.

Boxed Text

Bold indicates maps.

MAP LEGEND

BOUNDARIES

··························· International
··························· Provincial, State
··························· Regional, Suburb

HYDROGRAPHY

························· Coastline
························· River, Creek
························· Lake
························· Canal

Building
Urban Area

ROUTES & TRANSPORT

························· Freeway
························· Highway
························· Major Road
························· Minor Road
························· Unsealed Road
························· City Freeway
························· City Highway
························· City Road
························· City Street, Lane

························· Pedestrian Mall
························· Tunnel
························· Train Route & Station
························· Metro & Station
························· Tramway & Tram Stop
························· Cable Car or Chairlift
························· Walking Track
························· Walking Tour
························· Ferry Route & Terminal

AREA FEATURES

························· Park, Gardens
························· Cemetery

························· Market
························· Mountain Range

MAP SYMBOLS

☻ **FLORENCE** ············· Large City
● **Lucca** ····················· City
● Miniato ················· Large Town
● Galleno ·········· Town or Village

● ············· Point of Interest

▪ ················· Place to Stay
⛺ ················· Camp Site
🚐 ············· Caravan Park
⬒ ················· Hut or Chalet
▼ ················· Place to Eat
⬚ ················· Pub or Bar
⬢ ················· Picnic Area

⊠ ························· Airport
························· Ancient or City Wall
⬓ ············· Archaeological Site
⊖ ························· Bank
⬈ ························· Beach
🚏 ⬓ ··········· Bus Stop, Station
⬓ ············· Castle or Fort
⌂ ························· Cave
⬓ ⬒ ········· Church or Cathedral
⬓ ························· Cinema
⬚ ························· Embassy
⚓ ························· Fountain
⊕ ························· Hospital
⬓ ············· Internet Cafe

▲ ············· Mountain or Hill
⬓ ························· Museum
⬓ ············· National Park
⬓ ························· Palazzo
⬓ ························· Parking
⬓ ············· Police Station
⬛ ············· Post Office
⚐ ························· Ski Field
⬓ ············· Swimming Pool
⬓ ············· Synagogue
⬓ ························· Telephone
⬓ ························· Theatre
❶ ········· Tourist Information
⬓ ························· Trail Head

Note: not all symbols displayed above appear in this book

LONELY PLANET OFFICES

Australia
Locked Bag 1, Footscray, Victoria 3011
☎ 03 8379 8000 fax 03 8379 8111
email: talk2us@lonelyplanet.com.au

USA
150 Linden St, Oakland, CA 94607
☎ 510 893 8555 TOLL FREE: 800 275 8555
fax 510 893 8572
email: info@lonelyplanet.com

UK
10a Spring Place, London NW5 3BH
☎ 020 7428 4800 fax 020 7428 4828
email: go@lonelyplanet.co.uk

France
1 rue du Dahomey, 75011 Paris
☎ 01 55 25 33 00 fax 01 55 25 33 01
email: bip@lonelyplanet.fr
www.lonelyplanet.fr

World Wide Web: www.lonelyplanet.com *or* **AOL keyword: lp**
Lonely Planet Images: lpi@lonelyplanet.com.au